HANDBOOK OF EMPIRICAL SOCIAL WORK PRACTICE

HANDBOOK OF EMPIRICAL SOCIAL WORK PRACTICE

Volume 2

Social Problems and Practice Issues

Edited by
John S. Wodarski and Bruce A. Thyer

John Wiley & Sons, Inc.

New York • Chichester • Weinheim • Brisbane • Singapore • Toronto

The Library of Congress has catalogued as follows:

Library of Congress Cataloging-in-Publication Data

Handbook of empirical social work practice / edited by Bruce A. Thyer
    and John S. Wodarski.
      p.   cm.
    Includes bibliographical references and index.
    Contents: v. 1. Mental disorders—v. 2. Social problems and
practice issues.
    ISBN 0-471-15361-3 (cloth : alk. paper).—ISBN 0-471-15363-X
(set : alk. paper)
    1. Social case work.   2. Psychiatric social work.   I. Thyer,
Bruce A.   II. Wodarski, John S.
HV43.H316   1998
361.3′2—dc21   97-15312
                                                     CIP

Volume 2, edited by John S. Wodarski and Bruce A. Thyer.
ISBN 0-471-15362-1

Printed in the United States of America
10 9 8 7 6 5 4 3 2 1

Contributors

THOMAS A. ARTELT, MSW
School of Social Work
University of Georgia
Athens, Georgia

ROBERT BIDWELL, PhD
Department of Pediatrics
University of Hawaii
Honolulu, Hawaii

ANNA CELESTE BURKE, PhD
College of Social Work
The Ohio State University
Columbus, Ohio

D. ROSEMARY CASSANO, MSW, PhD
School of Social Work
University of Windsor
Ontario, Canada

NAMKEE G. CHOI, PhD
School of Social Work
State University of New York at Buffalo
Buffalo, New York

KRISTIN C. COLE, MS
School of Social Work
Columbia University
New York, New York

NURIA M. CUEVAS, PhD
College of Medicine
Northeastern Ohio University
Rootstown, Ohio

SHERRY CUMMINGS
School of Social Work
University of Georgia
Athens, Georgia

KEVIN L. DEWEAVER, PhD
School of Social Work
University of Georgia
Athens, Georgia

CATHERINE N. DULMUS, ACSW
School of Social Work
State University of New York at Buffalo
Buffalo, New York

ANNATJIE C. FAUL, PhD
School of Social Work
Rand Afrikaans University
Johannesburg, South Africa

MARVIN D. FEIT, PhD
School of Social Work
The University of Akron
Akron, Ohio

VIRGINIA L. FITCH, PhD
School of Social Work
The University of Akron
Akron, Ohio

M. E. BETSY GARRISON, PhD
School of Human Ecology
Louisiana State University
Baton Rouge, Louisiana

CHARLESA A. HANN-DOWDY, MSSA, LISW
School of Social Work
The University of Akron
Akron, Ohio

MICHAEL J. HOLOSKO, MSW, PhD
School of Social Work
University of Windsor
Ontario, Canada

Although controversy continues to rage regarding the strengths and weaknesses of *DSM-IV* as a diagnostic tool and its role in a complete social work assessment, it is undeniable that this one work remains the most influential book in contemporary mental health practice. We cannot conceive of a well-trained clinical social worker who is not thoroughly conversant with the use of the *DSM-IV* (and aware of its problems).

Accordingly, Volume 1 follows the diagnostic outline found in *DSM-IV.* After an introductory chapter entitled "First Principles of Empirical Social Work Practice," which establishes the conceptual underpinnings of the book, each of the remaining 22 chapters deals with one (sometimes two) of the major so-called mental disorders found in *DSM-IV.* We hope that this will facilitate its use as a reference tool. Does the client meet *DSM-IV* criteria for Panic Disorder with Agoraphobia? If so, turn to Chapter 15 to learn the best methods to complete your assessment and to develop a treatment plan. Is Bulimia Nervosa a part of the picture? Then Chapter 22 will prove useful for the same purposes.

We are acutely aware of the limitations of this approach. Clients and their families are more than sets of diagnostic criteria. The so-called mental disorders (which really should be labeled *behavioral, affective, and intellectual disorders,* to avoid an unwarranted etiological inference, in our opinion) exist within a complex system of the client's biological structure (the body) and physical and psychosocial worlds, and the interactions among these entities. A prescriptive approach to treatment, which is encouraged by the *DSM-IV* framework, can discourage, to some extent, a thorough functional analysis of a problem in situation. In particular, marital and family dynamics are not usually well developed using the *DSM-IV* system. This is why we believe that an accurate *DSM-IV* diagnosis is a part of a, but is not a complete, social work assessment. Make no mistake, the blind application of particular interventions—no matter how well supported by empirical research—is never a part of the picture of professional social work practice. Empirical research *informs,* it does not dictate; it supplements, not replaces, clinical judgment. Social work is not yet a well developed interventive science, and art alone is an insufficient foundation on which to base one's professional practice. Rather, it is the judicious integration of both science and art that we believe should characterize contemporary empirical social work practice.

DSM-IV presently contains several hundred formal diagnoses. Space limitations prevent us from including more than two dozen of those most commonly encountered in contemporary clinical social work practice. We apologize for those omitted and promise to partially rectify the situation should we be so fortunate as to succeed to a second edition. We welcome constructive suggestions from readers to improve the work in the future.

Of course, social work practice encompasses far more than treating individual clients suffering from one or more of the *DSM-IV* disorders. Many psychosocial problems experienced by individuals do not lend themselves to the *DSM-IV* format, and many problems transcend practice with individuals and entail organizational, institutional, or community-level interventions. Thus Volume 2 of this *Handbook of Empirical Social Work Practice,* subtitled *Social Problems and Practice Issues,* addresses additional selected areas of social work practice. Again, there are far more problems than we could possibly include, so we winnowed out topics on the basis of the amount of empirical research that is presently available to guide practice. Some very important areas are quite undeveloped in this respect, such as community organization and policy practice; therefore, we were unable to address them. As scientific foundations for practice emerge in these fields, our hope is to include them in future editions, as well.

We gratefully acknowledge the valuable lessons taught to us by our clients, students, peers, and families, which have helped to shape our views regarding the immense constructive contributions of empirical research to social work practice. In particular we recognize those voices in the early years of the development of the social work profession that called for the accurate measurement of social problems, for proceduralized interventions that could be taught to others, and for the ongoing evaluation of social work services at all levels. Only now is their vision becoming fulfilled. It is to these little-recognized pioneers of empirical social work practice that we respectfully dedicate this book.

Bruce A. Thyer
Athens, Georgia

John S. Wodarski
Buffalo, New York

REFERENCES

American Psychiatric Association. (1989). *Treatments of psychiatric disorders.* Washington, DC: Author.

American Psychiatric Association. (1994). *Diagnostic and statistical manual of mental disorders* (4th ed.). Washington, DC: Author.

Ammerman, R. T., Last, C. G., & Hersen, M. (Eds.). (1993). *Handbook of prescriptive treatments for children and adolescents.* Boston: Allyn & Bacon.

Brandell, J. (1997). *Theory and practice in clinical social work.* New York: Free Press.

Dorfman, R. (Ed.) (1988). *Paradigms of clinical social work.* New York: Brunner/Mazel.

Giles, T. R. (Ed.) (1993). *Handbook of effective psychotherapy.* New York: Plenum Press.

Hayes, S. C., Follette, V. M., Dawes, R. M., & Grady, K. E. (Eds.) (1995). *Scientific standards of psychological practice: Issues and recommendations.* Reno, NV: Context Press.

Roberts, R., & Nee, R. (Eds.) (1970). *Theories of social casework.* Chicago: University of Chicago Press.

Turner, F. (Ed.) (1986). *Social work treatment* (3d ed.). New York: Free Press.

Contents

PART I

Social Problems

Chapter 1

SOCIAL PROBLEMS: A COST-EFFECTIVE PSYCHOSOCIAL PREVENTION PARADIGM

John S. Wodarski

The cost of social problems and the negative consequences are extensive and well documented. From a cost-benefit perspective, the interventions the social service system has chosen are extremely costly and highly unproductive for both client and practitioner in terms of targets, timing of intervention, ages, and contexts. Social, cognitive, and academic skills that adults must master should provide the focus for intervention from a life-span development perspective. This chapter reviews various elements of the public health model that should set the stage for interventions. A review and analysis of centering social problems underscores the need for cost-effective preventive efforts. First, the personal and societal costs of teen pregnancy, substance abuse, child maltreatment, and racial disparities are analyzed. Then the personal, social, economic, and political benefits of prevention are discussed. Next are elucidated the preventive models of service delivery. The chapter concludes with specific applications and discussions.

PREVENTION VERSUS REMEDIATION

Much has been written about the many problem behaviors of the young and the undesirable consequences thereof. Teenagers' experimentation with drugs and alcohol can lead to overindulgence and abuse. Serious short-term and long-term effects include risk taking and daredevil behaviors that increase risks to mental and physical health, including accidents, which are a leading cause of death among adolescents. Likewise, risk taking may increase the incidence of irresponsible sexual activity, which eventuates in venereal disease, unwanted pregnancy, and premature parenthood. Prevention during the adolescent developmental period would reduce these serious physical and social problems (Hamburg & Takanishi, 1989; Malow, West, Williams, & Sutker, 1989; Schinke, Orlandi, Forgey, Rugg, & Douglas, 1992).

Prevention is especially appropriate to dealing with the problems of the young. Prevention provides an early developmental focus for intervention, which may forestall development of future problems. The need for effective and efficient intervention programs is analyzed in this chapter by reviewing the personal and societal costs of teen pregnancy, substance abuse, child maltreatment, and racial disparities. These problems usually intensify later and become harder to alter, thereby increasing the need for investments of time and money. Prevention provides a view of the person that is optimistic. The approach is economic and mass-oriented rather than individual-oriented, and it seeks to build health from the start rather than to repair damage that has already been done.

The life skills training intervention model is proposed as the treatment of choice. This model has rationale and elements in common with other prevention programs that are based on a public health orientation. Such prevention programs consist of three essential components: education, skills training, and practice in applying skills. The Teams-Games-Tournaments (TGT) model consists of the same components as other prevention programs, except for an additional component: It uses peers as parallel teachers. Data to support social workers' use of the life skills and Teams-Games-Tournaments models are reviewed later in this chapter.

The prevention approach to intervention has implications for the traditional role of the human services practitioner and for the timing of the intervention. The prevention approach places major emphasis on the teaching and skills-building components of the intervention process (Hawkins, Catalano, & Miller, 1992; Jackson & Hombeck, 1989; Wodarski & Bagarozzi, 1979). Practitioners do not take a passive role in the intervention process, but instead attempt to help clients learn how to exert control over their own behaviors and over the environments in which they live. Professional knowledge, expertise, and understanding of human behavior theory and personality development are used by the practitioner in the conceptualization and implementation of intervention strategies. Since their training equips them to evaluate scientifically any prevention procedure they have instituted, there is continual assessment of the prevention process.

NEED FOR PREVENTION PROGRAMS

Deficit-ridden state and local governments are cutting back prevention programs in order to balance their budgets. However, this proves to be cost-ineffective on every level. One informative example of this unfortunate policy is the curtailing of family planning services and teen pregnancy programs. Specifically, savings in public medical costs alone are estimated to be $4.40 for each $1 spent in contraceptive services to the typical clinic patient (Forrest & Singh, 1990). Savings in income support and social services are greater yet. Almost 10 million women of reproductive age have no insurance, and more than 5 million women are insured under plans that do not provide, largely for financial reasons, maternity coverage (U.S. General Accounting Office [U.S. GAO], 1990d). State insurance commissioners should pressure planning services. Teens, single women, and poor women, who have the highest incidence of low-birth-weight (LBW) babies, are most likely to use publicly funded family services (National Center for Health Statistics [NCHS], 1990b) and these women tend to have far more unwanted pregnancies (NCHS, 1990a).

The largely disorganized publicly funded family planning system we now have provides contraceptive services for about 4.5 million women, most of whom are at high risk for unplanned pregnancies. Without these services there would be an estimated 1.2 million additional unintended pregnancies each year and over 500,000 additional births (Forrest and Singh, 1990). Infant mortality rates (IMRs) would only be greater. Federal and state governments spend approximately $400 million annually for contraceptive services. They save, according to the Guttmacher Institute (1985), approximately $1.8 billion on services that would have to be rendered to those women who would otherwise give birth. These trends underscore the importance of supporting, rather than cutting, prevention and early prevention programs.

SOCIAL PROBLEMS: A REVIEW AND ANALYSIS

Teenage Pregnancy

The high incidence of teenage pregnancy is the result of a decrease in the average age of menses, combined with increasing sexual activity among adolescents (Chilman, 1979; Flick, 1986; Schinke, 1978). According to the American Medical Association (AMA, 1991), medical and social science research on adolescents has revealed disturbing trends. Many health problems are affecting adolescents at younger ages. For example, the decline in age at first intercourse (and delay in contraceptive use by young, sexually active adolescents) has produced increased rates of sexually transmitted diseases (STDs) among adolescents.

By the time they are 18 years old, 65% of boys and 51% of girls are sexually active. Approximately 50% of American adolescents do not use contraceptives the first time they have intercourse. And half of premarital pregnancies occur within the first 6 months after sexual initiation. Each year 11% of adolescent women become pregnant, and 4% have an abortion. Adolescents who become pregnant while in high school are more likely to drop out of school, become dependent on welfare, and become single parents. Between 1950 and 1985 the nonmarital birth rate among adolescents younger than age 20 increased 300% for Whites and 16% for Blacks. Approximately 2.5 million adolescents have had an STD, and 1 in 4 sexually active adolescents will contract an STD before graduating from high school. STD rates are substantially higher among Black adolescents.

The cost borne by Medicaid for a birth to a teenager age 14 or younger has been calculated as $3,494, the cost for 15- to 17-year-olds is $3,224, and for 18- and 19-year-olds, it is $2,696, exclusive of pediatric care (Armstrong & Waszak, 1990).

The National Research Council estimates that, for each year a first birth is delayed, a family's income when the mother reaches age 27 is increased by $500. Thus every year a first birth is delayed (up to age 20), the chances of a woman and her family having an income below poverty level are reduced by about 22%. The Children's Defense Fund reports that women who first give birth as teens have about half the lifetime earnings of women who first give birth in their twenties (Armstrong & Pascale, 1990). Three major national surveys found the incidence of poverty among families begun by a teen birth to be 20%, 50%, and 60% greater than among families in which mothers gave birth to their first child at a later age (Furstenberg, Brooks-Gunn, & Morgan, 1987). The Center for Population Options (CPO) determined that the federal government spent $21.6 billion in 1989 on families begun by teen mothers. This expenditure includes $10.4 billion for Aid to Families with Dependent Children (AFDC), $3.4 billion for food stamps, and $7.7 billion for Medicaid. Based on the assumption that families begun by a teen birth comprise 53% of the welfare-recipient population, they consume 53% of the funding of these programs.

The following is the projected cost to the federal government of a family begun by a teen birth over the following 20 years, again including only three major benefit programs. Reflected in the calculations are the observations that (a) approximately 1 in 3 teen mothers receives welfare, (b) the average length of time a woman who begins her family as a teen remains on welfare is 2.5 years, (c) the probability a teen mother will receive public assistance declines over her lifetime, and (d) the younger a women is when she first gives birth, the more children she can be expected to have.

All considered, the CPO estimated that a family begun by a teenage mother in 1989 cost taxpayers an average of $16,975 by the time that baby reaches age 20. This figure, however, is deceptively low because it represents an average across all first births to adolescent mothers, even though only one third of the families begun by a teen birth actually receive welfare. More informatively, the CPO projects that the government will spend an average of $50,925 over 20 years on each family begun in 1989 by a teen birth that enrolled in public assistance. Presumably, that figure is averaged down by the families who drop out of the welfare system. The CPO estimates that the families begun in 1989 by a teen birth will have cost the public treasury $6.4 billion by the year 2009.

HIV/AIDS

More than two thirds of adolescents with AIDS were infected through sexual contact with adults. Although only 440 people with AIDS (fewer than 1%) are between ages 13 and 19, the prevalence of HIV infection among adolescents is a source of concern. Because it takes an estimated 5 to 10 years for the HIV infection to result in AIDS, many young adults who have AIDS contracted the virus as adolescents.

Approximately 20% of people identified as having AIDS are between ages 20 and 29 (AMA, 1991).

AIDS is expensive in terms of pain, suffering, premature mortality, fear, anxiety, and grief. It costs lovers their partners, parents their children, and children their parents. It is also costly in monetary terms. The United States spent about $10 billion on HIV-related activities in 1991. Federal government expenditures alone totaled $3.46 billion—$1.245 billion for research, $1.346 billion on medical care, $567 million for education and prevention, and $305 million in income support to AIDS victims (Office of Management and Budget [OMB], 1990). Federal expenditures on AIDS from 1982 to 1991 totaled almost $12 billion (NCHS, 1990b; OMB, 1990). Since the federal government contributes approximately one third of the total spent on AIDS, the total spending during that time approached $36 billion.

Hellinger (1990) estimates the direct medical costs of AIDS in 1991 to have been $5.8 billion, with the cost of treating an HIV-infected person averaging $5,150 yearly and the cost of treating a patient with full-blown AIDS averaging $32,000 yearly (Foreman, 1991).

Forecasts of the future costs of AIDS and HIV vary. Foreman (1991) estimated total personal care costs (drug, physician, hospital, and nursing home costs) to be $8.5 billion (in 1985 dollars) in 1991. They also projected an additional $2.3 billion to be spent on nonpersonal care activity (research, testing, education, and support services). Windenwerder and Associates estimated federal spending on HIV-related illnesses to reach $4.3 billion in 1992 and total national expenditures to be three times that. Hellinger (1990) estimated the cumulative lifetime medical care expenses (in 1988 dollars) for all people diagnosed with AIDS to be $4.3 billion in 1990, $5.3 billion in 1991, $6.5 billion in 1992, and $7.8 billion in 1993. He additionally projected that expenditures for medical care alone to AIDS patients in 1994 would total $10.4 billion (Foreman, 1991). Altogether, in 1989 alone, private insurers paid over $1 billion in AIDS-related health and life insurance claims, 71% more than in 1988 (Carrol, 1989). In spite of the armed forces' policy of discharging HIV-infected persons, the U.S. General Accounting Office (U.S. GAO) projects that AIDS will cost the U.S. military and veterans' health care system $3 billion by the end of this decade (U.S. GAO, 1990a).

The Centers for Disease Control (CDC) estimates that over 500,000 persons in this country are HIV infected and do not know it (K. Golan, Center for Disease Control Press Office, oral communication, August 1991). Thus the costs of HIV-related expenses are expected to continue rising until some type of cure or solution is found.

Substance Abuse

The United States has become a chemical culture (Morrison, 1985). The use and abuse of chemical substances exact an incalculable cost for substance abusers and nonabusers alike. Drug abuse–related deaths, injury, disease, family upheaval, and emotional disturbance are consequences that cannot be measured in monetary figures. In 1987, it was estimated that 100,000 to 120,000 deaths are directly attributable to substance abuse, and another 120,000 to 150,000 deaths are substance abuse related. Even more alarming, in 1988, 6% of 12- to 17-year-olds consumed alcohol daily, 4% used marijuana daily, and 0.5% used cocaine daily (AMA, 1991).

Adolescence is a time of growth, stress, and change. This developmental stage affects not only the adolescent but his or her family as well. Adolescents, while in the natural process of establishing autonomy and identity, begin to separate from parents and experiment with a variety of behaviors and lifestyle patterns (Belvin, 1983). During this period, the relative importance of family and peers begins to shift. The peer group becomes more central for the adolescent, who begins to rely more heavily on peers for support, security, and guidance (Belsky, Lerner, & Spanier, 1984). Establishing peer relationships and acceptance are the hallmarks of adolescence. Consequently, the needs to gain acceptance, approval, and praise are greater during adolescence than at any other time in life (Morrison, 1985).

Many adolescents experience confusion and turmoil as they strive to achieve autonomy. Because of this turmoil and confusion, adolescents often perceive taking psychoactive substances as one of their few pleasurable options (Morrison & Smith, 1987). According to Morrison (1985), the use and abuse of mood-altering chemical substances are now an integral part of growing into adulthood in the United States. Morrison notes that two thirds of high school students use drugs and alcohol with regular frequency, and 85% of these students use drugs and alcohol at least three times a week. Additionally, 65% to 70% of junior high school students use drugs and alcohol two to three times weekly (Morrison, 1985).

Long-range consequences of teenage substance misuses include the failure to formulate goals for the future (Goodstadt & Sheppard, 1983) and stigmatization following an arrest while under the influence of drugs. The labeling of an adolescent under these circumstances can result in loss of stature, opportunity, and personal self-esteem (Mayer & Filstead, 1980). Patterns of substance abuse also have significant health consequences (Prendergast & Schafer, 1974). Yet more teenagers die in alcohol- and drug-related motor vehicle accidents than from any disease. One fourth of all alcohol- and drug-related motor vehicle fatalities involve males ages 16 to 19 (Morrison, 1985). Tragically, drug overdoses also result in 88% of all adolescent suicides.

Drug-related problems begun in adolescence, or earlier, mount to staggering proportions as young addicts or abusers age. Recent estimates of cost are not yet available. However, in 1989 the Justice Department estimated the social costs generated by each addict to have been about $200,000 per year (Cook, 1989). The costs associated with drug use are much greater today than at the time of the 1989 analysis for several reasons. Federal spending for drug control was $1.6 billion in

1985, it was $10.5 billion in 1991, and $11.7 billion was requested for 1992 (U.S. Department of Health and Human Services [U.S. DHHS], 1990a; Office of National Drug Control Policy [ONDCP], 1991). Drug-related criminal justice costs have since skyrocketed. According to Rice and colleagues, 26% of our total policy protection expenditures can be attributed to drug-related crime (U.S. DHHS, 1990a, modified). Only 1,500 cases of the costly disease AIDS were attributed to drug use in 1985; by 1990 the number was 8,248 and growing rapidly (NCHS, 1990a). Yet an even greater source of increasing costs is the rise in the use of crack cocaine.

Recent examples from San Francisco underscore the magnitude of the problem.

- Police incidents involving cocaine increased 278% (cost: $9.80 million).
- Felony court cases specifically tied to cocaine possession or sales (61% of total cases) increased 218% (cost: $5.80 million).
- Juvenile cocaine-related arrests increased 440% (cost: $4.58 million).
- Jailing (mostly of people arrested for crack) increased 21% (cost: $15.50 million).
- The number of adults released on probation to the drug diversion program increased 21% (cost: $1.01 million).
- Felony lawyers in the public defender's office spent almost 50% of their time representing people charged with cocaine-related offenses (cost: $1.60 million).
- Foster care cases involving children of addicted parents increased 148% (cost: $22.18 million).
- The number of addicts in treatment for crack increased 144% (cost: $3.00 million).
- The number of infants born who tested positive for drugs increased 73% (cost: $3.50 million).
- The demand for adult health services increased substantially (cost: $4.72 million).

The total economic costs to the nation of alcohol misuse were estimated by Rice and colleagues to have been $70.3 billion in 1985, a year in which 94,765 deaths were attributed to alcohol (U.S. DHHS, 1990a). Miller estimates that an additional $100 billion a year in costs, far more than the $2.9 estimated by Rice and colleagues, are associated with alcohol-related crashes.

The costs can be extremely burdensome. A National Institute on Drug Abuse (NIDA) study found that American firms spend at least 25% on substance-abusing employees' wages responding to their performance deficiencies (Lodge, 1987).

- Alcohol is involved in 40% of industrial fatalities and 50% of industrial accidents.
- The accident rate among employees with a drinking or drug problem is four to six times higher than that of nonabusing employees.
- Absenteeism among employees with a drinking or drug problem is five to eight times higher.
- Medical claims are three times higher in substance-abusing families.
- The productivity of employees with a drug or alcohol problem is 25% to 40% less; yet they bring four times as many grievances.

Lodge informs us, in addition, that:

- Alcohol-abusing employees are late to work three times more often than other employees.
- Alcohol-abusing employees request early dismissal or days off 2.2 times more often.
- Employees with alcohol problems are involved in on-the-job accidents 3.6 times more often.
- Substance-abusing employees are five times more likely to file workers' compensation claims.

The National Council on Compensation Insurance estimates that substance abuse cost American business $16 billion in workers' compensation alone in 1987 (Kaigham, 1989). Two thirds of substance-abuse workplace costs are generally attributed to alcohol use. Firms whose workforces tend to be older incur a greater proportion of alcohol-related costs.

The total cost to society of drug abuse was $44.1 billion, whereas for alcohol it was $70.3 billion. Core costs (medical, morbidity, and morbidity-related costs) for drug abuse were $10.6 billion for 1989, during which 6,118 deaths were attributed to drugs, including possible suicides and accidental poisoning unrelated to illicit drug use. Core costs for alcohol were $58.2 billion, yet alcohol-attributed deaths numbered 94,765 (U.S. DHHS, 1990a).

Smoking

Cigarette smoking is the single most preventable cause of death in the United States. It is directly responsible for one in six deaths—22% of all deaths among men and 11% of all deaths among women (U.S. DHHS, 1989). Over 434,000 persons died from smoking-related causes in 1988, including 142,836 from cancer, 200,802 from cardiovascular diseases, and 82,857 from respiratory diseases (CDC,

1991). An estimated 30% of all cancer deaths, 87% of lung cancer deaths, 21% of deaths from coronary heart disease, 18% of stroke deaths, and 82% of deaths from chronic obstructive pulmonary disease are attributed to cigarette smoking (U.S. DHHS, 1989). Americans spent a record-breaking $44 billion on tobacco products in 1990—$41.8 billion on cigarettes alone (Grise, 1991). Cigarette industry profits have also set records. They totaled $7.2 billion in 1989, 10% greater than in 1988 (Saloman Brothers, 1990). The average compounded growth rate is 15.6%. The Office of Technology Assessment (OTA) estimates that smoking-related productivity losses in 1985 were probably about $43 billion, but may have run as high as $61 billion (OTA, 1985). Warner estimated that nonsmokers pay 62% of the economic costs of cigarette smoking (OTA, 1985). If that is true, the external costs of smoking in 1985 may have been as much as $22 billion in health care and as great as $38 billion in lost productivity.

The other costs of smoking that are most obviously internalized are the health consequences—the pain, suffering, disability, and death—smoking entails. These health consequences also involve monetary expenses, representing about 6% of all U.S. health care expenditures (OTA, 1985). According to the OTA, total smoking-related health care costs in 1985 were approximately $22 billion, perhaps as much as $35 billion. Over two thirds of that were incurred on behalf of persons under 65 years of age. Government spending on smoking-related illness approximated $3.5 billion for Medicare, $0.7 billion for Medicaid, and $0.4 billion for veterans' health, but may have been as high as $5.4 billion, $1.1 billion, and $0.6 billion for those programs, respectively. These figures are far greater today. The consumer price index (CPI) for medical care rose 56% from 1985 to 1991 alone (U.S. Department of Labor, 1992). Only a small portion of these costs is borne by the smoker in the form of direct payments, medical deductibles, contributions to health insurance, and tax payments that support government-funded health care. Most of the expense is collectively shared by coworkers, employers, and taxpayers.

Children at Risk for Abuse

From 1980 to 1986, the reported incidence of child abuse and neglect increased by 66% from 9.8 to 16.3 children per 1,000 (National Center on Child Abuse and Neglect, 1988). An explosion of public interest campaigns and media coverage has created a sense of urgency in addressing the problem. Numerous studies have documented the effect of maltreatment on children. The National Clinical Evaluation Study (NCES) described in Daro (1988) is the most comprehensive. In its evaluation of maltreated children under age 13, the study made the following findings:

- Approximately 30% suffered chronic health problems.
- Approximately 30% displayed cognitive or language disorders.

- Approximately 22% had learning disorders requiring special education.
- Approximately 50% had been disciplined at school for misconduct or poor attendance.
- Approximately 50% suffered severe socioemotional problems such as low self-esteem, lack of trust, or low frustration tolerance.
- Approximately 14% engaged in self-mutilative or self-destructive behavior.

The immediate costs of protecting maltreated children include the costs of prevention, investigation, intervention, and treatment. Federal and state child protection expenditures totaled $3.5 billion in 1987 (Daro, 1988). The Massachusetts Department of Social Services (MDSS) alone spent $415 million for child protective services in 1990 (MDSS, 1990).

Other Children at Risk

Five major studies of births in the United States, Canada, and Wales found that 21% to 30% of the incidence of low birth weight was due to maternal cigarette smoking (U.S. DHHS, 1989). Research has also shown that smoking cessation during pregnancy can partly reverse the reduction in infant birth weight (Hebel, Fox, & Sexton, 1988).

An estimated 3.2% of pregnant women drink alcohol while pregnant, resulting in an estimated incidence of 59 fetal alcohol syndrome (FAS) babies per 1,000 live births (Abel & Sokol, 1987). As the incidence of fetal alcohol effect (FAE) babies among these women is four times that (Abel, 1984), approximately 30% of the babies of women who drink very heavily during pregnancy suffer lifelong debilitating consequences.

The racial and ethnic differentials are startling. The incidence of FAS babies among Native Americans is a shocking 29.9 per 1,000 live births. Among Blacks, it is 6.0; among Whites, 0.9; among Hispanics, 0.8; and among Asian Americans, 0.3 (Chavez, Cordero, & Boccera, 1989). Studies show that on some Indian reservations up to 25% of the children suffer from FAS or FAE (Krauthammer, 1989).

Just as the afflicted children pay the price of others' drinking behavior, so do we all. The estimated economic costs of FAS were $1.84 billion in 1988 (U.S. DHHS, 1990a). Slightly more than 10% was for medical treatment. The rest was for residential care and support services for persons with mental retardation from prenatal alcohol exposure. Binkeley estimates the total lifetime economic costs of one FAS child to be $1.4 million (Streissguth et al., 1991).

Over 11% of the population admit to some cocaine use; 1.4% admit to using crack (NIDA, 1991). NIDA also found that 9% of all females have used cocaine at some point; 0.8% have used crack. Among Black women, the figures are 7.5% and 1.8%. Estimates of the national incidence of cocaine-exposed babies vary. The ONDCP estimates that 100,000 cocaine-exposed babies are born each year (U.S. GAO, 1990b). The National Association for Prenatal Addiction Research and Education estimates that 375,000 drug-exposed babies are born each year, most of whom have been exposed to cocaine (U.S. GAO, 1990b).

The short-run medical costs of LBW deliveries are typically $14,000 to $30,000 (U.S. GAO, 1990b). Since cocaine-exposed babies tend to be very small and very premature, they frequently need neonatal intensive care, which can run to $3,000 per day. Inner-city hospitals report that their facilities are operating at above capacity, with 50% to 70% of the babies in their neonatal intensive care units cocaine affected (Revkin, 1989; Gilliam, 1989). Nationally, we spend $2.6 billion on neonatal intensive care each year (Thompson, 1990). The Florida Department of Health and Rehabilitative Services estimates that the total service costs to age 18 for each drug-exposed child who suffers significant physiologic or neurologic impairment will be $750,000 (U.S. GAO, 1990c).

The U.S. GAO estimates that 280,000 pregnant women were in need of drug treatment services in 1990. Less than 11% received care even though the National Drug Control budget provided $32.6 million for the treatment of pregnant addicts (U.S. GAO, 1990c; ONDCP, 1991). Almost $46 million was provided in 1991, and another $52.4 million was requested in 1992 (ONDCP, 1991). However, this too will likely prove insufficient.

Racial Disparities

An examination and comparison of social indicators—rates of unemployment, delinquency, substance abuse, and teenage pregnancy—show that Blacks were relatively worse off in the 1990s than in the 1960s. Collaborative efforts among educators, parents, communities, and social service and law enforcement agencies are needed to develop preventive approaches to these interrelated problems (Harrison, Wodarski, & Thyer, 1996).

Blacks are 23% more likely than Whites to abstain from drinking. The prevalence of alcohol consumption among Black youth is far less than that among White youth, and only 4% of Blacks admit heavy drinking compared to 5% of Whites (NIDA, 1990). Yet Blacks experience far more social and medical problems associated with heavy drinking than do Whites (U.S. DHHS, 1990b). The unexpected disparity in adverse consequences may perhaps be explained by the greater underreporting of drinking among Blacks, variations in drinking patterns, or racial differences in biological vulnerability to alcohol. The age-adjusted death rate for alcohol-induced causes among the Black population is 2.7 times that among the White population (NCHS, 1990a).

A 1987 study conducted by the Philadelphia Perinatal Society found that in one low-income Black neighborhood, 20% of women failed to get adequate prenatal care (PNC), 16% of the babies were of low birth weight, 40% had mothers age 17 or less, and 85% had mothers who were not married. The infant mortality rate (IMR) was 30 per 1,000 live births. The situation was even worse in many other poor Black neighborhoods—more than 1 in 4 women received little or no PNC, and IMRs were as high as 42 per 1,000 live births (Fitzgerald, 1989).

Even though American IMRs have fallen a great deal during this century, the relative position has deteriorated dramatically. In 1918, the United States ranked 6th out of 20 countries reporting comparable data. However, by 1986, that standing had fallen to 13th out of the original 20 countries and 22nd out of all those reported by the World Health Organization (WHO). Ahead of the United States was almost all of Western Europe plus Canada, Hong Kong, Singapore, and Japan (Massachusetts Task Force on Infant Mortality, 1990).

In 1975, the total U.S. IMR stood at a historical low of 16.1 deaths per 1,000 live births. The figure for White babies was 14.2; for Black babies it was 26.2 (NCHS, 1990a). Even though these rates were almost half what they had been 25 years earlier, in comparison to countries reporting to the WHO, the United States still had needless infant deaths, especially among Blacks. Thus the surgeon general, in a 1979 report, set a standard for improving infant survival rates in the 1980s. The goal was an overall IMR of 9.0 with an IMR no greater than 12.0 for any ethnic or racial groups by 1990 (NCHS, 1990b).

The U.S. GAO estimates that implementation of the Canadian health care system would save the United States $3 billion annually after meeting the increased demands for health care that would result (U.S. GAO, 1991). Senator Edward M. Kennedy claimed that 40% of the U.S. population had no health care coverage or had inadequate coverage in 1991. The 1989 Current Population Survey found that over 13% of the total U.S. population had no insurance coverage. Non-Hispanic Whites comprised a majority of the uninsured, although this group had the lowest rate, 10%. Almost 20% of non-Hispanic Blacks and 40% of Mexican Americans had no insurance (Travino, Mayer, Valdez, & Stroup, 1991). Most minorities that are insured are covered by private policies; the remainder are covered by Medicaid. Puerto Ricans and Blacks are most likely to be insured by Medicaid, with rates of 33% and 23%, respectively. By contrast, only 4.5% of Whites are Medicaid recipients.

Most Americans under age 65 are covered by employer- or union-provided plans, but these are not without price. Health care costs to business increased more than 800% from 1970 to 1987, worsening overall inflation (U.S. GAO, 1990c). Costs increased almost 22% in 1990 alone for the firms surveyed by Foster Higgins, an employee benefits consulting agency. The cost to taxpayers had also increased. Spending for Medicare increased 14% in 1989 to a total of over $100 billion; spending for Medicaid increased 12% to a total of $54.5 billion, 34% of which was spent on the elderly (NCHS, 1990b).

Health care is expensive. Its cost has been growing both absolutely and relatively. Medical costs increased at an average annual rate of 8% during the 1980s, while the overall consumer price index increased an average of 4.7% annually and median family income increased an average of 5% (NCHS, 1990b; U.S. Bureau of the Census, 1990).

BEHAVIORAL SOCIAL WORK: A MEANS TO A SOLUTION

The preceding discussion suggests a new focus on solving social problems—one that must center on theory, assessment, intervention, and outcomes. We propose that behavioral social work offers a means of training practitioners for the solution of social problems. Behavioral social work involves the systematic application of intervention derived from learning theory and supported by empirical evidence to achieve behavior changes in clients. The behavioral social worker must possess both theoretical knowledge and an empirical perspective regarding the nature of human behavior and the principles that influence behavioral change. The worker also must be capable of translating this knowledge into concrete behavioral operations for practical use in a variety of practice settings. In order to be an effective practitioner, therefore, the behavioral social worker must possess a solid behavioral science knowledge base as well as a variety of behavioral skills. Moreover, a thorough grounding in research methodology will enable the clinician to evaluate therapeutic interventions, a necessary requisite of practice. Since the rigorous training of behavioral social workers equip them to assess and evaluate any interventive procedures that they have instituted, there is continual evaluation that provides corrective feedbacks to the practitioners. For behavioral social workers, theory, practice, and evaluation are all part of one intervention process. The arbitrary division of theory, intervention, and research, which does not facilitate therapeutic effectiveness and improved clinical procedures, is eliminated.

Knowledge Base

The central emphasis of behavioral social work is on employing empirically supported procedures that are aimed at the solution of the client's difficulties. The body of knowledge that the behavioral practitioner needs to possess in order to be an effective agent of change includes:

1. A thorough understanding of the scientifically derived theories of human learning as they relate to human behavior, which research shows are necessary conditions, but not sufficient in themselves, for therapeutic change

2. The ability to make accurate behavioral assessments that include the specification of those conditions that are antecedent and consequential to the problem behaviors under consideration

3. The ability to formulate behaviorally relevant and specific treatment goals

4. The ability to implement effectively a treatment plan designed to modify those target behaviors identified by the clients as problematic

5. The ability to evaluate objectively any treatment procedure and outcome and to formulate new treatment strategies when those that had been formulated originally have proven ineffective

Assessment

An effective intervention addresses assessment prior to initiation of change. Rapid assessment techniques have become increasingly popular with practitioners and agencies alike. This trend in the use of rapid assessment techniques has been associated with the recent request by funding agencies to have evidence that clients are reaching their stated goals and that programs are effective in treating their clients. Both practitioners and agencies have realized the contribution of rapid assessment instruments in meeting these two aims. Accurately assessing clients' needs and evaluating the effectiveness of programs for clients are two necessary objectives.

Social workers have begun to identify the utility of rapid assessment instruments to collect large quantities of and better quality data. Studies have consistently found that these instruments are easily administered, are cost-effective, and can provide reliable client data (McMahon, 1984; Streever, Wodarski, & Lindsey, 1984). In addition, these assessment instruments are more objective than a personal interview, in that the personal biases of the worker are reduced and the subjective nature of assessment as a whole is also decreased. Flowers, Booraem, and Schwartz (1993) found that clients who were given rapid assessment instruments throughout treatment made more improvement on their goals, terminated from treatment less often, and were in general more satisfied with treatment. These instruments have also been noted to obtain more information from clients in a shorter amount of time. Consequently, these instruments are more efficient as well as more accurate.

Social workers who work with children and multiproblem families need to assess multiple sources of data across and beyond family systems. For social workers who work with abused and neglected children, the need for accurate and reliable information is even more critical because of the serious decisions that must be made (Rittner & Wodarski, 1995). Adequate assessment is a prerequisite to effective treatment and preventive interventions. At the present time, many social service workers use clinical interviews, personal judgment, and assumptions to make decisions about services, treatment needs, and placement.

IMPLEMENTATION OF CHANGE STRATEGY

Level of Intervention

Social work has been characterized historically as a profession that emphasizes one-to-one relationships with clients to achieve behavioral change (Glenn & Kunnes, 1973; Ryan, 1971; Wodarski, 1995). However, the profession has seldom addressed itself adequately to the appropriateness of the various service-delivery mechanisms for certain types of clients. Few empirical studies have delineated the parameters or criteria for determining whether one-to-one or group-level treatment is best for achieving behavioral change in a given situation.

Individual Treatment versus Group Treatment

Even though in recent years focus on group treatment for clients has intensified as a result of various conceptualizations that place a heavy emphasis on the roles that clients' peers and significant others play, relatively few clients are treated in this manner as compared with those treated in casework. Yet the methods for placement of clients in casework services contain a number of obvious deficiencies.

The casework relationship is unlike most situations faced in daily interaction. In contrast, the provision of services in groups offers the following benefits. The group interactional situation more frequently typifies many kinds of daily interactions. Services facilitating the development of behaviors that enable people to interact in groups are likely to better prepare them for participation in larger society, that is, to help them learn social skills necessary to secure reinforcement (Feldman & Wodarski, 1975). For example, training in relaxation, systematic desensitization, assertiveness, and parenting skills can all occur in one-to-one contexts. From the perspective of social learning theory, however, it is posited that if a behavior is learned in a group context, it is likely to come under the control of a greater number of discriminative stimuli; therefore, greater generalizations of the behavior can occur for a broader variety of interactional contexts.

There are additional substantiated rationales for working with individuals in groups. Groups provide a context where behaviors can be tested in a realistic atmosphere. Clients can get immediate peer feedback regarding their problem-solving behaviors. They are provided with role models to facilitate the acquisition of requisite social behavior. Groups provide a more valid locus for accurate diagnosis and a more potent means for changing client behavior (Meyer & Smith, 1977; Rose, 1977).

These theoretical rationales indicate that treating clients in groups should facilitate the acquisition of socially relevant behavior. In addition, group treatment is equally effective as individual service; thus, managed care will support the use of groups to provide service. However, criteria need to be developed concerning who can benefit from group treatment. Such knowledge will be forthcoming only when adequately designed research projects are executed in which clients are assigned randomly to individual and group treatment to control for confounding factors, such as type of behavior, age, sex, income level, and academic abilities.

In instances where an individual does not possess the necessary social behaviors to engage in a group, a one-to-one treatment relationship may provide the best treatment context. For example, many antisocial children would be lost quickly in a group simply because they do not have the essential social behaviors for interaction. Likewise, in the case of children with hyperactivity disorders, working on an individual basis might be necessary until their dysfunctional behaviors are controlled enough to allow them to participate in a group context. However, as soon as they develop the necessary social skills, therapeutic changes are likely to be further facilitated if they can be placed in a group (Jacobs & Spardin, 1974).

Macrolevel Intervention

If, following an assessment, a change agent decides that a client is exhibiting appropriate behaviors for his or her social context but that a treatment organization or institution is not providing adequate reinforcers for appropriate behaviors or that it is punishing appropriate behavior, the change agent must then decide to engage in organizational or institutional change. This may involve changing a social policy, changing bureaucratic means of dealing with people, or other strategies. To alter an organization, the worker will have to study its reinforcement contingencies and assess whether he or she has the power to change these structures so that the client can be helped.

In social work practice, the primary focus has been on changing the individual. Practitioners must restructure their thinking. "Inappropriate" behavior exhibited by a client must be examined according to who defined it as inappropriate and where requisite interventions should take place. Future research should provide various means of delineating how human behavior can be changed by interventions on different levels, thus providing the parameters for micro- and macrolevel interventions. The obvious question that will face social workers is how to coordinate these multilevel interventions (Goldfried & Davison, 1994).

Generalization and Maintenance of Behavior Change

Interventions at the macrolevel are increasingly more critical, since follow-up data collected 5 years later on antisocial children who participated in a year-long behavior modification program, which produced extremely impressive behavioral changes in the children, indicate that virtually none of the positive changes were maintained. Possibly, maintenance could be improved when change is also directed at macrolevels.

Considerable study is needed to delineate those variables that facilitate the generalization and maintenance of behavior change. These may include substituting naturally occurring reinforcers, training relatives or other individuals in the clients' environment, gradually removing or fading the contingencies, varying the conditions of training, using different schedules of reinforcement, and using delayed reinforcement and self-control procedures (Kazdin, 1975; Wodarski, 1980). Such procedures will be employed in future sophisticated and effective social service–delivery systems.

Home visits, which were once the focus of practice, may also be employed in the future. Positive features of home visits include the fact that they provide the opportunity to assess family interactions more adequately, increase the probability of involving significant others in the treatment process, offer the opportunity to delineate attitudinal differences and how they affect therapy, and can increase the worker's influence potential (Behrens & Ackerman, 1956; Freedman, 1967; Hollis, 1972; Mickle, 1963; Moynihan, 1974; Richmond, 1971).

Empirically Based Treatment Technologies

Treatment technologies consist of behavioral approaches to the solution of interpersonal problems, which have impressive, accumulating empirical histories. Numerous data-based behavioral technologies are available for workers to use in helping clients acquire necessary behaviors to operate in their environments. Every year more data support the successful history of behavior modification practice with children classified according to hyperactivity, autism, delinquency, and retardation, and adults classified according to antisocial behavior, retardation, neurosis, and psychosis (Goldfried, Greenberg, & Marmar, 1990; Thyer, 1995).

Client Outcomes

The first requisite for the use of research in practice is the delineation of the possible outcomes for the client. The specification of outcomes is critical because outcomes determine the data that will be measured and the criteria that will be needed to evaluate an empirical intervention (Graycar, 1979; Lindsey, Wodarski, & Streever, 1986; Rossi & McLaughlin, 1979; Wodarski, Hudson, & Buckholdt, 1976). Discussions with other professionals about the appropriateness of various outcomes and an adequate review of the available literature help make possible the elucidation of outcomes. It is evident that professional and clients' values, theoretical orientation, agency goals, sociopolitical factors, available resources, and practice context affect the chosen outcomes (Wodarski, 1977).

SPECIFIC APPLICATIONS TO ADOLESCENTS: AN EMPIRICALLY BASED PROTOTYPE FOR PREVENTION

Peers

For teenagers, actions detrimental to health frequently occur in situations involving peers. The influence of peer groups on adolescent behavior is well known (Sherif & Sherif, 1964) and, for many teenagers, strong social pressure provokes participation in peers-sanctioned behaviors such as smoking, abuse of substances, and sexual intercourse. Although teenagers may understand health risks involved in these activities, this understanding is insufficient to counter the social significance of indulging. Research (McAlister, Perry, & Maccoby, 1979, p. 650) conducted jointly at Stanford and Harvard universities underscores this point:

> Behaviors detrimental to health are embedded in a complex milieu of social forces that often overwhelms educated rationality. . . . Even if a young person develops a negative attitude toward unhealthy behaviors, she or he may not possess the skills to resist strong social pressures to conform with peers who do not share that attitude.

Specific cognitive and behavioral skills are needed to resist external pressures and to successfully negotiate interpersonal encounters where pressure occurs (Hawkins, Catalano, Gillmore, & Wells, 1989). Adolescents often lack these skills, not because of individual pathology, but for developmental reasons. Age brings increased opportunity to engage in previously unknown or prohibited activities. Lack of experience and prior learning opportunities hamper youths' abilities to deal with new situations and new behavioral requirements. Sexual experimentation is an example. In national surveys, a significant number of 15- to 17-year-olds reported becoming sexually involved because it seemed to be expected of them and they did not know how to refuse (Cvetkovich & Grote, 1976). Lack of interpersonal skill is also implicated in teenagers' frequent nonuse of contraception (Kovar, 1979; Zelnik & Kantner, 1977). Research links failure to use contraception with failure to acquire critical assertive and communication skills (Campbell & Barnlund, 1977; Mindick, Oskamp, & Berger, 1978). These findings suggest that teenagers may know about and value birth control, but, embarrassed and lacking skill, they may be unable to obtain it or to negotiate its use with sexual partners.

A similar inability to resist external pressure and lack of skill in handling critical interpersonal situations has been associated with cigarette smoking and drug and alcohol misuse among youth (Roy & Shields, 1979). In short, a growing body of work suggests that practitioners can profitably focus prevention and health promotion efforts on teaching adolescents skills for coping with risk-related interpersonal situations.

Progress in preventing behavior that is detrimental to health is painfully slow (McAlister et al., 1979). Confusion exists as to what constitutes prevention education (Matus & Neuhring, 1979). Therefore, primary educational prevention programs are poorly supported through policy and funding (Broskowski & Baker, 1977). In addition, because preventive educational intervention is frequently poorly designed, with vague goals compounding the difficulties, prevention program effects are hard to evaluate, further diminishing the likelihood of public and legislative support. A new conceptualization is required if prevention and health promotion services are to become effective components of service systems (Kean, 1989).

An accurate database is available to provide rational and empirical support for the development of prevention and health education programs for adolescents. This is based on the Skills Training Interventive Model and the use of Teams-Games-Tournaments (TGT), a teaching method with a successful empirical history.

The Life Skills Training Interventive Model

The skills training model described here has rationale and elements in common with other preventive approaches based on a public health orientation (Caplan, 1964) and is variously called *graded pre-exposure* (Epstein, 1967), *immunization* (Henderson, Montgomery, & Williams, 1972), *psychological inoculation* (McGuire, 1964), *behavioral prophylaxis* (Poser, 1970, 1979), and *stress inoculation* (Meichenbaum, 1975). Whatever the label, the interventive goal is skill building to strengthen adolescents' resistance to harmful influences in advance of their impact. Three components compose this preventive model: health education, skills training, and practice applying information skills in troublesome situations.

Health Education. That adolescents need accurate information to make informed choices is clear. Equally clear is the inadequacy of simply exposing teenagers to facts about unhealthy consequences of certain behavior. One fault with past health education programs is their assumption that exposure to training materials guarantees learning. Information-only programs have had few long-lasting effects (Haggerty, 1977; Marsiglio & Mott, 1986). Accurate perception, comprehension, and storage of new information is a complex process dependent on individual receptivity and on the nature of the information presented (Mahoney, 1974). Particularly among younger adolescents, perceptual errors such as selectively ignoring, misreading, or mishearing certain facts or selectively forgetting information can create discrepancies between facts presented and facts received and remembered. The model proposed here addresses this potential problem by asking teenagers to periodically summarize presented content in written and verbal quizzes. Correct responses are then reinforced and errors detected and clarified. Also, peers are used as teachers, thus enhancing their commitment to healthy behaviors.

A second critical issue overlooked in traditional health education programs is helping youth relate specific facts about observable risks to themselves and to their own lives. Called *relational thinking* (Mahoney, 1974), this is the process by which abstract information becomes part of an individual's everyday reality. This relational or personalization process is best accomplished by actively involving adolescents in gathering and assimilating information. Examples include special information-collecting assignments (interviewing community resources and conducting minisurveys) and experimental exercises requiring verbalization of facts and choices in personal terms ("Each time I have sex and don't use birth control, I risk pregnancy"). Also helpful for information personalization are direct discussions of illusions and faulty thinking patterns used to conveniently ignore important health facts (e.g., "It can't happen to me"; "I can quit anytime I want to"; "I never have an orgasm, so I don't have to worry about getting pregnant").

Skills Training.   Even personalized information is of little value if adolescents lack the skills to use it. Translating health information into everyday decision making and behavior involves cognitive and behavioral skills. The model thus emphasizes skills for making effective short- and long-term decisions and assertive and communication skills needed to implement decisions.

Cognitive skills training is adapted from research on problem solving (D'Zurilla & Goldfried, 1971; Spivack, & Shure, 1974). Especially for adolescents, problem behavior is associated with peer norms and expectations. Realistic decisions about how to act must, therefore, consider responses of significant others. The ability to anticipate both interpersonal and health consequences of behavior, generate alternative action strategies, and arrive at the best choice are all crucial to health-promotive decision making. Again, training focused on sexual behavior provides an example. Following discussion of birth control advantages and disadvantages, adolescents anticipate possible difficulties using this information in social situations— for instance, not knowing when or how to initiate discussion of birth control with dating partners. The problem is examined in detail and major issues are identified, such as selecting appropriate times and places for discussion, handling personal embarrassment, and dealing with partner reactions. Adolescents generate several possible plans, specifying when, where, and how the discussion could occur. They predict the probable outcome of each plan and select the most feasible one.

Training also focuses on behavioral skills necessary to transform decisions into action. Based on established assertive and communication skills-training procedures (Lange & Jakubowski, 1976; Schinke & Rose, 1976), training presents verbal and nonverbal aspects of good communication to help adolescents learn to initiate difficult interactions, practice self-disclosure of positive and negative feelings, refuse unreasonable demands, request changes in another's behavior, ask others for relevant information and feedback, and negotiate mutually acceptable solutions.

Practice Applying Skills.   In the final and most important phase of the model, adolescents practice applying skills in a variety of potentially risky interpersonal situations. Extended role-played interactions provide adolescents with opportunities to recall and make use of health information, decision-making techniques, and communication skills, as in the following vignette. You are at a party with someone you've been dating for about 6 months. The party is at the home of someone whose parents are gone for the weekend. There is a lot of beer and dope, and couples are going into the upstairs bedrooms to make out. Your date says, "Hey Lisa and Tom have gone upstairs. It's real nice up there—let's go—come on."

In role playing, teenagers practice responding to increasingly insistent demands and receiving feedback, instructions, and praise to enhance performance. Practice in applying skills also takes the form of homework assignments involving written contracts to perform certain tasks outside the training environment—such as meeting with a family-planning counselor or initiating discussion of birth control with a dating partner.

Another example of applying skills is contained in the drug-refusal training aspects of the comprehensive health curriculum (Hawkins et al., 1989). The basic aim of drug-refusal training is to help students develop more effective ways of dealing with social pressures to consume drugs. Specific situations are practiced in which individuals apply pressure to persuade others to consume excessive amounts of drugs. Students practice reactions to statements such as: "One drink won't hurt you"; "What kind of friend are you?"; or "Just have a little one, I'll make sure you won't have any more."

Components of appropriate reactions are taught, such as: (a) to look directly at the pusher when responding, (b) to speak in a firm, strong tone with appropriate facial expressions and body language, (c) to offer an alternative suggestion such as "I don't care for a beer, but I'd love a Coke", (d) to request that the pushers refrain from continued persuasion, and (e) to change the subject by introducing a different topic of conversation.

Although all phases of the interpersonal skills training model can be conducted with individuals, groups provide the most efficient and effective training context for this final practice phase. Group settings allow teenagers to try out skills with various partners, give feedback and encouragement to each other, and learn from a variety of models.

The Teams-Games-Tournaments (TGT) Model

The most important socialization agent in adolescents' lives are their peers, with schools providing a natural environment for peer influence. Virtually all attempts to educate teenagers about health topics have taken an educational lecture model approach aimed at the general education of all teenagers. Nearly all instruction in educational techniques is aimed at the individual pupil, ignoring the potential usefulness of the peer group in motivating students to learn and to acquire new skills or behaviors. Evaluative data indicate, however, that the effectiveness of such an approach is minimal. Over the past three decades, a substantial amount of research has been conducted on learning groups. This research has suggested that learning teams in classrooms have uniformly positive effects on students.

The TGT technique, developed through two decades of research at the Johns Hopkins University Center for Social Organization of Schools, is an innovative, small-group teaching technique. The method is grounded in current theory; applies to diverse problems, populations, and settings; and provides clear criteria for evaluating program effects. The technique alters the traditional classroom structure and gives each student an equal opportunity to achieve and to receive positive reinforcement from peers by capitalizing on team cooperation, the popularity of games, and the spirit of competitive tournaments. Group reward structures set up a learning situation wherein the performance of each group member furthers the overall group goals. This has been shown to increase individual members' support for group performance, to increase performance itself under a variety of similar circumstances, and to further enhance the group's goals. The use of the group reward structure with adolescents is significant in that it capitalizes on peer influence and reinforcement, which are considered to be two of the most potent variables in the acquisition, alteration, and maintenance of prosocial behavior in youth (Buckholdt & Wodarski, 1978). Moreover, it facilitates learning among low academic achievers who have less attachment to prosocial norms and peers, a group that is at greater risk to develop health problems. Data indicate that TGT is a viable method for educating adolescents about health-related concerns. It has been found successful in helping children and adolescents acquire and retain knowledge in such areas as reading, arithmetic, and social studies, as well as in the health-related areas.

Peer relationships play a significant role in the adolescent's socialization and health behavior. Thus, the information is provided in a group context to help students practice necessary social skills to develop adequate behavior in regard to their health. Moreover, TGT capitalizes on the power of peers to influence the acquisition and subsequent maintenance of behavior. TGT capitalizes on peers as teachers, and this changes the normative peer structure to support healthy behavior and increases the attachment high-risk peers have to prosocial norms and peers (Buckholdt & Wodarski, 1978).

ISSUES

Family Intervention

Data indicate that parents whose adolescents are at risk of engaging in actions detrimental to their health face multiple social and psychosocial difficulties. The clearest empirical finding with regard to such adolescents seems to be the lack of consistency by the parent or parents in the handling of their child and the consequent lack of effectiveness in managing the child's behavior in a manner that facilitates his or her psychological and social development. It has also been pointed out that another common feature of relationships between parents and adolescents at risk is unrealistic expectations by the parents regarding appropriate behavior for their child (Howing, Wodarski, Kurtz, & Gauding, 1990; Patterson & Forgatch, 1987).

Another empirical finding of substance is the high degree of strain evident in families with children at risk. Family interaction patterns have been characterized as primarily negative; that is, parents engage in excessive amounts of criticism, threats, negative statements, and physical punishment, and a corresponding lack of positive interaction such as positive statements, praise, and positive physical contact (Zigler, Taussig, & Black, 1992). In view of this finding, a comprehensive prevention approach should include appropriate interventions that teach knowledge about the problems adolescents face, communication skills, problem solving, and conflict resolution to family members. Each intervention package must have an attractive and effective parent curriculum.

Timing of the Intervention

Recent research executed on various populations indicated that intervention should occur in the fourth, fifth, and sixth grades to psychologically inoculate children for the risks that they are going to face. All of the interventions discussed within this manuscript should be executed as early as possible. Ideally, booster sessions would occur as children move into junior high and high school. These booster sessions should include procedures for the maintenance and generalizations of behaviors such as training relatives or significant others in the child's environment, training behaviors that have a high probability of being reinforced in natural environments, varying the conditions of training, gradually removing or fading the contingencies, using different schedules of reinforcement, and using delayed reinforcement and self-control procedures (Wodarski & Wodarski, 1992).

Curriculum

Curriculum updates should occur periodically. Material that is included in the curriculum should be easily comprehended and presented in an attractive manner. All updates should include information that is relevant for the skills that are being acquired. Moreover, role-playing exercises that involve overlearning and repetition should be included. Such exercises make up the requisites of relevant curricula. The social skills training paradigm offers social workers an excellent procedure for preparing adolescents to live successfully in contemporary U.S. society. The curricula are particularly relevant to social group work since data indicate that peers play a strong role in the acquisition of either social or dysfunctional behaviors. The small-group learning techniques that are elucidated here capitalize on using peers as teachers. Thus, social workers are provided with viable techniques that can build on peer structures to help adolescents acquire necessary social behaviors to deal competently with the requisites of adolescent development.

CONCLUSION

Many prevention research programs have similar methodological complications: difficulty in adhering to a strict, randomized, controlled trial design; high attrition of participants; lack of documentation of fidelity in delivering the intervention; lack of multiple measures of outcomes from multiple sources; and insufficient long-term follow-up, which can prevent the collection of outcome data on the incidence of multiple disorders. In addition, there is wide variability regarding whether a program with positive outcomes will go on to field trials or be adopted as a service program, can provide good leads regarding intervention, and would profit from being evaluated experimentally.

Heller (1996) further argue that the mental health professions have created a trap for themselves by ignoring prevention and focusing exclusively on treatment. This is because treatment rhetoric fosters the illusion that societal problems are being solved. Yet, despite the statistics about the number of people who have been seen and helped by mental health services, most people eventually come to understand that increased treatment activity does not reduce the incidence of new cases of disorder. Although individual patients might benefit in the long run society as a whole is not better off as a result of this large investment. Thus the term for the implementation of an empirically based preventive approach is long past.

The alternative strategy, targeting interventions at persons who are at risk for mental disorders, has also been explored for both physical and mental health. The crucial advance is to recognize the links between this strategy and the universal strategy. In the Stanford heart studies, persons at high risk for heart disorder were recruited for more intensive face-to-face health training. Likewise, in the Baltimore study, children with attention difficulties were recruited for more intensive interventions. Indeed, the National Institute of Mental Health (NIMH, 1995) report noted that failure to respond to a universal intervention might itself be an important indication for including individuals in more intensive targeted interventions.

REFERENCES

Abel, E. L. (1984). *Fetal alcohol syndrome and fetal alcohol effect.* New York: Plenum Press.

Abel, E. L., & Sokol, R. J. (1987). Incidence of fetal alcohol syndrome and economic impact of FAS-related anomalies. *Drug and Alcohol Dependence,* pp. 51–70.

American Medical Association. (1991). *Profiles of adolescent health: Vol. 2. Adolescent health care: Use, costs, and problems of access.* Washington, DC: Author.

Armstrong, E., & Pascale, A. (1990). *Adolescent sexuality, pregnancy and parenthood. The Facts.* Washington DC: Center for Population Options.

Armstrong, E., & Waszak, C. (1990). *Teenage pregnancy and too-early childbearing; Public costs, personal consequences.* Washington, DC: Center for Population Options.

Behrens, M., & Ackerman, N. (1956). The home visit as an aid in family diagnosis and therapy. *Social Casework, 37*(1), 11–19.

Belsky, K. J., Lerner, R. M., & Spanier, G. B. (1984). *The child in the family.* New York: Random House.

Belvin, G. J. (1983). Prevention of adolescent substance abuse through the development of personal and social competence. In T. Glynn, C. Surkefeld, & J. Sudford, (Eds.), *Preventing adolescent drug abuse: Intervention strategies* (DHHS Publication No. [ADM] 83-1280). Washington, DC: U.S. Government Printing Office.

Broskowski, A., & Baker, F. (1977). Professional, organizational, and social barriers to primary prevention. *American Journal of Orthopsychiatry, 44,* 707–719.

Buckholdt, D. R., & Wodarski, J. S. (1978). The effects of different reinforcement systems on cooperative behaviors exhibited by children in classroom contexts. *Journal of Research and Development in Education, 12,* 50–68.

Campbell, B. K., & Barnlund, D. C. (1977). Communication patterns and problems of pregnancy. *American Journal of Orthopsychiatry, 47,* 134–139.

Caplan, G. (1964). *Principles of preventive psychiatry.* New York: Basic Books.

Carrol, W. (1989). *AIDS-related claims survey: Claims paid in 1989.* Washington, DC: American Council of Life Insurance Association of America.

Centers for Disease Control (CDC). (1991). Premarital sexual experience among adolescent women in the United States 1970–1988. *Morbidity and Mortality Weekly Report, 39*(51), 929–931.

Chavez, G. F., Cordero, J. F., & Boccera, J. E. (1989). Leading congenital malformations among minority groups in the United States 1981–1986. *Journal of the American Medical Association, 261*(2), 205–209.

Chilman, C. S. (1979). *Adolescent sexuality in a changing American society: Social and psychological perspectives.* Washington, DC: U.S. Government Printing Office.

Cook, J. (1989, November). The paradox of antidrug enforcement. *Forbes, 13,* 108–120.

Cvetkovich, G., & Grote, B. 1976, May, *Psychosocial development and the social problem of teenage illegitimacy.* Paper presented at the Conference on Determinants of Adolescent Pregnancy and Childbearing, Elkridge, MD.

Daro, D. (1988). *Confronting child abuse: Research for effective program design.* New York: Plenum Press.

D'Zurilla, T. J., & Goldfried, M. R. (1971). Problem solving and behavior modification. *Journal of Abnormal Psychology, 78,* 101–126.

Epstein, S. (1967). Toward a unified theory of anxiety. In D. Mahar (Ed.), *Progress in experimental personality research:* Vol. 4. New York: Academic Press.

Feldman, R. A., & Wodarski, J. S. (1975). *Contemporary approaches to group treatment.* San Francisco: Jossey-Bass.

Fitzgerald, S. (1989, May 16). Many go without prenatal care, city finds. *Philadelphia Inquirer,* p. 8.

Flick, L. H. (1986). Paths to adolescent parenthood: Implications for prevention. *Public Health Report, 10*(2), 132–147.

Flowers, J., Booraem, C., & Schwartz, B. (1993). Impact of computerized rapid assessment instruments on counselors and client outcome. *Computers in Human Services, 10*(2), 9–18.

Foreman, J. (1991, June 20). Care costs may nearly double by 1994. *Boston Globe,* p. 12.

Forrest, J. D., & Singh, S. (1990). Public sector savings resulting from expenditures for contraceptives services. *Family Planning Perspectives, 22*(1), 6–15.

Freedman, R. D. (1967). The home visit in child psychiatry: Its usefulness in diagnosis and training. *Journal of the American Academy of Child Psychiatry, 6,* 276–279.

Furstenberg, F. F., Jr., Brooks-Gunn, J., & Morgan, S. P. (1987). Adolescent mothers and their children in later life. *Family Planning Perspectives, 19*(4), 142–151.

Gilliam, D. (1989, July 31). The children of crack. *Washington Post.*

Glenn, M., & Kunnes, R. (1973). *Repression or revolution? Therapy in the United States today.* New York: Harper.

Goldfried, M., & Davison, G. (1994). *Clinical behavior therapy.* New York: Wiley.

Goldfried, M., Greenberg, L., & Marmar, C. (1990). Individual psychotherapy: Process and outcome. *Annual Review of Psychology, 4,* 659–688.

Goodstadt, M. S., & Sheppard, M. A. (1983). Three approaches to alcohol education. *Journal of Studies on Alcohol, 94*(2), 362–380.

Graycar, A. (1979). Political issues in research and evaluation. *Evaluation Quarterly, 3,* 470–471.

Grise, V. N. (1991, April). Economic importance of the U.S. tobacco industry. In U.S. Department of Agriculture, *Tobacco: Situation and Outlook Report* (pp. 30–34).

Guttmacher Institute. (1985). *Report on adolescent pregnancy.* New York: Author.

Haggerty, R. J. (1977). Changing lifestyle to improve health. *Preventive Medicine, 6,* 276–280.

Hamburg, D. A., & Takanishi, R. (1989). Preparing for life: the critical transition of adolescence. *American Psychologist, 44*(5), 825–827.

Harrison, D. F., Wodarski, J. S., & Thyer, B. A. (1996). *Cultural diversity and social work practice* (2nd ed.). Springfield, IL: Thomas.

Hawkins, J. D., Catalano, R. F., Jr., Gillmore, M. R., & Wells, E. A. (1989). Skills training for drug abusers: Generalization, maintenance, and effects on drug use. *Journal of Consulting and Clinical Psychology, 57*(4), 559–563.

Hawkins, J. D., Catalano, R. F., and Miller, J. Y. (1992). Risk and protective factors for alcohol and other drug problems in adolescence and early adulthood: Implications for substance abuse prevention. *Psychological Bulletin, 112*(1), 64–105.

Hebel, J. R., Fox, N. L., & Sexton, M. (1988). Dose response of birth weight to various measures of maternal smoking during pregnancy. *Journal of Clinical Epidemiology, 4*(5), 483–489.

Heller, K. (1996). Coming of age of prevention science: Comments on the 1994 National Institute of Mental Health–Institute of Medicine prevention reports. *American Psychologist, 51,* 1123–1127.

Hellinger, F. J. (1990). Updated forecasts of the costs of medical care for persons with AIDS. *Public Health Reports, 105*(1), 1–12.

Henderson, A. S., Montgomery, I. M., & Williams, C. L. (1972). Psychological immunization: A proposal for preventive psychiatry. *Lancet, 13,* 1111–1112

Hollis, F. (1972). *Casework: A psychosocial therapy.* New York: Random House.

Howing, P. T., Wodarski, J. S., Kurtz, D. R., & Gauding, J. M. (1989). The empirical base for the implementation of social skills training with maltreated children. *Social Work, 35*(5), 460–467.

Jackson, A. W., & Hombeck, D. W. (1989). Educating young adolescents: Why we must restructure middle grade schools. *American Psychologist, 44*(5), 831–836.

Jacobs, A., & Spardin, W. W. (1974). *The group as agent of change: Treatment, prevention, and personal growth in the family, the school, the mental hospital and the community.* New York: Behavioral Publications.

Kaigham, H. V. (1989, July). Substance abuse abuses: The bottom line. *Pension World,* pp. 16–19.

Kazdin, A. E. (1975). Covert modeling, imagery assessment, and assertive behavior. *Journal of Consulting and Clinical Psychology, 43*(5), 716–724.

Kean, T. H. (1989). The life you save may be your own: New Jersey addresses prevention of adolescent problems. *American Psychologist, 44*(5), 828–830.

Kovar, M. G. (1979). Some indicators of health-related behavior among adolescents in the United States. *Public Health Reports, 94,* 109–118.

Krauthammer, C. (1989, June 9). Worse than "Brave New World"; Newborns permanently damaged by cocaine. *Philadelphia Inquirer,* p. 11.

Lange, A. J., & Jakubowski, P. (1976). *Responsible assertive behavior.* Champaign, IL: Research Press.

Lindsey, E., Wodarski, J. S., & Streever, K. (1986). Assessing social agency functions: A model. *Journal of Behavior Therapy and Experimental Psychiatry, 18*(1), 51–60.

Lodge, J. H. (1987). *Drug and alcohol abuse in the workplace.* New York: Marcel Dekker.

Mahoney, M. J. (1974). *Cognition and behavior modification.* Cambridge, MA: Bellinger.

Malow, R. M., West, J. A., Williams, J. L., & Sutker, R. B. (1989). Personality disorders classification and symptoms in cocaine and opioid addicts. *Journal of Consulting and Clinical Psychology, 57*(6), 765–767.

Marsiglio, W., & Mott, F. L. (1986). The impact of sex education on sexual activity, contraceptive use and premarital pregnancy among American teenagers. *Family Planning Perspective, 18*(4), 151–162.

Massachusetts Department of Social Services. (1990). *Child abuse fact sheets.* Boston.

Massachusetts Task Force on Infant Mortality. (1990). *Unfinished business; Poverty, race and infant survival in Massachusetts.* Boston.

Matus, R., & Neuhring, E. M. (1979). Social workers in primary prevention: Action and ideology in mental health. *Community Mental Health Journal, 15,* 33–40.

Mayer, J. E., & Filstead, W. L. (1980). Adolescence and alcohol: A theoretical model. In J. Mayer & W. Filstad (Eds.), *Adolescence and Alcohol.* Cambridge, MA: Bellinger.

McAlister, A. L., Perry, C., & Maccoby, N. (1979). Adolescent smoking: Onset and prevention. *Pediatrics, 63,* 650–658.

McGuire, W. J. (1964). Inducing resistance to persuasion: Some contemporary approaches. In L. Berkowitz (Ed.), *Advances in experimental social psychology:* Vol. 1. New York: Academic Press.

McMahon, R. (1984). Behavior checklists and rating scales. In T. H. Ollendick & M. Hersen (Eds.), *Child behavioral assessment: Principles and procedures* (pp. 80–105). New York: Pergamon Press.

Meichenbaum, D. (1975). Self-instructional methods. In F. Kanfer & A. Goldstein (Eds.) *Helping people change.* New York: Pergamon Press.

Meyer, R. G., & Smith, S. S. (1977). A crisis in group therapy. *American Psychologist, 32,* 638–643.

Mickle, J. (1963). Psychiatric home visits. *Archives of General Psychiatry, 9,* 379–383.

Mindick, B., Oskamp, S., & Berger, D. E. (1978, August). *Prediction of Adolescent Mental Health.* Paper presented at the meeting of the American Psychological Association, Toronto, Canada.

Morrison, M. A. (1985). *Adolescence and vulnerability to chemical dependence, Insight 1.* Atlanta, GA: Ridgeview Institute.

Morrison, M. A., & Smith, T. Q. (1987). Psychiatric issues of adolescent chemical dependence. *Pediatric Clinics of North America, 34*(2), 461–480.

Moynihan, S. K. (1974). Home visits for family treatment. *Social Casework, 55*(10), 612–617.

National Center for Health Statistics. (1990a). Advance report of final mortality statistics 1988. *Monthly Vital Statistics Report, 39*(7), supplement.

National Center for Health Statistics. (1990b). *Health: United States, 1989* (DHHS Publication No. [PHS] 90-1232). Hyattsville, MD: Author.

National Center on Child Abuse and Neglect. (1988). *Research symposium on child neglect.* Washington, DC: Author.

National Institute on Drug Abuse. (1990). *National Household Survey on Drug Abuse: Main Findings 1988.* (DHHS Publication No. [ADM] 90-1682). Rockville, MD: Author.

National Institute on Drug Abuse. (1991). *National Household Survey on Drug Abuse: Population Estimates 1991.* (DHHS Publication No. [ADM] 91-1732). Rockville, MD: Author.

National Institute of Mental Health Committee on Prevention Research. (1995, May). *A plan for prevention research for the National Institute of Mental Health* (A report to the National Advisory Mental Health Council). Washington, DC: Author.

Office of Management and Budget. (1990). *Budget of the United States Government; Fiscal Year 1991.* Washington, DC: U.S. Government Printing Office.

Office of National Drug Control Policy. (1991). *National Drug Control Strategy: Budget Summary.* Washington, DC: U.S. Government Printing Office.

Office of Technology Assessment. (1985). *Smoking Related Deaths and Financial Costs.* Washington, DC: U.S. Government Printing Office.

Patterson, G. R., & Fergatch, M. S. (1987). *Parents and adolescents living together. Part 1: The basics.* Eugene, OR: Castalia.

Poser, E. G. (1970). Toward a theory of "behavioral prophylaxis." *Journal of Behavior Therapy and Experimental Psychiatry, 1,* 39–43.

Poser, E. G. (1979). Issues in behavioral prevention: Empirical findings. *Advances in Behavior Research and Therapy, 2,* 1–25.

Prendergast, T. J., Jr., Schafer, E. S. (1974). Correlates of drinking and drunkenness among high school students. *Quarterly Journal of Studies on Alcohol, 35*(1), 232–242.

Revkin, A. C. (1989, September). Crack in the cradle. *Discover,* pp. 62–69.

Richmond, M. E. (1971). *Social diagnosis.* New York: Russell Sage Foundation.

Rittner, B., & Wodarski, J. (1995). Clinical assessment instruments in the treatment of child abuse and neglect. *Early Childhood Development & Care, 106,* 43–58.

Rose, S. D. (1977). *Group therapy: A behavioral approach.* Englewood Cliffs, NJ: Prentice Hall.

Rossi, R. J., & McLaughlin, D. H. (1979). Establishing evaluation objective. *Evaluation Quarterly, 3,* 331–346.

Roy, T., & Shields, R. (1979). Alcohol education in school of social work. *Social Work in Education, 1,* 43–53.

Ryan, W. (1971). *Group therapy: A behavioral approach.* Englewood Cliffs, NJ: Prentice Hall.

Saloman Brothers. (1990). *Stock Research: Tobacco.* New York: Jan. report.

Schinke, S. P. (1978). Teenage pregnancy: The need for multiple casework services. *Social Casework, 59*(7), 406–410.

Schinke, S. P., Orlandi, M. A., Forgey, M. A., Rugg, D. L., and Douglas, K. A. (1992, July). Multicomponent, school-based strategies to prevent HIV infection and sexually transmitted diseases among adolescents: Theory and research into practice. *Research on Social Work Practice, 2*(3).

Schinke, S. P., & Rose, S. D. (1976). Interpersonal skills training in groups. *Journal of Counseling Psychology, 23,* 442–448.

Sherif, M., & Sherif, C. W. (1964). *Reference groups: Exploration into conformity and deviation of adolescents.* New York: Harper & Row.

Spivack, G., & Shure, M. B. (1974). *Social adjustment of young children.* San Francisco: Jossey-Bass.

Streever, K., Wodarski, J., & Lindsey, E. (1984). Assessing client change in human service agencies. *Family Therapy, 11,* 163–173.

Streissguth, A. P., Aase, J. M., Clanen, S. K., Randels, S. P., LaDue, R. A., & Smith, D. F. (1991). Fetal alcohol syndrome in adolescents and adults. *Journal of the American Medical Association, 265*(15), 1961–1967.

Thompson, D. (1990, June). Should every baby be saved? *Time,* p. 11.

Thyer, B. A. (1995). Effective psychosocial treatments of children: A selected review. *Early Child Development and Care, 106,* 137–147.

Travino, F. M., Mayer, M. E., Valdez, R. B., & Stroup-Benham, C. A. (1991). Health insurance coverage and utilization of health services by Mexican Americans, Mainland Puerto Ricans and Cuban Americans. *Journal of the American Medical Association, 265*(2), 233–237.

U.S. Bureau of the Census. (1990). *Statistical abstract of the United States, 1990* (110th ed.). Washington, DC: U.S. Government Printing Office.

U.S. Department of Health and Human Services. (1989). *Reducing the health consequences of Smoking: 25 years of progress. A report of the Surgeon General* (DHHS Pub. No. [CDC] 89-8411). Rockville, MD: Author.

U.S. Department of Health and Human Services. (1990a). *The economic costs of alcohol and drug abuse and mental illness; 1985.* Rockville, MD: Author.

U.S. Department of Health and Human Services. (1990b). *Seventh special report to the U.S. Congress on alcohol and health.* Rockville, MD: Author.

U.S. Department of Labor. (1992). *CP/ detailed report for November 1991. Bureau of Labor Statistics* (Report ISSN 0095-926X). Washington, DC: Author.

U.S. General Accounting Office. (1990a). *Defense health care: Effects of AIDS in the military* (CAO/HRD-90-39). Washington, DC: Author.

U.S. General Accounting Office. (1990b). *Drug-exposed infants: A generation at risk* (GAO/HRD-90-138), Washington, DC:

U.S. General Accounting Office. (1990c). *Health insurance: Availability and adequacy for small businesses* (GAO/T-HRD-90-33). Washington, DC:

U.S. General Accounting Office. (1990d). *Home visiting: A promising early intervention strategy for at-risk families* (GAO/HRD-90-83). Washington, DC:

U.S. General Accounting Office. (1991). *Canadian health insurance: Lessons for the United States* (GAO/HRD-91-90). Washington, DC: Author.

Wodarski, J. S. (1977). The application of behavior modification technology to the alleviation of selected social problems. *Journal of Sociology and Social Welfare, 4*(7), 1055–1073.

Wodarski, J. S. (1980). Procedures for the maintenance and generalization of achieved behavioral change. *Journal of Sociology and Social Welfare, 7*(2), 298–311.

Wodarski, J. S. (1995). Guidelines for building research centers in schools of social work. *Research on Social Work Practice, 5*(3), 383–398.

Wodarski, J. S., & Bagarozzi, D. A. (1979). *Behavioral social work.* New York: Human Sciences Press.

Wodarski, J. S., Hudson, W., & Buckholdt, D. (1976). Issues in evaluative research: Implications for social work practice. *Journal of Sociology and Social Welfare, 4*(1), 81–113.

Wodarski, J. S., & Wodarski, L. A. (1992). *Curriculums and practical aspects of implementation: Preventive health service for adolescents.* Lanham, MD: University Press of America.

Zelnik, M., & Kantner, J. F. (1977). Sexual and contraceptive experience of young unmarried women in the United States, 1976 and 1971. *Family Planning Perspectives, 9,* 55–71.

Zigler, E., Taussig, C., & Black, C. (1992). Early childhood intervention: A promising preventative for juvenile delinquency. *American Psychologist, 47*(8), 997–1006.

Chapter 2

CHILD MALTREATMENT

Peter Lyons

OVERVIEW

Our understanding of child maltreatment has increased markedly since the radiologist Caffey (1946) first noticed a correlation between multiple long bone fractures and subdural hematoma in infants. This was followed by Kempe's contribution, which focused attention on the battered child syndrome in the 1960s (Kempe, Silverman, Steele, Droegemueller, & Silver, 1962). Currently, the literature recognizes four major types of maltreatment: physical abuse, physical neglect, emotional maltreatment, and sexual abuse (National Association of Public Child Welfare Administrators, 1988). Child physical abuse and neglect, the twin foci of this chapter, are often coterminal, but independent, entities, with separate, though similar, etiologies and trajectories (Belsky, 1993; Lyons, Doueck, & Wodarski, 1996; McDonald & Marks, 1991). In reviewing the empirical literature on the treatment of physical abuse and neglect, one should make frequent distinctions between the two, (e.g., physical abuse as event, neglect as condition; physical abuse as commission, neglect as omission). However, the two are dealt with simultaneously here, as many studies have combined both types of maltreatment. In addition, physical abuse and neglect are often comorbid manifestations (Belsky, 1993).

Child maltreatment is a significant problem in the United States. Its significance derives from its prevalence and the serious consequences of maltreatment for individuals, families, and neighborhoods and for society as a whole. It has been suggested that child abuse is fundamental in three ways: first, it is correlated with a broad range of other social problems; second, it is a sensitive marker of the strength of the social fabric; third, it denies the worth of children (Melton & Flood, 1994). It is clear that for individuals there are very profound negative sequelae. These include psychological, social, academic, and emotional problems and deficits (Graziano & Mills, 1992; Howing, Wodarski, Kurtz, & Gaudin, 1989; Malinosky-Rummell & Hansen, 1993).

Incidence

When the battered child syndrome was first promulgated, it was estimated to be affecting about 300 hospitalized children (Kempe et al., 1962). This proved to be a gross underestimation of the true extent of the problem. Since the 1960s the number of reported victims of all types of maltreatment has steadily increased. By 1984, 1.7 million children were reported as victims, 2.4 million were reported in 1989, and 2.9 million were reported in 1993 (Ards & Harrel, 1993; Curtis, Boyd, Liepold, & Petit, 1995; McCurdy & Daro, 1993; National Center on Child Abuse and Neglect [NCCAN], 1988; NCCAN, 1995). Allowing for duplicated counts, an estimated 2.3 million individual children were subjects of report in 1993 (NCCAN, 1995). Of these, just over 1,000 were fatalities related to child maltreatment (NCCAN, 1995). Curtis and his colleagues have estimated, based on several national reports, that approximately 18,000 serious disabilities and 141,000 serious injuries arise annually from maltreatment (Curtis et al., 1995). In 1993, about 24% of victims suffered from physical abuse and about 48% from neglect (NCCAN, 1995).

Definition of Child Abuse and Neglect

This proliferation of reports is also a function of the malleable definition of the phenomenon. The Child Abuse Prevention and Treatment Act (CAPTA) of 1974, while establishing broad parameters for defining child abuse and neglect, gave autonomy to individual states to articulate their own definitions. Consequently, there is some agreement in extreme cases about what is and what is not child maltreatment. This precision fades, however, with the complexity of cases, in which decisions are often not between optimal parenting and abuse, but between shades of behavior (Howing & Wodarski, 1992).

Abuse has been defined as the degree to which parents may use inappropriate or aversive strategies to control their child or children; *neglect* has been defined as the degree to which parents provide little stimulation or structure or fail to provide minimal standards of nurturing and caregiving in the crucial areas of education, nutrition, supervision, health care, emotional availability, and general safety (Wolfe, 1987). This definition encapsulates the twin concepts of commission (abuse) and omission (neglect) that often characterize these two phenomena.

Hutchison (1990) has suggested that definitions of maltreatment have been developed to meet four interrelated purposes: social policy and planning, legal regulations, research, and case management. Confusion surrounding the definition of maltreatment is in part a function of the variety of competing explanations for its causes. It is generally recognized that maltreatment is multicausal and multiply determined, although there is no such agreement about the relative weight or combination of these multiple contributors (Lyons et al., 1996; McDonald & Marks, 1991). A recent review identified 46 causal models for child maltreatment

(Tzeng, Jackson, & Karlson 1991). The definitional consequences of these competing ontologies for the treatment of physical abuse and neglect are manifold. Selection of treatment is often determined by theoretical subscription or orientation, thus setting the parameters for intervention. In order to minimize these impediments, Wells (1994, p. 443) has suggested that a prerequisite for the future child protection research agenda is the development of "commonly accepted, sufficiently specific definitions of maltreatment and injury that can be used uniformly in the field."

ASSESSMENT METHODS

The nonunitary nature of child abuse and neglect suggests that they require multimethod, multisource assessment and intervention. There are also special circumstances surrounding the assessment of child maltreatment (e.g., social desirability in self-report measures and reactivity in observation), which reinforce the need to seek convergent findings across multiple sources. It is recommended that the clinician select from a variety of assessment procedures dictated by the unique features of each individual case.

The primary concern in any assessment of child abuse and neglect must be the assessment of immediate risk to the child. This is particularly salient in light of the finding from a review of 89 demonstration projects that one third or more of the participant parents maltreated their children while involved in treatment (Cohn & Daro, 1987). On occasion, the child or children must be removed prior to further assessment and treatment. Currently, several empirically derived risk assessment instruments are available (e.g., Baird, 1988; Johnson & L'Esperance, 1984; Weedon, Torti, & Zunder, 1988), although none of these has a sufficient level of predictive accuracy to allow for sole dependence in decision making (Lyons et al., 1996). In addition, these models have been derived to evaluate reports to Child Protection Services, rather than for use in a clinical setting, although they may provide a useful adjunct to clinical judgment.

Having addressed the initial determination of child safety, the objective of parenting assessment should be the determination of "functional parenting competencies" (Grisso, 1986; p. 201) based upon what the parent or caregiver understands, believes, knows, does, and has the capacity to do. This implies that, in addition to parental assumptions about child needs and their knowledge of parenting, the current and potential future behavior of the parent becomes central to clinical assessment. Furthermore, Belsky (1993) posits that "physical abuse and neglect are multiply determined by factors operating at multiple levels of analysis" (p. 427), thus suggesting that the developmental context, the immediate interactional context, and the broader context (community, culture, and evolution) should all be examined.

Structured Clinical Interviews

The modal form of clinical assessment is the interview, and to the extent that the factors raised by Belsky (1993) are addressed, this may be appropriate. However, as a vehicle for obtaining information in situations of family violence, the interview often suffers from respondent distortion, self serving, or social desirability bias and poor recall (Ammerman & Hersen, 1992). In an effort to guide clinicians in the assessment of abusive families, Ammerman and his colleagues devised the Child Abuse and Neglect Interview Schedule (CANIS; Ammerman, Hersen, & Van Haselt, 1988). This was originally developed for use with disabled children. However, it is designed to assess maltreating behaviors such as corporal punishment, physical abuse, and history of maltreatment, and is utilizable with the general population.

Structured interviews may also consist of various combinations of existing instruments. In choosing empirical measures, the clinician should have a clear understanding of the purpose of the assessment, the type of information required, the interventions available, and the family's strengths and cultural background, as well as the applicability of measures with diverse populations. A complete review of measures is beyond the scope of this chapter; however, Rittner and Wodarski (1995) have recently detailed many of the empirical assessment measures available for clinical use in child abuse and neglect. They categorized the measures under the headings parental assessment, child assessment, family level measures, marital assessment, environmental level measures, and ecological measures. They also provide information on the availability of each instrument and the length of time to administer.

Computerized Assessment Methods

The advent and availability of personal computers has made the collection and analysis of client information a much more accessible and flexible task. There are many computer programs available for clinical use; however, most do not have available psychometric information. Two measures with extensive psychometric information available are listed below; both are available in computerized format.

One measure of general individual and family functioning is the Multi-Problem Screening Inventory (MPSI; Hudson, 1990), which provides the clinician with a 334-item scale measuring 27 dimensions of family and individual functioning. Subscales addressing physical and nonphysical abuse, depression, self-esteem, partner problems, child problems, and family problems, as well as numerous other issues, are contained in this instrument.

A measure more directly focused on children is the Child Well-Being Scales (Magura & Moses, 1986) a multidimensional measure of potential threats to the well-being of children. The scales include both child and family measures and were originally designed as an outcome measure for child welfare services, rather than for clinical assessment. However, a computerized form of the scales has been in use as a clinical decision-making tool since the early 1990s (Lyons, Doueck, & Koster, 1995).

Self-Report Methods

In cases of child abuse and neglect there is an almost inevitable tendency to social desirability bias in self-report measures, deriving from the significance of assessment and treatment for the parent's future capacity to continue in the parenting role. This reinforces the need for triangulation in assessment to ensure accuracy and veracity. The Child Abuse Potential Inventory (CAPI; Milner, 1986), as well as being the most extensively researched instrument of its kind, has a validity index designed to detect biased or random response patterns. This 160-item inventory is intended to differentiate physically abusive parents from parents who are not abusive physically. The scale includes items related to distress, rigidity, child problems, family problems, unhappiness, loneliness, negative self-concept, and negative concept of the child. The CAPI is one of the few instruments available with published validation and cross-validation information. This measure also has cross-validated data available in Spanish translation for the abuse scale.

Although not yet as extensively researched as the CAPI, several other self-report instruments are worthy of note. The Parenting Stress Index (PSI; Abidin, 1986) is designed to assess the extent of parenting-related stressors. Although used more as a program evaluation tool, it has been used successfully with abusive parents. The Parent Opinion Questionnaire is an 80-item instrument that assesses the extent to which parents may hold unrealistic expectations about the developmental abilities of their children. Azar and her colleagues found significant scoring differences on this instrument with abusive as opposed to nonabusive parents (Azar, Robinson, Hekimian, & Twentyman, 1984).

Observation Methods

Several available observational procedures are designed to assess selected behaviors or qualities of the parent-child interaction. These include the 100-item Home Observation Measurement of the Environment (HOME; Caldwell & Bradley, 1978), which assesses the quality of stimulation in the child's early environment. Two versions of this instrument are available: for children from birth to age 3 and for children from ages 3 to 6. This scale consists of some self-report items; however, the majority are based on observation of the parent and child.

An observational system designed specifically to evaluate parent control strategies was developed by Schaffer and Crooke (1979, 1980). Examination of the parent-child interaction system using this model yields the classic, tripartite, antecedent child behavior–parent control–consequent child behavior model.

Some caution is merited in the use of observation measures, as they require extensive training for reliable use. In addition, many were developed for research, rather than clinical purposes. Even so, the items they reflect are often key to understanding the nature of the parent-child interaction. In a review of the research on variables that may affect parent-child behaviors during observations, Haynes and Horn (1982) noted that reactive effects may not preclude the validity of such assessments. In contrast, some research suggests that demand characteristics do impact observational assessment by depressing the frequency of negative interactions (Kavanaugh, Youngblade, Reid, & Fagot, 1988). Clearly, there is a need for caution in the interpretation of observational measures. Wolfe (1988) has suggested that this type of observation is most reliably performed in the family home or a structured setting such as a clinic, and that interactions should optimally involve the whole family, taking place over multiple sessions.

Rating Scales

The Childhood Level of Living Scale (CLLS; Polansky, Chalmers, Buttenweisser, & Williams, 1981) is a 99-item behavior rating scale developed as a measure for scaling the essential elements of child care and neglect of children under age 7. Subscales include positive child care, state of home repair, negligence, household maintenance, health care, encouraging competence, consistency of discipline, and coldness. This scale is particularly useful in assessing chronicity and severity of caretaking deficits.

Physiological Methods

Social desirability bias is less of an issue if physiological measures of arousal responses are used. Physiological measurements of arousal may be taken in response to audio- or videotaped material, or in vivo exposure to problematic child behavior, infant crying, and so forth (Frodi & Lamb, 1980). As an adjunct, to complement parent self-report, physiological measures may indicate underreporting or underrecognition of negative responses.

Family Strengths

The family or individual need concentration of many assessment measures means they are often deficit focused. This can tend to color the perspective of the clinician, as well as further stigmatizing already demoralized parents. Therefore, it is crucial that clinicians take into account the strengths and potential resources possessed by families. These may include interpersonal skills; affective involvement; supportive friends, family, and neighbors; motivation; or other compensatory characteristics. "Positive attributes provide a context for understanding the severity and implications of problematic parenting features, and they provide a basis on which future parenting competence can be built" (Budd & Holdsworth, 1996, p. 12).

EFFECTIVE SOCIAL WORK INTERVENTIONS

Unlike neglect, which is often a readily observable condition, child abuse is most often a private phenomenon. This makes it almost impossible to observe, at least until after the event. Consequently, most child abuse treatment programs are aimed at the amelioration of the correlates of maltreatment, such as parent-child conflict, anger, vulnerability to stress, and social isolation, rather than maltreatment per se.

Reflecting the multicausal nature of child abuse and neglect, many of the empirically validated interventions that follow consist of multiple components offered simultaneously, to parents, children, and families, in both group and nongroup settings. Additionally, many of the studies contrast two types of interventions (CBT and Multi-Systemic therapy, casework and play therapy, parent training and family therapy, etc.). Therefore, the following sections are divided between child-focused interventions, parent-focused interventions, and multiple-component interventions. However, overlap and duplication of one or other components has led to some arbitrary allocation based on the predominant component.

Child-Focused Interventions

Concern and some consternation have been expressed at the lack of research on children who have suffered child abuse and neglect (Fantuzzo, 1990). Graziano and Mills (1992) have argued cogently that there is a large body of literature on the treatment of the general population of those with childhood psychological complaints, which may be very similar to the complaints of those who have been maltreated, and that this expertise should be brought to bear on the needs of the maltreated child. The focus in child abuse treatment has generally been on the parents, with very little research directed toward the development of treatment interventions for children (Fantuzzo, 1990).

Although it is appropriate that parents should be held accountable for child abuse and neglect and that a significant proportion of societal efforts should be targeted at helping them alter their behavior, there seems to be an unreasonable and unacceptable paucity of research into the treatment needs of their children.

Even so, there are now a handful of studies, primarily therapeutic day treatment and peer-mediated social skills, that provide some preliminary guidance in interventive choice to redress the deficits sustained through maltreatment. In the first of several studies, Culp, Heide, and Richardson (1987) compared 35 maltreated children under age 6 with a matched control group. The treatment group had been in a cognitive developmental–based, therapeutic day treatment program for an average of 7.6 months. Posttreatment scores were compared across the groups with significant developmental differences in favor of the treatment. The posttest-only comparison is a relatively weak design to draw firm conclusions about the impact of the program; however, in the second analysis, pre and post scores for the treatment group were used and indicated significant gains.

In another of the Culp group studies, the perceived competence and social acceptance of a group of 17 maltreated children in day treatment were compared with those of a matched comparison group of 17 other children (Culp, Little, Letts, & Lawrence, 1991). The study reported significant improvement in perceived competence and social acceptance for the treatment group, as compared to their own pretreatment scores and the scores of the no-treatment group.

As is common with many studies of child abuse and neglect, other services were also provided to the parents of these children. While this is socially desirable, it makes for some difficulty in identifying the precise contribution made by individual components of the intervention.

In another series of child-focused studies, Fantuzzo, Jurecic, Stovall, Hightower, Goins, & Schachtel (1988) compared peer and adult social initiation procedures designed to increase positive social behavior in a sample of maltreated children. The sample consisted of 36 preschool children (28 boys and 11 girls) who either had experienced maltreatment (physical abuse or neglect) or were thought to be at high risk of maltreatment. The treatment conditions consisted of a peer-initiated social interaction, adult-initiated social interaction, and a control group. Each condition consisted of eight sessions over an approximate 3- to 4-week period. The peer condition was significantly more effective in improving positive social behaviors. One other finding of this study is worthy of note. The adult treatment condition was not superior to the control condition; in fact, the oral and motor responses in this condition were lower after treatment. This suggests that the positive initiation of the adults may have suppressed that of the participants in this condition.

Four withdrawn preschoolers who had been victims of neglect were treated in a related study (Fantuzzo, Stovall, Schachtel, Goins, & Hall, 1987). Using a combined reversal and multiple-baseline design, the authors assessed an intervention in which two maltreated children with high levels of prosocial behavior were trained to initiate positive interaction with the withdrawn children. The results indicated an improvement in prosocial behavior in both treatment and generalization settings.

In a study established to replicate these findings, Davis and Fantuzzo (1989) used an alternating treatment design with two withdrawn, non-maltreated participants, two withdrawn, neglected participants, and three, aggressive, abused participants. Using alternating play sessions with a peer and an adult, during the treatment phase, the peer and adults made programmed social initiations to the child. During the baseline and follow-up phases, no positive initiations were made, but confederates responded strongly to child-initiated play interactions. The neglected children made improvements in the level of their interactions. The aggressive children, however, ultimately showed improved interactions with adults, but showed an increase in noncooperative and hostile behavior with peers.

This latter finding highlights with some specificity the need for prescriptive treatments based on client characteristics. These programs also demonstrate some preliminary success in meeting child victim needs in relation to prosocial behavior, self-concept, and cognitive development. Services to children may also make some contribution to breaking the intergenerational transmission of abuse.

Parent-Focused Interventions

Parent Training.   The form of intervention for parents appearing most frequently in the empirical literature is parent training. This has been presented in videotaped demonstrations, discussion, modeling, and role playing and is allied with contingency contracts. Sessions often include information on human development, child management, and problem solving, as well as instruction, modeling and rehearsal, and self-control strategies (relaxation training and use of self-statements). The training is based on a social learning model targeted at problems in child management and child development, and in the literature has often been accompanied by home visits in order to facilitate generalization.

In an early study, Denicola and Sandler (1980) used a combination of parent training and self-control training with two minority families, in both of which the mothers had been charged with child abuse. They were able to demonstrate a reduction in aversive behavior and a corollary increase in prosocial behaviors evident at 3-month follow-up.

This was further developed in three studies by David Wolfe and his colleagues (Wolfe, Edwards, Manion, & Koverola, 1988; Wolfe & Sandler, 1981; Wolfe, Sandler, & Kaufman, 1981), which also utilized parent training. The first study (Wolfe & Sandler, 1981) used parent training and contingency contracting with three abusive mothers. Using a two-variable withdrawal design, the authors were able to demonstrate a reduction in high-risk interactions, stable at 3-, 8- and 12-month follow-up. In the second study (Wolfe, Sandler, & Kaufman, 1981), families who had been identified as at risk for abusive situations, following investigation or suspicion of abuse by a child welfare agency, received parent training. This was a controlled study in which the first group of families received the treatment and subsequent families were allocated to a waiting-list control group. Parent training was provided in 2-hour sessions on a weekly basis for 8 weeks. The control group received the standard package of services normally provided by the child welfare agency. Direct observation of the treatment group indicated improved child management skills. However, measures of child behavior and worker ratings did not indicate any differences, although none of the treated families had been reported or suspected of abuse at 1-year follow-up.

Some of the outstanding issues in this research—nonrandom assignment, pretest differences, small sample size, no follow-up comparison group—were addressed in an expanded version of this program (Wolfe et al., 1988). Thirty mother-child dyads, who were subject to supervision by a child protection agency, were randomly assigned to one of two conditions: The control group received information from the child protection agency; the treatment group received the same information and behavioral parent training.

Posttreatment, 3-month, and 1-year follow-up data were obtained. Results indicated that parent training was associated with reductions in child behavior problems as reported by the mother. Caseworker evaluations at 1-year follow-up also favored the treatment group. Interestingly, home observations of target behaviors did not confirm the gains reported by mothers or caseworkers. The authors point out that structured observation may provide more relevant and efficient information than unstructured observations of parent-child interactions.

One of the issues of concern in the treatment of child abuse and neglect is the impact of the legal system on therapeutic accessibility. Irueste-Montes and Montes (1988) examined the effects of voluntary versus court-mandated participation in a child abuse and neglect treatment program. The treatment for parents consisted of a weekly parent training group and, for the children, a therapeutic day care program. Based on pre and post improvements for each group, scored on an observational checklist, the authors concluded that both groups of parents increased the level of praise directed at the children, reduced their level of criticism, but continued to attend to their children's annoying behavior. In other words the court-ordered nature of some of the parents' involvement did not adversely impact their participation.

Brunk, Henggeler, and Whelan (1987) made a comparison of group-based parent training with multisystemic therapy. Multisystemic therapy is based upon the belief that behavior problems are both multiply determined and multidimensional (Brunk et al., 1987). As a result, the intervention in this study varied based upon individual family needs and strengths. Family therapy techniques, such as reframing, joining, and tasks aimed at family restructuring, were included in all cases. Many of the families also received parent education, information about appropriate expectations, marital therapy, advocacy services, coaching, and emotional support. This component was delivered in the family home. Forty-three families, from each of which at least one parent had been investigated for abuse or neglect, were randomly assigned to one of the treatment conditions.

Families in both conditions revealed reduced stress, reduced severity of problems, and fewer psychiatric symptoms. Multisystemic therapy was associated with more effective restructuring of parent-child relations. Parent training was more effective at reducing the number of identified social problems. It is interesting that the setting in which each of these components was delivered appears to have provided some secondary gain. For example, the group treatment condition appears to have been associated with improved social relations, and multisystemic therapy, delivered in the client's home, with greater generalization.

These interventions have demonstrated some efficacy in the remediation of high-risk and aversive behavior, child behavior problems, and criticism, as well as improving child management skills, increasing praise, and increasing prosocial behavior. What is more, many of the changes maintained through to follow-up, and none of the studies reported further incidents of abuse in this period. Training parents in the application of learning theory–based child management skills is the most widely reported empirical intervention. Building on this, other behavioral and cognitive-behavioral approaches have been applied.

Behavioral and Cognitive-Behavioral Interventions.   Whiteman, Fanshel, and Grundy (1987) reported a study with 14 people from a public agency who had "some credible evidence" of physical abuse and 40 people from a private agency who were thought to be at risk of abuse. Subjects were divided into four different treatment conditions and a control group. The control group continued to receive service from the agencies, but did not receive the treatment interventions, which were cognitive restructuring, relaxation procedures, problem solving, and a composite package consisting of all three interventions. Treatment took place in the client's own home and was provided by doctoral students, all of whom had graduate degrees in social work.

Results indicated that the composite treatment was the most effective in alleviating anger. However, the authors suggest that the relaxation technique might be omitted from the composite package, as individually it was the least effective. This treatment package is very encouraging, because the gains were made in only six sessions.

Another study that tested the efficacy of time-limited, cognitive-behavioral, group-based treatment is reported by Barth, Blythe, Schinke, and Schilling (1983). Parents who had been referred by the state child protection agency met for eight twice-weekly group sessions led by graduate social work students. A nonequivalent comparison group was recruited from a well-baby clinic; however, this group had some significant pretest differences. The comparison group did not receive the self-control training.

The parents were taught self-control training, consisting of early recognizing of cues to provocative situations, identifying the signs of anxiety or anger, pausing and taking deep breaths, employing alternative thoughts and actions, and rewarding their own self-coping behavior. This material was presented in a group format, with the self-control training consisting of several components aimed at increasing the number of calming self-statements. Another component was aimed at identifying and practicing actions that are not compatible with anger, and at relaxation training. One further component consisted of communication training.

Results indicated that social interaction was increased, although this is likely to have been an intended but secondary gain of the group format. Parents' evaluation of their own irritability, nervousness, and calm, as measured by a paper-and-pencil test, showed that the treatment-group anger levels declined more than those of the control group, although this is possibly explained by pretreatment differences. Similar differences were noted as measured by performance on role plays of parent-child interactions, with treatment parents demonstrating their ability to remain calm under provocation. However, as Wolfe et al. (1988) noted, there is no substitute for in-home, real-life observations.

A recent study (Kolko, 1996) combined the monitoring of high-risk behaviors during the course of treatment with a comparison of child and parent CBT and family therapy. Participants were randomly assigned to one of the two treatment conditions. CBT was provided for both children and parents by separate therapists using similar treatment protocols. Treatment for the children covered stressors and violence, coping and self-control, and interpersonal skills. The parent treatment included stress and the use of physical punishment, attributions, self-control techniques, and behavioral principles. The family therapy conditions emphasized family functioning and relationships, the enhancement of cooperation, motivation, and an understanding of coercive behavior.

In addition to 12 one-hour-per-week clinic sessions, each condition involved home sessions following every one or two clinic sessions. These home sessions provided the opportunity for review and application of the skills and knowledge developed in the clinic sessions.

Participants in this study consisted of 38 physically abused children from age 6 to age 13 and their caregivers. Twenty-nine of the families were referred by CPS. Results indicated that CBT parents and children reported less use of physical discipline during treatment and greater reduction in family problems. In addition, the average length of time until the first use of force or physical discipline was nearly twice as long for the CBT condition.

In a study designed to test the impact of a program to help abused children modify aggressive and increase cooperative behavior, Timmons-Mitchell (1986) reported on a sample of 16 physically abused children between ages 3 and 13 and their parents. Measures were taken after each session of the 15-week program. Treatment consisted of both cognitive and behavioral components designed to address self-awareness, empathy, behavior management, and developmental awareness. Weekly group meetings, lasting 2½ hours, in which the parent and child groups met simultaneously, followed a structured program of activities. Parental activities included learning to praise themselves and their children, learning time out as an alternative to physical discipline, stress reduction, and interpersonal skills. Activities for the children varied by age but included art activities, discussion of their fears of being abused, guidelines on how to keep safe, and suggestions for how to ask for help. Points were awarded based on the child's level of cooperation and ability to abide by simple group rules. The author reported an initial increase in aggressive behavior fol-lowed by a significant increase in cooperative behaviors.

A British study combining treatment for parents with treatment for children made a comparison between a focused casework approach and structured play therapy (Nicol et al., 1988). This theory-driven study used a randomized design with 38 families in which physical abuse had taken place. Through attrition, this was reduced to only 21 families by completion. Families were randomly assigned to each condition; treatment lasted 6 to 8 weeks, with three sessions per week for the focused casework group and two sessions per week lasting 2 to 3 months for the play therapy group. Focused casework was essentially behaviorally oriented, task-centered casework utilizing instruction, reinforcement by the therapist, mod-eling, confrontation, and problem analysis. The findings showed support for the use of the focused casework approach, which appeared to lessen coercive behav-iors and improve positive behaviors.

As is common with many studies of child abuse and neglect, these studies suf-fered from having dissimilar comparison groups and high rates of attrition. How-ever, they offer some promising directions for treatment, being associated with reduction in anger, greater self-control, reduced irritability, reduced coercion, and increased cooperative behaviors. In addition, there was some secondary gain in reduced social isolation, arising from the group format used in certain of the inter-ventions.

Parent Education.   A study by Golub, Espinosa, Damon, and Card (1987) used a video-based group format to provide parent education. The videotape, *Hugs and Kids: Parenting Your Pre-schooler,* consists of 13 episodes showing common parent-child interaction problems and several options for how to deal with them (Golub et al., 1987). Of the alternative endings, one is clearly inappropriate and likely to lead to violence.

Participants in this weekly program were largely clients who had been referred by the court because of abusive, neglectful, or high-risk behavior or because the child had been removed from the home for some other reason. Results of client response to a videotaped vignette indicated that, compared to a pretest, participants suggested fewer coercive strategies, more positive power responses, and a general reduction in proposed physical punishment. Although the results show that the par-ents learned something from the program, this does not measure whether the par-ents' actual behavior changed.

Ecobehavioral Interventions (Project 12 Ways).   In the treatment of child neglect, several studies from Project 12 Ways, a multifaceted, in-home assessment and treatment service, are worthy of note. Many of the interventions described to ameliorate neglect are, of necessity, very practical in nature; however, this should in no way detract from their contribution to improved well-being for the children involved. For example, in an effort to improve the personal hygiene and cleanliness of two children ages 5 and 9, the authors report the use of a multifaceted intervention (Rosenfield-Schlicter, Sarber, Bueno, Greene, & Lutzker, 1983). Several treatment phases involving different combinations of treatment (counselor visits, contingent allowance, laundry assistance) were compared with the normal routine in a single-system design. The phases that combined all three strategies produced the highest cleanliness score, assessed by teacher ratings.

Two studies that improved the home safety and cleanliness of client families utilized a treatment and education program also from Project 12 Ways (Tertinger, Greene, & Lutzker, 1984; Barone, Greene, & Lutzker, 1986). The first of these (Tertinger et al., 1984) targeted the reduction of hazards, such as poisons, fire, electricity, suffocation, and firearms. The program was generally successful in the reduction of serious hazards in the homes of six families. The treatment component in this study consisted of information about hazards and making them inaccessible to children, as well as feedback regarding the number and type of hazards present in the home. An elaboration of this program (Barone et al., 1986) used a 35-mm slide presentation, rather than the personalized educational component, as well as stickers, a home safety review manual, safety plates, and electrical tape. Using a multiple-baseline design across the homes and unannounced follow-up visits, the researchers were able to report zero hazards in each home.

A common feature of child neglect is the inability or unwillingness of parents to provide a clean enough home environment. Three families presenting with this problem were assessed using a specifically designed measure, the Checklist for Environments to Assess Neglect (CLEAN; Watson-Perczel, Lutzker, Greene & McGimpsey, 1988). In a successful effort to improve the personal hygiene and cleanliness of the families who had been adjudicated for child neglect, the authors established multiple baselines using various behavioral techniques, feedback positive reinforcement, and shaping. Following "several months of active intervention with each family" (p. 77) conditions in the three homes improved.

Application of a multifaceted, ecobehavioral approach to the prevention of child physical abuse has also been reported (Campbell, O'Brien, Bickett, & Lutzker, 1983). In-home treatment, consisting of stress reduction, parent training, and behavioral marital counseling, was assessed in a single-subject design and determined to be effective in reduction of the mother's migraine headaches and the development of a less coercive environment.

An overall examination of the ecobehavioral services provided by Project 12 Ways (Lutzker & Rice, 1984) looked at the reincidence and recidivism data from a random sample of former clients, compared with a sample of non-Project clients. Both groups were involved with CPS and had at least one previous incident of child abuse or neglect, or were considered at high risk for such behavior. Results of this study indicated that families who had received service from the Project were less likely to be reported for repeat incidents in the 1-year follow-up period. Services offered by the Project during this period included "parent-child training, stress reduction, self-control, social support, assertiveness training, basic skills" . . . "leisure time, health maintenance and nutrition," . . . "home safety" . . . "job placement," marital counseling, and alcohol referral (p. 520).

Social Network Interventions.   In an NCCAN-funded study, Gaudin and his colleagues assessed the effectiveness of social network interventions to reduce neglect, to increase the size and supportiveness of informal support networks, and to improve parenting knowledge and skills (Gaudin, Wodarski, Arkinson, & Avery, 1990/91). A culturally diverse sample of families from existing CPS caseloads, in which neglect had been verified, were randomly assigned to one of two conditions. The control group (36 families) received traditional agency services. The treatment group (52 families) received a multicomponent intervention consisting of: (a) direct interventions in the family members' existing relationships to improve the family support network, (b) mutual aid groups, (c) volunteers, (d) the development of relationships with "functionally adequate" (p. 105) neighbors, and (e) social skills training. The median intervention period was 10 weeks and the range was 2 months to 23 months.

Results indicated that the combination of the Social Network Intervention Program and intensive casework, advocacy, and case management was successful at 6- and 12-month follow-up in strengthening informal networks and in improving the parenting adequacy of low-socioeconomic-status (SES), neglectful families in both urban and rural settings. The authors stress that, although the research had initially posited the use of the program as an alternative to conventional casework, their experience with this program suggested that it would be more appropriately utilized as an adjunct to traditional services.

SUMMARY

The empirical literature on the treatment of physical abuse and neglect consists of several broad types: child-focused interventions aimed at social and cognitive development; parent-focused interventions, primarily behavioral and cognitive-behavioral; social network interventions; and multiservice or multicomponent treatments. However, the current empirical evidence is still preliminary. These studies contained numerous methodological weaknesses, often arising from the sensitivity and difficulty of research in this area. There was considerable variance in terms of how physical abuse and neglect were reported. This was also true for demographic characteristics of clients, referral source, and severity and duration of maltreatment. A major problem with several of the studies was the lack of follow-up to determine the maintenance of any change made in the treatment phase. The small sample sizes and absence of appropriate controls all contribute to a degree of healthy caution in selecting interventions. Differential dropout rates were also a major problem, as group differences may have been due to differences in the remaining participants rather than in the treatment itself. Unfortunately, but predictably, the extant research seems to indicate that those likely to remain in treatment are the most motivated and the least chronic child abusers (Johnson, 1988; Yates, Hull, & Huebner, 1983).

There are also significant gaps in our knowledge. For example, most of the studies involving parents were aimed at mothers, even though fathers and others are associated with significant numbers of abusive incidents (NCCAN, 1995). Nor were there any empirical interventions dealing with macrolevel or socioeconomic variables, although the multiservice and social network interventions may have something to offer in this regard in the future. Substance abuse and culturally diverse treatments are also noticeably absent. Even the intervention with the most empirical support (parent training) necessitates being able to specify the cause of maltreatment; also, the intervention recipient must be capable of learning the appropriate skills. As an illustration, none of these interventions is clinically tested with the seriously psychiatrically disturbed client. In fact, this was an exclusion criterion in many of the studies.

With the possible exception of parent training, the current state of the empirical literature makes it virtually impossible to determine the precise impact of individual treatment components. In addition, treatment success has been defined differently, often measured by the learning of a particular behavior, skill, or knowledge, rather than its utilization in a real-world setting, or by the assessment of future abuse. In essence, most of these studies focused on corollary outcomes and because none of these studies identified abuse as the dependent variable, there are no substantial conclusions to be drawn about which treatment eliminated abuse. Progress has undoubtedly been made, however, with behavioral and cognitive-behavioral interventions clearly emerging as the treatment of choice for many child, parent, and family-level problems associated with child abuse and neglect.

REFERENCES

Abidin, R. R. (1986). *Parenting stress index manual.* Charlottesville, VA: Pediatric Psychology Press.

Ammerman, R. T., & Hersen, M. (1992). Current issues in the assessment of family violence. In R. T. Ammerman & M. Hersen (Eds.), *Assessment of family violence: A clinical and legal source book* (pp. 3–10). New York: Wiley.

Ammerman, R. T., Hersen, M., & Van Hasselt, V. B. (1988). *The Child Abuse and Neglect Interview Schedule (CANIS).* Pittsburgh, PA: Western Pennsylvania School for Blind Children.

Ards, S., & Harrel, A. (1993). Reporting of child maltreatment: A secondary analysis of the national incidence surveys. *Child Abuse and Neglect, 17,* 337–344.

Azar, S. T., Robinson, D. R., Hekimian, E., & Twentyman, C. T. (1984). Unrealistic expectation and problem-solving ability in maltreating and comparison mothers. *Journal of Consulting and Clinical Psychology, 52,* 687–691.

Baird, C. (1988). Development of risk assessment indices for the Alaska Department of Health and Social Services. In T. Tatara (Ed.), *Validation research in CPS risk assessment: Three recent studies* (pp. 85–121). Washington DC: American Public Welfare Association.

Barone, V. J., Greene, B. F., & Lutzker, J. R. (1984). Home safety with families being treated for child abuse and neglect. *Behavior Modification, 10,* 93–114.

Barth, R. P., Blythe, B. J., Schinke, S. P., & Schilling, R. F. (1983). Self control training with maltreating parents. *Child Welfare, 62,* 313–325.

Belsky, J. (1993). Etiology of child maltreatment: A developmental-ecological analysis. *Psychological Bulletin, 114,* 413–434.

Brunk, M., Henggeler, S. W., & Whelan, J. P. (1987). Comparison of multi-systemic therapy and parent-training in the treatment of child abuse and neglect. *Journal of Consulting and Clinical Psychology, 55,* 171–178.

Budd, K. S., & Holdsworth, M. J. (1996). Issues in clinical assessment of minimal parenting competence. *Journal of Clinical Child Psychology, 25*(1), 2–14.

Caffey, J. (1946). Multiple fractures in the long bones of infants suffering from chronic subdural hematoma. *American Journal of Roentgenology, 56,* 163–173.

Caldwell, B. M., & Bradley, R. H. (1978). *Home observation for measurement of the environment.* Little Rock: University of Arkansas.

Campbell, R. V., O'Brien, S., Bickett, A. D., & Lutzker, J. R. (1983). In-home parent training, treatment of migraine headaches, and marital counseling as an ecobehavioral approach to prevent child abuse. *Journal of Behavior Therapy and Experimental Psychiatry, 14,* 147–154.

Cohn, A. H., & Daro, D. (1987). Is treatment too late: What ten years of evaluation research tell us. *Child Abuse & Neglect, 1*(3), 433–442.

Culp, R. E., Heide, J., & Richardson, M. T. (1987). Differential developmental progress of children in day treatment. *Social Work, 32,* 497–499.

Culp, R. E., Little, V., Letts, D., & Lawrence, H. (1991). Maltreated children's self concept: Effects of a comprehensive treatment program. *American Journal of Orthopsychiatry, 61*(1), 114–121.

Curtis, P. A., Boyd, J. D., Liepold, M., & Petit, M. (1995). *Child abuse and neglect: A look at the states.* Washington, DC: Child Welfare League of America.

Davis, S. P., & Fantuzzo, J. W. (1989). The effects of adult and peer social initiations on the social behavior of withdrawn and aggressive pre-school children. *Journal of Family Violence, 4,* 227–248.

Denicola, J., & Sandler, J. (1980). Training abusive parents in child management and self-control skills. *Behavior Therapy, 11,* 263–270.

Fantuzzo, J. W. (1990). Behavioral treatment of the victims of child abuse and neglect. *Behavior Modification, 14*(3), 316–339.

Fantuzzo, J. W., Jurecic, L., Stovall, A., Hightower, D., Goins, C., & Schachtel, D. (1988). Effects of peer social initiations on the social behavior of withdrawn maltreated pre-school children. *Journal of Consulting and Clinical Psychology, 56*(1), 34–39.

Fantuzzo, J. W., Stovall, A., Schachtel, D., Goins, C., & Hall, R. (1987). The effects of peer social initiations on the social behavior of withdrawn maltreated pre-school children. *Journal of Behavior Therapy and Experimental Psychiatry, 4,* 357–363.

Frodi, A. M., & Lamb, M. (1980). Child abusers' responses to infant cries. *Child Development, 51,* 238–241.

Gaudin, J. M., Wodarski, J. S., Arkinson, M. K., & Avery, L. S. (1990/91). Remedying child neglect: Effectiveness of social network interventions. *Journal of Applied Social Science, 15,* 97–123.

Golub, J. S., Espinosa, M., Damon, L., & Card, J. (1987). A videotape parent education program for abusive parents. *Child Abuse & Neglect, 11,* 255–265.

Graziano, A. M., & Mills, J. (1992). Treatment for abused children: When is a partial solution acceptable? *Child Abuse & Neglect, 16*(2), 217–228.

Grisso, T. (1986). *Evaluating competencies: Forensic assessments and instruments.* New York: Plenum.

Haynes, S. N., & Horn, W. F. (1982). Reactivity in behavioral observation: A review. *Behavioral Assessment, 4,* 369–385.

Howing, P. T., & Wodarski, J. S. (1992). Legal requisites for social workers in child abuse and neglect situations. *Social Work, 37*(4), 330–335.

Howing, P. T., Wodarski, J. S., Kurtz, D. P., & Gaudin, J. M., Jr. (1989). Methodological issues in child maltreatment research. *Social Work Research & Abstracts, 25*(3), 3–7.

Hudson, W. W. (1990). *The multi-problem screening inventory.* Tempe, AZ: WALMYR.

Hutchison, E. D. (1990). Child maltreatment: Can it be defined? *Social Services Review, 6,* 60–78.

Irueste-Montes, A. M., & Montes, F. (1988). Court-ordered vs. voluntary treatment of abusive and neglectful parents. *Child Abuse & Neglect, 12,* 33–39.

Johnson, W. B. (1988). Child-abusing parents: Factors associated with successful completion of treatment. *Psychological Reports, 63,* 434.

Johnson, W., & L'Esperance, J. (1984). Predicting the recurrence of child abuse. *Social Work Research & Abstracts, 20*(2), 21–26.

Kavanaugh, K. A., Youngblade, L., Reid, J. B., & Fagot, B. (1988). Interactions between children and abusive versus control parents. *Journal of Clinical Child Psychology, 17,* 132–142.

Kempe, C., Silverman, F., Steele, B., Droegemueller, W., & Silver, H. (1962). The battered child syndrome. *Journal of the American Medical Association, 181,* 17–24.

Kolko, D. J. (1996). Clinical monitoring of treatment course in child physical abuse: Psychometric characteristics and treatment comparisons. *Child Abuse & Neglect, 20*(1), 23–43.

Lutzker, J. R., & Rice, J. M. (1984). Project 12 Ways: Measuring outcome of a large in-home service for treatment and prevention of child abuse and neglect. *Child Abuse & Neglect, 8*(4), 519–524.

Lyons, P., Doueck, H. J., & Koster, A. J. (1995). Computerized risk assessment: Implementation of the Child Well-Being Scales. In T. Tatara (Ed.), *Eighth national roundtable on CPS risk assessment and family systems assessment: Summary of highlights.* Washington, DC: APWA.

Lyons, P., Doueck, H. J., & Wodarski, J. S. (1996, September). Risk assessment for child protective services: A review of the empirical literature on instrument performance. *Social Work Research, 20*(3), 143–152.

Magura, S., & Moses, B. S. (1986). *Outcome measures for child welfare services: Theory and applications.* Washington, DC: Child Welfare League of America.

Malinosky-Rummell, R., & Hansen, D. J. (1993). Long-term consequences of childhood physical abuse. *Psychological Bulletin, 114,* 68–79.

McCurdy, K., & Daro, D. (1993). *Current trends in child abuse reporting and fatalities: The results of the 1992 Annual Fifty State Survey (Working paper number 808).* Chicago: National Center on Child Abuse Prevention Research.

McDonald, T. P., & Marks, J. (1991). A review of risk factors assessed in child protective services. *Social Services Review, 65,* 112–132.

Melton, G. B., & Flood, M. F. (1994). Research policy and child maltreatment: Developing the scientific foundation for effective protection of children. *Child Abuse and Neglect, 18*(Suppl. 1), 1–28.

Milner, J. S. (1986). Assessing child maltreatment: The role of testing. *Journal of Sociology and Social Welfare, 13,* 64–76.

National Association of Public Child Welfare Administrators. (1988). *Guidelines for a model system of protective services for abused and neglected children and their families.* Washington, DC: American Public Welfare Association.

National Center on Child Abuse and Neglect. (1988). *Study findings. Study of national incidence and prevalence of child abuse and neglect: 1988 (DHHS# 105-85-1702).* Washington, DC: U.S. Government Printing Office.

National Center on Child Abuse and Neglect. (1995). *Child maltreatment 1993 reports from the states to the National Center on Child Abuse and Neglect.* Washington, DC: U.S. Government Printing Office.

Nicol, A. R., Smith, J., Kay, B., Hall, D., Barlow, J., & Williams, B. (1988). A focused casework approach to the treatment of child abuse: A controlled comparison. *Journal of Child Psychology and Psychiatry, 29*(5), 703–711.

Polansky, N. A., Chalmers, M. A., Buttenwieser, E., & Williams, D. P. (1981). *Damaged parents: An anatomy of child neglect.* Chicago: University of Chicago Press.

Rittner, B., & Wodarski, J. S. (1995). Clinical assessment instruments in the treatment of child abuse and neglect. *Early Child Development and Care, 106,* 43–58.

Rosenfield-Schlichter, M. D., Sarber, R. E., Bueno, G., Greene, B. F., & Lutzker, J. R. (1983). Maintaining accountability for an ecobehavioral treatment of one aspect of child neglect. *Education and Treatment of Children, 6,* 153–164.

Schaffer, H. R., & Crooke, C. K. (1979). Maternal control techniques in a directed play situation. *Child Development, 50,* 989–996.

Schaffer, H. R., & Crooke, C. K. (1980). Child compliance and maternal control techniques. *Developmental Psychology, 16,* 54–61.

Tertinger, D. A., Greene, B. F., & Lutzker, J. R. (1984). Home safety: Development and validation of one component of an ecobehavioral approach. *Journal of Applied Behavior Analysis, 17,* 159–174.

Timmons-Mitchell, J. (1986). Containing aggressive acting out in abused children. *Child Welfare, 65,* 459–468.

Tzeng, O., Jackson, J., & Karlson, H. (1990). *Theories of child abuse and neglect: Differential perspectives, summaries, and evaluations.* New York: Praeger.

Watson-Perczel, M., Lutzker, J. R., Greene, B. F., & McGimpsey, B. J. (1988). Assessment and modification of home cleanliness among families adjudicated for child neglect. *Behavior Modification, 12*(1), 57–81.

Weedon, J., Torti, T. W., & Zunder, P. (1988). Family risk assessment matrix: Research and evaluation. In T. Tatara (Ed.), *Validation research in CPS risk assessment: Three recent studies.* (pp. 3–43). Washington, DC: American Public Welfare Association.

Wells, S. J. (1994). Child protective services: Research for the future. *Child Welfare, LXXIII*(5), 431–444.

Whiteman, M., Fanshell, D., & Grundy, J. F. (1987). Cognitive-behavioral interventions aimed at anger of parents at risk of child abuse. *Social Work, 32*(6), 469–474.

Wolfe, D. A. (1987). *Child abuse: Implications for child development and psychopathology.* Newbury Park, CA: Sage.

Wolfe, D. A. (1988). Child abuse and neglect. In E. J. Mash & L. G. Terdal (Eds.), *Behavioral assessment of childhood disorders* (pp. 627–669). New York: Guilford Press.

Wolfe, D. A., Edwards, B., Manion, I., & Koverola, C. (1988). Early interventions for parents at risk of child abuse and neglect: A preliminary investigation. *Journal of Consulting and Clinical Psychology, 56,* 40–47.

Wolfe, D. A., & Sandler, J. (1981). Training abusive parents in effective child management. *Behavior Modification, 5,* 320–335.

Wolfe, D. A., Sandler, J., & Kaufman, K. (1981). A competency based parent training program for abusive parents. *Journal of Consulting and Clinical Psychology, 49,* 633–640.

Yates, A., Hull, J. W., & Huebner, R. B. (1983). Predicting the abusive parent's response to treatment. *Child Abuse & Neglect, 7,* 37–44.

Chapter 3

EDUCATIONALLY DISADVANTAGED CHILDREN

Catherine N. Dulmus
John S. Wodarski

Current school spending figures place the United States first in the world among industrialized countries in the dollar amount spent per child on public education (National Center for Education Statistics, 1991). Unfortunately, the United States also continues to lead other developed countries in rates of teen pregnancy, single parenthood, and poverty (Hobbs & Lippman, 1990). These problems, along with substance abuse, truancy, and violence in our schools place America's youth at risk of dropping out without obtaining the minimal education and skills that the job market demands of them today. Manning and Baruth (1995) state:

> The number of children and adolescents who are at risk today and the potential consequences of these learners being at risk are causes for educators' immediate concern and attention. There are many indicators of children and adolescents being at risk: They are dropping out of school without hope of future education or gainful employment; they are becoming parents and/or victims of sexually transmitted diseases; they are becoming addicted to drugs and alcohol; they are becoming lower achievers at all educational levels; and they are living in poverty, often with little hope of breaking out of poverty's confines. (p. 4)

Shanker (1994) reports that the biggest problem facing U.S. educators today is massive underachievement among all students throughout the system, at all levels. An April 1983 report entitled *A Nation at Risk* was released which warned that the United States is "menaced by a rising tide of mediocrity" in its schools and education system and that the nation had best make every effort to set matters right or it will be in serious trouble (Finn & Walberg, 1994).

Students in the United States continue to rank near the bottom of industrialized countries in achievement scores. The school-year length remains at 175 to 180 days, the shortest among industrialized nations even though research supports a longer school year. Adjusting for inflation, per-student costs have increased more than fivefold between 1940 and 1990, from $878 to $5,292 (National Center for Education Statistics, 1991), with less advantageous student outcomes for the investment.

Children who do not complete their high school educations have disadvantages in a high-tech society such as that of the United States. Although a variety of risk factors are associated with dropping out of school, this chapter's discussion is limited to the following: underachievement, truancy, teen pregnancy, substance abuse, juvenile violence, and poverty. In addition, empirically based interventions are discussed.

OVERVIEW

Public schools in the United States were instituted after the War of Independence by political and educational leaders of the time in order to educate the new nation's children to assume the responsibilities of citizenship in a democracy (Goodlad, 1994). The U.S. Constitution leaves to the states the responsibility for developing and guiding public education. This has resulted in great variability in the programs and practices of the thousands of schools in the United States, with certain school districts providing better education than others for their students.

School conditions must be considered when examining educationally disadvantaged children. Sometimes school conditions can actually create disadvantages for at-risk students through inappropriate instruction, competitive learning environments, ability grouping, and hostile classroom environments (Manning & Baruth, 1995).

Societal factors also contribute to the problem, as children and adolescents are often pushed to engage in adult behaviors and consumer habits. The tendency of U.S. society to be racist and sexist and to discriminate against culturally diverse groups, females, and people with disabilities adds to the educational disadvantages of these children and adolescents. Personal factors associated with educational disadvantages on the part of an individual student might include a lower self-concept, a lower ability level, a lack of motivation, and a decision to experiment with drugs and alcohol (Manning & Baruth, 1995)

Certainly social workers are concerned about educationally disadvantaged children. School social workers' days are often spent addressing problems that interfere with student learning among such children. Educationally disadvantaged children fill social workers' caseloads in a variety of social work settings. Often, many of the adults social workers encounter were once educationally disadvantaged children themselves.

DROPPING OUT OF SCHOOL

Experts increasingly realize that completion of high school is the absolute minimum educational level necessary to prepare youngsters for the vast majority of jobs in the modern U.S. economy. During 1988, 11% of students older than age 14 dropped out of school (U.S. Bureau of the Census, 1990). Muha and Cole (1991) report that each year's high school dropouts cost $296 billion in lost productivity and forgone taxes during the course of their lifetimes. The unemployment rate for those who drop out is more than 25% and, of those who find employment, two thirds earn only minimum wage (Muha & Cole, 1991). There is an overrepresentation among school dropouts of students from some minority groups, which has contributed to growing concern that large segments of the U.S. population may be isolated from mainstream social, political, and economic life if they fail to attain the basic education represented by the high school diploma (Natriello, 1995).

Natriello (1995) reports that factors associated with dropping out of school are many, but can be classified by at least three different types of antecedents: characteristics of individual students, characteristics of their schools, and the wider environments in which both the students and the schools exist. Characteristics of individuals that can be linked to nonattendance at school include racial and ethnic minority status, poor school performance, low self-esteem, low socioeconomic status, delinquency, a history of substance abuse, pregnancy, a non-English-speaking family, a single-parent family, and a family that is less involved in the educational process (Ekstrom, Goerta, Pollack, & Rock, 1986; Rumberger, 1983).

The United States has a dropout rate of 700,000 children per year (Karlsberg, 1989). Smith (1988) estimates that 12 million youngsters will become high school dropouts by the year 2000. The implications are serious. Students who drop out are five times more likely to face unemployment than those with diplomas (U.S. Census Bureau, 1989), and those from diverse cultures fare even worse in the job market (Muha & Cole, 1991).

The following section examines specific risk factors associated with an increase in the number of children who drop out of school, becoming educationally disadvantaged youth.

RISK FACTORS

Underachievers

As previously stated, the achievement scores of students in the United States continue to rank near the bottom among those of students from industrialized countries. Underachievement, or failing to achieve at one's potential, is a common problem facing both students at risk for educational disadvantages and their educators (Manning & Baruth, 1995). In 1985, 30.3% of 15-year-old males and 25.2% of 15-year-old females were one or more grade level behind in school (Children's Defense Fund, 1988). Murphy (1990) reports that 18% of U.S. high school seniors read at least 4 years below grade level, approximately 13% of 17-year-olds may be functionally illiterate, and 50% of 13-year-olds do not have a good grasp of elemental scientific concepts. Among high school seniors, nearly 40% lack the ability to draw logical inferences from written material, 20% cannot write a persuasive essay, and 33% cannot correctly solve multistep mathematical problems. Up to 20% of all students are retained in grade at least once at some time in their school careers (Meisels & Liaw, 1993), and, on average, 25% of students drop out of high school (National Center for Education Statistics, 1991). Underachieving students who do not learn to their potential are often educationally disadvantaged children. They do not acquire the necessary knowledge and skills to be gainfully employed upon graduating from school, which negatively impacts their future.

Poverty

The United States has the highest poverty rate of all industrialized nations. More than 12 million children in the United States, or about 1 in 5, is poor, and this number is likely to grow. Children are about twice as likely as any other group to be poor (Children's Defense Fund, 1991). Children and adolescents in female-headed families are five times as likely to be poor than those in married-couple families. Slightly more than half of all poor children now live in families headed by females (Children's Defense Fund, 1991). One fourth of the children in the United States spent part or all of their early, developmentally critical years living in poverty (Erwin, 1996).

The task of educating children of poverty has long been recognized as difficult. Knapp and Shields (1990) state:

> Many of these children and adolescents perform poorly on academic tasks. Likewise, the school, serving large numbers of these children and adolescents, faces a variety of problems that pose barriers to providing high-quality education such as high rates of mobility among learners' families, a high prevalence of severe emotional and behavioral problems among students, large number of students with limited English proficiency, low staff morale, and inadequate facilities and resources. (p. 19)

It is no wonder that poor teenagers are three times more likely to drop out of school than nonpoor teenagers (Children's Defense Fund, 1991).

Teen Pregnancy

About half of American teenagers are sexually active by the time they leave high school, and one in four young women has experienced a pregnancy (Kenny, 1987). Between 1960 and 1992, the birth rate for American teenagers rose nearly 200% (Schinke, 1997). It was estimated in 1985 that roughly 1 million teenage girls become pregnant every year, resulting in 600,000 live births and 378,500 pregnancies terminated by abortion (Guttmacher Institute, 1985). Presently, 1 in 10 babies is born to an unmarried teenage mother in the United States (Center for the Study of Social Policy, 1993). American teenagers under age 15 are 15 times more likely to give birth than their peers in other Western nations (Buie, 1987).

Schinke (1997) reports the social costs of teenage childbearing and parenthood as tremendous, stating, "Teenage mothers have more health problems, attain less education, and realize lower wages" (p. 5). Of unmarried teens who give birth, 73% will be on welfare within 4 years (Carnegie Council on Adolescent Development, 1989). Barth, Middleton, and Wagman (1989) summarized the evidence on youth pregnancy, stating that 20% of all teens have unintended pregnancies, with teenage pregnancy remaining the major reason for students leaving school. Eighty percent of all teenage mothers report that their pregnancies were not wanted.

Teenage mothers are more likely to become welfare recipients, less likely to finish high school, and less likely to marry than other women (Ellwood, 1988). Forty-seven percent of girls who drop out of school because they are pregnant never return to school (Schorr, 1988). When adolescents' schooling is disrupted by pregnancy, their financial futures are limited not only for themselves, but also for their offspring.

Juvenile Violence

The United States has the highest homicide rate in the world (Fingerhut & Kleinman, 1990). Each day in the United States, 9 children are murdered, 30 children are wounded with guns, and 307 children are arrested for violent crimes (Children's Defense Fund, 1993). Children and adolescents are twice as likely as adults to be victims of crime (Manning & Baruth, 1995). One survey found that from 1982 to 1984, youths from age 12 to age 19 were the victims of 1.8 million violent crimes and 3.7 million thefts per year (Vandrer Zanden, 1989). The Office of Technology Assessment (1991) reports that adolescents in the United States are more likely to be victims of violent crimes than individuals from other age groups.

In recent years, youths age 18 and younger have accounted for about 20% of all arrests for violent crime in the United States, 44% of all arrests for serious property violations, and 39% of overall arrests for serious crime (Manning & Baruth, 1995). Earls (1994) reports that 20% of all adolescents report having engaged in at least one violent act prior to age 18. Incidents of violence committed by adolescents have now become almost routine and commonplace (Rapp & Wodarski, in press). How does this increase in juvenile violence impact education in U.S. schools?

Manning & Baruth (1995) report that approximately 28,200 students are physically attacked in U.S. secondary schools each month. In addition, almost 8% of middle school and high school students missed at least 1 day of school per month because they were afraid to go to school. About one third of all violent crimes against younger teenagers and 83% of the thefts occur in school, whereas older teenagers are the victims of 14% of the violent crime and 42% of the thefts at school (Vandrer Zanden, 1989). How can young people focus on achieving an education when they are victims or perpetrators of violence in their schools?

Truancy

Truancy is defined as an unlawful absence from school without the parents' knowledge or permission (Hersov & Berg, 1980). Schultz (1987) defines truancy as excessive unexcused absences. Truancy directly affects students, educational institutions, and society in general (Bell, Rosen, & Dynlacht, 1994). It is estimated that 10% to 19% of school children are truant (Sommer, 1985). Rood (1989) reports that on a given Monday, the average absence rate in many urban high schools is 73%.

The most obvious and immediate implication of truancy is reflected in the truant's academic deficits. If students are not attending school, it is virtually impossible for them to receive the instruction they need to earn passing grades and graduate from high school (Bell et al., 1994). Also associated with truancy are juvenile criminal behavior, loitering, vandalism, and drug and alcohol abuse (Schultz, 1987). Truancy is further associated with lower status occupations, less stable career patterns, and more unemployment in adulthood (Gray, Smith, & Rutter, 1980). Truancy is highly correlated with school dropout rates (Rutter, Maugham, Mortimore, & Ouston, 1979).

Substance Abuse

The use and abuse of alcohol and other drugs by adolescents are significant problems today and continue to drain communities in the United States of human potential and financial resources (Johnson, O'Mallery, & Bachman, 1994). In 1988, 6% of 12- to 17-year-olds consumed alcohol daily, 4% used marijuana daily, and 0.5% used cocaine daily (American Medical Association, 1991). In a recent national survey, 51% of high school seniors reported using alcohol in the past 30 days (Johnson, O'Malley, & Bachman, 1994).

Substance use among adolescents appears to be influenced by a multitude of factors, including peers, family, school environment, and community. Education-related risk factors for substance abuse include poor school performance and lack of commitment to school (Hawkins, Catalano, & Miller 1992), low perceived expectations for education or career options, the marginal quality of the educational environment, and limited access to educational and career options (Dryfoos, 1990).

EFFECTIVE INTERVENTIONS

Educationally disadvantaged children should be assessed for identified risk factors, and empirically proven interventions, as they exist, should be carried out (Dulmus

& Wodarski, 1996). To date, preventive interventions to address many risk factors are suggested by the literature. The prevention approach to intervention has implications for the traditional role of social work practitioners and the timing of the intervention (Wodarski, Smokowski, & Feit, 1996). The prevention approach places major emphasis on the teaching and skills-building components of the intervention process (Wodarski & Bagarozzi, 1979). Social workers do not take a passive role in the intervention process, but instead attempt to help clients learn how to exert control over their own behaviors and over the environments in which they live (Wodarski et al., 1996). Prevention is especially appropriate to dealing with the problems of adolescence. The following section reviews prevention approaches to handling the issues of poverty, teen pregnancy, juvenile violence, truancy, and substance abuse as they affect educationally disadvantaged children.

Poverty

The best single predictor of future academic performance is early academic performance. Prevention of learning problems depends on early intervention and should occur before children from low-income households, who are at greater risk for such problems, reach elementary school (Durlak, 1995). Head Start, an early education program targeted for preschool children living in poverty, has been successful in addressing academic problems associated with poverty (Arnold, 1990). Head Start is based on encouraging or developing the inherent adaptive abilities of children. A multicomponent program, it includes early childhood education, home visits, parenting education, and socialization, which may assist some children in developing or maintaining resiliency. Even Start, a recent federally funded demonstration project, is a family literacy program that holds promise for children and families from disadvantaged backgrounds. Although it is similar to Head Start, it is more comprehensive and intensive, working with the entire family until the youngest child reaches age 8. This provides long-term programming and support to vulnerable children and their families (Dulmus & Wodarski, 1997).

Teen Pregnancy

Schinke (1997) reports that, to date, most teen pregnancy prevention programs have been ineffective. Although programs have focused on trying to help teenagers avoid unprotected intercourse in an attempt to delay childbearing, a report from the U.S. General Accounting Office (1995) concludes that teen pregnancy prevention programs have not been successful in preventing first or subsequent pregnancies.

Effective school-based prevention programs identified by Kirby et al. (1994) share five common components: (a) focusing on behavioral goals that lead to pregnancy prevention, (b) using learning principles to guide intervention, (c) informing youths about risks and prevention of unprotected intercourse through experiential activities, (d) addressing social and media influences, and (e) reinforcing norms against unprotected sex. Each of these components, combined with cognitive-behavioral approaches, such as educational materials and skills-building exercises, has had limited success in teen pregnancy prevention programs.

Schinke (1997) states, "New directions are needed to meet the challenges of reaching, engaging, and impacting today's youth with pregnancy prevention content" (p. 8). He further states that teen pregnancy involves multiple dimensions that require multiple solutions. He suggests that matching prevention programs to different adolescent populations, grouped according to risk, may hold greater promise. Further research is necessary to develop such programs.

Juvenile Violence

Both micro and macro approaches are currently recommended to address risk factors associated with juvenile violence. On a micro level, Wodarski and Hedrick (1987) provide an interdisciplinary preventive practice approach, which utilizes an educational, behavioral, and cognitive model that targets fourth- and fifth-grade students. It combines individual, family, and school in a school-based model that targets known risk factors for juvenile violence. The model has four major components: cognitive anger control, problem-solving strategies, peer skills development, and substance abuse education. Additionally, it has a parental component that further strengthens this model.

Rapp and Wodarski (in press) report that individual and family interventions will do little to ameliorate juvenile violence without the help of the community, which necessitates the need for macro interventions also. They recommend after-school recreational activities, sports clinics, job skills and training workshops, educational tutoring, and social activities as means of prevention. The use of metal detectors and an increase in security personnel in schools have been shown to decrease the incidence of weapons possession and conflicts between students (Wilson & Howell, 1995). Additional recommended macro approaches to prevent juvenile violence include community policing and legislation specific to the sale and possession of firearms (Rapp & Wodarski, in press).

Truancy

Because truancy is a problem with multiple causes and impacts, interventions for truant behavior have been targeted at three areas: the individual truant, the family of the truant, and the educational institution (Bell et al., 1994).

Individual interventions to date have targeted low self-esteem, conduct disorders, nonconformist behaviors, lower academic abilities and lack of motivation (Bell et al., 1994). In-school suspension incorporating counseling, writing therapy, and contingency contracting (Miller, 1986) and supportive instruction (Grala & McCauley, 1976) have been shown to improve school attendance and attitudes toward school.

A family intervention typically attempts to either alter a dysfunctional family situation or simply achieve more parental involvement in the child's education (Bell et al., 1994). School-based interventions have decreased truancy through lottery systems for perfect attendance (Rogers, 1980), contingency contracting (Brooks, 1974), and revised attendance policies (Duckworth, 1988). It is important that any truancy prevention program be multimodal, incorporating the individual, the family, and the school.

Substance Abuse

Although some progress has been made in the prevention of adolescent substance abuse, the problem remains a critical one for society (Wodarski & Smyth, 1994). When concentrating on the prevention of adolescent substance abuse, it is essential that intervention goals be clearly defined and that an appropriate target audience for intervention be selected (Bukoski, 1991). Programs would be more successful if they emphasized early intervention, drug resistance skills training, parent involvement, peer involvement, healthy school climate, social and life skills training, and communitywide planning, intervention, and coordination (Schinke, Botvin, & Orlandi, 1991). In addition, current research points toward a prevention model that is a multifaceted, ecological approach to dysfunctional adolescent behavior as holding much promise (Norman & Turner, 1993).

Because children and adolescents spend the major portion of their youth in the school setting, schools may be the sensible place to implement prevention programs (Wodarski & Smyth, 1994). A unique adolescent education program that is easily administered in a school setting is Teams-Games-Tournaments, or TGT (Wodarski, 1988). The TGT technique is an innovative, small-group teaching technique. Research (Chambers & Abrami, 1991; Niehoff & Mesch, 1991; Wodarski, 1988) has shown the TGT method to be a highly effective prevention strategy for alcohol and drug abuse. The TGT technique has been developed and proven an effective classroom method for adolescents. According to the developer, and supported by research data, TGT is especially helpful in teaching adolescents about behavior that puts them at high risk for educational disadvantage. It is also helpful in teaching adolescents how to make better decisions regarding these behaviors. Using the TGT technique, all students have an opportunity to succeed because all students compete against members of other teams who are at similar achievement levels. Points earned by low achievers are just as valuable to the overall team as points earned by high achievers. By using peer influence in a positive way (Swadi & Zeitlin, 1988), TGT capitalizes on one of the primary elements in an adolescent's life, thereby increasing social attachments and facilitating the acquisition of knowledge and behavior change (Wodarski & Wodarski, 1993). When compared with those receiving traditional instruction or no instruction, participants in the TGT method achieved superior results on the self-report indexes; they increased their drug and alcohol knowledge; and they showed a reduction in drinking behavior, positive shifts relating to drinking and driving, reduced impulsivity, and improved self-concept (Wodarski, 1988).

Macro approaches are also necessary in the prevention of substance abuse among youth. Raising the alcohol purchase age to 21 has resulted in a decrease in alcohol-related highway deaths to date among both adults and youth. Data suggest that in states where a lower blood-alcohol limit for adolescent drinking drivers has been legislated, alcohol-related crashes among youth have decreased (Hingson, 1993).

The literature indicates that a multifaceted, comprehensive approach to substance abuse among youth, incorporating multiple systems, is recommended.

CONCLUSION

Schorr (1988) states, "In today's world, a youngster who leaves school unable to read, write, and do simple arithmetic faces a bleak future. When a substantial proportion of boys and girls leave school uneducated, the rest of us face a bleak future too" (p. 7). Not completing high school results in decreased long-term income and lack of employment opportunities.

Many adolescents are not completing high school today for a variety of reasons. Others are graduating but lack the necessary literacy skills to obtain gainful employment. The impact this has on both the individual and society as a whole is astounding. Multifaceted prevention programs are recommended to address many of the risk factors associated with educationally disadvantaged children, in an attempt to decrease the number of students who drop out of school and to increase the literacy skills among our youth. Social workers must continue to address the risk factors associated with educationally disadvantaged children in the United States and develop empirically based interventions to assist their young clients.

REFERENCES

American Medical Association. (1991). *Profiles of adolescent health: Vol. 2. Adolescent health care: Use, costs, and problems of access.* Washington, DC: Author.

Arnold, E. L. (1990). *Childhood stress.* New York: Wiley.

Barth, R. P., Middleton, K., & Wagman, E. (1989). A skill building approach to preventing teenage pregnancy. *Theory Into Practice, 28*(3), 183–190.

Bell, A. J., Rosen, L. A., & Dynlacht, D. (1994). Truancy intervention. *The Journal of Research and Development in Education, 27*(3), 203–211.

Brooks, B. D. (1974). Contingency contracts with truants. *Personal and Guidance Journal, 52,* 316–320.

Buie, J. (1987). Teen pregnancy: It's time for the schools to tackle the problem. *Phi Delta Kappan, 68,* 737–740.

Bukowski, W. J. (1991). A framework for drug abuse prevention research. In C. G. Leukefeld & W. J. Bukoski (Eds.), *Drug abuse prevention intervention research: Methodological issues* (NIDA Research Monograph 107, DHHS Pub. No. ADM 91-1761, pp. 7–28). Rockville, MD: National Institute on Drug Abuse.

Carnegie Council on Adolescent Development. (1989). *Turning points: Preparing American youth for the 21st century.* Washington, DC: Author.

Center for the Study of Social Policy. (1993). *Kids count data book 1993: State profiles of child well-being.* Washington, DC: Author.

Chambers, B., & Abrami, P. C. (1991). The relationship between student team learning outcomes and achievement, causal attributions, and affect. *Journal of Educational Psychology, 8*(1), 140–146.

Children's Defense Fund. (1988). *Making the middle grades work.* Washington, DC: Author.

Children's Defense Fund. (1991). *Child poverty in America.* Washington, DC: Author.

Children's Defense Fund. (1993). *Annual report: The state of America's children.* Washington, DC: Author.

Dryfoos, J. G. (1990). *Adolescents at risk: Prevalence and prevention.* New York: Oxford University Press.

Duckworth, K. (1988). Coping with student absenteeism. *The Practitioner, 14,* 1–14.

Dulmus, C. N., & Wodarski, J. S. (1996). Assessment and effective treatments of childhood psychopathology: Responsibilities and implications for practice. *Journal of Child and Adolescent Group Therapy, 6*(2), 75–99.

Dulmus, C. N., & Wodarski, J. S. (1997). Prevention of childhood mental disorders: A literature review reflecting hope and a vision for the future. *Child and Adolescent Social Work Journal, 14*(3), 181–198.

Durlak, J. A. (1995). *School-based prevention programs for children and adolescents.* Thousand Oaks, CA: Sage.

Earls, F. (1994). Violence and today's youth. *The Future of Children, 4,* 10–23.

Ekstrom, R. B., Goerta, M. E., Pollack, J. M., & Rock, D. A. (1986). Who drops out of high school and why? Findings from a national study. *Teachers College Record, 87,* 356–373.

Ellwood, D. T. (1988). *Poor support: Poverty in the American family.* New York: Basic Books.

Erwin, E. J. (1996). *Putting children first: Visions for a brighter future for young children and their families.* Baltimore, MD: Paul H. Brookes.

Fingerhut, L. A., & Kleinman, J. C. (1990). International and interstate comparisons of homicide among young males. *Journal of the American Medical Association, 265,* 3292–3295.

Finn, C. E., & Walberg, H. J. (1994). *Radical education reforms.* Berkeley, CA: McCutchan.

Goodlad, J. I. (1994). *What schools are for?* (2nd ed.). Bloomington, IN: Phi Delta Educational Foundation.

Grala, C., & McCauley, C. (1976). Counseling truants back to school: Motivation combined with a program for action. *Journal of Child Psychology and Psychiatry and Allied Disciplines, 24,* 607–611.

Gray, G., Smith, A., & Rutter, M. (1980). School attendance and the first year of employment. In L. Hersov & I. Berg (Eds.), *Out of school* (pp. 321–339). New York: Wiley.

Guttmacher Institute. (1985). *Report on adolescent pregnancy.* New York: Author.

Hawkins, J. D., Catalano, R. F., & Miller, J. Y. (1992). Risk and protective factors in alcohol and other drug problems in adolescence and early adulthood: Implications for substance abuse prevention. *Psychological Bulletin, 112*(1), 64–105.

Hersov, L. A., & Berg, I. (Eds.) (1980). *Out of school.* New York: Wiley.

Hingson, R. (1993, June). *The effect of lowered BAC limits in state* per se *DUI laws on crash statistics.* Paper presented at the annual conference of the Research Society on Alcoholism. San Antonio, TX.

Hobbs, F., & Lippman, L. (1990). *Children's well-being: An international comparison.* Washington, DC: U.S. Bureau of the Census.

Johnson, L. D., O'Malley, P. M., Bachman, J. G. (1994). *National survey results on drug use from The Monitoring the Future Study, 1975–1993: Vol. I, Secondary school students* (National Institute on Drug Abuse. NIH Publication No. 94-3809). Washington, DC: U.S. Government Printing Office.

Karlsberg, E. (1989, January). School dropouts: Dead-end ahead. *Teen, 24–27.*

Kenny, A. M. (1987). Teen pregnancy: An issue for schools. *Phi Delta Kappan, 68*(10), 728–736.

Kirby, D., Short, L., Collins, J., Rugg, D., Kolbe, L., Howard, M., Miller, B., Sonenstein, F., & Zabin, L. S. (1994). School-based programs to reduce sexual risk behaviors: A review of effectiveness. *Public Health Reports, 109,* 339–360.

Knapp, M. S., & Shields, P. M. (1990). Reconceiving instruction for the disadvantaged. *Phi Delta Kappan, 72,* 753–758.

Manning, M. L., & Baruth, L. G. (1995). *Students at risk.* Boston: Allyn & Bacon.

Meisels, S. J., & Liaw, F. R. (1993). Failure in grade: Do retained students catch up? *Journal of Educational Research, 87,* 69–77.

Miller, D. (1986). Effects of a program of therapeutic discipline on the attitude, attendance, and insight of truant adolescents. *Journal of Experimental Education, 55,* 49–53.

Muha, D. G., & Cole, C. (1991). Dropout prevention and group counseling: A review of the literature. *The High School Journal, 74*(2), 76–79.

Murphy, J. (Ed.). (1990). *The educational reform movement of the 1980's.* Berkeley, CA: McCutchan.

National Center for Education Statistics. (1991). *The state of mathematics achievement: NAEP's 1990 assessment of the nation and the trial assessment of the states* (Report No. 21-ST-04). Washington, DC: U.S. Government Printing Office.

Natriello, G. (1995). Dropouts: Definitions, causes, consequences, and remedies. In P. W. Cookson & B. Schneider (Eds.), *Transforming schools* (pp. 107–127). New York: Garland.

Niehoff, B. P., & Mesch, D. J. (1991). Effects of reward structures on academic performance and group processes in a classroom setting. *Journal of Psychology, 125*(4), 457–467.

Norman, E., & Turner, S. (1993). Adolescent substance abuse prevention programs: Theories, models, and research in the encouraging 80's. *Journal of Primary Prevention, 14*(1), 3–20.

Office of Technology Assessment. (1991). *Adolescent health.* U.S. Congress, Washington, DC: Author.

Rapp, L. A., & Wodarski, J. S. (in press). Juvenile violence: The high risk factors, current interventions, and implications for social work practice. *Journal of Applied Social Sciences.*

Rogers, D. C. (1980). Stepping up school attendance, *NASSP Bulletin, 64,* 21–25.

Rood, R. E. (1989). Advice for administrators: Writing the attendance policy. *NASSP Bulletin, 73,* 21–25.

Rumberger, R. (1983). Dropping out high school: The influences of race, sex, and family background. *American Educational Research Journal, 20,* 199–220.

Rutter, M., Maugham, B., Mortimore, P., & Ouston, J. (1979). *Fifteen thousand hours: Secondary schools and their effects on children.* London: Open Books.

Schinke, S. P. (1997). Preventing teenage pregnancy. *Journal of Human Behavior in the Social Environment, 1*(1), 53–66.

Schinke, S. P., Botvin, G. J., & Orlandi, M. A. (1991). *Substance abuse in children and adolescents: Evaluation and intervention.* Newbury Park, CA: Sage.

Schorr, E. B. (1988). *Within our reach: Breaking the cycle of disadvantaged.* New York: Doubleday.

Schultz, R. M. (1987). Truancy: Issues and interventions. *Behavioral disorders, 12,* 175–130.

Shanker, A. (1994). National standards. In C. E. Finn & H. J. Walberg (Eds.), *Radical Education Reforms* (pp. 3–27). Berkeley, CA: McCutchan.

Smith, R. (1988). *America's shame, America's hope: Twelve million youth at risk.* New York: Charles Stewart Mott.

Sommer, B. (1985). What's different about truants? A comparison study of eighth-graders. *Journal of Youth and Adolescence, 14,* 411–423.

Swadi, H., & Zeitlin, H. (1988). Peer influence and adolescent substance abuse: A promising side? *British Journal of Addiction, 83*(2), 153–157.

U.S. Bureau of the Census (1989). *Statistical abstracts of the United States: 1988* (108th ed.). Washington, DC: U.S. Government Printing Office.

U.S. Bureau of the Census. (1990). *Statistical abstracts of the United States: 1990* (110th ed.). Washington, DC: U.S. Government Printing Office.

U.S. General Accounting Office. (1995). *Welfare dependency: Coordinated community efforts can better serve young at-risk teen girls.* Gaithersburg, MD: Author.

Vandrer Zanden, J. W. (1989). *Human development* (4th ed.). New York: Alfred A. Knopf.

Wilson, J., & Howell, J. (1995). Comprehensive strategy for serious, violent, and chronic juvenile offenders. In J. Howell, B. Krisberg, J. Hawkins, & J. Wilson (Eds.), *Serious, violent, and chronic juvenile offenders.* Thousand Oaks, CA: Sage.

Wodarski, J. S. (1988). Teaching adolescents about alcohol and driving. *Journal of Alcohol and Drug Education, 33*(3), 54–67.

Wodarski, J. S., & Bagarozzi, D. A. (1979). *Behavioral social work.* New York: Human Services Press.

Wodarski, J. S., & Hedrick, M. (1987). Violent children: A practice paradigm. *Social Work in Education, 10,* 28–42.

Wodarski, J. S., Smokowski, P. R., & Feit, M. D. (1996). Adolescent preventive health: A cost-beneficial social and life group paradigm. In J. S. Wodarski, M. D. Feit, & J. R. Ferrari (Eds.), *Adolescent health care* (pp. 1–40). New York: Haworth Press.

Wodarski, J. S., & Smyth, N. J. (1994). Adolescent substance abuse: A comprehensive approach to prevention intervention. *Journal of Child & Adolescent Substance Abuse, 3*(3), 33–58.

Wodarski, J. S., & Wodarski, L. A. (1993). *Curriculums and practical aspects of implementation: Preventive health services for adolescents.* Lanham, MD: University Press.

Chapter 4

VIOLENCE IN THE SCHOOLS

Lisa A. Rapp
John S. Wodarski

OVERVIEW

Violence has been a long-term tragedy in the United States. It has invaded multiple aspects of every American's life. No one has been immune from the negative effects of violence; it has been an equal opportunity offender. Unfortunately, children have been the most victimized by violence. That is, they have perpetrated the most violence and have been the recipients of the greatest number of violent acts (Johnson & Johnson, 1995; Rapp & Wodarski, in press). Recent reports suggest that adolescents are more than twice as likely to be the victims of violent crimes than are individuals over age 20 (American Psychological Association [APA], 1993). Between 1980 and 1991, violent crime toward young people increased by about 30%; especially prevalent have been the increases in the rates of murder, rape, and aggravated assault (Goldstein, Harootunian, & Conoley, 1994). These heightened levels of violence have quickly found their way onto high school and even junior high school campuses. As violence increases, so does the pressure on schools to ensure student safety and orderly conduct. Schools have struggled with new policies and practices to reduce this violence, but many have come up short (Johnson & Johnson, 1995). With this being the case, it seems clear why violence on school grounds has incurred such prominent attention from educators, social workers, and parents.

Prior to the 1960s, student misbehavior was considered to be a minor problem; when it did occur it often involved gum chewing, swearing, and running in the halls. However, by the late 1980s, student aggression had changed and increased to a dramatic level. Serious concern from parents and educators increased as school crime and assaults rose by 35% in New York City schools and weapons became more popular than pencils. Statistics have indicated that approximately 3 million crimes occur every year on school campuses. That is equal to 16,000 per day or one crime every 6 seconds (Soriano, Soriano, & Jimenez, 1991). Surprisingly, the greatest number of school crime increases has occurred at the elementary school level. In 1991, one in five elementary school teachers reported being verbally abused by students and 8% reported being physically threatened by students (Goldstein, Harootunian, & Conoley, 1994). Approximately 5,200 of the nation's 1 million secondary school teachers are physically attacked at school every month (Hranitz & Eddowes, 1990).

Most violence in America's schools is committed by students and directed at other students. In 1992, 14% of high school students had been threatened with a weapon at school (Soriano, Soriano, & Jimenez, 1991). Investigators at the University of Michigan in 1993 found that 29% of eighth graders were threatened at school; 19% of those were threatened with a weapon (Batsche & Knoff, 1994). Besides observable threats with weapons and physical violence, there has been an increase in overall bullying or intimidating behavior by students. This broader form of aggression has also been found to result in fear and anxiety in students and teachers.

Aggression in the school setting not only infringes on students' rights for safety, it also infringes on students' rights to be educated. It is obvious that an aggressive atmosphere can hinder school performance for victims and perpetrators. Learning can be close to impossible if students are worried about being attacked or jumped in the halls. Likewise, students are also more likely to avoid the entire problem by avoiding school all together. Approximately 8% of urban junior and senior high school students missed at least one day of school a month because they were afraid to go to school (Hranitz & Eddowes, 1990).

To gain a complete understanding of the issues of school violence, it is necessary to examine all types of violence that occur in the schools. A limited definition prohibits the comprehension of the negative and hostile climate that is present in many schools today.

BULLYING

Bullying is defined as a chronic form of aggression in which one or more students physically, psychologically, or sexually harass another student repeatedly over time. Typically, the action is unprovoked and the bully is considered to be more powerful than the victim (Batsche & Knoff, 1994). It has been found that approximately 75% of adolescent students were bullied at least once during their school years. Many students indicate that bullies are one of their chief concerns with regard to school.

This form of aggression often starts in elementary schools and tends to affect a large number of students. Bullying may start with simple name-calling, but it can be the precursor to later, more severe, physical and sexual aggression (Stein, 1995). Unfortunately, bullying is often ignored by educators, who may feel that it is a normal part of growing up. However, if bullying were addressed in its beginning stages, many future incidents of physical and sexual aggression could be avoided. According to Johnston, O'Malley, & Bachman (1993) incidents of bullying have increased in number and severity over the past few years. This form of aggression also includes students bullying teachers.

Chronic bullying produces many negative effects in the victims. Logically, victims of this type of aggression have been found to have high levels of anxiety and fearfulness at school and at home. Many times these students respond to bullying by using withdrawal or escape behaviors such as avoiding certain areas of the school, skipping school, running away, or committing suicide. These victims may also respond with aggressive behaviors such as fighting or bringing weapons to school. Overall, this type of aggression results in students fearing and avoiding school, making academic achievement close to impossible for them.

PHYSICAL AGGRESSION

Physical aggression by a student can result in pain, injury, fear, and, in some cases, even death for the victim. Physical aggression can be inflicted with or without a weapon. This type of aggression on school campuses mirrors the violence that is occurring in communities across the country. There is an unfortunate deficiency of statistics for these incidents of violence on school campuses, because incidents that occur during school hours are less likely to be reported to the police and currently there is no national database for homicides that happen on school grounds (Furlong & Morrison, 1994). The limited data that we do have suggest that this type of aggression is on the rise.

Of 2,700 Illinois high school students who were surveyed, 8% reported being cut during the 1989–1990 school year. Likewise, 4% of those students indicated that they had been shot at during that same year (Illinois Criminal Justice Information Authority, 1991). A small number of students accounts for a large majority (46.4%) of these physical altercations (Furlong & Morrison, 1994).

Students and teachers who have been victims of physical aggression often exhibit severe symptoms of posttraumatic stress disorder (PTSD), anxiety disorders, and depression. Students who commit this type of aggression often evince anxiety and depression themselves (Rapp & Wodarski, 1997). Aggressive students usually have exhibited aggression previously at home and within the community. Most often, these incidents occur in school districts where there are high levels of unemployment, crime, poverty, and hopelessness.

MINORITY VIOLENCE

Studies on violence, both in the community and on or around school grounds indicate that youth of color are the most often victimized by violence. Racial minorities, especially African Americans and Latinos, are also the perpetrators of a large number of violent acts (Soriano, Soriano, & Jimenez, 1991). Nationally, Latino males have the highest homicide victimization rate, with African American males a close second. Native American males have a homicide victimization rate which is 3 to 4 times higher than that for Whites (Hechinger, 1992). These minority students most often live in neighborhoods with the highest percentages of homelessness, poverty, joblessness, crowded schools, and individuals who embody racial stereotypes, factors that have repeatedly been linked to violence. Particular cultures are not to be considered causes of violence; however, different values, cultures, and ethnicities that come together within schools and communities highlight racism, classism, and sexism. These variables frequently incite violence.

American schools are rapidly changing to include diverse ethnic groups and multiple languages. Unfortunately, little time has been spent to educate students and teachers about cultural diversity and cross-cultural communication. This has led to devastating consequences in many school districts.

VIOLENCE TOWARD GAY, LESBIAN, AND BISEXUAL YOUTH

Studies have shown that not only is violence toward gay, lesbian, and bisexual youth common, but it has also increased by 127% in the past 6 years (D'Augelli & Dark, 1994). Other studies conducted across the country indicate that gay, lesbian, and bisexual youth endure a wide range of violent victimization including harassment, threats, verbal abuse, sexual assault, physical assault, and murder (National Gay and Lesbian Task Force Policy Institute, 1992; Pilkington & D'Augelli, 1995). Between 33% and 49% of lesbians and gay males responding to surveys reported being victimized in junior and senior high schools (Berrill, 1990). Many youths reported mental health problems, safety fears, and discomfort because of this victimization (D'Augelli & Dark, 1994).

Gay, lesbian, and bisexual youth are often subject to violence due to homophobia and because of the association of homosexuals with the HIV epidemic. These youths also have fewer social supports and are therefore more vulnerable as targets of abuse. For some youths who have not formally disclosed their orientation, victimization may force an unexpected disclosure to those who are unaccepting of their sexual orientation. Consequently, these youths may experience a secondary victimization through their attempts to obtain help. In fact, more than 1 in 20 youths reported that they had suffered some form of victimization from their own teachers (Pilkington & D'Augelli, 1995). Schools need to be ready to respond and protect youths who choose to disclose their orientation. Training for educators, as well as curricula designed to reduce bigotry, need to be incorporated into school practices.

JUVENILE GANGS

Typically, juvenile gangs tend to generate problems off school grounds and in the community. However, juvenile gangs have recently started to permeate school confines and create serious dangers for students and school personnel. Although many gang members do not attend school, they still affect students and school personnel safety when gang clashes occur within the school building, on the campus, or in close proximity to the school. Oftentimes, gangs use schools as prime recruiting grounds for membership (Wheeler & Baron, 1994). Most conflicts occur when members of opposing gangs attend the same school. Gang conflicts may involve weapons, thus escalating the clashes in a lethal manner.

According to Goldstein, Glick, Carthan, and Blancero (1994), there are approximately 2,000 gangs in the United States located throughout urban, suburban, and rural settings. These gangs are made up mostly of males; however, the number of independent female gangs is increasing (Goldstein, 1991). Youths join gangs for many reasons, including peer friendship, pride, sense of identity, increased self-esteem, excitement, attempts to gain resources and drugs, and family tradition (Goldstein & Soriano, 1994). Most of these motivations are normal developmental tasks for all adolescents. However, juveniles who join gangs are attempting to complete these developmental tasks through inappropriate means. Recently, gang behaviors have become more complex and lethal because of the use of firearms. Drive-by shootings, schoolyard slayings, and in-house burglaries are all common behaviors of contemporary gangs.

Juvenile gangs are a source of heightened concern for schools. Students who are gang members pose the greatest risk for creating school disturbances, violence, and property destruction. Younger students are usually the most common prey for gang recruitment. Refusal to join the gang often results in threats, coercion, and severe violence toward the student. Besides potentiating physical harm, gang behaviors can also induce fear and anxiety in children and school staff. Severe and chronic threats and violence can result in PTSD symptoms, anxiety, depression, feelings of hopelessness, and aggression. Students in schools that face these problems will have difficulty not only on an academic level, but also on an interpersonal and behavioral level. In other words, violence breeds multiple and complex psychosocial problems for youth and adult victims. The schools have no choice but to address this.

GUNS

Firearms have contributed significantly to the substantial increase in the number and severity of violent episodes in the past few years. Between 1987 and 1989, the incidence of homicides by shootings rose 79% for teenagers, with approximately 3 out of 4 youthful murderers using guns (U.S. Department of Justice, 1992). This increase has been partly blamed on the easy access and easy use of automatic and semiautomatic weapons.

There are approximately 200 million privately owned guns in the United States, and it has been estimated that 270,000 are brought to school every day (Center to Prevent Handgun Violence, 1990). Callahan & Rivara (1992) reported that 20% of the 9th- through 12th-grade students surveyed carried a weapon to school in the preceding month. Those students who did not own a handgun reported that they could obtain one quickly and without much hassle. In fact, over half of these youths said they could get a gun from family members and 33% reported that they could obtain a gun from someone on the streets. Handgun ownership has been related to involvement in deviant behavior, gang membership, drug use, and assault and battery (Callahan & Rivara, 1992). News reports analyzed between 1986 and 1990 found that 65 students and 6 school personnel were killed on school grounds and 201 were severely wounded by gunfire; 242 hostage situations were also reported (Center to Prevent Handgun Violence, 1990).

Youths packing handguns on school grounds have forced school administrations into using extreme measures to ensure the safety of other students and staff. Security guards, metal detectors, and trained dogs are some of the means that have been employed. These procedures have been somewhat successful in the reduction of the number of weapons within school buildings, but they have not stopped the overall violence in schools or on school grounds.

DRUGS

Drug use has been found to directly contribute to violent behavior. Individuals and groups who use controlled substances are more likely to become aggressive at minor provocation. Studies have indicated that in 60% of homicides, the perpetrator, the victim, or both used alcohol (Eron & Slaby, 1994). Drugs also increase violence in an indirect manner by users committing violent acts to obtain drugs and also by sellers committing violence to protect drug turf (Eron & Slaby, 1994). Drugs present a critical motivation as well as a tremendous economic opportunity for youths who reside in impoverished communities. Many youths view the drug trade as their only hope of financial gain, despite its dangers and illegality.

Sheley, McGee, and Wright (1992) report that drug sales are strongly associated with violence and occur most often around inner-city schools. Drugs have been a problem in the schools for many years. Their presence has been related to violence in two ways: (a) Drugs have caused an increased incidence of violence and (b) drugs have exacerbated the level of aggression that already existed. Schools need to be aware of the factors that lure adolescents toward controlled substances. They need to be prepared to handle substance abuse and substance selling, in addition to gangs, guns, and violence. These are the ingredients that, when combined, result in student and school personnel victimization.

ASSESSMENT

A formal assessment of the type and level of violence that is occurring in and around school grounds is required before a school system can begin to implement interventions and systemwide changes in policy and practice. Every school district will be different—some schools may have only minor violence problems that need to be addressed before major problems occur, while other schools will require swift, potent interventions. Some schools may require interventions that will confront the issues of violence against minorities and substance abuse, while other schools may require interventions for bullying and homophobia.

A comprehensive evaluation should include an assessment of bullying, weapons, substance abuse, gangs, and physical altercations. Assessments should also include review of violent acts against minorities, women, and homosexuals. Assessments should describe when and where violence occurs (e.g., at school events, on the bus, on the way home from school). Attendance records and discipline records should be analyzed as well as the overall school climate (Stephens, 1994).

Assessments need to be completed separately for each school level or building. There are two reasons for this. First, middle school children may be experiencing different types of violence from those which high school youth experience. Studies have indicated that younger students may be more likely to be victimized by bullying behaviors, while older students may be victimized by multiple and more severe types of violence. Therefore, developmental stages need not be forgotten during evaluation. Second, school buildings, although in the same district, may be located on different gang turf or in areas with varying substance abuse rates. Therefore, such schools may have very different problems that need to be addressed.

Assessments need to be given to multiple individuals. Students, educators, parents, school social workers, school staff, local probation workers, and local mental health workers should be included in assessments (others can be included if necessary). These individuals will help provide an accurate understanding of the violence problem within a particular school. Definitions should be clear and measurable.

Whenever possible, standardized assessment instruments should be utilized. These are currently available for students and parents; however, there are no systemwide standardized assessment instruments for schools to utilize to evaluate their systems and the level of violence exhibited in their schools. Thus, schools need to devise their own questionnaires or pay consultants to complete the assessments. Upon completion of the assessments, school administrators, as well as school social workers, can determine the combination of interventions that will be appropriate for their schools and tailor specific interventions to their students', parents', and community's needs.

SCHOOL-BASED INTERVENTIONS

Schools are no longer what they used to be; schools are no longer safe. Instead of educating, teachers spend an inordinate amount of time and energy subduing altercations, resolving conflicts, and managing disruptive behavior (Johnson & Johnson, 1995). Instead of improving school programs and policies, principals' time is consumed with student discipline, weapon control, and handling gang conflicts. As a result, schools are not able to effectively educate students and prepare them for careers and adult life. The schools are not at fault; school staff and teachers have not been trained in violent behavior management and school administrators are usually ill-prepared to handle these types of problems. However, schools can no longer view the education of children as their only objective. Schools now need to intervene with students to reduce violence.

The following empirically based interventions have been found to be effective in school districts across the country. The programs discussed here are only a fraction of the programs available and utilized on a daily basis. Schools interested in beginning such interventions should investigate multiple programs and curricula before proceeding.

PREVENTION

Stopping serious violence before it occurs is the main goal of prevention programs. In many school districts that are not yet overrun with violence, prevention will be the main intervention used. Prevention programs should include students, parents, educators, school personnel, administrators, and community members. Interventions should include skills training, violence policy and practice modifications, and school environment changes. In other words, for prevention efforts to be successful, interventions must be employed at multiple levels of school functioning, not just at the level of individual behavior modification.

Prevention programs for students, parents, and educators can be adapted from any combination of the interventions that will be discussed later. However, there are two well-known prevention interventions that have proven effective in outcome research. These are Second Step: A Violence Prevention Curriculum (Committee for Children, 1992) and The Violence Prevention Curriculum for Adolescents (Prothrow-Stith, 1987). The first curriculum is targeted for preschool through grade-five students. It is designed to reduce impulsivity and aggressive behavior and increase social competence (Larson, 1994). The second curriculum (for adolescents) focuses on developing values against fighting, using alternative methods to resolve conflicts, role playing, and using videotapes. The first curriculum has been found to be more effective thus far, because it commences prevention interventions with children at a younger age.

Prevention methods should be implemented at the system level in addition to the curricula mentioned above. Again, the most effective prevention program will target as many levels as possible, with as many individuals as possible.

1. *Emergency drills.*   Every school building should develop and practice emergency drills for violent crises (gunfire in the school building, gang altercation in the building, etc.). These drills should be practiced frequently to reduce hysterical behaviors and to prevent as many injuries as possible. Regular updates and in-service training should be held (Wheeler & Baron, 1994).

2. *Visitor screening.*   Establish an effective visitor screening process to prevent unwanted or dangerous individuals from coming on the grounds. Only one entrance should be open for visitors and a sign-in process should be utilized. A security task force, either professional or made up of volunteers and school staff, could coordinate this and also patrol the school building (Stephens, 1994).

3. *Safe grounds.*   Eliminate potentially dangerous environmental designs. Eliminate hiding places, increase lighting, and install more telephones and convex mirrors to improve the ability to supervise. Increase supervision by staff at all times. Teachers should monitor the halls, and community volunteers should be used.

4. *Parents.*   Involve parents in as many aspects of safety planning as possible. Recruit them as volunteers for special events, as hall monitors, or as safety task force members. Their involvement and support are crucial. Encourage them to emphasize no violence at home as well as at the schools.

5. *School crime reporting.*   Colleges and universities are required by law to collect and record campus crime data. Although K–12 schools are not mandated to do this, this procedure can provide information about persons, groups, times, and places that are related to violence and crime. School administrators can use this information to assess the overall violence in the school and to make adjustments as needed.

6. *School pride.*   Every student should feel a sense of pride and ownership toward the school. Recruit students or have them organize groups or clubs to generate ideas and activities for violence reduction. Positive peer pressure can be effective.

As previously mentioned, in-school violence interventions should be chosen based on the needs of the students and the issues present within each individual school building. Multiple curricula such as those discussed below should be considered, because each curriculum may not address all of the problems of each school. Modifications need to be addressed at the system and individual level.

ANTIBULLYING INTERVENTION

Besag (1989) has developed a complete curriculum for addressing the problem of bullying in schools. This curriculum includes individual and group interventions for victims, bullies, and their parents. The curriculum focuses on a social learning approach, because bullying has been identified as a learned behavior. Changing aggressive behaviors and improving communication, social skills, and problem-solving skills are the main objectives. Victims are also part of the intervention. The focus for these children is empowerment. In other words, self-esteem improvement is emphasized by teaching social skills and communication skills. Positive role models are provided and new friendships are encouraged. Victims are taught how to stand up to bullies without fighting. Parents of victims and bullies attend groups with their children so that they can reinforce these skills at home.

When improvements have been noted by both the victim and the bully, sessions including both children can be conducted to address the problem. Problem solving, cooperation, and negotiation should be encouraged. Behavior modification plans for both the victim and the bully can also be utilized to reinforce and shape positive behavior.

The curriculum described here is very flexible in that it can be utilized by social workers at both individual and group levels. Depending upon the seriousness and extent of the problem within the school building, group interventions may be more efficient. This program can also be targeted to any age level and can work with the victim and the perpetrator individually or with both children if necessary.

Another promising intervention used for bullying was conducted by Olweus (1991). This program encompassed parents, children, and teachers by providing educational components about bullying. In addition, the program developed and helped enforce school rules regarding bullying and made efforts to protect and support victims (Kazdin, 1994). The influences at the micro- and macrolevels have been found to be the greatest strengths of the program.

ANTIAGGRESSION INTERVENTIONS

There are numerous interventions that target aggression. Several that have been empirically proven as effective in the schools are discussed here. The first is the

Problem-Solving Training Program (Sarason & Sarason, 1981). This program was developed especially for high school students and is delivered during their health class over the course of 13 weeks. The intervention focuses on learning nonaggressive solutions through the use of modeling and role playing. Negotiation and communication skills are also incorporated to solve common social problems. Another curriculum, entitled the Positive Youth Development Program (Caplan et al., 1992) provides a 20-session curriculum to middle school children. Emphasis is placed on stress management, self-esteem, assertiveness, problem solving, health information, and social networks. These skills are considered to be critical for reducing and preventing aggression.

The Anger Coping curriculum is an 18-session program for fourth to sixth graders (Lochman, Lampron, Gemmer, & Harris, 1986). This intervention trains children in self-instruction, perspective taking, physiological cues to anger, social problem solving, and goal setting (Larson, 1994). This program utilizes role playing and videotaping and comes with a treatment manual that includes specific objectives and procedures for each session. This intervention has been used in school districts across the country.

The Positive Adolescents Choice Training (PACT) program, developed by Hammond (1991), specifically targets African American youth to reduce their disproportionate risk for becoming victims or perpetrators of violence (Kazdin, 1994). There are three major components that are taught over the 20-week sessions of this program: social skills training, anger management, and violence awareness education (Larson, 1994). Culturally sensitive videotapes are used to exhibit appropriate negotiation, problem-solving, and communication techniques. Outcome studies have shown good success with this program.

The Peer Culture Development Program (National School Resource Network, 1980) was developed to enhance the leadership and interpersonal skills between youths. This program has been used in elementary and high schools to alter peer interaction patterns. The program attempts to reduce negative peer influences and student alienation, and to increase self-esteem, school interest, and the support of conventional rules. This program can be specifically used to help reduce the problem of gangs in schools. This intervention may reduce the recruitment rate of young children into gangs if these children are able to resist negative peer influences. Gang involvement will also be reduced if students feel a strong responsibility for themselves, have adequate self-esteem, and are positively involved with school. Schools facing a gang problem may wish to adapt this program into their curricula.

SEXUAL ORIENTATION EDUCATION

Schools have a responsibility to educate children and that includes education about individuals with different sexual orientations. Schools are oftentimes faced with conflicts, including aggression toward students who are homosexual or bisexual. One of the reasons for this is that students often have very little understanding about different sexual orientations and consequently form stereotypes and biases. One of the most important interventions that a school can use to reduce violence against homosexual or bisexual youth is an education curriculum. This curriculum should focus on the education of students as well as that of parents and school personnel. School personnel especially need training and information about homosexual and bisexual issues. School administrations should reinforce a strong attitude condemning violence on the basis of sexual orientation. Common stereotypes and discriminatory practices should be identified and addressed immediately. School policies and practices should be regularly reviewed to ensure that all students are protected from discrimination.

Support groups for homosexual and bisexual youths should be established within the school, and heterosexual youths should attend some of these meetings to gain an understanding of the problems and discrimination homosexual and bisexual youths face on a daily basis (D'Augelli & Dark, 1994). The needs of homosexual and bisexual youths should be incorporated into school service planning. Likewise, schools should network with outside agencies, supports, and services that are located within the community, because these programs are usually more developed than school programs (D'Augelli & Dark, 1994).

MULTICULTURAL INTERVENTIONS

Studies have repeatedly urged schools and agencies to develop multicultural violence prevention and intervention programs (Yung & Hammond, 1994). To date, few of these programs have been developed or empirically evaluated. However, intervention programming needs to be sensitive toward differing values, cultural mores, and beliefs that minority youths espouse. Intervention programs that are not sensitive will most likely have little effect on reducing violence by minority youths.

Training for nonminority youths and school personnel regarding multicultural issues should be mandatory. Curricula in schools should consistently educate students about minority cultures to dispel common inaccurate beliefs and myths. Unfortunately, minorities have been the most likely to be victimized in schools and communities. Student ignorance, behavioral misunderstanding, and intolerance have been some of the causes for this victimization. By the year 2000, nearly one third of young people entering schools in the United States will be from minority groups (Wheeler & Baron, 1994). Until multicultural training is implemented in the schools, violence against and by minority youths will not be reduced.

DRUG ABUSE INTERVENTION

As previously indicated, drug use and drug trafficking by adolescents have increased the rate of violence by a substantial margin (Slaby, Barham, Eron, & Wilcox, 1994). Schools can help lower the level of drug abuse by providing education and prevention curricula. These curricula should be started in the early elementary school grades and continued through grade 12 for more effective outcomes. Curricula should be developmentally appropriate for each grade level and should include information about substances as well as the skills necessary to abstain from use (Wodarski & Feit, 1995). Youths who have been identified as having problems with substances will need more intensive treatment and should be referred to an outside agency that specializes in use and addiction.

One prevention program that has evinced positive results is the Teams-Games-Tournaments (TGT) Substance Abuse and Violence Prevention Program. Youths between ages 12 and 18 can be targeted for this program, which teaches knowledge about substances and violence, in addition to coping and problem-solving skills. The curriculum is presented using games and tournaments so children have fun while they are learning critical skills and techniques. Modeling, role playing, and videotapes are also incorporated.

THE ROLE OF TEACHERS

Educating youth today is a completely different profession than it was two decades ago. Teachers have been forced to incorporate social worker, police officer, and mediator into their job title. Less and less time is left for actual education. However, skills that are crucial for teachers are rarely taught to them in college. Instead, teachers are often thrown into positions with few, if any, of the skills required to successfully contain student behavior.

Schools in the process of implementing prevention or intervention programs need to take the time to train teachers. Teachers need to be skilled in behavior modification, conflict resolution, and negotiation. Additionally, multicultural training is essential, as is training regarding homosexuality and bisexuality. Teachers also need training in self-defense, which should include verbally deescalating provocative students and physically defending themselves. Teachers have a right to be safe in their work environments and to protect themselves from students who become aggressive with them.

Schools need to provide teachers with clear policies regarding violence, before violence becomes a problem within the school. Schools should also not expect teachers to be security guards—their talents lie in educating and their time should be focused on that task. Therefore, if necessary, schools should hire professional security guards to handle physical altercations and weapon control.

Finally, students who are entering the field of education should be aware that other skills and duties besides educating youth will be required of them. They should be made aware that there may be some physical risk involved in becoming a teacher.

THE ROLE OF PARENTS

Parents also need skills training, and schools may be more accessible sites than local agencies at which to hold training classes. Groups of parents should be taught the same skills as teachers and students, with behavior modification and child management emphasized. The ability to recognize symptoms of drug and alcohol use in children should also be incorporated. Parents should be encouraged to reinforce the school's policies of no violence at home.

Capable and willing parents should be recruited to teach these skills to parents. Other parents can take turns volunteering as hall monitors, dance chaperons, school grounds monitors, and bus aids. The more involved parents are, the more they will incorporate nonviolence into their home lives with their children.

An effective program to reduce or prevent violence in the school requires a unified front by the adults working with students, including parents, teachers, school personnel, coaches, and school social workers. All adults must work together with students to reduce school violence.

SCHOOL SOCIAL WORKERS

School social workers have a responsibility to assess, design, implement, and evaluate programs for the prevention or reduction of violence within their schools. School social workers should serve as advocates for their students by requesting school administrators to have schoolwide violence assessments completed. Individuals should not wait until multiple acts of violence occur before they evaluate their schools. A study conducted by Astor, Behre, Fravil, and Wallace (1997) indicated that most school social workers and school personnel did not believe they had a violence problem in their school and did not classify a violence problem until a severe or lethal form of violence occurred. Unfortunately, school administrators or social workers who wait this long may have a larger problem on their hands than they thought. It is recommended that all schools (elementary included) have a complete evaluation of their violence problems (type and level).

Once the results from an evaluation have been obtained, social workers should identify the types of interventions that are necessary for their school buildings. In addition, they should take lead roles in finding ready-made interventions or designing new ones.

Practicing social workers also have the resources (or can obtain them) to implement programs. Basic skills, including problem solving, negotiation, and conflict resolution, are common interventions for students and adults who meet with social workers. Therefore, social workers should be the ones to train school personnel, teachers, and parents. Afterward, interventions for the students can be implemented.

Depending on the size of the school, social workers may need to recruit local agency social workers to help them with the large task of implementation. Some school districts may need to hire additional social workers to assist with the implementation of violence programs. Such programs should later be incorporated into the curricula of the schools and all students should participate in them.

Schools have a unique opportunity to implement interventions more effectively than local community agencies. The reasons for this are that they have a captive audience of students who cannot skip appointments, parents may have fewer transportation problems for school appointments, interventions can be implemented immediately when conflicts arise, and all parties can be included in interventions. The opportunity to reduce school violence should not be disregarded or underestimated.

Schools have an obligation to ensure the safety of their students and staff, as well as to provide them with a positive learning environment. School social workers who have most, if not all, of the training and skills necessary to implement safety or violence prevention programs should serve as advocates for these programs in their schools. Although such programs still require refinement, they have been shown to be effective in impeding further violent tragedies in schools.

REFERENCES

American Psychological Association. (1993). *Violence and youth: Psychology's response.* Washington, DC: Author.

Astor, R., Behre, W., Fravil, K., & Wallace, J. (1997). Perceptions of school violence as a problem and reports of violent events: A national survey of school social workers. *Social Work, 42*(1), 55–68.

Batsche, G., & Knoff, H. (1994). Bullies and their victims: Understanding a pervasive problem in the schools. *School Psychology Review, 23*(2), 165–174.

Berrill, K. (1990). Anti-gay violence and victimization in the United States: An overview. *Journal of Interpersonal Violence, 5,* 274–294.

Besag, V. (1989). *Bullies and victims in schools: A guide to understanding and management.* Milton Keynes, PA: Open University Press.

Callahan, C., & Rivara, F. (1992). Urban high schools, youth, and handguns. *Journal of the American Medical Association, 267,* 3038–3042.

Caplan, M., Weissberg, R., Grober, J., Sivo, P., Grady, K., & Jacoby, C. (1992). Social competence promotion with inner-city and suburban young adolescents: Effects on social adjustment and alcohol use. *Journal of Consulting and Clinical Psychology, 60,* 56–63.

Center to Prevent Handgun Violence. (1990). *Caught in the crossfire: A report on gun violence in our nation's schools.* Washington, DC: Author.

Committee for Children. (1992). *Second step: A violence prevention curriculum.* Seattle, WA: Author.

D'Augelli, A., & Dark, L. (1994). Lesbian, gay and bisexual youths. In L. Eron, J. Gentry, & P. Schlegel (Eds.), *Reason to hope: A psychosocial perspective on violence and youth.* Washington, DC: American Psychological Association.

Eron, L., & Slaby, R. (1994). Introduction. In L. Eron, J. Gentry, & P. Schlegel (Eds.), *Reason to hope: A psychosocial perspective on violence and youth* (pp. 1–24). Washington, DC: American Psychological Association.

Furlong, M., & Morrison, G. (1994). Introduction to miniseries: School violence and safety in perspective. *School Psychology Review, 23*(2), 139–150.

Goldstein, A. (1991). *Delinquent gangs: A psychological perspective.* Champaign, IL: Research Press.

Goldstein, A., Glick, B., Carthan, W., & Blancero, D. (1994). *The prosocial gang.* Newbury Park, CA: Sage.

Goldstein, A., Harootunian, B., & Conoley, J. (1994). *Student aggression: Prevention, control, replacement.* New York: Guilford Press.

Goldstein, A., & Soriano, F. (1994). Juvenile gangs. In L. Eron, J. Gentry, & P. Schlegel (Eds.), *A reason to hope: A psychosocial perspective on violence and youth.* Washington, DC: American Psychological Association.

Hammond, R. (1991). *Dealing with anger: Givin' it. Takin' it. Workin' it out.* Champaign, IL: Research Press.

Hechinger, F. (1992). *Fateful choices: Healthy youth for the 21st century.* New York: Carnegie Corporation of New York.

Hranitz, J., & Eddowes, E. (1990). Violence: A crisis in homes and schools. *Childhood Education, 67*(1), 4–7.

Illinois Criminal Justice Information Authority. (1991). Trends and issues: Interim report. *Educational and Criminal Justice in Illinois.* Chicago: Author.

Johnson, D., & Johnson, R. (1995). *Reducing school violence through conflict resolution.* Alexandria, VA: Association for Supervision and Curriculum Development.

Johnston, L., O'Malley, P., & Bachman, J. (1993). *Monitoring the future study for Goal 6 of the National Education Goals: A special report for the National Education Goals panel.* Ann Arbor: University of Michigan's Institute for Social Research.

Kazdin, A. (1994). Interventions for aggressive children. In L. Eron, J. Gentry, & P. Schlegel (Eds.), *Reason to hope: A psychosocial perspective on violence and youth* (pp. 341–382). Washington, DC: American Psychological Association.

Larson, J. (1994). Violence prevention in the schools: A review of selected programs and procedures. *School Psychology Review, 23*(2), 151–164.

Lochman, J., Lampron, L., Gemmer, T., & Harris, S. (1986). Anger-coping intervention with aggressive children: A guide to implementation in school settings. In P. Keller & S. Heyman (Eds.), *Innovations in Clinical Practice: A Source Book* (Vol. 6, pp. 339–356). Sarasota, FL: Professional Resources Exchange.

National Gay and Lesbian Task Force Policy Institute. (1992). *Anti-gay/lesbian violence, victimization & defamation in 1991.* Washington, DC: Author.

National School Resource Network. (1980). *Peer culture development* (Technical Assistance Bulletin 28). Washington, DC: National School Resource Network.

Olweus, D. (1991). Bully/victim problems among school children: Basic facts and effects of a school based intervention program. In D. J. Pepler & K. H. Rubin (Eds.), *The development and treatment of childhood aggression* (pp. 411–448). Hillsdale, NJ: Erlbaum.

Pilkington, N., & D'Augelli, A. (1995). Victimization of lesbian, gay, and bisexual youth in community settings. *Journal of Community Psychology, 23,* 34–56.

Prothrow-Stith, D. (1987). *Violence prevention curriculum for adolescents.* Newton, MA: Education Development Center, Inc.

Rapp, L., & Wodarski, J. (in press). Juvenile violence: The high risk factors, current interventions, and implications for social work practice.

Rapp, L., & Wodarski, J. (1997). The comorbidity of conduct disorder and depression in adolescents: A comprehensive interpersonal treatment technology. *Family Therapy, 24*(2), 81–100.

Sarason, I., & Sarason, B. (1981). Teaching cognitive and social skills to high school students. *Journal of Consulting and Clinical Psychology, 49,* 908–918.

Sheley, J., McGee, Z., & Wright, J. (1992). Gun-related violence in and around the inner-city schools. *AJDC, 146,* 677–682.

Slaby, R., Barham, J., Eron, L., & Wilcox, B. (1994). Policy recommendations: Prevention and treatment of youth violence. In L. Eron, J. Gentry, & P. Schlegel (Eds.), *Reason to hope: A psychosocial perspective on violence and youth.* Washington, DC: American Psychological Association.

Soriano, M., Soriano, F., & Jimenez, E. (1991). School violence among culturally diverse populations: Sociocultural and institutional considerations. *School Psychology Review, 23*(2), 216–235.

Stein, N. (1995). Sexual harassment in school: The public performance of gendered violence. *Harvard Educational Review, 65*(2), 145–162.

Stephens, R. (1994). School violence prevention and intervention strategies. *School Psychology Review, 23*(2), 204–219.

U.S. Department of Justice (1992). *Uniform Crime Reports.* Washington, DC: U.S. Government Printing Office.

Wheeler, E., & Baron, A. (1994). *Violence in our schools, hospitals and public places: A prevention and management guide.* Ventura, CA: Pathfinder Publishing of California.

Wodarski, J., & Feit, M. (1995). *Adolescent substance abuse: An empirically based group preventive health paradigm.* New York: Haworth Press.

Yung B., & Hammond, R. (1994). Native Americans. In L. Eron, J. Gentry, & P. Schlegel (Eds.), *A reason to hope: A psychosocial perspective on violence and youth.* Washington, DC: American Psychological Association.

Chapter 5

ADOLESCENT SEXUALITY

John S. Wodarski

OVERVIEW

One of the most pressing social problems confronting our society is the increasing number of adolescents who are sexually active and who face the risk of the consequences of their sexual encounters. The statistics of teenage pregnancy are alarming (Franklin, 1988). The high incidence of teenage pregnancy is the result of a decrease in the average age of menses, combined with increasing sexual activity among adolescents (Chilman, 1979; Flick, 1986; Schinke, 1978). By age 18, 65% of boys and 51% of girls are sexually active. Moreover, approximately 50% of American adolescents do not use contraceptives the first time they have intercourse. It is not surprising then that half of premarital pregnancies occur within the first 6 months after initiation of sexual activity (Franklin, 1988).

Between 1950 and 1985 the nonmarital birthrate among adolescents younger than age 20 increased 300% for Whites and 16% for Blacks. It was estimated in 1985 that roughly 1 million teenage girls became pregnant every year, resulting in 600,000 live births and 378,500 pregnancies terminated by abortion (Guttmacher Institute, 1985). It was estimated at that time that 84% of the pregnancies were intended. In 1988, figures increased when it was estimated that 11% of adolescents became pregnant. An estimated 4% had abortions. For 1988, the latest year for which statistics are available, the National Centers for Disease Control in Atlanta, Georgia, reported that 1,005,299 babies—or 26% of U.S. newborns—were born to unmarried women. Sadly, the situation is not expected to improve. There is an expected increase to 2.2 million unplanned pregnancies by the year 2005, and a significant number of these will involve adolescents. Recidivism is an additional concern. It has been reported that 26% of the women who first gave birth at age 16 or younger gave birth a second time within 24 months (Story, 1987).

The decline in age at first intercourse (and delay in contraceptive use by young, sexually active adolescents) has produced increased rates of sexually transmitted disease among adolescents. Gonorrhea rates are actually higher among sexually active 15-year-olds than among 20- to 24-year-olds. Approximately 2.5 million adolescents have had sexually transmitted diseases (STDs), and 1 in 4 sexually active adolescents will have an STD before graduating from high school (American Medical Association [AMA], 1991).

Adolescents who become pregnant are ensuring for themselves and their babies a bleak future marked by interrupted education, inadequate vocational training, poor work skills, economic dependency and poverty, large single-parent households, and social isolation (Barth & Schinke, 1983). As Campbell (1968) commented, 90% of an adolescent's life script is written when she becomes a mother, and the story is often an unhappy one. Three out of four teenage mothers drop out of high school and only one in fifty finishes college. The cost to the teenage mother is high. Chances are increased that she and her baby will live in poverty. Moreover, the chances are great that the mother and baby will suffer ill health, as few pregnant teens obtain prenatal care.

Adolescent pregnancy is increasingly commonplace today and poses many difficulties for both the individuals involved and for society as a whole. Pregnant adolescents and their babies are at higher nutritional, health, social, and educational risk than the general population and are in need of comprehensive, interdisciplinary care (McAnarney, 1985). For programs to successfully address this problem, factors related to unintended pregnancies and consequences of teenagers' sexuality must be identified and understood. This chapter provides a review of current literature on these factors and consequences. Relevant prevention strategies are examined to furnish the rationale for a more comprehensive practice model to prevent unsafe sexual practices, sexually transmitted disease, and teenage pregnancies.

The High Cost of Teenage Sexuality

Teenage Pregnancies.   Each teenage pregnancy translates into a significant cost to the taxpayer, which is a major cause for concern. In 1985, for example, teenage pregnancy cost each U.S. taxpayer $16.65 in Aid to Families with Dependent Children (AFDC), Medicaid, and food stamps (Guttmacher Institute, 1985). In another example, the city of Baltimore spent about $179,500,000 in 1987 on AFDC, Medicaid, and food stamps for families that were begun when the mother was a teenager. Had these births been delayed until the mother was at least 20 years old, Baltimore would have saved almost $72,000,000 in public outlays (Santelli, Rosenblatt, & Birn, 1990). The cost borne by Medicaid for a birth to a teenager age 14 or younger has been calculated as $3,494; the costs for 15- to 17-year-olds is $3,224; and for 18- and 19-year-olds, it is $2,696, exclusive of pediatric care (Armstrong & Waszak, 1990).

The National Research Council estimates that for each year a first birth is delayed, the family income when the mother reaches age 27 is increased by $500.

Thus, every year a first birth is delayed (up to age 20), the chances of a women and her family having a poverty-level income are reduced by about 22%. The Children's Defense Fund reports that women who first give birth as teens have about half the lifetime earnings of women who first give birth in their twenties (Armstrong & Pascale, 1990). Three major national surveys found the incidence of poverty among families begun by teen births to be 20%, 50%, and 60% greater than among families of mothers who gave birth to their first child at a later age (Furstenberg, Brooks-Gunn, & Morgan, 1987).

The Center for Population Options (CPO) determined that the federal government spent $21.6 billion in 1989 on families begun by teen mothers. This includes $10.4 billion for AFDC, $3.4 billion for food stamps, and $7.7 billion for Medicaid. Based on the assumption that families begun by teen births comprise 53% of the welfare-recipient population, they consume 53% of the funding of these programs.

This represents the projected cost to the federal government over the subsequent 20 years of a family begun by a teen birth, again including only the three benefit programs. Reflected in the calculations are the observations that (a) approximately 1 in 3 teen mothers receives welfare, (b) the average length of time a woman who begins her family as a teen remains on welfare is 2.5 years, (c) the probability a teen mother will receive public assistance declines over her lifetime, and (d) the younger a woman when she first gives birth, the more children she can be expected to have.

All considered, the CPO estimates that a family begun by a teenage mother in 1989 will cost taxpayers an average of $16,975 by the time that baby reaches age 20. This figure, however, is deceptively low because it represents an average across all first births to adolescent mothers, even though only one third of families begun by a teen birth actually receive welfare. More informatively, the CPO projects that the government will spend an average of $50,925 over 20 years on each family, begun in 1989 by a teen birth, who enrolled in public assistance. Presumably, the figure is averaged down by the families who drop out of the welfare system.

The CPO estimates that the families begun in 1989 by a teen birth will have cost the public treasury $6.4 billion by the year 2009.

Teenage Sexually Transmitted Disease.   More than two thirds of adolescents with AIDS were infected through sexual contact with adults. The prevalence of HIV infection among adolescents is a source of concern. Because it takes an estimated 5 to 10 years for the HIV infection to result in AIDS, many young adults who have AIDS contracted the virus as adolescents. Approximately 20% of people identified as having AIDS are between ages 20 and 29 (AMA, 1991).

Contraceptive use has not kept up with adolescent coital activity. One significant reason for this may have to do with the development stage of the adolescent. The key to effective use of contraceptives may lie in a teen's cognitive ability to think abstractly—linking present behavior with future consequences, as well as recognizing the risks involved with unprotected sexual activity (Doctors, 1985). Many teens, especially younger ones, have not yet achieved this level of cognitive ability. See Chapter 6, "Preventing HIV Disease in Adolescents," for elaboration of the AIDS situation in the United States.

Current Expenditures.   AIDS is expensive. It is costly in terms of pain, suffering, and premature mortality, and in terms of fear, anxiety, and grief. It costs lovers their partners, parents their children, and children their parents. It is also costly in monetary terms. We spent about $10 billion on HIV-related activities in 1991. Federal government expenditures alone totaled $3.46 billion: $1.245 billion for research, $1.346 billion on medical care, $567 million for education and prevention, and $305 million in income support to AIDS victims (Office of Management and Budget [OMB], 1990). Federal expenditures on AIDS from 1982 to 1991 totaled almost $12 billion (National Center for Health Statistics [NCHS]; 1990s; OMB, 1990). Since the federal government contributes approximately one third of the total spent on AIDS, total spending during that time approaches $36 billion.

Hellinger estimates that the direct cost of AIDS will have been $5.8 billion in 1991, with the cost of treating an HIV-infected person averaging $5,150 yearly and the cost of treating a patient with full-blown AIDS averaging $32,000 yearly (Foreman, 1991).

Future Costs.   Forecasts of the future costs of AIDS vary. Foreman (1991) estimated total personal care costs (drug, physician, hospital, and nursing home costs) to be $8.5 billion (in 1985 dollars) in 1991. They projected an additional $2.3 billion to be spent on nonpersonal care activity (research, testing, education, and support services). Winkenwerder & Associates estimated federal spending on HIV-related illnesses to reach $4.3 billion in 1992 and total national expenditures to be three times that. Hellinger estimated the cumulative lifetime medical care expenses (in 1988 dollars) for all people diagnosed with AIDS to be $4.3 billion in 1990, $5.3 billion in 1991, $6.5 million in 1992, and $7.8 billion in 1993. He additionally projected that expenditures for medical care alone to AIDS patients in 1994 would total $10.4 billion (Foreman, 1991). In spite of the armed forces' policy of discharging HIV-infected persons, the U.S. General Accounting Office (U.S. GAO) projects that AIDS will cost the U.S. military and veterans' health care system $3 billion by the end of the 1990s (U.S. GAO, 1990).

Altogether, in 1989 alone, private insurers paid over $1 billion in AIDS-related health and life insurance claims, 71% more than in 1988 (Carrol, 1989).

The CDC estimated that over 500,000 persons in this country are HIV infected and do not know it (K. Golan, personal communication, August 1991). Thus, HIV-related expenses are expected to continue to increase until some type of cure or solution is found.

Social Consequences of Teenage Sexuality

Adolescents who engage in sexual activity are most likely to have lower grades in school, lower expectations of achievement, and lower levels of parental control, and to lack strong religious beliefs. They are likely to see their parents and peers in conflict. Many adolescents' mothers have low self-esteem and are inclined to be passive and hold traditional stereotypical views of male-female roles (Lockhart & Wodarski, 1990).

ASSESSMENT MEASURES

This section describes those measures that we have found helpful in evaluation of current interventions to reduce teenage pregnancy and sexually transmitted disease. We have chosen these measures based on the criteria of adequate reliability and ease of administration. A brief description of each is provided to assist professionals in determining whether to incorporate these assessment measures in evaluation.

Sex Knowledge

Sex Knowledge Test.   (Kirby, 1985.) This inventory is a 34-item, multiple-choice scale. It includes the following areas: adolescent physical development, adolescent marriage, the probability of pregnancy, birth control, and sexually transmitted disease. The test was developed after literature and overall goals of sexuality education were examined. The test-retest reliability of the knowledge test was determined by administering the test to 58 adolescents on two occasions, 2 weeks apart, and then calculating the correlation coefficient between their scores on the first administration and their totals on the second administration. The reliability is .89.

Behavior Inventory.   (Kirby, 1985.) Three aspects of behaviors were considered in developing the sex knowledge measures: the skills with which the behavior is completed, the comfort experienced during that behavior, and the frequency of that behavior. The Behavior Inventory measures these three aspects as demonstrated in:

1. Skills in taking responsibility for personal behavior
2. Social decision-making skills
3. Sexual decision making
4. Communication skills
5. Assessment skills

6. Birth control assertiveness skills

7. Comfort engaging in social activities

8. Comfort talking about sex and birth control

9. Comfort expressing concern and caring

10. Comfort being assertive sexually

11. Comfort having current sex life

12. Comfort getting and using birth control

13. Existence and frequency of sexual activity

14. Frequency of use of birth control

15. Frequency of communication about sex and birth control with parents

16. Frequency of communication about sex and birth control with friends

17. Frequency of communication about sex and birth control with boyfriends or girlfriends

The questions that measure skills use a 5-point scale; the questions that measure comfort use 4-point Likert-type scales. The questions measuring sexual activity, use of birth control, and frequency of communication ask how many times during the previous month the respondent engaged in the specific activity.

Test-retest coefficients indicate that the items have a great range of reliability coefficients. The scale measuring skills ranges from poor (.57) to excellent (.88). Scales measuring comfort range from a low of .38 (comfort getting and using birth control) to a high of .70 (comfort having current sex life). The questions involving sexual activity have excellent reliability. The questions about whether respondents have ever had intercourse had a reliability of 1.00. The items measuring frequencies of communication have an adequate, but not excellent, reliability (Kirby, 1985).

Attitude and Values Inventory. (Kirby, 1985.) This instrument includes 15 different scales, each consisting of 5-point Likert-type items measuring the following:

1. Clarity of long-term goals

2. Clarity of personal sexual values

3. Understanding of personal sexual values

4. Understanding of emotional needs

5. Understanding of personal social behavior

6. Understanding of personal sexual responses

7. Attitudes toward various gender role behaviors

8. Attitudes toward sexuality in life

9. Attitudes toward the importance of birth control

10. Attitudes toward premarital intercourse

11. Attitudes toward the use of pressure and force in sexual activity

12. Recognition of the importance of the family

13. Self-esteem

14. Satisfaction with personal sexuality

15. Satisfaction with social relationships

The reliabilities of the 15 different scales were determined in two different ways. First, the test-retest reliabilities were found by administering the questionnaire twice, at an interval of 2 weeks, to 51 participants in different programs, and then calculating the correlation coefficient between the first administration and the second administration of each scale. Second, the overall reliability of each scale was calculated by randomly selecting about 100 pretest and posttest questionnaires from each site, combining the questionnaires into a single file, and then calculating Cronbach's alpha for the items in each scale. Basically, using all of the measures of reliability, scales of the clarity of goals and values range from a coefficient of .54 to .90; scales addressing the understanding of needs, social behavior, and response range from .51 to .84; attitude scales range from .30 to .94; self-esteem scales range from .73 to .80; and satisfaction scales range from .64 to .88.

Youth HIV/AIDS Knowledge and Attitudes

The Knowledge, Attitudes, Beliefs, and Practice (KABP) is a standardized survey instrument developed by the World Health Organization (WHO) for measuring AIDS-related knowledge, attitudes, beliefs, and practices of adolescents (WHO, 1989). The instrument measures self-efficacy in avoiding pressure to have sex, in AIDS knowledge, and in attitudes and perceived social norms toward sexual intercourse. Behavior-specific questions elicit responses related to smoking, drug use, sexual intercourse, intention to engage in sexual intercourse in the next three months, and intention to use condoms when having sex (Seha, Klepp, & Ndeki, 1994).

Instructional Evaluation for Students.   (Kirby, 1985.) This class evaluation contains two parts. The first part asks the respondents to rate numerous teaching skills of the instructor, characteristics of classroom interaction, and program structure and materials. The second part asks participants to assess as accurately as possible the current or future effects of the course. In particular, it asks how the course affected their:

1. Knowledge

2. Understanding of personal behavior

3. Clarity of values

4. Attitudes toward birth control

5. Communication about sexuality

6. Communication with parents

7. Probability of having sex

APPROACHES TO PREVENTION

Past Approaches to Prevention

Despite extensive documentation of early childbearing consequences, efforts to prevent or ameliorate teenage pregnancy have been ineffective (Schinke, 1997; Stout & Rivara, 1989). One reason for this failure appears to be the lack of a complete conceptual framework for understanding and preventing this growing social problem. An extensive literature review reveals that, rather than recognizing the factorial complexity of the phenomenon, most approaches to understanding and preventing teenage pregnancy can be characterized as either reductionistic models stressing a single underlying explanation or developmental models emphasizing a normal adolescent maturational process (Schinke & Gilchrist, 1977). The reductionistic approach explains teenage pregnancy as resulting from one problem condition or factor that leads to a single, straightforward assumption: Given easy, low-cost access to sex and contraceptive education and services, adolescents will be informed, responsible, and self-regulating in avoiding unplanned pregnancies. Prevention, as emphasized in traditional sex education, attempts to change attitudes by exposing adolescents to the unattractive consequences of their behaviors. This so-called scare tactic approach has not been effective in preventing teenage pregnancies (Dryfoos, 1983; Gilchrist, Schinke, & Blythe, 1979).

The search for a pathology that underlies teenage sexual activities has directed many efforts and has guided many of the reductionistic prevention programs. Researchers have looked for personality correlates of adolescents' vulnerability to having intercourse (Goldfarb et al., 1977), pregnancy risk (Rosen & Ager, 1981), and decision making about childbearing (Perlman, Klerman, & Kinard, 1981). Research has uncovered little reason to suspect that adolescents' sexual behavior is pathological (Gilchrist, 1981; Gilchrist & Schinke, 1983; Litt, Cuskey, & Rudd, 1980; Olson, 1980; Schinke, 1979). Nevertheless, a host of social service programs for teenagers has been based on the pathological orientation. Unfortunately, pathologically oriented sex education programs have had little or no effect on adolescents' sexual behavior (Kirby, 1980; Reid, 1982; Zelnik & Kim, 1982).

The developmentalists, in contrast, have strongly stressed the complexity of multiple interactional factors that influence adolescents' behavior (Jones & Bonte, 1990). They suggest that situational, social, interpersonal, and maturational factors may interact to lead adolescents into premarital sexual activities and can be factors that prevent adolescents from effectively applying their contraceptive knowledge and understanding (Cvetkovich & Grote, 1980; Sandberg & Jacobs, 1971). Cvetkovich and Grote (1980) further suggest that female adolescents may be placed at pregnancy risk "not by any form of pathology, moral or otherwise, but, by a unique convergence of factors which are 'normal' to the lives of many" (p. 2). Adolescence is a period of growth that demands mastery of critical developmental tasks, two of which are learning sexual functioning (Wagner, 1970) and the relational nature of sexual activities (McAlister, Perry, & Maccoby, 1979). McAlister and his colleagues (1979) suggest that if prevention efforts are to be effective, their developers must consider factors that include the interpersonal aspects of risk taking, the social significance of many problem behaviors, and the role of peer pressure. In the Cvetkovich and Grote study (1980), females reported they became sexually active because they could not say no, because they wanted to please and satisfy their boyfriends, or because it seemed as though sexual activity was expected of them.

One major perspective of this approach suggests that adolescents acquire cognitive and behavioral skills to cope with the new opportunities and expectations accompanying physical and social maturity if they are to avoid behaviors detrimental to themselves and others. Additionally, this perspective suggests that adolescents need skills to transform knowledge or abstract information into personal decisions and personal decisions into overt behavior (Alemi, Cherry, & Meffert, 1989; Schinke, Gilchrist, & Blythe, 1980; Schinke, Gilchrist, & Small, 1979; Schoeman, 1990).

A second perspective used under the developmentalistic approach is that of values clarification. Chesler (1980) suggested, "In addition to needing accurate, unbiased information about contraceptive technology, teenagers need help in clarifying their values so that social behaviors are congruent with their moral codes" (p. 18). Although the data are not in, values-focused programs, which are aimed at values clarification, may have the potential of lowering teenage pregnancy and of transferring values to other developmental tasks teenagers are confronted with during this stage (Toohey & Valenzuela, 1982). However, earlier research on values clarification programs has indicated that this perspective has not helped teenagers improve their self-esteem, change their interpersonal relationships, or alter their sexual values or behavior (Lockwood, 1978).

Current Prevention Strategies

Prevention programs may be classified into three general groups: sex education and information, contraceptive services, and the broadening of life options such as general education and employment during pregnancy and after childbirth (Dryfoos, 1983). Sex education is considered the primary prevention strategy of teenage pregnancy.

Sex education is one prevention strategy of teenage pregnancy that offers two major advantages: It can reach all young people before they become sexually active, and information can be provided to them at relatively low cost through the school, churches, and other delivery systems. In the past, sex education attempted to help adolescents understand the physical changes accompanying puberty, the biology of reproduction, and the responsibilities of family life.

Several studies aimed at HIV/AIDS prevention have incorporated skills-building elements with some notable successes. According to Auslander (1993), short-term, information-only interventions are ineffective in increasing HIV/AIDS-related knowledge and reducing high-risk activities. She suggests that, in addition to information, youth need to acquire skills to apply what they have learned when faced with situations that place them at risk. She states further that adolescents need to learn specific interpersonal skills to resist peer pressure to engage in unsafe sexual practices and take drugs, and they need skills to negotiate less risky activities with friends or partners. Auslander reviews three studies that suggest that HIV/AIDS prevention programs based on a cognitive-behavioral framework hold some promise. In the first, Rotheram-Borus and coworkers (Rotheram-Borus & Koopman, 1991) focused on improving knowledge and coping skills through video and art workshops, information about community resources, and reduction of the number of individual barriers to safer sex. The frequency of engaging in high-risk patterns of sexual behavior decreased as the number of intervention sessions increased. In the second study, Jemmott, Jemmott, and Fong (1992) provided inner-city Black male youths with a 5-hour program designed to increase knowledge of STDs, reduce unsafe attitudes, and encourage problem solving related to risky sexual behavior through role playing, videotapes, games, and exercises. Their intervention resulted in greater knowledge, less risky attitudes, and less inclination to engage in risky behavior. Moreover, at 3-month follow-up, the adolescents were engaging in fewer occasions of sexual intercourse, had fewer sexual partners, used condoms more frequently, and engaged in anal intercourse less often than the adolescents in the control condition. Finally, Auslander (1993) compared a skills training format (role plays, practice, demonstrations) to a discussion-only format to reduce HIV risk among adolescents who engage in delinquent activities. They found that the discussion group format was equally as effective as the skills training group in imparting knowledge, changing attitudes, and increasing interpersonal skills to cope with HIV-risk situations. The skills-training format, however, was more effective in changing the youths' intentions to engage in HIV-risk behaviors.

Most Americans today believe that sex education should address the complex problems of human sexuality that teenagers face. But a few people still believe that sex education, particularly when it covers methods of contraception, actually increases teenagers' sexual activity, causes an upswing in unintended pregnancies, and undermines the family unit (Kenney & Orr, 1984). Consequently, sex education remains controversial, despite the enormous diversity of nationwide program offerings. Many parents and teenagers believe, however, that sex education plays an important role in the prevention of unwanted teenage pregnancies (Bachman, Johnston, & O'Malley, 1980; Gallup Opinion Index, 1978).

Sex education rarely involves parents as primary sex educators of their children (McAnarney & Schreider, 1984). Research has revealed that fewer than 20% of parents tell their teenage children about intercourse, discuss birth control, or provide them with sex education literature (Schinke & Gilchrist, 1984). McAnarney and Schreider (1984) suggest several reasons for this: (a) Parents may not have adequate information to share, (b) parents may not know how to educate their child about sexuality, (c) parents may be uncomfortable with the subject, and (d) adolescents may be uncomfortable when parents assume the roles of sex educators, especially if no discussion of the subject has occurred before puberty. Parents need to be prepared for their roles as sex educators before their children reach teenage years. Thus, an effective prevention program will include a parental component.

Very few sex education programs have been systematically evaluated (Kirby, 1985). With the exception of the aforementioned follow-up study by Jemmott, Jemmott, and Fong (1992), virtually no attempts have been made to conduct follow-up studies to ascertain the long-term effects of sex education on adolescents' knowledge, attitudes, and behavior. Evaluative studies of sex education have concluded that there was no evidence to support the belief that sex education would increase or decrease the sexual activities of teenagers (Kirby, Alter, & Scales, 1979; Stout & Rivara, 1989) or to support the claim that the decision to engage in sexual activities is influenced by sex education in school. However, females who are sexually active and had sex education that covered contraceptive methods appeared somewhat more likely to use contraceptives the first time they engaged in sexual intercourse. They also experienced fewer pregnancies than sexually active females who did not have formal sex education (Zelnik & Kim, 1982). A needed element of evaluative research of sex education programs is the study of the long-term retention of knowledge.

THE COMPREHENSIVE PARENT, PEERS, AND SCHOOL PREVENTION MODEL

Acknowledgment of a problem is the first step toward its resolution. Substantial research has been devoted to teenage pregnancy. Individuals who are associated with adolescents can demonstrate their concern about combating the problem of teenage pregnancy by developing prevention programs aimed at three groups: adolescents, parents, and schoolteachers and counselors. For effective pregnancy prevention training, information input and behavior change output must be considered. More important, training must address influential intervening variables, that is, cognitive and moral processes mediating the understanding and use of information in decision making. Thus, a comprehensive education program that gives teenagers, parents, and schoolteachers and counselors accurate sex education through a curriculum that is attractive, through social skills training in terms of assertiveness and problem solving, and through practice in applying this information in at-risk situations is needed.

Timing, Context, and Content

Research has indicated that if adolescents are to adopt the idea of pregnancy prevention, then sex education must be an integral part of their personal development and must begin before or during puberty (McAnarney & Schreider, 1984; Thornburg, 1981). In practice, most sex education curricula and programs have occurred too late in the developmental cycle (Blythe, Gilchrist, & Schinke, 1981; Gilchrist & Schinke, 1983; Gilchrist, Schinke, & Blythe, 1979; Schinke, 1982; Schinke, Blythe, Gilchrist, & Burt, 1981). Auslander (1993) suggests that it is imperative that prevention programs address the social environments and culture of the contexts in which adolescents interact. This involves educating the staff, the foster parents, the biological parents, and all institutions in which adolescents will reside. She states further that, to maintain attitudinal and behavior change over time, realistic and culturally specific prevention practices need to be consistently reinforced among youth within their social environment. Coie et al. (1993, p. 1019) state that "the public schools offer a logical setting for broad-scale prevention interventions because 9 of 10 children in our society are found there." Moreover, they suggest that schools provide the greatest access to children who may be reliably identified as being at risk, while at the same time providing access to those who might be overlooked in the risk assessment protocols. DiClemente (1993) adds that "the school is the only institution regularly attended by most young people, and virtually all youth attend schools before they initiate the behaviors that may place them at risk." The introduction of sex education prevention programs at the middle school level would be appropriate. This follows the suggestion by Doty and King (1985) that to have an impact on adolescent pregnancy rates and to circumvent our traditional practices of providing "too little, too late," sex education programs must begin to span preadolescence, early adolescence, and adolescence. Programs could be incorporated into health education courses or group discussions within local youth organizations associated with churches, as well as through other formal and informal community organizations (Doty & King, 1985).

Auslander (1993) reminds us that there is no one strategy that will be effective with all individuals. Rather, different strategies should be developed in response to the unique characteristics of the target population. She suggests that early prevention programs for youths who are not yet sexually active might be designed differently than those for youths who are sexually active, and interventions needed within schools would be different from those delivered in clinics.

Although it is often said that sex education programs should be values-free, Scales (1983) and McAnarney and Schreider (1984) have pointed out that sex education is not values-free. Each program and community, as well as the parents, will stress their beliefs, which are embodied in the program's goals (Scales, 1983). Therefore, the ideal program is grounded in a set of values. Students need not agree initially with these values, but they should be clearly stated so that they can make decisions based on a known standard. The following values will be incorporated into the prototypic sex education program:

1. Being a teen parent is not a good idea; it brings with it social, emotional, educational, financial, and medical consequences.
2. No one should be pressured into a sexual act against his or her will or principles.
3. Postponement of sexual intercourse should be strongly encouraged until adolescents have at least completed high school.
4. The double standards for males and females, which still exist in our society, are not to be condoned.
5. Having unprotected intercourse is like skydiving without a parachute—it is political, social, emotional, and financial suicide (Scales, 1983).

Peers

Prevention programs should assist adolescents in identifying and examining peer pressure and in exploring ways to make individual, deliberate decisions, especially since peers have a significant impact on each other's behaviors. According to DiClemente (1993), the use of peer educators as behavior change agents is perhaps the most underutilized prevention strategy. He adds that informed peer educators may be more credible sources of information and they communicate in a language that is more likely to be understood by their classmates. Thus, we posit that sex education should be offered through a peer group experience. Peer learning structures should create a learning situation in which the performance of each group member furthers the attainment of overall group goals. This increases individual members' support for group performance, strengthens performance under a variety of similar circumstances, and further enhances the attainment of group goals. Group reward structures capitalize on peer influence and peer reinforcement. These are considered to be some of the most potent variables in the acquisition, alteration, and maintenance of prosocial norms among youths (Buckholdt & Wodarski, 1978). Peer programs that foster a sense of self-worth, awareness of one's own feelings, and assertiveness will help adolescents learn to act in their own interests, with a stronger sense of control over their own lives. Moreover, a prevention program must be aimed at males as well as females. Adolescent males are presently less aware of the risks of pregnancy, less informed about contraceptives, and less supportive of the use of contraceptives than are females, and they have the most to learn from a sex education program (Freeman, 1978).

Parent Component

Parents greatly influence their children's behavior. Next to those of peers, parental involvement and communication are most critical and should be strengthened to help adolescents become more responsible. Yoshikawa (1994) suggests that prevention interventions that combine comprehensive family support with early education may bring about long-term prevention through short-term protective effects on multiple risks. In a survey by Yankelovich, Skelly, and White (1979), 84% of the parents of teenagers said it was up to them to teach their children about sex-related topics, even though they supported sex education in public schools. Although parents want to be involved in educating their children about sex-related topics, they find it very difficult (Fox, 1980; Fox & Inazu, 1980). Parents need the skills to establish open communication with their children regarding sexual issues. The main thrust of the program with parents should be toward enhancing communication skills between parents and children, because lack of communication has been consistently shown to have an effect on teenage sexual activities (Cvetkovich & Grote, 1980; Fox & Inazu, 1980; McAnarney & Schreider, 1984). Focusing on increasing parents' skills in communicating, especially in the areas of values clarification and moral consciousness and the relational aspect of sexuality, as well as other sex-related topics, should be a major part of the program for the parental group of the prevention model. Parents, who are often less informed than their teenagers (Dryfoos, 1982a, 1982b), need to be involved in prevention programs in order to become more informed and comfortable with discussing sexual issues with their children. Parental involvement is a necessary element of any successful prevention model so that accurate and open communication, as well as the learning process, can be supported at home. Furthermore, fathers should be present with their sons and mothers with their daughters.

SUMMARY

In order to alleviate the dilemma of teenagers having children, it is evident that the following points must be considered:

1. The timing of sex education is critical; sex education should occur in the middle school years.
2. Attractive curricula taught by qualified teachers are necessary.

3. Curricula should center particularly on gender roles, premarital sexual activity, contraception, abortion, AIDS, psychological issues (e.g., self-esteem and judgment), decision making, and problem solving. Moreover, curricula should include help-seeking strategies, life options, family relationships, and alternatives to pregnancy and parenting (Haslett, 1991; Herdt, 1989).

4. More research is needed on constitutional predisposition for risk taking and how such predispositions interact with the social contexts of adolescent development.

5. The incorporation of the peer group experience as a learning vehicle is necessary since peer norms influence sexual behavior (Benda and DiBlasio, 1991).

6. Sex education should involve the opportunity to practice appropriate behaviors for high-risk situations.

7. A final component of the comprehensive model should be the involvement of parents in the education of their children. One of the reasons that sex education has failed our youngsters is that educators have not employed enough foci to make it meaningful to them. The solution to the problem of pregnancy among teens requires an all-out effort by those societal forces capable of effecting change. Families, schools, peers, communities, businesses, and the media all possess powers to eradicate this social problem. The campaign cannot be waged from only one front, however; combined efforts are essential. The responsibility must be shared for both previous condoning of actions that have perpetuated the problem and for working toward mutual goals and solutions.

REFERENCES

Alemi, F., Cherry, F., & Meffert, G. (1989). Rehearsing decisions may help teenagers: An evaluation of a simulation game. *Computers in Biology and Medicine, 19*(4), 283–290.

American Medical Association. (1991). Adolescent health care: use, costs and problems of access. *Profiles of Adolescent Health: Vol. 2.* Chicago: Author.

Armstrong, E., & Pascale, A. (1990). *Adolescent sexuality, pregnancy, and parenthood: The facts.* Washington, DC: Center for Population Options.

Armstrong, E., & Waszak, C. (1990). *Teenage pregnancy and too-early childbearing: Public costs, personal consequences.* Washington, DC: Center for Population Options.

Auslander, W. (1993). Challenges in HIV prevention among youth: Abuse survivors and participants in delinquent behavior. *Prevention Forum, 13*(4), 12–17.

Bachman, J. G., Johnston, L. D., & O'Malley, P. M. (1980). *Monitoring the future: Questionnaire responses from the nation's high school seniors, 1978.* Ann Arbor: University of Michigan Institute for Social Research, Survey Research Center.

Barth, R. P., & Schinke, S. P. (1983). Coping with daily strain among pregnant and parenting adolescents. *Journal of Social Service Research, 7*(2), 51–63.

Benda, B. B., & DiBlasio, F. A. (1991). Comparison of four theories of adolescent sexual exploration. *Deviant Behavior, 12*(3), 235–257.

Blythe, B. J., Gilchrist, L. D., & Schinke, S. P. (1981). Pregnancy-prevention groups for adolescents. *Social Work, 26*(6), 503–504.

Buckholdt, D., & Wodarski, J. S. (1978). The effects of different reinforcement systems on cooperative behavior exhibited by children in classroom contexts. *Journal of Research and Development in Education, 12*(1), 50–68.

Campbell, A. (1968). The role of family in the reduction of poverty. *Journal of Marriage and the Family, 30*(2), 236–246.

Carrol, W. (1989). *AIDS related claims survey: Claims paid in 1989.* Washington, DC: American Council of Life Insurance Association of America.

Chesler, J. S. (1980). Twenty-seven strategies for teaching contraception to adolescents. *Journal of School Health, 50*(1), 18–21.

Chilman, C. S. (1979). *Adolescent sexuality in a changing American society: Social and psychological perspectives.* Washington, DC: U.S. Government Printing Office.

Coie, J. D., Watt, N. F., West, S. G., Hawkins, G., & David, J. (1993). The science of prevention: A conceptual framework and some directions for a national research program. *American Psychologist, 48*(10), 1013–1022.

Cvetkovich, G., & Grote, B. (1980). Psychosocial development and the social problem of teenage illegitimacy. In C. Chilman (Ed.), *Adolescent pregnancy and childbearing: Findings from research* (pp. 15–41; NIH Publication No. 81-2077). Washington, DC: Department of Health and Human Services.

DiClemente, R. J. (1993). Preventing HIV/AIDS among adolescents: Schools as agents of behavior change. *Journal of the American Medical Association, 279*(6), 760–762.

Doctors, S. R. (1985). Premarital pregnancy and childbirth in adolescence: A psychological overview. In Z. DeFries, R. C. Friedman, & R. Corn (Eds.), *Sexuality: New perspectives* (pp. 45–70). Westport, CT: Greenwood Press.

Doty, M. B., & King, M. (1985). Pregnancy prevention: A private agency's program in public schools. *Social Work in Education, 7*(2), 90–99.

Dryfoos, J. G. (1982a). Contraceptive use, pregnancy intentions and pregnancy outcomes among U.S. women. *Family Planning Perspectives, 14*(2), 81–94.

Dryfoos, J. G. (1982b). The epidemiology of adolescent pregnancy: Incidence, outcomes, and interventions. In I. Stuart & C. Wells (Eds.), *Pregnancy in adolescence: Needs, problems, and management* (pp. 27–47). New York: Van Nostrand Reinhold.

Dryfoos, J. G. (1983). Review of interventions in the field of prevention of adolescent pregnancy. Preliminary report to the Rockefeller Foundation [Monograph].

Flick, L. H. (1986). Paths to adolescent parenthood: Implications for prevention. *Public Health Report, 101*(2), 132–147.

Foreman, J. (1991, June). Care costs may nearly double by 1994. *Boston Globe,* p. 12.

Fox, G. L. (1980). The mother–adolescent daughter relationship as a sexual, socialization structure: A research review. *Family Relations, 29*(1), 21–80.

Fox, G. L., & Inazu, J. K. (1980). Patterns and outcomes of mother-daughter communication about sexuality. *Journal of Social Issues, 36*(1), 7–29.

Franklin, D. L. (1988). Race, class, and adolescent pregnancy: An ecological analysis. *American Journal of Orthopsychiatry, 58*(3), 339–354.

Freeman, E. (1978). Abortion: Subjective attitudes and feelings. *Family Planning Perspectives, 10*(3), 150–155.

Furstenberg, F., Brooks-Gunn, J., & Morgan, S. (1987). Adolescent mothers and their children in later life. *Family Planning Perspectives, 19*(4), 142–151.

Gallup Opinion Index, Report #156 (p. 28). (1978). Princeton, NJ: American Institute of Public Opinion.

Gilchrist, L. D. (1981). Group procedures for helping adolescents cope with sex. *Behavioral Group Therapy, 3*(1), 3–8.

Gilchrist, L. D., & Schinke, S. P. (1983). Counseling with adolescents about their sexuality. In C. S. Chilman (Ed.), *Adolescent sexuality in a changing American society* (pp. 230–249). New York: Wiley.

Gilchrist, L. D., Schinke, S. P., & Blythe, B. J. (1979). Primary prevention services for children and youth. *Children and Youth Services Review, 1*(4), 379–391.

Goldfarb, J. L., Mumford, D. M., Schum, D. A., Smith, P. E., Flowers, C., & Schum, C. (1977). An attempt to detect "pregnancy susceptibility" in indigent adolescent girls. *Journal of Youth and Adolescence, 6*(2), 127–143.

Guttmacher Institute. (1985, March 11). *Report on adolescent pregnancy.* New York: Author.

Haslett, D. C. (1991). *Sex education curricula for young teens: Implications for social work.* Unpublished dissertation, University of Illinois at Chicago.

Herdt, G. (Ed.), (1989). *Gay and lesbian youth.* New York: Haworth Press.

Jemmott, J. B., Jemmott, L. S., & Fong, G. T. (1992). Reductions in HIV risk-associated sexual behaviors among black male adolescents: Effects of an AIDS prevention intervention. *American Journal of Public Health, 82,* 372–377.

Jones, M. E., and Bonte, C. (1990). Conceptualizing community interventions in social service needs of pregnant adolescents. *Journal of Pediatric Care, 4*(4), 193–201.

Kenney, A. M., & Orr, M. T. (1984). Sex education: An overview of current programs, policies, and research. *Phi Delta Kappan, 65*(7), 491–496.

Kirby, D. (1980). The effects of school sex education programs: A review of the literature. *Journal of School Health, 50*(10), 559–563.

Kirby, D. (1985). Sexuality education: A more realistic view of its effects. *Journal of School Health, 55*(10), 421–424.

Kirby, D., Alter, J., & Scales, P. (1979, July). *An analysis of U.S. sex education programs and evaluation methods* (DHEW Publication No. CD-2021-79-DKFR). Washington, DC: U.S. Department of Health, Education, and Welfare.

Litt, I. F., Cuskey, W. R., & Rudd, S. (1980). Identifying adolescents at risk for noncompliance with contraceptive therapy. *Journal of Pediatrics, 96*(4), 742–745.

Lockhart, L., & Wodarski, J. (1990). Teenage pregnancy: implications for social work practice. *Family Therapy, 17*(1), 30–47.

Lockwood, A. (1978). The effects of values clarification and moral development criteria. *Review of Educational Research, 48*(3), 325–364.

McAlister, A. L., Perry, C., & Maccoby, N. (1979). Adolescent smoking: Onset and prevention. *Pediatrics, 63,* 650–658.

McAnarney, E. R., (1985). Adolescent pregnancy and childbearing: New data, new challenges. *Pediatrics, 75*(5), 973–975.

McAnarney, E. R., & Schreider, C. (1984). Identifying social and psychological antecedents of adolescent pregnancy. New York: William T. Grant Foundation.

National Center for Health Statistics. (1990). *Health: United States, 1989* (DHHS Publication No. [PHS] 90-1232). Hyattsville, MD: Author.

Office of Management and Budget. (1990). *Budget of the United States Government; Fiscal Year 1991.* Washington, DC: U.S. Government Printing Office.

Olson, L. (1980). Social and psychological correlates of pregnancy resolution among adolescent women: A review. *American Journal of Orthopsychiatry, 50*(3), 432–445.

Perlman, S. B., Klerman, L. V., & Kinard, E. M. (1981). The use of socioeconomic data to predict teenage birth rates: An exploratory study in Massachusetts. *Public Health Reports, 96*(4), 335–341.

Reid, D. (1982). School sex education and the causes of unintended teenage pregnancies: A review. *Health Education Journal, 41*(1), 4–11.

Rosen, R. H., & Ager, J. W. (1981). Self-concept and contraception: Pre-contraception decision making. *Population and Environment, 4*(1), 11–23.

Rotheram-Borus, M. J., & Koopman, C. (1991). Sexual risk behaviors, AIDS knowledge, and beliefs about AIDS among runaways. *American Journal of Public Health, 81,* 208–210.

Sandberg, E. C., & Jacobs, R. I. (1971). Psychology of the misuse and rejection of contraception. *American Journal of Obstetrics and Gynecology, 110*(2), 227–242.

Santelli, J., Rosenblatt, L., and Birn, A. E. (1990). Estimates of public cost for teenage childbearing in Baltimore city in FY 1987. *Maryland Medical Journal, 39*(5), 459–464.

Scales, P. (1983). Adolescent sexuality and education: Principles, approaches, and resources. In C. S. Chilman (Ed.), *Adolescent sexuality in a changing American society* (pp. 207–229). New York: Wiley.

Schinke, S. P. (1978). Teenage pregnancy: The need for multiple casework services. *Social Casework, 59*(7), 406–410.

Schinke, S. P. (1979). Research on adolescent health: Social work implications. In W. T. Hall & C. Y. Young (Eds.), *Health and social needs of the adolescent: Professional responsibilities* (pp. 320–351). Pittsburgh: University of Pittsburgh Graduate School of Public Health.

Schinke, S. P. (1982). School-based model for preventing teenage pregnancy. *Social Work in Education, 4*(2), 34–42.

Schinke, S. P. (1997). Preventing teenage pregnancy: Translating research knowledge. *Journal of Human Behavior in the Social Environment, 1*(1), 53–66.

Schinke, S. P., Blythe, B. J., Gilchrist, L. D., & Burt, G. A. (1981). Primary prevention of adolescent pregnancy. *Social Work with Groups, 4*(2), 121–135.

Schinke, S. P., & Gilchrist, L. D. (1977). Adolescent pregnancy: An interpersonal skill training approach to prevention. *Social Work in Health Care, 3*(2), 159–167.

Schinke, S. P., & Gilchrist, L. D. (1984). *Life skills counseling with adolescents.* Baltimore: University Park Press.

Schinke, S. P., Gilchrist, L. D., & Blythe, B. J. (1980). Role of communication in the prevention of teenage pregnancy. *Health and Social Work, 5,* 54–60.

Schinke, S. P., Gilchrist, L. D., & Small, R. W. (1979). Preventing unwanted adolescent pregnancy: A cognitive-behavioral approach. *American Journal of Orthopsychiatry, 49*(1), 81–88.

Schoeman, M. (1990). Sexuality education among black South African teenagers: What can reasonably be expected? *Curatimis, 13*(3-4), 13–18.

Seha, A., Klepp, K., & Ndeki, S. (1994). Scale reliability and construct validity: A pilot study among primary school children in Northern Tanzania. *AIDS Education and Prevention, 6*(6), 524–534.

Story, M. (1987). Nutrition issues and adolescent pregnancy. *Contemporary Nutrition, 12*(1), 1–2.

Stout, J. W., & Rivara, F. P. (1989). School and sex education: Does it work? *Pediatrics, 83*(3), 375–379.

Thornburg, H. D. (1981). The amount of sex information learning obtained during early adolescence. *Journal of Early Adolescence, 1*(3), 171–183.

Toohey, J. V., & Valenzuela, G. J. (1982). Values clarification as a technique for family planning education. *Journal of School Health, 53*(2), 121–125.

U.S. General Accounting Office. (1990). Defense health care: Effects of AIDS in the military (CAD/HRD-90-39). Washington, DC: Author.

Wagner, N. (1970). Adolescent sexual behavior. In E. Evans (Ed.), *Adolescents: Readings in behavior and development.* Hinsdale, IL: Dryden Press.

World Health Organization (1989). *Interview schedule for knowledge, attitudes, beliefs and practices on AIDS of young people* (WHO/GPA/SBR). Geneva: Author.

Yankelovich, Skelly, & White, Inc. (1979). *The General Mills American family report, 1978–79.* Minneapolis: General Mills.

Yoshikawa, H. (1994). Prevention as cumulative protection: Effects of early family support and education on chronic delinquency and its risks. *Psychological Bulletin, 115*(1), 28–54.

Zelnik, M., & Kim, Y. J. (1982). Sex education and its association with teenage sexual activity, pregnancy, and contraceptive use. *Family Planning Perspectives, 14*(3), 117–126.

Chapter 6

PREVENTING HIV DISEASE IN ADOLESCENTS

Charles W. Mueller
Robert Bidwell
Scott Okamoto
Eberhard Mann

Since its first appearance in 1981, acquired immunodeficiency syndrome (AIDS) has grown to have a profound impact on the world's adolescent and young adult population. It is presently the sixth leading cause of death among young people ages 15 to 24 and the leading cause of death among men ages 25 to 44 (Centers for Disease Control [CDC], 1995).

AIDS is a disease caused by the human immunodeficiency virus (HIV). For every individual who is symptomatic from AIDS, many more are infected but not yet symptomatic. HIV is transmitted from one person to another through direct exchange of blood, semen, or vaginal fluid. Once infected, an individual's immune system is invaded by the virus, and an active process of viral replication and immune cell destruction begins. Over time, often after many years, the immune system becomes compromised to a point where a person becomes vulnerable to repeated opportunistic infections affecting virtually any organ system. These infectious assaults, along with direct infection by HIV of the brain and other organs, ultimately result in death. Research continues to yield treatments that improve the quality of life for those infected with HIV. However, as there remains no cure, prevention continues to be the only option for decreasing mortality resulting from AIDS.

EPIDEMIOLOGY

Worldwide, there have been an estimated 4.5 million AIDS cases since the beginning of the pandemic (World Health Organization, 1995), with half of new cases

Note: This work was supported in part by a grant from the Robert E. Black Foundation and by NIH Grant RO1 MH47649-02.

appearing among 15- to 24-year-olds (Goldsmith, 1993). Three quarters of all infections have occurred through sexual intercourse. Over 90% have occurred in developing regions of the world, the majority in Africa. In the United States, a total of 513,486 persons have been diagnosed with AIDS as of December 1995 (CDC, 1995). It is estimated that 600,000 to 900,000 individuals may be infected with the virus but have not yet developed AIDS. Each year there are an estimated 40,000 to 80,000 new cases of AIDS. Over time, there have been changes in the epidemiology of HIV infection in the United States. Early in the epidemic, the great majority of AIDS cases resulted from male-to-male sexual contact. In the past decade, the proportion of cases due to male-to-male contact has decreased and percentages due to heterosexual contact and intravenous drug use, as well as cases among women, children, and ethnic and racial minorities, have increased. As of December 1995, 42% of cases were due to male-to-male contact, 26% from intravenous drug use, 11% from heterosexual transmission, and 5% due to combined male-to-male contact and intravenous drug use.

By the end of 1995, 2,354 adolescents ages 13 to 19 had been diagnosed with AIDS in the United States (CDC, 1995). Among young adults ages 20 to 24, there have been 18,955 additional cases. Because the latency period for HIV infection may be as long as 10 years or more, it is likely that most of those diagnosed with AIDS in their early 20s were infected as teenagers. Seroprevalence studies indicate that infection rates vary among differing populations of adolescents. The number of adolescents with AIDS increases markedly with age: 74% of all reported teenage cases are between ages 17 and 19, the rest are found among 13- to 16-year-olds (Lindegren, Hanson, Miller, Byers, & Onorato, 1994). Among heterosexual adolescents, rates for females are considerably higher than those for males. The incidence of HIV in young women giving birth has been fairly stable at approximately 1.6/1,000 but the figures are higher in urban centers. More pronounced among teenagers is the number of HIV-infected women: The male-to-female ratio is 2.1:1 compared to 7.8:1 in adults. Over half of infected female teenagers report heterosexual exposure to injecting drug users versus 36% of adults who report the same source of infection. Fewer infected male teens report homosexual contact (33%) than do young adults (64%; CDC, 1994). While HIV can be found in all regions of the country, the greatest proportion of infections is found in certain urban areas. For example, while only 3% of all U.S. teenagers live in New York City, 20% of all reported infected adolescents live there. Other HIV epicenters are New Jersey, San Francisco, Los Angeles, Chicago, Miami, and Puerto Rico (Sperling, Sacks, & Mayer, 1989). Opportunity for infection is thus much greater in these locales.

Certain groups of adolescents are at particularly high risk for HIV infection. They include gay, and male bisexual youth (Dean & Meyer, 1995); homeless and runaway adolescents (Allen et al., 1994); teenage drug injectors (Wendell, Onorato, McCray, Allen, & Sweeney, 1992), and crack users (Edlin et al., 1994).

African American and Latino youth are significantly more likely to be infected by HIV than are Caucasian youth. African American adolescents ages 13 to 19 constitute 14% of the total U.S. teenage population, but account for 37% of all teen AIDS cases. Similarly, Hispanic youth constitute 8% of the teenage population, but 19% of known teen AIDS cases (CDC, 1994).

HIV-RELATED KNOWLEDGE AND RISK BEHAVIOR

The vast majority of U.S. high school students report having received some form of HIV education, whereby, at a minimum, youth are told some basic biological facts, the major transmissions routes, and ways to avoid infection. Given these and related efforts (e.g., public service announcements; television, movie, and other mass media programming), it should come as no surprise that most adolescents are quite knowledgeable about HIV. Many recent surveys have shown that most adolescents possess fairly accurate knowledge about the major aspects of HIV infection. They know that AIDS is caused by the HIV virus that is transmitted through unprotected hetero- or homosexual intercourse or use of shared needles with infected persons. They realize that HIV infection may take many years before causing the symptoms of AIDS, and that it is not curable. Most teenagers can describe methods of protection from HIV infection, such as sexual abstinence, use of condoms, and avoidance of contaminated needles (Kirby, Short, & Collins, 1994; Lindegren et al., 1994; Osborne, Kistner, & Helgemo, 1993). In fact, adolescents, on average, seem to know more about HIV and AIDS than do most adults in the United States (Sweat & Levin, 1995). When knowledge mistakes occur, youth tend to think that some behaviors (e.g., kissing) or experiences (e.g., mosquito bites) are actual transmission routes (cf. Mueller et al., 1996).

Sexual activity among adolescents increased greatly between 1970 and 1990. For instance, in 1970, 29% of 15- to 19-year-old females reported premarital intercourse, and this rate increased to 52% by 1988. By 1990, about 10% of 13-year-olds had engaged in sexual intercourse. By age 15, one third of males and one fourth of females had engaged in sexual intercourse, and by age 18, almost all men (86%) and over half of all women were sexually active (Sonenstein, Pleck, & Ku, 1989).

Recent nationwide HIV education efforts have clearly increased adolescent knowledge and seem to have had some impact on sexual risk behavior in adolescents, primarily since 1990. Since 1990, the steep increase in adolescent sexual activity seems to have leveled off, at least for those adolescents attending high school. For example, from 1990 to 1993 there has been no consistent change in the percentages of high school students who reported having ever had intercourse, having had intercourse with more than four partners, and having had intercourse within the last 3 months (CDC, 1995). Concurrently, among sexually active high school students, condom use at last intercourse increased from 46.2% in 1991 to 52.8% in

1993. Other indicators of unprotected sex (e.g., sexually transmitted diseases and teenage pregnancies), all of which increased markedly between 1979 and 1990, have shown a gradual decrease since 1990 (National Health Statistics, 1996).

In summary, for the last 10 years the Centers for Disease Control and Prevention began to collaborate with local, state, and national educational and health agencies to develop HIV prevention programs for youth. All states in the United States now mandate HIV/AIDS education in public schools (Britton, DeMaurro, & Gambrell, 1992), mass media provide some HIV preventive messages, and public and private community agencies have developed HIV preventive services, often for specific groups of youth engaged in HIV risk behavior. However, the majority of sexually active teens, in spite of their knowledge about HIV and preventive behaviors, continue to engage in high-risk sexual activities. Most adolescents who use condoms do so only inconsistently. Estimates for regular and correct condom use among sexually active adolescents do not exceed 10% to 20% (Aral, 1991; Mosher & McNally, 1991). While there is some evidence on positive behavioral change, the rates of AIDS, sexually transmitted disease, and unprotected risky behaviors among adolescents remain unacceptably high. Interventions that go beyond knowledge development and demonstrably reduce risk behaviors need to be implemented.

ASSESSING HIV-RELATED RISK BEHAVIORS

Conducting a valid assessment of adolescent HIV-related risk behaviors can be tricky. In one-on-one clinical settings, practitioners should be trained to conduct sensitive, straightforward, and explicit interviews about sexuality and drug use. One useful strategy is to contextualize such questions into a more complete psychosocial screening assessment. Goldenring and Cohen (1988) developed the HEADSS method, whereby practitioners conduct a six-step interview focused on the *H*ome environment, *E*ducation and/or employment, peer *A*ctivities, *D*rug and alcohol use, *S*exuality, and *S*uicide/depression. Such an interview allows the adolescent to answer easier questions first, thereby allowing rapport to develop. Naturally, practitioners need to have adequately worked through their own comfort with these issues, especially as related to sexuality and substance use. Face-to-face interviews with adolescents are extremely vulnerable to distortion, especially when the practitioner is seen as judgmental or untrustworthy. In addition, the practitioner needs to be sure about how confidentiality is to be handled and must be ready to communicate this to the adolescent in a useful way.

As will be seen in the next section, most HIV prevention efforts have been conducted using small group interventions. Thus, individual face-to-face assessment interviews are not necessary or natural in many such prevention contexts. Indeed, given the availability of national (and often local) data on adolescent risk behavior, many prevention efforts are conducted without direct assessment of individual risk behavior. For instance, we know that over 50% of high schoolers in the United

States are sexually active and, of these, less than 50% consistently use condoms (Centers for Disease Control, 1992). Local data about sexual behavior can often provide a more specific picture. Together, local and national data sources should point to the need for prevention and give a rough estimate of the sexual and substance use behaviors of the participants of any intervention.

While behavioral epidemiology provides a general description of the target population's risk behavior profile, it does not replace specific assessments of the actual youth who will receive your intervention. Most demonstrably successful programs use paper-and-pencil questionnaires to assess the occurrence, frequency, and specific character of risk behaviors. Useful questionnaires are explicit (specifically identify types of sexual behavior, e.g., vaginal intercourse, anal intercourse, fellatio) and comprehensive (include all common sexual behaviors), specifically include options to indicate same-sex practices, include questions about the use of pregnancy and STD prevention practices, include similarly specific questions about substance use (including the use of needles for drug use and for tattooing and piercing), and indicate frequency or latency since last occurrence of the behavior (e.g., "How often have you participated in each of the following sexual behaviors during the last 30 days?"). Many successful programs also assess HIV-related risk reduction beliefs and skills (e.g., refusal skills) that are to be a focus of their intervention.

Practitioners interested in conducting such assessments can look at the published studies cited in the next section for descriptions or copies of successful assessment instruments. Once an instrument has been selected or multiple measures combined and trimmed for use, a useful practice is to convene one or more focus groups of adolescents to review the instrument for length, comprehension, and suitability, and to suggest alternative wording for overly technical language (e.g., changing "fellatio" to "oral sex, that is, putting your mouth on his penis and/or her vagina").

There remain controversies about the most reliable and valid ways to measure HIV-related risk in adolescents. However, paper-and-pencil questionnaires are probably more valid than face-to-face interviews and certainly seem to provide higher estimates of behaviors (cf. Vaughan et al., 1996). Regardless of the controversies, specific assessment of risk behaviors can be used to fine-tune the prevention program (e.g., based on the percentage of participants who are sexually active but inconsistent users of condoms) and can serve as a pretest, thereby allowing for posttest and follow-up evaluations.

EFFECTIVE SOCIAL WORK INTERVENTIONS

Preliminary Comments

Many clinic- and school-based adolescent HIV prevention studies that seem (or claim) to show positive intervention effects on risk behavior have major substantive or methodological limitations or both. As such, they often can just as easily be read as showing little or no effect. Problems relate to measurement, design, statistical analysis, and inferences from findings. Nevertheless, there are a limited number of reasonably solid empirical studies that measure behavior for some period of time after the intervention. From these studies, empirically based practice guidelines and conclusions can be derived.

The following conclusions and guidelines are based on published studies of adolescent prevention interventions focused specifically on HIV, which measured one or more risk behaviors, had a comparison group (i.e., used an experimental or quasi-experimental design), and had a delayed follow-up (1 month or more). Risk behaviors measured included sexual abstinence rates, delays in initiation of sexual intercourse, various forms of sexual intercourse, unprotected sex, sexual intercourse with multiple partners, use of condoms during sexual intercourse, coercive sexual experiences, variations on these categories (e.g., use of condoms with spermicide or unprotected anal intercourse with multiple partners), and injection drug use. Twenty-one studies met these criteria and were included in our analysis (Ashworth, DuRant, Newman, & Gaillard, 1992; Brown, Barone, Fritz, Cebollero, & Nassau, 1991; Huszti, Clopton, & Mason, 1989; Jemmott, Jemmott, & Fong, 1992; Kirby, Barth, Leland, & Fetro, 1991; Levy et al., 1995; Magura, Kang, & Shapiro, 1994; Main et al., 1994; Mansfield, Conroy, Emans, & Woods, 1993; Newman, DuRant, Ashworth, & Gaillard, 1993; Rickert, Gottlieb, & Jay, 1990; Rotheram-Borus, Koopman, Haignere, & Davies, 1991; Schinke, Gordon, & Weston, 1990; Slonim-Nevo, Auslander, Ozawa, & Jung, 1996; Slonim-Nevo, Ozawa, & Auslander, 1991; Smith & Katner, 1995; Stanton et al., 1996; St. Lawrence, Brasfield, et al., 1995; St. Lawrence, Jefferson, Alleyne, & Brasfield, 1995; Sunwoo et al., 1995; Walter & Vaughan, 1993). Of these, eleven found no significant impact on risk behavior (although nearly all found positive impacts on knowledge, attitudes, or other related behaviors, e.g., assertiveness). Ten studies found program impact effects on one or more risk behaviors. It is important that no study found strong behavioral effects across all aspects of risk behavior. Thus, there exists no single completely effective program or way to prevent HIV in adolescents. We will return to this theme after examining the most common characteristics of the ten relatively successful programs, making suggestions for designing and implementing a successful prevention program, and providing brief descriptions of a few of these programs.

Characteristics of Effective Programs

Programs that successfully influenced adolescent HIV risk behavior over time were of sufficient duration. Successful programs tended to have considerably longer interventions than those which did not influence risk behavior. In our review, programs that successfully impacted some aspect of risk behavior averaged about 10 hours of focused intervention contact with clients. Programs with no discernible impact on risk behavior averaged a little more than 3 hours. At a minimum, successful programs tended to provide 5 or more hours of focused intervention (above and beyond that provided through the usual school, media, and other societal mechanisms). Every long program did not and will not necessarily affect risk behavior, and many shorter programs seem to have beneficial effects on HIV-related knowledge and attitudes, if not risk behavior. However, short 1- or 2-hour additions to the standard AIDS education fare seem to have little impact on risk behavior, regardless of the format (e.g., discussion, videos, lectures, peer education, using persons living with HIV as presenters) or the location (e.g., a practitioner's office or a school classroom).

Nearly every successful program had clear, targeted goals and expectations concerning risk behavior. The most successful programs often targeted both abstinence or delay in initiation of intercourse *along with* safer sex precautions for those who are or who become sexually active. It is worth noting that these successful programs did not pit abstinence against safer sex and there is no evidence that adolescents want or need to have any such debate resolved on their account. Furthermore, there is very little evidence that conducting HIV prevention programs leads to increases in risk behavior (sexually related or otherwise). While there has been debate about whether general sex education programs have contributed to increased sexual activity in youth, there is no evidence of this in the modern AIDS prevention programs, including programs that make condoms available (cf. Sellers, McGraw, & McKinlay, 1994). In fact, there is some tentative evidence that HIV can serve as a potential link between adolescents and adults concerning sexuality (Mueller et al., 1996). Very few youth want to get infected (as compared to frequent ambivalent feelings about sexual maturation, pregnancy, etc.), and very few adults want them to either.

Understandably, programs that are focused on actual risk behavior seem to have stronger behavioral impacts. This may be a truism, but is less obvious in historical context. When transmission routes for HIV and the attendant risks these posed for adolescents were first understood, schools were the major service-delivery organizations to respond (probably because of their established history of struggling with health and sex education and their presence in the lives of most, though not all, youth). With hindsight, it seems almost preordained that the school systems would be best able to contribute to the educational component of HIV prevention. Along with public service announcements, media programs, and other community work, this (educational) need is being fairly well addressed. However, the standard educational system has often struggled with effecting behavioral change, particularly adolescent sexual behavior. As other professions (including social workers) have joined in the effort, state-of-the-art interventions, be they conducted in schools or elsewhere, have clearly evolved into programs with strong behavioral foci. As such, social work interventions with adolescents need to have strong behavioral components.

All successful programs incorporated some form of social learning principles. The majority of less successful programs did not do so or did so only in very indirect ways. A variety of social learning models have been used, including social inoculation theory, theory of reasoned action, cognitive-behavioral theories, problem-solving theory, behavioral skills theory, and more general social learning theory. Currently, there is insufficient evidence to determine the efficacy of interventions based on one versus another of these more specific models. However, programs that actively and explicitly use a limited number of specific social learning principles in the planning and implementation of the intervention are most effective. This seems to go along with the need for a clear focus and a clear plan on how to get there. Thus, the point for the practitioner is twofold. Use some specific form of social learning theory to explicitly inform the development of the intervention, and plan and conduct an intervention with fidelity to these ideas. There is no evidence that preventions based on alternative theoretical frameworks (e.g., self psychology, psychoanalysis, family dynamics, or didactic education) effectively reduce risk behavior over time.

Nearly all programs that influence risk behavior have a strong skills-development component, usually toward the end of the intervention. Less successful programs are much less likely to include specific skills-development activities. Different successful programs identify somewhat different skills; however, common foci of skills include avoidance of risk situations, development of assertion and refusal skills, sexual-communication and negotiation skills, accurate assessment of the benefits and risks of a particular behavior, and skills in the effective use of condoms.

Successful programs tend to be conducted in small and medium-sized peer groups. Group size has varied from 3 to 7 to about 20 to 25 (school classrooms). However, a larger percentage of successful programs (62%) used small groups ($n < 12$) than did the less successful programs (30%). Successful programs used standard group techniques designed to facilitate participant rapport, to clarify values and explore beliefs, and to directly practice new learned behaviors (e.g., active learning, sharing ideas, role playing). In summary, the use of small groups seems to increase the likelihood of successful risk reduction and probably encourages more effective use of rapport building, values clarification, norm development, and skills-based techniques. However, successful programs can be conducted in classroom-size groups, so long as other criteria are met.

One successful program took advantage of the naturally occurring social networks of peers (Stanton et al., 1996). Unlike most programs that formed groups based on other criteria (e.g., homeroom, admission to one or another social service program), this intervention identified teen cliques and used these cliques to form the intervention groups. Given that teens in peer networks share many common behaviors, including sexual activity, substance use, and other risk behavior (Kandel, 1978; Mueller, McGrady, & Vera, 1995; Myers, McGrady, Marrow, & Mueller, 1997), such clique-based groupings might increase impact or efficiency. However, more research is needed before the relative advantages and disadvantages of such an approach can be known.

Many successful programs used highly trained and sufficiently motivated facilitators. Some of the best programs provided 20 to 40 or more hours of facilitator training. Less successful studies tended to spend less time on facilitator training or made no mention of the extent of training. The best studies had trained observers check to be sure the facilitators delivered the agreed-upon program. Many studies allowed for self-selection of facilitators. This may be an important lesson: There is little evidence that forcing someone to be a facilitator (e.g., a schoolteacher chosen because she or he teaches a particular class) will lead to a quality program.

Contrary to some expectations, all of the successful programs reviewed used adult facilitators. This does not mean that peer-facilitated programs would not or do not work. There is simply not sufficient data to address this issue. However, adult-lead programs can have demonstrable impacts on adolescent risk behavior.

Many successful programs incorporate substantial local planning into the program development process. Such planning can include ethnographic inquiry (e.g., interviews and participant observations), pilot studies, and direct input from youth and adults in the community. While such procedures likely lead to a more culturally sensitive and localized program, they pose at least two hazards to the social worker. First, they prevent the relatively easy, direct application of a packaged prevention program that proved to be successful elsewhere. Second, such procedures can lead program developers away from the very characteristics found in empirically demonstrated successful programs. For example, some members of the community might not want any skills-development components.

Nearly all successful programs described strategies to actively connect with adolescents and to explore values and norms about responsible behavior. Most programs utilize group exercises to establish rapport among the youth and with the facilitators. This rapport is then relied upon to explore beliefs about risk behaviors and perceptions about norms concerning these behaviors. In particular, programs targeted for disenfranchised youth need to pay particular attention to developing such rapport. In many communities (but not all), early sexual risk behavior is correlated with other risk behaviors, such as substance use, school failure, and status offenses (Jessor, 1991; Lovely et al., 1994). Some comprehensive and well-planned HIV prevention programs targeted at such high-risk youth have not successfully influenced their HIV risk behavior. In fact, there is some evidence that programs targeted at high-risk youth need to be longer (probably 15 or more sessions) with even more emphasis on establishing rapport and developing healthier values and group norms. In short, disenfranchised youth need to be reengaged as part of the early steps in HIV prevention. Once accomplished, the remainder of the HIV prevention program can probably proceed in a fashion similar to those described herein.

Most successful programs work with similar aged peers in groups. Often, groups are based upon grade in school. Programs have been successful with a variety of ages, ranging from a mean of 11.3 years old to 17.8 years old (overall mean age equal to 14.5). Successful programs have been conducted with same- and mixed-gender groups. Within the successful programs, there is no compelling evidence that boys or girls benefit more from HIV prevention programs. Similarly, there is no evidence that Caucasian, African American, or Latino youth benefit more or less from such programs (although there remains little empirical research on other ethnic groups, including Asian American and Native American youth).

Very few studies have used booster sessions (individual or group interventions delivered sometime after the initial sessions). However, the impact of even the best HIV prevention programs often diminishes with time. Whether booster sessions would enhance maintenance of intervention gain remains an empirical question, and, in our opinion, one worth pursuing. One possible direction might focus on relapse prevention approaches borrowed from substance abuse intervention programs.

Contrary to prior reviews (Kirby et al., 1994), we found no compelling differential program impact on virgins versus nonvirgins, or abstinence and delayed initiation of sexual activity versus safer sex (e.g., use of condoms, restricting number of partners). Highly similar programs would at times produce a bigger impact on one or the other characteristic, in no clear convincing pattern. This may argue for a continued deemphasis on abstinence versus safer sex and support the seeming emerging idea of addressing both in the context of youth being knowledgeable about HIV; exploring choices, values, and norms; and learning specific technical, cognitive, and social skills to protect themselves.

Successful programs can be conducted within or outside the school. Health clinics, shelters, jails, and community organizations (e.g., recreation centers) have been the sites of successful programs. Very few programs have successfully integrated families into the HIV prevention intervention. Programs that have attempted to do so report difficulties sustaining family involvement. One program was fairly successful involving families by using homework assignments that explicitly directed students to interview parents about their own views on abstinence and birth control (Kirby et al., 1991). Once more programs successfully develop parental and family involvement components, empirical research will be able to examine the extent to which such involvement impacts on risk behavior outcomes.

DESIGNING AND IMPLEMENTING A SUCCESSFUL PROGRAM

Given the emerging evidence about effective HIV prevention for adolescents, a general state-of-the-art set of guidelines can be proposed. While much more research in this area is needed, the following design and implementation steps are supported by the existing literature:

1. Develop a commitment to a sufficiently intense and sufficiently long intervention program.

2. Conduct preliminary pilot and ethnographic work to better understand the local context of adolescent HIV risk, community attitudes, youths' prior experiences with HIV and HIV education, and barriers that might interfere with the development of effective skill-based behaviors that will help youths avoid or minimize risk. Pay particular attention to various ethnic and cultural values related to sexuality, and teen sexuality in particular.

3. Develop clear goals and objectives for the program. Be sure to keep a risk behavior focus. A sample goal might be to reduce HIV infection. Sample objectives could include some of the following: Increase adolescent abstinence, delay initiation of sexual intercourse, increase condom use for sexually active teens, decrease sexual intercourse with multiple partners, decrease unprotected anal intercourse, decrease sexual exploitation, decrease injection drug use, or decrease needle sharing.

4. Identify a social learning theoretical model that fits with your goals and objectives and your analysis of the context of risk behavior. Use only one or a few models (e.g, social inoculation theory, behavioral skills theory, protection motivation theory, theory of reasoned action) and be sure to clarify exactly what this model states. Given the current state of the research evidence, fidelity to the specific model is probably more important than the selection of one model over another.

5. Identify and review available existing adolescent HIV prevention programs. Examine their suitability to your context and goals. A few samples are provided in the next section.

6. Develop (or modify) a program with explicit connections to the theoretical model used and adjusted to the specific local context. Be sure that the planned program has sufficient focus on behaviors and the development of skills that can modify risk behaviors.

7. Identify and train motivated facilitators in the program. Pilot-test your procedures and solicit and incorporate facilitator and pilot participant feedback to fine-tune the intervention program.

8. Consider innovative additions (not yet empirically validated) such as creative family involvement, the use of booster sessions or relapse prevention techniques, or outreach to particularly disenfranchised youth. However, do not let any such innovations or modifications (see #2 also) take away from delivering a program that includes the empirically demonstrated criteria for success.

9. Consider evaluation of your intervention. Focus your intervention and your evaluation on behavior. Remember, there is still much that needs to be

learned about adolescent HIV prevention. You can become a part of the effort.

10. Review your intervention plan. Be sure that the complete plan fits specifically with your goals and objectives. Be sure you have trained and motivated facilitators delivering a sufficiently long, yet clear and focused, program, informed by specific, identified social learning ideas, tailored to your particular target population, with strong activities designed to develop group rapport, clarify values, and teach and practice risk reduction behaviors.

11. Implement the program with integrity. Make note of variations from the plan. Upon completion, review and revise the plan, as indicated.

SAMPLES OF SUCCESSFUL PROGRAMS

In our review of the empirical literature we found a number of effective programs, each with different characteristics, but with much in common. We have selected three sample model programs to describe in somewhat more detail, to give the reader a sense of how specific successful programs work.*

Reducing the Risk (RTR) is a 15-session high school classroom–based program (Kirby et al., 1991). It has an extremely strong behavioral skill emphasis with a good deal of modeling, role playing, and social skills development. The program also uses homework assignments that encourage parent-child discussion about abstinence and birth control. The curriculum is based upon three related theories. Following general social learning theory, youth are thought to learn through observing others and by actively practicing new skills. It is thought that youth will engage in these new behaviors once they understand what needs to be done, believe they can do it (e.g., delay intercourse or use a condom), and believe in the benefits of their actions. Social inoculation theory is analogous to physiological inoculation. Here, youth are taught to recognize and resist social pressure to engage in (unprotected) sexual intercourse. The social inoculation process has a heavy emphasis on role playing with progressively less assistance from others. Cognitive-behavior theory focuses on specific cognitive and behavioral skills to successfully negotiate risky situations. From this view, the RTR program emphasizes activities to personalize information about sexuality, reproduction, and contraception, along with training in decision making and assertive communication skills. RTR has been successfully administered in 10th-grade health classes in rural and urban areas. Self-selected high school health teachers participated in a 3-day training program before implementing the program.

---

*Those readers interested in reviewing these programs should obtain the empirical studies cited and contact those authors for program details.

Main et al. (1994) describe another 15-session skills-based program delivered in high school classrooms. The curriculum was organized around two interrelated theoretical models: social cognitive theory and the theory of reasoned action. Sessions were designed to address major components of these theories and most sessions emphasized skill acquisition. Three of the fifteen sessions focused on functional (i.e., useful in helping youth reduce risk) HIV-related knowledge, one session focused on teen vulnerability to HIV, two sessions focused on normative determinants of risky behaviors, one session focused on condom use, and *eight* focused on the development of skills designed to identify, manage, avoid, and leave risky situations. Teachers chosen to deliver the intervention first attended a 5-day, 40-hour training program. During this training, teachers practiced and modeled all sessions, both from the teachers' and the students' perspectives. In addition to the classroom HIV curriculum, schools were encouraged to implement school-based activities designed to reinforce the themes of the sessions (e.g., displaying posters throughout the school).

Stanton et al. (1996) developed and implemented a program housed in a community recreation center. The intervention was based on protection motivation theory, which considers both environmental and personal factors that combine to pose a health threat. The model considers both intrinsic and extrinsic rewards, perceived severity and vulnerability to threat, perceived likelihood that a particular action will reduce the threat, and the belief that one can engage in the desired behavior, even in the face of barriers to do so. The intervention is also informed by social network theory, which focused on already established natural peer groups as strong socializing forces. As such, the intervention was delivered to these peer groups (or cliques), rather than to randomly selected and assigned individuals. The intervention was developed over the course of 2 years of ethnographic inquiry and pilot testing. The final intervention design consisted of eight weekly sessions (each about 90 minutes) followed by one daylong session conducted at a separate rural campsite. Small group discussions, lectures, videos, games, role playing, and performing arts were used, each time with a specific focus on one or more components of the theoretical model. In the seventh session, youth developed community projects with specific target audiences and intervention messages, which were then implemented in the eighth session.

UNRESOLVED ISSUES AND FUTURE RESEARCH DIRECTIONS

While we were able to identify more and less successful HIV prevention programs, it is important to recognize that no single program was completely successful. Some programs seemed to have an impact on one aspect of risk behavior (e.g., consistent use of condoms), but not another (e.g., initiation of sexual intercourse). Indeed, there is a great need for improved, empirically demonstrated prevention methods. Even the successful programs, which involve a considerable investment of time and energy on the part of the interventionists, need to be improved, refined, and strengthened.

There is relatively little need for programs that are below the standards set forth here. Most youth know most of what they need to know about HIV. We should be sure that the existing delivery systems (e.g., schools, mass media) continue to provide this important educational program. However, we should not merely repeat the same messages to already knowledgeable youth. Instead, social workers (and others) who want to contribute to real reductions in HIV rates in youth and young adults should find ways to deliver high-quality programs guided by what has been described here.

Finally, there has been very little solid empirical literature on HIV prevention targeted at gay and lesbian youth (cf. Rotheram-Borus, Reid, & Rosario, 1994). Fortunately, there is an emerging scientific literature on the life experiences and risk behavior of these youth, who remain at particular risk for HIV (Rotheram-Borus & Koopman, 1991). As these experiences become better understood, empirically sound HIV prevention programs should emerge.

There remain many fruitful research areas in need of further exploration. The extent to which individual participant characteristics (gender, ethnicity, age, sexual orientation, prior sexual experience, extent of related risk behaviors, personality characteristics, family dynamics, etc.), program characteristics (family involvement, booster sessions, use of natural peer groups, group sizes, use of peer counselors, etc.), and other ecological factors (poverty, opportunity for success, community quality of life, etc.) influence program success should continue to be examined.

REFERENCES

Allen, D. M., Lehman, J. S., Green, T. A., Lindegren, M. L., Onorato, I. M., & Forester, W. (1994). HIV infection among homeless adults and runaway youth, United States, 1989–1992. *AIDS, 8,* 1593–1598.

Aral, S. Q. (1991). Sexual behavior and risk for sexually transmitted infections. *STD Bulletin, 10,* 3–10.

Ashworth, C. S., DuRant, R. H., Newman, C., & Gaillard, G. (1992). An evaluation of a school-based AIDS/HIV education program for high school students. *Journal of Adolescent Health, 13,* 582–588.

Britton, P. O., DeMaurro, D., & Gambrell, A. E. (1992). HIV/AIDS education for schools finds states make progress but work remains. *Siecus Report, 21,* 1–8.

Brown, L. K., Barone, V. J., Fritz, G. K., Cebollero, P., & Nassau, J. H. (1991). AIDS education: The Rhode Island experience. *Health Education Quarterly, 18,* 195–206.

Centers for Disease Control. (1992). Sexual behavior among high school students. *Morbidity and Mortality Weekly Report, 40,* 885–889.

Centers for Disease Control. (1994). AIDS among racial/ethnic minorities: United States, 1993. *Morbidity and Mortality Weekly Report, 43,* 653–655.

Centers for Disease Control. (1995). *HIV/AIDS surveillance report: Year-end report* (No. 7). Atlanta, GA: Author.

Dean, L., & Meyer, I. (1995). HIV prevalence and sexual behavior in a cohort of New York City gay men (aged 18–24). *Journal of AIDS, 8,* 208–211.

Edlin, B. A., Irwin, K. L., Faruques, S., McCoy, C. B., Ward, C., Serrano, Y., Inciardi, J. A., Bowser, B. P., Schilling, R. F., & Holmberg, S. D. (1994). Intersecting epidemics: Crack cocaine use and HIV infection among inner city youth adults. *New England Journal of Medicine, 331,* 1422–1427.

Goldenring, J. M., & Cohen, E. (1988). Getting into adolescent heads. *Contemporary Pediatrics,* 3–14.

Goldsmith, M. (1993). Invisible epidemic now becoming visible as HIV/AIDS pandemic reaches adolescents. *The Journal of the American Medical Association, 270,* 16–19.

Huszti, H. C., Clopton, J. R., & Mason, P. J. (1989). Acquired immunodeficiency syndrome educational program: Effects on adolescents' knowledge and attitudes. *Pediatrics, 84,* 986–994.

Jemmott, J. B., III, Jemmott, L. S., & Fong, G. T. (1992). Reductions in HIV risk-associated sexual behaviors among black male adolescents: Effects of an AIDS prevention intervention. *American Journal of Public Health, 82,* 372–377.

Jessor, R. (1991). *Beyond adolescence: Problem behavior and young adult development.* New York: Cambridge University.

Kandel, D. (1978). Homophily, selection and socialization in adolescent friendships. *American Journal of Sociology, 84,* 427–436.

Kirby, D., Barth, R. P., Leland, N., & Fetro, J. V. (1991). Reducing the risk: Impact of a new curriculum on sexual risk-taking. *Family Planning Perspectives, 23,* 253–263.

Kirby, D., Short, L., & Collins, J. (1994). School-based programs to reduce sexual risk behaviors: A review of effectiveness. *Public Health Report, 109,* 339–360.

Levy, S. R., Perhats, C., Weeks, K., Handler, A. S., Zhu, C., & Flay, B. R. (1995). Impact of a school-based AIDS prevention program on risk and protective behavior for newly sexually active students. *Journal of School Health, 65,* 145–151.

Lindegren, M. L., Hanson, C., Miller, K., Byers, R. H., & Onorato, I. M. (1994). Epidemiology of human immunodeficiency virus infection in adolescents, USA. *Journal of Pediatric Infectious Disease, 13,* 525–535.

Lovely, R., Liebow, E., Vera, M., McGrady, G., Mueller, C., Mann, E., & Klovdahl, A. (1994). *Ethnic youths' social network structure can inform HIV prevention.* Paper presented at the Xth International Conference on AIDS, Yokohama, Japan.

Magura, S., Kang, S.-Y., & Shapiro, J. L. (1994). Outcomes of intensive AIDS education for male adolescent drug users in jail. *Journal of Adolescent Health, 15,* 457–463.

Main, D. S., Iverson, D. C., McGloin, J., Banspach, S. W., Collins, J. L., Rugg, D. L., & Kolbe, L. J. (1994). Preventing HIV infection among adolescents: Evaluation of a school-based education program. *Preventive Medicine, 23,* 409–417.

Mansfield, C. J., Conroy, M. E., Emans, S. J., & Woods, E. R. (1993). A pilot study of AIDS education and counseling of high-risk adolescents in an office setting. *Journal of Adolescent Health, 14,* 115–119.

Mosher, W. D., & McNally, J. W. (1991). Contraceptive use at first intercourse, United States, 1965–1988. *Family Planning Perspectives, 23,* 108–116.

Mueller, C., Bidwell, R., Mann, E., Mew, S., Goo, C., Dunbar, H., & Lovely, R. (1996). Adolescent construction of HIV and HIV prevention. *Journal of HIV/AIDS Prevention and Education for Adolescents & Children, 1,* 13–27.

Mueller, C., McGrady, G., & Vera, M. (1995). *Using social network analysis to re-conceptualize adolescent HIV-risk.* Paper presented at the annual meeting of the Council on Social Work Education, San Diego, CA.

Myers, G. P., McGrady, G. A., Marrow, C., & Mueller, C. W. (1997). Weapon carrying among Black adolescents: A social network perspective. *American Journal of Public Health, 87,* 1038–1040.

National Health Statistics. (1996). *Trends in adolescent pregnancies and sexually transmitted diseases.* Washington, DC: Author.

Newman, C., DuRant, R. H., Ashworth, C. S., & Gaillard, G. (1993). An evaluation of a school-based AIDS/HIV education program for young adolescents. *AIDS Education and Prevention, 5,* 327–339.

Osborne, M. L., Kistner, J. A., & Helgemo, B. (1993). Developmental progression in children's knowledge of AIDS: Implications for education and attitudinal change. *Journal of Pediatric Psychology, 18,* 177–192.

Rickert, V. I., Gottlieb, A., & Jay, M. S. (1990). A comparison of three clinic-based AIDS education programs on female adolescents' knowledge, attitudes, and behavior. *Journal of Adolescent Health Care, 11,* 298–303.

Rotheram-Borus, M. J., & Koopman, C. (1991). Sexual risk behavior, AIDS knowledge, and beliefs about AIDS among predominantly minority gay and bisexual male adolescents. *AIDS Education and Prevention, 3,* 305–312.

Rotheram-Borus, M. J., Koopman, C., Haignere, C., & Davies, M. (1991). Reducing HIV sexual risk behaviors among runaway adolescents. *The Journal of the American Medical Association, 266,* 1237–1241.

Rotheram-Borus, M. J., Reid, H., & Rosario, M. (1994). Factors mediating changes in sexual HIV risk behaviors among gay and bisexual male adolescents. *American Journal of Public Health, 84,* 1938–1946.

Schinke, S. P., Gordon, A. N., & Weston, R. E. (1990). Self-instruction to prevent HIV infection among African-American and Hispanic-American adolescents. *Journal of Consulting and Clinical Psychology, 58,* 432–436.

Sellers, D., McGraw, S., & McKinlay, J. (1994). Does the promotion and distribution of condoms increase teen sexual activity? Evidence from an HIV prevention program for Latino youth. *American Journal of Public Health, 84,* 1952–1958.

Slonim-Nevo, V., Auslander, W. F., Ozawa, M. N., & Jung, K. G. (1996). The long-term impact of AIDS-preventive interventions for delinquent and abused adolescents. *Adolescence, 31,* 409–420.

Slonim-Nevo, V., Ozawa, M. N., & Auslander, W. F. (1991). Knowledge, attitudes and behaviors related to AIDS among youth in residential centers: Results from an exploratory study. *Journal of Adolescence, 14,* 17–33.

Smith, M. U., & Katner, H. P. (1995). Quasi-experimental evaluation of three AIDS prevention activities for maintaining knowledge, improving attitudes, and changing risk behaviors of high school seniors. *AIDS Education and Prevention, 7,* 391–402.

Sonenstein, F. L., Pleck, J. H., & Ku, L. C. (1989). Sexual activity, condom use and AIDS awareness among adolescent males. *Family Planning Perspectives, 21,* 152–158.

Sperling, R. S., Sacks, H. S., & Mayer, L. (1989). Umbilical cord blood sero-survey for human immunodeficiency virus in parturient women in a voluntary hospital in New York City. *Obstetrics and Gynecology, 73,* 179–181.

Stanton, B. F., Li, X., Ricardo, I., Galbraith, J., Feigelman, S., & Kaljee, L. (1996). A randomized, controlled effectiveness trial of an AIDS prevention program for low-income African-American youths. *Archives of Pediatrics & Adolescent Medicine, 150,* 363–372.

St. Lawrence, J. S., Brasfield, T. L., Jefferson, K. W., Alleyne, E., O'Bannon, R. E., III, & Shirley, A. (1995). Cognitive-behavioral intervention to reduce African American adolescents' risk for HIV infection. *Journal of Consulting and Clinical Psychology, 63,* 221–237.

St. Lawrence, J. S., Jefferson, K. W., Alleyne, E., & Brasfield, T. L. (1995). Comparison of education versus behavioral skills training interventions in lowering sexual HIV-risk behavior of substance-dependent adolescents. *Journal of Consulting and Clinical Psychology, 63,* 154–157.

Sunwoo, J., Brenman, A., Escobedo, J., Philpott, T., Allman, K., Mueller, J., Jaeger, J., Brown, L. K., & Cole, F. S. (1995). School-based AIDS education for adolescents. *Journal of Adolescent Health, 16,* 309–315.

Sweat, M. D., & Levin, M. (1995). HIV/AIDS knowledge among the U.S. population. *AIDS Education and Prevention, 7,* 355–372.

Vaughan, R. D., McCarthy, J. F., Walter, H. J., Resnicow, K., Waterman, P. D., Armstrong, B., & Tiezzi, L. (1996). The development, reliability, and validity of a risk factor screening survey for urban minority junior high school students. *Journal of Adolescent Health, 19,* 171–178.

Walter, H., & Vaughan, R. (1993). AIDS risk reduction among a multiethnic sample of urban high school students. *Journal of the American Medical Association, 270,* 725–730.

Wendell, D. A., Onorato, I. M., McCray, E., Allen, D. M., & Sweeney, P. A. (1992). Youth at risk: Sex, drugs and human immunodeficiency virus. *American Journal of Diseases of Children, 146,* 76–81.

World Health Organization. (1995). *The current global situation of the HIV/AIDS pandemic.* Geneva, Switzerland: Author.

Chapter 7 ────────────────────────────────

SUBSTANCE ABUSE

Nancy J. Smyth

OVERVIEW

Substance abuse is a serious social problem that can contribute to a wide range of other problems. This chapter provides an overview of empirically based social work as it relates to alcohol and other drug (AOD) problems, including those people with dual disorders, that is, AOD problems and coexisting psychiatric disorders. Prior to discussing the literature on assessment and intervention, operational definitions, prevalence rates, and social work's role are presented.

Operational Definitions

Substance Use and Problems. Any consumption of alcohol and other drugs (AOD) is considered substance use. However, whether the use of AOD is considered a problem depends on several factors, most of which are culturally defined, including the type of substance, the conditions under which it is used, who is using it, and the consequences of use (Jonas, 1992; Musto, 1992). For example, while the sale of alcohol to adults is currently legal in most of the United States, this wasn't always the case (Musto, 1992); therefore, alcohol use by adults is not automatically considered a problem. However, the use of alcohol by some special populations, such as pregnant women and adolescents, has been identified as a concern, as it has in certain situations, such as drinking and driving. While the occasional use of any illegal drug has not always been identified as a major problem, the past decade of U.S. policy on drugs has emphasized that both casual and regular users of drugs were considered part of the drug problem (Kleber, 1992).

Substance-Related Disorders. Substance disorders are divided into two major categories by the *Diagnostic and Statistical Manual,* fourth edition (*DSM-IV;* American Psychiatric Association [APA], 1994): substance use and substance-induced disorders. The latter includes such diagnoses as alcohol-withdrawal delirium, cocaine-induced psychotic disorder, and hallucinogen intoxication; the former includes two major categories of diagnoses, substance abuse and substance dependence, the second of which is considered more severe. This chapter focuses primarily on substance use, not substance-induced, disorders because they are more often the focus in social work. The terms *substance abuse, AOD abuse,* and *AOD problems* will be used interchangeably to include substance use disorders and substance use problems, including alcohol use disorders and problems. The terms *drug abuse* and *drug problems* will refer to substance use disorders other than those involving alcohol.

DSM-IV substance use diagnoses are applied according to the specific drugs abused; for each drug, one of two substance use disorder diagnoses, abuse or dependence, is possible. Therefore, an individual addicted to cocaine and alcohol is given the substance-specific diagnoses of cocaine dependence and alcohol dependence, instead of the more generic substance dependence (APA, 1994).

In order to qualify for a diagnosis of substance abuse, individuals must, within a 1-year time period, demonstrate a "maladaptive pattern of substance use" (APA, 1994, p. 182) that results in significant "impairment or distress" (APA, 1994, p. 182) in one of four ways: (a) failure, as a consequence of substance use, to adequately complete one's responsibilities in some significant life role or setting (e.g., work, school, family); (b) substance use in physically dangerous situations (e.g., drinking heavily and then driving, or operating heavy machinery while high on marijuana); (c) continuing to use AOD despite having social or interpersonal problems that result from, or are worsened by, drinking or using; and (d) experiencing repeated difficulties with the law as a result of substance use. Qualifying for substance dependence is an exclusion criterion for an abuse diagnosis.

A *DSM-IV* (APA, 1994) diagnosis of substance dependence is assigned if an individual experiences three or more of the following seven symptoms within a 1-year period: (a) withdrawal symptoms; (b) tolerance, that is, needing more of a substance to achieve the same effect or finding that the same amount of a substance has a markedly reduced effect; (c) using or drinking more than planned or for a longer period of time than was planned; (d) failed attempts to reduce or control use or a persistent wish to do so; (e) spending a lot of time acquiring alcohol or other drugs, drinking or using, or recovering from drinking or using; (f) decreasing or giving up "important social, occupational or recreational activities" (p. 181) due to substance use; and (g) continuing to drink or use in spite of the awareness that drinking or using causes or exacerbates an ongoing or recurring physical or psychological problem.

Dual Disorders.   Although the phrase *dual disorders* can be used to refer to any two coexisting disorders, it is often used, as it will be in this chapter, to refer to the co-occurrence of any substance use disorder with any major psychiatric disorder. The major psychiatric disorders most often considered in this category are schizophrenia and other psychotic disorders, mood disorders, anxiety disorders, and personality disorders, and sometimes dissociative and eating disorders.

Prevalence, Incidence, and Social and Financial Costs

Almost 19% of the U.S. adult (more than 18 years old) population report never drinking alcohol, 18.5% identify themselves as former drinkers, and 11.3% as lifetime infrequent drinkers, leaving slightly more than half (51.6%) of adults identifying themselves as current drinkers (Grant, 1994). Slightly more than one third (37.2%) of Americans age 12 and older report having used drugs illicitly at some point in their lifetimes, 11.8% in the past year, and 5.6% in the past month. The most commonly used illegal drug is marijuana, with 33.7% of the population (age 12 and older) reporting lifetime use, followed by cocaine (11.3%), hallucinogens (8.7%), and heroin (1.1%; Nonmedical use of psychotherapeutic drugs (e.g., stimulants, sedatives) is reported by 11.1% of the population (Substance Abuse and Mental Health Services Administration [SAMHSA], 1995).

Men generally have a drug use prevalence rate twice that of women, and overall, there are no significant differences in illicit drug use among Whites, Blacks, and Hispanics, White or Black (Rouse, 1995). With regard to alcohol, men are more likely than women to drink, and Whites more likely than Blacks or Hispanics, White or Black (SAMHSA, 1995). The overall rate of lifetime substance abuse or dependence is 26%, while the current rate (past year) is 11% (Rouse, 1995).

About 14% of the population between ages 15 and 54 qualify for a lifetime dual disorder, while 5% qualify in the past year (Rouse, 1995). However, among those people with a mental disorder, 39% met the lifetime criteria for dual disorder and 21% for the past year (Rouse, 1995). Among people with a substance use disorder, 52% met the lifetime criteria for a dual disorder, and 42% for the past year (Rouse, 1995).

Substance use and abuse play a significant role in many problems, including a wide range of medical diseases (including AIDS), accidental deaths and injuries, suicides and attempted suicides, homicides, family violence, criminal behavior, birth defects, and job productivity losses (Institute for Health Policy [IHP], 1993; National Institute on Alcohol Abuse and Alcoholism [NIAAA], 1994; Rouse, 1995). For example, 49.5% of all fatal crashes in 1990 were alcohol-related (NIAAA, 1994) and 35.3% of adult AIDS cases were attributed to injecting drug use (Rouse, 1995). While this is an alarmingly high rate, it reflects a 12.9% decrease since 1982 (NIAAA, 1994). Taken together, the direct and indirect economic costs of AOD problems in the United States were estimated at $165.6 billion for 1990 (Rouse, 1995). While figures for the social costs of dual disorders are hard to come by, a review of studies of heavy users of psychiatric services identified that patients with dual disorders were one of the subpopulations responsible for heavy service use (Kent, Fogarty, & Yellowless, 1995). By themselves, the social costs of mental health problems were estimated at $147.9 billion for 1990 (Rouse, 1995).

Relevance of Social Work's Involvement

Social workers can work to prevent and treat AOD problems in numerous ways, including through direct practice with individuals, groups, and families; administration; community-oriented practice; and social policy development. Since substance abuse may affect people in any number of ways, people with AOD problems (and their family members) often seek services for a wide range of presenting problems, including family conflict, depression, anxiety, financial difficulties, legal problems, declining performance in school or work, and physical disorders (Smyth, 1995). Therefore, social workers employed in all practice settings will frequently encounter clients who are experiencing substance-related problems, either as a result of their own use or because of substance abuse by someone they know. However, because clients may not see their AOD use as the cause of their difficulties, they may not volunteer information about AOD, so it is essential that all social workers be familiar with the effect of substance abuse on individuals and families and have some ability to screen for this problem.

Recently, social workers have shown increased interest in working with people with AOD problems and their families. For example, the National Association of Social Workers recently formed a special section for members interested in this field of practice ("Substance section," 1995). While the percentage of social workers providing service in substance abuse agencies is still relatively small, it has been slowly increasing; in 1991, social workers constituted 8.5% of the direct care staff in alcohol and drug treatment agencies (National Institute on Drug Abuse [NIDA]/NIAAA, 1993), a slight increase from the 1982 figure of 6.9% (NIAAA, 1983).

ASSESSMENT METHODS

Overview

As with all good social work practice, the assessment of substance abuse provides the foundation for case conceptualization and treatment planning. Substance abuse assessment should take place within the context of a comprehensive biopsychosocial assessment of clients and their environments. Factors such as social support, family environment, psychopathology, and employment all affect the client's probability of success in addressing an AOD problem (Moos, Finney, & Cronkite, 1990). As a general rule, the more aspects of clients' lives that are impaired, whether due to substance use or other problems, the more involved and comprehensive treatment will need to be.

A comprehensive AOD assessment includes the following (Sobell, Sobell, & Nirenberg, 1988): type of substances and how they are taken (e.g., nasally, intravenously, orally, by smoking); quantity and frequency; predominant situations and moods that precede, coincide with, and follow use (i.e., antecedents and consequences); withdrawal symptoms experienced; indications of tolerance (needing more of a substance to get the same effect); medical problems caused or exacerbated by use; psychosocial problems caused or exacerbated by use; length of client's substance abuse history; previous treatment experiences and response to these experiences; longest periods of abstinence; if applicable, relapse precipitants; social and environmental supports or barriers; and any other life problems. In addition, the cultural context of a client's use should be taken into consideration.

In addition to conducting clinical interviews, a variety of strategies can be used to facilitate the assessment process, including structured interviews, computerized assessment tools, self-report methods, observation, and biological methods. Unless indicated otherwise, all of the assessment instruments discussed here have demonstrated good psychometric characteristics; that is, they have demonstrated reliability and validity. Prior to discussing specific treatment methods, an overview of differential diagnosis principles for dual-diagnosis clients will be presented.

Differential Diagnosis of Dual Disorders

Clients with dual disorders can vary widely in their presentation, depending upon the severity and nature of each disorder (Evans & Sullivan, 1990; Fayne, 1993; First & Gladis, 1993). In particular, the practitioner should keep in mind that even small amounts of a particular drug can create problems for a person with serious mental illness (Cohen & Levy, 1992; Evans & Sullivan, 1990).

Assessing clients for dual disorders must take into account that AOD use, particularly chronic use, can cause psychiatric symptoms and mimic psychiatric disorders (APA, 1994; First & Gladis, 1993). Research on the reliability of psychiatric diagnoses indicates that current mood and psychotic disorders, as well as panic disorder, cannot be reliably diagnosed among clients with current substance use disorders (Bryant, Rounsaville, Spitzer, & Williams, 1992). For this reason, ideally, psychiatric diagnoses should be made when the client has been AOD free for a period of time. Recommendations for how long a client should be AOD free prior to diagnosis vary widely, from 3 weeks to 1 year (Evans & Sullivan, 1990; Zimberg, 1993), although there has been minimal research addressing this question. However, some research indicates that symptoms of anxiety and depression, while still clinically significant, drop to subclinical levels (i.e., levels insufficient to make a psychiatric diagnosis) within a couple of weeks of abstinence (Brown, Irwin, & Schuckit, 1991; Brown & Schuckit, 1988; Davidson, 1995; Strain, Stitzer, & Bigelow, 1991).

Because realities of practice and insurance reimbursement demand that diagnoses be assigned immediately, all diagnoses should be assigned provisionally and continually reevaluated as clients acquire more AOD-free time (Sederer, 1990). Careful history taking can also provide insight into a client's psychiatric status; the following characteristics may suggest the presence of a psychiatric diagnosis that will persist after a client is AOD free: presence of psychiatric symptoms prior to heavy or problematic AOD use, psychiatric symptoms that are not of the nature or type expected with the type of drug abused, psychiatric symptoms that persist well into periods of abstinence, family history of mental illness, and a history of trauma (Evans & Sullivan, 1990, 1995).

Structured Clinical Interviews

There are several structured clinical interviews that can be used in substance abuse assessment and treatment. The substance abuse sections of the Diagnostic Interview Survey (DIS; Robins, Helzer, Croughan, & Ratcliff, 1981) or of the Structured Clinical Interview for *DSM-IV* Axis I Disorders (SCID; First, Spitzer, Gibbon, & Williams, 1996) are often used to establish a reliable and valid diagnosis of substance abuse or dependence. A structured interview often used for treatment planning and for measurement of treatment outcome is the Addiction Severity Index (ASI; McLellan et al., 1992), which yields composite and severity scores in seven areas of client functioning: alcohol use, drug use, medical, employment, legal, family and social, and psychiatric. The DIS, SCID, and ASI also are used to identify clients with dual disorders. While the DIS and the SCID yield specific psychiatric diagnoses, the ASI yields a psychiatric severity score. Although it hasn't been tested widely, the ASI has demonstrated good reliability and validity with people with serious mental illness (Teitelbaum & Carey, 1996).

Computerized Assessment Methods

There are computerized versions available of many of the assessment scales discussed in this chapter. Among the structured interviews, a computerized version of the Diagnostic Interview Survey exists. The computerized version of the Timeline Followback (TLFB; Sobell & Sobell, 1995c), an AOD consumption assessment tool, greatly facilitates information collection and scoring. Many of the self-report assessment instruments, such as the Inventory of Drinking Situations (IDS; Annis, Graham, & Davis, 1987), also have computerized versions, so it is advisable to contact the source of the original version for an instrument in order to determine if one is available. Practitioners should evaluate the psychometric characteristics of computerized instruments separately from those of their noncomputerized counterparts (Finnegan, Ivanoff, & Smyth, 1991).

Self-Report Methods

Many self-report methods are used in the assessment and treatment of AOD problems and they can be conceptualized in three major categories: measures of consumption, screening and diagnostic measures, and treatment planning tools (Allen & Columbus, 1995). Self-reports are more likely to be accurate if interviews are conducted when clients are AOD free, confidentiality is ensured, and interviews are conducted in clinical or research settings, as opposed to legal settings (Sobell & Sobell, 1995a).

Psychiatric symptom scales (e.g., for depression, anxiety) are often used to assess the status of psychiatric symptoms among clients with dual disorders. Because discussion of these scales is beyond the scope of this chapter, readers are referred to the appropriate chapters in the *Handbook of Empirical Social Work Practice, Volume 1: Mental Disorders.*

Consumption Measures.

Common measures of AOD consumption include the Timeline Followback method (Sobell & Sobell, 1995b) and the use of diaries or self-monitoring logs (Miller, Westerberg, & Waldron, 1995). In addition, a range of alcohol quantity-frequency (QF) measures is available (see Room, 1990). All measures of alcohol consumption evaluate drinking in terms of the number of standard drinks. One standard drink is equivalent to 0.5 ounces of ethyl alcohol. Street drug use is more difficult to quantify, because the strength of a street drug can vary widely depending upon how it is prepared prior to sale on the street.

Diaries and drinking or drug use self-monitoring logs are useful for collecting current or prospective levels of AOD use from clients on a day-by-day basis. Log entries usually include information about: (a) the situations in which alcohol or drugs are consumed, (b) the client's moods or thoughts, and (c) the amount and type of alcoholic beverage or type of drug consumed (Allen & Columbus, 1995). In addition to providing information about consumption levels, this method provides useful information about drinking and drug use antecedents, which, in turn, can facilitate treatment planning. Information on AOD use antecedents can provide important insights into possible coexisting psychiatric disorders and can inform treatment planning for clients with dual disorders (Stasiewicz, Carey, Bradizza, & Maisto, 1996).

The TLFB method utilizes a calendar to collect detailed information about a person's past daily AOD use over a specific time period, anywhere from 30 days to 12 months prior to the interview (Sobell & Sobell, 1995b). Several memory aids are used to enhance accurate recall, and the TLFB can be administered by a trained interviewer or self-administered by clients in either paper-and-pencil or computerized formats (Sobell & Sobell, 1995b, 1995c).

Screening and Diagnostic Measures.   Screening and diagnostic measures aid in the determination of the existence and severity of an AOD problem. Screening measures are designed to detect people with problems who have not yet been identified as having AOD problems, for example, people seeking primary health care. For this reason, such measures are usually brief (Connors, 1995). Diagnostic measures are used to assess the severity of an AOD problem among clinical populations. There are some instruments, such as the Michigan Alcoholism Screening Test (MAST; Selzer, 1971) or the Drug Abuse Screening Test (DAST; Skinner, 1982), that are sometimes used for both screening and diagnosis.

Two common brief screening tools are the MAST for alcohol, the DAST for drugs, and the CAGEAID (Brown, 1992) for both. CAGEAID is the simplest of the screening tools; it involves asking the following four questions about alcohol or drug use (two positive responses are clinically significant):

C   Have you ever felt you ought to **C**ut down on your drinking or drug use?

A   Have people **A**nnoyed you by criticizing your drinking or drug use?

G   Have you ever felt bad or **G**uilty about your drinking or drug use?

E   Have you ever had a drink or used drugs first thing in the morning to steady your nerves or to get rid of a hangover or to get the day started (**E**ye-opener)? (Brown, 1992)

Diagnostic measures are used to assess the severity of an AOD problem; they are more often employed in situations where an AOD problem is already suspected, as in the case of evaluation interviews conducted in an addiction treatment clinic. Common diagnostic measures are the Alcohol Dependence Scale (ADS; Skinner & Horn, 1984), an instrument that assesses severity of alcohol dependence, the DrInC (Miller, Tonigan, & Longabaugh, 1995), a scale that measures the consequences of alcohol use, and the Personal Experience Inventory (PEI) for adolescents (Henly & Winters, 1988). Information from these measures can be useful in making some clinical decisions. For example, the ADS can be used to determine if a moderate drinking (versus abstinence) treatment goal is likely to be successful for a particular client (Skinner & Horn, 1984).

Treatment Planning Tools.   There are a plethora of assessment instruments that provide useful information in designing treatment plans. These tools provide information about clients' motivation to change and AOD relapse risk and self-efficacy, as well as other aspects of clients' substance-related behavior (Donovan, 1995).

One key factor that should be assessed is client motivation and readiness to change. The Stages of Change Readiness and Treatment Eagerness Scale

(SOCRATES; Miller & Tonigan, 1994) assesses clients according to the stages-of-change model developed by Prochaska and associates (Prochaska & DiClemente, 1984; Prochaska, DiClemente, & Norcross, 1992), a research-derived model of the five stages of change people go through in modifying addictive behaviors: precontemplation, contemplation, preparation, action, and maintenance. Research suggests that those clients who do best are in the preparation or action stages during intervention (Prochaska, DiClemente, et al., 1992; Prochaska, Norcross, Fowler, Follick, & Abrams, 1992). Clients in the earlier stages (precontemplation and contemplation) should receive interventions designed to move them into later stages (Prochaska, Norcross, et al., 1992; Miller & Rollnick, 1991).

The assessment of relapse risk is often done through examination of two aspects of clients' behavior: situational patterns of AOD use and self-efficacy, that is, beliefs about their ability to successfully maintain changes in their AOD use (Dimeff & Marlatt, 1995). Assessment instruments that are frequently used for these purposes are the Inventory of Drinking Situations (IDS; Annis, Graham, & Davis, 1987) and Inventory of Drug-Taking Situations (IDTS; Annis & Martin, 1985b) to assess AOD situational antecedents and the Situational Confidence Questionnaire (SCQ; Annis & Graham, 1988) and Drug-Taking Confidence Questionnaire (DTCQ; Annis & Martin, 1985a) to measure self-efficacy. Both scales are based upon the relapse research conducted by Marlatt and colleagues that identifies the following common situations for relapse risk: unpleasant emotions, physical discomfort, pleasant emotions, testing personal control and urges or temptations to use, conflict with others, social pressure to use, and pleasant times with others (Marlatt, 1985).

Self-Report Methods among Clients with Dual Disorders.

Almost no AOD screening or diagnostic scales exist that were developed specifically for people with serious mental illness (e.g., schizophrenia and bipolar disorder). In addition, the literature on the reliability and validity of AOD screening or diagnostic scales in psychiatric populations is relatively sparse. The MAST is, by far, the most widely evaluated measure among people with serious psychiatric problems and, while it has demonstrated good reliability in these populations, its validity varies widely across different studies (Teitelbaum & Carey, 1996). As a result, experienced practitioner-researchers recommend that assessment of this population rely on more idiosyncratic methods, such as functional assessment as outlined in Stasiewicz et al. (1996). Assessment instruments such as those identified under "Treatment Planning Tools" may be useful with this population, since they suggest functional relationships between AOD use, moods, and situational triggers (Stasiewicz et al., 1996; Teitelbaum & Carey, 1996). Finally, the TLFB has not been evaluated extensively in this population, but, when studied, it has demonstrated good reliability and validity (Teitelbaum & Carey, 1996).

Observational Methods

Observational methods are not used as frequently in the assessment and treatment of substance abuse as they are in clinical research, where observation in simulations, such as a simulated bar, may be used. The most common observational method relevant to practice is that of observing clients in role-play scenarios. While practitioners can develop client-specific scenarios, there are several role-play tests that have been developed for this purpose. One such instrument is the Alcohol-Specific Role Play Test (ASRPT; Monti et al., 1993), a ten-situation role play that is used to assess relapse risk in intrapersonal and interpersonal situations.

Physiological Measures

While there is a range of physiological tests used in AOD research, those tests used in practice tend to be urine tests, blood tests, alcohol breath tests, and liver functioning tests (Sobell et al., 1988). Drug use is most often evaluated through the use of urine tests. However, it should be kept in mind that these tests measure drug use, not the presence of a drug abuse problem, and there is a large amount of variation among drugs in the length of time each will stay in the body after cessation of use. While there are new drug tests available using hair and sweat, more research is needed to determine appropriate procedures for their use (Swan, 1995).

The alcohol breath test, or Breathalyzer, is a test that measures the amount of alcohol on the breath. This test often is used in clinical as well as legal settings to determine if an individual is under the influence of alcohol and is normally reported as a blood alcohol count (BAC) or blood alcohol level (BAL; Anton, Litten, & Allen, 1995). While there are no biological tests for alcoholism, there are some liver function tests that detect chronic alcohol intake, the most sensitive of which is gamma glutamyltransferase, or GGT (Anton et al., 1995). Unlike the Breathalyzer, which is often utilized by social workers and other nonmedical personnel, the GGT test tends to be utilized by medical personnel or researchers.

EFFECTIVE SOCIAL WORK INTERVENTIONS

There are many empirically validated approaches available for intervening with AOD problems. However, it has often been the case that substance abuse treatment agencies do not use treatment approaches that have research support; instead, many agencies have relied on approaches that either have not been effectively tested or have been shown to be less effective than other methods (Miller & Hester, 1986; Miller, Brown, et al., 1995).

Among the most important trends in AOD treatment research has been an emphasis on matching clients to treatments, that is, recognizing that no one treatment approach works for everyone (Allen & Kadden, 1995; Institute of Medicine [IOM], 1990a; McLellan & Alterman, 1991). A range of characteristics has been found to predict differential treatment outcome, including psychosocial, demographic, and AOD-related characteristics. Examples of relevant psychosocial characteristics are sociopathy, autonomy, locus of control, and social stability; important demographic variables include gender and age; and relevant AOD-related characteristics are the client's view of addiction, motivation to change, and urge to drink or use (Allen & Kadden, 1995). Although there is little research investigating the impact of treatment matching on treatment outcome, results from existing research are mixed, with some studies demonstrating important benefits to matching (McLellan et al., in press, as cited in NIDA, 1997; McLellan, Woody, Luborsky, O'Brien, & Druley, 1983) and another showing a minimal matching effect (Project MATCH Research Group, 1997).

Individual Therapies

Most substance abuse treatment settings provide some type of individual counseling, although most place a greater emphasis on group and self-help approaches (Straussner, 1993). There is a wide range of empirically validated individual treatment methods, the majority of which come from a cognitive-behavioral perspective (Miller, Brown, et al., 1995).

Brief intervention in alcohol problems is receiving increasing attention in the treatment literature, particularly for clients with low or moderate alcohol dependence; for this population it seems to be more effective than no treatment and as effective as more extensive treatment (Heather, 1995). Brief treatment most often involves some assessment of clients' drinking, followed by the provision of personalized feedback about their drinking; this can include a physician simply giving someone advice to cut down on drinking, as well as a clear message about the nature of sensible and problematic drinking (Babor, Ritson, & Hodgson, 1986). Motivational interventions are a specialized type of brief intervention designed to enhance people's commitment to changing their AOD use. The most well-known of these approaches, Motivational Interviewing (Miller & Rollnick, 1991), synthesizes elements of several effective motivational strategies. Outcome research on motivational interventions indicates that they are quite effective for alcohol problems (Miller, Brown, et al., 1995), and research extending investigation to drug problems found that a four-session treatment incorporating motivational interviewing can be effective for cocaine and marijuana problems, as well (Sobell, Sobell, Brown, Cleland, & Buchan, 1995).

Behavioral Self-Control Training (BSCT) is a treatment method that can be used for either abstinence or moderation goals and can be delivered in individual or group treatment formats (Hester, 1995b); moderation goals are not recommended for severe alcoholics (Hester, 1995b). The most recent innovation in

BSCT for alcohol problems is an interactive computer software program that teaches clients BSCT skills with minimal therapist involvement (Hester, 1995a). BSCT involves setting limits on drinking, self-monitoring of drinking, utilizing moderation strategies such as drinking rate control skills, using a self-reward, analyzing the antecedents for overdrinking, and developing coping skills to manage overdrinking trigger situations (Hester, 1995b). Overall, BSCT has strong empirical support for the treatment of alcohol problems (Hester, 1995b); those times when it hasn't performed well have been because it was compared to brief interventions (Miller, Brown, et al., 1995), suggesting it should be provided after efforts with brief intervention have failed (Hester, 1995b; Miller, Brown, et al., 1995).

Relapse prevention is a treatment approach that has been offered in individual, family, and group treatment formats, although it has been most consistently evaluated as part of group treatment (Dimeff & Marlatt, 1995). Therefore, it is discussed in the section on group therapies.

A pharmacological approach is the primary intervention for alcohol withdrawal (detoxification)—generally using benzodiazepines such as diazepam and chlorodiazepoxide (Anton, 1994). The most well-known drug used in treating alcoholism is disulfiram (Antabuse), a medication that causes illness if alcohol is ingested, which enhances treatment outcome when used in combination with other alcoholism treatment approaches (Fuller, 1995). Recent research on Naltrexone suggests that when it is used as an adjunct to treatment it can prevent alcoholism relapse (O'Malley et al., 1992; Volpicelli, Alterman, Hayashida, & O'Brien, 1992), and two other medications, buspirone and acamprosate, also hold promise for enhancing treatment outcome (Schuckit, 1996).

There is a wide range of pharmacological interventions for drug abuse. As with alcohol, medications are used for the treatment of acute withdrawal, when necessary, as in the treatment of opioid or sedative withdrawal. For opioid dependence, pharmacological interventions use either opioid replacement drugs, conceptualized as a type of hormone replacement, or opiate receptor antagonists, drugs that block the effects of opiates (O'Brien, 1996). Among the former are methadone, a synthetic opiate, and buprenorphine, a drug that also activates opiate receptors in the brain but which has a ceiling effect beyond which higher doses have no effect. While both medications are effective, methadone maintenance is the pharmacological intervention with the strongest empirical support (IOM, 1990b; O'Brien, 1996). However, it remains a controversial treatment because clients are maintained on this synthetic opioid medication, instead of being drug free (IOM, 1990b). A new, longer-acting opioid, LAAM, is currently being explored as an alternative to methadone. Naltrexone is the opiate antagonist with the most empirical support (O'Brien, 1996).

Clients do best on methadone if they receive other services, including on-site drug counseling and cognitive-behavioral or supportive-expressive psychotherapy (Crits-Cristoph & Siqueland, 1996; McLellan, Childress, Ehrman, O'Brien, &

Pashko, 1986; O'Brien, 1996; Woody, Luborsky, McLellan, & O'Brien, 1986), and family therapy, psychiatric care, and employment counseling (McLellan, Arndt, Metzger, Woody, & O'Brien, 1993). Additional on-site psychotherapy appears particularly important for people with high general psychopathology scores, as well as a depression diagnosis upon intake (Woody et al., 1984; Woody, McLellan, Luborsky, & O'Brien, 1985).

Pharmacologic interventions for cocaine dependence are currently under investigation. Preliminary studies indicated that a tricyclic antidepressant, desipramine, reduces craving and relapse; however, results from subsequent studies have been mixed (O'Brien, 1996). Promising preliminary studies on the effectiveness of serotonin reuptake inhibitors and buprenorphine (the partial opiate agonist) have been completed, but further research is needed to investigate the consistency of these findings (O'Brien, 1996; Treatment Outcome Working Group [TOWP], 1996).

Finally, research suggests that some people—for example, alcoholics with coexisting depression—may respond better to AOD treatment when placed on medications targeting their psychiatric disorder, although the research on this is mixed (e.g., Carroll, Nich, & Rounsaville, 1995; Nunes et al., 1993; Powell et al., 1995; Tollefson, Lancaster, & Montague-Clouse, 1991). While this is a given for dual-diagnosis clients with chronic psychiatric disorders, such as schizophrenia or bipolar disorder, it is an area for further research for clients with less severe dual disorders (Nunes & Deliyannides, 1993).

There is a range of other treatment strategies with empirical support. Most of these treatment methods reflect additional cognitive behavioral interventions for alcohol problems, including behavior contracting, cognitive therapy, aversion therapy (using covert sensitization or nausea-producing drugs), and use of self-help manuals that usually teach BSCT (Miller et al., 1995). In addition, a few treatment strategies show promise but need to be subjected to further investigation and replication (Miller, Brown, et al., 1995). Among these methods are acupuncture (Bullock, Umen, Culliton, & Olander, 1987), sensory deprivation (Cooper, Adams, & Scott, 1988), and developmental counseling (Alden, 1988).

Group Therapies

Although practitioners consider group therapy to be the treatment of choice for people with AOD problems (Galanter, Castaneda, & Franco, 1991), the comparative effectiveness of group versus other treatment modalities has not been systematically examined (Cartwright, 1987). One study of problem drinkers found no difference between the two treatment modalities, although group therapy clients achieved their gains earlier in treatment than those in individual therapy (Duckert, Amundsen, & Johnsen, 1992). Another study compared individual and group guided self-change treatment, a motivationally based, four-session BSCT intervention, and found no difference in AOD treatment outcome, retention in treatment, or client satisfaction between the two modalities (Sobell et al., 1995). For cocaine problems, research indicates that intensive group treatment (120 minutes five times a week) results in higher client retention rates than does standard group treatment (90 minutes twice a week), although the addition of individual therapy or family therapy to the standard group treatment also had this effect (Hoffman et al., 1994).

As was noted earlier, relapse prevention (RP) is often provided in the form of group treatment. Its components include self-monitoring drinking or drug use or urges to use, identifying high-risk situations, assessing the client's current coping skills and resources and self-efficacy, developing coping strategies and a plan to manage high-risk situations, and developing or strengthening lifestyle balance with regard to shoulds and wants (Dimeff & Marlatt, 1995). Research generally supports the effectiveness of RP (Dimeff & Marlatt, 1995; Carroll et al., 1994; Miller, Brown, et al., 1995). Some research suggests that RP is most likely to benefit people with moderate to severe alcohol dependence (Dimeff & Marlatt, 1995) or severe cocaine problems (Carroll, Rounsaville, & Gawin, 1991), and alcoholics with differentiated (versus undifferentiated) drinking profiles, that is, drinking that varies over different types of situations (Annis & Davis, 1989). RP with marijuana-dependent clients yielded marginally significant better results at 3 months' post-treatment, particularly for men, than those obtained by clients receiving supportive group therapy; however, these differences disappeared at later follow-ups (Stephens, Roffman, & Simpson, 1994).

Coping and social skills training (CSST; Monti, Rohsenow, Colby, & Abrams, 1995) for treating AOD problems has been most often delivered and investigated as a group intervention, although it has been adapted for individual treatment as well (Monti, Abrams, Kadden, & Cooney, 1989; Monti et al., 1995). These approaches usually include interpersonal and mood management skills, particularly as they relate to use (Monti et al., 1989, 1995). Topics might include coping with cravings and drinking- or drug-related thoughts, problem solving, managing anger, assertiveness, giving and receiving criticism, planning for emergencies, coping with a lapse, and managing negative thinking. CSST has strong empirical support for its effectiveness with alcoholics (Miller, Brown, et al., 1995; Monti et al., 1989). In addition, research suggests that it may be particularly effective for more severe alcoholics and for alcoholics with concurrent psychopathology (Monti et al., 1995), as well as cocaine abusers with depressive symptomatology (Carroll, Nich, & Rounsaville, 1995; CSST was provided in individual sessions).

Another group treatment is interactional group therapy for alcohol problems, developed by Getter (1984) and based on work by Yalom and colleagues (Brown & Yalom, 1977; Yalom, 1974); interactional group therapy has demonstrated important matching effects for specific types of alcoholics when compared to coping skills group treatment (Allen & Kadden, 1995). Alcoholics higher in either psychopathology or sociopathy were more likely to relapse in interactional group therapy as opposed to CSST, whereas alcoholics lower in these two characteristics, or who had high levels of cognitive impairment, were less likely to relapse in interactional group therapy (Cooney, Kadden, Litt, & Getter, 1991).

No discussion of group treatment would be complete without mention of self-help groups. The largest and most widely known self-help group is Alcoholics Anonymous (AA), but there are others, including Narcotics Anonymous (NA; for all types of drug addiction), Women for Sobriety (WFS), Rational Recovery (RR), Secular Organizations for Sobriety/Save Our Selves (SOS), and Self-Management And Recovery Training (SMART) Recovery (McCrady & Delaney, 1995; Horvath, 1996). The last three were created as self-help groups that, unlike AA and NA, would not include any references to God. For people with dual disorders, specialized groups, such as Double Trouble, exist (Zaslav, 1993).

While most substance abuse treatment professionals refer clients to AA and NA, there is no empirical evidence supporting the effectiveness of these groups as interventions themselves. Of all of the above-mentioned self-help groups, AA is the only one that has been subject to any outcome research (McCrady & Delaney, 1995). A review of studies examining AA's effectiveness as an adjunct to treatment did indicate that AA attendance was correlated with modest improvements in outcome (Emrick, Tonigan, Montgomery, & Little, 1993).

Marital and Family Therapies

The nature of effective marital and family treatment (MFT) for AOD problems varies depending upon whether the treatments are for alcohol problems or drug problems. For alcohol problems, almost all of the treatment research has focused on behavioral MFT, primarily with White male alcoholics (O'Farrell, 1995). For drug problems, most of the research has been on family treatment (FT) of youth AOD abuse (Crits-Christoph & Siqueland, 1996).

MFT for adult AOD problems can be divided into two major categories: interventions designed to work with spouses of treatment-resistant AOD abusers and interventions used when the AOD abuser is in treatment. FT for adolescent AOD abuse may focus on the entire family or on one or more members of the family. In addition, there are self-help groups for family members, although there are almost no data on the effectiveness of these groups.

MFT Interventions for Treatment-Resistant AOD Abusers.   The most commonly researched interventions for treatment-resistant AOD abusers are unilateral spouse interventions, that is, treatment approaches that focus on changing spouses' behavior as a vehicle for changing their partners' AOD use. Three such approaches currently exist: Unilateral Family Therapy (UFT; Thomas, 1994), Reinforcement Training (RT; Sisson & Azrin, 1986), and the Pressures to Change (PC) approach (Barber & Crisp, 1995). While both RT and UFT involve several

months of treatment, PC is only five or six sessions and currently has the most research support (Barber & Gilbertson, 1997). Preliminary trials evaluating UFT have supported its effectiveness in decreasing spouses' distress, increasing marital satisfaction, and facilitating alcoholics' entry into treatment (Barber & Gilbertson, 1997; O'Farrell, 1995; Thomas, Santa, Bronson, & Oyserman, 1987), and a pilot study comparing RT to supportive counseling or disease concept education plus referral to Al-Anon (a self-help group) found that RT was more successful in getting alcoholics both to enter treatment and to reduce their drinking prior to entering treatment (Sisson & Azrin, 1986). Investigations of the PC approach, whether provided in group, individual sessions, or a self-help manual, have found it to be more effective than either a control group or Al-Anon in engaging heavy drinkers into treatment (Barber & Gilbertson, 1996, 1997). When provided in individual treatment or a self-help manual, it also is effective at improving spouses' well-being (Barber & Gilbertson, in press, as cited in Barber & Gilbertson, 1997).

Two additional interventions have some data to suggest effectiveness, although both need more rigorous evaluation. The Johnson Institute Intervention (JII) model (Johnson, 1973), an approach that involves educating and preparing family members to confront the alcohol abuser, appears to help facilitate clients' entry into alcohol treatment (Liepman, Nirenberg, & Begin, 1989; Loneck, Garrett, & Banks, 1996), although it hasn't been compared with other unilateral models. The second approach with some promise of empirical support is disease concept–oriented group therapy for spouses of alcoholics. One study found that wives in this group treatment had less enabling and anxiety and greater self-concept than wives in a waiting-list control condition (Dittrich & Trapold, 1984). Neither of these two interventions has been researched in relationship to drug abuse.

MFT Interventions When the AOD Abuser Is in Treatment.   Most AOD treatment agencies treat couples by enrolling the spouse and AOD abuser in separate, concurrent treatment; however, no controlled studies evaluating the effectiveness of this treatment approach have been done (O'Farrell, 1995). Conjoint treatment approaches, especially Behavioral MFT (BMFT), which can be conducted with one couple or in a group, have quite a bit of empirical support. BMFT is more effective in treating alcoholics than treatment methods that do not include conjoint or family treatment, and adding relapse prevention sessions can minimize deterioration of treatment gains (O'Farrell, 1995). There is minimal controlled research on BMFT with drug-abusing clients, although the existing research suggests it also is an effective intervention for this population (Fals-Stewart, Birchler, & O'Farrell, 1996).

There also is some empirical support for nonbehavioral marital interventions. Specifically, the research suggests that the addition of couples group treatment to alcohol treatment is superior to standard alcohol treatment without couples treatment (Cadogan, 1973; Corder, Corder, & Laidlaw, 1972; McCrady, Paolino, Longabaugh, & Rossi, 1979).

Family Treatment of Youth AOD Abuse.   Some research supports the use of family treatment with adolescents with AOD problems. Strategic structural family treatment was more effective at engaging, in treatment, the families of Hispanic youth than was a comparison control group; however, no treatment outcomes were examined (Szapocznik et al., 1988). Additional outcome studies offer some support for multidimensional family therapy (Liddle & Dakof, 1993, as cited by Crits-Cristoph & Siqueland, 1996) and family systems therapy (Joanning, Quinn, Thomas, & Mullen, 1992) over adolescent group therapy, although the methodological limitations in these studies suggest the need for cautious interpretation of results.

Family Self-Help Groups.   Self-help groups for family members of alcoholics and of drug addicts also exist, specifically, Al-Anon and Nar-Anon (for adult family members), Alateen and Alatot (for children), and Al-Anon–Adult Children of Alcoholics (ACOA), for adults who grew up in alcoholic families (McCrady & Delaney, 1995). Of these groups, only Al-Anon has received any study, and that has been minimal (Barber & Gilbertson, 1997; O'Farrell, 1995). In the one small, controlled study comparing Al-Anon to the PC unilateral approach (Barber & Gilbertson, 1996), Al-Anon participants had fewer personal problems than control participants and PC group counseling participants, but not PC individual counseling participants. However, as was noted above, Al-Anon was not effective in helping spouses facilitate their partners' entry into treatment. Several uncontrolled, correlational studies have reported positive outcomes for wives who participated in Al-Anon (Barber & Gilbertson, 1997; O'Farrell, 1995).

Community

Community interventions can range from interventions that utilize environmental components in the treatment of individuals to interventions that target population subgroups or whole communities for intervention.

The Community Reinforcement Approach (CRA; Meyers & Smith, 1995; Smith & Meyers, 1995) is a broad-spectrum behavioral treatment method that utilizes environmental reinforcers (social, recreational, vocational, familial) to intervene in AOD problems. Treatment strategies are chosen from a wide array of options, including coping skills training, job-training, social clubs, marital therapy, relapse prevention, disulfiram, and social and recreational counseling, depending upon the assessment of the antecedents and consequences of an individual's AOD use. CRA has substantial empirical support for the treatment of alcohol dependence (Miller, Brown, et al., 1995) and preliminary empirical support for treatment of cocaine dependence (O'Brien, 1996; Smith & Meyers, 1995). Providing vouchers, contingent on clean urines, enhanced treatment outcomes with cocaine-abusing or -dependent and opiate-dependent clients enrolled in CRA treatment (Higgins et al., 1994; Silverman et al., 1996), as did the participation of cocaine clients' significant others (Higgins, Budney, Bickel, & Badger, 1994).

A very different type of community intervention can be found in the application of brief interventions to community settings such as hospitals and primary health care settings. These interventions may be conducted as part of health screening programs or regular physical exams, or in the context of a medical hospitalization. As with brief intervention in general, these community-based brief treatment approaches have excellent empirical support (Heather, 1995).

Intervention with driving under the influence (DUI) offenders is another focus for community intervention. A metanalysis of DUI remediation programs concluded that such programs are generally successful in preventing recidivism. The best combination of interventions was identified as education, psychotherapy, and probation contact (Wells-Parker, Bangert-Drowns, McMillen, & Williams, 1995). A new approach to intervening with multiple DUI offenders, the Probation Alcohol Treatment (PAT) approach, integrates alcoholism treatment and probation into a single intervention; research on the PAT program found that it reduced recidivism among repeat drinking and driving offenders ("Combination of alcohol treatment . . .", 1995).

A new type of intervention program, Drug Court, emerged in the late 1980s. Drug courts generally target nonviolent first offenders charged with drug and drug-related offenses, although, recently, more programs are targeting more serious drug offenders (Drug Court Clearinghouse and Technical Assistance Project [DCCTAP], 1996). Offenders are identified as early as possible, ideally after arrest, and are referred to intensive outpatient treatment, frequent urinalysis, frequent follow-up contacts with the judge, and a rehabilitation program providing vocational, educational, medical, and family services (DCCTAP, 1996). Evaluation data from the older drug courts indicate excellent retention and completion rates (70%) and reduced criminal justice recidivism rates (5% to 25% compared with the typical 45%; DCCTAP, 1996).

Workplace drug testing is another type of community strategy. It has been used as a mechanism to identify people in need of treatment and then to send them through employee assistance programs (EAPs) for assessment and treatment referral; the threat of job loss serves as leverage to coerce people with positive drug tests into treatment. A recent study evaluated the effectiveness of this strategy by comparing 6-month treatment outcomes for coerced EAP participants with those of voluntary EAP participants and found that the coerced participants with those of voluntary EAP participants and found that the coerced participants had somewhat better outcomes than voluntary participants (Lawental, McLellan, Grissom, Brill, & O'Brien, 1996). While there were some methodological problems with the study, the results are nonetheless promising.

Another promising community strategy, that of placing comprehensive substance abuse prevention programs in Boys and Girls Clubs located in public housing projects, was evaluated by Schinke and colleagues (Schinke, Orlandi, & Cole, 1992). Reductions in community crack use occurred following the implementation of these programs, while crack use levels stayed the same for control comparison sites (Schinke et al., 1992).

Finally, there is a wide range of residential settings for people with AOD problems, including halfway houses, self-run recovery homes, community residences, and therapeutic communities (TCs; Smyth, 1995), the latter being the subject of the most research. A therapeutic community is an intensive, highly structured, long-term (9 to 24 months) treatment program for those clients with serious drug problems who also require a total restructuring of personality and lifestyle. Research indicates that although TCs have very high dropout rates (only 25% remain longer than 3 months), good treatment outcomes are associated with longer lengths of stay and treatment completion (TOWP, 1996).

Many of the communitywide interventions for AOD problems focus on preventing the development of substance abuse, or primary prevention, as opposed to intervention with people with mild, moderate, or more serious AOD problems (NIAAA, 1994). These strategies are discussed in the prevention section.

Dual Disorders

Much of the literature on treatment of clients with dual disorders discusses three primary approaches to delivering services to this population: integrated, parallel, and sequential (Minkoff, 1991; Ries, 1994). Integrated intervention programs systematically address both problems under one roof—the staff are skilled in assessment and treatment of both disorders, and the disorders are treated together. Parallel intervention is the concurrent enrollment of an individual in two (or more) different programs (e.g., a mental health outpatient clinic and substance abuse halfway house). Sequential intervention is the enrollment of an individual in a second program at some point after completion of the first. Because this last option is appropriate only when treatment of one condition can be temporarily placed on hold (Smyth, 1996), discussion of service-delivery options is usually limited to the parallel versus integrated options. While there is a host of methodological problems with conducting research into the question of which of these two approaches is more effective, results from evaluation and services research, and one experimental study, all indicate that integrated treatment is the preferred approach. Research also indicates that, at least for those dually disordered individuals with severe mental illness, intensive case management improves treatment outcome (Drake, Mueser, Clark, & Wallach, 1996).

Prevention

Prevention interventions can target multiple system levels, from individuals and families, as in direct practice interventions, to communities, as in coordinated community programs, to an entire nation, as in social policies (NIAAA, 1994; NIDA, 1996; Wodarski & Smyth, 1994).

Policy Interventions.   Policy-level interventions vary considerably depending upon whether a drug is legal (Musto, 1992). Efforts to prevent alcohol problems can be divided into several categories, including policies targeting the supply or availability of alcohol, social controls on alcohol, and primary prevention programs (Moskowitz, 1989). Drug policies are usually divided into two major categories: supply reduction and demand reduction (Office of National Drug Control Policy [ONDCP], 1996). Supply reduction policies include the creation of special law enforcement units, special policing of high-intensity drug trafficking areas, and interdiction, or efforts to keep drugs from being smuggled into the United States. Demand reduction strategies include treatment and primary and secondary prevention programs (ONDCP, 1996).

Alcohol availability reduction approaches can encompass limiting the type and number of outlets where alcohol is sold, raising the prices of alcoholic beverages, limiting alcohol advertising, and limiting the sale and consumption of alcohol. While some data indicate that limiting the availability of alcohol is correlated with a reduction in alcohol consumption and alcohol problems (NIAAA, 1994; NIDA, 1996), methodological limitations in many of these studies do not allow for the identification of clear cause-effect relationships (Moskowitz, 1989). However, research on raising the minimum drinking age from 18 to 21 indicates that it has resulted in reduced alcohol consumption and reduced traffic crashes and fatalities among people under age 21 (Moskowitz, 1989; Toomey, Rosenfeld, & Wagenaar, 1996).

Social control approaches to reducing alcohol problems have focused on public intoxication laws and, more recently, drinking and driving laws. To date, there is good empirical support for increased enforcement of drinking and driving laws as a policy to reduce alcohol-related fatalities (Hingson, 1996; Moskowitz, 1989). In addition, the data supporting the effectiveness of alcohol server training interventions (i.e., for bartenders) on the prevention of alcohol impairment are promising (Moskowitz, 1989; NIAAA, 1996), although somewhat mixed (McKnight, 1996).

Rydell and Everingham recently compared policy strategies to control cocaine use; they found that supply-reduction strategies (such as source-country control, interdiction, and domestic enforcement, which account for 93% of federal, state, and local expenditures) are less cost-effective in reducing cocaine use than is treatment. Overall, they found that "an expenditure of $34 million on treatment could reduce cocaine use by as much as would an expenditure of $250 million on the least expensive of the three supply-control approaches, domestic enforcement" ("Cocaine use . . .", 1994, p. 3).

Community, Educational, and Skill-Building Interventions.   Primary prevention programs can consist of coordinated community strategies, educational programs, and skill building.

There is little research to support the effectiveness of mass media and education programs and some research to indicate that these programs can result in *increased* drinking and drug use (Moskowitz, 1989; NIDA, 1996; Schinke, Botvin, & Orlandi, 1991). At best, mass media and education programs appear to influence knowledge, but rarely behavior (Moskowitz, 1989; Schinke et al., 1991). In other cases, as with the introduction of warning labels on alcoholic beverages, mass education campaigns appear to have had no impact even on knowledge and awareness of the hazards of alcohol consumption (NIAAA, 1994).

Most of the few effective primary prevention interventions have been cognitive-behavioral approaches, primarily skills training programs, particularly for the prevention of adolescent AOD use and abuse (Botvin, Baker, Dusenbury, Botvin, & Diaz, 1995; NIAAA, 1994; NIDA, 1996; Schinke et al., 1991; Wodarski & Feit, 1993), and, more recently, reduction of alcohol use among blue-collar workers (Cook, Back, & Trudeau, 1996). Recent developments in prevention research suggest some promising new approaches. For example, a recent quasi-experimental evaluation of the impact of family skills training (FST) for African American drug-using parents and their children indicated that the parents experienced a reduction in drug use, while their children had a decrease in high-risk factors and an increase in protective factors (Aktan, Kumpfer, & Turner, 1996). In addition, multicomponent coordinated school- and community-based approaches, such as Project Northland and Project STAR, have also demonstrated promising results in reducing alcohol use among adolescents (NIDA, 1996).

SUMMARY

In conclusion, social workers have at their disposal a range of empirically validated interventions for substance abuse, and future research is likely to continue to expand the knowledge base. Effective intervention in any social problem requires attention to intervening with individuals, groups, families, communities, and with the society as a whole. This requirement places the social work profession, with its emphasis on multilevel, micro-to-macro practice, in an excellent position to provide leadership in combating this serious social problem.

REFERENCES

Aktan, G. B., Kumpfer, K. L., & Turner, C. W. (1996). Effectiveness of a family skills training program for substance abuse prevention with inner city African-American families. *Substance Use & Misuse, 31,* 157–175.

Alden, L. E. (1988). Behavioral self-management controlled-drinking strategies in a context of secondary prevention. *Journal of Consulting and Clinical Psychology, 56,* 280–286.

Allen, J. P., & Columbus, M. (Eds.). (1995). *Assessing alcohol problems: A guide for clinicians and researchers* (NIAAA Treatment Handbook, Series 4 NIH 95-3745). Bethesda, MD: U.S. Department of Health and Human Services.

Allen, J. P., & Kadden, R. M. (1995). Matching clients to alcohol treatments. In R. K. Hester & W. R. Miller (Eds.), *Handbook of alcoholism treatment approaches* (2nd ed., pp. 170–182). Boston: Allyn & Bacon.

American Psychiatric Association (1994). *Diagnostic and statistical manual of mental disorders* (4th ed.). Washington, DC: Author.

Annis, H. M., & Davis, C. S. (1989). Relapse prevention. In R. K. Hester & W. R. Miller (Eds.), *Handbook of alcoholism treatment approaches* (2nd ed., pp. 278–291). New York: Pergamon Press.

Annis, H. M., & Graham, J. M. (1988). *Situational confidence questionnaire (SCO-39) users guide.* Toronto: Addiction Research Foundation.

Annis, H. M., Graham, J. M., & Davis, C. S. (1987). *Inventory of drinking situations (IDS) user's guide.* Toronto: Addiction Research Foundation.

Annis, H. M., & Martin, G. (1985a). *Drug-taking confidence questionnaire.* Toronto, Canada: Addiction Research Foundation.

Annis, H. M., & Martin, G. (1985b). *Inventory of drug-taking situations.* Toronto, Canada: Addiction Research Foundation.

Anton, R. F. (1994). Medications for treating alcoholism. *Alcohol Health and Research World, 18,* 265–271.

Anton, R. F., Litten, R. Z., & Allen, J. P. (1995). Biological assessment of alcohol consumption. In J. P. Allen & M. Columbus (Eds.), *Assessing alcohol problems: A guide for clinicians and researchers* (NIAAA Treatment Handbook, Series 4 NIH 95-3745, pp. 31–39). Bethesda, MD: U.S. Department of Health and Human Services.

Babor, T. F., Ritson, E. B., & Hodgson, R. J. (1986). Alcohol-related problems in the primary health care setting: A review of early intervention strategies. *British Journal of Addiction, 81,* 23–46.

Barber, J. G., & Crisp, B. R. (1995). The pressures to change approach to working with the partners of heavy drinkers. *Addiction, 90,* 269–276.

Barber, J. G., & Gilbertson, R. (1996). An experimental study of brief unilateral intervention for the partners of heavy drinkers. *Research on Social Work Practice, 6,* 325–336.

Barber, J. G., & Gilbertson, R. (1997). Unilateral interventions for women living with heavy drinking. *Social Work, 42,* 69–78.

Botvin, G. J., Baker, E., Dusenbury, L., Botvin, E. M., & Diaz, T. (1995). Long-term follow-up results of a randomized drug abuse prevention trial in a white middle-class population. *JAMA, 273,* 1106–1112.

Brown, R. L. (1992). Identification and management of alcohol and drug disorders. In M. F. Fleming & K. L. Barry (Eds.), *Addictive disorders* (pp. 25–43). St. Louis: Mosby.

Brown, S. A., Irwin, M., & Schuckit, M. A. (1991). Changes in anxiety among abstinent male alcoholics. *Journal of Studies on Alcohol, 52,* 55–61.

Brown, S. A., & Schuckit, M. A. (1988). Changes in depression among abstinent alcoholics. *Journal of Studies on Alcohol, 49,* 412–417.

Brown, S., & Yalom, I. D. (1977). Interactional group therapy with alcoholics. *Journal of Studies on Alcohol, 38,* 426–456.

Bryant, K. J., Rounsaville, B., Spitzer, R. L., & Williams, J. B. W. (1992). Reliability of dual diagnosis: Substance dependence and psychiatric disorders. *The Journal of Nervous and Mental Disease, 180,* 251–257.

Bullock, M. L., Umen, A. J., Culliton, P. D., & Olander, R. T. (1987). Acupuncture treatment of alcoholic recidivism: A pilot study. *Alcoholism: Clinical and Experimental Research, 11*, 292–295.

Cadogan, D. A. (1973). Marital group therapy in the treatment of alcoholism. *Quarterly Journal of Studies on Alcohol, 34*, 1187–1194.

Carroll, K. M., Nich, C., & Rounsaville, B. J. (1995). Differential symptom reduction in depressed cocaine abusers treated with psychotherapy and pharmacotherapy. *The Journal of Nervous & Mental Disease, 183*, 251–259.

Carroll, K. M., Rounsaville, B. J., Nich, C., Gordon, L. T., Wirtz, P. W., & Gawin, F. (1994). *Archives of General Psychiatry, 51*, 989–997.

Carroll, K. M., Rounsaville, B. J., & Gawin, F. H. (1991). A comparative trial of psychotherapies for ambulatory cocaine abusers: Relapse prevention and interpersonal psychotherapy. *American Journal of Drug and Alcohol Abuse, 17*, 229–247.

Cartwright, A. (1987). Group work with substance abusers: Basic issues and future research. *British Journal of Addiction, 82*, 951–953.

Cocaine use: Trends and control strategies (1994, June). *Rand Drug Policy Research Center Newsletter, 3*, 3.

Cohen, J., & Levy, S. J. (1992). *The mentally ill chemical abuser: Whose client?* New York: Lexington Books.

Combination of alcohol treatment and probation shown to reduce criminal behavior by repeat DWI offenders. (1995). *Drinking, Drugs & Driving* (Research Note 95-3). Buffalo, NY: Research Institute on Addictions.

Connors, G. J. (1995). Screening for alcohol problems. In J. P. Allen & M. Columbus (Eds.), *Assessing alcohol problems: A guide for clinicians and researchers* (NIAAA Treatment Handbook, Series 4 NIH 95-3745, pp. 17–29). Bethesda, MD: U.S. Department of Health and Human Services.

Cook, R. F., Back, A. S., & Trudeau, J. (1996). Preventing alcohol use problems among blue-collar workers: A field test of the *working people* program. *Substance Use & Misuse, 31*, 255–275.

Cooney, N. L., Kadden, R. M., Litt, M. D., & Getter, H. (1991). Matching alcoholics to coping skills or interactional therapies: Two-year follow-up results. *Journal of Consulting & Clinical Psychology, 59*, 598–601.

Cooper, G. O., Adams, H. B., & Scott, J. C. (1988). Studies in REST: I. Reduced environmental stimulation therapy and reduced alcohol consumption. *Journal of Substance Abuse Treatment, 5*, 61–68.

Corder, B. F., Corder, R. F., & Laidlaw, N. D. (1972). An intensive treatment program for alcoholics and their wives. *Quarterly Journal of Studies on Alcohol, 33*, 1144–1146.

Crits-Christoph, P., & Siqueland, L. (1996). Psychosocial treatment for drug abuse. *Archives of General Psychiatry, 53*, 749–756.

Davidson, K. M. (1995). Diagnosis of depression in alcohol dependence: Changes in prevalence with drinking status. *British Journal of Psychiatry, 166*, 199–204.

Dimeff, L. A., & Marlatt, G. A. (1995) Relapse prevention. In R. K. Hester & W. R. Miller (Eds.), *Handbook of alcoholism treatment approaches* (2nd ed., pp. 176–194). Boston: Allyn & Bacon.

Dittrich, J. E., & Trapold, M. A. (1984). Wives of alcoholics: A treatment program and outcome study. *Bulletin of the Society of Psychologist in Addictive Behaviors, 3*, 91–102.

Donovan, D. (1995). Assessments to aid in the treatment planning process. In J. P. Allen & M. Columbus (Eds.), *Assessing alcohol problems: A guide for clinicians and researchers* (NIAAA Treatment Handbook, Series 4 NIH 95-3745, pp. 75–122). Bethesda, MD: U.S. Department of Health and Human Services.

Drake, R. E., Mueser, K. T., Clark, R. E., & Wallach, M. A. (1996). The course, treatment, and outcome of substance disorder in persons with severe mental illness. *American Journal of Orthopsychiatry, 66,* 42–51.

Drug Court Clearinghouse and Technical Assistance Project. (1996, May). *Summary assessment of the Drug Court experience* [Online]. Available: http://www/ojp/usdoj.gov/dcpo/assess.htm

Duckert, E., Amundsen, A., & Johnsen, J. (1992). What happens to drinking after therapeutic intervention? *British Journal of Addiction, 87,* 1457–1467.

Emrick, C. D., Tonigan, S., Montgomery, H., & Little, L. (1993). Alcoholics Anonymous: What is currently known? In B. S. McCrady & W. R. Miller (Eds.), *Research on alcoholics anonymous: Opportunities and alternatives* (pp. 41–79). New Brunswick, NJ: Alcohol Research Documentation, Inc., Rutgers University.

Evans, K., & Sullivan, J. M. (1990). *Dual diagnosis: Counseling the mentally ill substance abuser.* New York: Guilford Press.

Evans, K., & Sullivan, J. M. (1995). *Treating the addicted survivor of trauma.* New York: Guilford Press.

Fals-Stewart, W., Birchler, G. R., & O'Farrell, T. J. (1996). Behavioral couples therapy for male substance-abusing patients: Effects on relationship adjustment and drug-using behavior. *Journal of Consulting and Clinical Psychology, 64,* 959–972.

Fayne, M. (1993). Recognizing dual diagnosis patients in various clinical settings. In J. Solomon, S. Zimberg, & E. Shollar (Eds.), *Dual diagnosis: Evaluation, treatment, training, and program development* (pp. 39–53). New York: Plenum Press.

Finnegan, D. J., Ivanoff, A. M., & Smyth, N. J. (1991). A computer applications explosion: What practitioners and managers need to know. *Computers in Human Services, 8,* 1–19.

First, M. B., & Gladis, M. M. (1993). Diagnosis and differential diagnosis of psychiatric and substance use disorders. In J. Solomon, S. Zimberg, & E. Shollar (Eds.), *Dual diagnosis: Evaluation, treatment, training, and program development* (pp. 23–37). New York: Plenum Press.

First, M. B., Spitzer, R. L., Gibbon, M., & Williams, J. B. W. (1996). Structural clinical interview for DSM-IV Axis I disorders—patient edition (SCID-I/P, Version 2.0). New York: Biometrics Research Department.

Fuller, R. K. (1995). Antidipsotropic medications. In R. K. Hester & W. R. Miller (Eds.), *Handbook of alcoholism treatment approaches* (2nd ed., pp. 123–133). Boston: Allyn & Bacon.

Galanter, M., Castaneda, R., & Franco, H. (1991). Group therapy and self-help groups. In R. J. Frances & S. I. Miller (Eds.) *Clinical textbook of addictive disorders* (pp. 431–451). New York: Guilford Press.

Getter, H. (1984). Aftercare for alcoholism: Short-term interactional group therapy manual. Unpublished manuscript, Department of Psychology, University of Connecticut at Storrs.

Grant, B. F. (1994). Alcohol consumption, alcohol abuse and alcohol dependence. The United States as an example. *Addiction, 89,* 1357–1365.

Heather, N. (1995). Brief intervention strategies. In R. K. Hester & W. R. Miller (Eds.), *Handbook of alcoholism treatment approaches* (2nd ed., pp. 105–122). Boston: Allyn & Bacon.

Henly, G. A., & Winters, K. C. (1988). Development of problem severity scales for the assessment of adolescent alcohol and drug abuse. *International Journal of Addictions, 23,* 65–85.

Hester, R. (1995a). Behavioral self-control program for Windows (Version 3.0). Albuquerque, NM: Alcohol Self-Control Program.

Hester, R. K. (1995b). Behavioral self-control training. In R. K. Hester & W. R. Miller (Eds.), *Handbook of alcoholism treatment approaches* (2nd ed., pp. 148–159). Boston: Allyn & Bacon.

Higgins, S. T., Budney, A. J., Bickel, W. K., & Badger, G. J. (1994). Participation of significant others in outpatient treatment predicts greater cocaine abstinence. *American Journal of Drug and Alcohol Abuse, 20,* 47–56.

Higgins, S. T., Budney, A. J., Bickel, W. K., Foerg, F. E., Donham, R., & Badger, G. J. (1994). Incentives improve outcome in outpatient behavioral treatment of cocaine dependence. *Archives of General Psychiatry, 51,* 568–576.

Hingson, R. (1996). Prevention of drinking and driving. *Alcohol Health & Research World, 20,* 219–226.

Hoffman, J. A., Caudill, B. D., Koman III, J. J., Luckey, J. W., Flynn, P. M., & Hubbard, R. L. (1994). Comparative cocaine abuse treatment strategies: Enhancing client retention and treatment exposure. *Journal of Addictive Diseases, 13,* 115–128.

Horvath, A. T. (1996, July). Is SMART as effective as AA? *SMART recovery: news and views,* 1–2. Beachwood, OH: SMART Recovery.

Institute for Health Policy, Brandeis University (1993). *Substance abuse: The nation's number one health problem. Key indicators for policy.* Princeton, NJ: The Robert Wood Johnson Foundation.

Institute of Medicine (1990a). *Broadening the base of treatment for alcohol problems.* Washington, DC: National Academy Press.

Institute of Medicine (1990b). *Treating drug problems: Vol. 1.* Washington, DC: National Academy Press.

Joanning, H., Quinn, W., Thomas, F., & Mullen, R. (1992). Treating adolescent drug abuse: A comparison of family systems therapy, group therapy, and family drug education. *Journal of Marital and Family Therapy, 18,* 345–356.

Johnson, V. A. (1973). *I'll quit tomorrow.* New York: Harper & Row.

Jonas, S. (1992). Public health approach to the prevention of substance abuse. In J. H. Lowinson, P. Ruiz, R. B. Millman, & J. G. Langrod (Eds.) *Substance abuse: A comprehensive textbook* (2nd ed., pp. 928–943). Baltimore, MD: Williams & Wilkins.

Kent, S., Fogarty, M., & Yellowless, P. (1995). A review of studies of heavy users of psychiatric services. *Psychiatric Services, 46,* 1247–1253.

Kleber, H. D. (1992). Federal role in substance abuse policy. In J. H. Lowinson, P. Ruiz, R. B. Millman, & J. G. Langrod (Eds.) *Substance abuse: A comprehensive textbook* (2nd ed., pp. 32–38). Baltimore: Williams & Wilkins.

Lawental, E., McLellan, A. T., Grissom, G. R., Brill, P., & O'Brien, C. (1996). Coerced treatment for substance abuse problems detected through workplace urine surveillance: Is it effective? *Journal of Substance Abuse, 8,* 115–128.

Liepman, M. R., Nirenberg, T. D., & Begin, A. M. (1989). Evaluation of a program designed to help family and significant others to motivate resistant alcoholics into recovery. *American Journal of Drug and Alcohol Abuse, 15,* 209–221.

Loneck, B., Garrett, J. A., & Banks, S. M. (1996). A comparison of the Johnson intervention with four other methods of referral to outpatient treatment. *American Journal of Drug and Alcohol Abuse, 22,* 233–246.

Marlatt, G. A. (1985). Situational determinants of relapse and skill-training interventions. In G. A. Marlatt & J. R. Gordon (Eds.), *Relapse prevention: Maintenance strategies in the treatment of addictive behaviors* (pp. 71–127). New York: Guilford Press.

McCrady, B. S., & Delaney, S. I. (1995). Self-help groups. In R. K. Hester & W. R. Miller (Eds.), *Handbook of alcoholism treatment approaches* (2nd ed., pp. 160–175). Boston: Allyn & Bacon.

McCrady, B. S., Paolino, T. J., Jr., Longabaugh, R., & Rossi, J. (1979). Effects of joint hospital admission and couples treatment for hospitalized alcoholics: A pilot study. *Addictive Behaviors, 4,* 155–165.

McKnight, A. J. (1996). Server intervention to reduce alcohol-involved traffic crashes. *Alcohol Health & Research World, 20,* 227–229.

McLellan, A. T., & Alterman, A. I. (1991). Patient-treatment matching: A conceptual and methodological review with suggestions for future research. In R. W. Pickens, C. G. Leukefeld, & C. R. Schuster (Eds.) *Improving drug abuse treatment* (DHHS Publication No. ADM 91-1754, pp. 114–135). Washington, DC: National Institute on Drug Abuse.

McLellan, A. T., Arndt, I. O., Metzger, D. S., Woody, G. E., & O'Brien, C. P. (1993). The effects of psychosocial abuse treatment. *Journal of American Medical Association, 269,* 1953–1959.

McLellan, A. T., Childress, A. R., Ehrman, R., O'Brien, C. P., & Pashko, S. (1986). Extinguishing conditioned responses during opiate dependence treatment turning laboratory findings into clinical procedures. *Journal of Substance Abuse Treatment, 3,* 33–40.

McLellan, A. T., Kushner, H., Metzger, D., Peters, R., Smith, I., Grissom, G., Pettinati, H., & Argeriou, M. (1992). The fifth edition of the addiction severity index: Historical critique and normative data. *Journal of Substance Abuse, 9,* 199–213.

McLellan, A. T., Woody, G. E., Luborsky, L., O'Brien, C. P., & Druley, K. A. (1983). Increased effectiveness of substance abuse treatment. A prospective study of patient-treatment "matching." *The Journal of Nervous and Mental Disease, 171,* 597–605.

Meyers, R. J., & Smith, J. E. (1995). *Clinical guide to alcohol treatment: The community reinforcement approach.* New York: Guilford Press.

Miller, W. R., Brown, J. M., Simpson, T. L., Handmaker, N. S., Bien, T. H., Luckie, L. F., Montgomery, H. A., Hester, R. K., & Tonigan, J. S. (1995). What works? A methodological analysis of the alcohol treatment outcome literature. In R. K. Hester & W. R. Miller (Eds.), *Handbook of alcoholism treatment approaches* (2nd ed., pp. 12–44). Boston: Allyn & Bacon.

Miller, W. R., & Hester, R. K. (1986). The effectiveness of alcoholism treatment: What research reveals. In W. R. Miller & N. Heather (Eds.), *Treating addictive behaviors: Processes of change* (pp. 121–174). New York: Plenum Press.

Miller, W. R., & Rollnick, S. (1991). *Motivational interviewing.* New York: Guilford Press.

Miller, W. R., & Tonigan, J. S. (1994). *Assessing drinkers' motivation for change: The stages of change readiness and treatment eagerness scale (SOCRATES).* Unpublished manuscript,

Center on Alcoholism, Substance Abuse, and Addictions, University of New Mexico, Albuquerque.

Miller, W. R., Tonigan, J. S., & Longabaugh, R. (1995). *The drinker inventory of consequences (DrInC): An instrument for assessing adverse consequences of alcohol abuse. Test manual* (NIAAA Project MATCH Monograph Series, Vol. 4, NIH Publication No. 95-3911). Washington, DC: U.S. Government Printing Office.

Miller, W. R., Westerberg, V. S., & Waldron, H. B. (1995). Evaluating alcohol problems in adults and adolescents. In R. K. Hester & W. R. Miller (Eds.), *Handbook of alcoholism treatment approaches* (2nd ed., pp. 61–88). Boston: Allyn & Bacon.

Minkoff, K. (1991). Program components of a comprehensive integrated care system for serious mentally ill patients with substance disorders. In K. Minkoff & R. E. Drake (Eds.), *Dual diagnosis of major mental illness and substance disorder* (pp. 13–27). San Francisco: Jossey-Bass.

Monti, P. M., Abrams, D. A., Kadden, R. M., & Cooney, N. L. (1989). *Treating alcohol dependence: A coping skills guide.* New York: Guilford Press.

Monti, P. M., Rohsenow, D. J., Abrams, D. B., Zwick, W. R., Binkoff, J. A., Munroe, S. M., Fingeret, A. L., Nirenberg, T. D., Liepman, M. R., Pedraza, M., & Kadden, R. M. (1993). Development of a behavior analytically derived alcohol-specific role-play assessment instrument. *Journal of Studies on Alcohol, 54,* 710–721.

Monti, P. M., Rohsenow, D. J., Colby, S. M., & Abrams, D. B. (1995). Coping and social skills training. In R. K. Hester & W. R. Miller (Eds.), *Handbook of alcoholism treatment approaches* (2nd ed., pp. 221–241). Boston: Allyn & Bacon.

Moos, R. H., Finney, J. W., & Cronkite, R. C. (1990). *Alcoholism treatment context, process and outcome.* New York: Oxford University Press.

Moskowitz, J. M. (1989). The primary prevention of alcohol problems: A critical review of the research literature. *Journal of Studies on Alcohol, 50,* 54–88.

Musto, D. F. (1992). Historical perspectives on alcohol and drug abuse. In J. H. Lowinson, P. Ruiz, R. B. Millman, & J. G. Langrod (Eds.), *Substance abuse: A comprehensive textbook* (2nd ed., pp. 2–14). Baltimore, MD: Williams & Wilkins.

National Institute on Alcohol Abuse and Alcoholism. (1983). *National drug and alcoholism treatment utilization survey: September 1983 comprehensive report.* Rockville, MD: Alcohol, Drug Abuse, and Mental Health Administration.

National Institute on Alcohol Abuse and Alcoholism. (1994). *Eighth special report to the U.S. Congress on alcohol and health.* (NIH Publication No. 94-3699). Alexandria, VA: U.S. Department of Health and Human Services.

National Institute on Drug Abuse. (1996, October). Preventing alcohol abuse and related problems. *Alcohol Alert* (NIAAA Publication No. 34, PH/370, pp. 1–2). Bethesda, MD: U.S. Department of Health and Human Services.

National Institute on Drug Abuse. (1997, February). *Director's report to the National Advisory Council on Drug Abuse.* [Online]. Available: http://www.nida.gov/DirRep297/DirectorReport3.html

National Institute on Drug Abuse and National Institute on Alcohol Abuse and Alcoholism. (1993). *National drug and alcoholism treatment unit survey: 1991 main findings report* (DHHS Publication No. ADM 93-2007). Washington, DC: U.S. Government Printing Office.

Nunes, Jr., E. V., & Deliyannides, D. A. (1993). Research issues in dual diagnosis. In J. Solomon, S. Zimberg, & E. Shollar (Eds.), *Dual diagnosis: Evaluation, treatment, training, and program development* (pp. 287–309). New York: Plenum Press.

Nunes, E. V., McGrath, P. J., Quitkin, F. M., Stewart, J. P., Harrison, W., Tricamo, E., & Ocepek-Welikson, K. (1993). Imipramine treatment of alcoholism with comorbid depression. *American Journal of Psychiatry, 150,* 953–965.

O'Brien, C. P. (1996). Recent developments in the pharmacotherapy of substance abuse. *Journal of Consulting and Clinical Psychology, 64,* 677–686.

O'Farrell, T. J. (1995). Marital and family therapy. In R. K. Hester & W. R. Miller (Eds.), *Handbook of alcoholism treatment approaches* (2nd ed., pp. 195–220). Boston: Allyn & Bacon.

Office of National Drug Control Policy. (1996). *The national drug control strategy: 1996* (NCJ #160086). Washington, DC: Executive Office of the President.

O'Malley, S. S., Jaffe, A. J., Chang, G., Schottenfeld, R. S., Meyer, R. E., Rounsaville, B. (1992). Naltrexone and coping skills therapy for alcohol dependence. *Archives of General Psychiatry, 49,* 881–887.

Powell, B. J., Campbell, J. L., Landon, J. F., Liskow, B. I., Thomas H. M., Nickel, E. J., Dale, T. M., Penick, E. C., Samuelson, S. D., & Lacoursiere, R. B. (1995). A double-blind, placebo-controlled study of nortriptyline and bromocriptine in male alcoholics and subtyped by comorbid psychiatric disorders. *Alcoholism: Clinical and Experimental Research, 19,* 462–468.

Prochaska, J. O., & DiClemente, C. C. (1984). *The transtheoretical approach.* Homewood, IL: Dorsey Press.

Prochaska, J. O., DiClemente, C. C., & Norcross, J. C. (1992). In search of how people change: Applications to addictive behaviors. *American Psychologist, 47,* 1102–1114.

Prochaska, J. O., Norcross, J. C., Fowler, J. L., Follick, M. J., & Abrams, D. B. (1992). Attendance and outcome in a work site weight control program: Processes and stages of change as process and predictor variables. *Addictive Behaviors, 17,* 35–42.

Project MATCH Research Group. (1997). Matching alcoholism treatments to client heterogeneity: Project MATCH posttreatment drinking outcomes. *Journal of Studies on Alcohol, 58,* 7–29.

Ries, R. (1994). *Assessment and treatment of patients with coexisting mental illness and alcohol and other drug abuse* (Treatment Improvement Protocol Series No. 9, DHHS Publication No. SMA-94-2078). Rockville, MD: Center for Substance Abuse Treatment.

Robins, L. N., Helzer, J. E., Croughan, J., & Ratcliff, K. S. (1981). National Institute of Mental Health Diagnostic Interview Schedule. *Archives of General Psychiatry, 38,* 381–389.

Room, R. (1990). Measuring alcohol consumption in the United States: Methods and rationales. In L. T. Kozlowski, H. M. Annis, H. D. Cappell, F. B. Glaser, M. S. Goodstadt, Y. Israel, H. Kalant, E. M. Sellers, & E. R. Vingilis (Eds.), *Research advances in alcohol and drug problems* (Vol. 10, pp. 39–80). New York: Plenum Press.

Rouse, B. A. (Ed.) (1995). *Substance abuse and mental health: Statistics sourcebook* (DHHS Publication No. [SMA] 95-3064). Rockville, MD: U.S. Department of Health and Human Services.

Schinke, S. P., Botvin, G. J., & Orlandi, M. A. (1991). *Substance abuse in children and adolescents evaluation and intervention* (Vol. 22). Newbury Park, CA: Sage.

Schinke, S. P., Orlandi, M. A., & Cole, K. C. (1992). Boys & girls clubs in public housing developments: Prevention services for youth at risk. *Journal of Community Psychology* (OSAP

Special Issue. Programs for change: Office for Substance Abuse Prevention Demonstration Models), 118–128.

Schuckit, M. A. (1996). Recent developments in the pharmacotherapy of alcohol dependence. *Journal of Consulting and Clinical Psychology, 64,* 669–676.

Sederer, L. I. (1990). Mental disorders and substance abuse. In H. B. Milkman & L. I. Sederer (Eds.), *Treatment choices for alcoholism and substance abuse* (pp. 163–181). Lexington, MA: Lexington Books.

Selzer, M. L. (1971). The Michigan Alcoholism Screening Test: The quest for a new diagnostic instrument. *American Journal of Psychiatry, 127*(12), 1653–1658.

Silverman, K., Wong, C. J., Higgins, S. T., Brooner, R. K., Montoya, I. O., Contoreggi, C., Umbricht-Schneiter, A., Schuster, C. R., & Preston, K. L. (1996). Increasing opiate abstinence through voucher-based reinforcement therapy. *Drug and Alcohol Dependence, 41,* 157–165.

Sisson, R. W., & Azrin, H. H. (1986). Family-member involvement to initiate and promote treatment of problem drinking. *Journal of Behavior Therapy and Experimental Psychiatry, 17,* 115–121.

Skinner, H. A. (1982). The drug abuse screening test. *Addictive Behavior, 7,* 363–371.

Skinner, H. A., & Horn, J. L. (1984). *Alcohol dependence scale: Users guide.* Toronto: Addiction Research Foundation.

Smith, J. E., & Meyers, R. J. (1995). The community reinforcement approach. In R. K. Hester & W. R. Miller (Eds.), *Handbook of alcoholism treatment approaches* (2nd ed., pp. 251–266). Boston: Allyn & Bacon.

Smyth, N. J. (1995). Substance abuse: Direct practice. In R. L. Edwards et al. (Eds.), *Encyclopedia of Social Work* (19th ed., pp. 2328–2337). Washington, DC: National Association of Social Workers.

Smyth, N. J. (1996). Motivating persons with dual disorders: A stage approach. *Families in Society, 77,* 605–614.

Sobell, L. C., & Sobell, M. B. (1995a). Alcohol consumption measures. In J. P. Allen & M. Columbus (Eds.), *Assessing alcohol problems: A guide for clinicians and researchers* (NIAAA Treatment Handbook, Series 4 NIH 95-3745, pp. 55–73). Bethesda, MD: U.S. Department of Health and Human Services.

Sobell, L. C., & Sobell, M. B. (1995b). *Alcohol timeline followback (TLFB) users manual.* Toronto, Canada: Addiction Research Foundation.

Sobell, L. C., & Sobell, M. B. (1995c). *Timeline followback computer software.* Toronto, Canada: Addiction Research Foundation.

Sobell, L. C., Sobell, M. B., Brown, J. C., Cleland, P. A., & Buchan, G. (1995, November). *A randomized trial comparing group versus individual guided self-change treatment for alcohol and drug abusers.* Poster presented at the 29th annual meeting of the Association for Advancement of Behavior Therapy, Washington, DC.

Sobell, L. C., Sobell, M. B., & Nirenberg, T. D. (1988). Behavioral assessment and treatment planning with alcohol and drug abusers: A review with an emphasis on clinical application. *Clinical Psychology Review, 8,* 19–54.

Stasiewicz, P. R., Carey, K. B., Bradizza, C. M., & Maisto, S. A. (1996). Behavioral assessment of substance abuse with co-occurring psychiatric disorder. *Cognitive and Behavioral Practice, 3,* 91–105.

Stephens, R. S., Roffman, R. A., & Simpson, E. E. (1994). Treating adult marijuana dependence: A test of the relapse prevention model. *Journal of Consulting and Clinical Psychology, 62,* 92–99.

Strain, E. C., Stitzer, M. L., & Bigelow, G. E. (1991). Early treatment time course of depressive symptoms in opiate addicts. *The Journal of Nervous and Mental Disease, 179,* 215–221.

Straussner, S. L. (1993). Assessment and treatment of clients with alcohol and other drug problems: An overview. In S. L. Straussner (Ed.), *Clinical work with substance-abusing clients* (pp. 3–30). New York: Guilford Press.

Substance Abuse and Mental Health Services Administration (1995). *National household survey on drug abuse: Main findings 1993.* Rockville, MD: U.S. Department of Health and Human Services.

Substance section wins full status. (1995, October). *NASW News,* pp. 1, 10.

Swan, N. (1995, September/October). Sweat testing may prove useful in drug-use surveillance. In G. Soucy (Ed.), *NIDA Notes, 10* (NIH Publication No. 95-3478; pp. 10–11). Rockville, MD: National Institutes of Health.

Szapocznik, J., Perez-Vidal, A., Brickman, A. L., Foote, F. H., Santisteban, D., & Hervis, O. (1988). Engaging adolescent drug abusers and their families in treatment: A strategic structural systems approach. *Journal of Consulting and Clinical Psychology, 56,* 552–557.

Teitelbaum, L. M., & Carey, K. B. (1996). Alcohol assessment in psychiatric patients. *Clinical Psychology: Science and Practice, 3,* 323–338.

Thomas, E. J. (1994). Appendix B. The unilateral treatment program for alcohol abuse-background, selected procedures, and case applications. In J. Rothman & E. J. Thomas (Eds.), *Intervention research, design and development for human service* (pp. 427–447). New York: Haworth Press.

Thomas, E. J., Santa, C. A., Bronson, D., & Oyserman, D. (1987). Unilateral family therapy with spouses of alcoholics. *Journal of Social Service Research, 10,* 145–162.

Tollefson, G. D., Lancaster, S. P., & Montague-Clouse, J. (1991). The association of buspirone and its metabolite 1-pyrimidinylpiperazine in the remission of comorbid anxiety with depressive features and alcohol dependency. *Psychopharmacology Bulletin, 27,* 163–170.

Toomey, T. L., Rosenfeld, & Wagenaar, A. (1996). The minimum legal drinking age: History, effectiveness, and ongoing debate. *Alcohol Health & Research World, 20,* 213–218.

Treatment Outcome Working Group (1996). Treatment protocol effectiveness study. A white paper of the Office of National Drug Control Policy, Barry R. McCaffrey, Director. *Journal of Substance Abuse Treatment, 13,* 295–319.

Volpicelli, J. R., Alterman, A. I., Hayashida, M., & O'Brien, C. P. (1992). Naltrexone in the treatment of alcohol dependence. *Archives of General Psychiatry, 49,* 876–880.

Wells-Parker, E., Bangert-Drowns, R., McMillen, R., & Williams, M. (1995). Final results from a meta-analysis of remedial interventions with drink/drive offenders. *Addiction, 90,* 907–926.

Wodarski, J. S., & Feit, M. D. (1993). *Adolescent substance abuse.* Binghamton, NY: Haworth Press.

Wodarski, J. S., & Smyth, N. J. (1994). Adolescent substance abuse: A comprehensive approach to prevention intervention. *Journal of Child and Adolescent Substance Abuse, 3*(3), 33–58.

Woody, G. E., Luborsky, L., McLellan, A. T., & O'Brien, C. P. (1986). Psychotherapy as an adjunct to methadone treatment. In R. E. Meyer (Ed.), *Psychopathology and addictive disorders* (pp. 169–195). New York: Guilford Press.

Woody, G. E., McLellan, A. T., Luborsky, L., & O'Brien, C. P. (1985). Sociopathy and psychotherapy outcome. *Archives of General Psychiatry, 42,* 1081–1086.

Woody, G. E., McLellan, A. T., Luborsky, L., O'Brien, C. P., Blaine, J., Fox, S., Herman, I., & Beck, A. T. (1984). Severity of psychiatric symptoms as a predictor of benefits from psychotherapy: The Veterans Administration study. *American Journal of Psychiatry, 141,* 1172–1177.

Yalom, I. D. (1974). Group therapy and alcoholism. *Annals New York Academy of Sciences, 233,* 85–103.

Zaslav, P. (1993). The role of self-help groups in the treatment of the dual diagnosis patient. In J. Solomon, S. Zimberg, & E. Shollar (Eds.), *Dual diagnosis: Evaluation, treatment, training, and program development* (pp. 105–126). New York: Plenum Press.

Zimberg, S. (1993). Introduction and general concept of dual diagnosis. In J. Solomon, S. Zimberg, & E. Shollar (Eds.), *Dual diagnosis: Evaluation, treatment, training, and program development* (pp. 3–21). New York: Plenum Press.

Chapter 8

CRIME

Lisa A. Rapp
John S. Wodarski

OVERVIEW

High rates of crime and violence affect the lives of countless Americans every year. On an average day in 1995, 59 individuals died as a result of violence (Federal Bureau of Investigation [FBI], 1995), and 4,075 Americans received medical treatment for violence-inflicted injuries (Perkins, Klaus, Bastian, & Cohen, 1996). Each month the equivalent of more than a jumbo jet full of young people under age 18 are victims of homicide (Snyder, Sickmund, & Poe-Yamagata, 1996).

Americans have consistently rated crime and violence as the most imperative problem for the United States for the 3-year period from 1994 to 1996 (Bureau of Justice Statistics, 1996). Fear of criminal victimization is at an all-time high. These concerns by the U.S. public are justified when the facts are considered. Crime statistics from the FBI reveal that 13.9 million criminal offenses were reported in 1995. Approximately 12 million of these offenses were property crimes and 1.5 million offenses were violent crimes (U.S. Department of Justice, 1996). These statistics are somewhat inaccurate, in that they measure only officially reported crimes. The National Crime Victimization Survey (1995), which collects crime data from victims, estimates that there were approximately 39.6 million criminal offenses in 1995 (excluding murder). This total is a 1% decrease from 1994 (U.S. Department of Justice, 1996). Approximately 63% of all crimes are never brought to official attention.

Juveniles have played a critical, yet tragic, role in the nation's criminal and violent behavior. Juveniles were involved in 32% of all robbery arrests, 23% of weapon arrests, and 15% of murder and aggravated assault arrests in 1995 (Office of Juvenile Justice and Delinquency Prevention, 1997). While adult crime and violence appears to be mildly declining, juvenile crime and violence is increasing. From 1985 to 1994, the rate of murder committed by 14- to 17-year-olds increased by 172%. The arrest rates for juveniles ages 14 to 17 have now surpassed those for young adults ages 18 to 24 (Fox, 1996). By the year 2005, the number of juveniles ages 14 to 17 will increase by 20%. Even if the per capita rate of juvenile homicide remains the same, the number of 14- to 17-year-olds who will commit murder will increase simply because of changing demographics.

Costs

The costs of crime are astronomical. The total annual cost of crime has been estimated around $425 billion. This cost includes $90 billion for the criminal justice system and employees, $65 billion for private protection (alarms, security systems, etc.), $50 billion for urban decay (fleeing residents and lost jobs, etc.), $45 billion for property loss, $5 billion for medical care, and $170 billion for shattered lives (productivity losses, lost quality of life, etc., Farrell, 1993). Firearm-related injuries are especially costly. Acute medical care for patients with gunshot wounds has been estimated to cost over $30,000 per hospital visit (Kizer, Vassar, Harry, & Layton, 1995) and 80% of the costs are paid for by the taxpayers (Wintemute & Wright, 1992). It is no wonder that Americans report crime and violence to be their number one concern for the nation.

Minority Groups

Minority groups, especially African Americans, have been overrepresented as victims and perpetrators of crime and violence. Roscoe and Morton (1994) found a disproportionate representation from minority groups who were arrested, held in detention centers, and incarcerated in the United States. African Americans comprise approximately 12% of the population, but account for 26% of all arrests and 51% of all violent crime arrests. Blacks are 8.5 times more likely than Whites to go to prison (Pearson, 1994). African Americans are also disproportionately represented as victims of violence. Black youths between ages 14 and 24 comprise under 2% of the population, yet they are 17% of the victims of violence (Fox, 1996).

These statistics may have given the illusion that African Americans are to blame for crime and violence. However, studies have indicated that there is nothing inherent about the Black culture that provokes crime. Community characteristics, which include unemployment, family disruption, poor educational systems, and economic deprivation, are the factors that increase crime and violence (Pearson, 1994; Roscoe & Morton, 1994) and minority groups are disproportionately represented in these types of communities. Research indicates that approximately 41% of Black youths in Harlem are living below the poverty level and experience these maladaptive conditions conducive to crime (McCord & Freeman, 1990).

Corrections

The number of adults in the United States under some form of correctional supervision totaled more than 5.3 million at the end of 1995 (Brown, Gilliard, Snell, Stephan, & Wilson, 1996). This is nearly 2.8% of all adults in the United States. Currently, three quarters of these individuals are on probation and parole. This is a staggering number of adults who could be working, paying taxes, and taking care of their families. Officials predict that the rising incidence of juvenile crime and violence will continue to significantly increase the number of inmates. In the last two years, 79,417 new beds have been added to prisons in response to this increase. However, this is still not enough to meet the needs of the burgeoning inmate population. Making matters worse is the current increase in the number of juveniles who are transferred to the adult system and the increasing length of sentences given to criminals.

Juvenile facilities have encountered similar problems. A recent report on the conditions of confinement in U.S. juvenile detention and correctional facilities indicated that over 75% of the confined population were housed in facilities that violated one or more standards related to living space, including facility design, capacity, sleeping areas, and living unit size (Allen-Hagen, 1993). These institutions also were noted to have serious problems in education, rehabilitation, and treatment services, as well as safety and security (Allen-Hagen, 1993). Crowding in institutions has been found to be associated with institutional violence and suicidal behavior.

The idea of getting tough on crime has been a popular slogan with politicians who know how to influence and induce fear in the public. This retributive justice has increased the practice of treating juveniles like adults and has exhausted both the juvenile and adult correctional systems. The number of juveniles placed in crowded adult prisons has been estimated to be about 200,000 (Howell, Krisberg, & Jones, 1995). This type of justice has placed an emphasis on social control rather than rehabilitation and treatment.

The "three strikes" policy, which incarcerates individuals after their third offense, has also increased the inmate population. This policy tends to incarcerate individuals past the age of continued criminal activity. In other words, most criminals tend to reduce their crime by the end of their 20s and completely eliminate their criminal activity by their mid- to late 30s. The three strikes policy incarcerates individuals who tend to be near or at the end of their criminal careers. This policy makes a small dent in crime reduction at the cost of $5.5 billion for taxpayers.

Drug law violators have also been targeted with lengthy sentences. Most of the drug offenders are serving federally mandated sentences, which tend to be stiffer and tend to be even harsher for African Americans. These adults (who often have problems with drug use) are often locked away without rehabilitation or drug treatment. Consequently, they take up two thirds of the beds in the federal prison system (Carr, 1996) and they are not rehabilitated, so they are released with the expectation that they will not violate the law again. Thus, the recidivism rate for drug law offenders is extremely high.

Our current correctional system is overburdened and overwhelmed, therefore making it largely ineffective. This has fostered the general belief by politicians and the public that nothing works with regard to stopping crime and treating criminals. Rehabilitation has been forgotten and juveniles and adults have been placed at risk for abuse within the correctional system and for recidivism after the system.

New initiatives are desperately needed to reduce crime and violence. Prevention and treatment programs should be reexamined. New programs that target communities, drug involvement, and youths have begun to exhibit promising results. Several of these programs and policy initiatives will be discussed here.

ASSESSMENT

In order to effectively intervene to reduce crime and violence among juveniles and adults, comprehensive risk assessments should be completed. These assessments should be based on the risk factors that we know are inherent with criminal behavior. The following is a brief outline of the risk factors in the community, the family, the individual, and the school.

Community Risk Factors

1. Economically deprived areas with high levels of unemployment (Farrington, 1991)
2. Disorganized neighborhoods with high levels of crime and violence and low levels of supervision (Yoshikawa, 1994)
3. Availability of firearms (Rapp & Wodarski, in press; Reiss & Roth, 1993)
4. Media portrayals of violence (Donnerstein, Slaby, & Eron, 1994)

Family Risk Factors

1. Family management problems, including parenting and supervision (Rapp & Wodarski, in press; Yoshikawa, 1994).
2. Family conflict and violence (Farrington, 1991; Hawkins, Catalano, & Miller, 1992)
3. Parental attitudes favorable to crime and violence (Hawkins, Lishner, Jenson, & Catalano, 1987; Rapp & Wodarski, in press)

Individual Risk Factors

1. Early disruptive behaviors (Hawkins et al., 1987; Rapp & Wodarski, in press)
2. Impulsivity and risk taking (Hawkins et al., 1987)

3. Association with negative peers (Elliott, Huizinga, & Ageton, 1985)

4. Alcohol and drug use (Bushman & Cooper, 1990)

School Risk Factors

1. Academic failure and low level of commitment to school (Rapp & Wodarski, in press; Yoshikawa, 1994)

2. Early antisocial behavior in school (Farrington, 1991)

All individuals who engage in crime and violence will not have the same risk factors, and different factors will be more salient for some individuals than for others. Likewise, these factors may become more potent at different developmental ages and stages. These factors have been found to increase the risk of crime and delinquency as well as of other problem behaviors. Consequently, they should be assessed carefully for each individual. Clearly, the more risk factors an individual has, the more likely he or she will be of evincing criminal and violent behaviors.

RISK ASSESSMENTS

Risk assessment and classification refers to the process of evaluating offenders' current needs regarding treatment and their likelihood of reoffending. In other words, risks to themselves and the public must be assessed. The determined level of risk is then translated into the level of supervision or intervention recommended for the offender.

Previously, these assessments have been informal, highly discretionary, and inconsistent (Wiebush, Baird, Krisberg, & Onek, 1995). Oftentimes, these procedures were criticized as being inequitable, erroneous, and unreliable. Consequently, more structured and formalized procedures were developed to assist in decision making. These have included sentencing guidelines, standardized risk and need assessment instruments, and structured classification systems (Wiebush et al., 1995).

Three types of assessments have been developed that evaluate juvenile and adult offenders: risk assessment instruments, placement or custody assessments (juveniles only), and needs assessment instruments. These instruments will be briefly outlined here.

Risk assessment instruments are designed to estimate the likelihood that an offender will commit another offense. These instruments are generally used to determine the level of supervision or intervention most appropriate for the offender (Wiebush et al., 1995). Actuarial or historical data and clinical information are the two basic information sources used.

Placement or custody assessments go beyond the scope of recidivism. These instruments help to determine whether a youth should be placed in detention prior to a hearing, what type of placement or institution the youth should be placed in, and who should have custody of the youth (Wiebush et al., 1995).

The third type of evaluation instruments are needs assessments. These assessments have a slightly different role from those of the first two instruments. These assessments help staff identify what particular needs each offender has. These assessments drive the specific type of interventions given to offenders in and outside of institutions. For instance, substance abuse counseling, anger management, or employment skills may all be deficits that need to be addressed for a particular offender. These instruments help correctional staff develop an appropriate intervention plan for each offender.

In order for the correctional system to utilize the following alternative interventions, a clear, standardized assessment system must be in place. Interventions must match needs and risks of offenders. Offenders who are inappropriately assigned to interventions, no matter how innovative, will surely fail.

INTERVENTIONS

The system's response to the problem of serious crime and violence has been inconsistent. Some states have emphasized getting tougher on crime, while others have looked to prevention and rehabilitation as the answer. Lately, several alternative approaches to incarceration have been introduced. These alternatives include day reporting centers, boot camps, drug courts, and intensive supervision. Despite the variations in policy emphasis, there has been an emerging interest in developing a continuum of care (Wiebush et al., 1995). This continuum of care would move beyond traditional choices and would be able to match offenders with the level of treatment that would best meet their needs. The following is a brief introduction to some of these alternative approaches.

Prevention Programs

Creative thinking and innovative ideas have been encouraged in the attempt to reduce crime and violence. Prevention programs have been placed at the forefront in an effort to deter juveniles and young adults from becoming involved with crime.

Community Policing

Law enforcement administrators and academics using police research have generated the concept of community policing. Community policing does not address specific problems faced by law enforcement; rather, it calls for an all-encompassing change in the way police perform their duties (Carter, 1995). Community policing strategies vary depending on the needs and responses of the communities involved, although there are certain basic principles common to all community policing efforts. Essentially, community policing involves a collaboration between the police and the community to identify and solve community problems.

Crime statistics have indicated that the current system of crime fighting has failed to reduce crime (Community Policing Consortium, 1994). In fact, the organizational arrangement of most police stations has often isolated police officers from the communities they serve. This isolation tends to hamper crime-fighting efforts. Citizens often have the most information about the crimes that occur in their communities. Without strong ties to the community, police do not have access to this important information. Community policing offers a way for the police and the community to work together to resolve the serious problems that are ongoing within the community (Community Policing Consortium, 1994).

The two core components of community policing are community partnership and problem solving. These components address specific citizen concerns and provide more attentive police service. Plans to reduce crime or problems in the area are devised by citizens and police officers and are implemented by all.

Research has indicated that particular service amendments have been effective in reducing crime. Deployment of patrol officers that fluctuates depending on season, time of day, and geographic location was more effective than assigning patrol cars based on population ratios. One-officer patrol cars were just as effective and did not jeopardize officer safety. Prevention tactics worked in deterring and reducing crimes and teams of officers working together in cooperation were more comprehensive than nonteams (Carter, 1995).

Community policing is a prevention idea that can be tailored to meet each community's specific problems and needs. Community policing is not the answer to all problems and it may not be amenable to all communities. However, the concept provides a logical, comprehensive, preventive approach to police service delivery that relies on empirically based studies (Carter, 1995).

Second-Shift Schools

Second-shift schools are another prevention program that has been initiated in various schools throughout the nation. Schools that are located in troubled communities have begun to provide activities for youths after school hours. Activities include sports, arts, music, crafts, and various recreational activities, as well as assistance with homework. Second-shift programs begin directly after school and continue until 5 or 6 P.M. The intentions of the programs are to reduce associations with delinquent peers, increase the time spent in prosocial activities, improve social and leisure skills, and reduce the amount of time youths spend unsupervised (Fox, 1996). These programs have been found to be effective in reducing youths' involvement in criminal and delinquent activities (Brewer, Hawkins, Catalano, & Neckerman, 1995).

Empirical studies have found that juveniles tend to engage in delinquent activities between the hours of 3 and 8 P.M. (Fox, 1996). If prevention or other structured programs can be put into place during this time frame, crime and delinquent activities can be reduced among youth. Juveniles will also benefit from establishing a relationship with positive adult role models. Some second-shift school programs focus specifically on reducing crime and delinquency; others employ strategies for preventing gang involvement and drug abuse (Brewer, Hawkins, Catalano, & Neckerman, 1995). However designed, second-shift school programs can provide effective prevention for crime and delinquency for youths of all school ages.

Drug Courts

A number of innovative drug courts have reported success in reducing the levels of drug abuse, incarceration, and criminal recidivism among drug offenders (Tauber, 1994). Drug courts, which hear the cases of nonviolent drug offenders, are run by a judge who deals directly with the offender and usually decides on the type of rehabilitation program required. Offenders who are mandated to treatment are usually expected to commence that day. This process takes extensive coordination and team effort with community treatment programs (Tauber, 1994).

Coordinated comprehensive supervision is another key component of the program. Most offenders attend the drug court to beat incarceration. However, these programs are tightly supervised and maintained. Drug testing, immediate notice of treatment failures, and routine progress reports are utilized to keep track of offenders. For those offenders who require more intensive services, transfers to residential treatment centers are available.

Drug courts usually follow offenders over a longer period of time, and aftercare is considered a must. Drug court rehabilitations usually also include educational opportunities, employment training and placement, and housing and health assistance (Tauber, 1994).

Overall, the benefits of the drug court program include a reduction of the cost per defendant, added capability to incarcerate the most serious offenders, a reduction in police overtime and other witness costs, a reduction in grand jury and indictment costs, a lower percentage of those relying on public assistance, and a reduction of medical and social service costs (more drug-free babies; Office of Justice Programs, 1996). Further research will need to be conducted to evaluate the long-term benefits of these programs.

INTERMEDIATE-LEVEL SANCTIONS

Shock Incarceration and Boot Camps

Shock incarceration programs or boot camp prisons have recently been implemented throughout the nation. These programs have been at the forefront in the development of more effective correctional programs for juveniles and young adults. Shock incarceration programs have been advocated as a means to stop beginning offenders from continual criminal behavior. The structure of the boot camp or shock program is intended to shock or scare the offender into compliance. These programs focus on hard work, discipline, motivation, and structure. Many, though not all, also include intensive treatment to reduce drug use and criminal behavior (MacKenzie & Brame, 1995). These programs are expected to rehabilitate young adults in a rapid manner and maintain changes upon discharge.

Shock incarceration programs and boot camps are designed for a target population of nonviolent offenders under age 18. The programs usually run for 3 months followed by 6 to 9 months of community-based aftercare. The aftercare supervision assists youths in adjusting to the community; provides help in furthering educational, vocational, or employment training; and includes intensive supervision that gradually diminishes (Peterson, 1996).

The programs were originally developed to help reduce prison overcrowding as well as to reduce recidivism. Mixed results have been found. Overall, the alternative programs effectively reduced prison overcrowding. They also significantly reduced costs because of the shorter length of stay of offenders. Educational goals of offenders were improved, sometimes by almost two grade levels (Peterson, 1996). For those programs that did not include treatment components for offenders, recidivism rates were as high as those for juveniles released from prisons. In addition, aftercare programs that provided lower levels of supervision also had equal rates of recidivism to prisons (MacKenzie & Brame, 1995). Aftercare supervision was found to be one of the most important variables in reducing recidivism. The higher the level of intensity in supervision, the better the adjustment to the community and the less likely the offender was to repeat the offense.

The mixed results received by these programs suggests that they may be an effective alternative to prison for many young first offenders. However, substantial improvements need to be made to increase program effectiveness—namely, more intense interventions and effective aftercare follow-up.

Day Reporting Centers

Another intermediate sanction that has begun to gain some attention is day reporting centers. Day reporting centers are community-based corrections programs used to avoid imprisonment. These programs are intended to help reduce prison and jail overcrowding, provide treatment, and assist in community reintegration.

Day reporting can be defined as a highly structured nonresidential program that utilizes supervision, sanctions, and services (Diggs & Pieper, 1994). These programs confine and supervise offenders' activities while providing treatment and rehabilitation services. Offenders are also able to continue with their employment and educational goals. Offenders committed to these programs live at home and report daily, in person, to the center. They are expected to keep detailed itinerary notes on their daily travels, destinations, cohorts, and purposes. Offenders also call in several times a day. In addition, center staff call offenders to verify their whereabouts and to monitor them. Drug testing and counseling are mandatory components of the program.

Day reporting centers can be adaptable to many different populations; usually violent offenders are not included in these populations. However, the centers have been used as halfway-in and halfway-out steps. For instance, offenders who are in violation of their parole or probation may be placed in day reporting programs, or offenders who are released early from jail or prison may be placed in these programs prior to parole. The centers have also been used to monitor arrested individuals prior to trial.

Whatever the population of the programs, day reporting allows for the treatment and supervision of arrested individuals and convicted offenders in a setting that is more secure than probation or parole and less confining and expensive than incarceration (Diggs & Pieper, 1994). There is minimal outcome research to date, due to the infancy of the programs. But one program in Florida has shown an 84% success rate (Diggs & Pieper, 1994). Clearly, these community-based programs are worth considering in the attempts to reduce crime.

Drug Abuse Treatment during Community Supervision

Community supervision of offenders often involves monitoring offenders through meetings and telephone contact and assisting with employment or education. One critical component that has often been left out of this supervision has been drug abuse treatment. Research has indicated that treatment for drug-abusing offenders can be effective in reducing and eliminating drug use and in reducing recidivism (Evans, 1994; Prendergast, Anglin, & Wellisch, 1995). Yet, until recently, mandatory drug abuse counseling has not been included in community supervision. This is a very critical component for maintenance outside of jail or prison, especially considering that two thirds of offenders are currently in prison on drug-related charges.

Researchers have suggested that, to be effective, offenders' needs must be accurately assessed and matched to the correct type of drug abuse program. This program should also be considered as a mandatory part of the offenders' community supervision. In other words, consequences should be included if the offender does not attend and participate appropriately in treatment (Prendergast et al., 1995). Research has also indicated that these programs need to focus on long-term recovery with a high level of support for offenders.

Some offenders may require more intensive treatment, such as inpatient services. Several new facilities have recently been developed to address these needs. These new programs are designed to provide intensive drug abuse services to offenders who are on probation or parole (Evans, 1994). These facilities provide dormitory-style living for 9 months while offenders receive treatment. Upon discharge, intensive relapse prevention and aftercare programs are included and staff assist offenders in obtaining adequate housing and employment. These comprehensive types of programs have been shown to be effective in reducing drug use by offenders (Evans, 1994).

If we intend to utilize community supervision or intermediate sanctions as a method for reducing prison populations, costs, and recidivism, then we need to deliver comprehensive programs to offenders to meet their differing needs.

Treatment during Incarceration

Due to overcrowding and understaffing in prisons and jails, many institutions have been unable to provide treatment and services for the rehabilitation of inmates. New initiatives have been started with a focus on rehabilitating and preparing inmates for community living. These programs provide expanded services for inmates as they prepare to return to the community.

Education and Life Skills Programs

Many prisons have always provided GED classes for offenders; however, these classes are now being expanded to better meet the needs of inmates. For instance, several programs have been initiated to teach employability skills and job search skills. Information on writing resumes and obtaining and going on interviews is also included. Some inmate programs further include specific vocational training and actual part-time employment in the community (Bagley, 1996; Orosz, 1996). Computer skills are also being taught to increase inmates' employability.

Besides educational and employment components, most new programs include substance abuse treatment in individual and group formats, as well as stress and anger management. Programs that incorporate all of these interventions were found to be more successful in reducing recidivism when offenders are released. These programs were also found to increase employment and reduce substance abuse (Bagley, 1996; Orosz, 1996).

These programs have been found to be effective in improving the quality of life for participants. Consequently, they have helped renew interest in rehabilitation of inmates.

Drug Treatment

One of the few known factors about crime is that offenders are disproportionately substance abusers. The proportion of drug-using offenders among those arrested has never fallen below 60% and has reached 85% during some years (NIJ, 1996). Research studies have indicated that correctional drug treatment programs can have a substantial effect on the behavior of chronic drug-abusing offenders (NIJ, 1996).

Similar to services in the community, drug abuse treatment should match the needs of the inmate. Group versus individual treatment should also be chosen based on individual inmate needs. Studies have shown that improvements can still be made even when the inmate is mandated to treatment inside the institution. Consequently, some institutions are beginning to mandate treatment to reduce drug abuse and criminal acts after release (NIJ, 1996).

AFTERCARE

Aftercare programs are designed to assist newly released offenders with the transition back into the community. These community-based programs are similar to the already described intermediate sanctions; however, they focus on transitioning and adjusting. This can be an especially hard process when offenders have been imprisoned for many years. Most correctional systems place little emphasis on this part of correctional supervision, often believing their job is over when the inmate walks out the door. But after years of neglect, aftercare programming is starting to make a comeback.

The goals of aftercare include interventions that directly target the offender's needs. These usually include community-based treatment, continuity of care, offender assessment, and case management (Castellano, 1995). Aftercare programs build on the interventions the inmates were receiving in prison and reinforce the gains already made. These programs also tend to be lengthier than regular parole and fairly intensive. Another key component is the support services provided by ex-offenders and prison staff to the newly released offender. Group meetings as well as recreational activities are scheduled so the newly released offender does not feel alone and unsupported.

Parole supervision has come under increasing attack due to its ineffectiveness, and, consequently, services that provide better continuity of care have begun. These programs have not yet been evaluated. But it is expected that they will assist in reducing recidivism and in transitioning offenders back into the community.

CONCLUSION

The alternative and newly implemented programs described here have been developed as a result of prison overcrowding, astronomical costs to taxpayers, and the rising numbers of minorities and youth involved in crime and violence. These programs propose to make some important modifications in the correctional system as we know it. Some of the key concepts that these programs implement include prevention interventions, accurate assessment, appropriate intervention and level-of-supervision matching, rehabilitation, skill enhancement, drug abuse treatment, and community-level involvement. The empirical literature has begun to illustrate their effectiveness.

Prevention of criminal and violent behavior was touched on briefly in this chapter, yet an entire book could be devoted to the subject. Interventions that begin early, target known risk factors, and impact at the community level have shown promise. Prevention programs specifically developed for youth in disadvantaged communities have been particularly promising.

Although there has been a slight decline in adult crime, juvenile crime and violence have continued to escalate. Incarceration and get-tough policies have not controlled or reduced crime and violence. Prevention programs and alternative correctional programs may provide some opportunities to turn get-tough policies into get-treatment policies, which may be the long-lost component in reducing crime and violence.

REFERENCES

Allen-Hagen, B. (1993). *Conditions of confinement in juvenile detention and correctional facilities.* Washington, DC: Office of Juvenile Justice and Delinquency Prevention.

Bagley, C. (1996). A grassroots approach to reducing recidivism. *Corrections Today, 58*(5), 96–100.

Brewer, D., Hawkins, J., Catalano, R., & Neckerman, H. (1995). Preventing serious, violent, and chronic juvenile offending. In J. Howell, B. Krisberg, J. Hawkins, & J. Wilson (Eds.), *Serious, violent, & chronic juvenile offenders* (pp. 61–141). Thousand Oaks, CA: Sage.

Brown, J., Gilliard, D., Snell, T., Stephan, J., & Wilson, D. (1996). *Corrections populations in the United States, 1994.* Washington, DC: Bureau of Justice Statistics.

Bureau of Justice Statistics (1996). *Sourcebook of criminal justice statistics.* Washington, DC: U.S. Department of Justice.

Bushman, B., & Cooper, H. (1990). Effects of alcohol on human aggression: An integrative research review. *Psychological Bulletin, 107,* 341–354.

Carr, R. (1996). A debate over punishment and prevention. *Congressional Weekly Report, 54*(40), 2810–2814.

Carter, D. (1995, June). Community policing and D.A.R.E.: A practitioner's perspective. *BJA Bulletin,* 1–19.

Castellano, T. (1995). Aftercare. *Corrections Today, 57*(5), 1–8.

Community Policing Consortium (1994). *Understanding community policing: A framework for action.* Washington, DC: Bureau of Justice Assistance.

Diggs, D., & Pieper, S. (1994). Using day reporting centers as an alternative to jail. *Federal Probation, 58*(1), 9–12.

Donnerstein, E., Slaby, R., & Eron, L. (1994). The mass media and youth aggression. In L. Eron, J. Gentry, & P. Schlegel (Eds.), *Reason to hope: A psychosocial perspective on violence and youth.* Washington, DC: American Psychological Association.

Elliott, D., Huizinga, D., & Ageton, S. (1985). *Explaining delinquency and drug use.* Beverly Hills, CA: Sage.

Evans, D. (1994). Redefining community treatment programs can better serve offenders. *Corrections Today, 56*(3), 112–114.

Farrell, C. (1993). The economics of crime. *Business Week, 13,* 72–80.

Farrington, D. (1991). Childhood aggression and adult violence. In D. Pepler & K. Rubin (Eds.), *The development and treatment of childhood aggression* (pp. 5–29). Hillsdale, NJ: Erlbaum.

Federal Bureau of Investigation. (1995). *Crime in the United States.* Washington, DC: Author.

Fox, J. (1996). *Trends in juvenile violence.* Washington, DC: U.S. Department of Justice.

Hawkins, J., Catalano, R., & Miller, J. (1992). Risk and protective factors for alcohol and other drug problems in adolescence and early adulthood: Implications for substance abuse prevention. *Psychological Bulletin, 112,* 64–105.

Hawkins, J., Lishner, D., Jenson, J., & Catalano, R. (1987). Delinquents and drugs: What the evidence suggests about prevention and treatment programming. In B. S. Brown & A. R. Mills (Eds.), *Youth at high risk for substance abuse* (pp. 81–131). Rockville, MD: U.S. Department of Health and Human Services.

Howell, J., Krisberg, B., & Jones, M. (1995). Trends in juvenile crime and youth violence. In J. Howell, B. Krisberg, J. Hawkins, & J. Wilson (Eds.), *Serious, violent, & chronic juvenile offenders* (pp. 1–35). Thousand Oaks, CA: Sage.

Kizer, K., Vassar, M., Harry, R., & Layton, K. (1995). Hospitalization charges, costs, and income for firearm related injuries at a university trauma center. *JAMA, 273*(22), 1768–1773.

MacKenzie, D., & Brame, R. (1995). Shock incarceration and positive adjustment during community supervision. *Journal of Quantitative Criminology, 11*(2), 111–143.

McCord, C., & Freeman, H. (1990). Excess mortality in Harlem. *New England Journal of Medicine, 322,* 173–177.

National Crime Victimization Survey. (1995) *Preliminary findings.* Washington, DC: Bureau of Justice Statistics.

NIJ. (1996). *Drug and crime facts 1994* (Publication No. NCJ 154043). Washington, DC: Author.

Office of Justice Programs. (1996). *Summary assessment.* Washington, DC: Drug Resource Center, American University.

Office of Juvenile Justice and Delinquency Prevention. (1997). Juvenile arrests 1995. *Juvenile Justice Bulletin.* Washington, DC: Office of Justice Programs.

Orosz, C. (1996). LASER treatment changes criminal behavior. *Corrections Today, 58*(5), 74–78.

Pearson, D. (1994). The black man: Health issues and implications for clinical practice. *Journal of Black Studies, 25*(1), 81–98.

Perkins, C., Klaus, P., Bastian, L., & Cohen, R. (1996). *Criminal victimization in the United States, 1993, a national crime victimization survey report.* Washington, DC: U.S. Department of Justice.

Peterson, E. (1996). *Juvenile boot camps: Lessons learned.* Washington, DC: Office of Juvenile Justice and Delinquency Prevention.

Prendergast, M., Anglin, M., & Wellisch, J. (1995). Treatment for drug-abusing offenders under community supervision. *Federal Probation, 59*(4), 66–75.

Rapp, L., & Wodarski, J. (in press). Juvenile violence: Its high risk factors, current interventions and implications for social work practice. *Journal of Applied Social Sciences.*

Reiss, A., & Roth, J. (Eds.). (1993). *Understanding and preventing violence.* Washington, DC: National Academy Press.

Roscoe, M., & Morton, R. (1994). Disproportionate minority confinement. Washington, DC: Office of Juvenile Justice and Delinquency Prevention.

Snyder, H., Sickmund, M., & Poe-Yamagata, E. (1996). *Juvenile offenders and victims: 1996 update on violence.* Washington, DC: Office of Juvenile Justice and Delinquency Prevention.

Tauber, J. (1994). Drug courts: Treating drug-using offenders through sanction incentives. *Corrections Today, 56*(1), 28–35.

U.S. Department of Justice, Federal Bureau of Investigation. (1996). *Crime in the United States.* Washington, DC: FBI National Press Office.

Wiebush, R., Baird, C., Krisberg, B., & Onek, D. (1995). Risk assessment and classification for serious, violent, and chronic juvenile offenders. In J. Howell, B. Krisberg, J. Hawkins, & J. Wilson (Eds.), *Serious, violent, & chronic juvenile offenders.* Thousand Oaks, CA: Sage.

Wintemute, G., & Wright, M. (1992). Initial and subsequent hospital costs of firearm injuries. *Journal of Trauma, 33*(4), 556–660.

Yoshikawa, H. (1994). Prevention as cumulative protection: Effects of early family support and education on chronic delinquency and its risks. *Psychological Bulletin, 115,* 28–54.

Chapter 9

URBAN DECLINE AND FAMILY HOMELESSNESS

Namkee G. Choi

One of our most serious social problems, which has worsened in the past two decades, is the deterioration of housing and other living conditions in central cities and the resulting homelessness, especially among families with children. The number of the homeless is a matter of dispute between governments and advocates for the homeless (Kondratas, 1991; Mihaly, 1991). The number may not be in the millions, as estimated by homeless advocates, but most parties agree that it is at least in the hundreds of thousands, without even counting those who live doubled up with relatives or friends. Moreover, all data indicate that poor families, headed by mostly minority, young, single mothers with children, occupy an increasing share of the rank and file of the homeless (Rossi, 1994). A report by the U.S. Conference of Mayors estimated that more than one third of the homeless consisted of such families in the beginning of the 1990s (U.S. Conference of Mayors, 1990). Children are estimated to make up between one third and one half of the members of homeless families (Mihaly, 1991). Most studies of the homeless indicate that the number of homeless families and extremely poor families with children who are precariously housed and thus at risk of homelessness is also increasing.

The cost of human suffering due to homelessness is manifested in tens of thousands of poor families with children sleeping in temporary shelters or living doubled up with equally poor relatives or friends. Homeless children exhibit a host of academic, physical, and psychological problems that interfere with their proper development (Bassuk & Rosenberg, 1990; Rafferty, 1995). Insecurity, instability, and uncertainty about the next meal and bed undoubtedly cause enormous stress and anguish and overwhelm adults and children alike. Homeless and near-homeless families who move from one dangerous neighborhood to another in deteriorating central cities are also susceptible to crime and violence on the city streets.

Despite the deepening problems of urban deterioration and homelessness, however, the federal government has not been engaged in long-term, systematic solution of the problems, but has treated homelessness as a temporary problem that deserves no more than emergency relief in the form of temporary shelters and other temporary assistance. In the absence of systematic, structural government interventions to bring about urban revitalization and create enough permanent housing for the homeless and near-homeless, the number of homeless has been increasing and their plight continues.

Social workers have been diligently researching the causes and effects of homelessness and assisting the homeless not only to blunt the negative effects of homelessness on a daily basis, but to find permanent housing for them. Given the severity of the problem of homelessness and the underlying structural issues, however, social work interventions for the homeless need to be geared to effect more systemic changes to prevent homelessness among poor families. In this chapter, I first review homelessness, including its causes among families with children, its effects, and the status of policies and programs that have been designed to deal with it. I then recommend increased social work advocacy for affordable low-income housing and supportive services for poor families who are homeless or at risk of becoming so.

THE CAUSES OF HOMELESSNESS

Prior to the mid-1970s, a majority of the homeless were single, older males with substance (mostly alcohol) abuse and physical or mental health problems who lived in urban, skid-row neighborhoods and were rarely seen by the general public (Rossi, 1994). Most of those homeless men were not literally shelterless but lived in single-room-occupancy hotels or found beds in cheap accommodations (Rossi, 1994). Since the mid-1970s, however, homeless persons, both men and women, who were literally shelterless, became more numerous and visible on our city streets. Moreover, in the 1980s and into the 1990s, increasing numbers of poor families with children became homeless, and temporary homeless shelters serving both single adults and families have proliferated.

The current population of homeless, single adults, like their earlier counterparts, has much higher rates of mental illness, substance abuse, and jail or prison history than the domiciled population (McChesney, 1995). These disabilities may have been primary, and at least precipitating, factors causing these individuals' homelessness, as was the case of their counterparts in the 1950s and 1960s. Compared to their domiciled counterparts, the mostly single, minority-group women who head homeless families also have higher incidences of psychiatric hospitalizations prior to having become homeless, but the rates are in the single digits. Homeless mothers are also more likely than domiciled poor mothers to have abused drugs. Thus, mothers' drug abuse may have made poor families more vulnerable to homelessness (Baum & Burnes, 1993; Jencks, 1994; Weitzman, Knickman, & Shinn, 1992). But most studies show that family homelessness in the 1980s and the 1990s is primarily attributable to the increased number of poor people, especially poor, single-female-headed families and to the lack of affordable low-income housing units rather than to individual or behavioral deficits (DeAngelis, 1994; Johnson & Kreuger, 1989; Leonard, Dolbeare, & Lazere, 1989; McChesney, 1990; Rossi, 1989; Shinn & Gillespie, 1994; Timmer, Eitzen, & Talley, 1994). These two factors—the increase in the number of poor people, especially poor, minority, single-female-headed families, and the declining stock of affordable low-income housing units—are intertwined with the declining economic base and the deepening of racial segregation in many cities. Unless these structural barriers to improved living and housing conditions are dealt with, the plight of the homeless may not be alleviated. In sum, in terms of numbers, sociodemographic characteristics, and reasons for homelessness, today's homeless population is quite different from that of the 1950s and 1960s.

Poverty, Lack of Affordable Low-Income Housing, and Rent Burdens

Between 1975 and 1993, the poverty rate increased from 12.3%, or 25.9 million persons, to 15.1%, or 39.3 million persons. And the highest poverty rate was found among Black and Hispanic single-female householders with children younger than age 18: 57.7% of the Black families and 60.5% of the Hispanic families were poor in 1993. Among White, single-female-headed families, 39.6% were poor. (The number of poor, single-female-headed households with children increased across race and ethnicity lines between 1975 and 1993. A 188% increase, from less than 1 million in 1975 to 1.8 million in 1993, was recorded for Blacks; a 175% increase, from 1.3 million in 1975 to 2.1 million in 1993, was recorded for Whites; and a 245% increase, from 288,000 in 1979 to 706,000 in 1993, was recorded for Hispanics.) Of the 39.3 million poor persons in 1993, children living with female householders accounted for 9.1 million, as compared to 5.6 million in 1975 (U.S. Bureau of the Census, 1995).

The problem is not only the increased number of poor, single mothers with children but also the erosion of incomes and worsening poverty among this group over the years. For example, the average incomes of the poorest 20% of single mothers with children were at 33% of the poverty level in 1973 and 1979, but they were at 26% and 25% in 1983 and 1989, respectively. The average poor, female-headed family with children was surviving at only about half the poverty level in 1991 (Shinn & Gillespie, 1994). These millions of poor, female-headed families with children, together with increasing numbers of other poor families and individuals, are evidence that even the benefits of the robust economy in the mid- to late-1980s did not trickle down to those in the bottom economic strata.

To poor people, decent and affordable housing is an elusive goal that they cannot afford to achieve. Poor homeowners are likely to have a hard time paying their mortgages. But, through economic booms and busts, poor renters are likely to have an even tougher time trying to bear increasing rent burdens. That is, despite stagnant income among renter households, gross rents increased continuously for the past two decades. According to the State of the Nation's Housing report by the Joint Center for Housing Studies of Harvard University (1995), the median income of renter households, from 1970 to 1994, fell by 16% to $15,814 annually, while gross rents increased more than 11% to $403 monthly. Moreover, the largest rent increases were for units at the low end of the market. As a result, in 1990 some 43% (5.4 million) of all low-income renters (with incomes of $10,000 or less) paid more than half of their income for rent.

Much of the rent hike is due to the fact that housing programs have been cut back since the 1980s, squeezing subsidized and low-cost (monthly rent of $300 or less) unsubsidized housing units, despite increasing numbers of poor renters. For example, net new federal commitments to provide assisted (or subsidized) housing averaged less than 100,000 units in the period from 1988 to 1993, down from 300,000 to 400,000 units in the late 1970s (Joint Center for Housing Studies, 1995). In most major cities, the waiting lists for Section 8 housing subsidy and public housing units stretch for years. The number of low-cost unsubsidized rental units has also declined below 1974 levels, which is inevitable given that, between 1973 and 1983 alone, the country permanently lost some 4.5 million affordable rental units through demolition or structural conversion to higher-priced housing (U.S. House of Representatives, 1990).

The mismatch between the decreasing supply of affordable low-income rental housing units and the increasing demand for these units, attributable to the increasing numbers of poor households and the erosion of real incomes among such households, has been proven in many studies to be the primary cause of homelessness in many cities (McChesney, 1990; Ringheim, 1993; Shinn & Gillespie, 1994). In Ringheim's study (1993) of Houston between 1976 and 1983, rent increased far in excess of inflation, while renter incomes stagnated, a pattern that explained increasing vulnerability to homelessness among extremely poor minority-group (especially Black) households with children, even amid massive vacancies in rental housing units. An analysis of 482 New York City families who were newly homeless showed that nearly half of them (43%) had been primary tenants in their own living quarters in the year prior to the shelter request and that 47% of the primary tenants had left their residences due to eviction or rent problems (Weitzman, Knickman, & Shinn, 1990).

Because of the tight low-income rental market, the failure rates of rental-assistance vouchers or certificates (the number of households failing to find affordable housing even with a voucher or certificate) reached 50% to 60% in big cities (U.S. House of Representatives, 1990). In spite of some preventive measures in the 1990 Cranston-Gonzalez National Affordable Housing Act (PL 101-625), tens of thousands of subsidized rental housing stocks will be lost as the federal contract with private developers runs out in coming years. Thus, in the absence of major public policy changes regarding low-income housing, the housing affordability crisis and the gross human suffering we have seen in the plight of the homeless will continue to affect tens of thousands of poor families with children.

Poor, single mothers who lack education and job skills often depend on public assistance as a major income source. But the real dollar value of Aid to Families with Dependent Children (AFDC) has declined almost by half since the mid-1970s. The increasing rent burden borne by these poor, single mothers on welfare indicates that affordability problems are disproportionately visited upon them and that these problems may be especially severe in situations where they have compounding physical or mental health problems or both to deal with. A comparison between homeless families and a representative sample of low-income family households in St. Louis city and county found that homeless families are significantly younger, never married, female-headed families of color. Housed and homeless families are not significantly different in number of children or in the educational level of the household head, but housed families are larger and have higher incomes, suggesting the presence of another adult earner (Johnson, McChesney, Rocha, & Butterfield, 1995). The extremely poor households headed by young, single females dependent on insufficient welfare benefits and the vagaries of the welfare bureaucracy or on low-paying, unstable jobs as their primary or sole source of income can be easily thrown into homelessness out of already precarious housing situations. As one single, homeless mother put it: "I am in a job and I spend $15 too much and my apartment is gone" (Choi & Doueck, 1996).

Urban Decline and Spatial Isolation of Poor Blacks

Increasing numbers of young, Black, single-female-headed households along with the concentration of poverty and the crisis of housing affordability among Black families are the logical consequences of the social and economic marginalization of central cities and the spatial segregation of poor Blacks in dilapidated inner-city neighborhoods where the tax base, quality of the public schools, and availability of social services are all declining. As Wilson (1987) has so powerfully illustrated, the deindustrialization that took away well-paying manufacturing and other low-skilled jobs from cities, combined with the outmigration of middle-class Blacks and Whites to the suburbs, has left poor Blacks concentrated in central cities with few jobs and services. Over the past few decades, the demand for poorly educated labor has declined markedly and the demand for labor with a higher level of education (e.g., high-tech information-processing white-collar jobs) has increased substantially. Because of their poor education, poor Blacks in central cities have not been able to gain access to these well-paying jobs (Kasarda, 1989; Wilson, 1987). Even minimum-wage jobs that do not require much education have not been easily accessible to poor, urban Blacks, who seldom have private means of transportation, because most, if not all, of these jobs have moved to suburbs.

Wilson showed that increased joblessness among young Black males over the past decades was positively correlated with the increased numbers of single-female-headed families, because the high rate of joblessness means that the availability of potential marriage partners who can afford raising a family has declined. At the same time that the number of employment opportunities available to males with lower skill levels was declining, the ages of sexual maturity and the initiation of sexual activity dropped considerably over the past few decades, thus exposing more young women to the risk of early pregnancy (Rossi, 1994). Also, poor educational preparation and long-term poverty often breed attitudes of fatalism, powerlessness, and hopelessness among these young men and women. On top of these attitudes, the reality of their dim prospects for the future is not a good incentive for young men and women to postpone sexual activities and childbearing (Joint Economic Committee, 1992).

Massey, Gross, and Shibuya (1994) confirmed that industrial changes and outmigration of the nonpoor to suburbs were indeed responsible for the residential segregation of poor Blacks in central cities in the early 1970s. But Massey et al. also showed that, in later years, racial discrimination in housing markets was a more powerful force that isolated Blacks economically and socially and contributed to the concentration of poverty in Black neighborhoods. That is, because of racial discrimination, both nonpoor and poor Blacks moving out of a poor Black neighborhood had a much higher probability of moving into another poor Black neighborhood than into a nonpoor neighborhood, Black or White. Poor Blacks, especially, tend to gravitate from one poor Black neighborhood to another, without much possibility of leaving these economically depressed and dilapidated areas. So the vicious cycle of joblessness, single parenthood, poverty, and welfare dependency continues. In the absence of any spatial and economic policies that would systematically reduce the social and economic deprivation of poor, urban Blacks, their plight has been worsening.

Concentration of poverty also implies a simultaneous concentration of crime, violence, family disruption, and educational failure (Massey, 1994; Massey et al., 1994). The disappearance of businesses—as sources of legitimate economic activities—has stimulated the influx of drugs and criminal activities (see Wacquant & Wilson, 1989). As these extremely harsh and disadvantaged neighborhood conditions are not conducive to maintaining even a minimal level of housing quality, they put much of the rental stock now occupied by low-income households at risk of loss. Although poor renters may pay a high share of their income for rent, their payments are generally insufficient to properly maintain old units (Joint Center for Housing Studies, 1995). Because of this problem as well as the falling property values that accompany escalating violence and worsening economic situations in the neighborhood, owners of rental units in poor neighborhoods often disinvest in the properties and foreclose or abandon units (Timmer et al., 1994). It is an irony that boarded-up houses and abandoned buildings have become increasingly common fixtures of central city landscapes at a time when increasing numbers of poor families are looking for shelter.

Because investment in the upkeep of rental units is often inadequate, poor families in central cities often live in substandard units. One study shows that substandard housing and landlords' refusal to fix the problems was cited as the primary reason for homelessness by as many as one fifth of the sample homeless families (Choi & Doueck, 1996). Apparently, the physical dilapidation of some units reached a point that threatened the daily survival of these families. Children were bitten by bugs and became sick in unheated apartment buildings. Moreover, the drug-related violence and crime that ravage poor, inner-city neighborhoods often drive families with children out to homelessness. In Choi and Doueck's study, 10% of the sample families attributed their homelessness directly to such life-threatening violence and crime in their neighborhoods, but most of the families who lived in cities also mentioned it as a contributing factor. Interviews with 100 homeless women with children staying in shelters in Richmond, Virginia, also identified excessive use of drugs and vandalism in the neighborhood as a reason for homelessness (Khanna, Singh, Nemil, Best, & Ellis, 1992). Because of the crushing effects of poverty, rent burdens, physical inadequacy of housing, and dangerous neighborhoods, many families in central cities are at risk of becoming homeless even if they are not currently so.

Unlike unattached, homeless adults, homeless families seldom spend nights on the streets. Upon becoming homeless, many families double up with relatives or friends until they have overstayed their welcome, and then they go to family shelters. There most of them are assisted in finding housing. But lack of a private vehicle, limited welfare grants and earnings, and racial discrimination in housing markets usually send these families back to the same depressed, poor Black neighborhoods from which they came and in which they are likely to go through a revolving door of homelessness (see Choi & Doueck, 1996).

Mental Illness, Drug Abuse, and Domestic Violence

As mentioned, homeless mothers are more likely to have had a history of hospitalization for mental illness than are poor, housed mothers, but the rate is far lower than for those homeless individuals, both men and women, unaccompanied by children. A study of 677 New York City mothers who requested shelter and 495 poor, housed mothers showed that only 4% of the former as compared to 0.8% of the latter had ever experienced mental hospitalization (Weitzman et al., 1992). Studies based on probability or nonprobability samples of homeless, sheltered mothers in different locations (Bassuk & Rosenberg, 1988; Burt & Cohen, 1989) may show rates of psychiatric hospitalizations or prevalence of mental illness a little higher than found by Weitzman et al.'s study.

If there were enough affordable housing, mental illness of a mother or father alone would not force families onto streets or into shelters. Few studies of homeless families attribute homelessness directly to the mother's preexisting mental disorder. It appears that mothers with severe mental illness lose custody of their children because of their inability to take care of them before they become homeless. Mothers accompanied by children are thus not likely to become homeless solely or primarily because of mental disorder. But because of the shortage of affordable low-income housing and the resulting competition among the poor for it, mentally ill people are more likely to lose out in the competition and be vulnerable to homelessness than are poor people who do not have such a disability.

A very serious problem with the mental health of homeless mothers and children is that their homeless experiences are likely to not only exacerbate existing disorders but also cause all sorts of emotional distresses, notably depression and anxiety, which may interfere with normal daily functioning. Without adequate supportive services, many homeless families may thus have a tougher time coping with homelessness as well as impaired mental and emotional status.

With respect to substance abuse, most studies with comparison groups reported drug abuse two to eight times higher among homeless than among housed mothers, with the prevalence rates among homeless mothers fluctuating between 8% and 50% (see McChesney, 1995). The wide range may be due to the fact that most studies of homeless families are based on those staying in temporary shelters, some of which do not admit mothers with substance abuse problems. Unlike psychiatric disorders, drug abuse may have led some families to homelessness, because the habit eats up money that would otherwise be available for paying rent. Even when a substance abuse problem was caused by the family's friends or relatives who shared housing with the family, the family's risk of homelessness was elevated (Weitzman et al., 1992). In Choi and Doueck's study (1996), equal proportions of homeless mothers reported their own substance abuse and that of roommates, husbands or partners, or other relatives as the primary reason for homelessness.

Many poor mothers who have lived most of their lives in poor, inner-city neighborhoods are easy prey to the rampant crack epidemics in them. Even those who resisted were at high risk for being in a relationship with a substance abuser. In a study of 80 homeless mothers in Massachusetts shelters, more than 40% of the women reported that their most recent boyfriend or spouse was a substance abuser (Bassuk, 1992). When the man's alcohol or drug abuse problem spirals out of control, the woman usually leaves the relationship to avoid the physical abuse that usually accompanies a substance abuse problem. These women may double up with friends or relatives for a while, eventually ending up in homeless shelters. But homeless mothers often lack the social support that others can rely upon in times of hardship: Either their parents are dead, their parents and siblings do not live in the same geographic area, or they are estranged from their parents and siblings (Bassuk, 1990). Even parents or siblings who are willing to help are often in no position to do so, due to their own poverty and overcrowding (Choi & Doueck, 1996; Rossi, 1994).

Most studies report that homeless mothers are significantly more likely to have been abused as both child and adult than housed poor mothers (see McChesney, 1995), although one study found no such difference (Goodman, 1991). As to the role of domestic violence in precipitating homelessness among poor women, there are also different assessments. Bassuk's (1992) and Weitzman et al.'s (1992) studies report that despite high incidence of past victimization among homeless mothers, domestic violence only infrequently precipitated the current episode of homelessness. On the other hand, other studies (Hagen, 1987; Zorza, 1991) reported that domestic violence is a leading cause of homelessness among women with children. These different assessments may be due to the fact that some studies included but others excluded battered-women's shelters. Studies that did not include battered-women's shelters may have resulted in an undercount of battered women who became homeless (Steinbock, 1995).

Minority women and women living in poverty are at especially high risk of victimization by violence because they experience much higher rates of frequent, uncontrollable, and threatening life events than the general population (Browne, 1993). Urban decline, joblessness, poverty, drug and alcohol problems, and frequent family disruptions inevitably expose residents of most, if not all, ghettos to violence by strangers as well as by family members and friends. For poor, minority mothers who lack economic independence and are virtually imprisoned by their environment, "opportunities for improvement of living conditions or escape from threatening situations may be severely limited, and the level of protective resources is typically low" (Browne, 1993, p. 371). Thus, although domestic violence may be a direct cause of homelessness for many families, the relationship between domestic violence, poverty, and urban decline must not be forgotten.

THE EFFECTS OF HOMELESSNESS

The Effects of Homelessness on Families

Food, shelter, and clothing are basic human rights and necessities for a bare minimum standard of living. Deprivation of one or more of these basic necessities disrupts normal physical and emotional functioning. For a family, the loss of a shelter can cause especially serious problems, because it more often than not entails hunger and a lack of clothing at the same time. Loss of a home means a loss of most of the family's other belongings. The feeling of uprootedness, grief for a lost home, and the lack of the sense of security provided by having one's own home may also engender depression and anxiety even among the most resilient, impairing their ability to function normally. Once they become homeless, families face enormous difficulties in conducting their daily lives as usual. In fact, it is downright impossible to have an orderly life at a welfare hotel without cooking facilities but with illicit drug traffic or at a temporary shelter where families are required to take their meager belongings and leave during the day (because shelter staff are volunteers who have daytime jobs). Lack of privacy and rules that need to be followed in congregate living environments can be nerve-racking for both parents and children. The physical experience of a whole family's being compacted in a small space can be stifling and literally create breathing problems among both adults and children (Kozol, 1988).

Homelessness often causes family disruption, with separation between husband and wife as well as between parents and children. Some shelters may not admit all the family members because of a lack of space. Other family shelters bar men (sometimes including preteen or teenage boys) from staying with their female relatives and children, sending them to different shelters for homeless men or placing the adolescents in foster care. Studies also show that an increasing number of children are separated from their parents and placed in foster care solely or primarily because their families are homeless or living in inadequate or unsafe housing. Parents' lack of adequate housing was a major reason for placement of Black children in 30% of the foster care cases (U.S. House of Representatives, 1990).

Even if parents and children manage to stay together, the disruptive and traumatizing experience of homelessness impairs parental functioning. Most mothers are overwhelmed and depressed about being homeless and often have little energy left to mother their children consistently (Bassuk & Gallagher, 1990). When families are forced to cope with a myriad of crises on a daily basis, parents' capacity to provide protection and support and to respond to their children's needs may be eroded (Hausman & Hammen, 1993). When a family is placed in a temporary shelter and must share space with other families, the previously private interaction between the mother and her child(ren) is affected by its public and often scrutinized nature and is externally controlled by others, creating a sense of powerlessness in the mother: "The traditional role of mother as provider, family leader, organizer and standard setter was experienced by mothers as having vanished" (Boxill & Beaty, 1990, p. 60). Someone else decides when, what, and where the family will eat, wash up, and rest.

The lives of homeless families exiled in drug-infested welfare hotels or in temporary shelters of large cities, and the physical and mental price they pay for being homeless, have not been described as extensively as have either the circumstances that led to their homelessness or their sociodemographic characteristics. Only a few books (Kozol, 1988; Timmer et al., 1994) describe, through extensive contacts, how homeless families suffer from and cope with homelessness. Several other studies based on in-depth qualitative interviews with or participant observations of homeless mothers and children provide occasional windows through which a snapshot of their lives can be glimpsed (Bassuk & Gallagher, 1990; Berck, 1992; Boxill & Beaty, 1990; Choi & Doueck, 1996; McChesney, 1992). Most other studies of the effects of homelessness focus on children and are based on quantitative analyses of data on academic performance and physical and psychological health.

The Effects of Homelessness on Children

Even before they become homeless, children often have a variety of developmental and health problems that are mostly ascribable to extreme poverty. The poverty-stricken and violence-laden neighborhoods in which they live are not conducive to their healthy and normal development. Poor, single mothers have only limited resources to provide for their children and limited access to preventive—including prenatal—and curative health care. But loss of a home, the discontinuity of place of residence, and all other hardships that accompany homelessness can traumatize these poor children, exacerbating existing problems and creating a whole new set of them. Congregate and unsanitary living conditions in shelters put children at higher risk for rapid spread of infectious and communicable diseases. Once children become sick, the crowded living conditions in the shelters and welfare hotels do not provide an adequate curative environment, to say nothing of the lack of access to health care services. Health problems caused by dietary insufficiency, such as malnutrition, anemia, and overweight, are also more common among homeless children than among children in the general population (see Burg, 1994).

Studies have consistently found that homeless children are more often ill than their domiciled counterparts and that they suffer from both acute and chronic illnesses, especially upper respiratory disorders (including asthma), minor skin diseases, ear disorders, gastrointestinal problems, trauma, eye disorders, and infestations of lice (McNamee, Bartek, & Lynes, 1994; Wright, 1990, 1991). Compared to poor, housed children, homeless children also have higher rates of other poverty-related problems, including delayed immunizations, elevated lead levels, and iron deficiencies, which may be related to other unmeasured nutritional deficiencies (Bernstein, Alperstein, & Fierman, 1988, quoted in Rafferty & Shinn, 1991). Feeding children nutritionally balanced meals is a difficult task when the family lives in a welfare hotel without any cooking facility or in a temporary shelter that does not have a large operational budget.

Studies also report that a majority of homeless, preschool children exhibit developmental delays. The behaviors most frequently mentioned include short attention span, withdrawal, aggression, speech delays, sleep disorders, regressive behaviors, and immature motor behavior (Rafferty & Shinn, 1991). A study of homeless children in Massachusetts shelters reported that 47% of the preschoolers had at least one developmental delay and that their average score on the Simmons Behavior Checklist was significantly higher than the average scores for normal and emotionally disturbed children (Bassuk & Rubin, 1987).

Studies comparing homeless, preschool children with their poor, housed peers also indicate that homeless children have more cognitive and emotional problems. One study of children in Boston shelters showed that 54% of the homeless preschoolers, as opposed to 16% of their poor, housed peers, manifested at least one major developmental lag, measured by the Denver Developmental Screening Test, although the two groups were similar in scores on the Simmons Behavior Checklist (Bassuk & Rosenberg, 1990). Another comparison between preschool children residing in city shelters and their poor, housed peers showed that the homeless children exhibited slower development and more emotional-behavioral problems (Rescorla, Parker, & Stolley, 1991). DiBiase and Waddell's (1995) study of preschoolers participating in Head Start programs also found that homeless children showed significantly more problem behaviors, including symptoms of depression, social withdrawal, and schizoid behavior than did housed children. Moreover, homeless children generally perceived themselves as less cognitively, socially, and physically competent and as being less well accepted by their mothers than did housed children. Teachers also rated homeless children less cognitively competent than housed children, but rated the two groups similarly on peer relations and physical competence (DiBiase & Waddell, 1995).

Studies comparing school-age, homeless children and their poor, housed peers show mixed results. Ziesemer, Marcoux, and Marwell's (1994) study reported that previously homeless children were similar to low-income, mobile children in academic performance, adaptive functioning, and problem behaviors, although both groups had substantially more problems than the norm. Academically, almost two thirds of both groups were below the grade level. Rescorla et al. (1991) reported that homeless, school-age children scored significantly lower than their poor, housed peers in vocabulary, but that the two groups did not differ significantly in their block design and reading scores, although the latter scored somewhat higher. The homeless children were not significantly different from the poor, housed children in behavior problems. Zima, Wells, and Freeman's (1994) study of 169 homeless, school-age children in Los Angeles and Whitman, Accardo, Boyert, and Kendagor's (1990) study of homeless children in a St. Louis shelter also found that their language and reading skills were severely delayed.

The dislocation of children from their communities and their subsequent bouncing between shelters often require them to transfer into new schools (Rafferty, 1995). Children also skip school for lack of transportation to a new school, lack of proper school clothing (especially in areas with harsh winters), lack of immunization records, and bureaucratic problems that delay the transfer of school records or even lose them entirely (Dupper & Halter, 1994; Rafferty, 1995). Despite the 1990 federal mandate to remove the residency requirement in the best interest of homeless children, some states continue to impose the requirement in a manner that bars homeless children from attending their schools of origin or new schools in areas where the children are currently living (Rafferty, 1995). On top of the emotional trauma of being homeless and multiple developmental and health problems that predate their homelessness, these children are too often put at a serious academic disadvantage by having their education interrupted by such obstacles. Thus, it is not unexpected that a majority of school-age homeless, previously homeless, and poor mobile children must repeat grades or are failing or producing below-average work.

Considering the fact that homeless children have gone through negative life changes including the major loss of a home and separation from loved ones, friends, and familiar environment, it is not surprising that the majority of them suffer from severe anxiety and depression, as measured by the Children's Manifest

Anxiety Scale and the Children's Depression Inventory (Bassuk & Rosenberg, 1990; Bassuk & Rubin, 1987; Wagner & Menke, 1991; Zima et al., 1994). In Bassuk and Rubin's (1987) study, a majority of school-age, homeless children said that they think about killing themselves, but they would not. The acute stress associated with being homeless also contributes to depression among children. Nevertheless, only a minority of children had ever received psychiatric evaluation, to say nothing of treatment, because of their parents' lack of awareness of the children's problems and their lack of access to community mental health clinics (Zima et al., 1994).

Given these multiple barriers to proper cognitive and emotional development, homeless children face a severely compromised future. Lack of protective environment and the resulting sense of insecurity and loss of feelings of self-control and self-efficacy can lead to states of passivity and learned helplessness, especially as the chaos and environmental insults persist over time (Donahue & Tuber, 1995). Most homeless children are not able to stave off the trauma of living in overcrowded emergency shelters or violence-ridden welfare hotels, and "visions of academic achievement or career aspirations tend to get overshadowed by the harsh realities they face daily" (Donahue & Tuber, 1995, p. 251). Thus, the primary victims of homelessness are innocent children, who are crushed, physically and emotionally, by the weight of the trauma of homelessness and are unable to transcend the negative environment.

POLICIES AND PROGRAMS FOR HOMELESS FAMILIES WITH CHILDREN

Policy Responses

In 1987, triggered by widespread homelessness, the Stewart B. McKinney Homeless Assistance Act (PL 100-77) was passed with broad bipartisan support. Unfortunately, it has not addressed the fundamental problems of the low-income housing market. Instead of encouraging construction and rehabilitation of low-income housing units, opening them to homeless and other low-income people, the McKinney Act provides funds for emergency shelters, transitional housing, and temporary services for the homeless. This law is a notable example of federal policies and programs that continue to treat homelessness and the problems it brings as emergencies. The McKinney Act was expressly designed to be only a first, emergency response to homelessness and to meet the "critically urgent" needs of the nation's homeless (U.S. House of Representatives, 1993). These emergency-relief efforts no doubt alleviate suffering of the homeless, but they also tend to be "ad hoc, stopgap policies dealing, for the most part, only with manifestations of the problems" and to divert resources from long-term and fundamental solutions (Lipsky & Smith, 1989, p. 6).

The federal homeless-assistance policies are also fraught with the inflexibility of the government's regulations governing the Emergency Assistance (EA) portion of the AFDC program. That is, funds from the EA program are restricted to housing families only in temporary shelters for a limited period. It is an irony that a family evicted for nonpayment of rent will be housed in a shelter for over $3,000 a month, when the same amount could keep them in their apartment for more than a year (Dugger, 1993; Messinger, 1993).

The 1990 Cranston-Gonzalez National Affordable Housing Act revised the McKinney Act to make it more responsive to state and local situations. The core of the 1990 Act is the Housing Opportunity Partnerships (HOP) program, which mandates states and localities to build a long-term investment partnership with the private sector and to develop a strategy to expand the supply of affordable housing with preference to rehabilitation of substandard stock. Another aspect of the act, HOPE initiatives, would help low-income families buy public housing and other foreclosed property owned by HUD, provide supportive services to voucher recipients, provide rental assistance and supportive services for homeless persons with disabilities, and so on (U.S. Senate, 1990). Despite its good intention and plan, however, the level of appropriation under the act has been far short of what is needed to increase low-income housing stocks, to prevent homelessness, and to help homeless families obtain permanent housing. Lack of federal dollars and initiatives also translates into lack of state-sponsored programs aimed at prevention of homelessness. The curtailment of various social service budgets and the resulting budget shortfalls, as well as a general lack of political will, explain the lack of state programs for prevention of homelessness (Johnson & Hambrick, 1993).

Under President Bill Clinton, the Interagency Council on the Homeless, which had been created by Title II of the McKinney Act, was charged with developing federal strategies to break the cycle of homelessness. The council proposed a continuum-of-care approach, which was borrowed from the mental health field: Under this approach, a local board, with financial support from the U.S. Department of Housing and Urban Development (HUD), was supposed to provide a set of services ranging from shelters and mental health and substance abuse services to permanent housing and strategies to prevent homelessness (Johnson & Cnaan, 1995; U.S. Department of Housing and Urban Development [HUD], 1994). But in 1994 the council was defunded and made part of the White House Domestic Council, and, starting with fiscal year 1995, the programs were funded from HUD's operations budget (Hombs, 1994). To date, however, the local board has not materialized, but the council is responsible for providing a federal forum and coordinating 18 federal agencies to combat homelessness.

Another important federal funding source for homeless assistance is the Federal Emergency Management Agency (FEMA). FEMA's Emergency Food and Shelter (EFS) Program funds the purchase of food, consumable supplies essential to the operation of shelters and mass-feeding facilities, per diem sheltering cost, small equipment, the limited leasing of capital equipment, utility and rent or mortgage assistance to people on the verge of becoming homeless, first month's rent to help families and individuals move out of shelters or other precarious circumstances and into a stable environment, emergency lodging, and minor rehabilitation of shelter facilities (Hombs, 1994). As illustrated by its title, EFS is specifically designed for emergency needs for food and shelter.

Despite the direct relationship between housing and the changing structure of the urban economy, however, there has been a complete absence of concerted efforts to revitalize central cities in the 1980s and 1990s. The past two decades can indeed be characterized by "bipartisan federal disengagement from the cities," and urban policy under the Reagan and Bush administrations relied heavily upon economic development shaped by private investment decisions and a tax reform package that required state and local governments to raise more of their own revenues to deal with problems in cities (Ames et al., 1992, pp. 208–209). The status of our central cities has continued to decline under the Clinton administration with its sole program aimed at helping American cities, "empowerment zones," but an empty slogan (Fainstein & Fainstein, 1995).

Shelters, Transitional Housing, and Welfare Hotels

The most notable program that has sprung out in response to the increasing numbers of homeless families since the mid-1980s was the opening of an extensive number of family shelters. An up-to-date and accurate count of family shelters in the country does not exist, with the most recent information dating back to 1988, the year that HUD conducted a nationwide probability survey of shelters. The survey estimated a few more than 5,000 (an increase from 1,900 in 1984) shelters, 39% of which were family shelters serving 20,000 to 30,000 family groups nightly. All family shelters are nonprofit, supported by a combination of public—from FEMA, Community Development Block Grant (CDBG), and other federal, state, and local sources—and private funds. More than 85% of the family shelters provide some form of counseling, and an even higher proportion offer housing and other entitlement services through referrals to other agencies (Rossi, 1994; Weinreb & Rossi, 1995).

In addition to family shelters (which are usually temporary in terms of duration of the families' stay), transitional housing facilities (which provide longer-term housing along with services that prepare the families to enter the conventional housing market) have also become available. The transitional housing is the result of the view that many homeless families need training in skills of budgeting and parenting as well as rehabilitation from substance abuse if they are to avoid further episodes of homelessness (Rossi, 1994).

In large cities, so-called welfare hotels are also contracted out by local social service departments to house homeless families for short or long periods. Since there are virtually no supportive services in these hotels except the families' occasional contact with social services departments or agencies regarding permanent housing or other needs, they have the atmosphere of warehouses for the homeless.

Shelters help homeless families by providing a roof over the heads of thousands who might otherwise be sleeping on the streets. As mentioned, however, shelters are not fundamental or long-term solutions to homelessness, because they do not add permanent housing units or improve conditions in our cities, and they may in fact divert money from housing construction and rehabilitation and from other social services and financial assistance for the poor (Ferlauto, 1991). Moreover, shelter-based programs create unintended yet severe problems: Helping sheltered families tends to give them benefits that similarly situated poor families who do not enter or are denied a homeless shelter do not get (Berlin & McAllister, 1994). In a tight housing market, the housing service that sheltered families receive gives them a competitive edge over other poor families not served by a shelter. The flourishing of shelters also hides these poor families from the public by warehousing them and may help foster the perception that individual deficits rather than structural factors are responsible for their homelessness. Last but not least, congregating in one place families that have severe economic and other related problems creates an environment that is detrimental to the proper development of children. As discussed earlier, homeless children suffered before they became homeless and these helpless children deserve a better life than being warehoused in unsanitary, noisy, and unstable shelter environments.

SOCIAL WORK INTERVENTIONS

Previous research on homelessness, especially in mental health disciplines, has focused on personal deficits and pathologies, resulting in the medicalization of this devastating social problem and contributing to the depoliticizing of the problem (Snow, Anderson, & Koegel, 1994). Recently, however, with the increasing involvement of social workers and other social scientists with homeless families, their economic predicament has been highlighted and the need for macro intervention has been emphasized: As illustrated earlier, the primary cause of family homelessness is poverty and the lack of affordable housing units, not personal pathology of family members. Some families, of course, have mental and behavioral problems that precipitate their homelessness. Thus, supportive services are needed for the homeless, but homelessness cannot be prevented or eliminated without enough housing for the poor. Homeless families need permanent housing, and they should be able to afford it. Provision of permanent housing and the families' ability to afford such housing is also directly related to the revitalization of central cities and improved economic opportunities for poor minority groups in this society.

Although social workers are aware of these structural causes of homelessness, their involvement in dealing with day-to-day grievances and the devastating effects of homelessness on families often leave no time for dealing with structural issues. But social work practitioners and scholars need to go beyond emergency-based interventions with homeless families to advocacy and lobbying that would effect structural changes. In this section, I recommend social work interventions in the following areas to deal with structural problems as well as the enormous negative physical health, mental health, and educational effects of homelessness on families and children.

Expansion of Low-Income Housing Subsidies

A follow-up study of formerly homeless families in St. Louis showed that families who received a Section 8 placement were much less likely to become homeless again than those who did not (Stretch & Kreuger, 1992). Long waiting lists for Section 8 vouchers or certificates in most cities must be dealt with to prevent homelessness and to place homeless families in permanent housing as soon as possible. Rental- or mortgage-assistance programs for those who face a temporary financial crisis have also proven effective in preventing homelessness in Virginia (Johnson & Hambrick, 1993). In locations where the failure rate of Section 8 vouchers or certificates is high, a rental-assistance program similar to that in Virginia can be adopted.

Increased Funding for the CDBG and Restoration of Funding for Section 8 Substantial Rehabilitation and New Construction Programs

The federal government must restore its financial sponsoring of physical redevelopment and rehabilitation, designating funds to flow to areas most adversely affected by urban decline. Private and public partnership in building subsidized housing must be vigorously pursued.

Improved Programs to Preserve Existing Low-Income Housing

Municipal governments must adopt and enforce better property maintenance codes and take over abandoned property before disrepair becomes blight. State and city housing rehabilitation programs must also be targeted toward upkeep of existing low- or moderate-income rental properties with appropriate restrictions to prevent market upgrading (Schwartz, Bartelt, Ferlauto, Hoffman, & Listokin, 1992).

The Stuart B. McKinney Homeless Assistance Act for Permanent Housing

The focus of the McKinney Act on emergency shelters, transitional housing, and temporary services for the homeless must be replaced with that on short- and long-term rental subsidy for permanent housing, rehabilitation of abandoned buildings and houses, and enforcement of building codes in rental units in poor neighborhoods. That is, the funding under the act must be used to prevent homelessness rather than to supply emergency housing and services for the homeless. With the new preventive focus, the funding could then be used to assist those at risk of becoming homeless, reducing the pain and suffering of many poor families and saving taxpayers' money.

Grassroots Organizations for Permanent Housing

Grassroots organizations modeled after Habitat for Humanity must be used to increase homeownership among poor tenants by mobilizing them to rehabilitate abandoned or foreclosed units and by providing them with technical and legal assistance for property acquisition. The McKinney Act and HUD must subsidize such rehabilitation and homesteading programs.

More Efficient Management of Public Housing Projects

Due to concentration of poverty, many high-rise public housing projects in large metropolitan areas are characterized by austere living conditions and infested with drug-related violence and crime. Moreover, because of flagrant mismanagement by local housing authorities, some large cities have vacancy rates over 30% and many others have vacancy rates over 20%, while waiting lists run to years (Hinds, 1993). As evidenced by efficiently run public housing projects, however, the negative living conditions and mismanagement are not inherent weaknesses of public housing programs. Well-planned and -managed public housing projects can provide the most stable low-income housing. Construction of low-rise public housing projects scattered in mixed-income neighborhoods must follow the demolition of stand-alone high-rise projects in poor, isolated Black neighborhoods. HUD must enforce more stringent adherence to regulations by local public housing authorities.

Creation of Employment Opportunities for Inner-City Residents

When asked about how they were able to get out of homelessness, formerly homeless families said they had been helped most by an increase in income, the support of family and friends, and access to affordable housing (Dornbusch, 1993). Increase in income is most likely to come with employment. Creation of well-paying jobs and improvement of the employability of inner-city residents through skills-upgrading programs must be top priorities of urban policy. If a realistic hope of employment exists, people will be far more motivated to seek education and training (Fainstein & Fainstein, 1995). Low-wage workers who are not currently eligible for job-training programs directed at the unemployed or welfare recipients must be given opportunities to upgrade their skills.

Improvement of Placeability

The improvement of employability must be accompanied by improvement of placeability, which refers to "the perceived attractiveness of an applicant to an employer" (Wodarski, 1995, p. 3). The long-term unemployed or those who have not had substantial work history may need to brush up their job-seeking and interview skills to be able to identify and link with job openings and to increase employers' willingness to hire them. Once they land jobs, they may need to improve work performance skills and on-the-job social skills to increase their chances of keeping the jobs. Social workers need to provide the homeless and those at risk of becoming homeless with the comprehensive employment preparation and training in these job-related skills through a job club (see Wodarski, 1995).

Child Care and Transportation Services

Especially for single mothers, lack of child care is a major barrier to employment. Subsidized child care programs must be available for all those who need them. Parents who work in low-wage jobs often need child care services that offer extended or flexible hours, because work hours for many jobs stretch beyond the conventional nine-to-five schedule. Sick-child care services are also needed for parents with young children, especially when the parents are struggling with their new jobs. Frequent absence from work because of a sick child may lead to low productivity and dismissal. Children from poor families and deteriorating urban areas also need preschool or after-school programs that would stimulate their intellectual and developmental growth.

Availability and cost of transportation are frequently deciding factors in whether an individual can engage in an effective job search and take a job that is suitable for him or her. Because many cities have inadequate, poorly funded, and fragmented public transport systems, a significant number of potential workers from inner-city neighborhoods have been unable to avail themselves to jobs in the suburbs. Others have been forced to leave employment due to the cost and time involved in commuting. Without transportation, many homeless people also have a hard time finding housing and managing other aspects of their daily lives. A solution may be vouchers or transport coupons in cities with well-developed public transit systems. In other cities, if a major expansion of public transportation systems is too costly, a public-and-private-partnership venture such as Wisconsin's Job-Ride program, which transports low-income Milwaukee residents to suburban jobs (Nelson, 1993), needs to be developed. Also, zoning and financial incentives can be offered to regional and urban developers who can then cluster or plan to integrate public transport corridors with their developmental models (see Lowe, 1995).

Welfare Benefits, Earnings, and Health Care

To ensure the long-term economic independence of poor families currently receiving public assistance, they must be allowed to keep a higher proportion of their earnings and maintain their health benefits for a longer period before the public assistance benefits are reduced or entirely cut off. Under the Personal Responsibility and Work Opportunity Reconciliation Act of 1996 (which repealed the federal AFDC and replaced it with capped block grants to the states), each state has freedom to design its own welfare and welfare-to-work programs. Federal government must ensure that all states have adequate welfare-to-work programs that would promote long-term economic independence of poor families.

Racial Residential Desegregation

Federal support is needed to increase the spatial mobility of minorities in terms of both housing and transportation. To alleviate the residential segregation of poor Blacks in central cities, racial discrimination by real estate agents or prospective neighbors must be severely prosecuted. In addition, programs that would aggressively relocate individual families in subsidized suburban housing units are needed. To make this suburban transplant possible, however, public transportation must encompass suburban routes. As mentioned earlier, public housing units must be scattered in mixed-income neighborhoods in order to promote racial and class desegregation.

Alleviation of Drug-Related and Domestic Violence and Crime

Ridding low-income neighborhoods of drugs and drug-related violence and crime must go hand in hand with revitalization of their economic bases. Social workers' community organization skills can be used to mobilize residents of low-income neighborhoods into grassroots organizations to combat and alleviate drug-related violence. Residents of low-income neighborhoods where violence in the streets and domestic violence are problems must also be provided with stress management and anger control skills and nonviolent conflict resolution skills. Through various psychoeducational methods such as self-assessments, individual and group counseling, role play and corrective feedback, videotaped demonstrations, written materials, and positive reinforcement, individuals and groups need to be trained to build appropriate communication, social, and problem-solving skills as alternatives to aggression. Prevention of violence is much cheaper and more effective than dealing with the consequences of violence.

Assistance for Domestic Violence Victims

Women in abusive relationships need to be made aware of their legal rights and the supportive services and resources to which they can turn to ask for assistance. In conjunction with awareness of their rights, these women need to be taught assertiveness skills to exercise the rights and take necessary actions. The victims need to be connected to resources that would help them find stable housing, counseling for themselves and their children, and job-training programs that would assure their economic independence. Given the cost of sheltering victims of domestic violence, legislation must be introduced to hold perpetrators responsible for their behavior, both financially and legally.

Mental Health Services for Homeless and Precariously Housed Families

Outreach, combined with agency-based in- and outpatient services, and permanent housing with supportive services must be coordinated to provide stable lives for the mentally ill in the community. Linkage between housing and mental health services is needed to prevent homelessness among the mentally ill and to enable the homeless mentally ill to move back to permanent housing in the community as soon as possible. With the rising tide of managed care, it is especially important that the poor mentally ill receive quality services.

Substance Abuse Services for Homeless and Precariously Housed Families

As in the case of mental health services, outreach, combined with in- and outpatient drug and alcohol rehabilitation services and with supportive housing arrangements, appears to be the best approach. Emergency shelters must not just turn down drug and alcohol users but accept them and require them to participate in in-house or outside rehabilitation programs. For homeless and other poor mothers, participation in drug or alcohol treatment programs is often difficult because of a lack of child care. Child care must be provided to facilitate their participation and help them stay in treatment. The needs of those with co-occurring substance abuse and mental health disorders must be addressed.

Services to Homeless and Precariously Housed Children

Given the high incidence of depression and anxiety disorders among them, homeless and other poor children who need mental health evaluation must be connected to services and receive continuous monitoring and, if needed, treatment. Shelter or transitional housing staff must refer the children for these services; teachers and school nurses may also be encouraged to refer them to mental health agencies.

The many bureaucratic barriers (such as residency requirements and mishandling of school records) that face homeless and low-income, frequently mobile children when they try to go to school must be broken down. Remedial educational programs and recreational or social programs (with a supply of nutritious snacks) outside school hours must be open to these needy children. Improvement of transportation services for them is very important, as are school breakfast and lunch programs. Although schools cannot correct the damage done by poverty and unstable housing, they can be a sanctuary for many children by providing continuity in at least one important aspect of their lives. Homeless children should feel welcome at school, and greater sensitivity from school personnel toward them will go a long way to ease their pain.

Social workers, in cooperation with school counselors, may also need to develop school-based interventions for students that enhance understanding, tolerance, and respect for persons with diverse personal and financial backgrounds. Social workers can also provide in-service training for faculty and staff to increase their awareness of the specific academic and emotional needs of homeless children and to discuss appropriate interventions to promote these children's academic achievement and personal growth.

For best results, an interprofessional case management system for homeless and precariously housed school-age children needs to be established. The case management team can comprise a case manager–social worker stationed at a designated social service agency, a school counselor, a school nurse, shelter staff, and volunteers who would provide tutoring, group activities, and transportation. The case manager would identify homeless and precariously housed children, facilitate case management team meetings to establish and coordinate a system of needs assessment, service planning, and delivery of services such as referrals to health clinics and counseling, and monitor the effectiveness of services. The case management team would also advocate and make arrangements for specific services that are necessary for children's academic progress.

CONCLUSION

Homelessness will continue to haunt an increasing number of poor families unless we understand the relationship between housing and the changing structure of the urban economy. Low-income families face the double impacts of declining real income and increasing housing costs. As labor markets produce increasing wage and income disparities between rich and poor and as housing markets drive up rent and swallow up low-cost rental units, the poor will continue to wrestle with a crisis of housing affordability. The replacement of the AFDC with a new block grant, Temporary Assistance to Needy Families, to the states as of October 1996 also forces poor, minority, single mothers with children to deal with increasingly punitive welfare policies. The imposition of a 5-year (or less) lifetime limit on welfare benefits, without a simultaneous increase in employment opportunities and child care, is expected to only worsen the financial hardship of these poor families (Zedlewski, Clark, Meier, & Watson, 1996). Increasing poverty will drive an increasing number of families into homelessness.

Under these economic circumstances, no amount of effort geared to providing mental health and substance abuse services alone is likely to prevent homelessness among poor families and individuals. We have to tackle the root causes of homelessness. Revitalization of central cities, improved education and job training of poor residents of these cities, and rehabilitation and construction of low-income housing may sound like unrealistic measures in the current political and fiscal climate. But these projects can be largely self-financing and even profitable, if prudent planning and coordination of resources among federal, state, and local governments and with the private sector are adopted. When successfully implemented, urban revitalization that includes housing construction and rehabilitation is a revenue-generating venture for obvious reasons: Jobs will be created and tax bases will be expanded. What we lack is not money but political will. All levels of our governments have been saturated with neoconservatism, which pits rich against poor.

Because they are often the first to be called upon to help families with children cope with special needs and the daily crises that result from homelessness, social workers have witnessed the suffering of these families. In addition to the daily practice that aims at finding housing and improving the physical and mental health of each family on a micro scale, social workers must engage in macro-scale interventions with larger systems. Social workers must advocate, lobby, and take political and legislative actions to call for structural changes that would help prevent homelessness.

REFERENCES

Ames, D. L., Brown, N. C., Callahan, M. H., Cummings, S. B., Smock, S. M., & Ziegler, J. M. (1992). Rethinking American urban policy. *Journal of Urban Affairs, 14*(3/4), 197–216.

Bassuk, E. L. (1990). Who are the homeless families? Characteristics of sheltered mothers and children. *Community Mental Health Journal, 26*(5), 425–434.

Bassuk, E. L. (1992). Women and children without shelter: The characteristics of homeless families. In M. J. Robertson & M. Greenblatt (Eds.), *Homelessness: A national perspective* (pp. 257–264). New York: Plenum Press.

Bassuk, E. L., & Gallagher, E. M. (1990). The impact of homelessness on children. In N. A. Boxill (Ed.), *Homeless children: The watchers and the waiters* (pp. 19–34). Binghamton, NY: Haworth Press.

Bassuk, E. L., & Rosenberg, L. (1988). Why does family homelessness occur? A case control study. *American Journal of Public Health, 78,* 783–788.

Bassuk, E. L., & Rosenberg, L. (1990). Psychosocial characteristics of homeless children and children with homes. *Pediatrics, 85*(3), 257–261.

Bassuk, E. L., & Rubin, L. (1987). Homeless children: A neglected population. *American Journal of Orthopsychiatry, 57*(2), 279–286.

Baum, A. S., & Burnes, D. W. (1993). *A nation in denial: The truth about homelessness.* Boulder, CO: Westview.

Berck, J. (1992, Spring). No place to be: Voices of homeless children. *Public Welfare,* pp. 28–33.

Berlin, G., & McAllister, W. (1994). Homeless family shelters and family homelessness. *American Behavioral Scientist, 37*(3), 422–434.

Boxill, N. A., & Beaty, A. L. (1990). Mother/child interaction among homeless women and their children in a public night shelter in Atlanta, Georgia. In N. A. Boxill (Ed.), *Homeless children: The watchers and the waiters* (pp. 49–64). Binghamton, NY: Haworth Press.

Browne, A. (1993). Family violence and homelessness: The relevance of trauma histories in the lives of homeless women. *American Journal of Orthopsychiatry, 63*(3), 370–383.

Burg, M. A. (1994). Health problems of sheltered homeless women and their dependent children. *Health and Social Work, 19*(2), 125–131.

Burt, M. R., & Cohen, B. E. (1989). Differences among homeless single women, women with children, and single men. *Social Problems, 36,* 508–524.

Choi, N. G., & Doueck, H. J. (1996, February). Homeless families with children: Barriers to finding decent housing. Paper presented at the 42nd annual program meeting of the Council on Social Work Education, Washington, DC.

DeAngelis, T. (1994). Homeless families: Stark reality of the '90s. *The American Psychological Association Monitor, 25*(4), 1–39.

DiBiase, R., & Waddell, S. (1995). Some effects of homelessness on the psychological functioning of preschoolers. *Journal of Abnormal Child Psychology, 23,* 783–792.

Donahue, P. J., & Tuber, S. B. (1995). The impact of homelessness on children's level of aspiration. *Bulletin of the Menninger Clinic, 59,* 249–255.

Dornbusch, S. M. (1993). Some political implications of the Stanford studies of homeless families. In S. Matteo (Ed.), *American women in the nineties* (pp. 153–172). Boston: Northeastern University Press.

Dugger, C. W. (1993, July 26). Homeless shelters drain money from housing, experts say. *The New York Times.*

Dupper, D. R., & Halter, A. P. (1994). Barriers in educating children from homeless shelters: Perspectives of school and shelter staff. *Social Work in Education, 16*(1), 39–45.

Fainstein, S. S., & Fainstein, N. (1995). A proposal for urban policy in the 1990s. *Urban Affairs Review, 30*(5), 630–634.

Ferlauto, R. C. (1991, Summer). A new approach to low-income housing. *Public Welfare,* pp. 30–35.

Goodman, L. A. (1991). The prevalence of abuse among homeless and housed poor mothers: A comparison study. *American Journal of Orthopsychiatry, 61*(4), 489–500.

Hagen, J. L. (1987). Gender and homelessness. *Social Work, 32,* 312–316.

Hausman, B., & Hammen, C. (1993). Parenting in homeless families: The double crisis. *American Journal of Orthopsychiatry, 63*(3), 358–369.

Hinds, M. D. (1993, June 9). With help of federal rescue effort Philadelphia Housing Agency falters. *The New York Times.*

Hombs, M. E. (1994). *American homelessness: A reference handbook* (2nd ed.). Santa Barbara, CA: ABC-CLIO.

Jencks, C. (1994). *The homeless.* Cambridge, MA: Harvard University Press.

Johnson, A. K., & Cnaan, R. A. (1995). Social work practice with homeless persons: State of the art. *Research on Social Work Practice, 5*(3), 340–382.

Johnson, A. K., & Kreuger, L. W. (1989, November). Toward a better understanding of homeless women. *Social Work, 34,* 537–540.

Johnson, A. K., McChesney, K. Y., Rocha, C. J., & Butterfield, W. H. (1995). Demographic differences between sheltered homeless families and housed poor families: Implications for policy and practice. *Journal of Sociology and Social Welfare, 22*(4), 5–22.

Johnson, G. T., & Hambrick, R. S. (1993). Preventing homelessness: Virginia's homeless intervention program. *Journal of Urban Affairs, 15*(6), 473–489.

Joint Center for Housing Studies. (1995). *The state of the nation's housing 1995.* Cambridge, MA: Harvard University Press.

Joint Economic Committee. (1992). *Teenage pregnancy: The economic and social cost.* Hearing before the Subcommittee on Education and Health of the 102nd Congress of the United States. Washington, DC: U.S. Government Printing Office.

Kasarda, J. D. (1989). Urban industrial transition and the underclass. *Annals of the American Academy of Political and Social Sciences, 501,* 26–47.

Khanna, M., Singh, N. N., Nemil, M., Best, A., & Ellis, C. R. (1992). Homeless women and their families: Characteristics, life circumstances, and needs. *Journal of Child and Family Studies, 1*(2), 155–165.

Kondratas, A. (1991). Ending homelessness: Policy challenges. *American Psychologist, 46*(1), 1226–1231.

Kozol, J. (1988). *Rachel and her children: Homeless families in America.* New York: Crown.

Leonard, P. A., Dolbeare, C. N., & Lazere, E. B. (1989). *A place to call home: The crisis in housing for the poor.* Washington, DC: Center on Budget and Policy Priorities and Low Income Housing Information Service.

Lipsky, M., & Smith, S. R. (1989, March). When social problems are treated as emergencies. *Social Service Review, 63,* 5–25.

Lowe, M. (1995). Out of the car, into the future. In R. L. Kemp (Ed.), *America's cities: problems and prospects* (pp. 51–58). Brookfield, VT: Ashgate.

Massey, D. S. (1994, December). America's apartheid and the urban underclass. *Social Service Review, 68,* 471–487.

Massey, D. S., Gross, A. B., & Shibuya, K. (1994, June). Migration, segregation, and the geographic concentration of poverty. *American Sociological Review, 59,* 425–445.

McChesney, K. Y. (1990). Family homelessness: A systemic problem. *Journal of Social Issues, 46*(4), 191–205.

McChesney, K. Y. (1992). Homeless families: Four patterns of poverty. In M. J. Robertson & M. Greenblatt (Eds.), *Homelessness: A national perspective.* New York: Plenum Press.

McChesney, K. Y. (1995, September). A review of the empirical literature on contemporary urban homeless families. *Social Service Review, 69,* 429–460.

McNamee, M. J., Bartek, J. J., & Lynes, D. (1994). Health problems of sheltered homeless children using mobile health services. *Issues in Comprehensive Pediatric Nursing, 17,* 233–242.

Messinger, R. W. (1993, August 7). Out of hotels, into homes. *The New York Times.*

Mihaly, L. (1991). Beyond numbers: Homeless families with children. In J. H. Kryder-Coe, L. M. Salamon, & J. M. Molnar (Eds.), *Homeless children and youth: A new American dilemma* (pp. 11–32). New Brunswick, NJ: Transaction.

Nelson, T. M. (1993). Wisconsin picks up the tab. *Planning, 59*(12), 18–19.

Rafferty, Y. (1995). The legal rights and educational problems of homeless children and youth. *Educational Evaluation and Policy Analysis, 17*(1), 39–61.

Rafferty, Y., & Shinn, M. (1991). The impact of homelessness on children. *American Psychologist, 46*(11), 1170–1179.

Rescorla, L., Parker, R., & Stolley, P. (1991). Ability, achievement, and adjustment in homeless children. *American Journal of Orthopsychiatry, 61*(2), 210–220.

Ringheim, K. (1993). Investigating the structural determinants of homelessness: The case of Houston. *Urban Affairs Quarterly, 28*(4), 617–640.

Rossi, P. H. (1989). *Down and out in America: The origins of homelessness.* Chicago: University of Chicago Press.

Rossi, P. H. (1994). Troubling families: Family homelessness in America. *American Behavioral Scientist, 37*(3), 342–395.

Schwartz, D. C., Bartelt, D. W., Ferlauto, R., Hoffman, D. N., & Listokin, D. (1992). A new urban housing policy for the 1990s. *Journal of Urban Affairs, 14*(3/4), 239–262.

Shinn, M., & Gillespie, C. (1994). The roles of housing and poverty in the origins of homelessness. *American Behavioral Scientist, 37*(4), 505–521.

Snow, D. A., Anderson, L., & Koegel, P. (1994). Distorting tendencies in research on the homeless. *American Behavioral Scientist, 37*(4), 461–475.

Steinbock, M. R. (1995). Homeless female-headed families: Relationships at risk. In S. M. H. Hanson et al. (Eds.), *Single parent families: Diversity, myths and realities* (pp. 143–159). Binghamton, NY: Haworth Press.

Stretch, J., & Kreuger, L. W. (1992). Five-year cohort study of homeless families: A joint policy research venture. *Journal of Sociology and Social Welfare, 19*(4), 73–88.

Timmer, D. A., Eitzen, D. S., & Talley, K. D. (1994). *Paths to homelessness: Extreme poverty and the urban housing crisis.* Boulder, CO: Westview.

U.S. Bureau of the Census. (1995). *Income, poverty, and valuation of noncash benefits: 1993* (Current population reports, Series P60-188). Washington, DC: U.S. Government Printing Office.

U.S. Conference of Mayors. (1990). *A status report on hunger and homelessness in America's cities: 1990.* Washington, DC: Author.

U.S. Department of Housing and Urban Development. (1994). *Priority: Home!: The federal plan to break the cycle of homelessness* (HUD-1454-CPDU). Washington, DC: Author.

U.S. House of Representatives. (1990). *Public housing and Section 8 programs.* Hearing before the Subcommittee on Housing and Community Development of the Committee on Banking, Finance and Urban Affairs (Serial No. 101-91). Washington, DC: U.S. Government Printing Office.

U.S. House of Representatives. (1993). *Need for permanent housing for the homeless.* Hearing before the Subcommittee on Housing and Community Development of the Committee on Banking, Finance and Urban Affairs (Serial No. 103-21). Washington, DC: U.S. Government Printing Office.

U.S. Senate. (1990). *Cranston-Gonzalez National Affordable Housing Act* (P.L. 101-625; Senate Report No. 101-316). Washington, DC: U.S. Government Printing Office.

Wacquant, L. J. D., & Wilson, W. J. (1989). The cost of racial and class exclusion in the inner city. *Annals of the American Academy of Political and Social Sciences, 501,* 8–25.

Wagner, J., & Menke, E. (1991). The depression of homeless children: A focus for nursing intervention. *Issues in Comprehensive Pediatric Nursing, 14,* 17–29.

Weinreb, L., & Rossi, P. H. (1995, March). The American homeless family shelter "system." *Social Service Review, 69,* 86–107.

Weitzman, B. C., Knickman, J. R., & Shinn, M. (1990). Pathways to homelessness among New York City families. *Journal of Social Issues, 46*(4), 125–140.

Weitzman, B. C., Knickman, J. R., & Shinn, M. (1992). Predictors of shelter use among low-income families: Psychiatric history, substance abuse, and victimization. *American Journal of Public Health, 82*(11), 1547–1550.

Whitman, B. Y., Accardo, P., Boyert, M., & Kendagor, R. (1990). Homelessness and cognitive performance in children: A possible link. *Social Work, 35*(6), 516–519.

Wilson, W. J. (1987). *The truly disadvantaged.* Chicago: University of Chicago Press.

Wodarski, J. S. (1995). Employment interventions with adolescents. *Directions in Child & Adolescent Therapy, 2*(4), 3–15.

Wright, J. D. (1990). Homelessness is not healthy for children and other living things. In N. A. Boxill (Ed.), *Homeless children: The watchers and the waiters* (pp. 65–88). Binghamton, NY: Haworth Press.

Wright, J. D. (1991). Poverty, homelessness, health, nutrition, and children. In J. H. Kryder-Coe, L. M. Salamon, & J. M. Molnar (Eds.), *Homeless children and youth: A new American dilemma.* New Brunswick, NJ: Transaction.

Zedlewski, S., Clark, S., Meier, E., & Watson, K. (1996). *Potential effects of congressional welfare legislation on family income.* Washington, DC: Urban Institute.

Ziesemer, C., Marcoux, L., & Marwell, B. E. (1994). Homeless children: Are they different from other low-income children? *Social Work, 39*(6), 658–668.

Zima, B. T., Wells, K. B., & Freeman, H. E. (1994). Emotional and behavioral problems and severe academic delays among sheltered homeless children in Los Angeles County. *American Journal of Public Health, 84,* 260–264.

Zorza, J. (1991). Woman battering: A major cause of homelessness. *Clearinghouse Review,* pp. 421–429.

Chapter 10

UNEMPLOYMENT

Anna Celeste Burke

INTRODUCTION

Operational Definitions

Unemployment refers to the inability to gain entry into the labor market or to the "involuntary withdrawal from the workforce due to plant closures, layoffs, or other types of dismissals" (Leana & Feldman, 1991, p. 65). Since the mid-1970s, the U.S. economy has undergone dramatic changes, contributing to relatively high unemployment rates and large numbers of workers confronted with job loss. Between 1981 and 1988 alone, estimates are that 10.8 million U.S. workers experienced unemployment (Fraze, 1988). In the 1980s and 1990s it has also become increasingly difficult for young people to negotiate the transition from school to work (Mann, Miller, & Baum, 1995; Sum, Fogg, & Taggert, 1988). This is particularly true for young people with little education or training, but even those with college degrees find job acquisition more challenging (Sum et al., 1988). Modest growth and further economic restructuring are forecast for the next decade, meaning many more individuals will face unemployment (U.S. Department of Labor [U.S. DOL], 1996).

Extent and Costs of Unemployment

Figures provided by the U.S. government indicate that about 5.5% of the civilian labor force, or somewhere between 7 and 8 million individuals, are currently unemployed. Government-produced unemployment statistics do not, however, include all jobless workers:

> Those who are not actively looking for work or who are unable to work because of a physical or emotional disability may be excluded, as may be those who are working part-time or who have retired prematurely because they could not find full-time work. It has been estimated that the actual number of unemployed may be 50% higher than that indicated by official figures. (Kates, Greiff, & Hagen, 1990)

Thus, the number of unemployed may actually be closer to 10 or 15 million.

Estimates are that 2 out of 3 workers will experience unemployment at some point in their lifetimes (U.S. DOL, 1996). The likelihood of experiencing unemployment is greater for minority groups, women, immigrants, youth, and persons with disabilities. Moreover, members of these groups have more difficulty finding work when unemployed (Kates et al., 1990; Leana & Feldman, 1991, Snyder & Nowak, 1984).

On average, workers entering the labor force since the mid-1970s can expect to change jobs more times than those who entered the labor force in the three preceding decades. In recent years many jobs have emerged in the most highly competitive and least stable sectors of the economy. Small businesses have created a majority of new jobs in the United States for the last decade or so, but have a failure rate of about 50%. Since a majority of these jobs offer low wages and few benefits, workers have few resources to fall back on during transitions from one job to another. Workers in more well-established sectors of the economy are also more likely than their predecessors to have career patterns marked by lateral moves and reversals that require workers to reestablish themselves in existing careers or retool for entirely new ones.

Because work is so central to well-being in contemporary society, unemployment is a major source of concern. Since work provides access to material resources, economic deprivation is a major consequence of unemployment (Jacobsen, 1987). As the century ends, individuals without work will find it increasingly difficult to rely on the so-called safety net to meet even their most basic needs for food, shelter, and health care. Reductions in income subsidy, food stamps, Medicaid, and housing programs raise the stakes for getting and keeping a job. Work also meets various social, psychological, and emotional needs for individuals. For many adults it is a primary source of identity, status, and legitimacy. The inability to establish a significant attachment to the labor market early on greatly limits future earnings and increases the likelihood of subsequent episodes of unemployment (Parnes, 1982). Moreover, youth who want to work and are unable to do so are at increased risk for psychological distress, a deteriorating self-image, loss of commitment to conventional lifestyles, and antisocial attitudes and behaviors (Allen & Steffensmeier, 1989). At any age, job loss has been associated with a wide variety of negative physical and mental health consequences such as increased cardiovascular disease, hypertension, negative mood, hopelessness, depression, and anxiety (Dooley & Catalano, 1988; Kates et al., 1990; Kinicki and Latack, 1990; Vinokur & Caplan, 1987; Winefield, Tiggeman, & Winefield, 1990, 1991).

Efforts to put a dollar amount on the costs of unemployment typically include estimates of lost productivity, reduced consumption, and additional subsidy provided by taxpayers for unemployment compensation and other benefits for the unemployed. Needless to say, any such estimate runs into the billions of dollars very quickly. A 1% rise in unemployment, for example, has been estimated to add

$55 billion to the federal deficit. Given the range of health, social, and psychological problems associated with unemployment, such dollar estimates fall far short of representing the full impact of unemployment on individuals, their families, and the larger community.

Relevance of Social Work's Involvement

Although unemployment can have a devastating impact on individuals and their families, a number of factors can mitigate these negative effects. Reemployment appears to result in a reduction of negative symptoms and a return to previous levels of well-being (Turner, Kessler, & House, 1991). Demographic characteristics; developmental needs; previous physical and mental health history; and personal, social, and financial resources all interact with specific employment-related issues to determine the impact of the unemployment experience. Those who are seeking jobs for the first time, for example, may have very different needs from those who lose jobs after working for many years. Furthermore, circumstances tend to worsen significantly for the jobless as the period of unemployment lengthens (Sales, 1995).

Social workers have a vital role to play in facilitating entry and reentry by workers into the labor market. The broad-based approach to client assessment typical of a person-in-environment or ecological model is well-suited to assessing the needs of the unemployed. Traditional social work practice that combines a commitment to instrumental concerns with skillful use of clinical counseling techniques can have substantial benefits for unemployed clients and their family members. A major challenge for social workers, however, is to become more adept at identifying employment-related problems and more deliberate and effective in dealing with these matters. Further development of occupational or industrial social work as a field of practice is one way to involve more social workers in employment-related concerns. The scope of change in the labor market and the rapid transformation of social service systems in the United States means, however, that social workers in many practice settings must develop expertise with employment-related problems. Clients receiving services in a variety of systems are likely to be confronted with unemployment even if it is not the presenting problem or their primary reason for seeking services. Current trends in welfare reform that link benefits to work are already involving social workers more directly in the tasks of helping clients prepare, choose, find, and retain employment.

ASSESSMENT METHODS

A variety of specialized tools have been developed for assessing work-related attitudes, skills, and abilities. In addition, however, given the potential for unemployment to impact on health, psychological well-being, and marital and family relations, it is important to assess clients in these domains as well. Many standardized instruments that can be administered and scored by hand or by computer exist to assess clients in these areas. In addition, local adult education providers at high schools and community colleges and counselors in public and private employment agencies offer thorough assessment of education and vocational preparation.

Work History

Assessment with unemployed clients begins with a work history. At a minimum, a work history should include educational background and preparation for employment, work experience including the type and extent of previous employment, reasons for termination from prior position(s), and nature and extent of recent efforts to secure employment. A work history, especially in the context of a broader social history, can help specify the nature and extent of employment-related problems and put them in perspective. It provides the first opportunity to scope out client strengths, resources, and deficits, and may indicate that a preexisting or coexisting health, mental health, or substance abuse problem is standing in the way of a client's efforts to get and keep a job. A work history is the place to ascertain whether an episode of unemployment is an isolated event or part of a pattern of repeated terminations. It may also point to a specific deficit that a client needs to address, such as a language barrier, illiteracy, tardiness, or excessive absence.

The work history suffers from the same limitations associated with any self-report source. Corroborating information from a partner or some other family member, from employers or other referral sources, and from responses to standardized instruments is, of course, useful in developing clarity about employment issues. The work history is not a substitute for a structured clinical interview or psychiatric evaluation. Examination of mental health status or referral for psychiatric evaluation may be indicated by findings obtained from the work history or from responses to standardized instruments used to assess psychological well-being.

Education and Vocational Preparation

Hundreds of instruments exist to assess educational level and preparation for employment. These include tools for measuring achievement, aptitude, interest, and values and for matching client profiles to specific occupations and jobs. *Career Success: Tools for the 21st Century* (Oregon Career Development Association, 1994) is one compendium of such resources. Compendiums identify instruments, describe their specific uses, and, in many cases, cite published articles that review their psychometric properties and prior use. Tools vary not only in the specific areas they measure, but in their suitability for various age and grade levels or special populations, the format used to collect information, the number of items and length of time needed to collect the information, the costs associated with the purchase and scoring of instruments, and so on. Comparative information about nine computer-assisted career guidance (CACG) systems is also available (Sampson & Reardon, 1990, Sampson et al., 1990). Computerized systems save staff time and can involve clients more directly in vocational assessment.

The most critical issue during assessment is to get a clear sense of educational level and to identify deficits in basic skills. The inability to read, write, or carry out basic math calculations is a handicap in the current labor market. Even low-wage, entry-level jobs often require literacy skills, in contrast to entry-level jobs in previous decades that relied primarily on physical attributes of strength, stamina, or dexterity. Poor literacy skills may impact on the job acquisition process by making it impossible for a client to read job postings or fill out applications.

Grade attainment in school is not an adequate measure of basic educational achievement. Numerous tests are available, however, to gauge achievement. Those most commonly used by program participants in the Job Training Partnership Act include the Test of Adult Basic Education (TABE), the California Achievement Test (CAT), the Wide Range Achievement Test (WRAT), and the Adult Basic Learning Examination (ABLE). These instruments are used not only to appraise basic skills but to sort and assign individuals to appropriate programs, to diagnose or establish where learning should begin, to benchmark progress, and as posttests to measure gain from program participation (National Commission for Employment Policy, 1988). Many other tests exist to assess aptitude and interest. Further evaluation in these areas is recommended for clients who need help choosing an occupation or changing careers.

Work Attitudes and Values

Individuals vary in the value they place on work and their commitment to the employment role. Commitment to employment appears to be higher for married men with dependent children than for others (Jackson, 1994; Warr & Jackson, 1984). Persons who place greater value on work than on other roles are at greater risk for health and mental health problems during episodes of unemployment (Bartell & Bartell, 1985; Kasl & Cobb, 1979; Walsh & Jackson, 1995; Warr & Parry, 1982). A higher level of commitment to the work role is associated with greater motivation to find a job (Leana & Feldman, 1991), but may increase vulnerability to negative consequences from setbacks or delays in obtaining employment. Commitment to paid employment can be assessed with an eight-item measure developed by Rowley and Feather (1987).

Health and Mental Health Status

For many, the unemployment experience is "an emotional roller coaster, characterized by loss, grief . . . a sense of inadequacy, depression, lowered self-esteem, increased stress, social isolation, an increased tendency toward minor psychiatric illness, erratic mood shifts, and a progressive loss of optimism about finding employment" (Borgen & Amundson, 1990, p. 188). General psychological distress or untreated symptoms of a substance abuse or mental health problem can greatly inhibit an individual's capacity to deal with unemployment. Similarly, poor physical health is an obvious impediment to employment. Ideally, any psychological disorder, medical condition, or physical or psychological limitation should be identified and evaluated during the assessment process.

Job loss has been associated with increased risk for a variety of debilitating and even life-threatening disorders such as hypertension, stroke, and heart disease (Brenner, 1987; Moser, Fox, & Jones, 1984). Assessment of health status is vital and can best be accomplished with a physical exam. A thorough physical exam is warranted if the client has not had an exam within 6 months, is symptomatic, or has a personal or family history of cardiovascular problems. Specific attention should be paid to blood pressure and immunological and cardiovascular risk factors such as serum cortisol and cholesterol levels (Arnetz et al., 1991). Other chronic health problems should be monitored closely as well, since the stress of unemployment can exacerbate symptoms or disrupt management of chronic disorders such as diabetes (Kates et al., 1990). Checklists of ailments, somatic complaints, and measures of subjective health may also be used to assess and monitor health status.

Dozens of instruments exist to measure mental health and psychological well-being. Tools for measuring self-efficacy (Sherer et al., 1982), self-control (Rosenbaum, 1980), and self-esteem (Rosenberg, 1965) have all been widely used with unemployed and other types of clients. Low self-esteem is associated with mental health and substance abuse problems. More important, however, low self-esteem, self-efficacy, or self-control may inhibit clients from taking actions needed to deal with unemployment. The Mental Health Inventory (Viet & Ware, 1983) assesses general mental health (32 items) and cognitive impairment (6 items). The SCL-90-R is a self-report symptom checklist that includes subscales for depression, anxiety, and somatization as well as other major psychiatric disorders. This instrument has been widely used with both clinical and nonclinical populations. Norms and clinical cutpoints have been established for men and women and other subgroups (Derogatis, 1994). This tool is useful for monitoring mental health in nonclinical populations and can also be used as a screening device to identify individuals in need of referral for further psychiatric evaluation. A reduced set of 53 items referred to as the Brief Symptom Inventory (BSI) is also available for assessing mental health. Similarly, subscales for somatization, anxiety, and depression can be used independently for screening and to monitor change in symptom levels over time. Specific inventories developed by Beck and associates can be used to gauge hopelessness (Beck, Weisman, Lester, & Trexler, 1974) and depression (Beck, Ward, Mendelsen, Mock, & Erbaugh, 1961). Tools for assessing alcohol and drug involvement include the Michigan Alcoholism Screening Test

(MAST; Selzer, 1971), Index of Alcohol Involvement (IAI; MacNeil, 1991), and the McMullin Addiction Thought (MAT) Scale (McMullin & Gehlaar, 1990).

Financial Strain

Financial strain adds to the risk of negative health and mental health problems for unemployed individuals and their family members and can interfere with planning and decision making about the prospects for retraining or reemployment. In fact, financial strain has been identified as the single most damaging consequence of unemployment (Sales, 1995; Turner et al., 1991). An assessment of financial resources ought to identify immediate financial problems confronting clients, provide a basis for making realistic decisions about options to pursue further education or training or to seek reemployment, identify areas in which clients can make adjustments in expenditures or pursue other strategies to maintain a reasonable standard of living, and establish the length of time a household can maintain financial stability during a period of unemployment. A second wage earner, unemployment insurance, substantial savings, or assets that can be easily liquidated (e.g., stocks, bonds) are variables that can cushion the impact of job loss. How much an individual is bothered by or concerned about finances may not always be related to the actual availability of resources. Subjective financial strain can be measured using an instrument such as the eight-item Financial Concerns Scale (Mallinckrodt & Fretz, 1988).

Family and Partner Relationships

The dynamics of partner and family relations may shift dramatically with changes in employment status. Even couples and families with considerable resources are likely to experience increased financial strain as a result of job loss. In addition to financial strain, a change in employment status of one family member may radically alter roles, patterns of communication, and relationships. A variety of strategies exist to assess family distress, family functioning, and the quality of the partner or spouse relationship. The Dyadic Adjustment Scale (DAS), for example, is a 32-item instrument developed to assess the overall quality of dyadic relationships (Spanier, 1976; Spanier, Lewis, & Cole, 1975). Subscales on this instrument measure dyadic consensus, cohesion, and affection expression and satisfaction, and are widely used to measure the quality of relationships between partners (McGonagle, Kessler, & Schilling, 1992; Stein, Bush, Ross, & Ward, 1992).

The Family Assessment Device (FAD) uses a 60-item questionnaire to evaluate family functioning in relation to six dimensions: problem solving, communication, roles, affective responsiveness, affective involvement, and behavior control. Items included in this instrument also provide information about general family functioning (Epstein, Baldwin, & Bishop, 1983). The Family Crisis Oriented Personal

Evaluation Scale (F-COPES) is a 30-item instrument designed to assess family strategies for dealing with problems such as unemployment (McCubbin & Thompson, 1991). The Family Hardiness Index (FHI) serves a similar purpose, providing information about the capacity of the family to deal with the stresses of such major life events (McCubbin & Thompson, 1991).

EFFECTIVE SOCIAL WORK INTERVENTIONS

A protocol for assessment and intervention with unemployed clients encompasses more or less distinct phases or processes involving engagement and stabilization, goal setting and action planning, and implementation and termination. Follow-up is also advisable with individuals who have experienced employment-related difficulties. Although evidence suggests many individuals recover quickly from the negative effects of unemployment, other studies indicate increased risk for health and mental health problems 2 to 3 years following an episode of unemployment (Arnetz et al., 1991, Brenner, 1987; Moser et al., 1984).

Engagement and Stabilization

Engagement and stabilization actually begin during assessment, particularly if the same service provider is involved in both assessment and intervention. During this phase, primary tasks for the provider include efforts to establish rapport and convey empathy, overcome denial or debilitating negative thoughts and feelings, and resolve crises and achieve as much stability for clients as possible. Moderate self-disclosure by the service provider about his or her own experiences with unemployment and expressions of confidence about the ability to help others deal with these issues appear to heighten credibility and aid in rapport building (Caplan, Vinokur, Price, & van Ryn, 1989; Janis, 1982; Jourard, 1968; Meichenbaum, 1985).

Although responses to unemployment vary greatly, denial or an "initial vacation period" is common for many individuals early in the job loss experience (Borgen, Hatch, & Amundson, 1990). Denial can delay decision making and action, potentially extending the period of unemployment. Such a delay is disadvantageous because unemployed workers typically have fewer resources and less support as the period of unemployment lengthens (Sales, 1995). Clients overwhelmed by anger, guilt, and shame about their unemployed status may also be paralyzed into inaction.

Denial and self-blame can be countered by engaging clients in conversation about their unemployment experiences. Allowing clients to vent anger and express other negative sentiments may be helpful (Spera, Buhrfeind, & Pennebaker, 1994). Normalizing the unemployment experience by informing clients about the integral nature of unemployment to work in a dynamic economy can reduce stigma and provide relief to clients. "Plant closings, economic recessions, technological advances, global competition, new styles of work, and changing social relationships can all lead to a loss of jobs" (Kates et al., 1990, p. 5). Acknowledging the presence of such conditions and the challenges they pose for workers can counter client misattributions about the causes of unemployment. Clients should also be reassured that there are strategies and skills they can use to improve their prospects in the labor market, shifting their focus toward action to overcome their unemployed status. Success in this regard is likely to be predicated on discovering and correcting distorted cognitions and punitive self-talk, while helping clients identify and take responsibility for deficits they possess in employment-related knowledge, skill, motivation, or behavior.

Crisis resolution is central to stabilization of the client and client-family system. It is essential in this early period to identify and resolve crises provoked or uncovered by the unemployment experience. This is the point at which to deal with health, substance abuse, or mental health problems revealed during assessment, which can interfere with the client's ability to pursue employment-related goals. Problems related to family conflict and domestic violence should also be addressed, as should any legal or financial crises.

Case management skills, involving brokering and coordination of services, and advocacy on behalf of clients, can contribute to rapport building and stabilization. Service providers should ensure that unemployed individuals make full use of benefits and supports available to them such as unemployment compensation, extended health coverage from employer-paid or union-sponsored health benefit programs, or other public benefits such as food stamps, cash assistance, or public health insurance. Referral for financial planning or debt counseling may also be appropriate at this stage, particularly if financial matters have reached a crisis point. Individuals who have received lump-sum severance pay or who have had retirement savings refunded to them at termination should also be encouraged to seek financial counseling.

Case management is also useful for coordinating care and making sure that client needs are met as they change over time. This is particularly important for clients who need multiple services or in cases for which sequencing of services is warranted. Making appropriate referrals for specialized services that can help clients achieve employment-related goals is an integral function of case management. Such efforts are effective, however, only if clients follow through and are able to obtain the referred benefit or service. Advocacy may be particularly important to avoid delays in the receipt of services or to challenge the denial of benefits to clients. Unemployed clients may be reluctant to confront an agency about a delay out of fear that they will not get the services they need, or they may not understand the process for grieving a decision made by an agency to deny them benefits. Advocacy for unemployed clients may also include referral for legal assistance if a client appears to have been the victim of wrongful termination or some other form of malfeasance or discrimination in the labor market.

Goal Setting and Action Planning

During the goal-setting and action-planning phase, clients must make decisions about how to deal with their current joblessness. The primary decision unemployed clients face is whether to seek employment. The vast majority of unemployed individuals will opt to find work. In today's rapidly changing labor market, however, workers are increasingly likely to be confronted by the need to upgrade existing skills or to retool before seeking reemployment (Kates et al., 1990; Mann et al., 1995). Renewed emphasis on work as an adjunct or alternative to welfare and disability benefits means many more long-term unemployed or disadvantaged workers may be seeking assistance with employment-related decisions. Many of these individuals may lack basic educational or vocational skills and can often benefit by choosing to improve language and literacy skills, and by acquiring more specialized technical or vocational skills before seeking employment. This is especially true, however, if training in basic education leads to a year or more of postsecondary education (U.S. DOL, 1995).

A still small, but growing, number of persons may seek self-employment or withdrawal from the labor market as an alternative to retraining or job seeking. Individuals who decide not to pursue employment will need very different services and supports from those who want to find work. Moreover, those who want to try their hand at starting a new business face a very different set of challenges from those who opt for early retirement or who qualify for long-term disability.

It is important that findings from the assessment process be used to carefully evaluate the practicality of making the decision to pursue some goal other than finding a job. Although decisions are rarely irreversible, there are real limits to resources and their use can constrain subsequent decision making. Early retirement typically involves more adjustment than may be obvious. Clients may find it difficult to be realistic about their ability to make ends meet on the reduced income that typically accompanies retirement. Moreover, older workers often encounter more difficulty finding new employment, and an extended absence may make matters worse. The pursuit of additional education and training and the start-up of a new business both require a substantial investment of time, money, and personal resources. A great deal of risk is associated with the start-up of small businesses. Most fail, often because of unrealistic planning and inadequate resources. New businesses cannot be counted on as a source of income for individuals and their families for 5 years after they are established. Add to this 6 months or more of planning and it becomes clear that self-employment is not an immediate alternative to reemployment.

Once a choice has been made, clients need to develop an action plan. An individualized service plan (ISP) or some other similar device should be used to set out the terms of agreement between client and provider about the specific plan of action to be used to achieve employment-related goals. This action plan should set out goals, specify measurable objectives associated with client goals and the activities intended to achieve objectives and strategies for measuring progress toward objectives. It should also specify terms and conditions surrounding termination and, ideally, should include plans for recontact or follow-up at agreed-upon times.

Implementation Phase

Effective intervention efforts must blend knowledge acquisition and skill building specific to the vocational needs of clients, with supportive counseling and opportunities to reinforce cognitive and behavioral changes that will make it possible for unemployed clients to realize their goals. Convincing evidence indicates that extended periods without work create more problems for workers and their families (Sales, 1995). Notwithstanding earlier precautions about helping clients carefully evaluate the feasibility of choosing not to search for work, every effort should be made to move clients toward action in as short a time as possible.

Individual Intervention

Job Search Assistance.   A variety of well-established techniques exist that can help clients find employment quickly and without a reduction in the quality of the jobs obtained (Johnson & Wegmann, 1982). Indeed, some evidence suggests that job search assistance training can increase placement rates, decrease the length of time needed to find a job, and result in higher quality employment as indicated by hours worked per week, earnings, and wage rate (Caplan et al., 1989; Vinokur et al., 1991). In any case, effective job search assistance involves a short-term, highly focused set of activities aimed at helping workers find and get jobs. These activities can best be conceptualized as a set of planned behaviors (Ajzen, 1988) learned and carried out in the context of directive behavioral counseling. Counseling should be focused on teaching clients search behaviors in a safe, positive setting where they can learn and practice such skills.

Counseling about search behavior is rooted in helping clients develop a fundamental understanding about the concept of a labor market as a structure in which workers are queued, sorted, and selected for entry into various job openings. Distinctions are typically drawn between the primary and secondary sectors of the labor market and between the formal labor market and informal or hidden labor market. Primary-sector jobs tend to be located in larger, more well-established firms and offer better salaries and benefits and more opportunity for advancement, but they comprise a smaller proportion of available openings and generally carry more entry requirements than those in the secondary sector. Moreover, many jobs in both the primary and secondary sectors are never posted in the formal labor market. The concept of the so-called hidden labor market is used to represent the notion that positions are constantly being created by turnover or job growth, but most are filled before ever reaching newspaper ads or employment agency listings. Specific information about the local labor market, including areas of the economy that are shrinking and growing, is also useful to clients looking for work.

A variety of props, scripts, and practice or rehearsal opportunities are important to improving job acquisition skills. The résumé is a standard prop used in the implementation of a search strategy. Résumé preparation should stress identification and representation of behaviorally specific attributes that clients bring to the workplace, rather than listing vague, positive characteristics. Skill inventories can be used to help clients list marketable skills they have acquired, not only from previous employment but from hobbies and community activities. Examining the skills clients have acquired may extend the range or type of position a client is qualified to pursue. In addition to a well-written résumé, portfolios containing cover letters, reference letters, and thank-you letters to send to employers following an interview can all be used to bolster job acquisition efforts. Similarly, a standard application form, complete with well-thought-out answers to tough questions, can be included in such a portfolio and can serve as a model for completing applications on site.

Direct contact of employers is a key strategy for penetrating the hidden labor market and increasing the pool of possible job opportunities. Rather than waiting for jobs to be posted, clients should be encouraged to identify and contact establishments that might have positions appropriate to their interests and qualifications. Telephone book yellow pages and employer listings obtained from the chamber of commerce are common resources clients can use for this purpose. Once identified, employers should be contacted with inquiries about current or anticipated openings and the application process. Scripts are often useful guides for clients making telephone contact with potential employers (Johnson & Wegmann, 1982).

Clients may also use direct contact with employers to set up information interviews. During an information interview a client should not ask for a job. Instead, information interviews enable clients to learn more about a business or industry and gain greater clarity about the kind of setting in which they want to work. They also expand client networks and can result in referrals or recommendations for jobs in similar establishments. Employers have, on occasion, been known to create positions for clients when suitably impressed during information interviews or to offer them positions later. Such interviews are also typically less stressful than job interviews and can, at the very least, offer clients the opportunity to practice interviewing skills under low-risk circumstances (Johnson & Wegmann, 1982).

Direct contact of employers is only one of the ways in which clients can generate job leads. One of the most interesting and consistent findings from surveys of workers is the large number who report that friends, family members, or acquaintances helped them find the jobs they hold (Jones & Azrin, 1973; Sillikar, 1993). Typically, 2 out of 3 workers indicated they found their jobs through leads from friends, family members, or acquaintances. Formal sources, such as newspaper want ads or employment agency postings, were much less common sources of job referrals (Murphy & King, 1996). Thus, a network orientation to job finding has become an increasingly important part of job search assistance counseling. This means increasing the ability and willingness of clients to approach friends, relatives, and acquaintances with inquiries about job leads. Formulating and practicing such requests is an important precursor to actually using this strategy.

Self-presentation and interviewing skills are critical job search behaviors. Role playing and videotaping are commonly used strategies for providing clients with opportunities to practice and get feedback about their performance. This sort of rehearsal can be particularly important in preparing clients who are anxious about the interview situation. Videotaping can help clients review their performance to search for elements of their self-presentation, such as a nervous gesture, lack of eye contact, or a seemingly evasive or incongruent response, which might be interpreted as a danger signal by an employer (Caplan et al., 1989).

Danger signals, also sometimes referred to as *marginal utility signals,* are behaviors and background or status characteristics that employers regard as reducing the utility (i.e., the value) or increasing the risk of hiring a particular applicant. Role playing can help clients anticipate and respond to employer concerns about so-called marginal utility signals such as age, a gap in work history, termination from a previous job, or an identifiable disability (Johnson & Wegmann, 1982). Both younger and older workers will find it to their advantage to practice making positive statements about their age. For example, older workers can be counseled to emphasize that they bring maturity, dependability, depth of knowledge, sound judgment, and experience to the job. Young workers can tout the value of their enthusiasm, energy, flexibility, and openness to new ideas since they come to the workplace with few preconceptions. Together the client and service provider should identify and rehearse the best way to explain extended periods of unemployment or previous terminations, particularly when related to such sensitive matters as an accusation, arrest, or conviction for a criminal offense. Clients who are comfortable, forthright, and willing to take the initiative with their intentions "to learn from past mistakes" can make positive impressions on employers. This sort of rehearsal may also be particularly important to differently abled clients who must convey their willingness and ability to be productive employees, but must also speak frankly about accommodation needs. A recent study by Thompson and Dickey (1994) revealed that few individuals with disabilities felt they knew how to communicate with employers about these matters.

Supervised search is a core feature of effective job search assistance. Supervised search involves supporting and monitoring client involvement in search-related behavior once the core behaviors have been specified and acquired. Both the learning of job search–related behaviors and the motivation to put them into practice can be enhanced through consistent use of positive reinforcement, including verbal encouragement and acknowledgment, for attempted behaviors. A number of studies highlight the importance of search-related effort to job search success. Individuals who find jobs more quickly tend to engage in more job search–related behaviors indicated by the number of job leads generated, applications filed, and interviews completed (Caplan et al., 1989; van Ryn, & Vinokur, 1992).

Supervised search also involves helping clients track the number and type of search efforts they make. Clients should be advised to keep a weekly count of direct contacts with employers; information interviews completed; requests made of relatives, friends, and acquaintances for job leads; new job leads generated; résumés sent out; applications filed; job interviews obtained; contacts with employment agencies; and review of newspaper want ads. Weekly totals can be tabulated or graphed to provide counselor and client with a clear measure of effort.

In addition, supervised search can provide clients with the opportunity to debrief and reflect on search efforts, honing their search skills while receiving reinforcement and support. Overcoming setbacks has been demonstrated to have positive benefits for a variety of planned change activities (Janis, 1982; Meichenbaum, 1985). One of the consequences of trying harder may be that clients actually increase the amount of rejection they experience. Persistence in the face of such rejection is a key to eventual success in the labor market. Learning to cope with search-related setbacks involves anticipating situations in which a setback is likely to occur (e.g., a rejection from an employer after making an application or going to a job interview). Clients should be encouraged to generate alternatives to a dysfunctional response to setbacks such as reducing search efforts or failing to follow through on subsequent interviews. Alternatives might include seeking out support from a family member or friend or choosing among predetermined rewards that acknowledge the effort rather than the outcome. Clients should be positively reinforced for their efforts to anticipate, plan for, and cope with setbacks.

In addition to ongoing support and encouragement, clients may need a variety of material supports to carry out a job search (Johnson & Wegmann, 1982). Discussion between provider and client should occur, early on, about access to key search resources such as telephone, word processing, copying, postage, transportation to interviews, and a reliable system for retrieving messages. Service providers need to be explicit about the kinds of assistance they can offer clients and they need to be sure that clients have plans for how to get the other material supports they need.

Setting aside a designated space in the home to better organize and support the search effort is advisable. This strategy can also help reinforce the notion that searching for a job is a structured activity, requiring a full-time commitment until employment is obtained. Public employment agencies may offer some resources to unemployed clients who use their services. Libraries and adult education centers often offer low-cost access to word processors and copiers. An answering machine is a lower cost alternative for receiving messages than an answering service. Clients without access to an automobile will need special assistance in getting to interviews. Public transportation requires that clients allow more time to arrive punctually at an interview site and that they take care when scheduling more than one interview in a day. Renting or borrowing a car may be an alternative for some clients.

One of the great advantages of individualized intervention is the ability to tailor strategies to specific clients. Obviously, clients who come into counseling with well-written, recently revised résumés will not need to revise them again. Individualized intervention can also focus on unique client concerns that might inhibit or impede job search activity, such as anxiety related to the job interview. In some cases clients may benefit from developing additional skills related to problem solving, stress management, assertiveness, anger, and conflict management. Job search assistance is most effective, however, when focused on providing clients with training in specific search-related information and behaviors and motivating them to take action as quickly as possible. Several sessions held in close succession for a week or two to develop job search competencies are preferable to the more traditional model of weekly counseling sessions. Once the client has entered the supervised search stage, weekly sessions should be sufficient to monitor and maintain client progress.

Job Coaching.   Job coaching typically involves providing a broader range of assistance to unemployed individuals. For the job coach, intervention activities may encompass all aspects of employment: choosing, finding, getting, and keeping a job. Job coaches may also play a more active role in the job acquisition process, acting more like job developers by contacting employers on behalf of clients or encouraging an employer to create a position for a particular client. This aspect of job coaching requires service providers to acquire extensive knowledge of the local labor market and close ties to employers.

Job coaching is often integral to the success of supported employment for clients with a history of chronic unemployment, substance abuse, or mental illness. Supported employment may involve some employer accommodation to special needs of clients, but typically relies on coaches to monitor and support client performance in the workplace. The Work Personality Profile (WPP) is an instrument designed to measure basic work habits and work-related behaviors in employment settings (Bolton & Roessler, 1986). Situational assessments can yield a realistic sample of the individual's responses to a wide variety of stimuli relevant to task performance and interpersonal relationship demands on the job. Job coaches work with clients to handle issues as diverse as notification of an employer about an absence or tardiness, management of conflicts between clients and coworkers or supervisors, and resolution of problems with child care or transportation.

Mentoring.   Mentors are sometimes used to do many of the same things that job coaches do, but mentoring typically relies on establishing a special relationship between a client and a coworker or community volunteer rather than a paid, professional coach. A number of communities have formed mentoring programs to support and encourage individuals interested in changing careers or starting their own businesses. Social workers can make referrals on behalf of unemployed clients to such programs if they already exist in the community or can attempt to set up such a relationship on a more informal basis. The local chamber of commerce and service organizations such as Kiwanis can provide assistance in finding mentors or can be encouraged to start such a program if none exists in the community.

Self-Employment Assistance.   The Small Business Administration often sponsors workshops on start-up and operation of small businesses for aspiring entrepreneurs, many targeted at women and members of ethnic minorities. Self-employment assistance programs have been provided in some communities. These programs increased the percentage of unemployed individuals who actually started their own businesses, among those who expressed such an intention (U.S. DOL, 1995). Such activities also provide opportunities for networking and mentoring. Mentoring and networking are important because of the technical expertise and social support provided, but they can also facilitate acquisition of financial resources to start a new business.

Vocational Education and Career Counseling.   Vocational and career counseling are integral to achieving objectives related to remediation, retooling, or upgrading job-related skills. Clients who have chosen to pursue education or training as an alternative to employment will require guidance and support as they sort through the maze of options, paperwork, and deadlines associated with their participation. Such activities may be particularly challenging for an individual who may still be reeling from job loss or who has been out of school for some time.

Vocational counseling can provide clients with greater clarity about their aptitudes and interests; information about training requirements for specific occupations or jobs; eligibility and admission criteria for various programs; availability of financial assistance during the education or training period; estimates of the commitment (e.g., time, money, effort) required to participate in one program or another; and information about logistics such as scheduling, child care, or transportation. Unless service providers are familiar with the range of services available to clients, referral to a local adult education program, community college, or vocational rehabilitation specialist is the best way to provide clients with the technical information and assistance they need.

Apart from acquiring technical information about education and training options, clients may need supportive counseling to manage stress, stay motivated, and overcome anxiety about their capacity to perform in classroom settings. Individual counseling can be used as a supplement to classroom activities to help clients learn how to organize learning into smaller, more manageable steps, attaching recognition and reward to their accomplishments. Individualized intervention can also be used to focus on building specific skills that can enhance realization of education and training objectives such as time management, studying, and test taking.

Adjusting to Retirement or Disability.   The decision not to return to work has profound repercussions for most clients. A great deal of support may be required in order to adjust to an abrupt transition from worker to nonworker. Those who lose jobs permanently to illness or injury will likely need ongoing help adjusting to changes in their lives imposed by their conditions. Anticipating and developing strategies to compensate for losses associated with leaving the work role will be a central focus of individual intervention for clients who decide not work. Strategies will typically include developing alternative sources of social support, self-esteem, and structure. Part-time work or volunteer activities can greatly ease the transition and guard against social isolation and withdrawal.

Group Intervention

Group interventions for the unemployed are a mainstay of traditional approaches to intervention with this population. Almost any intervention activity that can be delivered to an individual client can be delivered in a group context. Traditionally, group interventions have been primarily didactic in nature, focusing on knowledge building, cognitive skills development, or both. Increasingly, however, groups have gained recognition as important sources of socialization and support for unemployed clients (Johnson & Wegmann, 1982).

Job Clubs and Support Groups.   Although job search assistance skills can be taught in the context of individual counseling, such training more commonly occurs in a group. The group context provides more opportunities for members to practice skill building and acts as a source of additional social support and contacts that can generate job leads (Sillikar, 1993). Job search assistance programs that combine targeted search behavior training with small-group interactions have been phenomenally successful in helping clients find work (Azrin, Flores, & Kaplan, 1975; Jones & Azrin, 1973; Murphy, & King, 1996; Rife & Belcher, 1994; Stidham & Remley, 1992; U.S. DOL, 1995).

Job clubs and similar groups, including both time-limited and open-ended groups, have demonstrated their value as a basis for providing mutual support as well as job search assistance training. Social support has been identified as an important mediator of the negative effects associated with stressful life events, including unemployment (Caplan et al., 1989, Kates et al., 1990). Unfortunately, since socialization and support are often tied to employment and employment-centered networks, job loss can result in diminished support at a point when such support is most needed. Mutual support from job search assistance groups may include instrumental support such as carpooling or exchange of child care. These groups can also provide clients with companionship, encouragement, and acknowledgment for success in performing search-related behaviors. Contact with others experiencing unemployment can assist in reducing stigma and other negative feelings associated with unemployment (Johnson & Wegmann, 1982).

Job search assistance training programs and support groups also provide clients with many of the material resources needed to develop search materials and carry out search activities. These include phone banks, word processors, copiers, stationery, and postage stamps. Many programs have offered clients stipends or assistance with the costs of transportation to the training site or to potential employers. These groups also offer unemployed clients a structured setting in which to learn and carry out search activities, and provide staff to consult about issues that come up during the supervised search period.

Recruitment strategy is a major consideration for providers of job search assistance training in groups. A variety of strategies may be required in order to reach unemployed workers, including media announcements, referrals from local human service agencies, public employment services, unions, and businesses. Drop-off can be expected in the numbers of individuals who are eligible to participate, express interest in participating, and actually join the group. It is not unreasonable to recruit two or three times the number of clients intended to join the group.

Vocational Education and Job-Training Programs.   Classroom training is a mainstay of intervention for clients interested in additional education or training. Such programs run the gamut from remedial education in basic language and literacy skills and preparation for the General Equivalency Diploma (GED) to include more specialized vocational training for specific jobs or occupations and postsecondary education leading to a 2-year or 4-year degree. Basic education focuses on literacy training in the three Rs and may supplement classroom teaching with computer-assisted programs that enable unemployed persons to pursue more individualized learning objectives. These programs have succeeded in raising reading levels, improving writing ability and math skills, and preparing individuals to pass the test earning them the GED. Unfortunately, by themselves, such programs have demonstrated little ability to improve job prospects, benefits, or earnings among the unemployed (U.S. DOL, 1995). Unless they are closely linked to local employers, short-term (3 to 6-month) vocational training programs seem not to improve employment outcomes.

Long-term job training and postsecondary education, on the other hand, significantly improve the life chances of the unemployed. More extensive and costly training programs such as the Job Corps have been demonstrated to improve employment rates, earnings, and employment retention and reduce the likelihood of problems with the law (Allen & Steffensmeier, 1989; U.S. DOL, 1995). Even greater benefits accrue to those who earn 2-year or 4-year degrees. The gap in earnings between workers with high school diplomas and bachelor's degrees widened dramatically in the 1980s (U.S. DOL, 1995). Postsecondary education increases earnings 6% to 12% for every year acquired and, even without obtaining a degree, results in better employment outcomes. It is advisable to help clients place participation in short-term, basic education or job-training programs within this broader context. The greatest benefit of basic education and acquisition of the GED is the fact that it increases the likelihood that an individual will pursue postsecondary education.

Marital and Family Intervention

A primary aim of marital and family counseling or psychoeducation with one or more families ought to be to foster open communication at all stages during client assessment and intervention. Family roles and relationships may be significantly disrupted by changes in the employment status of a family member (Broman, Hamilton, & Hoffman, 1990). Ideally, the spouse or partner, and other family members of unemployed clients, should be carefully evaluated and other members of the family ought to receive services as needed. Special attention should be paid to a family member who has developed somatic symptoms, who exhibits a sudden change of mood or behavior, or who develops specific problems at home, work, or school.

Psychoeducation for unemployed clients, their partners, and their families can be important to maintaining the integrity and stability of the client system. Such services provide information to family members about the psychosocial impact of job loss on the unemployed member and possible repercussions for family interactions. Psychoeducation can increase awareness among family members about when to seek help for additional family members who show signs of increased distress and about the kinds of services and supports available to them. Such efforts should also be used to activate support for the unemployed client. Family members can show support by becoming involved in the important decisions that clients have to make about their employment-related options, and can offer tangible and intangible support to the unemployed clients once they have developed an action plan. Clients engaged in job search, for example, can benefit from partners and family members who understand that looking for a job is a full-time job, countering misplaced expectations that the unemployed client is free to assume additional household duties or child care responsibility.

Group sessions for families can serve many of the same functions that support groups offer to unemployed clients. These include opportunities to interact with others sharing similar feelings and experiences, potentially reducing the stigma and other negative feelings experienced by families when one of their members loses a job. Support groups can counter tendencies for some families to experience increased isolation from the loss of work-related social relationships. In addition, family support groups can foster mutual support, increasing tangible supports through carpooling, child care exchange, and so on.

Marital and family counseling can also be used to identify and resolve problems that develop over the course of the unemployment episode or elude detection during the assessment process. Marital and family counseling should encourage flexibility and adaptability among families and should help them to develop and maintain a positive outlook while the unemployed client is making strides toward realizing employment-related goals. Families may need particular help in this regard when the period of unemployment is extensive (i.e., greater than 6 months), the unemployed member takes a lower status or lower paying job, or the unemployed member decides to withdraw from the labor force. Skill-oriented counseling can also be used to teach partners and family members better ways to communicate with one another or to manage conflict provoked by unemployment. Such skills can benefit families during the period of unemployment and can also be of value to the family well after employment issues have been resolved. It is also advisable to involve partners and family members in termination and follow-up activities.

Termination and Follow-up

The termination process can add clarity to accomplishments and bring closure to the unemployment experience and the intervention process. Both individuals and their family members should be encouraged to reflect on and summarize positive outcomes, highlighting successes and acknowledging contributions of partners and family members. A number of job clubs and other training programs have adopted more formal termination activities, often with a ceremonial or celebratory character, to mark transitions for clients when they finish training, launch a new business, or find a job. Of course, milestones like completing a training program, earning the GED, and finding a job need to be acknowledged even if they do not coincide with termination. Moreover, termination with clients adjusting to disability or retirement may have less obvious markers or milestones of progress, but warrants a similar congratulatory response.

Many programs have developed alumni groups and sponsor reunions as opportunities to follow up with individuals. Plans for follow-up should be revisited at termination and should be aimed at ensuring adequate opportunity to evaluate the need for further intervention. This may be particularly important for the downward status mover, that is, an individual who finds new employment, but in a much less prestigious or lucrative position (West, Nicholson, & Rees, 1990). In addition, follow-up allows for further evaluation of the effectiveness of intervention efforts. Both termination and follow-up are appropriate points to readminister tools used to assess clients and their families.

Community Prevention and Intervention Efforts

Supporting Employment Transitions.   Communities have a variety of options to support workers and their families while they are unemployed. Perhaps the single most important factor is maintaining the financial integrity of unemployed individuals and their families during a period of unemployment. Unemployment insurance is a primary mechanism for providing workers with financial support during job transitions, although only 1 or 2 out of every 3 workers are eligible for unemployment insurance. Unemployment compensation provides coverage for a maximum of 6 months, although many states have provisions for supplemental coverage (U.S. DOL, 1996). Twenty-six weeks may not be long enough in particularly hard-hit areas or during periods when unemployment rates reach into the double digits. Legislative language that automatically triggers extended benefits when unemployment reaches a preset target has been proposed as an efficient strategy for dealing with compensation under such conditions.

Individual development accounts (IDAs) have been identified as a means for encouraging workers to upgrade their skills or retool so they remain employable in a constantly changing labor market. Like individual retirement accounts (IRAs), IDAs are proposed as tax-free savings accounts set up by workers for further education or training. Proposals have also been made to change the rules associated with IRAs to allow their use for similar purposes.

Gaps and discontinuities in health care coverage are also a major source of concern in most communities. In the United States, most health care coverage is tied to employment, and job loss typically means the loss of health care coverage. This is particularly problematic given the fact that unemployment poses increased health and mental health risks for workers and their families. Moreover, the Clinton administration has recently taken action intended to guarantee that insurance companies cover so-called preexisting conditions when workers move from one job to another. The fear of being denied coverage for such conditions has prevented many workers from leaving a job for a better position.

Community Planning Initiatives.   Better community planning can contribute to lower unemployment and to better support for those who become unemployed. Most communities suffer from insufficient integration of economic development, workforce development, and human services planning. Discontinuities between job training and vocational education programs and opportunities in the local labor market greatly limit the usefulness of education and training programs, and make job placement much more difficult (U.S. DOL, 1995). One-stop service centers have been promoted as a way to develop a seamless, client-driven system, providing a single point of entry for assistance with employment-related problems (Downs, 1991). Such centers have been proposed as one way to better integrate and coordinate support for education and training programs with health and human services, bridging the gap between social services and human resources development and economic planning.

REFERENCES

Ajzen, I. (1988). *Attitudes, personality, and behavior.* Chicago: Dorsey.

Allen, E. A., & Steffensmeier, D. J. (1989). Youth, underemployment and property crimes: Differential effects of job availability and job quality on juvenile and young adult arrest rates. *American Sociological Review, 54*(1), 107–123.

Arnetz, B. B., Brenner, S. O., Levi, L., Hjelm, R., Petterson, I., Wasserman, J., Petrini, B., Eneroth, P., Kallner, A., Kvetnansky, R., & Vigas, M. (1991). Neuroendocrine and immunologic effects of unemployment and job insecurity. *Psychotherapy and Psychosomatics, 55,* 76–80.

Azrin, N., Flores, T., & Kaplan, S. (1975). Job finding club: A group assisted program for obtaining employment. *Behavior Research and Therapy, 13,* 17–22.

Bartell, M., & Bartell, R. (1985). An integrative perspective on the psychological response of women and men to unemployment. *Journal of Economic Psychology, 6,* 27–49.

Beck, A. T., Ward, C. H., Mendelsen, M., Mock, J., & Erbaugh, J. (1961). An inventory for measuring depression. *Archives of General Psychiatry, 4,* 561–571.

Beck, A. T., Weisman, A., Lester, D., and Trexler, L. (1974). The measurement of pessimism: The Hopelessness Scale, *Journal of Consulting and Clinical Psychology, 42,* 861–865.

Bolton, B., & Roessler, R. (1986). *Manual for the Work Personality Profile.* Fayetteville, AR: University of Arkansas, Arkansas Research and Training Center in Vocational Rehabilitation.

Borgen, W. A., & Amundson, N. E. (1990). New challenges for career development: Methodological implications. In R. A. Young & W. A. Borgen (Eds.), *Methodological approaches to the study of the career* (pp. 185–196). New York: Praeger.

Borgen, W. A., Hatch, W. E., & Amundson, N. E. (1990). The experience of unemployment for university graduates: An exploratory study. *Journal of Employment Counseling, 27,* 104–112.

Brenner, S. (1987). Economic change, alcohol consumption and heart disease mortality in nine industrialized countries. *Social Science Medicine, 25,* 119–132.

Broman, C. L., Hamilton, V. L., & Hoffman, W. S. (1990). Unemployment and its effects on families: Evidence from a plant closing study. *American Journal of Community Psychology, 18,* 643–659.

Caplan, R. D., Vinokur, A. D., Price, R. H., and van Ryn, M. (1989). Job seeking, reemployment, and mental health: A randomized field experiment in coping with job loss. *Journal of Applied Psychology, 74*(5), 759–769.

Derogatis, L. R. (1994). *SCL-90-R: Administration, scoring, and procedures manual.* Minneapolis, MN: National Computer Systems.

Dooley, D., & Catalano, R. (1988). Recent research on the psychological effects of unemployment. *Journal of Social Issues, 44,* 1–12.

Downs, Shirley. (1991). *Streamlining and integrating human resource development services for adults.* Washington, DC: National Governors' Association.

Epstein, N. B., Baldwin, L. M., & Bishop, D. S. (1983). The McMaster family assessment device. *Journal of Marital and Family Therapy, 9,* 171–180.

Fraze, J. (1988, January). Displaced workers: Oakies of the 80's. *Personnel Administrator, 33,* 42–51.

Jackson, P. R. (1994). Influences on commitment to employment and commitment to work. In A. Bryson & S. McKay (Eds.), *Is it worth working? Factors affecting labour supply* (pp. 110–121). London: Policy Studies Institute.

Jacobsen, D. (1987). Models of stress and meanings of unemployment: Reactions to job loss among technical professionals. *Social Science Medicine, 24,* 13–21.

Janis, I. L. (Ed.). (1982). *Counseling on personal decisions: Theory and research on short-term helping relationships.* New Haven, CT: Yale University Press.

Johnson, M., & Wegmann, R. (1982). *Job search training for youth.* Salt Lake City, UT: Olympus.

Jones, R., & Azrin, N. (1973). An experimental application of a social reinforcement approach to the problem of job finding. *Journal of Applied Behavior Analysis, 6,* 345–353.

Jourard, S. M. (1968). *Disclosing man to himself.* Princeton, NJ: Van Nostrand.

Kasl, S., & Cobb, S. (1979). Some mental health consequences of plant closings and job loss. In L. Ferman & J. Gordus (Eds.), *Mental health and the economy* (pp. 255–299). Kalamazoo, MI: Upjohn Institute for Employment Research.

Kates, N., Greiff, B. S., & Hagen, D. Q. (1990). *The psychosocial impact of job loss.* Washington, DC: American Psychiatric Press.

Kinicki, A. J., & Latack, J. C. (1990). Explication of the construct of coping with involuntary job loss. *Journal of Vocational Behavior, 36,* 339–360.

Leana, C. R., & Feldman, D. C. (1991). Gender differences in responses to unemployment. *Journal of Vocational Behavior, 38*(1), 65–77.

MacNeil, G. (1991). A short-form scale to measure alcohol abuse. *Research on Social Work Practice, 1,* 68–75.

Mallinckrodt, B., & Fretz, B. R. (1988). Social support and the impact of job loss on older professionals. *Journal of Counseling Psychology, 35,* 281–286.

Mann, A. R., Miller, D. A., & Baum, M. (1995). Coming of age in hard times. *Journal of Health & Social Policy, 6*(3), 41–57.

McCubbin, H. I., & Thompson, A. I. (Eds.). (1991). *Family assessment inventories for research and practice.* Madison, WI: University of Wisconsin.

McGonagle, K. A., Kessler, R. C., & Schilling, E. A. (1992). The frequency of marital disagreements in a community sample. *Journal of Social and Personal Relationships, 9,* 507–524.

McMullin, R. E., and Gehlaar, M. (1990). *Thinking and drinking: An exposé of drinkers' distorted beliefs.* Wheelers Hill, Victoria, Australia: Marlin Publications.

Meichenbaum, D. (1985). *Stress inoculation training: A clinical guidebook.* New York: Pergamon Press.

Moser, K., Fox, A., & Jones, P. R. (1984). Unemployment and mortality in the OPCS longitudinal study. *Lancet, 8,* 1324–1328.

Murphy, G. C., & King, N. J. (1996). Australian data supporting validity claims of Azrin's Job Club program to reduce unemployment. *The Behavior Therapist, 19*(7), 104–106.

National Commission for Employment Policy. (1988). *Survey of basic skills remediation practices in the JTPA youth programs.* Unpublished document.

Oregon Career Development Association. (1994). *Career success: Tools for the 21st century.* Salem, OR: Oregon State Department of Education.

Parnes, H. (1982). *Unemployment experiences of individuals over a decade.* Kalamazoo, MI: Upjohn Institute for Employment Research.

Rife, J., & Belcher, J. (1994). Assisting unemployed older workers become re-employed: An experimental evaluation. *Research on Social Work Practice, 4,* 3–13.

Rosenbaum, M. (1980). A schedule for assessing self-control behaviors: Preliminary findings. *Behavior Therapy, 11,* 109–121.

Rosenberg, M. (1965). *Society and the adolescent self-image.* Princeton, NJ: Princeton University Press.

Rowley, K. M., & Feather, N. T. (1987). The impact of unemployment in relation to age and length of unemployment. *Journal of Occupational Psychology, 60,* 323–332.

Sales, E. (1995). Surviving unemployment: Economic resources and job loss. *Social Work, 40*(4), 483–491.

Sampson, J. P., Jr., & Reardon, R. C. (1990). Evaluating computer-assisted career guidance systems: Synthesis and implications. *Journal of Career Development, 17,* 143–149.

Sampson, J. P., Jr., Reardon, R. C., Humphreys, J. K., Peterson, G. W., Evans, M. A., & Dombrowski, D. (1990). A differential feature-cost analysis of nine computer assisted career guidance systems (3rd ed.). *Journal of Career Development, 17,* 81–112.

Selzer, Melvin L. (1971). The Michigan Alcoholism Screening Test: The quest for a new diagnostic instrument, *American Journal of Psychiatry, 127,* 89–94.

Sherer, M., Maddox, J. E., Mercandante, B., Prentice-Dunn, S., Jacobs, B., & Rogers, R. W. (1982). The Self-Efficacy Scale: Construction and validation. *Psychological Reports, 51,* 663–671.

Sillikar, S. A. (1993). The role of social contacts in the successful job search. *Journal of Employment Counseling, 30*(1), 25–34.

Snyder, K., & Nowak, T. C. (1984). Job loss and demoralization: Do women fare better than men? *International Journal of Mental Health, 13,* 92–106.

Spanier, S. (1976). Measuring dyadic adjustment: New scales for assessing the quality of marriage and similar dyads. *Journal of Marriage and the Family, 38,* 15–28.

Spanier, S., Lewis, R. A., & Cole, C. A. (1975). Marital adjustment over the family life cycle. *Journal of Marriage and the Family, 37,* 275–362.

Spera, Stephanie P., Buhrfeind, Eric, D., and Pennebaker, James W. (1994). Expressive writing and coping with job loss. *Academy of Management Journal, 37*(3), 722–733.

Stein, C. H., Bush, E. G., Ross, R. R., & Ward, M. (1992). Married couples in relation to marital satisfaction and individual well-being. *Journal of Social and Personal Relationships, 9,* 365–383.

Stidham, H., & Remley, T. (1992). Job club methodology applied to a workforce setting. *Journal of Employment Counseling, 29,* 69–76.

Sum, A., Fogg, N., & Taggert, R. (1988). *Withered dreams: The decline in the economic fortunes of young, non-college educated male adults and their families* (Report to the William T. Grant Foundation Commission on Family, Work, and Citizenship). New York: William T. Grant Foundation.

Thompson, A. R., & Dickey, K. D. (1994). Self-perceived job search skills of college students with disabilities. *Rehabilitation Counseling Bulletin, 37*(4), 358–370.

Turner, J. B., Kessler, R. G., & House, J. S. (1991). Factors facilitating adjustment to unemployment: Implications for intervention. *American Journal of Community Psychology, 19*(4), 521–542.

U.S. Department of Labor. (1995). *What's working (and what's not)*. Washington, DC: U.S. Department of Labor, Office of the Chief Economist.

U.S. Department of Labor (1996). *Labor force statistics from the current population survey* [On-line]. Available: Bureau of Labor Statistics Homepage, cpsinfo@bls.gov

van Ryn, M., & Vinokur, A. D. (1992). How did it work? An examination of the mechanisms through which an intervention for the unemployed promoted job-search behavior. *American Journal of Community Psychology, 20*(5), 577–597.

Viet, C. T., & Ware, J. E. (1983). The structure of psychological distress and well-being in general populations. *Journal of Consulting and Clinical Psychology, 51,* 730–742.

Vinokur, A., & Caplan, R. D. (1987). Attitudes and social support: Determinants of job-seeking behavior and well-being among the unemployed. *Journal of Applied Social Psychology, 17,* 1007–1024.

Vinokur, A. D., Price, R. H., & Caplan, R. D. (1991). From field experiments to program implementation: Assessing the potential outcomes of an experimental intervention for unemployed persons. *American Journal of Community Psychology, 19*(4), 543–562.

Walsh, S., & Jackson, P. R. (1995). Partner support and gender: Contexts for coping with job loss. *Journal of Occupational and Organizational Psychology, 68,* 253–268.

Warr, P. B. (1987). *Work, unemployment and mental health.* Oxford, England: Oxford Science Publications.

Warr, P. B., & Jackson, P. R. (1984). Men without jobs: Some correlates of age and length of unemployment. *Journal of Occupational Psychology, 57,* 77–85.

Warr, P. B., & Parry, G. (1982). Paid employment and women's psychological well-being. *Psychological Bulletin, 91,* 498–516.

West, M., Nicholson, N., & Rees, A. (1990). The outcome of downward managerial mobility. *Journal of Organizational Behavior, 11,* 119–134.

Winefield, A. H., Tiggemann, M., & Winefield, H. R. (1990). Factors moderating the psychological impact of unemployment at different ages. *Personality and Individual Differences, 11*(1), 45–52.

Winefield, A. H., Tiggemann, M., & Winefield, H. R. (1991). The psychological impact of unemployment and unsatisfactory employment in young men and women: Longitudinal and cross-sectional data. *British Journal of Psychology, 82*(4), 473–486.

Chapter 11

MARITAL CONFLICT, DOMESTIC VIOLENCE, AND FAMILY PRESERVATION

M. E. Betsy Garrison
M. A. Keresman

This chapter examines the empirical literature concerning family preservation. In this chapter, the term *family preservation* is being used in the nominal sense to answer the question, What do we know about keeping families together? Our definition of family preservation does not include governmental legislation, such as the Family Preservation Act, or interventions specific to Intensive Family Preservation Services (For more information about either of these two topics, the reader is directed toward Garrison and Blalock [1996], and Keresman, Zarski, & Garrison [in press]).

When discussing families, the supposition must be made that not only do a multitude of problems exist in family life, but these problems interrelate. While, hypothetically, the problems of families may be separated, in reality, family problems are not distinct. Rarely, if ever, does family intervention involve the diagnosis, treatment, or both of a single, unrelated symptom, problem, or disorder. Often, for effective and long-term intervention, problems must be treated on multiple levels with a variety of therapeutic strategies.

Due to this multiplicity and interrelatedness, every chapter of this handbook has relevance to family preservation. So as not to duplicate the other chapters, however, we intentionally focus on family problems and disorders not explicitly discussed elsewhere in the book. Thus, we discuss marital conflict in terms of not only how couple members are affected, but also how family life impacts the health and well-being of the children. We do not address specific problems, such as chemical dependency, juvenile delinquency, and eating disorders, even though these problems affect family preservation, and we discuss family violence strictly in

Note: The research for this chapter was supported in part by the School of Human Ecology, the College of Agriculture, Louisiana State University, and the Louisiana State University Agricultural Center. Approved for publication by the Director of the Louisiana Agricultural Experiment Station as manuscript number 97-25-0242. We express our appreciation to Christina Barras, Nhan Thai, and Renior Young for their assistance with this chapter.

terms of domestic or spousal abuse, rather than child abuse, sibling abuse, or elder abuse, even though these problems, obviously, affect family preservation.

MARITAL CONFLICT

Definition

This chapter's discussion of marital conflict includes research on various stages of troubled marriages to the extent that couples have sought help, have been referred to various social service agencies, or were solicited to participate in studies that provided some type of assessment, psychoeducation, or intervention. The terms *marital discord, marital distress,* and *marital dissatisfaction* are used interchangeably in this body of literature and are included in our discussion of marital conflict.

Prevalence, Incidence, and Costs

Presumably, all marriages involve some degree of marital conflict, given that life is inherently stressful and that all relationships involve some degree of dissension. It is estimated that half of all marriages begun in the United States today will end in dissolution by divorce and approximately 60% of these marriages will involve children (U.S. Bureau of the Census, 1995).

For several years now, marital conflict has been identified as a risk factor for health and mental problems and a major disruption in the workplace (American Psychological Association, 1990). Bray and Jouriles (1995) discussed the cost-effectiveness of marital therapy and noted that the majority of marital therapies that have been empirically evaluated are relatively brief in duration and below the standard 20-session limit imposed by health insurance companies. Using an average cost of $60 to $100 per session, an average course of marital therapy would cost between $600 and $1,000. As stated by Bray and Jouriles, "Even twice this amount seems certainly less than the cost of a divorce and pales in comparison to the costs of many medical procedures" (1995, p. 469).

Social Work Involvement

In a recent review of the literature, Bray and Jouriles (1995) stated that marital conflict and divorce are associated with multiple family problems that negatively affect the well-being of family members. The authors state their belief that the "reduction of marital conflict and the prevention of divorce should represent high priorities for modern families" (p. 462). Marital and family therapy is caught up in the current health care revolution and demands to demonstrate the effectiveness and cost-effectiveness of their interventions are being made (Pinsof & Wynne, 1995).

These demands present a challenge to family social workers to keep investigating and implementing interventions that meet the therapeutic needs of the growing number of people who are affected by marital conflict, divorce, and remarriage. Family social workers need to continue the struggle to balance their own Code of Ethics from the National Association of Social Workers (NASW) and standards of practice with the demands of the health care system for therapeutic and cost-effective interventions. Bagarozzi suggests that "social workers become advocates for the American family in this era of managed care" (1995, p. 101).

Assessment Methods

In an article by Boughner, Hayes, Bubenzer, and West (1994), marital and family therapists reported that the two most commonly used assessments for all types of marital and family therapy were the Minnesota Multiphasic Personality Inventory-2 (MMPI-2) and the Myers-Briggs Type Indicator (MBTI). These instruments are typically given to individual members of the marital couple and interpreted separately. Information is provided by the publishers of these instruments on how couple profiles may be derived from the individual scores. Please refer to the article mentioned above for further information. Three other instruments commonly used to assess marital and family issues were reviewed that are more systemic in nature and measure relational rather than individual personality issues. These instruments are described in the following sections.

Dyadic Adjustment Scale (DAS). The DAS, developed by Spanier (1976, 1989), is a 32-item self-report assessment that measures the marital adjustment of couples with a total score and scores on four subscales: dyadic consensus, dyadic satisfaction, dyadic cohesion, and affectional expression. Spanier (1976, 1989) reports good reliability and validity for the DAS. The instruments manual are available from Western Psychological Services.

Recent studies used the DAS in combination with several other instruments to: (a) examine the role of family and marital conflict in adolescent functioning (David, Steele, Forehand, & Armistead, 1996), (b) predict the perceived quality of marital adjustment from general to relationship-specific beliefs (DeBord, Romans, & Krieshok, 1996), and (c) determine marital adjustment in parents of children with cancer (Dahlquist, Czyzewski, & Jones, 1996).

Marital Satisfaction Inventory (MSI). The MSI, developed by Snyder (1981), consists of 280 true-false, self-report items on 11 scales: conventionalization (social desirability), global distress, affective communication, problem-solving communication, time together, disagreements about finances, sexual dissatisfaction, role orientation, family history of distress, dissatisfaction with children, and conflict over children. Scheer and Snyder (1984), Snyder (1981), and Snyder, Wills, and

Keiser (1981) report good reliability and validity, including the ability to discriminate between clinical and nonclinical populations. MSI instruments and manual are available from Multi-Health Systems, Inc.

Recent studies used the MSI in combination with other instruments: (a) in a validation study of the Family of Origin Scale (Ryan, Kawash, Fine, & Powel, 1994), (b) to investigate the effects of parenting children with disabilities (Hornby, 1995), and (c) in examining factors of marital satisfaction among African American and Nigerian American couples (Durodoye, 1997).

Child Behavior Checklist (CBCL).   The CBCL is a 118-item parent-report scale designed to measure parents' perceptions of the behavioral problems and symptoms of children ages 4 to 18 (Achenbach, 1991). A Teacher's Report Form and a Youth Self-Report Form are also available. In a family systems approach, requesting the perceptions of parents, teachers, and youths is an important part of the assessment process. A computerized profile as well as the instruments and manual are available from University Associates in Psychiatry, Burlington, VT 05401.

Recent studies attest to the use of the CBCL as well as its reliability and validity (e.g., Macmann, Barnett, & Lopez, 1993). These studies include: (a) identifying children at risk for problem behaviors (Fagot, 1995), (b) comparing the CBCL with the Diagnostic Interview Schedule for Children (Jenson, Watanabe, Richters, & Roper, 1996), and (c) evaluating children with attention-deficit hyperactivity disorder (Wiedenhoff, 1994).

Effective Interventions

The Premarital Relationship Enhancement Program (PREP) was used by Van Widenfelt, Hosman, Schaap, and van der Staak (1996) as a preventive intervention program. The PREP is a cognitive-behaviorally oriented intervention derived from a behavior-competency model of marital success (for a more comprehensive description, refer to Renick, Blumberg, & Markman, 1992). Although the program was originally designed for couples who are marrying for the first time, it is also applicable to remarital couples. Special issues can be incorporated into the treatment that help integrate children from a previous marriage into a new family system (Markman, Floyd, Stanley, & Lewis, 1986).

Cognitive Marital Therapy (CMT) was the treatment used by Waring, Stalker, Carver, and Gitta (1991) in a study of 41 couples with severe marital discord. CMT is a structured, time-limited intervention that includes mutual self-disclosure. The treatment includes a nine-step summary of instructions to marital or family therapists as well as a five-step protocol of things not to do. The *CMT Training Manual* and videotapes of the techniques are available from the authors (Waring et al., 1991).

A study using behavioral marital therapy was designed by Gray-Little, Baucom, and Hamby (1996). The researchers examined the association of marital power type to marital adjustment and response to behavioral marital therapy in distressed couples. Besides receiving behavioral marital therapy, couples received various combinations of emotional expressiveness training and cognitive restructuring. Results indicated that wife-dominant couples improved the most, reporting increased marital satisfaction and demonstrating improved communication.

Kurkowski, Gordon, and Arbuthnot (1993) used a brief educational intervention to reduce the number of times divorced parents put their children in the middle. High school students were given a 32-item questionnaire that contained descriptions of situations in which parents may have put their child in the middle. Letters were sent home to parents stating that they unknowingly put their children in the middle and were advised to reduce the frequency of times these situations occurred. The outcome indicated that students in the intervention group improved more than those in control groups, and an unexpected outcome was their expression of happiness in having been able to sit down and talk as a family.

The Children First Program (CFP) was evaluated by Kramer and Washo (1993). This program was developed to help groups of divorcing parents become more sensitive to their children's needs. Parents attend two 90-minute sessions, conducted one week apart, in which they view videotaped vignettes. Also included in the program is a talk by a local judge and discussions led by a trained moderator. The program was found to have both positive and negative outcomes. On the positive side, parents found the CFP to be helpful and thought it would benefit other divorcing parents. Negative aspects presented themselves at followup—when parents perceived their children to be better adjusted to divorce. Respondents related these findings to the passage of time since marital separation rather than to participation in the program. The study suggested that the CFP may hold greater benefits for parents who report higher levels of conflict with their former spouses.

Another evaluation was conducted by Hughes, Clark, Schaefer-Hernan, and Good (1994) determining the effectiveness of a newsletter intervention for divorced mothers. The intervention consisted of a series of several newsletters that addressed issues identified as important to single mothers immediately following divorce. Each newsletter provided information based on current research knowledge that would help children adjust to the divorce. Specific practical suggestions were given to mothers as well as suggestions for further reading. Results indicated that over half of the participants read the newsletter from cover to cover and reported that they felt more hopeful and confident as a result of reading this material. The authors pose an important challenge to researchers and family life educators to create newsletters that are effective in helping families through this difficult transition.

Dillon and Emery (1996) evaluated the long-term effects of divorce mediation and resolution of child custody disputes. Nine years previous to the study, separated parents were randomly assigned to either a mediation group or to a traditional adversarial group. Results indicated that noncustodial parents assigned to mediation reported having more frequent current contact with their children as well as greater involvement in current decisions about them. Parents in the mediation group also reported more frequent communication about their children during the period since dispute resolution. This study supports a growing trend in the laws that are forcing parents to determine their own custody arrangements, which opens the door to even more divorce and family mediation, an area in which many family social workers are well-trained.

DOMESTIC VIOLENCE

Definition

Compared with other areas of social work, family violence is an extremely young field of study (Finkelhor, Hotaling, & Yllo, 1988) that has primarily investigated the prevalence of the types of family violence, risk factors associated with family violence, and the effects of family violence on its victims. For an excellent review article, the reader is directed to Dwyer, Smokowski, Bricout, and Wodarski (1995). For the purposes of this chapter, domestic violence is the emotional abuse, physical abuse, or both between adult members of a nuclear family or intimate system (Carden, 1994). This definition excludes violence toward elders and children. Other terms in the literature include spouse abuse, intimate violence, and relationship violence (Davis, 1995). There is little common agreement about what constitutes an act of domestic violence. The common thread is reference to an unjust exercise of force by a spouse or partner for the purpose of domination, abuse, or coercion (Dwyer et al., 1995).

Prevalence, Incidence, and Costs

There are startling statistics pertaining to domestic violence. Approximately 95% of victims are women, which means that 3 to 4 million American women are battered each year by husbands and partners, and about 1 in 4 women is likely to be abused by a partner in her lifetime. Domestic violence is the leading cause of injuries to women ages 15 to 44. These figures convert to financial costs to American businesses at the rate of $3 billion to $4 billion a year due to lost time, increased health costs, higher turnover, and low productivity (Glazer, 1993; U.S. Senate Judiciary Committee, 1992).

In the seminal National Family Violence Surveys (Gelles & Straus, 1988; Straus & Gelles, 1986), some kind of spousal violence was found in 16% of the homes in the year prior to the survey, and 28% of the couples reported marital violence at some point in their marriages. Gelles and Straus (1990) estimated that the annual incidence rate of physical assault on a spouse was 161 victims per 1,000 couples in their study of 5,349 couples. The rate of wife beating, defined as one or more violent acts that pose a serious risk of injury, was 34 victims per 1,000 couples or an estimated 1.8 million seriously assaulted wives per year in the United States. Gelles and Straus (1990) argue that their seemingly high estimates are actually low when nonreporting is taken into consideration. Although husband abuse is not particularly uncommon, wife abuse has consistently been found to have more detrimental effects than has husband abuse. In the therapy arena, two thirds of the couples in marital and family therapy engaged in some form of violence in the year prior to treatment (Sexual Assault Support Services, 1996).

The cost of domestic violence is staggering in terms of marital dissatisfaction and psychological and physical health problems (Holtzworth-Munroe & Stuart, 1994). In fact, mental health and nonmedical costs may be greater than the cost of treating physical injuries (Gelles & Straus, 1990). Other costs that must be accounted for include police services, social services, legal services, and imprisonment or another type of institutionalization.

Social Work's Involvement

A social worker is legally obligated to become involved in domestic violence cases. The Code of Ethics, outlined by the National Association of Social Workers, states that social workers are to intervene in cases of abuse or when imminent harm is evident (NASW Code of Ethics, 1995). If a social worker has knowledge of incidents of abuse, he or she is ethically and legally bound to report the abuse to the appropriate authorities. In the event a social worker does not uphold the Code of Ethics, he or she is legally liable for lack of involvement. For a more comprehensive review of the legal issues related to domestic violence, the reader is directed to Saunders (1995).

Assessment Methods

In an article by Aldarondo and Straus (1994), five self-report instruments that assess physical violence in couple relationships were reviewed. An additional self-report instrument found in the literature was the Abusive Behavior Inventory (ABI). These assessments are described in the following sections.

Conflict Tactics Scales.   One of the most widely used assessments is the self-report Conflict Tactics Scales (CTS) developed by Straus (1979, 1990). The CTS has been used in numerous studies involving more than 70,000 participants from diverse cultural backgrounds and in at least 20 countries (Straus, Hamby, Boney-McCoy, & Sugarman, 1996).

Based on conflict theory, the CTS measures both the extent to which partners in a dating, cohabiting, or marital relationship engage in psychological and physical attacks on each other and also their use of reasoning or negotiation to deal with conflicts. The CTS does not measure attitudes about conflict or violence nor the causes and consequences of using different tactics (Straus et al., 1996).

The original CTS had 19 items that represented a total scale and four subscales: minor violence, severe violence, verbal aggression, and reasoning. The CTS has been very recently revised (Straus et al., 1996) to include 39 items that represent five subscales: physical assault, psychological aggression, negotiation (both emotional and cognitive), injury, and sexual coercion. The new version is referred to as the Revised Conflict Tactics Scales (CTS2) and has: (a) additional items to enhance content validity and reliability, (b) revised wording to increase clarity and specificity, (c) better differentiation between minor and severe levels of each scale, (d) new scales to measure sexual coercion and physical injury, and (e) a new format to simplify administration and reduce response sets. According to Straus et al. (1996), permission to reproduce the CTS2 will be granted without charge for research purposes if a researcher agrees to carry out and report psychometric analyses or to provide the authors with the data.

The Index of Spouse Abuse (ISA).   The ISA, developed to quickly measure both physical and nonphysical abuse, consists of 30 items and has good reported reliability and validity (Hudson & McIntosh, 1981). While this assessment provides useful information about the psychological maltreatment of women, it offers limited information concerning physical violence and does not detect minor forms of physical violence (Aldarondo & Straus, 1994). Readers interested in this assessment are directed to Hudson and McIntosh's (1981) article.

A newer version of the assessment, renamed the Partner Abuse Scales, has been developed and measures both physical and nonphysical abuse on the Partner Abuse Scale: Physical (PASPH) and Partner Abuse Scale: Non-physical (PASNP), respectively (Hudson, 1990). Both the PASPH and the PASNP each contain 25 items with 7-point Likert-type scaling. Initial reliability and validity estimates are good, including the ability to discriminate between abused and nonabused women (Attala, Hudson, & McSweeney, 1994).

The Wife Abuse Inventory (WAI).   The WAI, designed to identify both men and women at risk of abuse (Lewis, 1985), asks women to rate their partners and themselves on a number of "family management matters" that primarily focus on causes and consequences of abuse rather than on abusive behavior (Aldarondo & Straus, 1994). Readers interested in this assessment are directed to Lewis's (1985) article.

The Severity of Violence Against Women Scales (SVAWS).   The SVAWS (Marshall, 1992), as the name indicates, were developed to assess the severity of violence against women. Initial factor analysis of this 49-item assessment yielded nine scales: symbolic violence, mild threats, moderate threats, serious threats, minor violence, mild violence, moderate violence, sexual violence, and serious violence (Marshall, 1992). Although the SVAWS are potentially useful to researchers and clinicians, there is presently no information on their validity and reliability (Aldarondo & Straus, 1994). Readers interested in this assessment are directed to Marshall's (1992) article.

The Relationship Conflict Inventory (RCI).   The RCI (Bodin, 1992), developed as part of the efforts of the Task Force on Diagnosis and Classification of the Family, a division of the American Psychological Association, consists of 114 items that measure levels of verbal and physical abuse among couples in treatment. Although the psychometric properties of the RCI are unknown, the RCI should be of interest to systemic family therapists, given the clinical and theoretical basis of its development (Aldarondo & Straus, 1994). The RCI is available from its author, Bodin, at the Mental Research Institute in Palo Alto, California.

The Abusive Behavior Inventory (ABI).   The ABI (Shepard & Campbell, 1992) was developed for the Domestic Abuse Intervention Project (DAIP) because existing assessments such as the CTS did not conceptualize abuse in terms of power and control. The ABI is a 30-item self-report instrument that women complete concerning their partners' behavior 6 months prior to the intervention. According to its authors, initial research suggests that the ABI is a reliable and valid assessment (Shepard, 1993). The ABI is available for duplication as an appendix in Pence and Paymar's (1993) book.

Effective Interventions

According to Yegidis (1992), couple or family therapy is usually useful only when the violent behavior is under control or when the abuser is receiving separate treatment. Once the violence is brought under control (as verified by the victim), couple counseling focuses on replacing mutual dependency with respect, teaching stress and anger management skills, and improving communication. Cognitive restructuring techniques have been found helpful for both abusive husbands and abused wives (Yegidis, 1992).

Many critics contend that conjoint counseling places women at risk of violence. In spite of this criticism, Gelles advocates conjoint therapy. He reported success rates in excess of 90% for couples staying in treatment for a 2-year period (Gelles & Conte, 1990). Yegidis (1992) advocates the use of support groups for all types of family abuse victims, while other scholars (e.g., Dwyer et al., 1995; Edelson & Tolman, 1992) champion the use of an ecological approach.

In 1992, The Family Violence Project of the National Council of Juvenile and Family Court Judges identified 18 "State-of-the Art" programs. Their report describes each program and includes whom to contact for further information. Exemplary comprehensive programs identified were Minneapolis's Domestic Abuse Project, Baltimore's House of Ruth, Cleveland's Templum project, Denver's

Project Safeguard, and Maui's Family Court of the Second Circuit and Alternatives to Violence program. These programs all included (a) services to victims, (b) services to batterers, (c) teamwork with prosecutorial units and law enforcement, (d) coordination of or participation in community response, (e) advocacy to change laws and procedures affecting victims of domestic violence and their children and abusers.

To date, many recently developed domestic violence programs and models have not been empirically evaluated, including developments by Dutton (1992), Edelson & Eisikovits (1996), Jackson and Dilger (1995), Peled, Jaffe, and Edleson, (1995), Pressman and Sheps (1994), and Walker (1994). In a follow-up evaluation of 12 support groups for women victims of domestic assault, Tutty, Bidgood, and Rothery (1993) found significant improvements in self-esteem, belonging support, locus of control, less traditional attitudes toward marriage and the family, perceived stress, and marital functioning. They also found significant decreases in both physical and nonphysical abuse for women currently living with their spouses.

Group Therapy.   Group therapy interventions tend to focus on anger management or anger control. One such intervention was developed by Deschner, McNeil, and Moore (1986) to treat couples by group methods to control anger in order to break battering cycles. The groups, limited to 14 to 16 members, met weekly for 10 weeks for approximately 2½ hours.

The authors note that time out is an appropriate strategy at most phases. An evaluation of the program indicated that it was successful in lowering the number of arguments, decreasing the anger intensity of batterers, and improving marital quality. An overwhelming majority of the couples (over 85%) contacted for follow-up (at both 8-month and 1-year intervals) had avoided further battering (Deschner et al., 1986).

More recently, Pence and Paymer (1993) developed a group education model for men who batter. Referred to as the Duluth Model, or Domestic Abuse Intervention Project (DAIP), both batterers (men) and victims (their partners) participated in weekly educational sessions. To complement their Power and Control Wheel with the spokes of intimidation; emotional abuse; isolation; minimizing, denying, and blaming; children; male privilege; and economic abuse, an Equality Wheel was developed with the spokes of negotiation and fairness, nonthreatening behavior, respect, trust and support, honesty and accountability, responsible parenting, shared responsibility, and economic partnership. The curriculum was developed around these spokes and involves the use of control logs and action plans. As with many intervention programs, DAIP has had short-term effectiveness, but limited long-term success. In later phases of DAIP, both men and women reported lower rates of abuse, and lower rates of abuse were reported at a 1-year follow-up of battered women. In an examination of abusive behavior as documented by police and court records over a 5-year follow-up period, however, 40 out of 100 men were identified as recidivists.

Community Interventions.   A variety of community interventions have evolved to address the problem of domestic violence. One such intervention developed to implement the Illinois Domestic Violence Act is Family Options. This program refers 911 calls involving domestic violence to the Family Options Program. The Family Options team is composed of two social workers, two community advocates, and one lawyer (Caputo & Moynihan, 1986).

The social workers assess a family's problems and identify its needs. The social workers also review service needs, such as job training, substance abuse treatment, and child care, and help a family identify support services that could be obtained through the extended family and community (Caputo & Moynihan, 1986).

The community advocates help victims with the complicated legal process. The community advocates work in conjunction with the assistant state's attorney in helping a victim obtain orders of protection or any other type of order necessary for assistance. The lawyers represent the victims during the actual court proceedings (Caputo & Moynihan, 1986).

Prevention.   Thus far, the empirical evidence shows that there is very little prevention of domestic violence, providing a challenge for family social workers to work with the larger systems (health care, legal, community resources, multimedia, etc.) researching and implementing effective domestic and family violence prevention programs. While not a primary prevention approach, screening for family violence is certainly advisable for all types of therapeutic interventions. There are several factors associated with family violence, including gender, social class, stress, unemployment, history of violence, dependence or jealousy, social isolation, poverty, substance abuse, and mental illness including depression and low self-esteem (Aldarondo & Straus, 1994; Gelles, 1994).

CONCLUSIONS

The purpose of this chapter was to examine the empirical literature concerning family preservation. Included in this chapter were studies that involved empirically based interventions. Certainly, many empirically based, but not clinical, studies of family preservation exist, as do studies of nonempirically based interventions.

Although this chapter has focused on dysfunctional aspects of family life, we conclude by discussing functional aspects of family life. In a recent study by Kaslow and Robinson (1996), 57 couples who had been married between 25 and 46 years reported the following primary reasons for remaining married: (a) the belief that marriage is a partnership for life, (b) love, (c) a sense of responsibility toward the partner, (d) an enjoyment of their established lifestyle and the wish not to change it, (e) religious convictions about the sanctity of marriage, (f) a sense of closeness resulting from shared experiences throughout life, (g) an appreciation of closeness and comfort with each other, and (h) a continuing attraction to the partner. These reasons correlate with the nine basic dimensions of a strong, healthy family developed by family therapists: (a) adaptive ability, (b) commitment to family, (c) communicativeness, (d) encouragement of individuals, (e) expression of appreciation, (f) religious or spiritual orientation, (g) social connectedness, (h) clear roles, and (i) shared time (*Family Therapy News,* 1990, p. 8). Three additional dimensions included in the literature are: (a) clear boundaries, (b) cooperation, and (c) task negotiations (Kaslow & Robinson, 1996).

It seems to us that individuals, therapists, and scholars may take one of two views, pessimistic or optimistic, concerning the future of the American family. Rigorous empirical support for either view is sorely lacking. A person with a pessimistic view focuses on dysfunctional aspects of family life and believes that American families are declining. A person with an optimistic view, on the other hand, focuses on functional aspects of family life and believes that American families are changing. The authors definitely hold an optimistic view of the strength and resiliency of the American family and believe in an unlimited potential for positive growth and change. Which view do you hold concerning the future of the family?

REFERENCES

Achenbach, T. M. (1991). *Manual for the Child Behavior Checklist/4-18 and 1991 Profile.* Burlington, VT: University of Vermont Department of Psychiatry.

Aldarondo, E., & Straus, M. A. (1994). Screening for physical violence is couple therapy: Methodological, practical, and ethical considerations. *Family Process, 33,* 425–439.

American Psychological Association. (1990). *Practitioner Focus, 4,* 7.

Attala, J. M., Hudson, W. W., & McSweeney, M. (1994). A partial validation of two short-form partner abuse scales. *Women & Health, 21*(2/3), 125–139.

Bagarozzi, D. A. (1995). Evaluation, accountability and clinical expertise in managed mental health care: Basic considerations for the practice of family social work. *Journal of Family Social Work, 1(2),* 101–116.

Bodin, A. M. (1992). *Relationship conflict inventory.* Palo Alto, CA: Mental Research Institute.

Boughner, S. R., Hayes, S. F., Bubenzer, D. L., & West, J. D. (1994). Use of standardized assessment instruments by marital and family therapists: A survey. *Journal of Marital and Family Therapy, 20(1).* 69–75.

Bray, J. H., & Jouriles, E. N. (1995). Treatment of marital conflict and prevention of divorce. *Journal of Marital and Family Therapy, 21(4),* 461–473.

Caputo, R. K., & Moynihan, F. M. (1986). Family options: A practice/research model in family violence. *Social Casework, 67,* 460–465.

Carden, A. D. (1994). Wife abuse and the wife abuser. Review and recommendations. *The Counseling Psychologist, 22,* 539–582.

Dahlquist, L. M., Czyzewski, D. I., & Jones, C. L. (1996). Parents of children with cancer: A longitudinal study of emotional distress, coping style, and marital adjustment two and twenty months after diagnosis. *Journal of Pediatric Psychology, 21,* 541–544.

David, C., Steele, R., Forehand, R., & Armistead, L. (1996). The role of family conflict and marital conflict in adolescent functioning. *Journal of Family Violence, 11,* 81–91.

Davis, L. V. (1995). Domestic violence. *Encyclopedia of Social Work, Vol. 1* (19th ed., pp. 780–789). Washington, DC: National Association of Social Workers Press.

DeBord, J., Romans, J. S., & Krieshok, T. (1996). Predicting dyadic adjustment from general and relationship-specific beliefs. *Journal of Psychology, 130,* 263–280.

Deschner, J. P., McNeil, J. S., & Moore, M. G. (1986). A treatment model for batterers. *Social Casework, 67,* 55–60.

Dillon, P. A., & Emery, R. E. (1996). Divorce mediation and resolution of child custody disputes: Long-term effects. *American Journal of Orthopsychiatry, 66,* 131–140.

Durodoye, B. A. (1997). Factors of marital satisfaction among African American and Nigerian male/African American female couples. *Journal of Cross-Cultural Psychology, 28,* 71–80.

Dutton, M. A. (1992). *Empowering and healing the battered woman: A model for assessment and intervention.* New York: Springer.

Dwyer, D. C., Smokowski, P. R., Bricout, J. C., & Wodarski, J. S. (1995). Domestic violence research: Theoretical and practice implications for social work. *Clinical Social Work Journal, 23,* 185–197.

Edelson, J. L., & Eisikovits, Z. C. (1996). *Future interventions with battered women and their families.* Thousand Oaks, CA: Sage.

Edelson, J. L., & Tolman, R. M. (1992). *Intervention for men who batter: An ecological approach.* Newbury Park, CA: Sage.

Fagot, B. I. (1995). Classification of problem behaviors in young children: A comparison of four systems. *Journal of Applied Developmental Psychology, 16,* 95–106.

Family Therapy News. (1990, July/August). Healthy families featured in Washington conference, p. 8.

Finkelhor, D., Hotaling, G. T., & Yllo, K. (1988). *Stopping family violence: Research priorities for the coming decade.* Newbury Park, CA: Sage.

Garrison, M. E. B., & Blalock, L. B. (1996). Intensive family preservation services. *Journal of Prevention & Intervention in the Community, 14,* 101–114.

Gelles, R. J. (1994). Family violence, abuse, and neglect. In P. C. McKenry & S. J. Price (Eds.), *Family and change: Coping with stressful events* (pp. 262–280). Thousand Oaks, CA: Sage.

Gelles, R. J., & Conte, J. R. (1990). Domestic violence and sexual abuse of children. *Journal of Marriage and the Family, 52,* 1045–1058.

Gelles, R. J., & Straus, M. A. (1988). *Intimate violence: The causes and consequences of abuse in the American family.* New York: Simon & Schuster.

Gelles, R. J., & Straus, M. A. (1990). The medical and psychological costs of family violence. In M. A. Straus & R. J. Gelles, *Physical violence in American families: Risk factors and adaptations to violence in 8,145 families* (pp. 425–430). New Brunswick, NJ: Transaction.

Glazer, S. (1993). Violence against women. *CO Researcher, 3,* 171.

Gray-Little, B., Baucom, D. H., & Hamby, S. L. (1996). Marital power, marital adjustment, and therapy outcome. *Journal of Family Psychology, 10,* 292–303.

Holtzworth-Munroe, A., & Stuart, G. L. (1994). Typologies of male batterers: Three subtypes and the differences among them. *Psychological Bulletin, 116,* 376–497.

Hornby, G. (1995). Effects on fathers of children with Down syndrome. *Journal of Child & Family Studies, 4,* 239–255.

Hudson, W. W. (1990). *Partner abuse scales.* Tempe, AZ: Walmyr Publishing Co.

Hudson, W. W., & McIntosh, S. R. (1981). The assessment of spouse abuse: Two quantifiable dimensions. *Journal of Marriage and the Family, 43,* 873–888.

Hughes, R., Clark, C. D., Schaefer-Hernan, & Good, E. S. (1994). An evaluation of a newsletter intervention for divorced mothers. *Family Relations, 43,* 298–304.

Jackson, M., & Dilger, R. (1995). An empowering approach to women's domestic violence groups. *Australian Social Work, 18,* 51–59.

Jenson, P. S., Watanabe, H. K., Richters, J. E., & Roper, M. (1996). Scales, diagnoses, and child psychopathology, II: Comparing the CBCL and the DISC against external validators. *Journal of Abnormal Child Psychology, 24,* 151–168.

Kaslow, F., & Robinson, J. A. (1996). Long-term satisfying marriages: Perceptions of contributing factors. *The American Journal of Family Therapy, 24,* 153–170.

Keresman, M. A., Zarski, J. J., & Garrison, M. E. (in press). An exploration of family environment, adolescent perceptions, and home-based intervention. *Journal of Family Social Work.*

Kramer, L., & Washo, C. A. (1993). Evaluation of a court-mandated prevention program for divorcing parents. *Family Relations, 42,* 179–186.

Kurkowski, K. P., Gordon, D. A., & Arbuthnot, J. (1993). Children caught in the middle: A brief educational intervention for divorced parents. *Journal of Divorce and Remarriage, 20*(3/4), 139–151.

Lewis, B. Y. (1985). The wife abuse inventory: A screening device for identification of abused woman. *Social Work, 30,* 32–35.

Macmann, G. M., Barnett, D. W., & Lopez, E. J. (1993). The Child Behavior Checklist/4-18 and related materials: Reliability and validity of syndromal assessment. *School Psychology Review, 22,* 322–333.

Markman, H. J., Floyd, F. J., Stanley, S. M., & Lewis, H. C. (1986). Prevention. In N. S. Jacobson and A. S. Gurman (Eds.), *Clinical handbook of marital therapy* (pp. 173–195). New York: Guilford Press.

Marshall, L. L. (1992). Development of the Severity of Violence Against Women Scales. *Journal of Family Violence, 7,* 103–121.

NASW Code of Ethics. (1995). Washington DC: NASW Publications.

National Council of Juvenile & Family Court Judges. (1992). *Family violence: State-of-the-art programs.* Reno: National Council of Juvenile & Family Court Judges.

Peled, E., Jaffe, P. G., & Edelson, J. L. (1995). *Ending the cycle of violence: Community responses to children of battered women.* Thousand Oaks, CA: Sage.

Pence, E., & Paymer, M. (1993). *Education groups for men who batter: The Duluth model.* New York: Springer.

Pinsof, W. M., & Wynne, L. C. (1995). The effectiveness and efficacy of marital and family therapy: Introduction to the special issue. *Journal of Marital and Family Therapy, 21*(4), 341–343.

Pressman, B., & Sheps, A. (1994). Treating wife abuse: An integrated model. *International Journal of Group Psychotherapy, 44,* 477–498.

Renick, M. J., Blumberg, S. L., & Markham, H. J. (1992). The Prevention and Relationship Enhancement Program (PREP): An empirically based preventive intervention program for couples. *Family Relations, 41,* 141–147.

Ryan, B. A., Kawash, G. F., Fine, M., & Powel, B. (1994). The Family of Origin Scale: A construct validation study. *Contemporary Family Therapy, 16,* 145–159.

Saunders, D. G. (1995). Domestic violence: Legal issues. *Encyclopedia of Social Work, Vol. 1* (19th ed., pp. 789–795). Washington, DC: National Association of Social Workers Press.

Scheer, N. S., & Snyder, D. K. (1984). Empirical validation of the Marital Satisfaction Inventory in a nonclinical sample. *Journal of Community and Counseling Psychology, 52,* 88–96.

Sexual Assault Support Services. (1996). *Domestic Violence* [On-line]. Available: gladstone.uoregon.edu/service

Shepard, M. (1993). Evaluation of domestic abuse intervention programs. In E. Pence & M. Paymer (Eds.), *Education groups for men who batter: The Duluth model* (pp. 163–168). New York: Springer.

Shepard, M., & Campbell, J. (1992). The abusive behavior inventory: A measure of psychological and physical abuse. *Journal of Interpersonal Violence, 7,* 291–305.

Snyder, D. K. (1981). *Marital Satisfaction Inventory (MSI) manual.* Los Angeles: Western Psychological Services.

Snyder, D. K., Wills, R. M., & Keiser, T. W. (1981). Empirical validation of the marital satisfaction inventory: An actuarial approach. *Journal of Consulting and Clinical Psychology, 49,* 262–268.

Spanier, G. B. (1976). Measuring dyadic adjustment: New scales for assessing the quality of marriage and similar dyads. *Journal of Marriage and the Family, 32,* 15–28.

Spanier, G. B. (1989). *Manual for the dyadic adjustment scale.* North Tonawanda, NY: Multi-Health Systems.

Straus, M. A. (1979). Measuring intrafamily conflict and violence: The Conflict Tactics (CT) Scales. *Journal of Marriage and the Family, 39,* 75–88.

Straus, M. A. (1990). The Conflict Tactics Scale and its critics: An evaluation and new data on validity and reliability. In M. A. Straus & R. J. Gelles, *Physical violence in American families: Risk factors and adaptations to violence in 8,145 families* (pp. 49–73). New Brunswick, NJ: Transaction.

Straus, M. A., & Gelles, R. J. (1986). Societal change and change in family violence from 1975 to 1985 as revealed by two national surveys. *Journal of Marriage and the Family, 48,* 1–15.

Straus, M. A., Hamby, S. L., Boney-McCoy, S., & Sugarman, D. B. (1996). The revised Conflict Tactics Scales (CTS2): Development and preliminary psychometric data. *Journal of Family Issues, 17,* 283–316.

Tutty, L. M., Bidgood, B. A., & Rothery, M. A. (1993). Support groups for battered women: Research on their efficacy. *Journal of Family Violence, 8,* 325–343.

U.S. Bureau of the Census. (1995). Statistical abstract of the United States (115th ed.). Washington, DC: Author.

U.S. Senate Judiciary Committee. (1992). *Violence against women.* Washington, DC: Government Printing Office.

Van Widenfelt, B., Hosman, C., Schaap, C., & van der Staak, C. (1996). The prevention of relationship distress for couples at risk: A controlled evaluation with nine-month and two-year follow-ups. *Family Relations, 45,* 156–165.

Walker, L. E. (1994). *Abused women and survivor therapy: A practical guide for the psychotherapist.* Washington, DC: American Psychological Association.

Waring, E. M., Stalker, C. A., Carver, C. M., & Gitta, M. Z. (1991). Waiting list controlled trial of cognitive marital therapy in severe marital discord. *Journal of Marital and Family Therapy, 17,* 243–256.

Wiedenhoff, A. R. (1994). Use of two behavior rating scales with mothers and teachers in the evaluation of children with attention-deficit hyperactivity disorder. *Dissertation Abstracts Int., 54(10-B), 5415.*

Yegidis, B. L. (1992). Family violence: Contemporary research findings and practice issues. *Community Mental Health Journal, 28,* 519–530.

Chapter 12

THE IMPACT OF RACE IN SOCIAL WORK PRACTICE

Marvin D. Feit
Nuria M. Cuevas
Charlesa A. Hann-Dowdy

Race, those genetically transmitted physical characteristics that lead to the categorization of individuals or groups of people, impacts every aspect of human life. The way in which an individual views the world is related to his or her race in the same way race is related to how others view him or her. Although many significant events have been aimed at improving race relations in this country, preconceived ideas or stereotypes based on race prevail. According to Davis (1978), *prejudice* is the attitude of feelings and behavioral intentions that are unfavorable toward a group or its individual members. *Discrimination* refers to a behavioral response, precipitated by prejudice, that is unfavorable to members of an ethnic or racial group (Brislin, 1981; McLemore, 1983). Both prejudice and discrimination, as a consequence of race, dominate society and, as might be expected, often dramatically affect social work practice. This chapter will examine the impact of racial differences in social work practice.

OVERVIEW

Social work has historically emphasized the importance of diversity in the worker-client relationship. However, most of the recent research in the profession has emphasized the study of other aspects of social work practice. At the same time, disciplines such as psychology and psychiatry have produced research with greater emphasis on relationship factors such as race and gender, on the therapeutic alliance, and on counseling outcomes. Greene, Jensen, and Harper-Jones (1996) indicate that "virtually all therapeutic approaches are equally effective and that the one thing essential to therapeutic success, regardless of theoretical orientation, is a good working relationship between the clinician and the client" (p. 172). Coady (1993) notes that "over the past two decades, the most striking and consistent empirical findings in individual psychotherapeutic research have been the non-significant outcome differences among various therapies" (p. 292).

Empirical evidence indicates that race and gender are key variables that affect the helping relationship and can produce clinician bias. For example, psychiatric evaluations are primarily based on a patient's history, basic personality, and current mental state. According to Wade (1993), the emphasis given to one item of information or the importance attached to an incident is dependent on the beliefs, value judgments, understanding, and knowledge of the psychiatrist. Diagnosis and subsequent care can often be a result of the differences in race, gender, age, and ethnicity between worker and client. In this chapter we focus on race and gender, for they are often the most volatile, with race being a dominant theme in our society.

Other studies have supported the contention that racial bias exists in the assessment and diagnosis of mental illness (Jenkins-Hall & Sacco, 1991; Jones, 1982). For example, some studies indicate that White professionals may misconstrue uncooperative behavior among Latinos as evidence of psychosis (Rendon, 1974; Smith Kline Corporation, 1978). Others suggest that instances of paranoid behavior exhibited by Blacks when interacting with White therapists are indicative of coping behavior exhibited by many African Americans in response to discriminatory life experiences (Pavkov, Lewis, & Lyons, 1989). Jones (1982) found that White therapists generally rated their Black clients as more psychologically impaired than did Black therapists. Furthermore, when diagnosed with psychotic or affective disorders, minority-race clients are more likely to be labeled as having a chronic syndrome than an acute episode (Sata, 1990).

Similarly, the field of psychology has studied race with reference to client-therapist interaction. Carkhuff and Pierce (1967) found that the race and social class of both the patient and the therapist were significantly related to the depth of the patient's self-exploration. Additionally, in the 1970s psychologists began to study the issue of gender stereotyping, in particular, gender stereotypes that determine differential and discriminatory treatment of female and male clients by clinicians.

One aspect of social work practice is based on acknowledging and accepting the phenomenon of difference. Nonetheless, differences between client and social worker race or gender may hinder the working relationship, indicating that these differences must continue to be addressed. Minority-group clients often tend to be less trusting in the helping relationship than nonminority clients. This lack of trust is usually based on lifetime experiences of prejudice, discrimination, and oppression, as well as daily slights, not easily recognized by people from the nonminority segment of society. Historically, people of color have encountered racism in this country based solely on the pigmentation of their skin. The lack of acceptance of difference in skin color has created a society that groups people according to their racial similarities as determined visually. Sager, Brayboy, and Waxenburg (1972) suggest that "this latent reserve of racism, this submerged sense that the black man is 'different,' not governed by the white's warm, human emotions or worthy motivations, is part of our American heritage" (p. 417).

Also of significance to the process and outcome of helping are the genders of the social worker and the client. In the same way that a White worker may be unable to experience the social realities of being Black, Asian, or Native American, a male practitioner may have equal difficulty understanding issues specific to women, such as menopause or miscarriage; likewise, a female worker may have the same difficulty discerning societal pressures placed upon a man.

Despite the underlying value in social work that encourages respect for diversity, little empirical data is available in this field regarding the impact of variables such as the race and the gender of the client and the worker on the helping process. One reason for the limited amount of empirical evidence with regard to race may be the difficulty with its definition. If race is treated as an independent variable, many problems arise. For example, since race can't be manipulated, its viability as an independent variable is extremely limited. Unlike gender, race is not a dichotomous variable that can be placed into mutually exclusive categories. Additionally, race is subject to an individual's self-classification. Finally, the concept of race is often intertwined with the concepts of culture, ethnicity, and social class. Hayes-Bautista et al. (1992) note that *minority* is a policy construct, and Montes, Eng, and Braithwaite (1995) note:

> Through sociopolitical fiat, our society has set the boundaries for defining minority groups and how they are to participate in this society. . . . The implication for minority health is that it is not being born into a minority group that is a risk factor, it is being a member of a minority group in this society. (p. 248)

For these reasons, race as a research category compromises the objectivity of scientific inquiry.

Despite having limited value as an independent variable and a scientific concept, race has extremely important social connotations (Applebome, 1995; Dinero, 1996; Wheeler, 1995). Since differences are noticeable and people are treated differently based on noticeable differences, one must acknowledge that the practical aspects of race and gender cannot be ignored. A major concern is how differences between the race and gender of the social worker and the race and gender of the client might impact the client-worker relationship and the outcome of the helping process. Some of the questions to consider are: To what extent can demographic factors affect the outcome of intervention? What is the combined effect of race and gender and do they elicit preconceived impressions (stereotypes) that may affect the client-worker relationship?

Our purpose is to determine the extent to which empirical research on race, that which is based on observation and study, can produce guidelines for social work practice. We define race as those genetically transmitted physical characteristics or features that lead to the categorization of individuals or groups of people based on these distinguishable physical characteristics or features. There appears to be an inherent need of society to clump all people with similar features and characteristics into one group. Any deviation of features or characteristics prescribed to one group causes confusion in society's classification of race. For example, let us consider a fair-skinned, light-eyed Black person. The fair skin and light eyes could lead society to the racial categorization of White. If this same individual happens to be biracial, that is he or she has parents of two different races, the classification becomes even more difficult for society. Indeed, it raises serious questions about the reliability of public health vital statistics (Hahn, 1992; Hahn, Mullinare, & Teutsch, 1992).

Historically, mainstream society has been supported by law in justifying classification of race based on bloodlines. However, in our era of liberalism, particularly in the social work profession, race is much more subject to an individual's self-classification. The field of child welfare asks biracial children or their parents to identify the race of the child. Additionally, biracial children are often forced to self-classify their race as they conform to peer pressure and identity formation.

In contrast, gender is a much easier variable to define. It is those biological physical traits that enable one to classify an individual into a mutually exclusive category of male or female. Gender also affects perceptions and behaviors, and it is important to learn how worker and client differences might affect the social work helping process. Such research leads to insight on methods to improve the effectiveness of the worker with clients of different genders and races.

ASSESSMENT METHODS

Research indicates that demographic factors affect the outcomes of the helping process. Members of ethnic groups are particularly distinguishable by characteristics such as race, skin color, and language. At the point of initial contact, both worker and client are making impressions of one another based upon these distinguishable characteristics. Additionally, both the worker and the client are bringing their own values, beliefs, and preconceived ideas to the initial encounter.

In their article "Fear of Black Strangers," St. John and Heald-Moore (1995) pose this question: "Do public encounters with black strangers evoke more fear than public encounters with white strangers?" St. John and Heald-Moore use the factorial survey method to examine how fearful survey respondents would be of encounters with persons of different combinations of age, race, and gender in a variety of contexts. A sample of 416 respondents was randomly chosen from the R. L. Polk Directory for Oklahoma City. Each of the respondents was asked to evaluate five vignettes in which characteristics of persons encountered and the contexts in which encounters took place were randomly assigned. Respondents were then asked to rate their levels of fear on a 4-point scale, from *not afraid* to *extremely afraid*. Their findings indicate that White encounters with Black strangers evoke more fear than White encounters with White strangers independent of the age and gender of the persons encountered, the contexts in which the encounters take place, and the ages and genders of the persons experiencing the encounters. The combined additive effects of the races, ages, and genders of the strangers encountered indicate that Whites are most fearful of Black males in their late teens or early twenties. Further, it made no difference to Whites if the Black strangers were encountered in safe or fearful contexts.

Baldwin and Hopkins (1990) conducted preliminary research focused on developing a scale designed to discriminate between African American and European American subjects on differences in basic cultural worldview. The authors initiated a research program intended to explore the development of a cross-cultural instrument for assessing cultural differences based on the worldview paradigm. An assessment called the Worldview Scale was developed empirically from a larger pool of worldview items. In its development, the Worldview Scale was first administered to 34 Black and 34 White college students, who were asked to respond to each statement as quickly and honestly as they could. Each item was then analyzed. The overwhelming majority of Whites responded in the Eurocentric direction, while the majority of Blacks responded in the Africentric direction. The results yielded a 26-item scale to be used in a pilot study.

The pilot study was implemented in the same manner. The scale was administered to 94 Black students attending the same university used in the preliminary testing (a predominantly Black school) and 87 White students from the predominantly White university used in the preliminary testing. Both groups comprised males and females between ages 17 and 52. The Black group consisted of 29 males and 65 females, while the White group contained 28 males and 59 females. The larger number of subjects were between ages 17 and 24. Seven Black and four White female subjects were in their 30s, one Black and two White subjects were in their 40s, and one White subject was 52 years of age.

The results indicate that a different worldview and cultural orientation exists between African Americans and European Americans. Black respondents' Worldview Scale scores tended to reflect a distinct African American worldview orientation, while White students' scores reflected the distinct Eurocentric worldview orientation. According to Baldwin (1985), a European American worldview is characterized by "humanity versus nature" and "survival of the fittest" assumptions. The thrust of these principles is toward achieving mastery and control over nature. Thus survival entails gaining control over, dominating, suppressing, and altering the natural arrangements of objects. Those who exhibit the greatest dominance over nature are those most fit to survive. In contrast, the basic assumption underlying the African American worldview is the notion of "oneness or harmony with nature" and "survival of the group." These principles emphasize a striving to maintain a *complementary coexistence* with the universe and prioritizing the maintenance or survival of the group as a whole versus that of the individual (p. 42).

With this in mind, we ask if an individual's perception of the world affects his or her perception of a problem? If so, how is the problem identified and defined in the helping process when the worker is White and the client is from a minority group? According to its principles, the European American worldview is in direct opposition to the African American worldview. Can a non-minority-group person who has been taught the value of competition and survival of the fittest relate to the value of teamwork and survival of the group in the African American worldview? Often, minority-group clients view this competitive, superior attitude of the European American orientation with mistrust.

Watkins, Terrell, Miller, and Terrell, (1989) examined the effects of cultural mistrust on African Americans' expectations about counselor credibility and competence. Specifically, they were interested in the effects of cultural mistrust on (a) subjects' perceptions of the counselor's credibility, (b) subjects' perceived confidence in the counselor to help them solve four problem areas of anxiety, shyness, inferiority feelings, and dating difficulties, and (c) subjects' perceived willingness to return for a follow-up visit to the counselor.

Using a $2 \times 2 \times 2$ (subject sex $\times$ subject mistrust level $\times$ counselor race) factorial design, 60 Black male and 60 Black female undergraduate students were administered six different questionnaires and scales over a 2-week period. Based on data gathered in the first sessions, participants were divided into groups according to their levels of mistrust (high or low) for the second set of scales.

The results were that highly mistrustful Blacks viewed White counselors as less credible and less likely to be able to help them with the four problem areas of anxiety, shyness, feelings of inferiority, and dating difficulties. The four problems focus primarily on self-definition and relationship issues that highly mistrustful Black students may have real difficulty in discussing with a White counselor, thereby being unable to maximally use the counseling relationship.

Several studies have been done on the influences of race on the psychotherapeutic relationship, with special emphasis on premature termination (Griffith, 1977; Proctor & Rosen, 1981, Terrell & Terrell, 1984). Findings indicate that Black clients who have been assigned to White counselors are more likely to terminate counseling prematurely than White clients.

Davis, Strube and Li Chin Cheng, (1996) suggest that racism appears to affect men more than women. In their experimental research design, they assigned 120 undergraduate college students to 4-person, same-sex groups with varying racial compositions: 1 Black and 3 Whites, 2 Blacks and 2 Whites, and 3 Blacks and 1 White. Each group was given decision-making tasks to perform. Later, individual members of the groups were interviewed by Davis and Strube to gather information on the individual's satisfaction with group performance, confidence in group decisions, and willingness to work with the group in the future. The findings indicate that men had the most difficulty working in groups with equal numbers of Blacks and Whites. Women appeared able to reach a resolution without negative conflict.

EFFECTIVE SOCIAL WORK INTERVENTIONS

Most of the literature addressing race as a factor in the therapeutic relationship focuses upon the White therapist–Black client relationship, neglecting to recognize other minority or ethnic groups. Racial and ethnic differences between the helping professional and the client are factors that create problems in the relationship of all minority-group clients, not just Black clients. Race continues to have a significant impact on relationships—both personal and professional. Despite the apparent progress of the last three decades, serious racial problems and inequities remain as we approach the next century. In addition, minority-group populations are increasing faster than the White American population. During the 1980s the African American population grew by 13%, the Native American population by 38%, the Hispanic population by 53%, and the Asian population by 107% (Barringer, 1991). With this growth in racial diversity, it is likely that racial differences between helping professionals and clients will intensify and will be addressed as a matter of necessity.

Lum (1996) asserts that minority-group clients often approach formal, professional social service organizations with varying degrees of skepticism, caution, and resistance. They have usually exhausted all other resources for help when they enter a social service organization (Redhorse, Lewis, Feit, & Decker, 1978). People from minority groups tend to be much more reluctant to approach human service agencies that are controlled and dominated by Whites. Lum suggests that social workers must overcome the resistance of clients from racial and ethnic minority groups that is caused by general mistrust of White-dominated systems by establishing trust on an individual level. Social workers who are prejudiced, inexperienced, or inadequately trained may tacitly accept racist attitudes by unconsciously condoning stereotypes of minority-group clients. Given this possibility, it becomes crucial that the social work profession address these and other differences at the onset of service to the client. The social workers must be willing to examine their own racial attitudes and values, as well as be willing and able to address differences between themselves and their clients.

In her book, *Black Families in Therapy,* Boyd-Franklin (1989) states that "race is a lens through which many black people view the world, and by extension the therapist, be she or he black or white" (p. 96). Boyd-Franklin illustrates that every Black client or family will check out the social worker (whether Black or White) in terms of appearance, race, skin color, clothing, perceived social class, language, and a range of more subtle clues such as warmth, genuineness, respect for the client, willingness to hear the client's side, patronizing attitudes, condescension, judgments, and human connectedness (p. 96). Race is likewise a lens through which many therapists (often unconsciously) view Black families. A therapist's values and perceptions have significant impact on his or her frame of reference and work as a therapist.

Boyd-Franklin suggests it is imperative that the social workers and therapists explore their own cultural identities, family values, beliefs, and prejudices before beginning work with clients who are different from themselves. Being a supporter of the Bowenian school of family therapy, she suggests that therapists begin by exploring their own families of origin. It is in the family of origin that an individual learns values and beliefs. As the family member has increasing interaction with the environment outside of the family of origin, these values and beliefs are challenged. Over time, the family member rejects and abandons some family-of-origin values and beliefs, but accepts and maintains others. Clinicians should examine which parts of their own family cultures they have accepted and rejected.

Boyd-Franklin further advises that cultural sensitivity training should incorporate the therapist's sharing of his or her own family genogram. She suggests that the sharing occur in a group setting or in supervision. This practice facilitates two ends: (a) the sharing of personal and family values and (b) the developing of the concept that there is no such thing as *the* Black family, *the* Jewish family, *the* Irish, Hispanic, or Asian Family. *All* families have similar life experiences; the difference is in how *the* family lives the experiences.

Mizio (1972) suggests that, because White social workers have never experienced the deprivations and injustices that minority-group clients have faced and continue to face, they may unconsciously withdraw from the pain of gaining intimate knowledge of the minority-group client's life. Mizio believes that, unless White social workers can "accept the ugliness of racism without being overwhelmed by guilt," they cannot help minority-group clients (p. 84). This acceptance of the ugliness of racism requires that social workers understand clients' behavioral manifestations of the effects of racism, which may be directed at them. Anger and resentment about the impacts of racism may be displaced on White social workers because they are from a nonminority group and have been spared the ugliness of racism. The anger and resentment are no more personal toward social workers than the acts of racism were the social workers' personal actions. However, because White social workers have not had the same life experiences with regard to race, it becomes imperative that they have the ability to connect to the feelings of those associated with racism. Although social workers cannot abolish the clients' anger and resentment, they can help them to constructively channel the anger so that clients are able to obtain what they want or need for themselves or their group.

Kadushin (1972) further supports Mizio's thoughts by asking: "How can the white worker imagine what it is like for the black client to live day after day in a society that grudgingly, half-heartedly, and belatedly accords him the self-respect, dignity and acceptance that are his right as a person or, more often, refuses outright to grant them to him? How can the worker know what it is like to live on intimate terms with early rejection, discrimination, harassment, and exploitation?" (p. 88). Kadushin also acknowledges that the relaxed atmosphere and comfortable interaction needed for a good interview are hampered when the Black client "feels accusatory and hostile as the oppressed and the white worker feels anxious and guilty about his complicity with the oppressor" (p. 89).

Psychotherapy, the practice of using the therapeutic relationship between the client and the practitioner to resolve client symptoms or problems, recognizes that cultural variables may affect an individual's ability or willingness to establish a therapeutic relationship. In general, the issue of matching clients and treatment techniques to enhance the likelihood of obtaining desired outcomes has received extensive discussion and widespread endorsement in psychotherapy (Szapocznik, Scopetta, Aranalde, & Kurtines, 1978). Paul (1969) has argued that the psychotherapy outcome research should focus on ascertaining which treatment by whom is most effective for a person with specific characteristics and problems in a particular set of circumstances.

Szapocznik, Scopetta, Aranalde, and Kurtines (1978) conducted a study based on the assumption that to develop therapeutic models that will effectively attract and maintain clients in therapy, the clients' cultural backgrounds must be understood. The study used a Value Orientation Scale similar to the work of Kluckhohn and Strottbeck to contrast cultural differences between Cuban immigrants and Anglo Americans. The scale was administered to 325 subjects, including 120 (37%) males and 205 (63%) females, 220 (67.7%) Cuban immigrants, 65 (20%) Anglo Americans, 12 (3.7%) non-Cuban Latinos, and 28 (8.6%) Black Americans.

The results were that Cubans tended to prefer lineality, subjugation to nature, and present time, and not to endorse idealized humanistic values; whereas, the Anglo Americans tended to prefer individuality, mastery over nature, and future time, and to endorse idealized humanistic values. Based on these findings, the authors suggest that these values be taken into consideration when designing psychosocial service-delivery systems for different groups. The social worker or therapist must validate the Cuban immigrant's preference for lineality by recognizing that his or her role is perceived by the client as a position of authority. Therefore, the therapist should assume responsibility and take charge of the therapist-client relationship. However, the social worker or therapist must recognize that the Cuban client will adhere to naturally occurring hierarchical systems (the family, teachers, probation officers, etc.) that should be enlisted in the treatment process of the client. Szapocznik et al. (1978) state that it is the breakdown of the lineal structural relational patterns within the family that contribute to instances of dysfunction in young Cuban clients. They further support this concept by citing clinical experience that suggests that desired therapeutic outcomes are reached most expediently by restoring the lineal-hierarchical relational structure in the family.

Additionally, the therapist should consider Cubans' sensitivity to environmental social pressures, particularly high levels of need for approval. The present study found that Cuban clients tend to perceive themselves as unable to control or modify their environmental circumstances. When environmental pressures or tensions seem to be a source of client dysfunction, ecological therapeutic interventions aimed at restructuring the interactions of the clients with their environments are necessary.

Finally, treatment of the Cuban client should be here-and-now or present oriented. The Cuban client usually approaches treatment as the result of the onset of a crisis and expects the therapist to provide immediate problem-oriented solutions to the problem(s). The culturally sensitive social worker or therapist must develop a treatment model that utilizes crises to promote growth and reorganize interpersonal relations. Treatment models that emphasize history or are past oriented do not jibe with the Cuban value structure.

Psychotherapy as an intervention with Asian clients is possible if some adjustments to the technique are used. Several authors (Chang & Kim, 1973; Hsu & Tseng, 1972; Kinzie, 1981; Lambo, 1974; Santopietro, 1981) suggest that the traditional Western-culture orientation of psychotherapy must be transformed for use with Asians. Psychological intervention is not accepted within this group and defies many of its cultural values. Therapists working with Asian clients must be aware of cultural values and of ways to work with them, rather than against them. For instance, because many families do not believe in psychiatry, Carlin and Sokoloff (1985) suggest that it is helpful to begin as a teacher when working with them. Asian culture tends to emphasize the wisdom and status of elders or those in positions of authority. Therefore, the therapist is viewed as such and should exhibit this in the therapeutic relationship. The therapist is expected to take charge of decision making and not expect the client to think or act independently—as this defies the Asian value of interdependence. Additionally, a therapist should recognize that emotional expression by the client to the therapist (a stranger) is rare.

The practitioner should also have an understanding of what a client believes in, will fight for, and will cherish. It is necessary for the therapist to develop a knowledge of the client's personal values if he or she is to develop a client-centered treatment approach. This perspective is consistent with the focus that practitioners must have when working with any client.

With the Asian population, preference is given to medication over just talking. In fact, it is often for psychosomatic reasons that an Asian seeks help. It is much more acceptable within the culture to seek help for physical ailments than for mental or emotional concerns. Asian medical concepts, although differing among the various ethnic groups, tend to be influenced by Chinese culture. Chinese tradition emphasizes a theory of disease caused by an imbalance of cosmic forces—yin and yang. Chinese medicine, holistic in its approach, focuses on function rather than structure of the body and is preoccupied with the restoration of balances (Lin, 1980; Singer, 1976). Additionally, there is a folk tradition in which illness, particularly mental illness, may result from an offense against deities or spirits (Kinzie, 1985). Mental or emotional illness of one member of the family attracts attitudes of fear, rejection, and ridicule directed at the entire family. Therefore, developing somatic disorders may be a more effective and legitimate way to request help.

Despite more willingness to seek medical attention and a preference for medication over talk therapy, many Asian clients have not been compliant with medication treatment. Kinzie (1985) found that a typical pattern is for patients to stop the medicine soon after they have shown some improvement. When checking blood levels of 35 patients who were being treated with antidepressant medicine, he found that almost two thirds were simply not taking their medication at all or were doing so on such a sporadic basis as to have nondetectable levels (p. 124).

In his book, *Ethnicity in Social Group Work Practice,* Davis (1984), draws attention to the fact that by the year 2000 approximately 30% of the population of the United States will be from non-White minority groups (p. 3). This likelihood, combined with a corresponding disproportionate growth in their need for public social services and a relative decline in resources to hire persons to deliver services to those in need, requires that social workers be trained to work effectively in small groups.

Nakao and Lum (1977) report that Asian American psychotherapists prefer to see their clients in individual psychotherapy rather than in group therapy. Some psychotherapists feel that the individual approach is less threatening to an Asian American who has enough difficulty talking about problems to one stranger, let alone several. However, Chu and Sue (1984) suggest that group work may be quite beneficial to Asian Americans. The client who values interdependence and cooperation may gain much from the strength and support of the group. The group may resemble the family, as all members work collectively to solve one member's problems. The extent to which the therapist identifies with Asian American values will reflect his or her approach regarding treatment. Additionally, the extent to which the therapist is able to tune in to the client's cultural values will significantly affect the client's compliance with treatment.

At times, a group can be less threatening than individual psychotherapy. In individual psychotherapy, all of the therapist's attention is directed to the client and the client may feel pressure to interact with the therapist. In the group setting, the client chooses to interact with the practitioner and chooses what problems and feelings to share. Therefore, Asian clients, who may be reluctant to talk about family members in ways that imply disrespect, are likely to prefer being group members.

When describing the Asian Pacific American population, it is important to be cautious about making generalizations. It is a population comprising many different ethnic groups. Various groups within the Asian population have similarities to and differences from other groups within the population. With this in mind, group work with people of common backgrounds would be most effective.

Similarly, within the Latino and Hispanic population there are diverse groups with differing characteristics. Over the past two decades, studies concerning the use of group work practice with Mexican Americans and Puerto Ricans have been conducted. Hynes and Werbin (1977) found group practice to be successful in helping patients deal with loneliness and severe somatic distresses when county transportation was used to bring Spanish-speaking clients to the group. Herrera and Sanchez (1976) reported successful use of a behavioral group approach in the treatment of Spanish-speaking Mexican American men and women. Levine and Padilla (1980) reported favorable results in a number of studies reviewed on group counseling with Hispanic children, adolescents, and young adults.

Comas-Diaz's (1981) experimental study of a control group, a cognitive therapy group, and a behavior therapy group represents one of the few empirically designed group work studies with Hispanics. This study found that low-income Puerto Rican women who participated in either cognitive group therapy or behavior group therapy showed significant reductions in depression compared to the control group that received no treatment. There were no significant differences found between the behavior and cognitive group approach. Fernandez-Pol (1978), in her empirical research, found that Puerto Ricans of lower socioeconomic classes who adhered to Latin American family values had less psychopathology than Puerto Ricans who were more acculturated.

Based on their clinical experience and on a review of the efforts of others, Acosta and Yamamoto (1984) suggest that group work practice with Hispanic Americans could be beneficial. However, they recommend some issues to be considered before inviting the Hispanic American to a group. First, the therapist should consider client characteristics such as sex, socioeconomic status, and level of acculturation. Second, consideration should be given to the client's diagnosis, personality characteristics, and treatment needs to assure the best possible fit between the client and the group. The authors' clinical experiences validate the effectiveness of providing early educational explanations to Hispanic American clients about the group work process. In addition, it has further proven to be an advantage to provide short-term group treatment and to encourage clients to make a commitment to their own progress.

Native American culture has traditionally focused on a variety of group activities involving families, clans, and tribal groups. Ritual ceremonies and rites of passage are celebrated in some tribal groups with extended family and friends. Many of these activities are similar, but again, we must recognize that each individual tribal group is unique.

Very few empirical data are available on the use of group work practice with Native Americans. Edwards, Edwards, Daines, and Eddy (1978) conducted a study with young Native American girls on the development of social skills in the group setting. This experience proved to be rewarding for the young women who participated in the group and for all members of their families who participated in some of their group activities.

Edwards and Edwards (1984) suggest that there are several types of groups that can be utilized with Native Americans. Educational groups could be beneficial at various levels, including assertiveness training, adult education, and skills development training. Therapy groups addressing drug and alcohol problems and social, behavioral, and personal problems could also be effectively utilized. Women's groups and men's groups could address some of the current issues relevant to Native American women and men, such as parenting issues, the development of cultural and tribal identity, and intertribal or mixed marriages. Task groups can be helpful in addressing issues related to unemployment, housing for the aged or handicapped, and provision of appropriate role models for Native American children.

Although many Native American people prefer to work with Native American social workers, many non-Indian social workers have enjoyed success in their social work interventions with Native Americans (Edwards & Edwards, 1984). It is important to understand the values of each individual Native American client and each individual tribal group. Family ties, bonds, and expectations vary considerably among the various tribal groups in the United States. Tribal customs and preference for native language or the English language also depend upon the individual tribe. Therefore, it becomes necessary for the social worker to study the values, customs, and traditions of the tribal group with whom he or she will be working prior to beginning work with the Native American.

Brown (1984) used the small group as a medium of intervention with low-income Black youths in a junior high setting. Using the reciprocal model of Schwartz, Brown developed and implemented a group to address the issues of poor grades, negative attitudes toward school, defiance of authority, and suspicion of drugs and truancy. Occurring racial and ethnic confrontations were also an issue of concern. Brown's group experience demonstrated that the small group can be beneficial to Blacks and that self-concepts, social competencies, and psychosocial-educational skills can be enhanced with this population through the use of the small group. Additionally, this group experience provided some practice wisdom and insights that Brown thinks are applicable to group work with Blacks in general. Among them are: (a) the need to view and evaluate members' behavior in light of their experiences in American society; (b) the use of action-oriented techniques; (c) a focus on enhancing self-concepts, improving coping skills, and gaining a sense of empowerment; (d) the need for the group social worker to be comfortable with self-disclosure; and (e) the need of the social worker to be prepared for testing and challenging by the group before the relationship is established.

Boyd-Franklin (1989) suggests a multisystems approach to working with Black families and couples. She contends that structural family therapy provides a comprehensive model of intervention with Black families that can be effectively employed in combination with other approaches. The problem-solving aspect of the structural approach makes it particularly useful in working with Black families in that it is focused, clear, concrete, and directive. For multiproblem families who feel powerless to change their lives, this approach can help the family to identify and prioritize its problems and provides a sense of empowerment and accomplishment as problem resolution is achieved. This approach also assists in engagement of the family as it emphasizes improving the current situation rather than focusing on the past, which can be intrusive and can interfere with the development of a relationship between the family and the social worker.

Boyd-Franklin identifies the Bowenian model as the second approach applicable to Black families. This approach has two primary aspects that make it particularly useful in working with Black families: (a) It provides strategies for exploring extended family dynamics, and (b) It provides a theoretical framework that can be useful in developing hypotheses about family dynamics. Boyd-Franklin suggests that the structural approach be utilized initially with the family to establish credibility of the worker by helping to resolve a problem. Then, in the middle phase of the intervention process, the Bowenian approach can be used to learn the real structure of the family.

Finally, Boyd-Franklin suggests that paradoxical, strategic, and systemic approaches can be used effectively with Black families when incorporated into an overall multisystems approach. She does advise that these approaches be used cautiously and with planning.

Szapocznik (1995) states that structural family therapy has been validated as a strategy to use in the prevention, early intervention, and treatment of behavior problems, including substance abuse and other behavior-related problems. Pioneered by a team of Hispanic and Latino professionals working with inner-city Puerto Rican and African American families in the late 1960s, structural family therapy was adopted by the Spanish Family Guidance Center in 1975 as an effective approach to be used by the center. Since 1975, the center has conducted important research and demonstration projects showing the effectiveness of the approach with Cubans and non-Cuban Hispanics in the Miami area. This approach has been widely used with Hispanic and Latino families throughout the United States and Puerto Rico. The basic concepts focus on the kinds of family interactions that encourage, permit, or maintain undesirable behaviors. Family empowerment is facilitated by giving families the skills to interact in new, successful ways to bring about the desired outcome(s).

COMMUNITY AND PREVENTION

Programa Mama, a community-based outreach model for addicted Hispanic and Latino women, seeks to intervene with women who use drugs during pregnancy. Although the project has identified specific strategies to use with Hispanic and Latino women, it was developed for racially and ethnically diverse populations and is an important model for working with addicted women and communities of color. Programa Mama, in affiliation with Boston City Hospital, assists women in initiating and successfully continuing the process of recovery from addiction by addressing the existing barriers to care. The program teaches women how to access services and supports engagement with drug treatment, prenatal care, and other needed services. The intervention consists of: (a) community outreach, (b) case management, referral, and advocacy, (c) health education and recovery support groups, (d) parenting skills enhancement, and (e) concrete support services such as transportation, child care, food, and clothing.

Intervention, whether individual, family, or community-directed, should serve as one form of a solution to social problems, but by no means the only problem resolution activity. Osborne and Feit (1992) provide empirical evidence on the importance of using race in medical research with correlation to social and economic considerations. Considerable thought and planning should be given to preventing the problem from occurring initially. Price and Smith (1985) indicate that if primary prevention programs are to take their place in the array of services at the local level, research and evaluation efforts are needed, not only to demonstrate program effectiveness, but to continually improve the ability to research underserved populations. Silverman (1985) proposes that, whether the focus of the primary prevention activity is reactive or proactive, it is essential that it be characterized by "specific actions directed at specific populations for specific purposes" (p. 174).

This brings us back to the notion that, whether emphasizing prevention or intervention, it is essential that social work approaches focus on the diversity of people. Proctor and Davis (1994) illustrate how the racially dissimilar social worker and client approach each other with little understanding of and with unfounded assumptions about each other. In their article, "The Challenge of Racial Difference: Skills for Clinical Practice," the authors validate that challenges to the helping relationship do exist based upon racial differences between the social worker and the client. However, there is no evidence that suggests that racial dissimilarity impairs treatment outcome (Davis & Proctor, 1989). In fact, there is supporting evidence that experienced, sensitive, and skilled practitioners can work effectively with racially dissimilar clients (Proctor & Davis, 1994).

It is critical to note that Davis and Proctor found no evidence that racial dissimilarity impairs treatment outcome. Additional research to confirm this finding is needed, as many anecdotal observations suggest otherwise. For example, it seems logical that social workers who are not able to communicate that they understand a good deal of the emotional impact of racism will have erected barriers to effective helping. While racial dissimilarity may not make it possible to fully understand a client's experience, it is very likely that social workers who demonstrate they are making a solid effort to understand that experience and its impact on clients create a climate for effective helping. Indeed, this is the type of supporting evidence Proctor and Davis note, which is consistent with being an experienced, sensitive, and skilled practitioner.

Proctor and Davis suggest some guidelines for practice with racially dissimilar clients. First, practitioners should recognize that racial stresses are rooted in society and that they should critically examine their own exposure to minority communities and cultures. When their own exposure is limited, social workers should be informed, they should be exposed to other ethnic cultures and histories, and they should be comfortable with difference. Furthermore, the social worker has the responsibility of acquiring skills to enhance client comfort, to foster trust, to convey understanding, to communicate professional competence, and to express caring and goodwill.

Social workers must move beyond the levels of construct, such as working with White families, Asian families, Native American families, or African American families, and they must learn to partialize situations into the present context—for example, to understand the extent to which a family is typical of the group it appears to represent. Baldwin and Hopkins (1990) suggest that there is a specific African American worldview orientation and a contrasting European American worldview orientation. However, this is not to assume that all White families behave in a manner that is stereotypical of the Eurocentric worldview or that all African Americans behave according to the stereotypically Africentric worldview orientation. As Boyd-Franklin (1989) illustrated previously, individual family members will pick and choose which family values, traditions, behaviors, and culture they want to maintain and which they will discard or replace. The task for the social worker is to understand which pieces of the culture the family has maintained and which pieces are stereotypically insensitive to the family. Only then is the worker considered to be culturally sensitive and practicing from a culturally specific perspective.

Lopez et al. (1989) propose a developmental model to teach cultural sensitivity to student therapists. In a seminar setting, doctoral counseling or clinical psychology students were asked to keep weekly journals describing how they considered cultural issues in their clinical practice. The weekly journal assignment proved to be beneficially stimulating in addressing many complex cultural issues. From these discussions came the idea that students were proceeding in stages as they increased their cultural sensitivity. Lopez et al. identify the stages as such: Stage 1 is an unawareness of cultural issues; Stage 2 is a heightened awareness of culture; Stage 3 is the burden of considering cultural issues; and Stage 4 is moving toward the integration of culture in a student's clinical work. The authors propose that these stages allow therapists to understand how to develop this sensitivity. Accordingly, these stages can be used to monitor the progress of clinicians learning how to provide culturally sensitive psychotherapy.

The issue of race in social work practice and research continues to be perplexing and volatile. Racial dissimilarity is a normative occurance in social work practice, reflecting that of society, yet there are few empirically based research efforts that provide guidelines for professional practice. There is evidence that a willingness to openly address issues in racial and cultural diversity provides the basis for treatment outcomes that do not adversely affect the quality of intervention.

REFERENCES

Acosta, F. X., & Yamamoto, J. (1984). The utility of group work practice for Hispanic Americans. In L. Davis (Ed.), *Ethnicity in social group work practice* (pp. 63–73). New York: Haworth Press.

Applebome, P. (1995, February 20). Scientists call race irrelevant. *The Beacon Journal,* pp. A1, A4.

Baldwin, J. A. (1985). Psychological aspects of European cosmology in American society. *The Western Journal of Black Studies, 9*(4), 216–223.

Baldwin, J. A., & Hopkins, R. (1990). African-American and European-American cultural differences as assessed by the worldviews paradigm: An empirical analysis. *The Western Journal of Black Studies, 14*(1), 38–52.

Barringer, F. (1991, March). Census shows profound change in racial makeup of the nation: Shift toward minorities since 1980 is sharpest. *The New York Times,* A-1, A-8.

Boyd-Franklin, N. (1989). *Black families in therapy: A multisystems approach.* New York: Guilford Press.

Brislin, R. W. (1981). *Cross-cultural encounters: Face-to-face interaction.* New York: Pergamon Press.

Brown, J. (1984). Group work with low-income Black youths. In L. Davis (Ed.), *Ethnicity in social group work practice* (pp. 111–124). New York: Haworth Press.

Carkhuff, R. R., & Pierce, R. (1967). Differential effects of therapist race and social class upon patient depth of self-exploration in the initial clinical interview. *Journal of Consulting Psychology, 31,* 632–634.

Carlin, J., & Sokoloff, B. (1985). Mental health treatment issues for Southeast Asian refugee children. In T. C. Owan (Ed.), *Southeast Asian mental health: Treatment, prevention, services, training, and research* (pp. 91–112). Rockville, MD: National Institute of Mental Health.

Chang, S. C., & Kim, K. (1973). Psychiatry in South Korea. *American Journal of Psychiatry, 130,* 667–669.

Chu, J., & Sue, S. (1984). Asian/Pacific-Americans and group practice. In L. Davis (Ed.), *Ethnicity in group work practice* (pp. 23–36). New York: Haworth Press.

Coady, N. (1993, May). The worker-client relationship revisited. *Families in Society: The Journal of Contemporary Human Services,* pp. 292–297.

Comas-Diaz, L. (1981). Effects of cognitive and behavioral group treatment on the depressive symptomatology of Puerto Rican women. *Journal of Consulting and Clinical Psychology, 49,* 627–632.

Davis, F. J. (1978). *Minority-dominant relations: A sociological analysis.* Arlington Heights, IL: AHM Publishing.

Davis, L. (Ed.). (1984). *Ethnicity in social group work practice.* New York: Haworth Press.

Davis, L., & Proctor, E. (1989). *Race, gender, and class: Guidelines for practice with individuals, families, and groups.* Englewood Cliffs, NJ: Prentice Hall.

Davis, L., Strube, M. J., & Li Chin Cheng. (1996, September). Differential effects of racial composition on male and female groups: Implications for group work practice. *Social Work Research, 20*(3), 157–166.

Dinero, T. E. (1996). Selected practical problems in health and social research. *Journal of Health and Social Policy, 8*(1), 1–7.

Edwards, E. D., & Edwards, M. E. (1984). Group work practice with American Indians. In L. Davis, (Ed.), *Ethnicity in social group work practice* (pp. 7–21). New York: Haworth Press.

Edwards, E. D., Edwards, M. E., Daines, G. M., & Eddy, F. (1978). Enhancing self-concept and identification with "Indianness" of American Indian girls. *Social Work with Groups, 1*(3), 309–318.

Fernandez-Pol, B. (1980). Culture and psychopathology: A study of Puerto Ricans. *American Journal of Psychiatry, 137*(6), 724–726.

Greene, G., Jensen, C., & Harper-Jones, D. (1996, March). A constructivist perspective on clinical social work with ethnically diverse clients. *Social Work, 41*(2), 172–180.

Griffith, M. (1977, February). The influences of race on the psychotherapeutic relationship. *Psychiatry, 40,* 27–40.

Hahn, R. A. (1992). The state of federal health statistics on racial and ethnic groups. *Journal of the American Medical Association, 267*(2), 268–271.

Hahn, R. A., Mulinare, J., & Teutsch, S. M. (1992). Inconsistencies in coding of race and ethnicity between birth and death in infants. *Journal of the American Medical Association, 267*(2), 259–263.

Hayes-Bautista, D., et al. (1992). *No longer a minority: Latinos and social policy in California, 1940 to 1990.* Los Angeles: UCLA Chicano Studies Research Center.

Herrera, A. E., & Sanchez, V. (1976). Behaviorally oriented group therapy: A successful application in the treatment of low-income Spanish-speaking clients. In M. R. Miranda (Ed.), *Psychotherapy with the Spanish-speaking: Issues in research and service delivery (73-84).* Monograph 3. Los Angeles: Spanish Speaking Mental Health Research Center, University of California.

Hsu, J., & Tseng, W. (1972). Intercultural psychotherapy. *Archives of General Psychiatry, 27,* 700–706.

Hynes, K., & Werbin, J. (1977). Group psychotherapy for Spanish-speaking women. *Psychiatrics Annals, 7,* 622–627.

Jenkins-Hall, K., & Sacco, W. P. (1991). Effect of client race and depression on evaluations by white therapists. *Journal of Social and Clinical Psychology, 10,* 322–333.

Jones, E. E. (1982). Psychotherapists' impressions of treatment outcome as a function of race. *Journal of Clinical Psychology, 38,* 722–731.

Kadushin, A. (1972, May). The racial factor in the interview. *Social Work,* pp. 88–98.

Kinzie, J. D. (1981). Evaluation and psychotherapy of Indochinese refugee patients. *American Journal of Psychotherapy, 35,* 251–261.

Kinzie, J. D. (1985). Overview of clinical issues in the treatment of Southeast Asian refugees. In T. C. Owan (Ed.), *Southeast Asian mental health: Treatment, prevention, services, training, and research* (pp. 113–135). Rockville, MD: National Institute of Mental Health.

Lambo, T. A. (1974). Psychotherapy in Africa. *Psychotherapy and Psychosomatics, 24,* 311–326.

Lin, K. M. (1980). Traditional chinese medical beliefs and their relevance for mental illness and psychiatry. In A. Kleinman & T. Y. Lin (Eds.), *Normal and abnormal behavior in Chinese culture.* Dordrecht, Holland: D. Reidel.

Levine, E. S., & Padilla, A. M. (1980). *Crossing cultures in therapy: Pluralistic counseling for the Hispanic.* Monterey, CA: Brooks/Cole.

Lopez, S. R., Grover, K. P., Holland, D., Johnson, M., Kain, C., Kanel, K., Mellins, C. A., & Rhyne, M. C. (1989). Development of culturally sensitive psychotherapists. *Professional Psychology: Research and Practice, 20*(6), 369–376.

Lum, D. (1996). *Social work practice with people of color: A process stage approach* (3rd ed.). Pacific Grove, CA: Brooks/Cole.

McLemore, S. D. (1983). *Racial and ethnic relations in America.* Boston: Allyn & Bacon.

Mizio, E. (1972, May). White worker-minority client. *Social Work,* pp. 82–86.

Montes, J. H., Eng, & Braithwaite, R. L. (1995, March/April). A commentary on minority health as a paradigm shift in the United States. *American Journal of Health Promotion, 9*(4), 247–250.

Nakao, S., & Lum, C. (1977). *Yellow is not white and white is not right: Counseling techniques for Japanese and Chinese clients.* Unpublished master's thesis, University of California, Los Angeles.

Osborne, N. G., & Feit, M. D. (1992). The use of race in medical research. *Journal of the American Medical Association, 267*(2), 275–279.

Paul, G. L. (1969). Behavior modification research: Design and tactics. In C. M. Franks (Ed.), *Behavior therapy: Appraisal and status.* New York: McGraw-Hill.

Pavkov, T., Lewis, D., & Lyons, J. (1989). Psychiatric diagnoses and racial bias: An empirical investigation. *Professional Psychology: Research and Practice, 20*(6), 364–368.

Price, R. H., & Smith, S. (1985). *A guide to evaluating prevention programs in mental health.* Washington, DC: Superintendent of Documents, U.S. Government Printing Office.

Proctor, E., & Davis, L. (1994, May). The challenge of racial difference: Skills for clinical practice. *Social Work, 39*(3), 314–323.

Proctor, E., & Rosen, A. (1981). Expectations and preferences for counselor race and their relation to intermediate treatment outcomes. *Journal of Counseling Psychology, 28*(1), 40–46.

Redhorse, J. G., Lewis, R., Feit, M. D., & Decker, J. (1978, February). Family behavior of urban American Indians. *Social Casework, 59*(2), 67–72.

Rendon, M. (1974). Transcultural aspects of Puerto Rican mental illness. *International Journal of Social Psychiatry, 20,* 297–309.

Sager, C. J., Brayboy, T. L., & Waxenburg, B. R. (1972). Black patient–white therapist. *American Journal of Orthopsychiatry, 42,* 415–423.

Sata, L. (1990, April). *Working with persons from Asian backgrounds.* Paper presented at the Cross-Cultural Psychotherapy Conference, Hahnemann University, Philadelphia.

Santopietro, M. C. S. (1981). Indochina moves to Main Street: How to get through to a refugee patient. *RN, 44*(1), 43–48.

Silverman, M. (1985). Preventive intervention research: A new beginning. In T. C. Owan (Ed.), *Southeast Asian mental health: Treatment, prevention, services, training, and research* (pp. 169–181). Rockville, MD: National Institute of Mental Health.

Singer, K. (1976). Cross-cultural dynamics in psychotherapy. In J. H. Masseman (Ed.), *Social Psychiatry, Vol. III. The range of normal in human behavior.* New York: Grune & Stratton.

Smith Kline Corporation. (1978). *Cultural issues in contemporary psychiatry: The Asian-American.* Philadelphia: Author.

St. John, C., & Heald-Moore, T. (1995). Fear of Black strangers. *Social Science Research, 24,* 262–280.

Szapocznik, J. (1995). Structural family therapy. In J. Szapocznik (Ed.), *A Hispanic/Latino family approach to substance abuse prevention* (pp. 41–74). U.S. Department of Health and Human Services.

Szapocznik, J., Scopetta, A., Aranalde, M., & Kurtines, W. (1978). Cuban value structure: Treatment implications. *Journal of Counseling and Clinical Psychology, 46*(5), 961–970.

Terrell, F., & Terrell, S. (1984). Race of counselor, client sex, cultural mistrust level, and premature termination from counseling among Black clients. *Journal of Counseling Psychology, 31*(3), 371–375.

Wade, J. C. (1993, October). Institutional racism: An analysis of the mental health system. *American Journal of Orthopsychiatry, 63*(4), 536–544.

Watkins, E., Terrell, F., Miller, F., & Terrell, S. (1989). Cultural mistrust and its effects on expectational variables in Black client–white counselor relationships. *Journal of Counseling Psychology, 36,* 447–450.

Wheeler, D. L. (1995). A growing number of scientists reject the concept of race. *The Chronicle of Higher Education 4, 1*(23), A8–A9, A15.

Chapter 13

PRACTICE APPROACHES WITH OLDER CLIENTS

Nancy P. Kropf
Sherry Cummings
Bhuvana Sukumar

OVERVIEW

Since the turn of the last century, the increase in the number of older adults has been dramatic. In the early 1900s, when the current cohort of elders was born, only 5% of the population was over the age of 65 (*Aging America,* 1991). Today, there are more than 33 million people over the age of 65 in the United States, which represents 12.7% of the total population (U.S. Bureau of the Census, 1996). The trend toward an increasingly older population is expected to continue, as a greater number of adults live into late life. Because of their multiple needs that often include medical, social, and financial assistance, social work practitioners in all service settings can expect to work with greater numbers of older adults in coming years.

This chapter will provide an overview of empirical practice approaches with older adults. Due to the diversity of practice issues in work with older clients, various approaches focus on different practice outcomes. Certain interventions have prevention objectives, with goals of keeping older adults as physically, socially, and psychologically healthy as possible. Other intervention approaches are remedial, with the goal of restoring functioning after the onset of a certain type of problematic condition (e.g., death of spouse, onset of chronic health problem). Finally, some approaches provide support in progressive and irreversible situations such as dementia care or terminal illness. Intervention approaches discussed in this chapter are practice with individual clients, groups and families of older adults, and community prevention programs.

ASSESSMENT METHODS

Due to the number of different treatment programs for older adults, numerous assessment methods and instruments are found in outcome research with these clients. While some of the instruments used in assessment are specifically constructed for use with an older population (e.g., the Geriatric Depression Scale), the majority are used with adults of various age groups. This section will summarize assessment procedures by outcome, organized in the categories of health and physical functioning, psychiatric conditions, and social functioning and well-being.

Health and Physical Functioning

Overall physical functioning of older adults is commonly measured by the Physical Activities of Daily Living (Duke University, 1978), which measures an older adult's level of functioning across several physical domains. This instrument can be administered to older adults or their care providers, or observational assessment can be performed by a rater. Physical health status has been measured by several self-report instruments. These include the Sickness Impact Profile (Bergner, Bobbitt, Carter, & Gilson, 1981) and the Perceived Health Questionnaire (Pfeiffer, 1976), both of which measure the impact of health conditions on an individual.

For specific health problems, self-reports tend to be used. These methods include sleep or headache journals that calculate the incidence of a condition over the course of a specified time period. Entries may also include the perceived severity or duration of the condition.

In sleep disorders, polysomnography (PSG) is also used. A PSG rates brain wave activities, respiration, and limb movement. These assessments are performed in a sleep laboratory and evaluated by an experienced technician.

Psychiatric Conditions

The two most common psychiatric conditions that are included in outcome studies of older adults are depression and anxiety. Numerous instruments have been used to measure both diagnostic conditions, the majority of which are self-ratings scales or indexes. A listing of the instruments that were used in the research studies included in this chapter are presented in Table 13.1.

Social Functioning

Several measures have also been used to assess areas of social competence with older adults. Many use self-report methods that measure a dimension of social

Table 13.1   Measurement of Depression and Anxiety

Depression	
Instrument	Reference
Beck Depression Inventory	Beck, Ward, Mendelson, Mock, & Erbaugh, 1971
Epidemiological Studies Depression Scale	Radloff, 1977
Geriatric Depression Scale	Yesavage et al., 1983
Hamilton Depression Scale	Hamilton, 1967
Schedule for Affective Disorders and Schizophrenia	Endicott & Spitzer, 1978
Wakefield Self-Rating Depression Scale	Snaith, Ahmed, Mehta, & Hamilton, 1971
Zung Depression Scale	Zung, 1965
Anxiety	
Instrument	Reference
Affective Adjective Checklist Anxiety Index	Zuckerman and Lubin, 1960
Beck Anxiety Inventory	Beck, Epstein, Brown & Steer, 1988
Hamilton Anxiety Scale	Hamilton, 1959
Spielberger Self-Evaluation Questionnaire	Spielberger, Gorsuch, & Lushene, 1967
State Trait Anxiety Inventory	Spielberger, Gorsuch, Luchene, 1970

connection or quality of life. Table 13.2 lists those instruments that have been included in the research reported in this chapter.

Other competencies are measured by certain types of outcome conditions as a result of participating in a treatment protocol or training situation. Examples of these measures are higher degree of knowledge about a certain subject (e.g., late-life alcoholism, accident prevention) or obtaining a particular outcome such as securing a job.

Table 13.2   Measures of Social Functioning

Dimension	Instrument	Reference
Coping	Folkman & Lazarus Ways of Coping	Folkman & Lazarus, 1980
	Health Specific Family Coping Index	Choi, LaVohn, & Christensen, 1983
	Revised Ways of Coping Scale	Vitaliano, Russo, Carr, Maiuro & Becker, 1985
Life Satisfaction	Life Satisfaction Index	Neugarten, Havighurst, & Tobin, 1961
Loneliness	UCLA Loneliness Scale	Russell, Peplau, & Ferguson, 1978
Morale	Philadelphia Geriatric Center Morale Scale	Lawton, 1975
Stress	Perceived Stress Scale	Cohen, Kamarck, & Mermelstein, 1983
Well-being	Bradburn's Affect Balance Scale	Bradburn, 1969

EFFECTIVE SOCIAL WORK INTERVENTIONS

Interventions with Older Individuals

As people age, they often experience some type of physical health problem. Psychosocial interventions are used to help older clients in relieving health symptoms or increasing positive health behaviors. Psychiatric concerns are also areas for intervention, especially depression and anxiety. (Chronic mental illness in older adults, including dementia, will be specifically covered in another chapter.) In addition, older clients may face difficulties in adjusting to new environments, such as moving into a nursing home facility.

Health Conditions. One health problem that affects older adults is chronic headache. A study of 14 older adults (mean age $M = 66.7$ years) who suffered from migraine or tension headaches combined cognitive therapy with biofeedback and relaxation training to reduce pain (Nicholson & Blanchard, 1993). Each participant attended twelve 90-minute sessions. Cognitive therapy included instruction and practice of techniques to reduce stress and increase problem-solving abilities. Headache activity was measured by a daily diary in which each participant scored headache activities four times per day (0 = *no headache* to 5 = *incapacitating headache*). At the conclusion of the treatment, 50% of the sample achieved clinically significant reductions in headache activities.

A second health-related area involves sleep disturbances. Unfortunately, sleep disorders are commonly treated by medications, which can cause problems for older adults, including dependence, drug interactions, and increased potential for falls. In order to alleviate certain potentially harmful consequences, a sample of older adults ($n = 7$, $M = 61.9$ years) with insomnia was treated individually with relaxation therapy (4 weeks duration, then discontinued) followed by cognitive-behavioral therapy for 4 weeks (Edinger, Hoelscher, Marsh, Lipper, & Ionescu-Pioggia, 1992). Outcomes included objective measures such as number of awakenings, total sleep time, and time in bed, and subjective measures included perception of sleep difficulty and sleep quality. The findings indicated that relaxation therapy had little effect on either objective or subjective sleep outcomes. However, cognitive-behavioral therapy produced significant positive changes in sleep patterns. Furthermore, these gains were maintained at 3-month posttreatment.

In another study, however, relaxation was effective in treating sleep disorders. In a single-subject study, a 73-year-old female with intermittent insomnia was taught relaxation techniques to decrease experiences of nocturnal awakenings (Piercy & Lohr, 1989). Awakening was operationalized as an instance when the client was unable to return to sleep after a 15-minute interval. The client underwent a training protocol that lasted for 6 weeks. During the relaxation training, scores decreased and indicated clinical significance in diminishing nocturnal awakenings.

Depression and Anxiety.   Other studies have investigated outcomes of interventions on psychiatric conditions of older clients. In research on depression, one study compared three treatment modalities (cognitive, behavioral, brief psychodynamic) on depressive episodes (Gallagher-Thompson, Hanley-Peterson, & Thompson, 1990). Ninety-one older adults (M = 67.07 years) were randomly assigned to one of three treatment groups or a delay treatment group (6 weeks before starting therapy). All participants received 16 to 20 individual therapy sessions over four months. Data were gathered at 3, 6, 12, 18, and 24 months. At the conclusion of therapy, 52% of the sample were no longer clinically depressed using the Schedule for Affective Disorders and Schizophrenia (SADS) Change interview. There were not significant differences by modality. By 2-years posttreatment, 70% of the participants were not clinically depressed, with no differences by treatment group.

Cognitive-behavioral treatment has been found to be effective with anxiety in older clients. In a study using 10 older adults (M = 73 years), the participants were involved in individual therapy sessions (mean number of sessions = 8) to relieve panic and phobic symptoms (King & Barrowclough, 1991). The intervention consisted of cognitive restructuring, controlled breathing training, and educational information about panic responses. Anxiety was measured by the Beck Anxiety Inventory (BAI) and self-report data on frequency and intensity of panic symptoms. The subjective data showed significant decline at 3- and 6-month posttreatment (p = .002). While not significant, scores on the BAI were in the direction of symptom reduction.

A desensitization approach was successful in treating a dog phobia of a 70-year-old woman (Thyer, 1981). The woman had two harmful encounters with large dogs (an attack and an incident in which she fell), which resulted in a phobia that prevented her from walking in her neighborhood. The client engaged in five sessions with a therapist who gradually exposed her to anxiety-evoking stimuli, beginning with exposure to a small dog. By the last session, the client was exposed to two large dogs without significant anxiety. Telephone contact at 3 and 6 months after termination determined that the client remained symptom free.

A study of older hospitalized patients evaluated reminiscence in decreasing preoperative anxiety (Rybarczyk & Auerbach, 1990). In this research, 104 men (M = 65.7 years) in a Veterans Administration hospital were assigned one of three situations: a reminiscence interview in which they recounted past life events, a present-focused interview in which they discussed events of their present life, or a no-treatment situation. Both types of interviews lasted about 60 minutes. The research included two outcome measures: anxiety, measured by the State-Trait Anxiety Inventory (STAI), and coping, measured by the Coping Self-Efficacy Inventory developed specifically for this research. The pretest was performed in the morning of the interview, and posttest data were collected the same evening. The patients who received reminiscence interviews had significantly lower anxiety scores at posttest than the other two groups ($p < .001$). Additionally, reminiscence patients had higher coping scores than did the other groups ($p < .001$).

Adjustment Disorders.   Adjustment difficulties of older adults have also been successfully treated with cognitive-behavioral approaches. Rapp et al. (1989) report a single-subject design (A-B-A-B) to decrease helpless behavior in an older aphasic male residing in a nursing home. Social contingencies were changed to increase his participation in his physical and occupational therapy regime. The therapists instituted a social praise program in which he was reinforced for completing his therapy regime within a specific time frame. By the end of the intervention, the resident had increased his participation in physical therapy (measured in number of minutes of treatment) by 23% and occupational therapy by 56.5% (measured by number of times attending sessions).

Cognitive-behavioral therapy has also been used to enhance functioning in an acute care setting (Lopez & Mermelstein, 1995). Patients who were at risk for poor recovery participated in individual therapy sessions ($n = 21$, $M = 70$ years). "At risk" was defined as being depressed (measured by the Center for Epidemiological Studies Depression Scale), anxious (measured by the Profile of Mood States), stressed (measured by the Perceived Stress Scale), or having poor coping skills (measured by the Folkman and Lazarus Coping Scale and the Revised Ways of Coping Scale). All participants met with their therapists about three or four times per week, for 30 minutes each session. At discharge, the participants' levels of depression and avoidance had decreased significantly.

Adjustment difficulties of elders in community settings have also been evaluated. In one outcome study, 52 elders of limited mobility were randomly assigned to one of three treatment protocols: a 6-week life review program, an equivalent number of "friendly visits," or neither intervention (Haight, 1992). The mean age of the sample was 76 years and all participants were receiving homebound services such as in-home meals. The study included the four outcome measures of life satisfaction measured by the Life Satisfaction Index, well-being measured by Bradburn's Affect Balance Scale, depression operationalized by the Zung Depression Scale, and the Activities of Daily Living Inventory. After 8 weeks, the participants who received life review showed significant gains on life satisfaction and well-being. Retesting after 1 year revealed that these participants continued to improve in life satisfaction, while the individuals who received the other treatment protocols remained the same.

Group Therapies

Group work is a common modality in the treatment of the elderly. Just as the elderly are a heterogeneous population, so are the groups that address their needs. While many elderly are healthy and seek to remain active in their postretirement years, others struggle with physical and cognitive disabilities, medical illness, and loss. In response, a large variety of groups have been developed and are currently used to address the challenges faced by the elderly and their family members. The following section will highlight those studies that utilized more rigorous research designs or those that demonstrated potential for creatively meeting elders' needs through a group modality.

Medical and Functional Disabilities.   An 8-week structured group to address the management of chronic pain was developed and tested by Subramanian (1991). The purpose of the group was to reduce participants' ($n = 32$, $M = 62$) subjective perception of pain and increase their physical and psychosocial functioning in spite of the actual presence of pain. Participants were randomly assigned to cognitive behavioral treatment groups or to a wait-list group. The cognitive behavioral groups, ranging in size from 5 to 7 members, met weekly for 2 hours over a period of 8 weeks. Treatment groups incorporated relaxation training, cognitive restructuring, and social skills training. The Sickness Impact Profile and the Profile of Mood States were used to measure the impact of this treatment. Results showed that at posttest the treatment group improved significantly on measures of physical and psychosocial functioning and on mood status compared to the wait-list group and to pretest measures.

A cognitive-behavioral group approach was also utilized for the treatment of late-life insomnia. Morin, Kowatch, Barry, and Walton (1993) randomly assigned 24 community-dwelling elders ($M = 67$ years) to a group treatment or to a wait-list control group. All participants had struggled with insomnia for an average of 13 years. The group treatment included a behavioral component (sleep restriction and stimulus control), a cognitive component (altering dysfunctional beliefs about sleep and the impact of sleep loss), and an educational component about food, nutrition, and exercise. Participants met weekly in groups of 4 to 6 persons for 8 weeks, in 90-minute sessions. Polysomnography, sleep diaries, ratings by significant others and by the patients, and psychological measures such as the Beck Depression Scale (BDI), the Profile of Mood States, and the State-Trait Anxiety Scale were utilized to measure partipants' pre- and posttest functioning. Those subjects participating in the cognitive-behavioral groups showed a significant decrease in the amount of awake time after sleep and greater sleep efficiency when compared to the control group. These improvements were maintained at 3- and 12-month follow-ups.

Evans and colleagues tested the efficacy of telephone group therapy for disabled community elders. In separate studies, legally blind veterans (Evans & Jaureguy, 1982) and physically disabled outpatients (Evans, Smith, Werkhoven, Fox, & Pritzl, 1986) were randomly assigned to cognitive-behavioral telephone groups or to a control group condition. The average age of participants in the studies was 61.7 years and 62.4 years, respectively. In both studies, the treatment groups focused on the development of behavioral goals, goal achievement, the use of positive reinforcement, and problem solving. Three participants and a telephone counselor participated in group telephone therapy 1 hour a week for 8 weeks. Before the designated appointment time, group participants were called and placed on the same trunk line so that a group discussion could follow. The Wakefield Self-Rating Depression Scale, the Ellsworth Personal Assessment of Role Skills (Ellsworth, 1975), the UCLA Loneliness Scale, and the Life Satisfaction Index were all used to measure treatment efficacy. Both studies revealed a significant decrease in loneliness. While there was also a decrease in depression, this did not reach a significant level.

Depression and Anxiety.   A variety of group methods are utilized to treat community-dwelling elders who suffer from depression and anxiety. Most of the studies focusing on this topic have utilized a cognitive-behavioral approach. A research project conducted by Steuer et al. (1984) examined the impact of both cognitive-behavioral and psychodynamically oriented groups. Noninstitutionalized elders, ($M = 66$ years), who had suffered from depression for 2 months to 15 years, were randomly assigned to cognitive-behavioral groups or to psychodynamic group psychotherapy. The former groups used cognitive and behavioral strategies to change behavior and modes of thinking. Techniques included the use of weekly activity schedules, mastery and pleasure logs, the recording and examination of cognitive distortions, and the generation of new ways of perceiving life. The latter groups were based on psychoanalytic concepts such as insight, transference, and resistance. All groups met twice a week for 10 weeks and then once a week for 26 weeks for a total of 46 sessions over a period of 9 months. Each session lasted 90 minutes. The Hamilton Depression Scale, the Hamilton Anxiety Scale, the Zung Self-Rating Depression Scale, and the BDI were administered as pretests and then again at 4, 8, 12, 26, and 36 weeks. Results revealed that participants in both types of group treatment experienced a significant decline in depression and anxiety across time.

Beutler et al. (1987) compared the impact of treating depressed elders with group cognitive therapy, with medication (alprazolam), and with a combination of the two. Elders assigned to cognitive therapy groups met for 90 minutes per week for a period of 20 weeks. Some of the elders in the therapy groups also received the medication, while others did not. Elders not in group treatment received either medication only or medication and support. Depression, using the Hamilton Rating Scale for Depression and the BDI, cognitive distortions using the Cognitive Error Questionnaire (Beck, Rush, Shaw, & Emery, 1979), and sleep efficiency based on polysomnographic recordings were all measured at pre- and posttest periods. A significant decrease in depression was found for all cognitive therapy groups, regardless of medication status. However, no significant change was revealed for those who received medication but did not participate in the therapy groups.

DeBerry, Davis, and Reinhard (1989) found that a relaxation-meditation group was effective in decreasing anxiety. Participants in a relaxation-meditation group received progressive relaxation combined with meditative imagery. A second treatment group received cognitive restructuring and assertiveness training, while a third group received no treatment and served as a control Thirty-two participants ($M = 68.9$ years) met in treatment groups or a control group twice weekly for 10 weeks. The results of this study indicate that relaxation-meditation group treatment is effective in reducing anxiety. No significant change was found for the cognitive restructuring or control groups.

Studies have also explored the efficacy of group treatment for depressed nursing home residents. Hussian and Lawrence (1981) tested the relative impact of problem-solving groups, social reinforcement of activity groups, and a group combination of the two. Group treatments were relatively brief, lasting for five sessions, 30 minutes per session, over a 2-week period. Participants in the problem-solving groups were taught problem definition and formulation, generation of alternatives, and decision-making skills. Those in the social reinforcement groups received reinforcement from staff for attendance, participation, and interaction. The BDI was used to measure participants' levels of depression at pretest, after the first and second weeks of treatment, and at a 3-month follow-up. After 2 weeks, the problem-solving groups evidenced a significant decline in depression when compared with both of the other groups. However, the effects did not last posttreatment. At the 3-month follow-up, no significant difference was found between groups.

Dhooper, Green, Huff, and Austin-Murphy (1993) also utilized a group problem-solving approach in the treatment of depressed nursing home residents. Sixteen depressed, cognitively intact residents ($M = 77.6$ years) were randomly assigned to a treatment or a control group. A combination of problem-solving and reminiscence was used in the treatment group to counteract social isolation and increase participants' ability to cope with nursing home life. Groups met once a week over a 9-week period. Depression was measured through the administration of the Zung Depression Scale at pre- and posttest intervals. A significant difference was found in the depression levels of the problem-solving group when compared with the control group.

Quality of Life of Healthy Community-Dwelling Elders.

A variety of groups have emerged to meet the needs and enhance the lives of community-dwelling elders. While the goals and techniques utilized by these groups vary, the assumptions of such groups are based on the belief in elders' capacity for continued learning, growth, and development. Lopez and Silber (1991) developed and tested a group treatment designed to increase elders' ability to deal with stressful situations in their lives. Thirty-nine elders ($M = 72$ years) were recruited from the community and randomly assigned to a stress inoculation group, an information/control group, or a no-treatment control condition. Participants assigned to the group conditions received training 2 hours per week over a 6-week period. Those in the stress inoculation group received information on and skill-building training in stress relaxation techniques, which were rehearsed through role plays and imagery. Those in the information/control group were provided with information but did not receive training. Elders assigned to all conditions completed a Perceived Health Questionnaire, the Affective Adjective Checklist Anxiety Scale, the STAI, and an Acquisition Test developed by the authors to measure the participant's ability to cope with stress. Those in the stress inoculation group performed significantly better on the Acquisition Test and showed a significant decline in anxiety when compared to those in the control groups. No difference in perceived health was found among the groups.

Effectiveness of mutual aid mental health groups designed for isolated, low-income elderly were tested by Rosen and Rosen (1982). A purposive sample of elders was recruited to participate in the mutual aid groups, non–mental health comparison groups (elders who were not in at-risk conditions), and control group composed of at-risk elders. The average age of the 117 participating seniors was 70 years. The mental health mutual aid groups were held in senior centers and met once a week for 12 to 15 months. The groups focused on issues of loss and isolation, emphasized commonalities, and encouraged participants to remain in contact with one another between sessions. Measures of social isolation, activity, and morale, adapted from the Older American Resource and Service (OARS) Multi Dimensional Functional Assessment were administered as pre- and posttests. Evidence of social, physical, and psychological functioning was gathered before and after the treatment by means of in-depth interviews with the participants. Those in the mental health groups experienced a significant increase in perceived health and a decrease in loneliness when compared to the control group. The level of functioning of the mental health treatment group increased to a level comparable to that of the non–mental health comparison group at posttest.

Groups for well-functioning older adults were developed to increase problem-solving skills (Zgliczynski, 1982). Volunteers at senior centers were randomly assigned to multimodal behavioral therapy (MBT) groups or to a wait-list control group. The MBT groups met once a week for 75 minutes over an 8-week period. Problem identification, specification, and -solving skills were demonstrated and applied to participants' particular concerns. The Philadelphia Geriatric Center Morale Scale and a Problem Checklist designed for the study were administered at pre- and posttest intervals. Results revealed that MBT group participants experienced a significant decline in the number of problems and a significant gain in morale when compared with control group members.

Another area of concern for some older adults is regaining employment after a job loss. Rife and Belcher (1994) evaluated a Job Club program to assist older workers ($n = 52$, $M = 58$ years) in regaining employment. The participants were randomly assigned to the Job Club group ($n = 26$) or the control group ($n = 26$), which was served by the state government job service and community referral program. The Job Club ran workshops on job search topics specifically targeted toward older adults, including skill-building activities such as goal setting, interviewing, writing résumés, and completing employment applications. Participants in the control group received services that are regularly available in the community for unemployed persons. They were interviewed 1 week before receiving services and at the end of 4, 8, and 12 weeks of participation. Results indicated that participants in the Job Club intervention group had a significantly higher employment rate, a higher job retention rate, a higher income, and more hours of work than those in the control group.

Older Family Members.   Over the past two decades there has been growing recognition of the unique dynamics present in late-life families. While all families undergo change related to members' aging processes, most studies have focused on those families struggling with caregiving responsibilities. In a recent study, Mittelman et al. (1995) tested the impact of multimodal treatment on the depression levels of caregivers who provided care for moderately to severely impaired spouses. Participants were randomly assigned to either a treatment group or a control group condition. Those in the treatment group received two individual and four family counseling sessions within 4 months of entrance into the program. After the completion of the counseling sessions, participants took regular part in support group meetings. In addition, those in the treatment group were provided with informal consultation with family counselors. Those in the control group received resource information upon request but no formal counseling or intervention. The Geriatric Depression Scale was used to measure caregivers' depression levels prior to treatment and at 4-, 8-, and 12-month intervals. Results demonstrated that caregivers in the treatment group reported decreased levels of depression, which occurred initially at the 8-month period.

Chiverton and Caine (1989) also explored the effectiveness of group treatment to assist caregiving spouses. Forty spouses ($M = 71$ years) of patients with Alzheimer's disease were randomly assigned to an educational group or a control group condition. The educational groups comprised 3 to 6 spouses and met for three sessions over a 3- to 4-week period. The 2-hour sessions consisted of didactic material followed by group discussion. Information about the disease process, changing roles and responsibilities, communication skills, behavioral management techniques, and available resources was presented and discussed. The Health Specific Family Coping Index for Non-Institutional Care was used to measure caregivers' psychosocial and physical health problems prior to and after treatment completion. After the intervention, the treatment group had significantly higher scores on coping and emotional competence than the control group did.

Lovett and Gallagher (1988) utilized groups to teach self-change and problem-solving skills to caregivers of frail elderly people. Caregivers ($n = 107$, $M = 59.3$

years) were randomly assigned to one of two psychoeducational groups or to a wait-list control condition. Groups met weekly, 2 hours per session, for a period of 10 weeks. Members of one group were taught self-change skills such as mood monitoring, identification of pleasant events, and progression in pleasant event activities. Members of the second group were taught problem-solving skills. All participants completed the Perceived Stress Scale, the BDI, the Schedule for Affective Disorders and Schizophrenia, and the Philadelphia Geriatric Morale Scale. Caregivers in both group treatment modalities experienced a significant reduction in stress and depression and an increase in morale. Caregivers assigned to the control group condition evidenced no changes.

A group program evaluated by Sullivan, Coffey, & Greenstein (1987) focused on care recipients rather than on the caregivers. Veterans experiencing anxiety, depression, and impaired coping ability were invited to participate in weekly half-day meetings for 10 weeks. The veterans ($n = 72$), all males, had an average age of 69 years. Vets and family members gathered for a period of socialization followed by an educational session. Afterward, the vets and the family members divided and met separately for supportive group therapy. The Philadelphia Geriatric Center Depression Scale was completed by the veterans at pre- and posttest periods, while information regarding behavioral changes was gathered from the veterans' records and staff members' weekly progress notes. Improvement in morale was significant for 21 veterans. Vets experiencing the greatest improvements were those who had normal scores at pretest. An increase in observed socialization skills was reported for all veterans.

Community Prevention Approaches

In order for older adults to remain functional in society, it is necessary for them to maintain an adequate level of psychosocial, economic, and physical well-being. Programs can maximize the quality of life by providing information and identifying lifestyle factors that can prevent or delay the onset of illnesses, disability, or other problems. This section includes community and prevention programs that have been found to be effective in promoting the health and well-being of older adults.

A major threat to older adults is home accidents. The SAFE (Study of Accidental Falls in the Elderly) project was designed to prevent in-home falls by providing information, physical conditioning programs, and in-home risk assessments (Hornbrook et al., 1994). Research on this community program consisted of 3,182 adults aged 65 and older who lived independently. Participants were randomly assigned to the intervention group ($n = 1,611$) and to the control group ($n = 1,571$). Home visits were conducted with both groups to assess and record the fall safety hazards. Participants in the intervention program were advised about home repair and participated in fall-prevention classes for four weekly sessions. These programs lasted for 90 minutes and included both information and exercise sessions. Outcomes were measured on a fall-incidence calendar. Results indicated that the odds of falling for the intervention group decreased by .85 when compared to the control group. These improvements were maintained at 23-month follow-up.

Another problem faced by some older adults is alcoholism, yet awareness of this addiction in the older population is low. An alcohol education program was offered to service providers and older adults and their families to educate them about alcoholism and to raise their awareness of this issue (Coogle, Osgood, Pyles, & Wood, 1995). A group of volunteers ($n = 132$) became facilitators after attending an 8-hour training session, then led educational sessions in local communities about alcoholism and older adults. Each session lasted 2 hours and included written, video, and lecture content. The sessions had 1,036 participants, all of whom completed a pre- and a posttraining knowledge test. A follow-up evaluation of the training was conducted at 10 months. Participants in these educational sessions had significant gains in alcohol-related knowledge at post- and follow-up testings.

Many older adults are involved with health care, yet often they do not have any advanced directives in case of an emergency situation. An education program was used to increase the use of living wills and durable powers of attorney by the elderly. High (1993) investigated the efficacy of these interventions in increasing the rates of completion of directives by older persons. A total of 431 participants were recruited and randomly assigned to a control group ($n = 120$) or an intervention group ($n = 311$). The members of the intervention group were then randomly assigned to six intervention strategy groups, each receiving different printed information about advanced directives. The remaining intervention groups received printed materials and also were invited to receive counseling and legal assistance to complete directives. Follow-up interviews were conducted 4 months after the intervention. The combination of having printed materials plus attending a meeting produced statistically significant increases in the use of advanced directives.

SUMMARY

In summary, various intervention approaches are helpful with older adults. Some methods have been successfully used in both individual treatment and group approaches, such as cognitive-behavioral therapy and relaxation. Outcome studies in physical and social functioning, as well as psychiatric conditions, indicate that practice with older adults can prevent and ameliorate problematic conditions that occur in late life. Demographics suggest that greater numbers of older adults will become clients of social work practitioners in coming years. Therefore, even greater efforts toward identifying and evaluating practice with older adults are necessary.

REFERENCES

Aging America: Trends and projections. (1991). Washington, DC: U.S. Senate Special Committee on Aging, American Association of Retired Persons, the Federal Council on the Aging, and the U.S. Administration on Aging.

Beck, A. T., Epstein, N., Brown, G., & Steer, R. A. (1988). An inventory for measuring clinical anxiety: Psychometric properties. *Journal of Consulting and Clinical Psychology, 56,* 893–897.

Beck, A. T., Rush, A. J., Shaw, B. F., & Emery, G. (1979). *Cognitive therapy of depression.* New York: Guilford Press.

Beck, A. T., Ward, C., Mendelson, M., Mock, J., & Erbaugh, J. (1971). An inventory for measuring depression. *Archives of General Psychiatry, 4,* 561–571.

Bergner, M., Bobbitt, R. A., Carter, W. B., & Gilson, B. S. (1981). The sickness impact profile: Development and final revision of a health status measure. *Health Care, 19,* 787–805.

Beutler, L. E., Scogin, F., Kirkish, P., Schretlen, D., Corbishley, A., Hamblin, D., Meredith, K., Potter, R., Bamford, C. R., & Levenson, A. I. (1987). Group cognitive therapy and Alprazolam in the treatment of depression in older adults. *Journal of Consulting and Clinical Psychology, 55,* 550–556.

Bradburn, H. (1969). *Structure of psychological well-being.* Chicago: Aldine.

Chiverton, P., & Caine, E. D. (1989). Education to assist spouses in coping with Alzheimer's disease. *Journal of the American Geriatrics Society, 37,* 593–598.

Choi, T., LaVohn, J., & Christensen, M. (1983). Health specific family coping index for noninstitutional care. *American Journal of Public Health, 73,* 1275–1277.

Cohen, S., Kamarck, T., & Mermelstein, R. (1983). A global measure of perceived stress. *Journal of Health and Social Behavior, 24,* 385–396.

Coogle, L. C., Osgood, N. J., Pyles, M. A., & Wood, H. E. (1995). The impact of alcoholism education on service providers, elders, and their family members. *Journal of Applied Gerontology, 14,* 321–332.

DeBerry, S., Davis, S., & Reinhard, K. E. (1989). A comparison of meditation-relaxation and cognitive/behavioral techniques for reducing anxiety and depression in a geriatric population. *Journal of Geriatric Psychiatry, 22,* 231–247.

Dhooper, S. S., Green, S. M., Huff, M. B., & Austin-Murphy, J. (1993). Efficacy of a group approach to reducing depression in nursing home elderly residents. *Journal of Gerontological Social Work, 20,* 87–100.

Duke University, Center for the Study of Aging and Human Development. (1978). *Multidimensional functional assessment: The OARS methodology* (2nd ed.). Durham, NC: Duke University Press.

Edinger, J. D., Hoelscher, T. J., Marsh, G. R., Lipper, S., & Ionescu-Pioggia, M. (1992). A cognitive-behavioral therapy for sleep-maintenance insomnia in older adults. *Psychology and Aging, 7,* 282–289.

Ellsworth, R. (1975). Consumer feedback in measuring the effectiveness of mental health programs. In M. Guttentag (Ed.), *Handbook of evaluation research* (pp. 239–274). London: Sage.

Endicott, J., & Spitzer, R. (1978). A diagnostic interview for affective disorders and schizophrenia. *Archives of General Psychiatry, 35,* 837–844.

Evans, R. L., & Jaureguy, B. M. (1982). Phone therapy outreach for blind elderly. *The Gerontologist, 22,* 32–35.

Evans, R. L., Smith, K. M., Werkhoven, W. S., Fox, H. R., & Pritzl, D. O. (1986). Cognitive telephone group therapy with physically disabled elderly persons. *The Gerontologist, 26,* 8–10.

Folkman, S., & Lazarus, R. S. (1980). An analysis of coping in a middle-aged community sample. *Journal of Health and Social Behavior, 21,* 219–239.

Gallagher-Thompson, D., Hanley-Peterson, P., & Thompson, L. W. (1990). Maintenance of gains versus relapse following brief psychotherapy for depression. *Journal of Consulting and Clinical Psychology, 3,* 371–374.

Haight, B. K. (1992). Long-term effects of a structured life review process. *Journal of Gerontology, 47,* P312–P315.

Hamilton, M. (1967). Development of a rating scale for primary depressive illness. *British Journal of Social and Clinical Psychology, 6,* 287–296.

Hamilton, M. (1959). The assessment of anxiety states by rating. *British Journal of Medical Psychology, 32,* 50–55.

High, M. D. (1993). Advance directives and the elderly: A study of intervention strategies to increase use. *The Gerontologist, 33,* 342–349.

Hornbrook, C. M., Stevens, J. V., Wingfield, J. D., Hollis, F. J., Greenlick, R. M., & Ory, G. M. (1994). Preventing falls among community-dwelling older persons: Results from a randomized trial. *The Gerontologist, 34,* 16–23.

Hussian, R. A., & Lawrence, P. S. (1981). Social reinforcement of activity and problem-solving training in the treatment of depressed institutionalized elderly. *Cognitive Therapy and Research, 5,* 57–69.

King, P., & Barrowclough, C. (1991). A clinical pilot study of cognitive-behavioral therapy for anxiety disorders in the elderly. *Behavioral Psychotherapy, 19,* 337–345.

Lawton, M. P. (1975). The Philadelphia Geriatric Morale Scale: A revision. *Journal of Gerontology, 30,* 85–89.

Lopez, M. A., & Mermelstein, R. J. (1995). A cognitive-behavioral program to improve geriatric rehabilitation outcome. *The Gerontologist, 35,* 696–700.

Lopez, M. A., & Silber, S. (1991). Stress management for the elderly: A preventive approach. *Clinical Gerontologist, 10*(4), 73–76.

Lovett, S., & Gallagher, D. (1988). Psychoeducational interventions for family caregivers: Preliminary efficacy data. *Behavior Therapy, 19,* 321–330.

Mittelman, M. S., Ferris, S. H., Shulman, E., Steinberg, G., Ambinder, A., Mackell, J. A., & Cohen, J. (1995). A comprehensive support program: Effect on depression in spouse-caregivers of Alzheimer's disease patients. *The Gerontologist, 35,* 792–802.

Morin, C. M., Kowatch, R. A., Barry, T., & Walton, E. (1993). Cognitive-behavioral therapy for late-life insomnia. *Journal of Consulting and Clinical Psychology, 61,* 137–146.

Neugarten, B., Havighurst, R., & Tobin, S. (1961). The measurement of life satisfaction. *Journal of Gerontology, 16,* 134–143.

Nicholson, N. L., and Blanchard, E. B. (1993). A controlled evaluation of behavioral treatment of chronic headache in the elderly. *Behaviour Therapy, 24,* 395–408.

Pfeiffer, E. (Ed.). (1976). *Multidimensional functional assessment: The OARS methodology.* Durham, NC: The Center for the Study of Aging and Human Development.

Piercy, J. W., & Lohr, J. M. (1989). Progressive relaxation in the treatment of an elderly patient with insomnia. *Clinical Gerontologist, 8*(4), 3–11.

Radloff, L. S. (1977). The CES-D Scale: A self-report depression scale for research in the general population. *Journal of Applied Psychological Measurement, 1,* 385–401.

Rapp, S. R., Mayo, L. L., Cole, P., Shires, C. L., Williams, R., Fowler, C. D., & Steen, C. (1989). Interdisciplinary behavioral geriatrics in long-term care: A controlled study. *Clinical Gerontologist, 8*(2), 35–42.

Rife, C. J., & Belcher, R. J. (1994). Assisting unemployed older workers to become reemployed: An experimental evaluation. *Research on Social Work Practice, 4,* 3–13.

Rosen, C. E., & Rosen, S. (1982). Evaluating an intervention program for the elderly. *Community Mental Health Journal, 18,* 21–33.

Russell, D., Peplau, L. A., & Ferguson, M. L. (1978). Developing a measure of loneliness. *Journal of Personality Assessment, 42,* 290–294.

Rybarczyk, B. D., & Auerbach, S. M. (1990). Reminiscence interviews as stress management interventions for older patients undergoing surgery. *The Gerontologist, 30,* 522–528.

Snaith, R. P., Ahmed, S., Mehta, S., & Hamilton, M. (1971). Assessment of the severity of primary depressive illness. *Psychological Medicine, 1* 143–149.

Spielberger, C. D., Gorsuch, R. L., & Luchene, R. E. (1970). *Manual for the State-Trait Anxiety Inventory.* Palo Alto, CA: Consulting Psychologists Press.

Spielberger, C. D., Gorsuch, R. L., & Lushene, R. (1967). *State-Trait Anxiety Inventory.* Palo Alto, CA: Consulting Psychologists Press.

Steuer, J. L., Mintz, J., Hammen, C. L., Hill, M. A., Jarvik, L. F., McCarley, T., Motoike, P., & Rosen, R. (1984). Cognitive-behavioral and psychodynamic group psychotherapy in treatment of geriatric depression. *Journal of Consulting and Clinical Psychology, 52,* 180–189.

Subramanian, K. (1991). Structured group work for the management of chronic pain: An experimental investigation. *Research on Social Work Practice, 1,* 32–45.

Sullivan, E. M., Coffey, J. F., & Greenstein, R. A. (1987). Treatment outcomes in a group geropsychiatry program for veterans. *The Gerontologist, 2,* 434–436.

Thyer, B. A. (1981). Prolonged in-vivo exposure therapy in the treatment of a 70-year-old-woman. *Journal of Experimental Psychiatry, 12,* 69–71.

U.S. Bureau of the Census (1996). *National Population Estimate.* Washington, DC: Author.

Vitaliano, P. P., Russo, J., Carr, J. E., Maiuro, R. D., & Becker, J. (1985). The ways of coping checklist: Revision and psychometric properties. *Multivariate Behavioral Research, 20*(1), 3–26.

Yesavage, J. A., Brink, T. L., Lum, O., Huang, V., Adey, M. B., & Leivor, V. O. (1983). Development and validation of a geriatric depression rating scale: A preliminary report. *Journal of Psychiatric Research, 17,* 27–49.

Zgliczynski, S. M. (1982). Multimodal behavior therapy with groups of aged. *Small Group Behavior, 13,* 53–62.

Zuckerman, M., & Lubin, W. (1960). *Affect Adjective Checklist.* New York: Educational and Industrial Testing Service.

Zung, W. W. K. (1965). A self-rating depression scale. *Archives of General Psychiatry, 12,* 63–70.

Chapter 14

RETIREMENT

Virginia L. Fitch
Marvin D. Feit
Nuria M. Cuevas
Lee R. Slivinske

Retirement in and of itself is not a social problem. However, it does require a series of changes and adjustments that may present problems for many elderly individuals. Social Security legislation in 1935 institutionalized retirement in U.S. society. Since that time, retirement has been inextricably linked in the public's perception with age 65 and eligibility for full Social Security benefits. Aging, in general, and retirement, in particular, have become associated with a loss of productivity and a decreased ability to work or engage in retraining (Mor-Barak & Tynan, 1993).

This chapter examines retirement as it is now understood through empirical research, its associated problems, and the implications for treatment and intervention that may be derived from research.

OVERVIEW

Early gerontological literature viewed retirement as leading to an identity crisis (Miller, 1965). Other studies now contradict that view. Although retirement, taken as the sole consideration, does not directly alter life satisfaction, self-esteem, or morale (Hanks, 1990; Palmore, Fillenbaum, & George, 1984), a variety of factors associated with it, such as the voluntary nature of the retirement decision, degree of financial security, health, and spousal and family support, may have a powerful impact (Bosse, Aldwin, Levenson, Spiro, & Mroczek, 1993; Bosse, Aldwin, Levenson, & Workman, 1991; Haug, Belgrave, & Jones, 1992).

Retirement is not a single event. Research has increasingly emphasized the importance of looking at retirement as an ongoing process that covers a temporal span beginning with preretirement and extending into the postretirement years (Hardy, 1996; Julia, Kilty, & Richardson, 1995; Quinn & Kozy, 1996). In the stereotypical retirement route, the worker exits from full-time employment in a career job and from the labor force in one move, usually at the normal retirement age. Retirement routes have become increasingly diverse over the last 30 years, with many of the exit patterns taking place over a prolonged time period. The range of possibilities includes early retirement, partial retirement, and moving into a second career, as well as diverse adaptations.

Quinn, Burkhauser, and Myers (1990) found that about 25% of male and non-married female wage and salary workers chose a transitional exit, consisting of a new job, part-time for some and full-time for others. A similar percentage of the self-employed did the same, while another quarter moved to part-time employment in their own career jobs. Other analyses have found partial employment to be important even among individuals in good health (Gustman & Steinmeier, 1984). The importance of partial employment tends to increase with age for men and for nonmarried women, though less so (Honig 1985; Honig & Hanoch, 1985).

Karp (1989) identified a person's 50s as the transitional decision-making decade for a sample of White male and female professionals. Retirement was found to have multiple meanings for the sample. It was typically viewed as less positive by those with unfinished agendas at work, those with a high degree of job satisfaction, those who did not perceive themselves as financially secure, and those in good health.

There is evidence that a preretirement process of gradual dissociation from work may take place for workers as they move closer to the age of retirement. Results from a pooled time-study analysis of 1,365 nonretired male workers ages 50 to 69 indicated that, regardless of age, their jobs were increasingly viewed as burdensome as they drew closer to retirement. Their jobs were more likely to be perceived as causing tension and fatigue (Ekerdt & DeViney, 1993).

Since the 1950s, the labor force participation of older workers has declined. Social Security initially defined early retirement eligibility as age 62 for women in 1956 and for men in 1961. A major impetus from the private sector in the form of early retirement incentive programs pushed the age of early retirement into the 50s for increasing numbers of older workers. A disparity seemed to exist between the direction taken by social policy and the decision making manifested in many retirement decisions. The 1983 Amendments to the Social Security Act will cause the normal retirement age to gradually increase to 66 and later to 67 (Chen, 1994; Quinn & Kozy, 1996). These and other recent changes were designed to increase the elderly labor supply. Some experts have suggested that the normal retirement age should be raised more quickly and even higher to 68 and later indexed to life expectancy with early eligibility for Social Security retirement benefits delayed until 65 (Chen, 1994; Mitchell & Quinn, 1996).

The dramatic drop in the proportion of older adults who remained economically active between 1950 and the 1990s appears unlikely to wane (Gendell & Siegel, 1992; Ruhm, 1995). Early retirement incentive programs have offered opportunities to retire at much earlier ages than stipulated by pension plans. While appearing to offer greater freedom of choice concerning the age of retirement, early retirement programs may be perceived as coercive, depending on the structure of the program. Since incentives for early retirement may be offered as part of downsizing, older workers may fear their jobs are in jeopardy and elect to take early retirement. A telephone survey of a random sample of 1,148 early retirees from General Motors found that the majority were satisfied with the timing of the opportunity for early retirement and with retirement experiences. Expressions of dissatisfaction were associated with special retirement incentive programs that were offered by management to avoid massive layoffs. Although offering generous benefits, they appeared to limit workers' control over the decision-making process. Although these early retirees were qualified for the highest level of benefits and were among the most healthy, they were more likely to express dissatisfaction than other early retirees (Hardy & Quadagno, 1995). Examination of the process that led to retirement is an important indicator of future adjustment. Even one that appears to offer maximum flexibility to the retiree can inform practitioners about another potential source of dissatisfaction with the retirement experience.

The trend toward early retirement has raised a number of key areas of concern. These include potential labor shortages, the ability or even willingness of society to provide retirement benefits for early retirees, and the need to postpone the age at which a person can receive full retirement benefits. These are issues that must be addressed through the forum of public policy.

Honig (1996) found that people form expectations of future retirement behaviors and engage in planning based on apparent current resources. Preretirement expectations of future retirement income, the net rewards to be derived from continued work, and the value of nonmarket time provide strong and precise estimates of current behavior, particularly for White men and women, and to a lesser degree for African American and Hispanic men and women.

Retirement involves both loss of the worker role and gain in terms of new, culturally transmitted rights, such as autonomy in the management of an individual's own time and duties (Atchley, 1976). Retirement outcomes are highly variable and thought to be influenced by the reason for retirement, whether it was voluntary or expected, the income adequacy, the presence of social support, the health of the retiree, spousal attitude toward retirement, education, work history and occupation, and values toward work (Atchley 1982; Bosse et al., 1993; Haug et al., 1992).

Much of our understanding of retirement decisions has come from research on retirement decisions by males (Beck, 1984; Burkhauser, 1980; Ekerdt, Bosse, & Mogey, 1980; Evans, Ekerdt, & Bosse, 1985). The male retirement decision has been found to be positively influenced by such factors as the pension and Social Security benefits of both spouses, if married, annuity payments, including many personal descriptors associated with receiving such payments, such as reaching the age of 62 or 65. Earnings of both spouses, on the other hand, have been found to have a negative impact on the decision (Anderson, Clark, & Johnson, 1980; Burkhauser, 1980; Hall & Johnson, 1980; Heckman, 1978).

Analyses of retirement decisions often overlook two factors: the intricacies of the retirement process and the segment of the employed population that does not retire. These analytical shortcomings were addressed in a study of male respondents consisting of both retirees and older continuing workers. Those who wanted to retire were found to be affected by family variables. Retirement was hastened by being married, having no children, and having the youngest child over age 21. The social appropriateness of retirement seemed to be influenced by the spouses' relative age. Having an older wife tended to speed up retirement, while having a younger wife tended to slow it down. This, plus the importance of pension amounts and higher wages, indicates that there are many considerations that lead to self-defined, voluntary retirements. The existence of a health limit (any disease or health condition that impedes but does not disable) not only increased the likelihood of retirement for health reasons but also for other reasons. This indicates that understanding the effect of health on retirement is far more complex than originally thought. It also suggests that examining the reasons for retirement provides only partial insight into retirement processes (Henretta, Chan, & O'Rand, 1992).

The majority of studies in this area have used married male subjects' reports of their spouses' earnings or employment status to examine these influences on the retirement decision (Evans et al., 1985; Hall & Johnson, 1980; Quinn, 1977). This approach has been discounted because decisions made by a husband and wife should be more appropriately examined as joint decisions (Clark, Johnson, & McDermed, 1980; Gratton & Haug, 1983; Shaw, 1984). An exception is provided by Campione (1987), who analyzed data on 187 married couples from the 1979 cohort of the University of Michigan's Panel Study of Income Dynamics. She found that the married woman's retirement decision is linked to her potential Social Security benefits, wage and pension wealth, age, the husband's wage wealth, and retirement status.

The involvement of social work is relevant to the problems associated with retirement. Social workers are uniquely prepared to address preretirement preparation and adjustment difficulties, as well as other problems arising in postretirement. Social workers also are influential in the development of social policy relating to work and retirement issues.

ASSESSMENT METHODS

Retirement has been conceptualized by many as consisting of several stages. These include a preretirement period characterized by the formulation of a consciousness about the meaning of retirement and leaving work, actually playing out the retirement role, and giving up the retirement role. Atchley (1972, 1980) identified six phases: The preretirement phase is the time during which the possibility of retirement is considered. It may evolve into planning for retirement, denying it, or just letting it happen. The honeymoon phase, occurring immediately after actual retirement, is one in which the individual attempts to engage in the things envisioned in preretirement. This phase ends for many as they begin establishing a retirement routine. The disenchantment phase may be experienced by some who feel let down after the honeymoon phase. Feelings of boredom, restlessness, or depression may be described. Reorientation is a phase during which some of those who have difficulty adapting to retirement reorient themselves to available alternatives for identity, socialization, and recreation. It should result in the development of a satisfying routine. During the stability phase, this daily routine becomes comfortable and consistent. Termination, the final stage, occurs for older adults who tire of the retirement role and take on another.

These phases have potential as a useful tool for assessment (Julia et al., 1995). Accurate identification of the current role phase can be used to guide the development of treatment options. For example, during the preretirement phase, preventive planning can be introduced to make the retirement decision as informed as possible. The disenchantment stage may indicate a need for helping the individual identify realistic avenues for involvement.

Other recognized assessment methods are notably absent in the empirical literature on retirement. Many gaps exist in our understanding of retirement. These are partly the result of limitations in the size and composition of samples studied. Comparatively little empirical research has been dedicated to the study of the retirement process in ethnic and racial minority groups (Gibson, 1991; Zsembik & Singer, 1990). Until very recently, the Retirement History Study (RHS), a survey of older adults during the period from 1969 to 1979, provided the primary basis for our current understanding about the retirement process. Because it included no married women and a limited number of people from minority groups, it contributed most to our knowledge about the retirement patterns of White males (Irelan, 1972).

Recently, the first wave of the Health and Retirement Study, a large, ambitious prospective longitudinal panel study, has become available for analysis. Undertaken to examine health and retirement processes (Juster & Suzman, 1995; Wallace & Herzog, 1995), interviews with approximately 13,000 older adults, including oversamples of approximately 2,000 African Americans and 1,200 Hispanics, were obtained. It offers greater opportunities for expanding the understanding of retirement among minority groups than was heretofore available. This will be particularly true as subsequent waves of data are made available (Jackson, Lockery, & Juster, 1996).

It has been speculated that the retirement process for ethnic and racial minority groups and for women may be quite different than for White males. A large number of older African Americans fail to report themselves as retired, despite their nonworking status. This has further caused them to be excluded from much retirement research. One investigation found that those who did not define themselves as retired either never had a full-time job or had a lifetime of sporadic employment extending into old age (Jackson & Gibson, 1985). Self-defined retirement also has been found to be inhibited by thinking of oneself as disabled and being in economic need (Gibson, 1987).

EFFECTIVE SOCIAL WORK INTERVENTIONS

Treatment is not directly addressed in the majority of retirement research, although possible applications of their findings are identified by some researchers. Empirical research tends to focus on understanding normal retirement rather than on treating its maladaptations. However, inferences to practice can be drawn from research outcomes. Important and underutilized roles for practitioners in the field of retirement may be identified as a result.

Individual Treatment

Retirement is not a crisis for most people. A host of studies provide evidence that it is a welcome and satisfying period of life for most people. Since it involves change, it requires some degree of adaptation. Most people adapt to the changes and achieve good adjustment. However, adjustment to retirement does not automatically occur. Retirees who describe themselves as dissatisfied and restless due to boredom and having time on their hands may benefit from interventions directed toward activity promotion. Several studies provide empirical support for the health-enhancing benefits of activity in later life (Dorfman, 1995; Herzog, House, & Morgan, 1991; McIntosh & Danigelis, 1995; Midanik, Soghikian, Ransom, & Tekawa, 1995; Mutran & Reitzes, 1984; Schmidt, 1993). Productive activity has been found to decline with increasing age, although health status and educational level reduce the magnitude of these declines. Part of the decline results from the termination of paid work and child care, although the degree of activity in volunteerism and unpaid work has been found to remain as high for older adults as for those younger (Herzog, Kahn, Morgan, Jackson, & Antonucci, 1989).

A three-site longitudinal study of community-dwelling older men and women ages 70 to 79 compared the change in productive activities among high-, medium-, and lower functioning cohorts. Hospital admission and stroke were identified as risk factors for declines in activity. Being older, functionally disabled at baseline, and married, and reporting increased mastery were found to protect against declines. However, African Americans, those expressing greater life satisfaction at baseline, and those reporting increased mastery were more likely to increase their productivity than Whites. Additional findings indicated that declines in old age may result more from economic incentives than from physical limitations. This suggests that helping adults enhance their economic profiles as well as promoting public policy reform of legislation such as tax laws could enable elderly people to achieve their potential and maintain higher levels of productivity as they age (Glass, Seeman, Herzog, Kahn, & Berkman, 1995). The importance of the two psychosocial predictors, increased mastery and life satisfaction, identified in this study suggests a possible focus of intervention. Changes in performance may be achieved by focusing on bringing about changes in efficacy cognition or improving skill proficiency.

Additional insight into the meaning of productive activity and its relevance to different groups of elders is provided by McIntosh and Danigelis (1995). They studied the impact of paid and unpaid productive activity outside the home on the affective dimension of subjective well-being for African American and White males and females. Paid work was found to have the least important effect on any of the four subgroups, while informal volunteering had the greatest. Formal religious participation was most important for improving the affect of older African American women, although their participation was not greater than that of others. Formal nonreligious participation was most important for reducing the negative affect of older African American men, while increasing the positive affect of older White men. Older African American men and older White women responded similarly to informal volunteering. It increased their positive affect and reduced their negative affect. Thus, it appears that activities could be used to address both dimensions of affect among older men and women. It also suggests that activities must be specific to group membership for affect to improve.

In her study of factors related to the subjective retirement of 305 nonworking, older Black persons, Gibson (1991) provides further support for this approach. Data from face-to-face interviews with participants from a national multistage probability sample were gathered. Their self-defined retirement was discouraged by discontinuous patterns of work and by an economic and psychological need for the disabled work role. She speculated that inefficacy and negative life experiences interact and lock people into self-defeating systems. Negotiations with the environment cease. She suggested that appropriate social interventions could be fashioned through identification of the mechanisms whereby individuals within the older Black population receive feedback on their capabilities.

The effects of retirement on physical and mental health have been the object of considerable empirical scrutiny. A 1-year prospective randomized trial, stratified for blue-collar and white-collar occupations, indicated that Type A behavior changed in the direction of Type B after a year of normal retirement. Moreover, the mental health of those identified as Type A improved with retirement. A program of regular vigorous exercise was related to a decrease in interpersonal sensitivity and hostility in Type A personalities and to a decrease in depression in both Type A and Type B personalities (Howard, Rechnitzer, Cunningham, & Donner, 1986).

An examination of the relationship between retirement and medical services utilization in a 10% random sample of participants ages 60 to 66 in a prepaid health care system found no significant differences between retirees and those electing not to retire in overall use of outpatient and inpatient services in the year following retirement. Those remaining employed reported higher usage of urgent care and emergency visits. The researchers concluded that retirement as a major life event did not seem to cause undue distress and morbidity (Soghikian, Midanik, Polen, & Ransom, 1991). Other research has supported their findings (Midanik et al., 1995; Shapiro & Roos, 1982).

On the other hand, increased utilization of health services by retirees was noted in the research of Boaz and Muller (1989). Two differences in the studies that may have affected the findings are the socioeconomic makeup of the samples and the retirement time period studied. The Soghikian et al. study of HMO membership looked at only the first year of retirement and their sample underrepresented those in the lower socioeconomic groups, while the Boaz and Muller study compared retirees to full-time, self-employed workers.

The relationship between retirement and physical and mental health has been found to vary by gender and minority-group membership. An examination of mental health among 222 retirees, approximately half male and half female, at pre-retirement, 6 months later after retirement, and 1 year later, found gender differences in the symptoms expressed at each data collection point (Richardson & Kilty, 1995). The relative poor health of African American men and women is a more important determinant of early labor force exit when compared with that of Whites. Health differences between them account for most of the racial gap in labor force attachment for African American men. For women, research findings indicated that Black women would have higher labor force participation than White women if they had similar health status. Furthermore, African Americans in good health were less likely to be able to have the same resources to permit them to freely choose whether to retire early. They had fewer financial resources, they were less able to count on a spouse's earnings, and the jobs held by males were less likely to include pension benefits. Both males and females were more likely to have physically demanding jobs for which good health was important and to experience greater difficulty in finding alternative employment (Bound, Schoenbaum, & Waidmann, 1996).

Limited or lack of retirement resources may compel people from minority groups who are in poor health to continue working past normal retirement age (Angel & Angel, 1996; Gibson & Burns, 1991). It is noteworthy that the low levels of health insurance coverage among employed members of minority groups, notably African Americans, Hispanics, and Mexican Americans, means that a large fraction will not receive supplemental insurance after retirement. Social workers helping those from minority groups deal with managed care will need to be aware of both the financial and nonfinancial barriers to health care. For Hispanics, these include language difficulties and cultural distance between the patient and health care providers, cultural views of health care as a luxury, and reference group expectations (Angel & Angel, 1996).

A sizable proportion of older adults postpones retirement indefinitely or remains in the labor market after retirement. A study of variations in the labor market behavior of a nationally representative sample of men ages 45 to 59 at baseline included longitudinal data on surviving members of the original sample or their widows or relatives 24 years later (Parnes & Sommers, 1994). The surviving members of the original sample were ages 69 to 84. More than 1 in 6 were employed at the second interview and 1 in 5 reported working at some time in the preceding year. Approximately one third of the employed men indicated they worked full-time. Good health, a strong commitment to work, and a dislike for retirement were found to be associated with their continued employment. Employment also was positively related to having a working wife and educational attainment, but negatively related to age and level of income in the absence of work. It is noteworthy that few of those who were retired in the sample gave any hint of a desire to work.

From a practice viewpoint, maximizing opportunities for older adults who wish to retire as well as for those who wish to continue working expands individual opportunities for self-fulfillment and choice. Practitioners might consider encouraging employers to invest in the health and education of their employees as a means of encouraging them to remain economically active and productive. This could be carried out by the company itself in-house or through contracts with area providers. Employees, in turn, will feel better and have fewer absences. Their higher levels of educational attainment will open more opportunities for higher pay and more intrinsically satisfying work opportunities (Parnes & Sommers, 1994).

A study by Hirshorn and Hoyer (1994) on private-sector hiring and utilization of retirees suggests that practitioners dealing with the employment of older adults would do well to match specific retiree needs with company needs. Skill and reliability factors were specified by a large number of firms with 20 to 249 employees as major reasons for seeking retirees. Many firms interviewed in the study did not have the necessary skills in-house to find and hire these individuals. Moreover, retirees usually were unaware of the employment possibilities in firms of any size. The researchers suggested that pointing out the disadvantages of hiring younger workers, including their higher training costs, greater probability of premature exit, and greater likelihood of filing grievances, offers a promising tactic to encourage firms to hire retirees.

The importance of economic preparation for retirement should be emphasized to older workers and their families. This is particularly critical for women and members of minority groups who are divorced, widowed, or in second marriages (Holden & Kuo, 1996; Kart, Longino, & Ullman, 1989). The protection provided by social legislation, such as marital property reform and the survivorship rules of public and private pension and insurance programs, is based on the traditional standard of couples in a lifelong marriage. Yet couples in a first marriage make up only 25% of Black households and less than half of White and Hispanic households. An examination of the marital histories of women and men on the verge of retirement found that currently widowed or divorced households and couples in which the prior marriage of one spouse ended in widowhood or divorce have significantly lower incomes and assets than those couples in a first marriage. This remains true for both Black and White households (Holden & Kuo, 1996). Previous research suggests this may result from underinsuring against the future economic consequences of widowhood and the striking declines in family income that occur for women having the highest family income prior to divorce or widowhood (Holden & Kuo, 1996; Holden & Smock, 1991).

Other research suggests that interventions directed toward individuals' initial reactions to retirement may be helpful. The formal rituals usually held to mark the transition from worker to retiree have been found to be less helpful in negotiating this period than the informal rites initiated by friends and family. Postretirement travel has also been noted as helpful (Savishinsky, 1995). The preference for informal celebrations and travel may indicate that they offer the new retiree reassurance of the compensation to be derived from existing relationships and new activities. The proclivity of retirees to spend money on transportation, health, entertainment, and trips immediately after retirement has been examined as a temporary economic adjustment to a major life-cycle change (Rubin & Nieswiadomy, 1995). However, for some retirees, such proclivity may assume more importance to their psychosocial adjustment to retirement. Continued reliance on costly recreational activities may eventually place a strain on the retiree's finances. In such cases, the practitioner may need to teach the client the social and problem-solving skills needed to take on new roles and activities. At the same time, the practitioner must continue to respect the client's values about social, economic, and personal issues.

Group Treatment

Preretirement planning and postretirement counseling can be carried out very effectively through group intervention. Research provides clear indications of a need for preretirement planning whereby emphasis is placed on dealing with the economic, social, and psychological aspects of retirement. Those who prepare are more aware of their postretirement needs and exhibit higher morale, more favorable attitudes toward retirement, and less longing for their jobs (Teaff & Johnson, 1983). Despite the growth of employee assistance programs (EAPs) in corporations, such programs may have limited ability to provide retirement planning because of their need to relate employees' problems to the organization's business plans. They function more as the organization's representative than the employees' (Googins & Davidson, 1993).

Although retirement planning is offered by some large companies, most workers do not have access to it. Still others may not participate because they have not begun to consider retirement as a part of their future. Preretirement planning groups need to be more available and accessible to all workers, but particularly to women and minority groups. African Americans are an extremely vulnerable group in this regard. They are more disadvantaged than Whites in almost every aspect of retirement (Haywood, Friedman, & Chen, 1996).

The relationship between subjective retirement and subjective disability was examined on a probability sample of 305 nonworking African Americans ages 55 and over. The economically needy were found to be the most likely to be subjectively disabled. However, economic need did not significantly decrease the tendency toward subjective retirement, indicating a stronger indirect than direct influence. Psychological need increased the proclivity toward subjective disability and, through that, inhibited subjectivity retirement (Gibson, 1991). Although the research oversampled Whites and the middle class while undersampling African Americans, individuals with no college education, and incomes under $25,000, the findings suggest that preretirement planning may help anticipate and reduce some of the strains, including financial, associated with retirement. Planning also could be directed toward maintaining and strengthening old roles that will continue into the retirement years, as well as identifying new roles and activities.

Although traditionally these seminars have focused on financial preparation, their content should be considered carefully to ascertain their appeal to all groups. Prior knowledge of the demographic characteristics of seminar participants also can be helpful in matching the content of the course to likely retirement needs. For example, Richardson and Kilty (1992) recommend that greater emphasis be placed on making successful financial investments and planning for postretirement employment for predominantly African American groups. Obstacles to their participation should also be assessed, because their participation rates are lower than those of Whites (Beck, 1984).

Although reduction of financial strain is essential to retirement satisfaction, preretirement groups have a much broader practice potential than simply helping with financial planning. They can help workers enhance their postretirement self-esteem by planning meaningful new roles and activities in retirement and strengthening existing roles that will continue into retirement (Reitzes, Mutran, & Fernandez, 1996).

Although some experts believe that planning should ideally begin in early middle age (Hancock, 1990), it may need to occur at different points. Employed people can be encouraged to participate in retirement planning groups as a way to develop concrete plans and address any negative feelings about retirement. They may need help in dealing with feelings of loss as they approach retirement and even in overcoming avoidance of retirement in those highly committed to work. Some workers will deny retirement until they are forced to think about it for health or other reasons such as caregiving. A support group composed of retirees and soon-to-be-retired people may provide a means of facilitating preparation for the psychosocial changes that will come after leaving work (Reitzes et al., 1996).

Marital and Family Treatment

The importance of family and the spousal relationship is suggested by a host of studies exploring the complex relationship between retirement satisfaction, gender, and various characteristics of the marital relationship. Being married as opposed to never having been married seems to be more significant in explaining men's satisfaction in retirement, even though marital status has such a profound impact on women's income level (Meyer, 1990).

Szinovacz (1996) studied the impact of married couples' employment-retirement patterns on marital quality and found that marital quality was perceived as being lower by couples with the husband retired and the wife still employed. Wives who remained employed after their husbands' retirement exhibited significantly lower marital satisfaction than wives whose marriages were characterized by any other combination of employment status (Lee & Shehan, 1989). The impact of retirement on marital quality has been found to be influenced by a range of preretirement factors. These include characteristics of the husband's job, the division of labor, social support, and marital quality (Myers, 1996).

Calasanti (1996) examined whether the male model based on men's experiences could be used, as it has been traditionally, to assess women's satisfaction in retirement. The sample consisted of 1,031 retirees ages 62 to 75 taken from survey years 1973 to 1990 of a national survey using a combination of block quota and full probability sampling techniques. She found persistent gender differences in life satisfaction in retirement. Marital status, health, and, to a lesser extent, education were important for the life satisfaction of retirees who were more occupationally self-directed and ideationally flexible (nonfemale occupations). She concluded that gender defines the context of such employment structures as reliance on relationships with coworkers. These employment structures, in turn, lead to important differences in life satisfaction in retirement.

In particular, research on the importance of domestic work arrangements to older wives' well-being offers some understanding of the dynamics underlying complaints of depression or marital concerns in older women. A study by Pina and Bengtson (1995) explored the relationship between the division of household labor and retirement-aged wives' well-being. The wife's perception of spousal support was treated as a mediating variable. The sample consisted of 144 primarily White, working- to middle-class married women, ages 54 to 74, currently married between 1 and 56 years. All sample participants reported that both they and their husbands were physically able to carry out household chores. Results indicated that the relationship between a couple's division of household responsibilities and the wives' well-being was mediated by perceptions of spousal support. Wives with husbands who engaged in more domestic work reported greater satisfaction with their support. They also were less likely to report that their husbands made too many demands on them. Wives employed full-time were more likely to report dissatisfaction with the support received from a husband who contributed less to domestic chores than were wives who were primarily homemakers. However, the relationship between a lack of equity in domestic contributions and wives' perceptions of spousal support did not vary by the husband's retirement status.

The actual division of responsibility in domestic labor arrangements is not altered substantially by retirement (Ward, 1993). Usually older women continue to have primary responsibility. Men may increase their involvement in household chores but not to as great an extent as both spouses expect (Robinson & Spitze, 1992). The complexity of the relationship between spouses' employment or retirement status and involvement in domestic work suggests the existence of unequal power in the marital relationship. Szinovacz and Harpster (1994) found that employed husbands with retired wives were able to secure an advantageous division of housework in their favor, either through the greater involvement of their wives or their own lower involvement. Employed wives appeared unable to enlist greater involvement from their husbands, regardless of whether they were retired. The researchers speculated that any power shift resulting from the husband's retirement was not sufficient to bring about a more equitable division of domestic responsibilities.

These findings offer clear implications for practitioners working with older couples. They should be mindful of their domestic work arrangements as possible problem sources, particularly when the wives present complaints of marital problems or depression. Examination of their perceptions of spousal support and demands may indicate potential areas for change. The effectiveness of marital treatment may be increased by examining how expectations and perceptions of domestic divisions of labor and support are communicated. This may highlight ways in which the couple can negotiate mutually satisfying arrangements (Pina & Bengtson, 1995).

Community

The importance of the local environment to elders has been the subject of empirical scrutiny and debate in recent decades. Retirement migration research offers some understanding of the meaning of location for retired people. Although elderly persons are no more likely to return to their regions of birth than is any other segment of the general population (Rogers, 1990), a substantial number do migrate. Most of those who do migrate begin contemplating the move at some point prior to retirement. A longitudinal examination of motives for elderly migration among 930 noninstitutional movers over age 70 revealed that health was not the dominant motive. Respondents were divided in their responses among the five other motives examined: affiliation, economic security, comfort, functional independence, and getting on with life after a family crisis. Changing physical disability and instrumental disability were related to mobility only for those who reported health as a motive for moving—about 19% of the sample (De Jong, Wilmoth, Angel, & Cornwell, 1995).

In their research, Haas and Serow (1993) conceptualized retirement migration as a process. Factors *pushing* migrants versus those *pulling* them were examined for 586 migrant households in western North Carolina via telephone survey. Push factors referred to physical and social factors that detracted from the community of origin, while pull factors were those that made potential host locations attractive. Pull factors, the most salient to the households studied, were primarily environmental amenities (climate and scenic beauty) and secondarily activity amenities (recreation and cultural attractions). Financial issues were of limited importance regardless of income level. Approximately half of the sample selected the area after considering other destinations, based on its amenities. Those who chose the destination specifically were more likely to indicate ties to the community through friends but not family.

One finding uncovered in the aforementioned study was somewhat disturbing because it suggested that the migrants as a group were in the new community, but not a part of it. Although migrants contributed to the community through participation in voluntary organizations and political activities, their social contacts usually were with other migrants. Those with church denominational affiliations like those in the area or those with local family were more likely to report friendships with those native to the area (Haas & Serow, 1993). It may be that increasing age and illness will necessitate a second move for those without local family and a support system to provide informal caregiving if the host community fails to provide the services needed as migrants grow less capable of living independently.

Using the 1980 public-use microdata sample of the U.S. Census, Longino and Smith (1991) conducted an analysis of retirement migration patterns among African Americans. Two primary migration patterns were observed among them: provincial return migration resulting from earlier southern settlement followed by regional labor force outmigration and a regional counterstream migration pattern leaving the South. The two groups did not differ educationally or economically. A possible explanation, proposed by the researchers, is that many of those returning to the South do so to provide care for frail parents, after which they may return to the North. Those leaving the South differed in that they typically were older, were more often widowed, and tended to live dependently upon arriving at their destinations. Research on the motives for African Americans' retirement migration is needed.

Increasingly, research documents the movement of older adults out of the central cities and into the suburbs. This trend is expected to continue (Golant, 1990). The graying of the suburbs raises questions about the nature of the relationship between location and perceptions of life quality or well-being. Although having limited generalizability, in one study of elderly tenants in public housing, environmental characteristics were found to be better predictors of friendship behavior, activity patterns, and housing satisfaction than were personal characteristics (Lawton & Nahemow, 1979).

Reitzes, Mutran, and Pope (1991) studied a national sample of 1,654 retired men ages 60 to 74 living in central city, suburban, or nonmetropolitan areas. They examined three issues regarding their psychological well-being: differences in well-being by location, the comparative importance of location to well-being when considered with other variables, and the indirect influences of location through other factors such as activities. Analysis revealed that retired men living in the central cities had the lowest levels of well-being and suburban dwellers had the highest. Location differences also were found to be associated with differences in health, income, social support, and participation. Retired central city men were in better health, had fewer assets, and participated in fewer informal activities, while retired nonmetropolitan men had the worst health but more extensive networks. Retirees in the suburbs were better off financially, better educated, and the most active in informal activities.

Implications for community practice can be drawn from these research studies. Although the community does not determine the behavior or mental health of older people, their well-being is influenced through the presence or absence of opportunities for informal and recreational activities as well as other types of involvement (Reitzes et al., 1991). These findings imply that the type of interventions needed by elderly retirees may be determined, at least in part, by urban versus nonmetropolitan dwelling. As increasing disability limits independent mobility, such as access to or use of a car by central city dwellers, affordable transit services for disabled elderly people could increase their participation in informal activities. The development of new opportunities for formal and informal activities could enlarge their networks as they become increasingly decimated by the loss of people with whom they customarily interacted.

Nonmetropolitan dwellers appear most in need of health promotion activities in the earlier years of retirement. As they age, increasing the availability and accessibility of health services could enhance their well-being as well as their health. Use of these services and other services also depends on retirees' knowledge of their existence, eligibility requirements, procedures for accessing them, and recognition of having the problem.

Quality of life also may be influenced by the existence of barriers to elders who, after moving to a community, find themselves unaccepted. Increasing disability may limit their access to places, people, and activities at a modest distance. Practitioners in host communities will want to be aware of the personal and social characteristics of older migrants and cognizant of their changing needs over time. Interventions aimed at drawing them into the community will strengthen the community and ease tensions that must inevitably exist between two cultures dwelling in the same geographical area. Furthermore, it will enable the community to be proactive in developing services for all its citizens.

Effective interventions that would bring the two coexisting cultures together and appeal to older adults in both would be activity programs. Churches of various denominations could serve as referral sources or even alternating hosts for the activities, along with other organizations that migrants are known to frequent. Referrals that would yield a mix of those who migrated to the area and those who are native to it would provide a common meeting ground for forming more extensive social networks than those currently available to both.

Prevention

The Anderson-Newman framework of the determinants of health service utilization includes health attitudes and beliefs as part of the predisposing factors that may have a bearing on need, recognition, or service usage (Andersen & Newman, 1973). This component of the model has been rarely examined, with the exception of a study by Strain (1991). She examined the relative importance of general health beliefs on older adults' use of formal health services among a random sample of 743 Canadians ages 60 and over. Those who expressed more skepticism about medicine were likely to make fewer visits to the doctor. Individuals with a stronger belief in the importance of health maintenance activities utilized a greater array of health services at least once in the year preceding the study. However, they did not necessarily engage in a greater volume of service use.

These research findings suggest that educating individuals on the value of preventive health measures may encourage them to access the health care system when the need arises. Health promotion and illness prevention activities appear to increase awareness of initial symptoms at an early point at which the treatment required may be only minimal. This may account for the utilization of a greater array, but not a higher volume, of health services among the individuals in the aforementioned study.

Health maintenance activities may assume even greater importance for prevention in the future. Awareness of the increasing costs of retiree health insurance may encourage the narrowing or elimination of employer-sponsored coverage in some firms (Clark, Ghent, & Headen, 1994; Jensen & Morrisey, 1992).

More support for the importance of health promotion and illness prevention activities is provided by a study of the factors associated with physical function among retirement-age African American men and women (Clark, Callahan, Mungai, & Wolinsky, 1996). Slightly more than half of the 957 women in the sample reported some problems with physical function compared to one third of the 649 male respondents. The physical function variable was composed of participants' responses to a series of questions about difficulty with body movements. Among their findings, several warrant special consideration. The rate of high-risk behaviors in the sample is particularly disturbing. These included smoking (40% for men, 24% for women), alcohol abuse among men, and obesity among women. Most of the factors associated with difficulty in physical function in the study sample could potentially have been prevented or managed. The researchers concluded that understanding and managing these risks among African Americans should be a primary public health goal.

The importance of such a goal cannot be overstated. However, a prospective study by Hayward et al. (1996) suggests that implementing activities to achieve this goal may not be enough. A cohort-based nationally representative sample of 5,020 men ages 45 to 59 was followed for 17 years. The analysis indicated that race inequities in retirement resulted from health inequities, including the higher disability and mortality rate of African Americans. These, in turn, reflected social class disadvantages that may be more appropriate long-term public policy goals.

In the meantime, social workers may use these findings to promote higher levels of educational attainment and develop health promotion activities for African Americans. Educational programs could focus on promoting awareness of the specific risks of smoking, alcohol abuse, and being overweight among African Americans. Inclusion of such education, beginning with preschool and continuing through high school, could prevent many of the chronic diseases in later life that are associated with high-risk behaviors. Specific prevention activities and interventions could be developed for other target groups based on their risk factors.

The positive relationship between alcohol dependence and chronic stress indicates another potential target for prevention. Late-onset heavy drinking has been found to be associated with chronic stress from the stressors of aging in a general population of older adults. Retirement was indicated as a stressor in the study (Welte & Mirand, 1995). Stress management has been directed toward managing the stressors of the workplace. The potential stressful aspects of retirement have been largely ignored. Incorporating stress management techniques into preretirement planning seminars may be used to promote the development of proactive responses.

The influences of preretirement worker and spouse identities on postretirement self-esteem were studied in a group of 300 retired workers. Through telephone interviews, the researchers found evidence for the existence of continuity between their pre- and postretirement self-esteem. They found that preretirement self-esteem served as a foundation for current self-esteem. Furthermore, preretirement commitment to the worker role and identity and to the spouse role contributed to postretirement self-esteem indirectly through preretirement self-esteem (Reitzes et al., 1996). Workers appear to enter retirement with some direction from their past to guide them in this new stage in their lives. This suggests that new coping skills learned in preretirement can foster positive adaptation to retirement.

In summary, it appears possible to minimize the negative effects of retirement by adequate preparation. Social workers may develop or take part in community programs that emphasize retirement planning. They also should use their knowledge of the broad impact of retirement to expand the focus of retirement planning. When addressing problems that may be produced or affected by retirement, the changes, losses, and unmet expectations of the individual or couple should be explored to determine appropriate interventions.

REFERENCES

Anderson, K. R., Clark, L., & Johnson, T. (1980). Retirement in dual career families. In R. L. Clark (Ed.), *Retirement policy in an aging society.* Durham, NC: Duke University Press.

Andersen, R., & Newman, J. F. (1973). Societal and individual health determinants of medical care utilization in the United States. *The Millbank Memorial Fund Quarterly, 51,* 95–124.

Angel, R. J., & Angel, J. L. (1996). The extent of private and public health insurance coverage among adult Hispanics. *The Gerontologist, 36*(3), 332–340.

Atchley, R. (1972). *The social forces in later life.* Belmont, CA: Wadsworth.

Atchley, R. (1976). *The sociology of retirement.* New York: Wiley/Schenkman.

Atchley, R. (1980). *Social forces and aging.* Belmont, CA: Wadsworth.

Atchley, R. (1982). Retirement: Leaving the world of work. *Annals of the American Academy of Political and Social Sciences, 464,* 120–131.

Beck, S. H. (1984). Retirement preparation programs: Differentials in opportunity and use. *Journals of Gerontology: Social Science, 39,* S596–S602.

Boaz, R. F., & Muller, C. F. (1989). Does having more time after retirement change the demand for physician services? *Medical Care, 27,* 1–15.

Bosse, R., Aldwin, C., Levenson, M., Spiro, A., & Mroczek, D. (1993). Changes in social support after retirement: Longitudinal findings from the Normative Aging Study. *Journals of Gerontology: Social Sciences, 48*(2), S210–S217.

Bosse, R., Aldwin, C., Levenson, M., & Workman, D. (1991). How stressful is retirement? Findings from the normative aging study. *Journals of Gerontology: Social Sciences, 46*(1), 9–15.

Bound, J., Schoenbaum, M., & Waidmann, T. (1996). Race differences in labor force attachment and disability status. *The Gerontologist, 36*(3), 311–321.

Burkhauser, R. V. (1980). The early acceptance of Social Security: An asset maximization approach. *Industrial and Labor Relations Review, 33,* 484–492.

Calasanti, T. M. (1996). Gender and life satisfaction in retirement: An assessment of the male model. *Journals of Gerontology: Social Sciences, 51*(1), S18–S29.

Campione, W. A. (1987). The married woman's retirement decision: A methodological comparison. *Journals of Gerontology: Social Science, 42*(4), 381.

Chen, Y. P. (1994). Equivalent retirement ages and their implication for Social Security and Medicare financing. *The Gerontologist, 34*(6), 731–735.

Clark, D. O., Callahan, C. M., Mungai, S. M., & Wolinsky, F. D. (1996). Physical function among retirement-aged African American men and women. *The Gerontologist, 36*(3), 322–331.

Clark, R. L., Ghent, L. S., & Headen, A. E. (1994). Retiree health insurance and pension coverage: Variations by firm characteristics. *Journals of Gerontology: Social Sciences, 49*(2), S53–S61.

Clark, R., Johnson, T., & McDermed, A. (1980). Allocation of resources by married couples approaching retirement. *Social Security Bulletin, 43,* 3–17.

De Jong, G. F., Wilmoth, J. M., Angel, J. L., & Cornwell, G. T. (1995). Motives and the geographic mobility of very old Americans. *Journals of Gerontology: Social Sciences, 50*(6), S395–S404.

Dorfman, L. T. (1995). Health conditions and perceived quality of life in retirement. *Health & Social Work, 20*(3), 192–199.

Ekerdt, D. J., Bosse, R., & Mogey, J. M. (1980). Concurrent change in planned and preferred age for retirement. *Journals of Gerontology: Social Science, 35*(2), S232–S240.

Ekerdt, D. J., & DeViney, S. (1993). Evidence for a preretirement process among older male workers. *Journals of Gerontology: Social Sciences, 48*(2), S35–S43.

Evans, L., Ekerdt, D. J., & Bosse, R. (1985). Concurrent change in planned and preferred age for retirement. *Journals of Gerontology: Social Science, 40*(3), S368–S374.

Gendell, M., & Siegel, J. S. (1992). Trends in retirement age by sex, 1950–2005. *Monthly Labor Review, 115,* 22–29.

Gibson, R. C. (1987). Reconceptualizing retirement for black Americans. *The Gerontologist, 27,* 691–698.

Gibson, R. C. (1991). The subjective retirement of black Americans. *Journals of Gerontology: Social Sciences, 46*(4), S235–S242.

Gibson, R. C., & Burns, C. J. (1991). The health, labor force, and retirement experiences of aging minorities. *Generations, 15,* 31–35.

Glass, T. A., Seeman, T. E., Herzog, A. R., Kahn, R., & Berkman, L. F. (1995). Change in productive activity in late adulthood: MacArthur Studies of Successful Aging. *Journals of Gerontology: Social Sciences, 50*(2), S65–S76.

Golant, S. M. (1990). The metropolitanization and suburbanization of the U.S. elderly population. *The Gerontologist, 30*(3), 80–85.

Googins, B., & Davidson, B. N. (1993). The organization as client: Broadening the concept of employee assistance programs. *Social Work, 38*(4), 477–484.

Gratton, B., & Haug, R. (1983). Decision and adaptation: Research on female retirement. *Research on Aging, 5,* 59–76.

Gustman, A. A., & Steinmeier, T. L. (1984). Partial retirement and the analysis of retirement behavior. *Industrial and Labor Relations Review, 37,* 403–415.

Haas, W. H., & Serow, W. J. (1993). Amenity retirement migration process: A model and preliminary evidence. *The Gerontologist, 33*(2), 212–220.

Hall, J., & Johnson, T. (1980). Determinants of planned retirement age. *Industrial and Labor Relations Review, 33,* 241–254.

Hancock, B. L. (1990). *Social work with older people.* Englewood Cliffs, NJ: Prentice Hall.

Hanks, R. S. (1990). The impact of early retirement incentives on retirees and their families. *Journal of Family Issues, 11,* 424–437.

Hardy, M. A. (1996). Symposium III: Employment, economic status, and retirement. *The Gerontologist, 36*(3), 361–362.

Hardy, M. A., & Quadagno, J. (1995). Satisfaction with early retirement: Making choices in the auto industry. *Journals of Gerontology: Social Sciences, 50B*(4), S217–S228.

Haug, M., Belgrave, L., & Jones, S. (1992). Partner's health and retirement adaptation of women and their husbands. *Journal of Women and Aging, 43*(3), 5–29.

Hayward, M. D., Friedman, S., & Chen, H. (1996). Race inequities in men's retirement. *Journals of Gerontology: Social Sciences, 51B*(1), S1–S10.

Heckman, J. J. (1978). The life cycle and household decision making: A partial survey of recent research on the labor supply of women. *American Economic Association, 68,* 200–207.

Henretta, J. D., Chan, C. G., & O'Rand, A. M. (1992). Retirement reason versus retirement process: Examining the reasons for retirement typology. *Journals of Gerontology: Social Sciences, 47*(1), S1–S7.

Herzog, A. R., House, J. S., & Morgan, J. N. (1991). Relation of work and retirement to health and well-being in old age. *Psychology and Aging, 6,* 202–211.

Herzog, A. R., Kahn, R. L., Morgan, J. N., Jackson, J. S., & Antonucci, T. C. (1989). Age differences in productive activities. *Journals of Gerontology: Social Sciences, 44*(3), S129–S138.

Hirshorn, B. A., & Hoyer, D. T. (1994). Private sector hiring and use of retirees: The firm's perspective. *The Gerontologist, 34*(1), 50–58.

Holden, K. C., & Kuo, H. D. (1996). Complex marital histories and economic well-being: The continuing legacy of divorce and widowhood as the HRS cohort approaches retirement. *The Gerontologist, 36*(3), 383–390.

Holden, K. C., & Smock, P. J. (1991). The economic costs of marital dissolution: Why do women bear a disproportionate cost? *Annual Review of Sociology, 17,* 51–78.

Honig, M. (1985). Partial retirement among women. *Journal of Human Resources, 20,* 613–621.

Honig, M. (1996). Retirement expectations: Differences by race, ethnicity, and gender. *The Gerontologist, 36*(3), 373–382.

Honig, M., & Hanoch, G. (1985). Partial retirement as a separate mode of retirement behavior. *Journal of Human Resources, 20,* 21–46.

Howard, J. H., Rechnitzer, P. A., Cunningham, D. A., & Donner, A. P. (1986). Change in Type A behavior a year after retirement. *The Gerontologist, 26*(6), 643–649.

Irelan, L. M. (1972). Retirement History Survey: Introduction. *Social Security Bulletin, 35*(11), 3–8.

Jackson, J. S., & Gibson, R. C. (1985). Work and retirement among the black elderly. In Z. Blau (Ed.), *Current perspectives on aging and the life cycle* (Vol. 1) Greenwich, CT: JAI Press.

Jackson, J. S., Lockery, S. A., & Juster, F. T. (1996). Introduction: Health and retirement among ethnic and racial minority groups. *The Gerontologist, 36*(3), 282–284.

Jensen, G. A., & Morrisey, M. A. (1992). Employer-sponsored postretirement health benefits: Not your mother's Medigap Plan. *The Gerontologist, 32*(5), 693–703.

Julia, M., Kilty, K. M., & Richardson, V. (1995). Social worker preparedness for retirement: Gender and ethnic considerations. *Social Work, 40*(5), 610–620.

Juster, F. T., & Suzman, R. (1995). An overview of the Health and Retirement Study. *The Journal of Human Resources, 30*(Suppl.), S7–S56.

Karp, D. A. (1989). The social construction of retirement among professionals 50–60 years old. *The Gerontologist, 29*(6), 750–760.

Kart, C. S., Longino, C. F., & Ullmann, S. G. (1989). Comparing the economically advantaged and the pension elite: 1980 Census Profiles. *The Gerontologist, 29*(6), 745–749.

Lawton, M. P., & Nahemow, L. (1979). Social areas and the well-being of tenants in housing for the elderly. *Multivariate Behavioral Research, 14,* 463–484.

Lee, G., & Shehan, C. (1989). Retirement and marital satisfaction. *Journal of Gerontology: Social Sciences, 44,* S226–S230.

Longino, C. F., & Smith, K. J. (1991). Black retirement migration in the United States. *Journal of Gerontology: Social Sciences, 46,* S125–S132.

McIntosh, B. R., & Danigelis, N. L. (1995). Race, gender, and the relevance of productive activity for elders' affect. *Journals of Gerontology: Social Sciences, 50*(4), S229–S239.

Meyer, M. H. (1990). Family status and poverty among older women: The gendered distribution of retirement income in the United States. *Social Problems, 37,* 551–563.

Midanik, L. T., Soghikian, K., Ransom, L. J., & Tekawa, I. S. (1995). The effect of retirement on mental health and health behaviors. *Journal of Gerontology: Social Sciences, 50*(1), S59–S61.

Miller, S. J. (1965). The social dilemma of the aging leisure participant. In A. Rose and W. Petersen (Eds.), *Older people and their social world.* Philadelphia: Davis, 263–331.

Mitchell, O. S., & Quinn, J. F. (1996). *Final report of the Technical Panel on Trends and Issues in Retirement Savings.* Washington, DC: Advisory Council on Social Security.

Mor-Barak, M. E., & Tynan, M. (1993). Older workers and the workplace: A new challenge for occupational social work. *Social Work, 38*(1), 45–55.

Mutran, E., & Reitzes, D. G. (1984). Intergenerational support activities and well-being among the elderly: A convergence of exchange and symbolic-interaction perspectives. *American Sociological Review, 49,* 117–130.

Myers, S. M. (1996). Men's retirement and marital quality. *Journal of Family Issues, 17*(3), 336–357.

Palmore, E. B., Fillenbaum, G., and George, L. (1984). Consequences of retirement. *Journal of Gerontology, 39*(2), 109–116.

Parnes, H. S., & Sommers, D. G. (1994). Shunning retirement: Work experience of men in their seventies and early eighties. *Journal of Gerontology: Social Sciences, 49*(3), S117–S124.

Pina, D. L., & Bengtson, V. L. (1995). Division of household labor and the well-being of retirement-aged wives. *The Gerontologist, 35*(3), 308–317.

Quinn, J. F. (1977). Micro-economic determinants of early retirement: A cross-sectional view of white married men. *Journal of Human Resources, 12,* 329–346.

Quinn, J. F., Burkhauser, R. V., & Myers, D. A. (1990). *Passing the torch: The influence of economic incentives on work and retirement.* Kalamazoo, MI: Upjohn Institute for Employment Research.

Quinn, J. F., & Kozy, M. (1996). The role of bridge jobs in the retirement transition: Gender, race, and ethnicity. *The Gerontologist, 36*(3), 363–372.

Reitzes, D. C., Mutran, E. J., & Fernandez, M. E. (1996). Preretirement influences on postretirement self-esteem. *Journals of Gerontology: Social Sciences, 51*(5), S242–S249.

Reitzes, D. C., Mutran, E., & Pope, H. (1991). Location and well-being among retired men. *Journal of Gerontology: Social Sciences, 46*(4), S195–S203.

Richardson, V., & Kilty, K. M. (1992). Retirement intentions among black professionals: Implications for practice with older black adults. *The Gerontologist, 32*(1), 7–16.

Richardson, V., & Kilty, K. M. (1995). Gender differences in mental health before and after retirement: A longitudinal analysis. *Journal of Women & Aging, 7,* 19–35.

Robinson, J., & Spitze, G. (1992). Whistle while you work? The effect of household task performance on women's and men's well-being. *Social Science Quarterly, 73,* 844–861.

Rogers, A. (1990). Return migration to region of birth among retirement-age persons in the United States. *Journal of Gerontology: Social Sciences, 45*(3), S128–S134.

Rubin, R. M., & Nieswiadomy, M. L. (1995). Economic adjustments of households on entry into retirement. *Journal of Applied Gerontology, 14*(4), 467–482.

Ruhm, C. J. (1995). Secular changes in the work and retirement patterns of older men. *Journal of Human Resources, 30*(2), 362–385.

Savishinsky, J. (1995). The unbearable lightness of retirement: Ritual and support in a modern life passage. *Research on Aging, 17*(3), 243–259.

Schmidt, D. T. (1993). Health watch: Health promotion and disease prevention in primary care. *Methods of Information in Medicine, 32,* 245–248.

Shapiro, E., & Roos, N. P. (1982). Retired and employed elderly persons: Their utilization of health care services. *The Gerontologist, 22*(1), 187–193.

Shaw, L. (1984). Retirement plans of middle-aged married women. *The Gerontologist, 24*(3), 154–159.

Soghikian, K., Midanik, L. T., Polen, M. R., & Ransom, L. J. (1991). The effect of retirement on health services utilization: The Kaiser Permanente retirement study. *Journal of Gerontology: Social Sciences, 46*(6), S358–S360.

Strain, L. A. (1991). Use of health services in later life: The influence of health beliefs. *Journal of Gerontology: Social Sciences, 46*(3), S143–S150.

Szinovacz, M. (1996). Couples' employment/retirement patterns and perceptions of marital quality. *Research on Aging, 18*(2), 243–368.

Szinovacz, M., & Harpster, P. (1994). Couples' employment/retirement status and the division of household tasks. *Journal of Gerontology: Social Sciences, 49*(3), S125–S136.

Teaff, J., & Johnson, D. (1983). Preretirement education: A proposed bill for tuition tax credit. *Educational Gerontology, 9,* 31–36.

Wallace, R. B., & Herzog, A. R. (1995). Overview of the health measures in the Health and Retirement Study. *Journal of Human Resources, 30*(suppl.), S84–S107.

Ward, A. (1993). Marital happiness and household equity in later life. *Journal of Marriage and the Family, 55,* 427–438.

Welte, J. W., & Mirand, A. L. (1995). Drinking, problem drinking and life stressors in the elderly general population. *Journal of Studies on Alcohol, 56,* 67–73.

Zsembik, B. A., & Singer, A. (1990). The problem of defining retirement among minorities: The Mexican Americans. *The Gerontologist, 30*(5), 749–757.

Chapter 15

PROMOTING SELF-MANAGEMENT OF CHRONIC MEDICAL PROBLEMS

Jan Ligon

CHRONIC MEDICAL PROBLEMS

A recent study published by the Harvard School of Public Health (Murray & Lopez, 1996) forecasts that chronic medical conditions will replace infectious diseases as the primary global health concern by the year 2020. Published on behalf of the World Bank and the World Health Organization, the study projects that deaths from infectious diseases will decline from 17.2 million in 1990 to 10 million in 2020. At the same time, as the world's population continues to age and medical technology advances, health-related expenditures are likely to move from infectious to chronic conditions.

The combined influences of a shift in emphasis to chronic medical conditions, an aging population, and a continuing reform of the health care system may significantly change the role of social workers in health care. Regardless of future changes in the health care system, former U.S. Surgeon General C. Everett Koop (1996) believes that "one thing seems certain, the economics of health care will mean that patients are going to have less time with their doctors" (p. 69).

CHANGING ROLES IN HEALTH CARE

According to Wodarski, Wodarski, Nixon, and Mackie (1991), prior to the 1960s "reliance on the family physician as primary change agent was reasonable and necessary" (p. 20) because of the focus on infectious diseases. However, the authors note that as the predominant area of health problems began shifting to chronic conditions, which are often related to unhealthy lifestyles, the health care system began "to include active client responsibility in the treatment of disease and the maintenance of health" (p. 20).

As noted by Wodarski et al. (1991), "interdisciplinary fields are forming as traditional boundaries between disciplines break to accommodate the biopsychosocial model" (p. 21). Instead of waiting for a physician's instructions, patients are actively participating as informed partners in tandem with other resource persons, including medical personnel, social workers, psychologists, dietary and exercise consultants, and other paraprofessionals and volunteers.

This chapter provides information concerning methods that have been found to be effective in the self-management of four common chronic medical problems: (a) diabetes, (b) arthritis, (c) headache and low back pain, and (d) asthma. In addition, information is provided concerning effective components of self-management programs, which may be helpful to social workers in designing patient education and self-management programs.

PROMOTING SELF-MANAGEMENT

As the role of the patient moves away from that of relying on the professional as expert and the predominant area of medical problems shifts to chronic conditions, the ability to self-manage a wide range of health problems will become increasingly important. Social workers Ivanoff and Stern (1992) define self-management as "the naturally occurring process by which individuals identify and solve problems in the absence of external intervention" (p. 32). As noted earlier by Vattano, although patients "may be taught by professionals, the client assumes major responsibility for their operation in helping himself or herself" (1978, p. 113). Lorig (1996) agrees and describes self-management as being more complex than education alone, "in that it assists patients in gaining skills and, more important, gaining the confidence to apply these skills on a day-to-day basis" (p. xiv).

KEY ASPECTS OF SELF-MANAGEMENT PROGRAMS

Clark et al. (1991) identify three elements that are essential to the effective self-management of chronic medical problems: (a) adequate information, (b) "activities aimed at management of the condition," and (c) the ability to "maintain adequate psychosocial functioning" (p. 6) through the management of feelings associated with the medical condition. In addition, patients must deal with a number of specific tasks, which are also noted (Clark et al., 1991).

Adequate patient information must be made available to patients so that informed self-management decisions can be made. Such information is available in many different forms and languages. Although written materials are the most common, valuable information is available through other formats, including audio- and videotapes and the Internet. This information will help patients accomplish such tasks as understanding symptoms and triggers, using medication correctly, and managing crises.

It is important that social workers address any impairments to patient under-standing, such as language, poor reading ability, visual or hearing impairments, or cognitive limitations, in order that the patient understands the information to the fullest possible extent. Physicians may not provide adequate coverage of this essen-tial element of patient care. In a 1995 study, patients experiencing chronic medical problems were interviewed to gather information that would help to "enrich the approach to patient education through the views of patients" (Lacroix, Jacquemet, & Assal, 1995, p. 301). Medical problems addressed in the study included hyper-tension, back pain, asthma, chronic obstructive pulmonary disease, diabetes, and several other conditions. Numerous patients identified poor communication with physicians as a significant barrier to their treatment.

Patients interviewed in the study reported that physicians used language that was not comprehensible, that there was a lack of access to relevant information, and that they experienced poor communication with physicians (Lacroix et al., 1995). For example, one patient reported feeling "like a person relegated to the side," while another patient reported that nurses, on the other hand, "are listening to us and lend us support" (p. 303). In addition to nurses, social workers and other health professionals are increasingly involved in the role of educating patients about their chronic medical conditions.

Self-management activities are behavioral steps or actions that are taken by patients based on the knowledge they have obtained about their conditions. Strecher, DeVellis, Becker, and Rosenstock (1986) note that it is important for self-management programs to remove "the mysticism of change" (p. 90) by keeping programs simple and understandable. The social worker's role is to enhance the patient's ability to self-manage. Therefore, the patient, not the social worker, should become the expert on his or her condition. Self-management activities are helpful in dealing with a number of tasks, including eating properly, exercising, making decisions about symptoms and medications, and avoiding such harmful behaviors as smoking or abuse of alcohol and other substances.

Psychosocial functioning must be maintained in order for the patient to continue to self-manage his or her medical condition. Vattano (1978), a social worker, wrote about the need for self-management skills in dealing with stress and anxiety. In addition, people with chronic medical problems may also experience feelings of isolation, depression, and hopelessness. Interventions may be helpful to patients in accomplishing such tasks as adapting to work, managing emotions, and enhancing relationships with others (Clark et al., 1991).

SELF-MANAGEMENT TREATMENT COMPONENTS

Patient education, medical self-management skills, and psychosocial self-management skills are three common components of many effective self-management programs. Social workers will likely experience a great deal of variance in their patients, not only with respect to their specific medical problems, but also relative to levels of functioning, cognitive ability, and motivation to self-manage their problems. Therefore, it is important to understand the subtleties of each medical problem and to work with patients at their own pace and level of motivation to change.

Patient Education

In order to self-manage a chronic medical problem, the patient must first obtain sufficient medical knowledge about the problem to be able to make treatment decisions when the condition becomes exacerbated. Lorig (1996) provides extensive information on patient education and its role in self-management and states that "changes in knowledge may be necessary before we can change behaviors or health status" (p. xiv). She goes on to note, however, that "just because someone has correct knowledge does not mean he or she will change" (p. xiv).

The social worker can contribute greatly to the effort to educate the patient. First, information can be provided that is not only adequate but is also in a form that the person can comprehend. Second, social workers can assist in obtaining any necessary equipment that is needed to monitor medical conditions as well as in teaching the patient how to use it correctly. Third, supportive resources can be provided, such as telephone help lines or emergency services, for the patient to use as a backup when needed. Finally, social workers can support their patients by providing feedback and positive reinforcement as the medical knowledge is mastered.

Medical Self-Management Skills

Although medical self-management skills will vary by specific problem, Clark et al. (1991) found that there were categories that were common to many programs. The correct use of medication is a frequent task in managing chronic medical problems and would begin with patient education about the medications. Next, programs may teach patients to use such tools as self-monitoring logs, daily medication dispensers, and devices to measure symptoms. These skills target medical symptoms and often involve teaching not only patients but also other supportive persons. The data obtained can be used to decide whether to alter medication, connect with a backup resource, or go to an emergency facility.

Psychosocial Self-Management Skills

In addition to managing medical symptoms, many self-management programs incorporate skills for use in managing the feelings and emotions associated with chronic medical problems. Wodarski et al. (1991) provide information concerning a number of effective techniques that social workers might teach to patients, including biofeedback, exercise, relaxation training, and systematic desensitization. Social workers Ivanoff and Stern (1992) report that, of 14 studies with follow-ups of 6 months or longer, 9 "identified self-monitoring as an ongoing intervention component" (p. 33), and they further note that cognitive restructuring, self-instruction, and planning were used in the majority of the 14 studies. Certainly there may be overlap between medical and psychosocial techniques. In other words, becoming proficient at using a medical device to monitor symptoms may boost the patient's confidence. At the same time, learning to use relaxation techniques may help with the management of both physical symptoms and emotional characteristics.

Studies evaluating self-management programs have found that patients can be helped with a number of common chronic medical problems. As they become educated about their problems, learn medical and psychosocial management techniques, apply the knowledge on their own, and receive coaching and positive reinforcement from their social workers, patients can learn to effectively self-manage a wide range of conditions.

SELF-MANAGING SPECIFIC CHRONIC MEDICAL PROBLEMS

Social workers need a repertoire of potential tools and techniques in order to develop self-management programs that are congruent with patients' needs. However, a working knowledge of chronic medical conditions and the self-management programs that have been found to be effective for specific medical problems is also essential. Although not exhaustive, the following review of effective programs for diabetes, arthritis, headache and low back pain, and asthma provides strong support for the potential benefits of self-managing chronic medical problems. In addition, Table 15.1 provides a brief summary by problem of the programs studied.

Diabetes

Diabetes is caused by absent or ineffective insulin in the body, which causes high levels of glucose to appear in the blood. Diabetes can lead to serious complications, including high blood pressure, kidney disease, blindness, and the necessity of amputations. According to the National Institutes of Health (NIH; 1995) cardiovascular disease is 2 to 4 times more common in diabetics, who also have a 2.5-times higher risk of stroke. Although 6.2% of White adults in the United States are diagnosed with diabetes, the condition affects 11% of Puerto Rican Americans and 10% of both Mexican Americans and African Americans (NIH, 1995). The American Diabetes Association is an information resource at both the national and local levels.

Table 15.1   Studies of Self-Management of Chronic Medical Problems

Authors	Intervention components	Outcomes
Asthma		
Boulet, Boutin, Cote, Leblanc, & Laviolette (1995)	Self-management training for adults	Increased asthma knowledge and fewer visits to emergency room
Colland (1993)	Communication skills, education, and problem solving	Reduced anxiety, improved sleep, and fewer school absences
Harver (1994)	Verbal feedback	Improved ability to detect flow resistance to breathing
Wilson et al. (1993)	Small-group or individualized education program	Improved use of inhalers and better ability to control symptoms
Arthritis		
Davis, Busch, Lowe, Taniguchi, & Djkowich (1994)	Group instruction	Improved knowledge and perceived ability to self-manage
Keefe et al. (1990)	Relaxation, imagery, and cognitive restructuring	Lower levels of pain and less psychosocial disability
Lorig & Holman (1993)	Education, pain management, problem solving, and exercise	Lower pain, increased knowledge, and improved ability to self-manage
Taal et al. (1993)	Weekly contracting, goal-setting, and feedback	More practice of physical and relaxation exercises
Diabetes		
Glasgow et al. (1992)	Self-management training for patients over 60	Reduced calorie intake and reduced intake of fat
Glasgow, Toobert, Hampson, & Noell (1995)	Goal setting, feedback, and computer assistance	Weekly dietary goals achieved at a rate of 90% or higher
Pichert, Snyder, Kinzer, & Boswell (1994)	Anchored instruction for diabetics ages 9 to 15	Improved ability to link problem solving to decision rationales
Low Back Pain and Headache		
Holroyd & Penzien (1994)	Biofeedback and relaxation training	Significant reduction in levels of pain
Turner & Clancy (1988)	Goal setting, relaxation, imagery, and spouse training	Decreased physical and psychosocial disability

Treatment emphasizes blood-glucose level and diet monitoring, physical activity, and attention to medical and psychosocial factors (NIH, 1995). Jenkins (1995) provides an overview of behavioral management techniques used in a number of diabetes programs. Self-management skills can be successfully learned by patients and several studies have indicated that these skills can be improved, although patient differences may affect the choice of intervention. For example, Bradley (1994) identifies earlier studies that indicate that stress management may improve the psychological well-being of diabetics. On the other hand, a 10-week support group targeted to "improve blood sugar control and improve means of social support" (Oren, Carella, & Helma, 1996, p. 2) did not indicate significant results. Other programs that target specific populations and problems have been found to be significantly helpful to diabetics.

Pichert et al. (1994) studied the benefit of two 45-minute small-group teaching sessions using an anchored instruction technique for participants ages 9 to 15 who were recruited from a summer diabetes camp. Campers who received the instruction were able to link the rationale for disease-management guidelines to their sick-day management decisions at a significantly higher rate than were controls.

A 10-session self-management training program for patients over age 60 having Type II (non-insulin-dependent) diabetes was helpful to "a relatively hardcore group of patients who had a long history of diabetes and a number of chronic diseases besides diabetes" (Glasgow et al., 1992, p. 71). Participants were reached through an aggressive community effort that included free testing materials and a coupon that could be redeemed for free walking shoes. Weekly groups focused on dietary and exercise self-care issues and used goal setting, logs, weekly assignments, and problem-solving activities. Participants reduced total calorie intake levels as well as the percent of fat calories at significantly higher rates than did controls.

Diabetic patients who utilized an office-based program to improve dietary self-care were able to achieve their goals at a very high level of success (Glasgow et al. 1995). Using computer technology, including interactive video, patients received a behavioral intervention program followed by immediate feedback and goal setting specifically tailored to the individual patient. At 1-week follow-up, 90% of the patients reported achieving their goal and 96% were successful after 3 weeks.

Arthritis

Arthritis is a common chronic medical problem and is "the major cause of disability in the elderly and of admission to skilled nursing facilities" (Lorig & Holman, 1993, p. 18). There are different types of arthritis. Rheumatoid arthritis involves joint inflammation, with swelling, stiffness, and tenderness. Osteoarthritis, a degenerative joint disease, is the most common form of arthritis. The Arthritis Foundation is a resource for additional information at both the national and local levels. Several studies have demonstrated the effectiveness of arthritis self-management that is focused on learning to cope and live with the condition.

The Arthritis Self-Management Program (ASMP) is a patient education program developed at Stanford University in 1979 (Lorig, 1992) that consists of six 2-hour weekly sessions. Volunteers in the community are trained to teach the course, which is offered through local chapters of the Arthritis Foundation. The ASMP has been held in a wide range of community settings, including "senior centers, libraries, mobile home parks, churches, and shopping centers" (Lorig & Holman, 1993, p. 19).

The ASMP educates patients about the different forms of arthritis, the types and use of medications, exercises, cognitive pain management, and problem-solving skills. *The Arthritis Helpbook* (Lorig & Fries, 1995), a paperback text, provides additional information on the types of arthritis and medications and on goal setting and contracting, illustrates various exercises, and provides numerous tips on how to make daily tasks more manageable. In addition, *Arthritis* (Fries, 1995) is a reference text for use by teachers and trainers.

Outcome studies have found the ASMP to be very helpful to arthritis patients. An earlier outcome study (Lorig, Lubeck, Kraines, Seleznick, & Holman, 1985) found that after 4 months, patients randomized to the ASMP exceeded those in a control group in their knowledge and practice of self-management techniques and experienced lower levels of pain. The investigation also included a 20-month longitudinal study that found that frequency of exercise and "a significant decline in pain was sustained at 20 months" (p. 682). Lorig and Holman (1993) published a 12-year review of the ASMP noting that the outcomes of replication studies in Australia and Canada were "similar to those in the original experimental setting with a reasonable range of variability" (p. 25).

Although Kraaimaat, Brons, Geenen, and Bijlsma (1995) did not find a 20-hour cognitive-behavioral therapy group to be significantly helpful to rheumatoid arthritis patients, a 37-hour group instruction program in Canada was found to improve both knowledge about arthritis and the perceived ability to self-manage the condition (Davis et al., 1994). The Canadian program (Davis et al., 1994) is conducted by professionals, including social workers, rather than by trained volunteers like the ASMP (Lorig, 1992).

Patients with osteoarthritic knee pain who received pain-coping skills training were found to have significantly lower levels of pain and psychosocial disability than those in a control group who received patient education (Keefe et al., 1990). The intervention was conducted in small groups of 6 to 9 people and included training in a number of techniques, including relaxation, imagery, distraction, and cognitive restructuring. Participants also were taught how to break tasks into time periods of activity followed by rest, as well as how to schedule pleasant activities.

A group program for rheumatoid arthritis patients who participated in 10 hours of instruction was found to be significantly more helpful than controls (Taal et al., 1993). Participants demonstrated higher levels of knowledge, of practice of physical and relaxation exercises, of self-management behaviors, and of positive outcome expectations. The program was delivered by social workers and other professionals and included weekly contracting, goal setting, and feedback. Follow-up data indicated that after 14 months the researchers "still found strong effects on knowledge and the practice of physical exercises and a small effect on self-efficacy function" (Taal et al., 1993, p. 184).

Headache and Low Back Pain

Chronic low back pain and recurrent headache disorders are two common health problems that can account for large numbers of outpatient medical visits and serious economic losses, including the ability of patients to work (Holroyd & Penzien, 1994; Lackner, Carosella, & Feuerstein, 1996). Several behavioral techniques have been found to be helpful for both problems. For tension headaches, Holroyd and Penzien (1994) summarized 37 studies and found that biofeedback and relaxation training are equally effective and "have each yielded a nearly 50% reduction in tension headache activity" (p. 58). For migraine headaches, the researchers reported that a combination of biofeedback and relaxation training "yielded significantly larger reductions in migraine activity than either relaxation training or thermal biofeedback training alone" (p. 58). In a subsequent article, Penzien and Holroyd (1994) provide a practical summary of techniques involved in both relaxation and biofeedback training.

For chronic low back pain, Turner and Clancy (1988) reported that, at 12-month follow-up, patients who had received 16 hours of either operant behavioral or cognitive-behavioral treatment were helped equally. The operant behavioral group addressed pain and well behaviors and instructed spouses on how to positively reinforce well behaviors. Patients set behavioral goals, including exercise, that were progressively increased using a quota system. The cognitive-behavioral group received training in progressive relaxation, in the use of imagery, and in methods for altering maladaptive thoughts.

A component analysis conducted by Turner, Clancy, McQuade, and Cardenas (1990) compared the outcomes of patients who were randomly assigned to 16 hours of behavior therapy, to aerobic exercise, to a combination of both, or to a waiting-list control group. All three groups were found to have benefited at 6-month and 12-month follow-ups, although the groups receiving the combined behavioral and aerobic intervention reported the most significant reductions in self-reported levels of pain as well as in psychosocial disability. Behavioral treatment consisted of exploring pain and well behaviors, goal setting, homework assignments, and social reinforcement for completion.

Lackner, et al. (1996) tested the influence of self-efficacy expectations on the treatment outcome of patients having chronic low back pain disorders. The study investigated "functional self-efficacy expectations which refer to confidence judgements regarding the ability to execute or achieve tasks of physical performance" (p. 213). Results indicated that "performance-specific cognition may have greater explanatory power over disability than pain-specific ones" (p. 212). Keefe,

Dunsmore, and Burnett (1992) provide additional information on the efficacy of behavioral interventions for chronic pain.

Asthma

Asthma is a chronic medical problem caused by airflow obstruction in the bronchioles, which may lead to shortness of breath, wheezing, coughing, and tightness in the chest. The Centers for Disease Control and Prevention (CDC) report that asthma affects an estimated 14 to 15 million people in the United States. The death rate from asthma increased 118% from 1980 to 1993 for persons under age 25. Death and hospitalization rates are highest among African Americans, with death rates 6 times higher for Black males ages 15 to 24 than for Whites (CDC, 1996).

As noted by Buist and Vollmer (1994), "the number of hospitalizations and the amount of outpatient care required to treat asthma are substantial and rising" (p. 1584), and asthma occurs at a higher rate in poverty settings. CDC (1995) notes that "morbidity and mortality associated with asthma may be affected by patient compliance, patient education, and medical management" (p. 954). Buist and Vollmer (1994) note the need for the increased use of objective measures, for improved efforts in environmental control, and for "a partnership between patients and healthcare providers that includes health education" (p. 1585). At the national and local levels, the American Lung Association provides information and support concerning the growing problem of asthma. Programs to improve the self-management of asthma have been found to be effective for both adults and children.

One third of the 14 to 15 million people diagnosed with asthma in the United States are children and young adults under age 18 (CDC, 1996). Interventions and studies of programs to improve the self-management of asthma in children are extensive and are beyond the scope of this chapter. Rachelefsky (1987) provides a review of several self-management programs that have been helpful to children with asthma in reducing the frequency of asthma attacks, the numbers of school absences, and the numbers of both hospital emergency room visits and hospital inpatient days.

Children ages 8 to 13 who participated in a 10-hour educational training program (Colland, 1993) experienced significant changes when compared to controls, including a higher level of knowledge about asthma, a greater reduction in anxiety, a higher level of ability to use inhaled medications correctly, fewer sleep interruptions, and fewer school absences. The program used behavioral techniques and group therapy to teach self-management activities. A positive reward system was used for individuals and for the group as a whole to reinforce the completion of homework. In addition to self-management skills, participants learned how to communicate their needs when exposed to triggers, such as tobacco smoke. Problem-solving skills were practiced in role plays and in homework assignments. One year after the program ended, the experimental-group children demonstrated clinically significant differences in their ability to manage their asthma. Colland (1993) also reported that for parents of the children, "the burden of having a chronically ill child had been reduced as a result of the child's participation in the training program" (p. 150).

The Centers for Disease Control and Prevention (1996) note the need for environmental controls in conjunction with patient education and medical management. Buist and Vollmer (1994) further note that "environmental factors should be taken seriously" (p. 1585) in controlling asthma, particularly in poverty areas. Social workers can provide patients with a wide range of helpful information (Ingram & Heymann, 1993), including using plastic mattress covers, controlling dust mites, applying household cleaning tips, exterminating cockroaches, and reducing of numerous triggers, including cat allergen and cigarette smoke. One study (Huss et al., 1994) found that children ages 5 to 12 who had plastic covers on their mattresses had significantly fewer emergency room visits than children without the mattress covers.

The ability to detect flow resistance in breathing, an important factor in asthma self-assessment, was "improved significantly as a function of feedback experience" (Harver, 1994, p. 60). Boulet et al. (1995) compared participants and controls 1 year before and 1 year after a 2½-hour education and self-management training program for adult asthma patients and found that the intervention group had significant increases in asthma knowledge and the means to control it, as well as a significant reduction in emergency room visits.

Wilson et al. (1993) studied adult asthma patients who were randomly assigned to one of four groups, including a 6-hour small-group education program, three to five individually tailored sessions, a self-study workbook group, or a control group that did not include asthma education. Patients in the two treatment groups (small group or individual sessions) were found to report significant improvements in the bedroom environment, in the use of inhaler medications, in the control of symptoms, and in adherence to treatment. Although the use of a self-study workbook was not found to be helpful, small groups were found to "have significant beneficial effect for modest cost" (p. 575).

SUPPLEMENTARY INFORMATION

General overviews concerning patient education and self-management programs, including theoretical perspectives, are available (Clark et al., 1991; Lorig, 1996; Stretcher et al., 1986). Additional information on the techniques used in self-management programs are available elsewhere, including the use of goals and homework assignments (Shelton & Levy, 1981) and progressive relaxation training (Bernstein & Borkovec, 1973). Patient outcomes can be measured by using reliable and valid instruments available from original publications or from a two-volume sourcebook (Fischer & Corcoran, 1994). Self-anchored scales, the use of client logs, and behavioral observations are also described by Fischer and Corcoran (1994).

Additional information concerning specific medical problems, as well as other helpful resources and patient education materials, are available from numerous organizations, books, and the Internet. For example, the American Lung Association offers extensive information about asthma and has offices at both the national and local levels. The U.S. Department of Health and Human Services (1992) also offers materials on asthma. In addition, several well-written paperback books are available to provide helpful information about asthma not only to patients (Newhouse & Barnes, 1994; Weinstein, 1987), but also to parents of children with asthma (Plaut, 1988).

CONCLUSION

Former Attorney General C. Everett Koop, commenting on managed care and the sweeping changes in the delivery of health care, states that he is "convinced that patient education will help us solve the problems that lie before us" (1996, p. 69). Many chronic medical problems have a more adverse effect on poor and disadvantaged groups traditionally served by social workers, including children, minority groups, disabled people, and elderly people. Patient education alone is not sufficient and may not reach these vulnerable and needy populations.

Social workers offer a unique perspective, practical skills, and a commitment to helping others that is congruent to the assessment, development, implementation, and evaluation of effective programs to help patients with the self-management of chronic medical problems. Dissemination of information through publishing, workshops, conferences, and teaching opportunities is essential as the expertise to help patients continues to expand.

REFERENCES

Bernstein, D. A., & Borkovec, T. C. (1973). *Progressive relaxation training: A manual for the helping professions*. Champaign, IL: Research Press.

Boulet, L. P., Boutin, H., Cote, J., Leblanc, P., & Laviolette, M. (1995). Evaluation of an asthma self-management education program. *Journal of Asthma, 32*, 199–206.

Bradley, C. (1994). Contributions of psychology to diabetes management. *British Journal of Clinical Psychology, 33*, 11–21.

Buist, A. S., & Vollmer, W. M. (1994). Preventing deaths from asthma. *The New England Journal of Medicine, 331*, 1584–1585.

Centers for Disease Control and Prevention. (1995). Asthma—United States, 1982–1992. *MMWR, 43*, 952–955.

Centers for Disease Control and Prevention. (1996). Asthma mortality and hospitalization among children and young adults—United States, 1980–1993. *MMWR, 45,* 350–353.

Clark, N. M., Becker, M. H., Janz, N. K., Lorig, K., Rakowski, W., & Anderson, L. (1991). Self-management of chronic disease by older adults. *Journal of Aging and Health, 3,* 3–27.

Colland, V. T. (1993). Learning to cope with asthma: A behavioural self-management program for children. *Patient Education and Counseling, 22,* 141–152.

Davis, P., Busch, A. J., Lowe, J. C., Taniguchi, J., & Djkowich, B. (1994). Evaluation of a rheumatoid arthritis patient education program: Impact on knowledge and self-efficacy. *Patient Education and Counseling, 24,* 55–61.

Fischer, J., & Corcoran, K. (1994) *Measures for clinical practice: A sourcebook* (Vols. 1–2). New York: Free Press.

Fries, J. F. (1995). *Arthritis: A comprehensive guide to understanding your arthritis* (4th ed.). Reading, MA: Addison-Wesley.

Glasgow, R. E., Toobert, D. J., Hampson, S. E., Brown, J. E., Lewinsohn, P. M., & Donnelly, J. (1992). Improving self-care among older patients with type II diabetes: The "sixth something . . ." study. *Patient Education and Counseling, 19,* 61–74.

Glasgow, R. E., Toobert, D. J., Hampson, S. E., & Noell, J. W. (1995). A brief office-based intervention to facilitate diabetes dietary self-management. *Health Education Research, 10,* 467–478.

Harver, A. (1994). Effects of feedback on the ability of asthmatic subjects to detect increases in the flow-resistive component to breathing. *Health Psychology, 13,* 52–62.

Holroyd, K. A., & Penzien, D. B. (1994). Psychosocial interventions in the management of recurrent headache disorders: 1. Overview and effectiveness. *Behavioral Medicine, 20,* 53–63.

Huss, K., Rand, C. S., Butz, A. M., Eggleston, P. A., Murigande, C., Thompson, L. C., Schneider, S., Weeks, K., & Malveaux. (1994). Home environmental risk factors in urban minority asthmatic children. *Annals of Allergy, 72,* 173–177.

Ingram, J. M., & Heymann, P. W. (1993). Environmental controls in the management of asthma. *Immunology and Allergy Clinics of North America, 13,* 785–801.

Ivanoff, A., & Stern, S. B. (1992). Self-management interventions in health and mental health settings: Evidence of maintenance and generalization. *Social Work Research and Abstracts, 28,* 32–38.

Jenkins, C. D. (1995). An integrated behavioral medicine approach to improving care of patients with diabetes mellitus. *Behavioral Medicine, 21,* 53–65.

Keefe, F. J., Caldwell, D. S., Williams, D. A., Gil, K. M., Mitchell, D., Robertson, C., Martinez, S., Nunley, J., Beckham, J. C., Crisson, J. E., & Helms, M. (1990). Pain coping skills training in the management of osteoarthritic knee pain: A comparative study. *Behavior Therapy, 21,* 19–62.

Keefe, F. J., Dunsmore, J., & Burnett, R. (1992). Behavioral and cognitive-behavioral approachers to chronic pain: Recent advances and future directions. *Journal of Consulting and Clinical Psychology, 60,* 528–536.

Koop, C. E. (1996). Manage with care. *Time, 148*(14), 69.

Kraaimaat, F. W., Brons, M. R., Geenen, R., & Bijlsma, J. W. J. (1995). The effect of cognitive behavior therapy in patients with rheumatoid arthritis. *Behaviour Research and Therapy, 33,* 487–495.

Lackner, J., Carosella, A. M., & Feuerstein, M. (1996). Pain expectancies, pain, and functional self-efficacy expectancies as determinants of disability in patients with chronic low back disorders. *Journal of Consulting and Clinical Psychology, 64,* 212–220.

Lacroix, A., Jacquemet, S., & Assal, J. (1995). Patients' experiences with their disease: Learning from the differences and sharing the common problems. *Patient Education and Counseling, 26,* 301–312.

Lorig, K. (1992). *Arthritis self-help course.* Atlanta, GA: Arthritis Foundation.

Lorig, K. (1996). *Patient education: A practical approach.* Thousand Oaks, CA: Sage.

Lorig, K., & Fries, J. F. (1995). *The Arthritis Helpbook: A tested self-management program for coping with your arthritis.* Reading, MA: Addison-Wesley.

Lorig, K., & Holman, H. (1993). Arthritis self-management studies: A twelve-year review. *Health Education Quarterly, 20,* 17–28.

Lorig, K., Lubeck, D., Kraines, E. G., Seleznick, M., & Holman, H. R. (1985). Outcomes of self-help education for patients with arthritis. *Arthritis and Rheumatism, 28,* 680–685.

Murray, C. J., & Lopez, A. D. (1996). *The global burden of disease.* Cambridge, MA: Harvard University Press.

National Institutes of Health. (1995). *Prevalence of diabetes in the United States* (NIH Publication No. 96-3926). Washington, DC: National Institute of Diabetes and Kidney Diseases.

Newhouse, M. T., & Barnes, P. J. (1994). *Conquering asthma: An illustrated guide to understanding and care for adults.* Hamilton, Canada: Empowering Press.

Oren, M. L., Carella, M., Helma, T. (1996). Diabetes support group—study results and implications. *Employee Assistance Quarterly, 11,* 1–20.

Penzien, D. B., & Holroyd, K. A. (1994). Psychosocial interventions in the management of recurrent headache disorders: 2. Description of treatment techniques. *Behavioral Medicine, 20,* 64–73.

Pichert, J. W., Snyder, G. M., Kinzer, C. K., & Boswell, E. J. (1994). Problem solving anchored instruction about sick days for adolescents with diabetes. *Patient Education and Counseling, 23,* 115–124.

Plaut, T. F. (1988). *Children with asthma: A manual for parents.* Amherst, MA: Redipress.

Rachelefsky, G. S. (1987). Review of asthma self-management programs. *Journal of Allergy and Clinical Immunology, 80,* 506–511.

Shelton, J. L., & Levy, R. L. (1981). *Behavioral assignments and treatment compliance.* Champaign, IL: Research Press.

Stretcher, V. J., DeVellis, B. M., Becker, M. H., & Rosenstock, I. M. (1986). The role of self-efficacy in achieving health behavior change. *Health Education Quarterly, 13,* 73–91.

Taal, E., Riemsma, R. P., Brus, H. L., Seydel, E. R., Rasker, J. J., & Wiegman, O. (1993). Group education for patients with rheumatoid arthritis. *Patient Education and Counseling, 20,* 177–187.

Turner, J. A., & Clancy, S. (1988). Comparison of operant behavioral and cognitive-behavioral treatment for low back pain. *Journal of Consulting and Clinical Psychology, 56,* 261–266.

Turner, J., Clancy, S., McQuade, K. J., & Cardenas, D. D. (1990). Effectiveness of behavioral therapy for chronic low back pain: A component analysis. *Journal of Consulting and Clinical Psychology, 59,* 573–579.

U.S. Department of Health and Human Services. (1992). *Teach your patients about asthma: A clinician's guide* (NIH Publication No. 92-2737). Washington, DC: U.S. Department of Health and Human Services.

Vattano, A. J. (1978). Self-management for coping with stress. *Social Work, 23,* 113–199.

Weinstein, A. W. (1987). *Asthma: The complete guide to self-management of asthma and allergies for patients and their families.* New York: Ballantine.

Wilson, S. R., Scamages, P., German, D. F., Hughes, G. W., Lulla, S., Coss, S., Chardon, L., Thoms, R. G., Starr-Schneidkraut, N., Stanvacage, F. B., & Arsham, G. M. (1993). A controlled trial of two forms of self-management education for adults with asthma. *The American Journal of Medicine, 54,* 564–576.

Wodarski, J. S., Wodarski, L. A., Nixon, S. C., & Mackie, C. (1991). Behavioral medicine: An emerging field of social work practice. *Journal of Health and Social Policy, 3,* 19–43.

Chapter 16

HOSPICE CARE

Michael J. Holosko
D. Rosemary Cassano

Despite the facts that hospice care as we know it has been in existence for about 30 years in North America and that social work has been an integral part of it since that time, a review of the medical and psychosocial literature related to the effectiveness of social work practice in hospice care reveals the following: (a) there are very few empirical studies of social work practice; (b) those that are published generally lack methodological rigor; (c) there are few evaluations of hospice programs or services at all; (d) there are a predominance of theoretical, opinion-type, and exploratory studies—only remotely related to the effectiveness of social work practice; (e) there are frequent accounts of social work services, practice roles, and responsibilities that are written primarily by social work academics, not by practitioners working in this area; and, (f) the more rigorously controlled empirical investigations of practice effectiveness are found in the nursing literature more so than in that of medicine or social work. But in regard to the latter, however spotty the social work literature on practice effectiveness is, the medical literature is even spottier, in that few accounts of physician interventions and their relative effectiveness or outcomes are to be found.

This state of the art of the literature on social work effectiveness in this area is surprising, given: (a) the profession's long-standing history with hospice care; (b) that U.S. national accrediting standards have delineated a role for social work in hospice care since 1979 (National Hospice Organization, 1979); and (c) that the federal Tax Equity and Fiscal Responsibilities Act (1982) defines hospice care as "nursing care by or under the supervision of a registered professional nurse; medical social services under the direction of a physician; [and] counselling (including dietary counselling) with respect to care of the terminally ill individual and adjustment to his death" (pp. 359–360). As a result, this chapter examines the effectiveness of both social work and other disciplines in hospice care and is organized according to: (a) hospice versus traditional care, (b) social work's relevance to hospice care, (c) research on hospice patients, (d) research on caregivers of hospice patients, (e) effective non–social work interventions, and (f) the effectiveness of social work interventions.

OVERVIEW

Hospice versus Traditional Medical Care

Historically, hospice care has been designed to enhance the quality of the end of life. Its formal beginnings are attributed to the pioneering efforts of Dame Cicely Saunders, a British nurse, medical social worker, and physician who was distressed at the lack of attention given to dying patients in London hospitals and founded St. Christopher's Hospice in 1967 (Fish, 1992, p. 5). Presently, hospice programs in the United States number over 2,300 and their numbers grow annually. They are found in every state of the union (Office of Research and Demonstrations, 1994).

Hospice care offers several advantages over traditional hospital-based care for terminally ill patients. First, the overriding philosophy of hospice is palliative care (rather than cure), which extends the symptom-disease model of medicine into a holistic realm where physical care is normally offered for pain alleviation and psychological supports are simultaneously offered for patients, families, caregivers, loved ones, and significant others (Vachon, 1988). Paradis and Cummings (1986) indicate that the hospice movement since its inception has been "humanistic and holistic, focusing on the psycho-social as well as the physical needs of patients" (p. 370). Burger (1980) contends that *the* unique feature of hospice care is that "a dying patient should be free of physical, mental, social and spiritual pain in order that s/he may live as fully as possible" (p. 134).

Second, hospice care may be offered in a home-based environment (which it is about 80% of the time; Christakis & Escarce, 1996), in specialized inpatient care facilities (i.e., a palliative or hospice care facility), or in general inpatient facilities (i.e., hospitals or nursing homes). Characteristics of hospice care programs that set them apart from traditional health care programs include: (a) care is physician-supervised or -directed; (b) coordinated home and inpatient care is provided under a central hospice management; (c) there is concurrent symptom management of a physical, psychosocial, and spiritual nature; (d) interdisciplinary team care, usually including a physician, a nurse, a social worker, clergy, and volunteers is provided; (e) the patient and the family together comprise the primary unit of care; (f) volunteers are an increasingly important component of the overall care team; (g) there is normally 24-hour care; and (h) bereavement counselling is normally offered as a regular follow-up for family members (Fish, 1992, p. 405). Inpatient hospice programs are increasingly being offered on a day patient basis.

Although hospice care programs are unique and are different from traditional health care, they are not distinct from them. Arguably, the "care-ative" versus "curative" philosophical difference between hospice and health care may have caused the differences among hospices (Mor, 1987). However, their philosophy engenders a holistic (and, in turn, humanistic) view in which, foremost, physical comfort and then psychosocial support is offered to hospice patients and their families. Indeed, Lack (1977) noted some 20 years ago that "there is far too much talk . . . in this country about psychosocial and emotional problems, and far too little about making the patient comfortable. Counselling a dying person who is lying in a wet bed is ineffective" (p. 162).

The definition of *palliative care* approved by the National Hospice Organization (NHO) in 1988 is the standard that guides decisions about palliative care today.

> The NHO defines palliative care for terminally ill patients (those in advanced progressive stages of illness such as cancer, AIDS and other diseases) as treatment that enhances comfort and improves the quality of a patient's life. No specific therapy is excluded from consideration. The test of palliative treatment resides in the agreement by the attending physician, the patient, the primary care support, and the hospice team that the goals of the intervention are pain control, symptom management, quality of life enhancement and spiritual-emotional comfort for patients and their primary support. The decision to intervene or not with a palliative treatment is based on its ability to meet with the goals mentioned above rather than its effort on the underlying disease. Each patient's needs must continue to be assessed and all treatment options explored and evaluated in the context of the patient's values and symptoms. (Zinn, 1995, p. 137)

Thus, the philosophy of palliative care—the framework for hospice care—requires a personal acceptance of death and an acknowledgment that dying does not indicate a failure to provide good medical care but, more so, calls for an acquiescence that the curative treatment is no longer feasible. Thus, the terminal state is an integral process and is a time to reconcile issues so that patients, family, and support groups may better accept death with a minimum of physical, spiritual, and psychosocial anguish (Rousseau, 1995).

Social Work Relevance to Hospice Care

Ever since Mary Richmond (1917) coined the phrase "social conscience of the hospital" to describe hospital social workers in her seminal text *Social Diagnosis,* social workers have played a prominent role in the provision of health services in America. Social work's malleability, its psychosocial orientation, and its ability to perform essential roles that are different and unique from other health care roles (Bartlett, 1961) have positioned the profession as an integral and necessary part of the changing present and future health care service delivery system (Holosko, 1992). As Bracht (1978) stated, "social work's uniqueness comes from its persistent focus on the physical, social-psychological and environmental health needs of clients" (p. 13).

Since psychosocial care is a universal and defining feature of hospice care, over the years this component has solidly entrenched social work practice in hospice services and programs. The nature of this relationship is symbiotic, as social work and hospice care are intimately interrelated. McDonnell (1986) stated that the role of professional social work must be viewed as integral to hospice care and social workers' skills and knowledge are indispensable to effective hospice programs

(p. 225–226). As such, Quig (1989) reported that the interdisciplinary team is much more able to carry out its tasks and functions when the social worker is a part of that team (p. 23). Rusnack, Schaefer, and Moxley (1988) indicated that holistic social work values, humanism, the ecological perspective, and treating the client's system in the social environment provide an excellent fit between social work practice and hospice care. Indeed, Macdonald (1991) indicated that it is this very viewpoint of social work that helps distinguish hospice from mainstream terminal care. He went further to state that "from its consideration of the patient and family as the unit of care and its commitment to addressing the multiple needs of the individual, hospice practice demonstrates a philosophy adapted directly from the fundamental tenets of social work" (p. 275). As such, he indicated that the values and principles of social work practice are probably the greatest single influence on hospice theory and practice. McDonnell (1986) made this point more succinctly when he described hospice as "the embodiment of social values, principles and practice" (p. 225).

RESEARCH ABOUT HOSPICE PATIENTS

Demographics

Although hospice care is designed for any patient with any terminally ill diagnosis, the majority of patients are over age 65, are White, and have cancer. In 1992, the Centers for Disease Control and Prevention (CDCP) and the National Health Center for Statistics conducted the first national survey of approximately 2,100 hospice programs (home health agencies, hospices, and their patients) serving about 47,200 patients in the United States. Notable findings in this study were that 77% of the patients admitted to these programs were over age 65; 65% of the patients had first-listed diagnoses of malignant neoplasms (cancer); 10% of the patients were admitted with end-stage heart disease; 91% of the patients in the 12 months preceding this survey died while receiving hospice care; and the average length of hospice service was 60 days (Strahan, 1992). It is estimated that a further 10% to 15% of the patients admitted to hospice had AIDS, ALS, or end-stage renal disease (Zinn, 1995).

In 1982, Medicare began covering hospice care under the Tax Equity and Fiscal Responsibilities Act. Medicare pays for hospice support services on a per diem basis and provides coverage for two 90-day benefit periods, a subsequent 30-day period, and an indefinite period after 210 days while the patient is terminally ill (Rousseau, 1995, p. 786). Regulated Medicare benefits in licensed Medicare-certified hospices include medical and nursing care; physical, speech, and occupational care; social work counselling; home health and impatient services; medications and medical supplies; and durable medical equipment (Rhymes, 1990).

In 1994, about 221,849 beneficiaries received hospice care at a cost to Medicare of $1.32 billion (Christakis & Escarce, 1996). Christakis and Escarce analyzed the characteristics of 6,451 of these Medicare patients in five states in America, and found that 92.4% were White, the average age was 76.4 years, 50% were male, 80.2% had cancer of some type, the median survival rate was 36 days, and 15.6% died within 7 days after enrollment. The most common cancers were lung (21.4%), colorectal (10.5%), and prostate (7.4%). The authors concluded, among other things, that when Medicare patients enter hospice care they do so late in the course of their terminal illness (p. 172).

Regardless of whether patients are receiving Medicare, the need for hospice care grows annually in America, in particular for elderly patients and their families. Coupled with this is the overall growing number of elderly persons in proportion to the population as a whole, particularly in the over age 85 category (Holosko & Feit, 1996). This demographic trend will inevitably result in hospice care taking on a distinct gerontologic flavor—which appears to be happening at present, with the emergence of a number of hospice care in nursing home programs. This, in turn, will have implications for specialized education training and hospice care practice in a variety of disciplines (Crane, 1994; Wall, Rodriguez, & Saultz, 1992).

Characteristics and Utilization Patterns

Although the majority of studies on the characteristics and utilization patterns of hospice patients are secondary analyses of extant data, there are some that have collected primary data from patients in care. Given the current trend toward patient- and consumer-driven research in health and social services in North America, one may speculate that more consumer-oriented studies will appear in the literature in the near future (Holosko, 1997). Overall, the studies of characteristics and utilization patterns are descriptive in nature and do not use rigorous or controlled designs to any extent. Further, the majority cannot readily be generalized as they are typically bracketed geographically by either the hospice program or its locale (i.e., the region, city, or state).

The secondary analyses studies were usually concerned with assessing utilization patterns and patient needs, with determining how data on patients correlated to program care, or with assessing costs. In regard to utilization patterns, it appears that despite the proliferation of hospice care in America and its increasing popularity, individuals typically do not enter hospice until a late stage of terminal illness. As previously indicated, this delay appears to be greater for Medicare patients than for non-Medicare patients (Christakis & Escarce, 1996). Utilization also appears to be primarily affected by access and proximity to a program (Infeld, Crum, & Koshuta, 1990), indicating a decidedly urban bias to such programs and their services. That is, larger urban centers with well-integrated home health service components are more likely to be used than isolated, nonintegrated home health service programs (Smith & Reid, 1987).

In addition, the use of hospice care by different population groups—namely, by elderly patients with dementia, by AIDS patients, by fewer persons with a primary diagnosis of cancer as a proportion of admissions, and by different cultural groups—and growing participation in hospice care by HMOs are apparently trends that will continue in the future (Berry, Boughton, & McNamee, 1994; Infeld et al., 1990; Smith & Reid, 1987). Given the fact that hospice programs are designed to be based on home care, there is some indication that health care specialists already linked to the home, such as family physicians, should have more training to deal with the core issues of hospice, such as grief and loss, death and dying, and bereavement counselling (Wall et al., 1992). In regard to cost issues, rigorous overall cost analyses do not appear in the published literature. As a result, no definitive conclusions about the costs of hospice can yet be rendered with any certainty. However, some authors have been concerned with this lack of information and with speculation about cost-effectiveness, in particular, as it relates to Medicare and the elderly (Christakis & Escarce, 1996; Scitovsky, 1994). It is also apparent that future hospice care research requires more cost studies that have an empirical basis.

Although the primary data studies on characteristics and utilization patterns were generally inconclusive and reflected point-in-time analyses of patient opinions and attitudes, the surveys in the literature revealed the following: (a) general population samples show a limited awareness of hospice programs, but awareness is not correlated with use, as the programs are extensively utilized (Mor, Hendershot, & Cryan, 1989); (b) health care professionals are aware of hospice programs and encourage patients to use them (Kinzel, 1992); (c) professionals support the use of hospice care for a number of illnesses other than a primary diagnosis of cancer (Kinzel, 1992), namely AIDS (Miller, 1991) and end-stage dementia (Hanrahan & Luchins, 1995). As well, these studies revealed that specific features of hospice treatment itself—namely, its adaptable multidisciplinary home health care (Hansen & Evashwick, 1981); its focus on the psychological issues related to death, dying, and bereavement (Dobratz, 1995); its patient education on pain control in assisting with pain prevention and relief (Rimer, Kedziera, & Levy, 1992); its orientation to patient and family care satisfaction (Hays & Arnold, 1986); its person-centered comforting (Zimmerman & Applegate, 1992); and its help in dealing with denial in terminal illness (Conner, 1992)—were deemed positive attributes of hospice care from the perspective of patients, families, volunteers, and care providers.

Overall, patient physical symptoms are similar—usually pain (both the most frightening and the easiest to manage), extreme weakness, nausea, vomiting, loss of appetite, constipation, edema, and weight loss (Fish, 1992, p. 406). The diagnosis of terminal cancer frequently disrupts the patient and his or her lifestyle, family members, and loved ones (Dobkin and Morrow, 1986). Pollin (1984) states that normal living is replaced by conditional living—the realization that one cannot go on with one's life as planned (p. 28). Thus, as indicated by Fish (1992), patients encounter intense fears, anxieties, and frustrations that are both unexpected and unfamiliar (p. 407).

RESEARCH ON CAREGIVERS

Although a few researchers have challenged the prevailing assumption that hospice care is unique, the majority of studies on caregiver effectiveness clearly demonstrate that hospice care differs from hospital care; hospice-style care may not be unique to hospices; caregiver effectiveness varies from hospice to hospice; different outcomes of effectiveness are ascribed to different caregivers; few studies of effectiveness focus on what happens in day-to-day care procedures because of their emphasis on outcomes and interventions; and caregivers are truly valued, as they are the lifeblood of any hospice program. *Caregivers* here refers to either primary care persons (PCPs)—families, spouses, loved ones, social supports, neighbors, relatives, and significant others—or professional caregivers (PCs)—namely, nurses, physicians, psychologists, occupational therapists, pastoral careworkers, and volunteers. Social workers are consciously excluded in this latter group as their effectiveness is discussed in more detail in a later subsection of this chapter.

An overview of the empirical literature in this area renders the following conclusions. The majority of the research is foremost exploratory and quantitative-descriptive in nature, and generally is lacking in methodologic rigor. The methods used and the findings are limited in terms of their general applicability, as they are usually studies of the outcomes of interventions at a specific hospice. The majority used small convenience samples ($N < 50$); about one third employed the use of standardized measures to assess outcomes; and almost all showed very positive outcomes ascribed to caregivers in a variety of hospice settings. In terms of the critical mass of literature in this area, almost half the studies reviewed were about PCPs and approximately one fourth were about nurse caregiving, while the remaining studies (ranked in descending order of frequency) were about physicians, volunteers, and psychologists.

Primary Care Persons (PCPs)

Overall, the explicit goal of hospice care is maintaining the family and support system in patient care. As such, hospice programs typically advise, consult, liaise with, and support family caregivers rather than take on the day-to-day practical caregiving work themselves. As well, inpatient hospice care ideally involves a high level of visiting and actual care by friends, families, and relatives (Seale, 1989, p. 555). It has been shown that PCPs who carry the lion's share of home hospice care services report higher levels of involvement than those caring for patients in inpa-

tient hospice units (National Hospice Study, 1986). Similarly, Kane, Klein, Bernstein, Rothenberg, and Wales (1985) found that, overall, those caring for hospice
patients were more satisfied with their involvement in care than were those caring
for hospital patients, reiterating the point that hospice care differs from hospital
care from this perspective.

PCPs are normally involved in implementing a variety of aspects of hospice
care. This care is usually practical, occurs at home, is demanding in terms of time
and energy, and is highly interactive in nature. Indeed, both patients and PCPs
report the overall positive effects of such care in a variety of ways. Birenbaum &
Robinson (1991), in their study of family relationships among 48 families during a
child's terminal illness with cancer and 1 year following the child's death found
that caregiving parents perceived their family relationships as being different from
those of normal families and that hospital-based terminal care families presented
evidence of better family relationships than home-based terminal care families. In
a comparison of hospice to conventional care, Seale (1991) reported higher levels
of PCP satisfaction with hospice home nursing and inpatient hospice care than
with other forms of care. Similarly, Dawson (1991) reported that perceptions of
basic needs satisfaction regarding the role of the nurse in supporting family care
and overall satisfaction with PCP care were higher in hospice than in conventional
care settings. In an attempt to test the hypothesis that greater predeath lengths of
stay (LOS) in hospice would have a beneficial effect on bereavement adjustment,
Speer, Robinson, and Reed (1995) found no significant differences in bereavement
adjustment between caregivers with varying predeath LOS. They concluded that
bereavement resolution is a complex process and that cumulative medical illness
burden, impairment of the activities of daily living (ADL), and caregiver burden
need to be more fully determined.

In an effort to both understand and determine the efficacy of the PCP role in supporting hospice care programs, Kirschling, Tilden, and Butterfield (1990) developed and psychometrically scrutinized the variables of social support, reciprocity,
cost, and conflict with Tilden's Cost and Reciprocity Index (CRI). They concluded
that the CRI is a reliable and valid measure to use in assessing the experiences of
hospice family caregivers. Martens and Davies (1990), in an effort to understand
the work of patients and spouses in managing advanced-stage cancer at home,
reported that patients and spouses used both internal and external resources; the
external resources used were either physical or interpersonal in nature; and both
patients and spouses faced either inevitable or uncertain death by engaging in various types of goal-directed work, such as specific comfort-related activities, having
a pain-free day, hoping, and ADL. These authors concluded that understanding the
dimensions of such work has implications for health care professionals caring for
patients and families in palliative care.

In this context, Stetz and Hanson (1992), in their study of bereaved spouse caregivers, reported that although managing physical care was identified as most diffi-

cult, reflective thought about the difficulties in caregiving revealed that standing by or observing the slow deterioration of the ill spouse was perceived as most difficult. They reported that over 50% of the caregivers in their survey regretted that they had not sought out or utilized more resources to aid them in caregiving. Seale and Addington-Hall (1995) corroborated the complexities and difficulties facing PCP caregivers when they concluded that the PCPs of people who received hospice care were, if anything, more likely to feel that it would have been better if the patient had died earlier rather than prolonging death. In extending their analyses to support a position for euthanasia, these authors concluded that care judged to be good may do only little to counteract people's fears of dependency and, indeed, may serve to decrease feelings of autonomy (p. 581).

In the past decade in North America, the number of AIDS patients requiring hospice care has increased annually. The literature has indicated that such patients may require unique hospice care, or, more precisely, hospice care that accommodates their unique needs. For example, Baker and Seager (1991) compared the psychosocial needs of hospice patients with AIDS to those of patients with other terminal illnesses. They concluded that AIDS patients required significantly more psychosocial support than non-AIDS patients. Further, the nature of that support was different—family, neighbors, congregation, and hospice staff indicated that working with such patients was both more time-consuming and more stressful than working with non-AIDS patients. Similarly, Atkins and Amenta (1991) showed that families of AIDS patients had significantly more stress, more rules prohibiting emotional expression, lower trust levels, and more illness anxiety than families in the non-AIDS group. Finally, in this regard, Pomeroy, Rubin, and Walker (1995) conducted a quasi-experimental evaluation testing the effectiveness of a combined psychoeducational and task-centered group for family members of AIDS patients. They found that this group was effective in alleviating stress, perceived stigma, depression, and anxiety for such families.

Nursing Care

One of the major duties and responsibilities of the hospice care nurse is facilitating the overall quality of life for patients and their PCPs. The nurse, functioning as a member of the interdisciplinary hospice team, both provides an environment of comfort and security and directs care to the control and management of pain and other discomfort. It has been shown that nurses exhibit specific behaviors and provide interventions shown to be effective in hospice settings. However, less well known is the extent to which such interventions are unique or at all different in hospice versus traditional (hospital) care. Given the current trends in health care (i.e., toward more cost-effective community-based care) hospice nurses have been concerned with determining how their roles and responsibilities will be affected. For example, Amenta (1995) stated:

What do these changes mean for the hospice nurse? Surely, the managers of hospice programs will make the transitions as seamless as possible and will provide sufficient in-service education to prepare staff as they meet new conditions. And just as surely, hospice nurses will carry more patients, will be making visits of shorter duration, and will make more visits per day. Hospice nurses will need to develop more scrupulous hospice-specific charting skills, because documentation will be the key to maintaining the integrity of hospice care even if, and as, familiar structures melt away (p. 7)

In response to these concerns, Morris & Christie (1995a) developed a standardized inventory to determine the roles, responsibilities, and functions of hospice nursing in today's health care environment. In a prior article, which laid the conceptual framework for their assessment inventory, they made the case that "hospice services are underutilized for a variety of reasons, even though such services are efficacious not only for the dying patient, but also for the family. Home health care nurses are well placed to encourage hospice-appropriate clients to accept client care" (Morris & Christie, 1995b, p. 21). Hackman (1995) argued the same point from the perspective of case management and hospice nursing, showing them to be an ideal fit.

Overall, patient and PCP perceptions toward hospice nursing have been positive. For example, McGinnis (1986) showed that nursing behaviors related to the clients' psychosocial needs were perceived by PCPs as most helpful in promoting satisfaction with life, capacity for self-care, and maintenance of control. Similarly, Ryan (1992) assessed nursing behaviors perceived to be most and least helpful and found that behaviors that conveyed honesty, and the ability to answer questions, give clear explanations, provide information, and provide comfort were perceived as most helpful. Further, in terms of categories of perceived needs and nursing inventions to meet them, patients' psychosocial needs were of foremost importance, followed by caregivers' psychosocial needs and patients' physical needs (p. 28).

Finally, knowledge, skills, values, and attitudes are important in shaping the effectiveness of hospice nursing behaviors or interventions as described in the preceding. For example, Lev (1986) showed positive posttest outcomes in attitudes and behaviors when she administered a structured hospice nursing course to undergraduate and graduate nurses. Kinzel, Askew, and Godbole (1992) showed that nurses had slightly more positive attitudes about hospice care and its perceived benefits when compared with a sample of physicians, again suggesting a relationship between attitudes and behaviors and intervention outcomes.

Physician Care

All hospice patients in North America must be referred, attended, and discharged by a physician in order to be eligible for care in an accredited hospice. Interestingly, Dame Cicely Saunders, the renowned founder of the modern-day hospice movement, was a nurse, physician, and medical social worker—embodying the three professional roles of present-day hospice care. The majority of referrals to hospice are from oncologists, and physicians play the pivotal role in the physical care of hospice patients. Miller (1992) indicated that political and economic factors in North America, which set the parameters for existing health care trends, have contributed to the development of physician-supervised hospice care with less emphasis on direction from the medical director and more reliance on continued involvement by the original referring or attending physician (p. 27).

Further, Medicare legislation had initially stated that hospice would provide physician services to meet "the general needs of the patient." This was subsequently modified to require that hospice would provide only those "needs not met by the attending physician" (*Federal Register,* December 29, 1983). Miller (1992) outlined two working models for physicians in hospice: active and passive. The former involves an attending physician actively involved in patient care (i.e., referrals, house calls, and care of family members). The other involves basically turning the hospice care, as much as possible, over to the interdisciplinary team (p. 30). Either working model is determined by both the physician's personal orientation and the type of hospice care promoted by the organizational setting. Consequently, Vinciguerra et al. (1992) argued that, given the growth of hospice care in North America, the new patient groups presenting new challenges, and the medical, psychosocial, and financial benefits of hospice, physicians should maintain an active and prominent role in home hospice care.

In terms of medical knowledge, awareness, and attitudes, McQuade (1992) made a convincing case for more specialized physician education and training in the areas of interpersonal skills, human relationships, the life cycle, and death and dying. He noted the importance of these knowledge domains in effecting competent hospice care and indicated that "because exposure to death constitutes such a large portion of their professional lives, physicians either learn to grow and adapt to the pressures of death in practice or become dysfunctional and unhappy with the part of their practice that involves dying patients" (p. 71). Gochman and Bonham (1988) showed that, although the vast majority (about 91%) of the physicians in their sample were aware of hospice and were favorably disposed to it (90%), only 45% of the former group discussed hospice with their terminally ill patients, constituting a so-called discussion gap (their word choice) regarding this issue.

Psychological Services

Although psychologists have been prominent in research and writing in the field of thanatology, their professional involvement in hospice care is definitely lacking. This is primarily attributed to the fact that they are not, and never have been, included in accredited hospice staffing arrangements. However, the profession presumably has something to offer hospice settings in the areas of grief and bereavement, staff and volunteer training, patient counselling, supervision, education, research and evaluation, family support, and interdisciplinary team collaboration. As a result, Liss-Levinson (1982) presented a compelling case for their inclusion in hospice care. Unfortunately, the literature did not bear out her contention, as not a single research article on the effectiveness of psychological intervention was found in the review conducted for this chapter.

Volunteers

Given the current trends in hospice care and the fact that volunteers are the lifeblood of many hospice programs, there are only a few studies in the reviewed literature that assessed the effectiveness of volunteers. Generally, they concluded that volunteers are not only integral to hospice care, but are motivated by altruism and exhibit a set of behaviors that is complementary to overall hospice care. For example, Field and Johnson (1993) found that the majority of volunteers in their U.K. hospice survey were satisfied with their experiences as volunteers and felt that they were adequately supported and valued by the hospice program and its paid staff. Further, they had become volunteers mainly through contacts with friends, and a substantial minority were motivated by their own personal experiences with death. Finally, their contact with dying patients did not cause them any serious emotional problems (p. 1625).

Similarly, Caldwell and Scott (1994) showed that effective hospice volunteers (in Texas) were likely to be female and had above average incomes, were active in other volunteer activities, and were highly satisfied with volunteering; some were motivated by their own personal experiences with the death of a loved one. Their primary roles included direct patient care (60%), office assistance (22.4%), bereavement support (3.2%), and fundraising (2.6%). Finally, Lafer and Craig (1993) created a 27-item scale to evaluate the performance of hospice home care volunteers. This scale has four subsections, related to: (a) commitment to the program, (b) relationship to patient and family, (c) team member functions, and (d) self-awareness. Although derived from a national sample for item analysis, the reliability and validity of this measure remains to be determined.

EFFECTIVE NON–SOCIAL WORK INTERVENTIONS

Due to the patient population itself—in that the patients are dying; the standardized measures of certain variables can provide misleading results for this population; there is a covariance of physical and psychosocial manifestations of functional abilities of these patients; patients have a relatively brief involvement with hospice care; and assessment is difficult given the effects of nonresponse and almost no follow-up data—overall, the issue of assessing patient outcomes has been of some concern to researchers for a number of years (Mor, 1986). Coupled with these methodologic constraints is the overarching palliative philosophy of humanism and dignity as hallmark characteristics of hospice care—which provides for an organizational climate that is not necessarily conducive to a raft of empirical investigations. Despite these mitigating factors, studies on the effectiveness of non–social work interventions offered in hospice care are related to hospice care's two main components, relieving physical pain and discomfort and providing support for patients and their PCPs. In this body of literature, such interventions are generally deemed to be relatively successful.

The alleviation of physical pain and discomfort, as previously mentioned, is the first priority of hospice care. As one would assume, studies in this area appear primarily in nursing or medical journals (i.e., *Nursing Research, Nursing Management, Cancer,* and *Annals of Internal Medicine*) or specialized care journals (i.e., *The Hospice Journal* and *American Journal of Hospice and Palliative Care*). All of these studies generally have small sample sizes (<75), employ time series designs, use standardized clinical measures, and use comparison groups; they focus on assessing the effectiveness of a single pain alleviator (e.g., morphine), or they assess overall pain management programs in hospice care (e.g., quality assurance of pain assessments). In regard to the former, Lazarus, Fitzmartin, and Goldenheim (1990) showed that cancer patients perceived oral controlled-release morphine as being superior to their previous medications. Further, the benefits of less frequent dosing combined with the potent analgesic effects plus the aggressive use of laxatives resulted in a positive global quality of life for cancer patients in this study (p. 2). Wilkie, Lovejoy, Dodd, and Tesler (1990), in a study of patients with advanced-stage cancer, reported high concurrent validity with the Visual Analogue Scale and the Pain Intensity Number Scale in measuring the complex and subjective experiences of cancer pain intensity. Burish, Vasterling, Carey, Matt, and Krozely (1988) reported on the effective use of progressive muscle relaxation training (PMRT) to reduce the side effects of chemotherapy in cancer patients. McMillan and Tittle (1995) described the pain and pain-related symptoms among cancer and hospice patients and showed that despite their pain management regimens, both groups of patients still experienced much pain. In regard to the latter, Lee, McPherson, and Zuckerman (1992) proposed a patient-customized instrument for follow-up pain documentation, as they found that pain assessment and documentation were poorly done in the hospice setting they studied. Along the same lines, Lazerowich (1995), noting the trend in health care of fewer acute-care admission days and more home-based services, suggested the development of a hospice patient classification system linking resource consumption with outcome-of-care criteria.

In regard to the effectiveness of hospice care as related to providing support for patients and their families, the majority of studies in this area focus on assessing interactions related to grief and bereavement. For example, Rognlie (1989) showed positive effects of both short- and long-term bereavement support groups in a specific hospice program. Similarly, Longman, Linstrom, and Clark (1989) showed that the bereavement program of a hospice in Tucson, Arizona, was helpful to families for up to 2 years after the death of a loved one. From a related methodological point of view, McCanse (1995) developed and psychometrically scrutinized the McCanse Readiness for Death Instrument (MRDI), a reliable and valid measure for use in hospice care. Levy (1991), in an analysis of the Anticipatory Grief Inventory (AGI), showed that anticipating grief may be a risk factor for poor early bereavement adjustment. Millison (1995) presented an overview of the literature on spiritual care in hospice and showed its central importance to overall hospice care service delivery. Hays and Arnold (1986) reiterated the importance of consumer data—namely, patient and family satisfaction outcomes—in assessing the effectiveness of any hospice program or its services. Finally, Cody and Naierman (1990) showed that five hospices in metropolitan Washington, DC, that developed a collaborative hospital liaison program were more efficient at educating and maximizing referral sources, improving patient access to services, assisting in ensuring the long-term survival of hospice care, and saving on overall costs.

EFFECTIVE SOCIAL WORK INTERVENTIONS

A literature search yielded nine articles on social work practice interventions in hospices. Four of these are empirical studies (Amar, 1994; Kulys & Davis, 1986, 1987; Remsen, 1993). Three of the remaining five articles are conceptual (Macdonald, 1991; Rusnack et al., 1988, 1990) and two are descriptive (Fish, 1992; Stark & Johnson, 1983). Overall, from a methodological standpoint, all four empirical studies lack rigor. Three of these have sample sizes ≥ 100 (Kulys & Davis 1986, 1987; Amar, 1994) and only one utilized random sampling (Amar, 1994). All employed surveys with such data collection methods as structured interviews (Kulys & Davis, 1986; 1987), mailed questionnaires (Remsen, 1993), and case record analysis (Amar, 1994). Overall, the analyses of data in all studies lack inferential tests of statistical significance and are limited to frequency distributions. The four empirical studies focus on the role of the social worker in hospice settings as opposed to an examination of the effectiveness of social work practice. In sum, empirical research on social work practice in hospice is sparse, its general applicability is limited, and empirical research on the effectiveness of social work practice in hospice appears to be nonexistent.

In order to provide a context within which to examine social work practice in hospice settings, a brief review of social work's role in health care settings is provided. The role of the social worker in hospice then is examined in terms of direct and indirect practice roles and their effectiveness. Finally, the current state of knowledge regarding social work practice effectiveness in hospice care is summarized and directions for further research are offered.

Social Work Roles in Health Care Settings

A literature search yielded three empirical studies in the area of social work practice and health care (Lister, 1980; Shepard, Mayer, & Ryback, 1987; Vincent & Davis, 1987). All focus on describing the particular role of the social worker as opposed to the effectiveness of social work practice.

Erickson & Erickson (1992) provide a catalog of 34 roles for social workers in health care that range from *case finder* to *resource developer* to *practitioner-scientist.* In this account, the reader is alerted to the possible existence of additional roles not mentioned. Such breadth of practice roles may be considered a strength of social work in health care. Conversely, a lack of role clarity and specificity with regard to social work responsibilities and tasks may result (Caroff, 1988; Erickson & Erickson, 1992; Lister, 1980; Vincent & Davis, 1987).

Direct Practice Roles.   Direct practice roles require the social worker to interact directly with the patient, the family, and significant others. Fundamental to direct practice is the role of *assessor* (Caroff, 1988; Erickson & Erickson, 1992; Olson, 1986). In operationalizing this role, a focus is maintained on the patient in continued interaction with the family, the community, and the medical system (Caroff, 1988). Subsequent to assessment, the social worker in health care may carry out the role of *crisis interventionist* (Brengarth, 1981; Caroff, 1988). Alternatively, the social worker may select roles pertaining to intervention with the patient individually, or as part of a couple or a family (Caroff, 1988; Erickson & Erickson, 1992). At times, the social worker in health care may also intervene through the roles associated with the *group worker* (Brengarth, 1981). Thus, patients and their families may become members in a group constructed and led by the social worker for treatment purposes. In some health care settings, all of the aforementioned roles may be subsumed under the role of *clinician.*

Indirect Practice Roles.   Indirect practice roles may be grouped as follows: (a) roles pertaining to interdisciplinary practice, (b) roles pertaining to the service network, and (c) roles pertaining to knowledge building. In interdisciplinary health care settings, social workers perceive of themselves as the team members with expertise in the psychosocial components of health problems and the constructive use of the service network (Lister, 1980). Thus, the social worker is frequently presented as a *team builder* and a facilitator of intrateam communication (Brengarth, 1981). In extending this role, both Caroff (1988) and Kerson (1985) described the social worker as a teacher and educator for staff within health care settings.

Within the roles pertaining to the health service network, the *case manager* role predominates (Brengarth, 1981). In this role, the social worker carries coordination, referral, linkage, and advocacy responsibilities (Dinerman, 1979; James, 1986; Lister, 1980). In addition, the role of *resource developer* is emphasized by many authors (Brengarth, 1981; Caroff, 1988; James, 1986; Kerson, 1985). Participation as a *policy developer* and *analyst* for the service network as well as for workers' own health care facility is yet another social work role (Dinerman, 1979; James, 1986; Kerson, 1985). As well, *administrator* and *supervisor* roles are frequently carried by social workers in a variety of health care settings (Erickson & Erickson, 1992; Kerson, 1985).

Researcher and *practitioner-scientist* constitute the roles related to knowledge building (Erickson & Erickson, 1992; James, 1986; Kerson, 1985). As such, the establishment of a place to form research alliances was proposed as a means to facilitate the operationalization of research roles and to deal with the issues of the lack of both role clarity and specificity regarding social work practice in health care. As indicated by Kerson (1985):

> The old call for agency-based research has recently been heard again. Setting up a system for collective documentation could provide a catalyst for such research. Through its use people working on similar problems in agencies all across the country could begin to put together larger blocks of data about common subjects such as discharge planning, quality assurance, self-help, professional collaborating, and public health and prevention programs. In this way, documentation could become increasingly universal and new ways to document the contribution of social work might be found. (p. 305)

Social Work Roles in Hospice Care

From a role perspective, hospice care was conceptualized by Rusnack et al. (1988) as a *transition*. It is the period of passing from the patient's and family's previous life situation to their present life situation, to the death of the patient, and to the subsequent family situation. These authors hypothesized that the social worker in hospice care charts and facilitates a safe passage for the person in transition within a nurturing environment. The four phases of hospice care and the social work process provide the context for the enactment of both direct and indirect practice roles (Rusnack, Schaefer, & Moxley, 1990). These phases include: (a) hospice home care, (b) hospice inpatient care, (c) hospice extended care, and (d) hospice bereavement care. Interacting with these roles, the social work process, reflecting a proactive stance, consists of the following five steps: (a) identification of high-risk characteristics; (b) assessment of the patient, the social environment, and barriers to safe passage; (c) determination of a plan of action; (d) response to the situation of persons in hospice; and (e) evaluation or process analysis.

Direct Practice Roles.   Rusnack et al. (1988) conceptualized the primary roles of social workers in direct practice with patients and families as advocate, counsellor, educator, enabler, facilitator, and mediator. In addition, the social worker is a participant with patients and an assistant with families. Fish (1992) described direct practice roles as enabler and extender, comforter, interpreter, advocate, and teacher. Stark and Johnson (1983) saw the role of counsellor, utilizing individual, family, and group methods, as constituting social work's direct practice role in applying hospice concepts to an acute hospital oncology service.

In their study of 34 hospices, Kulys and Davis (1986) collected data from 34 hospice directors, 29 social workers, 33 nurses, and 30 volunteers regarding the provision of social services in hospices in Illinois. Their study focused on the frequency with which social services were provided. Twenty-seven social service components were surveyed and were categorized into four groups: (a) nursing, (b) case management, (c) social psychological roles, and (d) roles that assisted with daily living tasks. Social services were provided most frequently by nurses, followed by social workers and then by volunteers. Social workers were substantially more active than nurses (defined as "a greater than 40% difference") in only 2 of the 27 social service components. These two activities were financial counselling and civil legal assistance, both of which were located in the group of roles associated with daily living assistance. As a result, Kulys and Davis (1986) concluded that social workers working in hospices do not have a unique role in meeting the psychosocial needs of patients and their families. However, these findings may be questioned, as the 34 hospice directors used their own criteria to designate staff members to participate in the study. Also, the data analyses do not include any inferential tests of significance.

In a subsequent study, Kulys and Davis (1987) investigated whether social workers or nurses were *perceived* to be better qualified to perform certain social service tasks in hospices by hospice directors, nurses, social workers, and volunteers. The preferences of 34 hospice directors, 22 of whom were nurses, were assessed by asking whether a nurse or a social worker was deemed better qualified to perform 15 hospice program activities and interventions. Hospice directors considered social workers more qualified than nurses in one direct service role (for 33 of 34 directors), the provision of financial information. In 9 of 15 areas, nurses and social workers were considered equally qualified by at least half of the 34 directors. These nine areas of equal qualifications included the following four activities described in the direct practice roles of social workers: (a) facilitation of family communication, (b) counselling, (c) discharge planning, and (d) crisis intervention.

In this same study, the preferences of the 29 social workers, 33 nurses, and 30 volunteers were assessed by asking if a social worker or a nurse was better qualified to carry out an inventory (list) of 14 specific tasks and functions. Social workers perceived themselves as being more qualified than nurses in the eight activities usually included in their direct practice roles in hospice care. Nurses, however, saw themselves as being more qualified than social workers in six of these same eight activities: (a) evaluation of functional abilities, (b) provision of help to patients with emotional problems, (c) provision of help to families with emotional problems, (d) continuation of contact when death is imminent, (e) inducement of feelings of hope and acceptance, and (f) discussion of terminal illness with families. As well, nurses saw social workers as being more qualified in the assessment of emotional and social problems and in discharge planning.

This study (Kulys & Davis, 1987) had the same limitations as those documented for the previously noted one (Kulys & Davis, 1986). Its findings, however, suggested that nurses were expanding into areas that social workers had considered to be part of their direct practice roles in hospice care, and role blurring did indeed occur with the same frequency. Furthermore, nurses perceived themselves as being more qualified than social workers to carry out the majority of direct practice roles, ones normally deemed the exclusive province of social work.

Remsen (1993) examined the role of the nursing home social worker in terminal care. She hypothesized that the presence of policies and procedures for terminal care could be related to a decreased amount of stress for social workers. This study utilized a survey administered to 60 social workers in 14 nursing homes in the greater Milwaukee area. Profit and nonprofit, large and small, and city and suburban homes were included in the sample. Forty-six questionnaires were completed, comprising a response rate of 76.6%. Seventy-one percent of the social workers reported no policies or procedures. Thirty-three percent reported that terminal care was a source of stress; as a result, the main hypothesis was rejected. This rejection and the fact that 59% of the social workers felt that their role in terminal care had not even been discussed in the social service departments of their respective facilities led the author to question the extent to which social workers are actually involved in terminal care in nursing homes. As a result, social workers were urged to take an instrumental role in terminal care with residents and families to ensure safe passage and death with dignity.

Amar (1994) studied the role of the hospice social worker in nursing home settings by utilizing a random sample of 50 nursing home patients and 50 home care patients served by Hospice of the North Shore in the Chicago area. The nursing home patients were substantially older and frailer than the in-home patients. In addition, they were more likely to have had significant mental as well as physical impairments than the in-home patients. (Although these differences were described as "significant," no tests of significance were reported.) In describing practice implications, Amar stated that assessment of the patient and family system fit with the nursing home environment was important. Direct practice roles included assessment, counseling with patients and families, and conducting support groups for patients and families. A role for the hospice social worker with other nursing home residents who required bereavement care also was identified.

Indirect Practice Roles

Interdisciplinary Practice. The roles of advocate, collaborator, consultant, educator, maintainer, and sustainer are carried out by the hospice social worker and staff, according to Rusnack et al. (1988). Fish (1992) presented the hospice social worker as team member, consultant, and teacher to members of other disciplines, adding that "for an effective, smooth-functioning team, it is essential that team members accept that role blurring is inevitable" (p. 411). However, Macdonald (1991) indicated that there is a danger that such overlaps may encourage individuals to go beyond their professional competence. The roles of the social worker in interdisciplinary practice were described by Stark and Johnson (1983) as "collaboration, coordination and facilitation of team effort" (p. 67). Social workers also provided individual staff members with emotional support as needed and helped the staff maintain awareness of the patient, health care, and community interacting systems (Stark & Johnson, 1993).

Kulys and Davis (1986) asked the 29 social workers, 33 nurses, and 30 volunteers in their sample if they played an active role in a number of program activities. A greater number of nurses than social workers reported that they were involved in the following activities: staff development, staff support group, volunteer support group, staff orientation and training, and volunteer orientation. These findings compelled these researchers to ask "just how important are social workers in hospice care?" (Kulys & Davis, 1986, p. 454).

The majority of 34 hospice directors interviewed for Kulys and Davis's (1987) subsequent survey perceived nurses to be as qualified as social workers in the provision of staff development, staff support, and volunteer and staff training. However, the majority of social workers perceived themselves as being more qualified than nurses to communicate the needs of patients to the team. Conversely, the majority of the 33 nurses saw themselves as being more qualified than social workers to carry out this role.

Remsen (1993) recommended that the social worker in terminal care in a nursing home reinforce the team concept and carry a coordinating role for the optimum care of the residents. Thus, the social worker could participate in in-service or workshop education on terminal care issues and could offer emotional support to the staff. The social services department was described as taking "the initiative in setting terminal care as a priority and can model compassionate care in its development of staff training and support" (Remsen, 1993, p. 204).

Similarly, Amar (1994) saw the nursing home setting as offering the hospice social worker an opportunity for staff support groups and in-service training on psychosocial issues. The roles of advocacy and negotiation in the nursing home also were described. As well, team membership for the hospice social worker in the nursing home were seen as depending on the culture of the facility. The social worker must assess patterns of communication within the nursing home and between the home and hospice staff in order to determine the most constructive way to operationalize his or her role as a team member.

Roles Pertaining to the Service Network.   Rusnack et al. (1988) conceptualized the roles of the hospice social worker in relation to the service network as consultant, educator, innovator, liaison, mediator or negotiator, and organizer. Fish

(1992) also listed advocate, mobilizer, and teacher roles for the linkage of the hospice social worker to the service network. The social worker's role in hospice was seen by Fish (1992) as having potential for expansion into management, planning, policy development, education, and involvement in legislation. Macdonald (1991) articulated a potential role for hospice social workers as community organizers and political activists.

Kulys and Davis (1986) found that both hospice nurses and social workers were actively involved in case management. However, 60% of social workers and 75% of nurses provided the same eight of the nine services comprising case management. Further, a greater number of nurses than social workers reported involvement in supervision. A greater number of social workers, however, reported involvement in informal policy setting.

Subsequently, Kulys and Davis (1987) reported that a majority of hospice directors surveyed perceived social workers as being more qualified than nurses in using community resources. Nurses and social workers were seen as equally qualified for program development and advocacy by the majority of these directors. Social workers perceived themselves as being more qualified than nurses in the provision of information to other facilities, coordination of services, and contacting the clergy. Nurses perceived themselves as being more qualified than social workers to document discharge summaries and to contact the clergy. It should be noted, however, that while 52% of nurses saw social workers as best qualified to coordinate services, 48% of nurses saw themselves as better qualified than social workers to coordinate these same services.

Roles Pertaining to Knowledge Building.   Rusnack et al. (1990) stated that research is needed "to determine whether proactive social work interventions make a difference to the safe passage of terminally ill patients in hospice" (p. 117). Furthermore, social workers in hospices were to consider the use of single-subject designs (SSDs) and quasi-experimental designs to conduct empirically based practice (EBP). Fish (1992) indicated that research needs in hospice social work practice can range from effective ways to help children and adolescents cope with loss and grief to the use of humor as a coping mechanism. Macdonald (1991) encouraged hospice social workers to assert leadership in an applied research context. In turn, such leadership could facilitate the development of specificity in intervention as opposed to providing generic support. The effectiveness of hospice social work intervention could then be evaluated and the predictive capacity of assessments increased. The use of SSDs and psychometric assessment instruments to evaluate family dynamics and coping styles was also recommended. Social workers could readily integrate such EBP into referral, admission, and daily care tasks that occur in hospice. Kulys and Davis (1986) stated that "until it can be empirically demonstrated that social services provided by a social worker are 'superior' and result in 'better' patient-family outcomes than the social services provided by nurses, social workers will not be perceived as indispensable members of a hospice team" (p. 455). One year later, Kulys and Davis (1987) reiterated the need to conduct outcome studies in hospice social work to determine if social workers are more effective than nurses in the provision of social services. Similarly, Remsen (1993) articulated a need for further study of issues pertaining to nursing home social work with terminal care patients. Such research was seen as critical to ensure the provision of quality care to elderly residents.

In sum, a review of the literature pertaining to the effectiveness of social work practice in hospice care indicates that knowledge building in this area is in a beginning stage of development and empirical research of any kind is lacking. The need for empirical research focusing on the effectiveness of hospice social work, however, is continually documented throughout the literature. Strategies to integrate research into social work practice in hospices also have been outlined. It is quite evident that EBP could only assist in the provision of high-quality care to hospice patients and their families. In addition, EBP would bring greater clarity, specificity, and knowledge to the role of social workers in hospice care settings.

CONCLUSION

Hospice care is a growing area of practice in North America, and social work is an integral part of it. Despite this, the profession has not conducted much empirical research on practice effectiveness in hospice care. As indicated in this chapter, the social work literature is oriented more toward descriptive accounts of roles and responsibilities than toward the empirical testing of interventions or outcomes. We suggest that if social work is to evolve and determine its efficacy in this area, more empirically based practice studies should be conducted and disseminated. More research of this nature will not only enhance our practice knowledge in this area but will legitimize and guide our day-to-day practice in an informed way.

REFERENCES

Amar, D. F. (1994, May/June). The role of the hospice social worker in the nursing home setting. *The American Journal of Hospice & Palliative Care,* pp. 18–22.

Amenta, M. (1995). The challenge to hospice nurses for the future. *Home Health Care Nurse, 13*(5), 7–8.

Atkins, R., & Amenta, M. (1991). Family adaptation to AIDS: A comparative study. *The Hospice Journal, 7*(1/2), 71–83.

Baker, N., & Seager, R. (1991). A comparison of the psychosocial needs of hospice patients with AIDS and those with other diagnoses. *The Hospice Journal, 7*(1/2), 71–83.

Bartlett, H. (1961). *Social work practice in the health field.* New York: National Association of Social Workers.

Berry, D., Boughton, L., & McNamee, F. (1994). Patient and physician characteristics affecting the choice of home based hospice, acute care inpatient hospice facility or hospitals as last site of care for patients with cancer of the lung. *The Hospice Journal, 9*(4), 21–38.

Birenbaum, L., & Robinson, M. (1991). Family relationships in two types of terminal care. *Social Science Medicine, 32*(1), 95–102.

Bracht, N. (1978). *Social Work in Health Care.* New York: Haworth Press.

Brengarth, J. A. (1981). What is special about specialization? *Health and Social Work, 5*(2), 91–94.

Burger, S. (1980). Three approaches to patient care: Hospice, nursing homes, and social work. In M. Hamilton & H. Reid (Eds.), *A hospice handbook: A new way to care for the dying* (pp. 131–144). Grand Rapids, MI: W. B. Eerdmans.

Burish, T., Vasterling, J., Carey, M., Matt, D., & Krozely, M. (1988). Post-treatment use of relative training by cancer patients. *The Hospice Journal, 4*(2), 1–9.

Caldwell, J., & Scott, J. (1994). Effective hospice volunteers: Demographic and personality characteristics. *The American Journal of Hospice Care, 11*(2), 5–7.

Caroff, P. (1988). Clinical social work: Present role and future challenge. *Social Work in Health Care, 13*(3), 21–33.

Christakis, N., & Escarce, J. (1996). Survival of Medicare patients after enrollment in hospice programs. *New England Journal of Medicine, 335*(3), 172–178.

Cody, C., & Naierman, N. (1990). Evaluation of the cost effectiveness of a collaborative liaison program. *The Hospice Journal, 6*(3), 47–61.

Connor, S. (1992). Denial in terminal illness: To intervene or not to intervene. *The Hospice Journal, 8*(4), 1–15.

Crane, R. (1994, January/February). Intermittent subcutaneous infusion of opioids in hospice home care: An effective, economical, manageable option. *The American Journal of Hospice and Palliative Care,* 8–12.

Dawson, N. (1991). Need satisfaction in terminal care settings. *Social Science Medicine, 32*(1), 147–152.

Dinerman, M. (1979). In sickness and in health: Future social work roles. *Health and Social Work, 4*(2), 5–23.

Dobkin, P., & Morrow, G. (1986). Biopsychosocial assessment of cancer patients: Methods and suggestions. *The Hospice Journal, 2,* 37–57.

Dobratz, M. (1995). Analysis of variables that impact psychological adaptation in home hospice patients. *The Hospice Journal, 10*(1), 75–88.

Erickson, R., & Erickson, G. (1992). An overview of social work practice in health care settings. In M. J. Holosko & P. A. Taylor (Eds.), *Social work practice in health care settings* (pp. 3–19). Toronto, Ontario: Canadian Scholar's Press.

Federal Register. (1983, December). *48*(251).

Field, D., & Johnson, I. (1993). Satisfaction and change: A survey of volunteers in a hospice organization. *Social Service Medicine, 36*(12), 1625–1633.

Fish, N. M. (1992). Social work practice in hospice care. In M. J. Holosko & P. Taylor (Eds.), *Social work practice in health care settings* (pp. 403–419). Toronto, Ontario: The Canadian Scholar's Press.

Gochman, D., & Bonham, G. (1988). Physicians and the hospice decision: Awareness, discussion, reasons and satisfaction. *The Hospice Journal, 4*(1), 25–53.

Hackman, M. (1995, March). Case management and hospice nursing—a good fit. *Colorado Nurse,* 12–15.

Hansen, M., & Evashwick, C. (1981). Hospice: Staffing and cost implications for home health agencies. *Home Health Care Services Quarterly, 2*(1), 61–81.

Hanrahan, P., & Luchins, D. (1995). Access to hospice programs in end-stage dementia: A national survey of hospice programs. *Journal of American Geriatrics Society, 43,* 56–59.

Hays, R., & Arnold, S. (1986). Patient and family satisfaction with care for the terminally ill. *Hospice Journal, 2*(3), 129–150.

Holosko, M. J. (1992). Social work practice roles in health care: Daring to be different. In M. J. Holosko & P. Taylor (Eds.), *Social Work Practice in Health Care Settings* (pp. 21–33). Toronto, Ontario: The Canadian Scholar's Press.

Holosko, M. J. (1997, in press). Service user input—fact or fiction? A case example of the Trauma Program, Department of Rehabilitation, Sault Ste. Marie, Ontario. *The Canadian Journal of Program Evaluation, 11*(2), 111–126.

Holosko, M. J., & Feit, M. (1996). *Social work practice with the elderly* (2nd ed.). Toronto, Ontario: The Canadian Scholar's Press.

Infeld, D., Crum, G., & Koshuta, M. (1990). Characteristics of patients in a long term care hospice setting. *The Hospice Journal, 6*(4), 81–104.

James, C. S. (1986). Emerging issues for social work in American health care: Recent impressions. *Australian Social Work, 39*(2), 27–31.

Kane, R., Klein, S., Bernstein, L., Rothenberg, R., & Wales, J. (1985). Hospice role in alleviating the emotional stress of terminal patients and their families. *Medical Care, 23*(3), 189–197.

Kerson, T. S. (1985). Responsiveness to need: Social work's impact on health care. *Health and Social Work, 10*(4), 300–307.

Kinzel, T. (1992). Hospice care for the non-cancer patient: A survey of issues and opinions. *Loss, Grief and Care, 6*(2/3), 77–85.

Kinzel, T., Askew, M., & Godbole, K. (1992). Palliative care: Attitudes and knowledge of hospital based nurses and physicians. *Loss, Grief and Care, 6*(2/3), 85–95.

Kirschling, J., Tilden, V., & Butterfield, P. (1990). Social support: The experience of hospice family caregivers. *The Hospice Journal, 6*(2), 75–93.

Kulys, R., & Davis, M. A. (1986). An analysis of social services in hospices. *Social Work, 31*(6), 448–556.

Kulys, R., & Davis, M. A. (1987). Nurses and social workers: Rivals in the provision of social services? *Health and Social Work, 12*(2), 101–112.

Lack, S. (1977). The hospice concept—the adult with advanced cancer. In *Proceedings of the American Cancer Society—2nd national conference on human values and cancer* (pp. 160–166). Chicago: American Cancer Society.

Lafer, B., & Craig, S. (1993). The evaluations of hospice home care volunteers. *The Hospice Journal, 9*(1), 13–20.

Lazarus, H., Fitzmartin, R., & Goldenheim, P. (1990). A multi-investigator clinical evaluation of oral controlled-release morphine (MS Contin® Tablets) administered to cancer patients. *The Hospice Journal, 6*(4), 1–15.

Lazerowich, V. (1995). Development of a patient classification system for a home-based hospice program. *Journal of Community Health Nursing, 12*(2), 121–126.

Lee, D., McPherson, M., & Zuckerman, I. (1992). Quality assurance: Documentation of pain assessment in hospice patients. *The American Journal of Hospice and Palliative Care, 9*(1), 38–44.

Lev, E. (1986). Effects of course in hospice nursing: Attitudes and behaviors of baccalaureate school of nursing undergraduates and graduates. *Psychological Reports, 59,* 847–858.

Levy, L. (1991). Anticipatory grief: Its measurement and proposed reconceptualization. *The Hospice Journal, 7*(4), 1–28.

Liss-Levinson, W. (1982). Reality perspectives for psychological services in a hospice program. *American Psychologist, 37*(11), 1266–1270.

Lister, L. (1980). Role expectations of social workers and other health professionals. *Health and Social Work, 5*(2), 41–49.

Longman, A., Lindstrom, B., & Clark, M. (1989). Preliminary evaluation of bereavement experiences in a hospice program. *The Hospice Journal, 5*(2), 25–37.

Macdonald, D. (1991). Hospice social work: A search for identity. *Health and Social Work, 16*(4), 274–280.

Martens, N., & Davies, B. (1990). The work of patients and spouses in managing advanced cancer at home. *The Hospice Journal, 6*(2), 55–73.

McCanse, R. (1995). The McCanse Readiness for Death Instrument (MRDI): A reliable and valid measure for hospice care. *The Hospice Journal, 10*(1), 15–26.

McDonnell, A. (1986). *Quality hospice care: Administration, organization, and models.* During Mills, MD: Rynd Communications.

McGinnis, S. (1986). How can nurses improve the quality of life of the hospice client and family? An exploratory study. *The Hospice Journal, 2*(3), 23–36.

McMillan, S., & Tittle, M. (1995). A descriptive study of the management of pain and pain related side effects in a cancer and a hospice. *The Hospice Journal, 10*(1), 89–107.

McQuade, J. (1992). Physicians and death. *Loss, Grief and Care, 6*(2/3), 39–75.

Miller, R. (1991). Some notes on the impact of treating AIDS patients in hospice. *The Hospice Journal, 7*(1/2), 1–12.

Miller, R. (1992). Hospice: Who's in charge, and of what? *Loss, Grief and Care, 6*(2/3), 27–32.

Millison, M. (1995). A review of the research on spiritual care and hospice. *The Hospice Journal, 10*(5), 3–18.

Mor, V. (1986). Assessing patient outcomes in hospice: What to measure? *The Hospice Journal, 2*(3), 17–37.

Mor, V. (1987). *Hospice care systems: Structure, process, costs and outcome.* New York: Springer.

Mor, V., Hendershot, G., & Cryan, C. (1989). Awareness of hospice services: Results of a national survey. *Public Health Reports, 104*(2), 178–183.

Morris, R., & Christie, K. (1995a). Continuing education test. Initiating hospice care. Why, when and how? *Home Health Care Nurse, 13*(5), 27–28.

Morris, R., & Christie, K. (1995b). Initiating hospice home care. Why, when and how? *Home Health Care Nurse, 13*(5), 21–26.

National Hospice Organization (1979). *Standards of a Hospice Program of Care* (p. 14). McLean, VA: Author.

National Hospice Study. (1986). *Journal of Chronic Disease, 39*(1), 1–27.

Olson, M. (1986). Beyond specialization: Social work education and practice for health care and family life. *Journal of Social Work Education, 22*(2), 30–37.

Office of Research and Demonstrations. (1994). Health care financing. In *Report to Congress: High cost hospice care* (HCFA Publication No. 03360). Baltimore: Health Care Finance Administration.

Paradis, L., & Cummings, S. (1986). The evolution of hospice in America toward organizational homogeneity. *Journal of Health and Social Behavior, 27,* 370–386.

Pollin, I. (1984). The talk-interrupted dimension: Understanding the emotional components of a traumatic medical diagnosis. *The American Journal of Hospice Care, 1,* 28–31.

Pomeroy, E., Rubin, A., & Walker, R. (1995). Effectiveness of a psychoeducational and task-centered group intervention for family members of people with AIDS. *Social Work Research, 19*(3), 142–152.

Quig, L. (1989). The role of the social worker. *American Journal of Hospice Care, 6*(4), 22–30.

Remsen, M. F. (1993). The role of the nursing home social worker in terminal care. *Journal of Gerontological Social Work, 19*(3/4), 193–205.

Rhymes, J. (1990). Hospice care in America. *Journal of the American Medical Association, 264,* 369–372.

Richmond, M. (1917). *Social Diagnosis.* New York: Russell Sage Foundation.

Rimer, B., Kedziera, P., & Levy, M. (1992). The role of patient education in cancer pain control. *Hospice Journal, 8*(1/2), 171–191.

Rognlie, C. (1989). Perceived short and long term effects of bereavement support, group participation at the hospice of Petaluma. *The Hospice Journal, 5*(2), 39–52.

Rousseau, P. (1995). Hospice and palliative care. *Disease-a-Month, 41*(12), 774–835.

Rusnack, B., Schaefer, S., & Moxley, D. (1988). Safe Passage: Social work roles and functions in hospice care. *Social Work in Health Care, 13*(3), 3–19.

Rusnack, B., Schaefer, S., & Moxley, D. (1990). Hospice: Social workers' response to a new form of social caring. *Social Work in Health Care, 15*(2), 95–119.

Ryan, P. (1992). Perceptions of the most helpful nursing behaving in a home care hospice setting: Caregivers and nurses. *American Journal of Palliative Care, 9*(5), 22–31.

Scitovsky, A. (1994). The high cost of dying revisited. *The Millbank Quarterly, 72*(4), 561–591.

Seale, C. (1989). What happens in hospices: A review of research evidence. *Social Science Medicine, 28*(6), 551–559.

Seale, C. (1991). A comparison of hospice and conventional care. *Social Science Medicine, 32*(2), 147–152.

Seale, C., & Addington-Hall, J. (1995). Euthanasia: The role of good care. *Social Science Medicine, 40*(5), 581–587.

Shepard, P., Mayer, J. B., & Ryback, R. (1987). Improving emergency care for the elderly: Social work intervention. *Journal of Gerontological Social Work, 10*(3/4), 123–140.

Smith, M., & Reid, R. (1987). Integrating hospice and home health services: Analysis of strategic factors. *Home Health Care Services Quarterly, 8*(1), 87–102.

Speer, D., Robinson, B., & Reed, M. (1995). The relationship between hospice length of stay and caregiver adjustment. *The Hospice Journal, 10*(1), 45–58.

Stark, D. E., & Johnson, E. M. (1983). Implications of hospice concepts for social work practice with oncology patients and their families in an acute care teaching hospital. *Social Work in Health Care, 9*(1), 63–70.

Stetz, K., & Hanson, W. (1992). Alterations in perceptions of caregiving demands in advanced cancer during and after the experience. *The Hospice Journal, 8*(3), 21–34.

Strahan, G. (1992). *Overview of home health and hospice patients: Preliminary data from the 1992 National Home and Hospice Care Survey.* Hyattsville, MA: U.S. Department of Health and Human Services, Public Health Service, Centers for Disease Control.

Tax Equities Act (1982). *Tax Equity and Fiscal Responsibilities Act of 1982* (Pub. L. No. 97-248, pp. 359–360). Washington, DC: U.S. Government Printing Office.

Vachon, M. (1988) Counselling and psychotherapy in palliative/hospice care: A review. *Palliative Medicine, 2*(1), 36–50.

Vincent, P. A., & Davis, J. M. (1987). Functions of social workers in a home health agency. *Health and Social Work, 12*(3), 213–219.

Vinciguerra, V., Degnan, T., Sciortino, A., Carlton, D., Eng, M., & DeMarco, L. (1992). Why physicians should remain involved in home hospice care. *Loss, Grief and Care, 6*(2/3), 33–38.

Wall, E., Rodriguez, G., & Saultz, J. (1992). A retrospective study of patient care needs on admission to an inpatient hospice facility. *Journal of the American Board of Family Practice, 6*(3), 233–238.

Wilkie, D., Lovejoy, N., Dodd, M., & Tesler, M. (1990). Cancer pain intensity measurement: Concurrent validity of three tools—Finger Dynamometer, Pain Intensity Number Scale, Visual Analogue Scale. *The Hospice Journal, 6*(1), 1–13.

Zimmerman, S., & Applegate, J. (1992). Person-centered comforting in the hospice interdisciplinary team. *Communication Research, 19*(2), 240–263.

Zinn, C. (1995, May/June). Hospice: From grassroots to the mainstream. *The West Virginia Medical Journal, 91,* 136–138.

Chapter 17

TREATING CHRONIC GRIEF

Thomas A. Artelt
Bruce A. Thyer

OVERVIEW

Grief is an expected reaction to the death of a loved one. We grieve the loss of deceased persons and the relationships we shared with them. Bowlby (1980) noted that healthy grief enables one to surrender a physical attachment to a deceased person and that the grieving process helps the survivor to integrate the deceased into life through the survivor's memories and recollections of the deceased. Averill (1968) distinguished mourning from grieving. He defined *mourning* as the practice of culturally prescribed customs in response to a loss. *Grieving* consists of various biological and psychological changes that are triggered by that loss.

Persons who grieve may exhibit various avoidance or withdrawal behaviors. These actions serve to insulate or isolate the survivor from places, activities, and persons, among other things, that evoke memories of the deceased person and cause the survivor emotional pain. Through the process of healthy grieving, survivors are usually able to resume contacts with these places, activities, and persons within 6 to 12 months after the death of the significant person.

An individual's adjustment to the loss of another person through death has been defined as a progressive, linear process that presumes movement through various stages. Kübler-Ross (1970), one of the most widely read and cited authorities, called these stages *denial, anger, bargaining, depression,* and *acceptance.* It should be noted, however, that empirical research has failed to support the hypothesis that the grieving process is such a linear progression through these stages. Many individuals apparently fail to experience some of these so-called stages of grieving, and successful grieving does not appear to be dependent upon experiencing all of them in any particular sequence. Here is Bugen's view on these issues:

> The "stage" concepts of grieving contain a number of theoretical weaknesses and inconsistencies. First, the stages are not separate entities, but subsume one another or blend dynamically. Second, the stages are not successive; any individual may experience anger, for instance, prior to denial, or perhaps disorganization before shock. Third, it is not necessary to experience every stage. . . . Fourth, the intensity and duration of any stage may vary idiosyncratically among those who grieve. (Bugen, 1977, pp. 196–197).

A behavioral perspective on grief and loss, based upon contemporary social learning theory, notes that the grieving reaction is related to a reduction in the reinforcing activities experienced (including those provided by, or associated with, the deceased person) by the survivor. The support and care for the bereaved person from one's family, friends, community, and associational groups (religious congregation, professional groups, and health care providers) may help to facilitate grieving and resolve its impacts upon the survivor. However, these groups may also inadvertently inhibit the resolution of healthy grieving, particularly if, over the long term, they encourage the survivor to avoid or withdraw from anything that triggers memories of the deceased person and that serves to upset the survivor. A behavioral perspective does not claim that the preceding processes account for all of the phenomena labeled "chronic grief," but hypothesizes that they may be salient and should be explored in the assessment process (see Brasted & Callahan, 1984).

Consider the reinforcement dynamics related to grieving described by Gauthier and Marshall:

> Normally, the withdrawal of social attention from grieving behavior and shift to alternative responses is sufficient to reduce grief reactions. Occasionally, however, the grief reaction continues for so long that it becomes a source of worry to all concerned, and the individual seeks treatment. The most obvious cause for this "pathological" reaction . . . is that the griever continues to obtain attention for his sorrow. . . . While . . . pathological grievers often seek out new sources of sympathy as earlier sources are withdrawn, all too often the immediate family or friends either fail to withdraw attention for grieving or do not provide consistent encouragement for more adaptive behavior. Therefore, a rearrangement of the social consequences of the behavior of the bereaved person seems essential to effective treatment.

And

> Some families and friends, or even the bereaved person himself, may decide that the best course is to avoid a grief reaction altogether. In these circumstances, social attention is given to behaviors that do not permit grief to occur, including a careful avoidance of contact with thoughts, objects, or experiences that may remind the person of his loss. A common finding in the history of overwhelming and protracted grief reactions is the "conspiracy of silence," whereby friends and relatives withhold

information about the death, avoid discussing the dead person, remove all signs (clothes, photographs, etc.) of him or her, and forestall the involvement of the grieving person in the funeral and burial procedures. Although some control can be achieved by these efforts, it is difficult to exercise satisfactory control over his thinking. It is, therefore, likely that thoughts about the deceased person will occur with reasonable frequency. Because the grieving person has been led to believe that it is not good for him to think about the deceased, or because he cannot stand the pain produced by such a memory, his immediate reaction to these intrusive thoughts is to avoid them. This strategy, however, does not avert sadness. (Gauthier & Marshall, 1977, pp. 40–41)

Although the preceding account certainly possesses some degree of face validity, it remains a conceptual model, not an experimentally supported one. Behavioral science lacks a well-supported theory of normal bereavement, as well as one that adequately accounts for so-called pathological grief. Nevertheless, this has not inhibited sound research into developing operational definitions, some descriptive psychopathology, and treatments for morbid grieving. And, fortunately, as will be described, some effective therapies have emerged.

OPERATIONAL DEFINITIONS

Grief that persists for more than 12 months has been labeled as *pathological, chronic,* or *morbid* grief. It is frequently associated with the avoidance of people, places, objects, and conversations concerning the deceased person. Chronic grief has also been linked with physical and psychological complaints or symptoms that disrupt an individual's ability to carry on the activities of daily living.

Physical complaints also may include an increase or decrease in sleep patterns, a significant weight gain or loss, periods of daily tearfulness and crying, a lack of appetite, headaches, an increased use of tobacco, the abuse of alcohol or drugs, and fatigue. Psychological complaints have included a decreased affect; a general disinterest in one's life, job, family members, or leisure activities; feelings of depression; a generalized lack of energy; or intense feelings of guilt, anger, hostility, fear, and sadness. Such complaints have been noted to inhibit the performance of the grieving person's usual tasks within the family, workplace, and community. The incomplete resolution of morbid grief has also been associated with the survivor's suicidal ideations or suicide.

More specific diagnostic criteria compatible with the *Diagnostic and Statistical Manual* (fourth edition; *DSM-IV;* American Psychiatric Association [APA], 1994) system have been recently proposed, for a category labeled "Complicated Grief Disorder" (Horowitz et al., 1997). This latter description is consistent with what we have labeled "chronic grief" in the present chapter.

PREVALENCE, INCIDENCE, AND SOCIAL
AND FINANCIAL COSTS

Individuals who exhibit symptoms of chronic grief have been described as persons who complain of "persistent distress of over one year's duration which dated from the loss, or which had been greatly exacerbated by the loss" (cf. Mawson, Marks, Ramm, & Stern, 1981, p. 186). The consequences of bereavement are the obvious separation from the deceased person, the possible onset of post-traumatic stress disorder, or the onset of a major depressive disorder that inhibits or severely limits the person's psychosocial functioning, physical health, or psychological well-being.

The *DSM-IV* (APA, 1994) defines *bereavement* as a period of adjustment to the loss of a loved one. Symptoms that differentiate bereavement from a major depressive episode include the following: (a) The survivor feels guilty about things other than his or her own actions or inactions at the time of the deceased person's death, (b) the survivor has thoughts of death that differ from thoughts that would lead the survivor to believe that he or she would be better off dead or that he or she should have died with the deceased person, (c) the survivor exhibits a preoccupation with his or her own worthlessness, (d) the bereaved person exhibits psychomotor retardation or prolonged functional impairment, and (e) the survivor admits having hallucinatory experiences other than thinking that he or she hears the voice or sees the image of the deceased person.

Of crucial interest to social workers in treating persons with chronic grief is the survivor's history of depression. The criteria for a major depressive episode (MDE) include a severely depressed mood and a loss of interest or pleasure in life's activities that lasts for 6 months or more.

DSM-IV also indicates that there is a close relationship between the number of major depressive episodes and the likelihood that an individual would develop another MDE. Of persons with a history of one major depressive episode, there is a 50% to 60% chance that they would develop a second major depressive episode. If an individual experienced a second MDE, there is about a 70% chance that he or she would develop a third MDE. If the person had a third MDE, there is a 90% chance of having a fourth one.

The foregoing statistics are relevant because bereavement is a period during which such an episode may likely occur or *re*cur. It is important that the social worker evaluate chronic grief within the context of a possible history of MDE and offer effective treatment specific to clinical *depression* if the client meets the *DSM-IV* criteria for an affective disorder, as distinct from experiencing the features of chronic grief. It must be recognized that it can be quite difficult to reliably diagnose complicated grief, that is, chronic grief experienced in conjunction with other problems such as mood, anxiety, or personality disorders (see Marwit, 1996).

Chronic grief may be considered as a public health problem, the consequences of which can be quite severe (cf. Averill & Wisocki, 1981; Engel, 1961; Simos, 1977). Epstein, Weitz, Roback, & McKee (1975, p. 541) found that "the rate of dying is at least twice as great for widows and widowers at all age levels for a variety of diseases." The health risks for bereavement are most pronounced for those already in poor health and for older men. The economic, physical, psychological, and psychosocial costs of MDE related to chronic grief and bereavement are hard to quantify, but they are undoubtedly high in dollars devoted to physical health, mental health, and custodial care. Chronic grief is *not* a benign affliction.

RELEVANCE OF SOCIAL WORK'S INVOLVEMENT

Social work's emphasis on the person-in-situation aspects of understanding clients, characteristic of the ecological and behavioral models of practice, is highly functional when it comes to assessing and treating the client with chronic grief. This is important, given the large number of social workers engaged in fields of practice in which it is likely that they will encounter seriously bereaved individuals. For example, the current edition of the social work dictionary contains articles on social work practice in hospice settings (Richman, 1995), HIV/AIDS (Taylor-Brown, 1995), suicide (Ivanoff & Reidel, 1995; see also Boyle & Canady, 1997), dealing with bereavement and loss (McNeil, 1995), and making end-of-life decisions (Kaplan, 1995).

Potocky (1993) found, in a content analysis of nine programs that offered treatment to bereaved spouses suffering from chronic grief, that the programs generally neglected to consider interactional patterns among their clients, favoring instead isolated, intrapsychic treatment approaches such as conventional psychotherapy. Given that there is no empirical evidence of the efficacy of these techniques in helping clients recover from chronic grief, it would seem that much opportunity exists to improve social work services to the grieving.

ASSESSMENT METHODS

In general, we do not have very sophisticated or disorder-specific approaches to assessing the client experiencing chronic grief. A recent review concluded that "currently there is no standard approach to bereavement assessment, in either the clinical or research setting" (Stroebe, Hansson, & Stroebe, 1993, p. 460) and that there was a paucity of valid assessment instruments. However, we do review what we believe to be the current state of the art in assessing chronic grief.

The Clinical Interview

A treatment approach to morbid grief might best begin with a multidimensional, semistructured psychosocial interview with the client. Areas to assess include the client's history of physical and mental health (e.g., depression), the client's bereavement period, social functioning, social support network and living arrangements, employment and financial situations, legal concerns, risk factors for acute and chronic grief, and future plans. The clinical interview may also discuss clearly defined treatment plans, goals, and measurable outcomes. Depending upon the approach to treatment, it might be useful to use the clinical interview as a means of determining, with the client, the environmental and internal cues that exacerbate the grieving response. What objects, situations, or thoughts evoke the most acute pangs of grief? Examples are seeing the deceased person's clothing, personal effects, and photos; doing certain things alone (e.g., grocery shopping, attending church, seeing family or mutual friends) that used to be done together; and having particularly poignant memories. In some circumstances, it may be appropriate to ask the client to help in *prospectively* noting the grief-evoking cues, as opposed to retrospectively describing them to the social worker in the consulting room. A diary or log, which the client can bring along to the next appointment, may be helpful in this regard.

Self-Report Methods

Apart from the qualitative information gleaned from the clinical narrative provided by the client, it can be useful to undertake some simple techniques to quantify certain aspects of chronic grief as a preliminary to formal intervention, as well as to help assess client improvements over the course of treatment. Mawson et al. (1981) describe some methods to aid in this process. One is to ask clients, in the privacy of their own homes, to undertake certain short (e.g., 2-minute) tasks, such as looking at a picture of the deceased person or writing the deceased person a letter. The client then rates the distress the task caused them on a self-rating scale from 0 (*none*) to 5 (*extreme*). These numbers can provide an indicator to both assess the real grief-evoking cues and, if repeated several times during the course of treatment, to help supplement clinical judgments about whether the client is truly getting better.

Mawson et al. (1981) also developed a "physical symptoms of grief" scale, which lists 13 physical symptoms (e.g., crying) and has clients rate each symptom on a scale from 1 (*I almost never have this*) to 3 (*This is a severe problem*). The total of the scores the clients rate on the 13 items constitute a rough quantitative indicator of their physical grief reactions for the past week or so (between sessions). A similar scale was developed to assess the *affective* (as opposed to the physical) symptoms, listing possible reactions such as hostility, anger, and guilt, which could be similarly scored.

We believe that these techniques are excellent beginning methods for social workers to help assess the chronically grieving client. The specific items listed on such rating forms can be idiosyncratically tailored by the social worker to the unique and specific aspects of the survivor's individual grief reactions. While lacking in formal psychometric standards relating to reliability and validity, this approach seems one very useful way of "beginning where the client is at." It is also congruent with the advice given by Mary Richmond over 75 years ago: ". . . special efforts should be made to ascertain whether abnormal manifestations are increasing or decreasing in number and intensity, as this often has a practical bearing on the management of the case" (Richmond, 1935, p. 435).

Other specific aspects of grief may be assessed by using one or more focused rapid assessment instruments (RAIs). RAIs are brief, easy-to-read, -answer, and -score questionnaires and rating forms, which clients (and sometimes significant others) complete as a part of a comprehensive social work assessment. The two-volume compilation by Fischer and Corcoran (1994) is an excellent resource to consult in this regard. Among the RAIs reproduced in this book relevant to assessing chronic grief are various measures of depression, social support, self-esteem, guilt, loneliness, life satisfaction, social relationships, social avoidance and distress, and anger. Instruments for families, couples (for use with bereaved parents), and children and adolescents are also reproduced, along with scoring and validity information.

For example, Fischer and Corcoran (1994) include the *Generalized Contentment Scale* (GCS), which is actually a good measure of depression (developed by social worker Walter Hudson). One could administer this RAI at the beginning of social work treatment with a client and perhaps repeat it every 2 weeks or so, to glean a sense of therapeutic change. Or, if conducting a support group for chronically grieving surviving spouses, the social worker could ask all group members to complete the GCS at the first group session and once more when the group is terminated. In this manner, the pretest-posttest change in average scores could be used as one indicator of the effectiveness of the group therapy program.

These recommendations are actually used in practice and research. For example, studies by Lieberman and Yalom (1992) and Lieberman and Videka-Sherman (1986) evaluated the treatment of severe grief, using various symptom checklists and scales to measure drug and alcohol use, and used client-provided ratings (on a point scale from 1 to 7) of the most significant problem for a widow or widower, grief intensity, anger, social adjustment, role strain, and guilt, among other variables.

There does exist one measure specifically designed to assess chronic grief that seems to be the current gold standard among assessment instruments. This scale is known as the *Texas Inventory of Grief* (TIG). The TIG is a seven-item, self-rating, pencil-and-paper scale that purports to assess unresolved grief through the presence of grief-related symptoms within an individual (Faschingbauer, Devaul, & Zisook, 1977). The TIG measures the presence of emotional symptoms that reflect the presence of unresolved grief (e.g., crying, emotional upset, thoughts about the deceased person, refusal to accept the deceased person's death, sympathetic pain, identification with the deceased person, and annual upsets around the time of the deceased person's death date).

The authors of the TIG created a list of 13 statements that they believed were linked to, or symptomatic of, unresolved grief and incomplete grieving. Participants in the Faschingbauer et al. (1977) study that developed the TIG rated the presence of each symptom on a five-point Likert-type scale. Clients also documented the nature of their relationships with the deceased persons and the length of time that had passed since the persons died. The TIG is easy to administer and score by merely totaling the numerical scores for each question. The properly completed scale's scores can range from a low of 7 to a high of 35. We highly recommend the TIG as an assessment and evaluation tool for social work practice with bereaved persons, particularly when used in conjunction with client self-ratings, clinical interviews, and behavioral measures of grief.

TREATMENT

The treatment of the client suffering from chronic grief may occur through a variety of modalities—individual, small group, marital or family therapy, and even through larger scale community interventions (e.g., memorial services following natural or human-caused disasters). Various self-help groups have also become widely available, such as those provided by Mothers Against Drunk Driving and the Compassionate Friends (for the parents of a dead child). Unfortunately, little outcome research has been conducted on most interventions, leaving open the possibility that some therapies provided by social workers to the grieving may be ineffective or may even exacerbate bereavement. Molendijk's (1996) recent call for protocol-driven interventions to treat grieving children is a welcome development, inasmuch as a clear specification of the independent variable (treatment) is very helpful in conducting evaluation research.

Individual Therapies

The similarities between chronic grief and certain aspects of phobic disorders have been noted by some writers (e.g., Gauthier & Marshall, 1977; Ramsay, 1979). In both conditions, *brief* periods of exposure to evoking stimuli (environmental or internal cues that elicit grief or fear, respectively) cause emotional upset and avoidance behavior. With avoidance, the client temporarily feels better, which serves, according to the operant model called *negative reinforcement,* to strengthen avoidance. Attempts by others to soothe the distraught individual may also inadvertently reinforce emotional distress. This is important because phobic disorders are among those conditions for which a highly effective psychosocial treatment exists, called *exposure therapy* (ET; see Thyer, 1987). ET involves helping the client to *confront* for *lengthy* periods of time anxiety-evoking cues and remain in their presence until significantly calmer. This is usually done with the assistance of the social worker, who makes use of traditional clinical skills of support and empathy, as appropriate. After enough time passes (perhaps several hours, but usually much less), and the client is reasonably calm and composed, the session is terminated, and treatment is resumed next time. Most clients with specific phobias show substantial improvements in less than 10 hours of such prolonged exposure to anxiety-evoking cues, and in many cases complete cures are achieved.

An adaptation of exposure therapy known as *guided mourning* has been used in the treatment of chronic grief. In this formulation, the cues that exacerbate grief reactions are seen as similar to the anxiety-evoking stimuli of the phobic. The reactions of friends and family to the symptomatology of prolonged bereavement are analogous to the efforts made by a spouse to shelter his or her partner from frightening stimuli, and the solicitude provided when bereaved people are upset because of encountering reminders of the deceased people is similar to the comfort afforded phobic people when they weep and shudder after fearful encounters.

Guided mourning consists of two concurrent approaches to intervention, both undertaken after the social worker has completed his or her assessment and ascertained that the circumstances do indeed fit the picture of chronic or morbid grief. The first is psychoeducational in nature and consists of trying to determine if family members or friends are inadvertently perpetuating the client's experience of grief through solicitude and reinforcement, both positive (comfort, expressions of sympathy) and negative (avoiding naturally occurring opportunities to mention the deceased person, removing environmental cues that would remind the survivor of the deceased person, etc.). If such appears to be the case, then these individuals need to be instructed about the need to discontinue these efforts and to resume a normal life with respect to how they treat the bereaved person. This, of course, applies to clients experiencing incapacitating grief over long periods of time, beyond what is considered normal for the resolution of healthy bereavement.

The second approach is to undertake a series of guided exposure exercises, perhaps conducted in the social worker's office or in the client's own home. These exercises would consist of arranging for the client to experience *prolonged* exposure to mildly upsetting grief-evoking stimuli, such as reminiscing to photos of the deceased person, talking about the deceased person's good points, writing the person a goodbye letter, or visiting the grave to say goodbye. With the support of the social worker, these activities are continued so that emotional distress occurs, is fully experienced, and then subsides—as it almost assuredly will. (Dynamically oriented social workers will notice the similarities between this approach and those of the techniques called *catharsis* and *abreaction*.)

As one activity is encountered and experienced in a given session, it is repeated in subsequent sessions until it no longer evokes an abnormal grief response. Mild sadness is, of course, to be expected, as guided mourning (GM) is a treatment for *pathological* grief, not normal emotional reactions. Then the social worker and client move on to a second, perhaps somewhat more difficult, task. Between sessions with the social worker, the client is asked to repeat similar homework exercises at home, either alone or with a support person (the social worker can schedule time to consult by phone to see how things went).

Clinically, it is very useful to ask clients to assess their grief reactions on a scale from 1 (*none*) to 10 (*as upset as I have ever been*). Periodically throughout the guided mourning treatment sessions, clients should be asked for ratings of their grief. Typically, these will rise, reach a plateau, and then slowly subside, so that at the end of a session clients are actually *doing* the activity but are no longer visibly or internally upset (at least by their self-reports). Many times, clients will spontaneously remark how surprised they are at being able to do some activity they have studiously avoided because it made them upset and still be calm. This is incredibly therapeutic, and, of course, the social worker needs to appropriately reinforce the clients' efforts all along, praising them for their sturdiness and willingness to see sessions through until they are calm.

It is important to ensure that clients experience the full array of exposure to various aspects of grief-evoking cues, including the physical proximity and encountering of them, any cognitive cues (thoughts elicited during the exposure session), and affective responses experienced (weeping, grimacing, closing the eyes, etc.).

Guided mourning has been comparatively tested through a number of case studies, and through uncontrolled as well as controlled clinical trials. Ramsay (1976) and Callahan and Burnette (1989) each reported on one case treated with GM and positive results, as did Tilley (1985) and Schauss and Taylor (1992), who also employed some systematic measurements of the client's grief reaction and depression in the context of evaluating treatment using a single-case research design. Vogel and Peterson (1991) reported three narrative case studies of bereaved clients treated with GM, of whom two were essentially cured. Lieberman (1978) reported on its effective use with a series of 19 clients, and this was followed by Ramsay's (1979) published report of 23 cases, of whom, by Ramsay's judgments, 9 highly improved, 9 moderately improved, 4 slightly improved, 1 remained unchanged, and no one became worse. The average number of sessions required was nine, and the median number of sessions was five. The average length of time from initial bereavement to treatment was 11 years (median 2.5 years).

There have been two controlled clinical trials of guided mourning for chronic grief. In the first, conducted by Mawson et al. (1981), 12 patients were assigned to either guided mourning therapy or to a control condition (avoid all exposure to grief-evoking cues). Four of six patients who initially received GM (six 90-minute sessions over 2 weeks) significantly improved, whereas the antiexposure control patients did not, at 5 months' follow-up. This initial study was replicated by Sireling, Cohen, and Marks (1988), with 26 patients suffering from morbid grief.

Fourteen were randomly assigned to GM and twelve to antiexposure control treatment. GM treatment consisted of ten 60- to 90-minute sessions, with a follow-up at 9 months. Evaluations were conducted by independent assessors blind to the nature of the treatment each patient received. GM was significantly better at helping clients reduce avoidance and distress from bereavement cues than was antiexposure treatment.

Ramsay's chapter is an excellent clinical guide to flesh out the details of assessing bereaved clients in terms of their potential to receive treatment using GM. For example, Ramsay suggests:

> For those still grieving more than a year after the loss, one would have to assess the client's ability to withstand the stress of the treatment, the efficacy of the social network to support the client during treatment, and the possibilities open to the client for making a new life. A person with a long history of psychiatric problems prior to the loss would probably not be able to withstand the stress of the therapy; a widow with three young children and no close family to fall back on would not be a good candidate. . . ." (Ramsay, 1979, p. 229)

Of course, these are clinical impressions, not proven criteria of acceptability. Flannery (1974) finds behavioral methods to be well suited to and effective in helping elderly bereaved clients. Nevertheless, Ramsay (1979) is a superlative clinical guide to the conduct of guided mourning, which the social worker seeking to provide therapy to chronically bereaved clients should consult.

Sireling, Cohen, and Marks provide a case description of the treatment of one client using guided mourning:

> The therapist first explained the features of healthy grief and why Ann's (the client) was unhealthy, and reviewed events prior to mother's death. Areas of avoidance were noted (the bereavement avoidance profile)—cognitive (e.g., avoiding thoughts that she should have done more for mother), affective (e.g., blocking resentment that her mother should have confided in her that she was dying), and behavioral (e.g., mother's photo, books, and relatives). At the end of the first session, Ann was asked to confront some of these avoided cues during the next week. Subsequent sessions began by reviewing the exposure homework, exploring difficulties in carrying it out, and planning the next week's homework. New activities and relationships were encouraged. . . . Guided mourning tasks were prescribed both within sessions and between sessions as homework. They included facing hitherto avoided situations, e.g., 1) visiting the crematorium to look at smoke emerging from the chimney; 2) asking her grandmother to describe the body's appearance in the hospital chapel; 3) talking about her mother's final illness; 4) bringing mother's photograph to several sessions and looking at it for prolonged periods; 5) listing mother's positive and negative attributes (to elicit avoided anger with her); . . . 7) spending fixed periods in mother's bedroom; 8) wearing shoes and jewelry given by her mother. By the end of treatment the patient had carried out all prescribed homework tasks plus some others of her own devising,

e.g., sitting for 20 minutes in her mother's favorite chair. She was pursuing a new career, getting on well with her husband, and was not depressed or panicky. (Sireling, Cohen, & Marks, 1988, p. 124)

How much research constitutes credible scientific evidence is an important question. Psychoanalysts might contend that a series of published case histories lacking quantitative measures, but which provide narrative anecdotes supportive of curative claims, will suffice. Behavior analysts would like such individual cases presented in the context of well-controlled, single-case research designs, with reliable and valid outcome measures. Methodological purists may only be content with a series of independently replicated, large-scale controlled clinical trials. One standard recently established by the American Psychological Association's Task Force on Promotion and Dissemination of Psychological Procedures (Task Force, 1995) is that at least two good between-group design experiments demonstrating efficacy and possessing certain qualities (e.g., used well-proceduralized treatments) constitute adequate evidence to claim that a treatment is "well-established." By this criterion, guided mourning would seem to be a first-choice, empirically based treatment for use by social workers.

Paradoxically, guided mourning is used much less often than nonspecific psychosocial treatments such as individual dynamic psychotherapy or supportive treatments, both of which lack any evidence of efficacy apart from clinical anecdote. This is not to state, unequivocally, that these techniques are not clinically useful, but it does point out the need to subject these procedures to programs of clinical research similar to that which the GM procedure has undergone.

Group Therapies

Mutual self-help, support, or psychotherapy groups have reportedly been successful in moderating the effects the loss of a spouse may present to the surviving partner (Lieberman & Videka-Sherman, 1986). A study of bereaved spouses researched the benefits of a group treatment protocol (Lieberman & Yalom, 1992). It included a sample of bereaved surviving spouses ($n = 56$), the use of a brief, preventive treatment intervention for a randomly assigned number of participants within the study, a planned follow-up assessment 1 year after the study ended to assess its impact upon the participants, and the determination of whether those study participants who were considered to be at risk for psychiatric complications due to their bereavement were helped by this early treatment approach.

Lieberman & Yalom (1992) created four treatment groups with the 36 research participants. These groups met weekly for 8 weeks, with eight sessions. Group work was selected as the model of intervention because the authors believed that the surviving spouse's complaints, feelings of loneliness and isolation, role change, and existential issues were best addressed in a group format. It was hoped that the group could also help survivors establish a new social network and reduce feelings of social isolation. Each of the four groups was led by a team consisting of a male and a female cotherapist.

Group participants improved over control participants in self-esteem and decreased in single role strain. No differences between group and control participants were found with the variables of mental health and mourning, and no significant relationships in treatment-pathology interaction were observed. Lieberman & Yalom (1992) concluded that an individual's level of risk prior to entering therapy was not related to his or her clinical improvement. There was no support for the hypothesis that brief group psychotherapy would produce a greater benefit for at-risk participants than for at-risk control participants. Spousal bereavement decreased over time for most survivors, irrespective of their receipt of brief group psychotherapy.

Of course, the paucity of credible evidence of the effectiveness of group work interventions in relieving chronic grief does not necessarily mean that such treatments are ineffective, but it certainly does point out the need for additional outcome studies conducted by social workers and others in this area.

Community

Interventions after major disasters within the community may offer reassurance and hope to survivors. Through community events that encourage the acknowledgment of the disaster and structure a basic framework concerning the bereavement and healing periods, practitioners may offer some stress inoculation to citizens and begin the recovery process. Community-focused events such as dinners, concerts, memorial services, and dignified speeches from community leaders at community centers, religious organizations, aid societies, and schools may begin the healing process. The media and brief flyers might be allies in helping to publicize and define the range of possible grief reactions and to inform citizens about accessing the helping network. At present, such community-based efforts do not appear to have been empirically evaluated.

Prevention

Awareness of the life cycle from conception to death offers the opportunity to see grief and loss as significant responses within people who attach themselves to others. Grief is a response to the loss of a person with whom one shared an attachment. Health care providers, hospice-based caregivers, and mental health clinicians may anticipate this loss among their client's network of support and can establish supportive and informational linkages with these persons before the client's death. Social workers may anticipate this issue by creating an interdisciplinary coalition of caregivers who offer bereavement services, speak on bereavement issues, and publicize services for bereaved persons. However, as Lieberman and Yalom (1992, p. 118) noted, "There is no published research that satisfactorily answers the question of whether the majority of bereaved spouses might benefit from a preventive therapeutic intervention." Prior studies along these lines have simply been too methodologically flawed to permit firm conclusions (e.g., Vachon, Lyall, Rogers, Freedman-Letofsky, & Freeman, 1980; Williams & Pollack, 1979).

CONCLUSION

Treating persons who present with symptoms of chronic grief can be a rewarding field of practice for the social worker. Helping bereaved persons live amid and beyond feelings of loss touches the very core of professional social work practice. There is a growing clinical literature devoted to helping those suffering from chronic grief (e.g., Humphrey & Zimpfer, 1996), and, slowly, empirical research is supporting the efficacy of selected psychosocial therapies for this work. At present, the guided mourning approach seems to be the best supported treatment available for social workers to employ for their work with the bereaved. A promising area for research and practice will involve providing guided mourning treatment in the context of group therapy.

REFERENCES

American Psychiatric Association. (1994). *Diagnostic and Statistical Manual of Mental Disorders* (4th ed.). Washington, DC: Author.

Averill, J. R. (1968). Grief: Its nature and significance. *Psychological Bulletin, 70,* 721–748.

Averill, J. R., & Wisocki, P. A. (1981). Some observations on behavioral approaches to the treatment of grief among the elderly. In H. J. Sobel (Ed.), *Behavior therapy in terminal care: A humanistic approach* (pp. 125–150). New York: Ballinger.

Bowlby, J. (1980). *Attachment and loss: Loss, sadness, and depression* (Vol. III). New York: Basic Books.

Boyle, D. P., & Canady, K. (1997). Should social workers participate in assisted suicide? In B. A. Thyer (Ed.), *Controversial issues in social work practice.* Boston: Allyn & Bacon.

Brasted, W. S., & Callahan, E. J. (1984). A behavioral analysis of the grief process. *Behavior Therapy, 15,* 529–543.

Bugen, L. A. (1977). Human grief: A model for prediction and intervention. *American Journal of Orthopsychiatry, 47,* 196–206.

Callahan, E. J., & Burnette, M. S. (1989). Intervention for pathological grieving. *The Behavior Therapist, 12*(7), 153–157.

Engel, G. L. (1961). Is grief a disease? *Psychosomatic Medicine, 23,* 18–22.

Epstein, G., Weitz, L., Roback, H., & McKee, E. (1975). Research on bereavement: A selective and critical review. *Comprehensive Psychiatry, 16,* 537–546.

Faschingbauer, T. R., Devaul, R. A., & Zisook, S. (1977). Development of the Texas Inventory of Grief. *American Journal of Psychiatry, 134,* 696–698.

Fischer, J., & Corcoran, K. (Eds.) (1994). *Measures for clinical practice* (2nd ed.). New York: Free Press.

Flannery, R. B. (1974). Behavior modification of geriatric grief: A transactional perspective. *International Journal of Aging and Human Development, 1,* 197–203.

Gauthier, J., & Marshall, W. L. (1977). Grief: A cognitive-behavioral analysis. *Cognitive Therapy and Research, 1,* 39–44.

Horowitz, M. J., Siegel, B., Holen, A., Bonanno, G. A., Milbrath, C., & Stinson, C. H. (1997). Diagnostic criteria for Complicated Grief Disorder. *American Journal of Psychiatry, 154,* 904–910.

Humphrey, G. M., & Zimpfer, D. G. (1996). *Counseling for grief and bereavement.* Thousand Oaks, CA: Sage.

Ivanoff, A., & Reidel, M. (1995). Suicide. In R. L. Edwards (Ed.), *Encyclopedia of social work* (pp. 2358–2372). Washington, DC: NASW Press.

Kaplan, K. O. (1995). End-of-life decisions. In R. L. Edwards (Ed.), *Encyclopedia of social work* (pp. 856–868). Washington, DC: NASW Press.

Kübler-Ross, E. (1970). *On death and dying.* London: Tavistock.

Lieberman, S. (1978). 19 cases of morbid grief. *British Journal of Psychiatry, 132,* 156–163.

Lieberman, M. A., & Videka-Sherman, L. (1986). The impact of self-help group therapy on the mental health of widows and widowers. *American Journal of Orthopsychiatry, 56,* 435–449.

Lieberman, M. A., & Yalom, I. (1992). Brief group psychotherapy for the spousally bereaved: A controlled study. *International Journal of Group Psychotherapy, 42*(1), 117–132.

Marwit, S. J. (1996). Reliability of diagnosing complicated grief: A preliminary investigation. *Journal of Consulting and Clinical Psychology, 64,* 563–568.

Mawson, D., Marks, I. M., Ramm, L., & Stern, R. S. (1981). Guided mourning for morbid grief: A controlled outcome study. *British Journal of Psychiatry, 138,* 185–193.

McNeil, J. S. (1995). Bereavement and loss. In R. L. Edwards (Ed.). *Encyclopedia of social work* (pp. 284–291). Washington, DC: NASW Press.

Molendijk, K. M. (1996). A different perspective: Helping foster children grieve through the use of protocols. *Social Work Perspectives, 6*(1), 23–26.

Potocky, M. (1993). Effective services for bereaved spouses: A content analysis of the empirical literature. *Health and Social Work, 18*(4), 288–301.

Ramsay, R. W. (1976). A case study in bereavement therapy. In H. J. Eysenck (Ed.), *Case studies in behaviour therapy* (pp. 227–235). London: Routledge & Kegan Paul.

Ramsay, R. W. (1979). Bereavement: The behavioral treatment of the pathological grief. In P. Sjoden, S. Bates, & W. S. Dockens (Eds.), *Trends in Behavior Therapy* (pp. 217–248). New York: Academic Press.

Richman, J. M. (1995). Hospice. In R. L. Edwards (Ed.), *Encyclopedia of social work* (pp. 1358–1365). Washington, DC: NASW Press.

Richmond, M. (1935). *Social diagnosis.* New York: Sage. (Original work published in 1917)

Schauss, S. L., & Taylor, M. L. (1992, May). *Cognitive-behavioral treatment of pathological grief: A case example.* Paper presented at the annual convention of the Association for Behavior Analysis, San Francisco, CA.

Simos, B. G. (1977). Grief therapy to facilitate health restitution. *Social Casework, 58,* 337–342.

Sireling, L., Cohen, D., & Marks, I. M. (1988). Guided mourning for morbid grief: A controlled replication. *Behavior Therapy, 19,* 121–132.

Stroebe, M. S., Hansson, R. O., & Stroebe, W. (1993). Contemporary themes and controversies in bereavement research. In M. S. Stroebe, W. Stroebe, & R. O. Hansson (Eds.), *Handbook of bereavement* (pp. 457–476). New York: Cambridge University Press.

Task Force on Promotion and Dissemination of Psychological Procedures. (1995). Training in and dissemination of empirically-validated psychological treatments: Report and recommendations. *The Clinical Psychologist, 48*(1), 3–23.

Taylor-Brown, S. (1995). HIV/AIDS: Direct practice. In R. L. Edwards (Ed.), *Encyclopedia of social work* (pp. 1291–1305). Washington, DC: NASW Press.

Thyer, B. A. (1987). *Treating anxiety disorders.* Newbury Park, CA: Sage.

Tilley, S. (1985). Multiple phobias and grief: A case study. *Behavioural Psychotherapy, 13,* 59–68.

Vachon, M. L., Lyall, W. A., Rogers, J., Freedman-Letofsky, K., & Freeman, S. J. (1980). A controlled study of self-help intervention for widowers. *American Journal of Psychiatry, 137,* 1380–1384.

Vogel, W., & Peterson, L. E. (1991). A variant of guided exposure to mourning for use with treatment resistant patients. *Journal of Behavior Therapy and Experimental Psychiatry, 22,* 217–219.

Williams, W. V., & Pollack, N. P. (1979). Follow-up research on primary prevention: A model of adjustment in acute grief. *Journal of Clinical Psychiatry, 35,* 35–45.

PART II

Practice Issues

Chapter 18

PREVENTION

Steven P. Schinke
Kristin C. Cole

OVERVIEW

Prevention in the behavioral sciences and human services is supported more in theory than in practice. Although most behavioral scientists and clinicians recognize the value of and need for preventive services, few researchers and professionals are in fact engaged in studying or delivering those services. For their part, policymakers call for increased preventive services—aimed at such problems as substance use, AIDS and sexually transmitted diseases, child abuse, teenage pregnancy, and welfare dependence—but fail to appropriate adequate resources and legislation for prevention programs.

The appeal of prevention is patent. Preventing problems is more humane, more economic, potentially more effective, and certainly more enjoyable for professionals and clients than treating the untoward consequences of those problems. Yet developing, implementing, and evaluating prevention programs is difficult. Gaps between the concept and the practice of prevention in the behavioral sciences are particularly germane for preventive social work services.

RELEVANCE OF SOCIAL WORK INVOLVEMENT

By its nature, social work is a field confronted with rich opportunities for prevention. In the course of executing their professional duties, social workers encounter children and families at risk, persons involved with the criminal justice system, recovering substance users, and even organizations and entire communities—all of which could benefit from preventive services. Social workers find themselves in situations and environmental contexts that could not only benefit from prevention programs but that, in fact, cry out for the early ameliorative potential that a prevention effort may yield.

Across the spectrum of social work services, prevention is a logical intervention approach. Preventing problems is invariably easier, cheaper, and more humane than treating them after they happen. More than a few targets for prevention, particularly AIDS and sexually transmitted diseases, offer significant challenges to their treatment and amelioration. Efforts to reverse such refractory problems frequently meet with disappointment and failure. Because the consequences of many serious social and health problems are nearly irreparable, treatment offers a poor substitute for successful efforts to prevent the problems from the outset. Prevention, therefore, is less an option for social work and more a mandate for the provision of effective, efficient, and responsive services.

ASSESSMENT METHODS

Depending on the focus of prevention services, social workers can employ a range of assessment methods to quantify the nature of the problem and to direct potentially effective prevention programs. Those assessment methods are categorized as follows.

Structured Clinical Interviews

Clinical interviews are helpful to isolate the individual and environmental context for the target problem. Because prevention services seek to help clients forestall or altogether avoid future problems, assessment procedures in preparation for those services must search for prodromal conditions of the ultimate presenting problem. Effective structured clinical interviews will discover those conditions to direct subsequent prevention efforts. A program seeking to prevent AIDS and other sexually transmitted diseases, for example, will profit from interviews that compile not only information on sexual behavior among target young people, but also that gather clinically relevant information on documented correlates of that behavior. Clinical interviews might thus ask youths and appropriate adult informants about IV drug and other substance use, prostitution, homosexuality, bisexuality, and other associated factors that prior research has shown helpful in predicting future risky sexual behaviors.

Clinical interviews to lay the foundation for prevention programs should be structured to elicit empirically demonstrated correlates of these target problems and to generate useful data for program design. Thus, in the earlier example of assessment procedures for an AIDS and STDs prevention program, structured clinical interviews should ask respondents about optimal conditions for delivering prevention services. Respondents might be asked about the timing, length, and situational context for prevention services. Should the prevention program be delivered in school or in after-school settings? Should the program engage youths' families? How much time should be devoted to the program? By including these and similar questions in the structured clinical interview, social workers will optimize their opportunities to use this assessment method to inform a precise and responsive prevention effort.

Computerized Assessment Methods

Without offering significant advantages for the development of prevention programs, computerized assessment methods warrant inclusion in any comprehensive assessment system. Illustrative of the potential of these methods for prevention programs are findings from a study completed by Murray and Hannan (1990). The investigators employed a computer-assisted telephone interviewing (CATI) system to follow youths involved in smoking prevention programs. Through the added precision and ease of use of the CATI system, Murray and his colleague were able to track successfully several thousand youths for purposes of obtaining postintervention data on the efficacy of their prevention program. Absent the CATI systems, the investigators might not have gathered the rich follow-up data that allowed them to isolate the effects of their prevention program and suggest heuristic hypotheses to guide future research.

Self-Report Methods

Of all the extant assessment procedures, self-report methods remain the most heavily used. The reasons for the continued popularity of self-report assessments are several. Few other types of assessment methods offer the ease of administration, portability, low cost, and adaptability of self-report instruments. Among the options available to social work practitioners and researchers, self-report has the greatest diversity of existing psychometrically tested measures. Several thousand self-report instruments are accessible through the literature to reliably measure nearly any mental health, social, or behavioral topic imaginable. Consequently, the clinical and research literature contains myriad examples of self-reported indices as outcome variables for social work prevention programs.

Illustrative of those examples is a study by Schinke et al. in which elementary school–aged children participated in a prevention study aimed at reducing violence among inner-city residents in Washington, DC (Schinke, Jansen, Kennedy, & Shi, 1994). Children in the experiment took part in a brief intervention designed to impart problem-solving skills for avoiding violence and aggressive behavior, either as a perpetrator or as a victim. Prior to and after intervention delivery, children in the study completed a self-report schedule asking them to scale their agreement with a series of statements about risk taking, anger, aggression, violence, and adaptive, health-enhancing activities. The questionnaire was developed with a comparable sample of youths and had acceptable retest reliability. Its construct validity was suggested by the nature of its items, which were directly related to the violence prevention program. Analyses of youths' pretest to posttest responses to the questionnaire revealed differences in favor of the prevention program.

Observational Methods

Assessment procedures that allow social workers to observe and collect data on behavioral interactions related to prevention outcome offer distinct benefits. Among those benefits are the validity inherent in observing the behaviors targeted by the prevention program, the reduction in response bias as clients interact in naturalistic settings, and the ability to test interrater reliability within data collection teams. Furthermore, observation measures carry social relevance, because the investigator is expressly documenting the presence or absence of the problem that prompted the prevention program. If the social worker is planning a prevention program to reduce fighting and increase positive interactions among preschoolers, for example, he or she can gather through observational measures first-hand data on these behaviors. The social worker's confidence in the veracity of the resulting data may be greater than his or her faith in parallel data gleaned from self-reported responses gathered by teachers.

Observational data also lend themselves to archival retrieval and review through videotape recordings. Enjoying a long history of support in social work research, videotaped observational data have been employed to test the effectiveness of programs to prevent teenage pregnancy, child abuse, substance use, and other problems among adults and children (Moncher & Schinke, 1994; Schinke et al., 1994; Schinke, Moncher, & Singer, 1997; Schinke et al., 1992; Schinke, Singer, Cole, & Contento, 1997). Videotape recordings permit retrospective viewing and scoring in the laboratory setting. Data collected through videotape methods allow precise quantification of verbal and nonverbal parameters. And, relative to live behavioral observations, archival videotaped data are much easier to score for interrater reliability because they can be replayed again and again.

Physiological Measures

Representing a nascent type of assessment data method for social prevention programs, physiological measurements are most often adjuncts to self-report, observational, and other assessments. Typically, physiological assessment information is used as confirmatory evidence for the absence of a particular behavior or response targeted by a prevention program. For example, biochemical data collection is routinely part of evaluations to test the efficacy of interventions aimed at preventing tobacco, alcohol, or drug use (Moncher & Schinke, 1994; Schinke, Moncher, Holden, Botvin, & Orlandi, 1989; Schinke et al., 1990; Schinke et al., 1992; Schinke, Schilling, Gilchrist, Ashby, & Kitajima, 1989). Past studies of these prevention programs have collected samples of expired alveolar air, blood, urine, saliva, or hair to determine whether clients were using the target substances.

Albeit physiological measures can quantify clients' use of substances as well as their success in combating cardiovascular disease, certain cancers, and other health problems, these measures are typically employed in prevention programs to enhance the veracity of self-reports. That enhancement occurs when clients believe biochemical samples can reveal true levels of physiological phenomena or functioning. For example, smoking prevention studies routinely inform youths that biochemical sampling will disclose whether they are using tobacco. Youths are then asked for biochemical samples and asked to self-report their smoking. Studies of such biochemical enhancement procedures for self-reported behavior confirm that the illusion of physiological verification increases the accuracy of youth reports (Patrick et al., 1994; Pechacek et al., 1984).

EFFECTIVE SOCIAL WORK INTERVENTIONS

Much progress over recent years has been made to develop and test social work interventions for preventing a range of problems. By dint of the time frame for prevention programs, much of this progress is with youth-oriented interventions. Because young people have the most to gain from early lifestyle changes, prevention efforts for this population hold great promise. Even though adults can alter their behavior and thereby avoid later problems, many adult clients who fall within the purview of social work interventions have already adopted problem habits and lifestyles. For these clients, prevention efforts may happen too late. Youth, therefore, are appropriate recipients of most prevention programs in social work and in other behavioral sciences.

The ideal age span among youth for preventive intervention depends on the target problem. With most problems among young people occurring in the adolescent years, the preteen and early teenage periods are the focus of most prevention efforts. Beginning at about age 10 and lasting through the middle teen years, youths start the process through which they separate from their parents, develop independence, establish self-identity, and acquire skills to function as adults.

As youths move from childhood to adolescence, parental influence declines and is replaced by an increase in peer influence (Utech & Hoving, 1969). Increased reliance on peers further weakens parental influence and facilitates deviance (Jessor, 1984; Urberg & Robbins, 1983). Early adolescence is thus a time to experiment with new patterns of behavior (Bailey, 1992). Consequently, youths in early adolescence offer an efficient target for social work preventive intervention and behavioral risk reduction efforts.

Younger adolescents are eager for information about themselves and their bodies. Unfortunately, much information communicated to adolescents is either incorrect, misleading, or unhealthy. Prevention services can arm youth with accurate information that will help them to protect themselves and to feel more confident about their choices.

Group Therapies Rationale

Group intervention has relevance for prevention studies. A preventive intervention can exploit the natural group of the classroom or community to reinforce intervention messages. Targeting group norms is especially important, given the emerging importance of peer relationships for youth (Oetting & Beauvais, 1987; Oetting & Lynch, in press). According to theorists, peer clusters—which include friendship networks and dating dyads—not only account for the presence and type of risk taking among adolescents, but may also help youths reduce pressures and influences toward deviance. The therapeutic use of peer clusters in an intervention may enhance efforts to reduce adolescents' risks for problem behavior. By providing positive alternatives and by changing social norms, therapeutic peer clusters can be a source of social development.

The tasks involved in skills-based and social influence–based interventions rely upon groups for several reasons. Behavioral rehearsal, skills modeling, brainstorming, and identifying perceptions of normative behaviors all require groups of subjects. Peer reprisals appear more effective in extinguishing negative behaviors than similar sanctions from intervention leaders.

A classroom or community center has the obvious advantage of reaching a large number of youths at once. And given the urgent need for preventing such unhealthy behaviors as tobacco and other substance use, early pregnancy, and unprotected sex, and the lack of funding necessary to target specific individuals for this intensive work, group intervention as a prevention modality will likely be the norm for many years.

The vast majority of social work prevention programs reported in the literature have been delivered in small group contexts. Offering an efficient vehicle for intervention delivery, small groups also tap strengths of this clinical medium as identified by theory. Social learning theory and other cognitive-behavioral approaches suggest that, within group settings, clients have available role models, partners for behavioral rehearsals, and peer coaches for developing prevention skills (Bandura, 1986). Moreover, groups foster vicarious learning, as clients share with one another meaningful situations from their own lives. Assuming a commonality of experience among clients faced with the same target problem, these situations provide advance views of circumstances that all clients may someday encounter. Given the goal of prevention to help clients avoid entirely future problems, these advance views are an essential part of learning in groups.

Group Therapies Illustration

An illustrative group intervention was conducted by the authors to prevent tobacco use among Native American youth. Based on life skills and social influence models of prevention, the group intervention included material on bicultural competence, tobacco use knowledge, and cognitive and behavioral techniques for problem solving, communication and resistance, and stress and coping. Much of the curriculum involved interactive classroom work. In particular, subjects frequently participated in rehearsals of cognitive and behavioral techniques to avoid tobacco use.

A skills-community condition also received intervention designed to involve the community in the project. Under the intervention leader's guidance, skills-community condition youths staged various activities in which they modeled the skills they had learned in classroom intervention to their parents and other community members. Publications and posters produced by this condition's participants further educated their parents and other community members about the nature and purpose of the intervention effort.

A number of media were used to enhance group participation and cultural specificity in both skills-only and skills-community interventions. Traditional Native American legends and puppets helped initiate and enhance classroom discussion. For example, a Native American legend about the ceremonial use of tobacco was performed by participants with puppets. Following their performance, group leaders asked youths for alternative choices to using tobacco in other settings, ways to resist tobacco use, and ways to deal with the stress from refusing peers. To encourage group discussion, leaders routinely asked youths for their ideas, wrote them on the blackboard, and then asked the group to select and defend the best ideas among those offered by the group.

In the skills-community condition, subjects were also encouraged to discuss their learning experiences at home and in the community, and to practice what they had learned in the classroom in settings outside of school. In subsequent sessions, youths reported to the group about these attempts and then evaluated their efforts with the help of their classmates. Data from this study indicate that youths in the skills-community condition were slightly less likely to use tobacco than youths in the skills condition, and youths in both experimental conditions were less likely than their control group counterparts to use tobacco (Schinke, Moncher, et al., 1989).

Also employing small groups, Wodarski and his colleagues developed an adolescent education program that teaches youths about alcohol through games (Wodarski, Adelson, Tidball, & Wodarski, 1980; Wodarski & Hoffman, 1984). By emphasizing group rather than individual achievement, the method capitalizes on peer influence and increases social attachment to peers. Recent data support the effectiveness of this prevention strategy for alcohol abuse (Wodarski, 1987; Wodarski, 1988).

Community Intervention

Social work prevention programs in community settings have grown in recent years. Community venues for prevention offer distinct benefits. By serving clients in the setting within which they live and work, community programs can address the variables and influences that may account for the target problem for prevention. For example, a prevention effort aimed at substance use among youth can better modify such forces as liquor store access, police surveillance, and parental sanctions when the program is grounded in a community context rather than solely in a school setting (Schinke et al., 1992).

Intervening with at-risk youths in their communities has other advantages. Because the nonschool day is longer than the school day, scheduling intervention is easier due to the increased hours of opportunity. Frequently, researchers have trouble persuading school administrators and teachers to release class time for intervention. Working with community centers avoids this problem, and additionally provides weekend hours as possible intervention hours.

Many at-risk youths perceive the community center as a more neutral ground than their school. Unlike their mandated attendance at school, children in community centers choose to be there. What is more, youths who do not perform well in school may be disinclined to participate in an intervention that is delivered at school. Similarly, at-risk youths frequently have parents that had negative experiences with schools, thus making them averse to school-based efforts. The community center is free of such prejudices.

Community programs can also bring to bear multiple sources of prevention programming on members of the target client population. Insofar as they can impact more cognate areas of clients' lives, community programs can maximize the potency of a prevention effort. A program to prevent cardiovascular disease among residents in a community, for example, can engage print and electronic media, workplaces, health providers, and commercial establishments in spreading a consistent and coordinated intervention message (Farquhar, Fortmann, & Maccoby, 1984). Community prevention activities also have potential for sustaining program effects long after the activity has formally concluded. For instance, a citywide program to help young people avoid tobacco may also foster positive alternatives for youths in the form of after-school, recreational, and peer-support activities.

Community Intervention Illustration

A comparative study evaluated the effects of SMART Moves–enhanced Boys and Girls Clubs on children and adolescents who live in public housing projects. With or without SMART Moves (a drug abuse prevention program) Boys and Girls Clubs constitute a rich illustration of a community-based prevention program. The clubs provide daily programs for their members through individual services, small group programs, and drop-in activities. The Boys and Girls Clubs core program formally covers six areas: cultural enrichment, health and physical education, social recreation, personal and educational development, citizenship and leadership development, and environmental education. Boys and Girls Clubs services include reading classes, library activities, cooking and crafts groups, weight lifting, sports, and free lunch programs. Girls and boys take field trips and attend cultural events. Homework assistance, tutoring, computer instruction, home economics, and learning center activities are also available to club members.

Boys and Girls Clubs are typically housed in neighborhood recreational centers or other human service settings. Run by trained staff and volunteers familiar with neighborhood youth, Boys and Girls Clubs provide both formal and informal guidance and counseling. In addition to monitoring all club-related activities, staff take an active interest in members' lives by monitoring their attendance at school and reviewing their report cards. Staff also try to involve the members' parents in Boys and Girls Clubs programs specifically, and in their members' lives generally.

SMART Moves (Self Management and Resistance Training) is a participatory substance abuse prevention program developed by Boys and Girls Clubs of America and based on research conducted at Cornell University Medical College and the University of Southern California. The program builds on the structure and support systems of the Boys and Girls Clubs, targeting the specific pressures and challenges preteens and adolescents face. Community-oriented rather than individualistic, the program aims to educate parents and the community as well as the adolescent.

Our study compared substance abuse and other problem behavior rates among youth who live in public housing developments with newly established and SMART Moves–enhanced Boys and Girls Clubs, youth who live in public housing developments with existing Boys and Girls Clubs, and youth who live in public housing developments without clubs. The study sought to determine the overall impact the Boys and Girls Clubs might have on a housing development's environment, manifested in such areas as rates of criminal activity, drug dealing, vandalism, and parent involvement. In addition, the study evaluated the influence of clubs on youths' grades, truancy, and behavior problems in school.

Based on analyses of data collected from housing developments that have Smart Moves–enhanced Boys and Girls Clubs, regular Boys and Girls Clubs, or no clubs, several conclusions from the study were empirically warranted. Foremost among those conclusions was that, for adults and youths alike, Boys and Girls Clubs appear to be associated with an overall reduction in substance abuse, drug trafficking, and other drug-related criminal activity. The presence of crack cocaine was lowest in housing developments with Boys and Girls Clubs with the SMART Moves drug prevention programs. The ratings of drug-dealing activity were also the lowest in those housing developments served by Boys and Girls Clubs with the SMART Moves drug prevention program.

Evaluation results showed that housing developments with Boys and Girls Clubs with and without SMART Moves had fewer damaged units and less criminal activity than housing developments without any clubs. Boys and Girls Clubs' programs thus appear to improve the physical quality of life in housing developments, which seems to have boosted the morale of the development's residents and authority figures in the community.

Members of the evaluation team discovered through interviews that establishing Boys and Girls Clubs in housing developments encourages residents to organize and improve their communities. Boys and Girls Clubs stimulate communication between housing development residents, the police, housing authority managing personnel, and other community groups. The increase in communication seems to have enriched the social quality of life in the housing developments. This informal interaction and communication is perhaps the most important effect of the Boys and Girls Clubs and it is also the most difficult to measure.

Social support services are critical for poor youth, but comprehensive and sensitive prevention services for young people in housing developments are practically nonexistent. Housing development communities in particular need attention, community organization, and carefully designed intervention programs. Although the long-term impact of Boys and Girls Clubs in housing developments is yet to be seen and is difficult to measure, our evaluation affirmed the clubs' positive influence on and contribution toward developing strategies of preventive intervention for youth at risk for substance use and other problem behavior.

Family Intervention

The absence of family supports contributes to adolescents' problem behavior (Moncher, Holden, & Schinke, 1991; Pandina & Schuele, 1983; Wiess, 1988). Studies have shown an association between harsh parental discipline and children's subsequent behavioral problems. Other studies have found a relationship between parental support for health behavior and children's healthy habits (American Psychological Association, 1993; McLoyd & Wilson, 1990; Resnick, Chabliss, & Blum, 1993). Increased family conflict, decreased family management, decreased family rituals, decreased family cohesion, and low income have all been related to substance abuse (Bruce & Emshoff, 1992). Other data have demonstrated the positive influence of family psychoeducation and expanded social networks on children's health behavior (McFarlane, 1993). These data suggest the salubrious effects of including adolescents' families in preventive interventions.

Parent involvement can strengthen youths' learning through positive family interactions that support risk reduction efforts (Hawkins, Catalano, & Miller, 1992; Hawkins et al., 1992). Parents can include natural parents and other significant adult members of youths' lives. Interactive exercises should encourage parent-child communication not only around risk reduction content, but also around shared enjoyable activities.

Shared parent-child exercises can be introduced during family sessions or home-based exercises. For ethnic-racial minority groups, risk reduction research has found family sessions more effective than exercises completed at home for increasing parent participation and for changing youths' behavior (Perry, 1993).

In our previous work with family interventions, we found that parents valued activities focused on their needs, not only on their children's needs (Moncher, 1991). To that end, parent intervention might include events exclusively for youths' parents. Such parent sessions should have provisions for child care and transportation reimbursements. Parenting workshops might encompass child-management skills (e.g., negotiation, positive reinforcement) and ideas to help youths avoid tobacco, alcohol, drugs, and other problem behaviors. For example, because low levels of parental support and weak parental sanctions against using tobacco and alcohol are related to adolescent drug use (Jessor & Jessor, 1977), parents can practice communicating strong, consistent messages about abstinence from tobacco and alcohol use to their children. Parents might also learn that effective parenting consists of being warm toward one's children, engaging in a high degree of give and take, offering rational explanations of rules and limits, and affirming their children's qualities, coupled with setting clear standards for conduct (Baumrind, 1978).

Although generalizations are hazardous in describing such a varied population as parents of high-risk youth, our prior data suggests that these parents might be inordinately occupied with providing for their households and thus might have limited time for working with their children on prevention goals. Admittedly, many prevention activities presume a commitment on the part of parents that may not always be possible. But through the help of focus groups and consultants, the parent involvement component can be crafted to accommodate many parenting styles. For example, if key figures in the community believe that parent attendance at intervention sessions is unrealistic, workbook or video instruction can be created for shared parent-youth activities at home.

Culturally Sensitive Intervention

Increasingly, social workers and researchers are arguing that prevention strategies need to incorporate the traditions and rituals of the target ethnic-racial populations into the content and process of prevention programs. Emphasizing cultural pride, according to these investigators, is critical to attracting ethnic-racial minority-group youths' attention (Tucker, 1985). When attempting to prevent substance abuse in African American youth, for example, Knox (1985) recommends exploring sources of hope, strength, and spirituality in the African American community.

Warranting further study is the relative effectiveness of different intervention strategies for various target populations. Thus far, most prevention programs have been implemented with majority-culture youth, although some programs have focused on Native American youth (Gilchrist, Schinke, Trimble, & Cvetkovich, 1987; Schinke et al., 1988) and others with predominantly African American and Hispanic American students (Ellickson & Bell, 1990; Hansen, Johnson, Flay, Graham, & Sobel, 1988). Of those implemented with minority-group youth, few have been designed to address culturally specific risk factors.

Culturally sensitive prevention programs can be more relevant, meaningful, and important than programs that pay only cursory attention to cultural nuance. Social workers who sensitively and accurately assess cultural variables can have greater confidence that results were due to the intervention itself. Conversely, social workers whose methods ignore or minimize cultural issues may reach erroneous conclusions. Although the development and testing of culturally sensitive prevention interventions is particularly time consuming because of a lack of previous efforts, the rewards are great.

CONCLUSION

Whatever the venues that social service providers choose to use for delivering prevention services, they are without question warranted for today's youth. Now more than ever, our nation's youth are vulnerable to a host of threats to their well-being. Especially for youth who are denied supportive and caring parents and safe schools, and who live in distressed and disadvantaged communities, prevention services are necessary to help them to resist pressures to engage in unhealthy behaviors.

Adolescents need peer approval, role models, and social and recreational activities that allow them to exercise their increasing cognitive sophistication. They have needs for independence from their families, for opportunities for the development of self-esteem, for information, and for adult guidance. These are needs that exist in a number of different arenas of an adolescent's life and cannot be addressed through school-based education alone.

Thus, prevention approaches must be taken out of the classroom and built into other community-based events that voluntarily attract all types of adolescents. Numbers of researchers have cited the need for more alternative activities for youth to turn to instead of using drugs, dropping out of school, or committing crimes for their recreation.

There needs to be a greater outreach to, and more attention given to, the social networks that may be means of incorporating the institutionally alienated. There is a need for interventions targeting minority populations that would balance an awareness of their cultural needs with an understanding of the social dynamics of adolescence, which can stigmatize populations receiving special attention. Longitudinal studies have shown that adding even one of these components to the lives of at-risk youths or teenage parents contributes significantly to their chances of developing into happy, productive citizens.

REFERENCES

American Psychological Association. (1993). *Violence and youth: Psychology's response. Vol. 1: Summary Report of the American Psychological Association Commission on Violence and Youth.* Washington, DC: Author.

Bailey, S. L. (1992). Adolescents' multisubstance use patterns: The role of heavy alcohol and cigarette use. *American Journal of Public Health, 32,* 1220–1224.

Bandura, A. (1986). *Social foundations of thought and action: A social cognitive theory.* Englewood Cliffs, NJ: Prentice Hall.

Baumrind, D. (1978). Parental disciplinary patterns and social competence in youth. *Youth and Society, 9,* 239–276.

Bruce, C., & Emshoff, J. (1992). The Super II Program: An early intervention program. *Journal of Community Psychology, OSAP Special Issue,* pp. 10–21.

Ellickson, P. L., & Bell, R. M. (1990). Drug prevention in junior high. *Science, 247,* 1299–1305.

Farquhar, J. W., Fortmann, S. P., & Maccoby, N. (1984). The Stanford Five-City Project: An overview. In J. D. Matarazzo, H. A. Herd, N. E. Miller, & S. M. Weiss (Eds.), *Behavioral health: A handbook of health enhancement and disease prevention* (pp. 1154–1165). New York: Wiley.

Gilchrist, L. D., Schinke, S. P., Trimble, J. E., & Cvetkovich, G. (1987). Skills enhancement to prevent substance abuse among American Indian adolescents. *International Journal of the Addictions, 22*(9), 869–879.

Hansen, W. B., Johnson, C. A., Flay, B. R., Graham, J. W., & Sobel, J. L. (1988). Affective and social influences approaches to the prevention of multiple substance abuse among seventh grade students: Results from project SMART. *Prevention Medicine, 17,* 135–154.

Hawkins, J. D., Catalano, R. F., & Miller, J. Y. (1992). Risk and protective factors for alcohol and other drug problems in adolescence and early childhood: Implications for substance abuse prevention. *Psychological Bulletin, 112*(1), 112–121.

Hawkins, J. D., Catalano, R. F., Morrison, D. M., O'Donnell, J., Abbott, R. D., & Day, L. E. (1992). The Seattle social development project: Effects of the first four years on protective factors and problem behaviors. In J. McCord & R. Tremblay (Eds.), *The prevention of antisocial behavior in children* (pp. 139–161). New York: Guilford Press.

Jessor, R. (1984). Adolescent development and behavioral health. In J. D. Matarazzo, S. M. Weiss, J. A. Herd, N. E. Miller, & S. M. Weiss (Eds.), *Behavioral health* (pp. 69–90). New York: Wiley.

Jessor, R., & Jessor, S. L. (1977). *Problem behavior and psychosocial development: A longitudinal study of youth.* New York: Academic Press.

Knox, D. H. (1985). Spirituality: A tool in the assessment and treatment of Black alcoholics and their families. *Alcoholism Treatment Quarterly, 2,* 31–44.

McFarlane, W. R. (1993). *The multiple family group, psychoeducation and maintenance medication in the treatment of schizophrenia: Psychiatric outcomes in a multi-site trial.* Manuscript submitted for publication.

McLoyd, V., & Wilson, L. (1990). Maternal behavior, social support, and economic conditions as predictors of distress in children. In W. Damon (Ed.), *New directions for child development* (pp. 49–71). San Francisco: Jossey-Bass.

Moncher, M. S. (1991). Process and outcome evaluation of intervention curriculum to increase parent involvement with students in character development program. (Doctoral dissertation, Columbia University, 1990). *Dissertation Abstracts International.*

Moncher, M. S., Holden, G. W., & Schinke, S. P. (1991). Psychosocial correlates of substance abuse among youth: A review of current etiological constructs. *International Journal of the Addictions, 26,* 377–414.

Moncher, M. S., & Schinke, S. P. (1994). Group intervention to prevent tobacco use among Native American youth. *Research on Social Work Practice, 4,* 160–171.

Murray, D. M., & Hannan, P. J. (1990). Planning for the appropriate analysis in school based drug use prevention studies. *Journal of Consulting and Clinical Psychology, 58,* 458–468.

Oetting, E., & Beauvais, F. (1987). Peer cluster theory, socialization characteristics and adolescent drug use: A path analysis. *Journal of Counseling Psychology, 34,* 205–213.

Oetting, E. R., & Lynch, R. S. (in press). Peers and the prevention of adolescent drug use. In Z. Amsel & B. Bukoski (Eds.), *Drug abuse prevention: Sourcebook on strategies and research.* Westport, CT: Greenwood Publishing Group.

Pandina, R. T., & Schuele, J. A. (1983). Psychosocial correlates of alcohol and drug use of adolescent students and adolescents in treatment. *Journal of Studies on Alcohol, 44,* 950–973.

Patrick, D. L., Cheadle, A., Thompson, D. C., Diehr, P., Koepsell, T., & Kinne, S. (1994). The validity of self-reported smoking: A review and meta-analysis. *American Journal of Public Health, 84,* 1086–1093.

Pechacek, T. F., Murray, D. M., Luepker, R. V., Mittelmark, M. B., Johnson, C. A., & Shutz, J. M. (1984). Measurement of adolescent smoking behavior: Rationale and methods. *Journal of Behavioral Medicine, 7,* 123–140.

Perry, C. L. (1993, March 20). Review of CATCH findings on CVD risk reduction in urban and rural settings. Cornell University Medical College, New York, NY.

Resnick, M. D., Chabliss, S. A., & Blum, R. W. (1993). Health and risk behaviors of urban adolescent males involved in pregnancy. *Families in Society, 74,* 366–374.

Schinke, S. P., Jansen, M., Kennedy, E., & Shi, Q. (1994). Reducing risk taking behavior among vulnerable youth: An intervention outcome study. *Family and Community Health, 16*(4), 49–56.

Schinke, S. P., Moncher, M. S., Holden, G. W., Botvin, G. J., & Orlandi, M. A. (1989). American Indian youth and substance abuse: Tobacco use problems, risk factors and preventive interventions. *Health Education Research, 4,* 137–144.

Schinke, S. P., Moncher, M. S., & Singer, B. R. (1997). Native American youths and cancer risk reduction: Effects of software intervention. *Journal of Adolescent Health, 15,* 105–110.

Schinke, S. P., Orlandi, M. A., Botvin, G. J., Gilchrist, L. D., Trimble, J. E., & Locklear, V. S. (1988). Preventing substance abuse among American Indian adolescents: A bicultural competence skills approach. *Journal of Counseling Psychology, 35*(1), 87–90.

Schinke, S. P., Orlandi, M. A., Schilling, R. F., Botvin, G. J., Gilchrist, L. D., & Landers, C. (1990). Tobacco use by American Indian and Alaska Native people: Risks, psychosocial factors, and preventive intervention. *Journal of Alcohol and Drug Education, 35*(2), 1–12.

Schinke, S. P., Orlandi, M. A., Vaccaro, D., Espinoza, R., McAlister, A., & Botvin, G. J. (1992). Substance use among Hispanic and non-Hispanic adolescents. *Addictive Behaviors, 17,* 117–124.

Schinke, S. P., Schilling, R. F., Gilchrist, L. D., Ashby, M. R., & Kitajima, E. (1989). Native youth and smokeless tobacco: Prevalence rates, gender differences, and descriptive characteristics. *Journal of the National Cancer Institute, 8,* 39–42.

Schinke, S. P., Singer, B., Cole, K., & Contento, I. R. (1997). Reducing cancer risks among Native American adolescents: Cultural issues, intervention strategies, and baseline findings. *Preventive Medicine, 25,* 146–155.

Tucker, M. B. (1985). U.S. ethnic minorities and drug abuse: An assessment of the science and practice. *International Journal of the Addictions, 20,* 1021–1047.

Urberg, K., & Robbins, R. (1983). *Adolescent invulnerability.* Unpublished manuscript, Wayne State University, Detroit, MI.

Utech, D., & Hoving, K. L. (1969). Parents and peers as competing influences in the decisions of children of differing ages. *Journal of Social Psychology, 78,* 267–274.

Wiess, H. B. (1988). Family support and education programs: Working through ecological theories of human development. In H. B. Wiess & F. H. Jacobs (Eds.), *Evaluating family programs* (pp. 3–36). New York: Aldine De Gruyter.

Wodarski, J. S. (1987). A social learning approach to teaching adolescents about drinking and driving: A multiple variable follow-up evaluation. *Journal of Social Service Research, 10*(2/3/4), 121–144.

Wodarski, J. S. (1988). Teaching adolescents about alcohol and driving. *Journal of Alcohol and Drug Education, 33*(3), 327–344.

Wodarski, L. A., Adelson, C., Tidball, M., & Wodarski, J. S. (1980). Teaching nutrition by teams-games-tournaments. *Journal of Nutrition Education, 12*(2), 61–65.

Wodarski, J. S., & Hoffman, S. D. (1984). Alcohol education for adolescents. *Social Work in Education, 6*(2), 69–92.

Chapter 19

MEASUREMENT OF SOCIAL PROBLEMS

Walter W. Hudson
Annatjie C. Faul

Progress in the delivery of services, treatment, and intervention, as well as progress in developing a validated knowledge base, is completely dependent on the use of high-quality measurement tools. This chapter provides a description of several measurement tools for use in social work practice (and research) and provides references for others that can be obtained from a variety of sources. Also provided is a brief discussion of a computer application that enables practitioners and clients to gain easy access to a rich variety of assessment scales for measuring and monitoring problems in personal and social functioning. Before turning to the description of measurement tools, it is important to have a brief discussion of the microtheory of human problems that forms the basis of the assessment scales that are described in this chapter.

DEFINING PERSONAL AND SOCIAL PROBLEMS

There are many different orientations to social work practice, but a commonly observed, even dominant, theme is a focus on *problem solving;* one could legitimately describe social work as a practice-based problem-solving profession. There also are many different theoretical orientations and practice approaches to problem solving, but the issue here is one of being more explicit about what is meant by a *problem.* In other words, if social workers are going to measure personal and social problems, they must first be able to define what is meant by a *problem,* and that is the focus of this section.

Social workers have long been familiar with the measurement of such diverse client characteristics as physical attributes, biological characteristics, social attributes, knowledge, ability, achievement, attitudes, beliefs, values, personality, feelings, perceptions, behaviors, and a host of other commonly understood attributes and characteristics that are used as measurement constructs across the social and behavioral sciences. Moreover, a problem-solving orientation to the definition and conduct of social work practice had been a part of the language of the profession for at least two decades (Perlman, 1957) before Hudson (1981) suggested that problems in personal and social functioning represent definable measurement domains that are especially important to, and are all but unique within, social work.

The types of assessment scales—unidimensional and multidimensional—that are described and discussed in this chapter are those that are designed to measure the degree or severity of a separate and distinct problem in personal or social functioning. Each such scale (or subscale) is viewed, by analogy, as being little more than a thermometer (Hudson, 1982). A thermometer will measure the temperature of an object but it will give no information about the source, cause, or origin of the heat that produces the temperature. A thermometer will inform a physician of the presence of a fever, but it is useless in giving information about what caused the fever. In other words, high-quality measurement tools are indispensable for the advancement of science and practice, but we must understand what they cannot do as well as what they provide in terms of information.

All assessment scales that are designed to measure problems in personal and social functioning perform very much like a thermometer. They may do a good job of telling you that a client has a problem in the area addressed by a specific measure, and they may do a good job of telling you how serious the problem may be. However, assessment scales that are designed to measure the severity of problems in personal and social functioning will *not* provide any information whatsoever about the source or cause of the problems they measure, nor will they provide any information concerning what should be done to alleviate the problems. To continue the previous analogy, a thermometer is completely atheoretical with respect to theories about the causes of heat and the sources of heat that produce the temperature. Similarly, measures of personal and social functioning are completely atheoretical with respect to the cause and control of those problems.

For purposes of description it may be useful to consider the theory of molecular motion as a microtheory that describes the phenomenon of temperature, while a theory about the causes and sources of heat can be regarded as a macrotheory. In this context, the microtheory is useful in studying the behavior of thermometers. By analogy with the thermometer, the basic elements of a microtheory are presented for the definition and measurement of problems in personal and social functioning. Such a theory is useful for understanding the theoretical orientation of assessment scales that measure the degree or severity of personal and social functioning and how they function as measurement devices. No effort is made to develop or defend a macrotheory about the cause or origin of personal and social problems. For example, the Index of Family Relations (IFR; Hudson, 1990c; Hudson & Acklin, 1980) shown in Figure 19-1 will not help you understand *why* family stress has occurred or how it came into existence should you wish to construct a theory of family discord, therapy, or intervention. On the other hand, the IFR scale will provide valuable information about the severity of problems in the area

INDEX OF FAMILY RELATIONS (IFR)

Name: _____   Today's Date: _____

This questionnaire is designed to measure the way you feel about your family as a whole. It is not a test, so there are no right or wrong answers. Answer each item as carefully and as accurately as you can by placing a number beside each one as follows.

1 = None of the time
2 = Very rarely
3 = A little of the time
4 = Some of the time
5 = A good part of the time
6 = Most of the time
7 = All of the time

1. ____ The members of my family really care about each other.
2. ____ I think my family is terrific.
3. ____ My family gets on my nerves.
4. ____ I really enjoy my family.
5. ____ I can really depend on my family.
6. ____ I really do not care to be around my family.
7. ____ I wish I was not part of this family.
8. ____ I get along well with my family.
9. ____ Members of my family argue too much.
10. ____ There is no sense of closeness in my family.
11. ____ I feel like a stranger in my family.
12. ____ My family does not understand me.
13. ____ There is too much hatred in my family.
14. ____ Members of my family are really good to one another.
15. ____ My family is well respected by those who know us.
16. ____ There seems to be a lot of friction in my family.
17. ____ There is a lot of love in my family.
18. ____ Member of my family get along well together.
19. ____ Life in my family is generally unpleasant.
20. ____ My family is a great joy to me.
21. ____ I feel proud of my family.
22. ____ Other families seem to get along better than ours.
23. ____ My family is a real source of comfort to me.
24. ____ I feel left out of my family.
25. ____ My family is an unhappy one.

1, 2, 4, 5, 8, 14, 15, 17, 18, 20, 21, 23.

Figure 19-1. Index of Family Relations.

of family stress. It will do a good job of measuring the amount of stress in a family (as seen by the respondent) on a scale from 0 to 100, where low scores indicate the relative absence of a problem and higher scores indicate the presence of a more serious problem.

A microtheory about personal and social problems is best created and understood by first describing the basic approach to measurement that is most often used in the development of personal and social problem measures. The approach is straightforward and consists of little more than asking respondents to report the relative frequency of occurrence of the behavior, affect, or perception that is represented by the content of a specific scale item. For example, the fourth item of the Generalized Contentment Scale (GCS), a measure of depression, states, "I have crying spells"; the respondent is asked to report how frequently that behavior occurs on a scale from 1 to 7, where 1 equals *None of the time* and 7 equals *All of the time.* The item scores obtained from the items comprising the GCS are summed and transformed in order to obtain a total score that ranges from 0 to 100. If the obtained GCS score is both reliable and valid, we can claim that we have measured something called *depression,* but we cannot yet claim that we have measured a personal adjustment problem. The following microtheory about human problems provides a basis for making the claim that we have measured a human problem. The core ingredients of the microtheory of human problems consist of two fundamental axioms. These axioms state that: (a) Human problems do not exist until someone defines them, and (b) all human problems are defined in terms of a value base.

Two major implications of these axioms must be kept in mind when using measures of personal and social functioning. The first is that any conclusion about the presence of any personal or social functioning problem or disorder is always based on the value position of the person who draws the conclusion. That is, *a problem does not exist until someone defines it,* and problems are always defined *in terms of someone's value position.* This means that it is entirely possible—and is, in fact, not at all uncommon—for a practitioner to conclude that a client has a problem in some well-defined area of functioning but for the client to claim otherwise. Discrepancies of this nature can arise for at least two reasons. First, the practitioner and the client may be using different data or the assessment scale may not be reliable and valid. This is largely a technological failure that is nearly always easily corrected by selecting a different measurement tool or by repairing one that does not perform as expected or as required. The second reason for such discrepancies may be the fact that the practitioner and the client are using different value positions to draw conclusions about the presence of a problem in personal or social functioning.

It is especially important to understand the latter difficulty, which can be illustrated with a familiar example. It is not uncommon for a traffic court to refer someone to a human services professional for the treatment of alcohol abuse because the client was driving a vehicle while intoxicated. The practitioner might administer the Multi-Problem Screening Inventory (MPSI; Hudson, 1990a, 1990b; Hudson & McMurtry, 1997; Pike & Hudson, 1997) to the client and obtain a very high score on the alcohol abuse subscale, say, a score of 77. Under these circumstances the practitioner will conclude that the client has a drinking problem, and the court has already arrived at that conclusion. The client, on the other hand, may strongly assert that he or she does *not* have a drinking problem ("I can hold my liquor with the best of them") and is seeking help only because it was mandated by the court as a way to avoid harsh penalties. The facts in this case are indisputable, but the conclusions differ because the client and the practitioner are evaluating the facts from different value positions. The main point here is that there is little doubt about having measured alcohol consumption and its consequences, because the reliability and validity of the alcohol abuse subscale are strong enough to attest to that. However, one person sees a very high score as a problem and the other does not. The difference in interpretation is based on their different value positions.

CLINICAL CUTTING SCORES

Despite the foregoing, practitioners need to have some basis from which to interpret scores. This leads to the second implication of our microtheory about problems in personal and social functioning, which has to do with the task of establishing clinical cutting scores for each such measure. In a very serious way, it addresses the question of how big is *big?* In other words, how large must a score be on a particular assessment scale in order to properly conclude that *the client has a problem;* that the client has a *clinically significant* problem in the area being assessed? The word *properly* here must be understood in the context in which it is being used. At its core, the method for establishing clinical cutting scores is based entirely on the consensual judgment of experienced practitioners. This means, quite clearly, that the use of the clinical cutting scores provided for any assessment scale is an implicit decision to abide by the consensual judgments of those colleagues who participated in the establishment of the clinical cutting score. It is also a recognition that those consensual judgments have emerged from adherence to a common set of values with respect to the definitions of clinically significant problems in the area of personal and social functioning represented by the scale in question.

This microtheory of human problems has many other implications that cannot be discussed here. The major purpose for stating it is to alert users of problem-oriented assessment scales to the fact that the clinical cutting scores of such measures are by no means rigid points that discriminate the *sick* from the *well* or the *functional* from the *dysfunctional.* At best, they are guidelines that are useful in making well-informed decisions about the severity of clients' problems in a wide range of areas concerning personal and social functioning. This also means that social workers must exercise professional judgment whenever they have a strong basis for departing from the typical prescriptions that are offered for interpretation of the scores that are obtained from such measures.

In summary, problems in personal and social functioning do not exist unless and until someone defines them, and those definitions ultimately rest on someone's values. If a client obtains a very high score on a reliable and valid depression scale, the social worker can be confident that the respondent is experiencing a great deal of distress. The amount of distress needed to describe this as a problem is a value-based judgment, and that is a critical fact that never should be forgotten. Finally, assessment scales that measure the amount of distress in personal and social functioning never impart information about the source or cause of the problem that is being measured. By putting all of the foregoing together, a *problem measure* can be defined as an assessment scale that reliably and validly measures the magnitude of individual distress or discomfort in an area of personal or social functioning such that it is also possible to establish a meaningful clinical cutting score for that instrument.

THE STRENGTHS AND LIMITS OF PROBLEM MEASURES

It may be disappointing for some to recognize that measures of personal and social problems do not provide information about the source or cause of a problem and that they provide no information about how to develop a treatment plan or decide upon initial and subsequent intervention choices. These shortcomings may even raise the question of whether such measures should be used at all. In short, what is the value of knowing the severity of a client's problem once you have determined through other means that the client does have a serious problem that requires professional intervention? These are legitimate questions, and there are at least two good answers to them.

It is not difficult for a trained or even a beginning practitioner to determine that some clients have truly serious problems in one or more areas of concern. For example, if a client is referred to treatment because he seriously battered and hospitalized his wife during an episode of binge drinking, it is not difficult to determine that he has fairly serious problems in two or more areas of personal functioning. However, it is incredibly difficult for even the most experienced practitioner to accurately address the question of how serious the client's problem is, in virtually any area of assessment. It is sometimes very easy to see the consequences of the problem (e.g., the contusions on a battered spouse), but it is extremely difficult to see the magnitude of the problem. The simple reason for this is that affect, perception, and distress are very private experiences, and the practitioner simply cannot get inside the client's head to see how intense the problem is as it is felt and experienced by the client.

In a personal correspondence, for example, one of the authors' colleagues described a case wherein the client was interviewed in depth by two highly trained and very experienced therapists. Neither of them suspected or saw any evidence of suicidal ideation or serious levels of depression and therefore did not investigate these areas. However, the client was asked to complete the MPSI, which revealed a very elevated score on the suicide subscale. An immediate follow-up was then conducted with the client, who confirmed that he was severely depressed, dwelt on suicide, and already had a plan to carry it out. In yet another case, a therapist could not see that any progress was being made in the treatment of depression for an adolescent girl, and, as a result, he recommended the transfer of the case to a more experienced therapist. The client was very distraught by this; she claimed that she had made considerable progress, and she dropped out of treatment prematurely because she felt so misunderstood by the therapist. Although the therapist did not properly use the information, the client had completed the GCS four times during treatment, and the scores (computed and examined too late to be useful) showed unmistakable evidence of the client's declining depression.

Social workers must never forget that clients are the same social creatures as are therapists and that they often are reluctant to display the expressive behaviors (or do not know how to do so) that help observers to perceive and thereby better gauge a client's level of distress. Clients who are making considerable progress in dealing with marital problems may not exhibit clear evidence of their gains. Suicidal clients often are entirely too polite, or fearful, to display how close to a disaster they may be standing, and an enraged teenager may smile pleasantly to everyone around mere moments or hours before engaging in extreme acts of violence. Standardized assessment scales that reliably and validly allow clients to self-report the seriousness of their private anguish (personal and social problems) can often be used to avoid the serious oversights in the assessment of client problems that result in the use of inadequate or misguided interventions.

A second very important reason for using standardized measures of personal and social functioning relates to professional and fiscal accountability and to treatment monitoring and planning. At core here is the question of whether the client has changed with respect to the problem that is being treated. It is often the case that trained therapists and service providers can reliably determine that a client has improved with respect to the problem that is being dealt with, but it is virtually impossible to determine the magnitude of that change without the use of psychometrically sound measurement tools. It therefore becomes essential that the client's problem be measured, at a *minimum,* at two different points in time. A social worker may be completely confident, and completely accurate, in the claim that a client has experienced considerable improvement with respect to, say, the level of intrafamilial discord. However, unless that problem is actually measured at two points in time (e.g., at intake and at termination of services) the actual magnitude of the improvement cannot be determined with any accuracy at all. This means that social workers simply cannot be professionally accountable to themselves, to their clients, or to their superiors if they fail to use adequate measures of the problems that are brought to them for professional intervention.

USING ASSESSMENT SCALES IN PRACTICE

Short-Form Assessment Scales

During the early 1970s applied measurement theory was all but unheard of in social work practice, and few, if any, reliable and valid assessment scales were available for use in social work practice. That began to change in the early 1980s when Hudson (1982) introduced the first small collection of short-form scales that were designed to assess a variety of specific client problems and to monitor progress over time in nine different areas of personal and social functioning. Today there are many different summated assessment scales that have been shown to be reliable and valid (e.g., Fischer & Corcoran, 1994; Hudson, 1982, 1990a, 1990b; Nurius & Hudson, 1993), and you are urged to consult these references in order to gain access to them.

Before turning to specific examples of how to use such scales in practice, it is important to recognize that none of the assessment scales that are referred to or referenced in this chapter are measures of *pathology*. The measurement and treatment of psychopathology falls most appropriately in the domains of clinical psychology and psychiatry, and there is an enormous amount of literature available concerning assessment tools that measure psychopathology. While social workers respect the work of their colleagues in those fields and disciplines, it is essential to recognize that social work, as a practice-based, problem-solving profession, has never identified itself as having the assessment or treatment of psychopathology as even a minor focus within its professional domain (some social work practitioners do choose such a practice focus, but that is a personal choice and not one that is offered as part of professional social work training). To the contrary, social work's focus has been and continues to be the person functioning interactively within the environment and our proper focus is therefore upon the measurement, assessment, and treatment of problems in personal and social functioning. The measurement needs of social workers are strongly and properly focused on personal and social functioning, and that is the fundamental approach to measurement that is presented in this chapter.

With these caveats in mind, consider the client who is referred to you because of an initial diagnosis of severe depression. You might choose to use an instrument such as the GCS (Hudson, 1990c) because it is a reliable and valid measure of depression and it has a known clinical cutting score of 30. Suppose, further, that your client obtains an initial score of 80, which indicates a serious problem with depression—it is well above the clinical cutting score of 30. How useful to you is this information? It certainly tells you that your client is in great distress. Moreover, if you were to administer the GCS each week, you could monitor the magnitude of the problem over time to determine whether the problem is diminishing, remaining at the same level, or getting worse. Once you began treatment you could even impose a design on the data, to distinguish between a baseline phase and one or more treatment phases and so evaluate the effectiveness of the intervention. In the event that you are not familiar with the use of time-series designs for monitoring client problems, we urge that you consult that literature (e.g., Bloom, Fischer, & Orme, 1994; Hudson, 1982; Hudson & Faul, 1997; Nurius & Hudson, 1993) and incorporate it into your practice.

For the moment, however, consider as an example the GCS completed by a teenage girl that is shown in Figure 19-2. In that figure you will see the item responses to the GCS along with the computation of her total score. As noted ear-

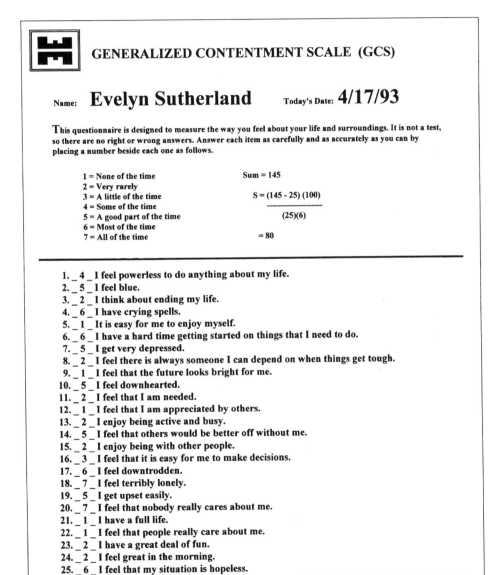

GENERALIZED CONTENTMENT SCALE (GCS)

Name: **Evelyn Sutherland**   Today's Date: **4/17/93**

This questionnaire is designed to measure the way you feel about your life and surroundings. It is not a test, so there are no right or wrong answers. Answer each item as carefully and as accurately as you can by placing a number beside each one as follows.

1 = None of the time
2 = Very rarely
3 = A little of the time
4 = Some of the time
5 = A good part of the time
6 = Most of the time
7 = All of the time

Sum = 145

$$S = \frac{(145 - 25)(100)}{(25)(6)}$$

= 80

1. _ 4 _ I feel powerless to do anything about my life.
2. _ 5 _ I feel blue.
3. _ 2 _ I think about ending my life.
4. _ 6 _ I have crying spells.
5. _ 1 _ It is easy for me to enjoy myself.
6. _ 6 _ I have a hard time getting started on things that I need to do.
7. _ 5 _ I get very depressed.
8. _ 2 _ I feel there is always someone I can depend on when things get tough.
9. _ 1 _ I feel that the future looks bright for me.
10. _ 5 _ I feel downhearted.
11. _ 2 _ I feel that I am needed.
12. _ 1 _ I feel that I am appreciated by others.
13. _ 2 _ I enjoy being active and busy.
14. _ 5 _ I feel that others would be better off without me.
15. _ 2 _ I enjoy being with other people.
16. _ 3 _ I feel that it is easy for me to make decisions.
17. _ 6 _ I feel downtrodden.
18. _ 7 _ I feel terribly lonely.
19. _ 5 _ I get upset easily.
20. _ 7 _ I feel that nobody really cares about me.
21. _ 1 _ I have a full life.
22. _ 1 _ I feel that people really care about me.
23. _ 2 _ I have a great deal of fun.
24. _ 2 _ I feel great in the morning.
25. _ 6 _ I feel that my situation is hopeless.

Copyright © 1993, Walter W. Hudson   Illegal to Photocopy or Otherwise Reproduce

5, 8, 9, 11, 12, 13, 15, 16, 21, 22, 23, 24.

Figure 19-2.   Example of a GCS.

lier, the GCS has a clinical cutting score of 30, so the obtained score of 80 unquestionably represents a clinically significant problem with depression. An interesting feature of the GCS is that it has two more clinical cutting scores, which are 50 and 70. When clients score above 50 it is most often the case that they are having some suicidal ideation, and when they score above 70 there is considerable concern for the possibility of a suicidal acting-out episode. Since this client scored 80 on the GCS, it would be very important that the practitioner immediately investigate the likelihood of a suicide attempt. The point here is that it is nearly impossible to obtain this level of assessment accuracy without the use of standardized assessment scales, and in cases such as this, an inaccurate assessment could have disastrous consequences.

Assessment scales such as the GCS can be powerful aids in the conduct and evaluation of intervention efforts. But do they help to formulate treatments or to identify proper and specific interventions? Not at all. If a client obtains a very low score on an instrument such as the GCS, that may very well indicate that you should not be offering that client any antidepressant interventions or providing mood-enhancing environmental changes. Low scores on reliable and valid personal and social functioning measurement scales are useful in telling you what *not* to treat. Such measures are also very useful in monitoring progress and evaluating treatment effectiveness in a global assessment of the client's problem (Hudson, 1996d). However, *no measurement scale can help you determine what to do to change the problem.* A measure of the severity of a specific problem in personal or social functioning is vital for treatment planning, but decisions concerning what to do about the problem must come from your knowledge of intervention theory, methods, and research—not from the obtained problem measure.

Space does not permit a review of the many different short-form assessment scales that are now readily available for use in practice. However, you should be aware that dozens of such instruments are available to measure such things as depression; problems with self-esteem, stress, and anxiety; drug and alcohol abuse; peer relationship problems; homophobia; sexual attitudes; family stress; marital and sexual discord; physical and nonphysical partner abuse; parent-child relationship problems; and sibling relationship difficulties, to name a few. Moreover, you can gain rapid access to a large number of these instruments by writing to coauthor Walter Hudson or through use of e-mail and the World Wide Web.* You may also consult the references cited earlier for an extensive list of assessment scales for use specifically in social work practice.

---

*A wide range of short-form unidimensional assessment scales, several new multidimensional assessment scales, and computer software to administer and score such scales can be obtained by writing to the WALMYR Publishing Co., PO Box 6229, Tallahassee, FL 32314-6229 or by sending e-mail to Scales@Walmyr.com. Sample copies of the scales and the computer software can also be downloaded from the World Wide Web at http://www.syspac.com/~walmyr/.

Multidimensional Assessment Scales

Short-form unidimensional assessment scales that focus on the measurement of personal and social functioning are powerful devices for use in both practice and research. However, by their very nature they are limited in utility because they provide a measure of only one problem at a time. This means that an assessment of several different problem areas requires the use of an entire battery of such short-form measures. If you wished to evaluate a client's difficulties in, say, 10 or 15 different areas and you used that many 25-item short-form scales, your client would be confronted with somewhere between 250 and 400 items, and you would be confronted with the management of 10 to 15 different scales. In other words, short-form assessment scales are not convenient to use when you need a broad-based assessment of a client's personal and social functioning status across a wide range of problem areas.

A much better approach to conducting broad assessments of client functioning would be to use a multidimensional assessment scale designed for that purpose. Unfortunately, social work researchers have not yet produced a wide variety of multidimensional assessment scales, although some work is now under way to partially remedy that deficit. A great deal of work must be done to remedy this assessment deficit, but one such measure that is currently available is the Multi-Problem Screening Inventory (MPSI). The disadvantage of instruments such as the MPSI is that they tend to be lengthy and are, therefore, more demanding in terms of administration and scoring. The advantage of such instruments is that they can provide an enormous amount of high-quality, reliable, and valid information about client functioning in a very brief period of time. The MPSI, for example, contains 334 items and takes about 30 to 45 minutes to complete. However, it produces information concerning 27 different areas of personal and social functioning. Moreover, it provides a multidimensional profile graph of the client's problem status, and such graphs are very powerful tools for use in diagnosis, treatment planning, and evaluation of client change or growth.

To illustrate with the maxim that a picture is worth a thousand words, consider the MPSI profile graph that is shown in Figure 19-3. If you choose to use the MPSI in working with your clients it is essential that you learn about its technical performance characteristics by consulting the *MPSI Technical Manual* (Hudson, 1990a). However, even when you know little or nothing about the performance of the MPSI, a mere glance at the profile graph in Figure 19-3 gives you an immediate grasp of the areas in which the client is having serious problems of personal or social functioning. Similarly, you also obtain an immediate grasp of those areas wherein the client is *not* having major difficulties, and those two simultaneously obtained visions of the client's problem status help you to more rapidly develop a treatment plan and problem-solving priorities for both initial and later work with the client.

Mary Test: Number MLT0478

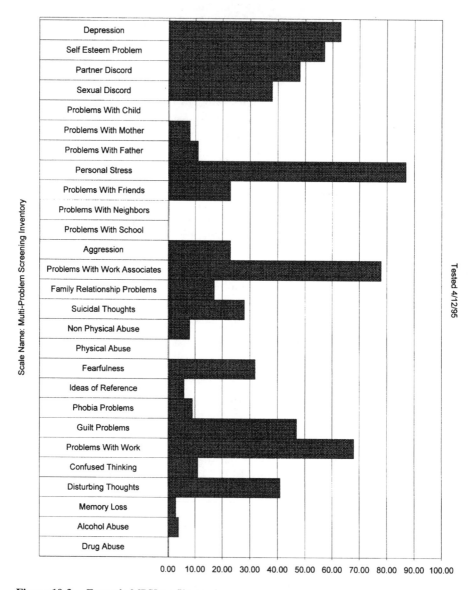

Figure 19-3.   Example MPSI profile graph.

As noted earlier, social work does not yet have a large battery of standardized multidimensional assessment scales for use in practice or in research, and, to the best of the authors' knowledge, the MPSI is the first such instrument to be made available specifically for use in social work. Other recently developed multidimensional assessment tools are the Family Assessment Screening Inventory

(FASI; Gabor, Thomlison, & Hudson, 1994) and the Inner Interaction Scale of Social Functioning (IISSF; Faul & Hanekon, 1994). Also available are the Brief Family Assessment Scale (BFAS; Hudson, 1996a), the Multidimensional Adolescent Adjustment Scale (MAAS; Hudson, 1996c), and the Brief Adult Assessment Scale (BASS; Hudson, 1997), which were developed as derivative instruments from the larger MPSI and FASI scales. The Gate Control Pain Management Inventory (GC-PMI; Hudson, Faul, & Sieppert, 1996) will soon be ready for use in practice, and still other multidimensional assessment tools will likely emerge over the next several years. The authors will gladly provide additional information about the preceding multidimensional assessment scales, samples can be downloaded from the World Wide Web at http://www.syspac.com/~walmyr/, and the next section describes a new computer-based technology that significantly expands our ability to conduct a rich variety of personal and social problem assessments and evaluations.

COMPUTERS IN THE SERVICE OF PRACTICE

Computer Assisted Assessment

The major purpose of this chapter is to discuss the measurement of personal and social problems, not computers. Yet, social workers can no longer ignore the fact that computers are playing an increasingly important role in the day-to-day conduct of social work practice, and that includes the tasks of measuring client problems, monitoring client progress over time, conducting multidimensional assessments of client problems, and evaluating the effectiveness of intervention and service-delivery efforts. This means that attention must also be given to developing computer support systems that will assist with the day-to-day realities of actually doing practice and that will also accommodate the measurement and assessment needs of all actors within the organization: clients, practitioners, supervisors, managers, administrators, and program evaluators. This section presents information about one system that will assist in these tasks through the use of a desktop computer.

It is not difficult to have a client complete a short-form assessment scale. It is also not difficult for a practitioner to administer, score, and interpret it. In fact, that is extremely useful to the client and the practitioner. It is also not difficult for a practitioner to prepare a simple time-series graph and plot the score results on the graph to monitor progress over repeated administrations of the same assessment scale. However, while all of these tasks are very simple to do (and minimal training is needed to do them), the challenge of engaging in these activities on a routine basis with *every* client is a very large one indeed. In fact, it may not be feasible unless special tools are provided to assist with scale administration, scoring, graphing, and large-scale data management using modern database management technology. The Microsoft Windows version of the Computer Assisted Social Services (CASS; Hudson, 1996b) system* can be used to do virtually all of that work, and more. It can easily score short-form and multidimensional assessment scales, it will produce time-series and multidimensional profile graphs, and it will manage all of your client records. The CASS software will even administer electronic copies of assessment scales to your clients through use of the Computer Assisted Assessment Package (CAAP) program; you can download a copy of the software from the World Wide Web (http://www.syspac.com/~walmyr/), or contact the authors to obtain a copy for use with your clients. But there is much more to computer-based assessment, and the following subsection introduces a new technology that significantly expands your capabilities with respect to the multidimensional assessment of client problems.

Multidimensional Assessment Groups (MAG) Technology

Despite the remarkably improved availability of measurement scales, practitioners often confront an important barrier in the use of those that are available. Consider the problems recently faced by a child welfare agency in the southwestern United States. The development team reviewed a large group of unidimensional and multidimensional assessment scales and finally located two that contained all of the intake assessment scales they wished to use. Unfortunately, they wanted to use only 7 of the subscales from the two parent measures, which together contained more than 50 subscales. Aside from the fact that there are important copyright issues involved in using parts of two different paper-and-pencil commercial assessment scales, the agency confronted very large logistical problems in identifying needed subscales, in putting them together as a usable instrument, and in developing a means of administering, scoring, interpreting, and graphing results while also managing the data for many different clients. The problems faced by that child welfare agency represent a major difficulty for many different service-delivery organizations, and measurement-oriented computer systems may help to solve these kinds of problems.

A recent development called Multidimensional Assessment Groups (MAG) technology (Hudson & Faul, 1996) provides practitioners with a computer based *designer assessment system* so that they can create a nearly unlimited number of different multidimensional assessment scales without ever having to write a single

---

*The Computer Assisted Social Services (CASS) software requires an IBM or compatible computer, Microsoft Windows, and a VGA color board and monitor. It can be downloaded from the World Wide Web at http://www.syspac.com/~walmyr/ or it can be obtained by writing to the WALMYR Publishing Co., PO Box 6229, Tallahassee, FL 32314-6229. Although the software is neither sold nor leased, please enclose a check or money order in the amount of $14.95 to cover the cost of materials, handling, and postage.

item.* In other words, computers can be used to introduce novel measurement applications that would be clumsy at best or virtually impossible if we must depend exclusively upon traditional paper-and-pencil formats and technologies. The MAG technology that is included with the CASS and CAAP software makes it incredibly easy for agencies and practitioners to develop and use multidimensional assessment scales that are uniquely tailored to the assessment needs of the specific client populations in their catchment areas. Moreover, all of the MAG scales developed through use of this technology are guaranteed to be reliable and valid even before the new scales have been developed and used. If you wish to learn more about this technology, you can read or print the article by Hudson and Faul (1996) within the MAGDK Help file that is provided as part of the CAAP program. You need only download the software from the World Wide Web.

FUTURE AGENDAS IN OUTCOME MEASUREMENT RESEARCH

Applied measurement theory is becoming increasingly important and useful in many different ways for the micro- and macrolevel human services professional. While much good work continues in basic psychometric research, psychometric science is currently rock solid and will not remain as the principal focus of applied measurement research. What is most needed are more assessment and evaluation tools that will provide a broader coverage of the measurement constructs that are useful to clients and service-delivery personnel.

A great deal of evaluation research conducted in the 1960s (and much that followed over the 35 years since) was driven by the fundamental question of whether proffered services actually provide useful services or help the client solve meaningful problems. Does social work work? It is a legitimate question and it must (and will) be addressed. But we must also address the equally important questions of whether quality assurance monitoring works, and whether the 800-pound gorilla we call *managed care* is going to sit properly and in the right place when it comes into the dwelling of social work. Much research is needed to determine whether methods, devices, policies, and procedures that are used to construct a quality assurance monitoring system (managed care) actually produce a useful outcome, or whether they misguide us and perhaps even choke off the opportunity of providing clients with useful assistance. At the moment, few believe that to be even a remote possibility, but these are nonetheless legitimate questions.

---

*The Multidimensional Assessment Groups (MAG) technology has been implemented for the first time within the Computer Assisted Social Services (CASS) system. It operates through use of the Computer Assisted Assessment Package (CAAP) program, which can be downloaded from the World Wide Web at http://www.syspac.com/~walmyr/.

Although the major thrust of this section is the future of measurement research and development, it is also important to identify the need for measurement education. Since many are becoming increasingly concerned about the stringent accountability requirements that are being imposed through the mechanism of managed care, there may be a rush to measurement never before seen, and at least two cautions are in order. The proper use of applied measurement theory in the field is not difficult. However, it does require training, and work must be done to determine how best to provide it. Most of what is needed in the way of practical training can be provided in a single day-long workshop, but much work must first be done to organize such workshops and to train personnel who can conduct them.

A second caution in response to a rush to measurement concerns the development and use of measurement tools. It is extremely easy to write some items on a sheet of paper, type them up, and call them a scale. If that is done by people who have no training or experience in basic psychometric theory, the results could be devastating at worst or simply useless at best. In short, the psychometric performance of measurement tools used in practice must be taken very seriously. It is quite surprising that there are many who believe they can develop a useful measurement tool when they cannot define, interpret, or calculate a reliability coefficient. Such behavior must not be encouraged or tolerated, and those who wish to explore the development of new measurement tools should, at a minimum, become thoroughly familiar with the work of Nunnally and Bernstein (1994).

There are many situations in which it is useful to employ client rating scales in place of client self-report measures. More research is needed to investigate the strengths and weaknesses of these two approaches. This chapter offers a general guideline that the authors believe should be followed, but its merits need to be examined through systematic research. That is, when the construct to be measured is a private event, affect, perception, or judgment, it is always wisest to use a client self-report measure. Observers who complete client rating scales simply cannot get inside the client's head to observe private events, thoughts, perceptions, affects, or judgments. However, when the measured construct is based largely on client *behavior* (what the client does), client rating scales that are completed by trained observers can be very useful, and more research is needed to investigate the relative merits of these two approaches to measurement.

CONCLUSIONS

This chapter provides what is hoped will be useful definitions of the constructs called personal and social problems. It also provides references for access to a very wide range of reliable and valid short-form and multidimensional assessment scales for use in evaluating the severity of client problems and in monitoring client problems over time to determine whether treatment or service plans should be maintained or altered. It also provides access to computer technology that will assist in the conduct of practice as well as in its evaluation. However, in closing this chapter the authors wish to make a few observations about assessment and evaluation that they think will be useful in the months and years ahead.

It is unfortunate but quite true that the practice of program evaluation and the demands for accountability have often contained an element of mean-spiritedness that is nearly always directed toward the practitioners who must do the actual day-to-day work of assisting clients to solve personal and social problems that range from the benign to the tragic in their magnitude and consequences. The delivery of social services (or therapy) is an organizational affair, and the responsibility for the quality of such services must be shared by all of the actors within the organization—by administrators, program evaluators, managers, and supervisors as well as by practitioners. The frontline practitioner cannot shoulder the entire burden of delivering effective social services and must not be allowed to bear sole responsibility for accountability with respect to practice effectiveness. Definitions and implementations of managed care and quality assurance management often exclude management, administration, and resource allocation authorities from having any culpability or responsibility for poor service outcomes. This view must end, because the failure to deliver effective social services is a responsibility that must be shared by all who contribute to the service-delivery organization.

If we can develop and maintain a sense of perspective about the intensely shared nature of accountability and responsibility for providing useful services to clients, then measurement tools, computers, and information management software systems can be useful and important aids that will help us do a better job at every level of the organization. If such tools are used by one group of actors to control, blame, or hold accountable another group of actors (e.g., practitioners), they will likely fail in their promise, and they will, no doubt, result in great harm to many. Clearly, the largest issues are not the state of the art with respect to measurement or computer technology but with respect to how we shall use them.

In conclusion, the authors wish to note that the single most important role of measurement in the delivery of services has nothing to do with accountability. Rather, the most important benefit of using standardized measures of personal and social problems is to obtain feedback information that can be used to evaluate the problem and to inform the direction of intervention, treatment, or service delivery. The feedback utility of monitoring client progress over time is the surest way known to correct inadequate interventions, to maintain or enhance interventions that are truly assisting with problem resolution, and to thereby increase the likelihood of a more positive outcome for the client. The measurement of personal and social problems is the technical core that makes that possible. Without it, there is and can be no such thing as professional practice or the development of an effective system of accountability.

REFERENCES

Bloom, M., Fischer, J., & Orme, J. G. (1994). *Evaluating practice: Guidelines for the accountable professional.* Boston: Allyn & Bacon.

Faul, A. C., & Hanekon, A. J. (1994). *Inner Interaction Scale of Social Functioning.* Pretoria, RSA: Perspective Training College (PO Box 1658, Silverton, 0127, Republic of South Africa).

Fischer, J., & Corcoran, K. (1994). *Measures for clinical practice.* New York: Free Press.

Gabor, P., Thomlison, B., & Hudson, W. W. (1994). Family Assessment Screening Inventory (FASI). Tempe, AZ: WALMYR.

Hudson, W. W. (1981). Development and use of indexes and scales. In R. M. Grinnell, Jr., (Ed.), *Social work research and evaluation.* Itasca, IL: F. E. Peacock.

Hudson, W. W. (1982). *The clinical measurement package: A field manual.* Homewood, IL: Dorsey Press.

Hudson, W. W. (1990a). *The MPSI technical manual.* Tempe, AZ: WALMYR.

Hudson, W. W. (1990b). Multi-Problem Screening Inventory (MPSI). Tempe, AZ: WALMYR.

Hudson, W. W. (1990c). *The WALMYR assessment scale scoring manual.* Tempe, AZ: WALMYR.

Hudson, W. W. (1996a). Brief Family Assessment Scale (BFAS). Tempe, AZ: WALMYR.

Hudson, W. W. (1996b). Computer Assisted Social Services (CASS). Tempe, AZ: WALMYR.

Hudson, W. W. (1996c). Multidimensional Adolescent Assessment Scale (MAAS). Tempe, AZ: WALMYR.

Hudson, W. W. (1996d). Professional practice for the 21st century: Information implications. In Steyaert, J. (Ed.), *Information technology and human services, more than computers?* Utrecht, Netherlands: Netherlands Institute for Care and Welfare/NIZW.

Hudson, W. W. (1997). Brief Adult Assessment Scale (BAAS). Tempe, AZ: WALMYR.

Hudson, W. W., & Acklin, J. D. (1980). Assessing discord in family relationships. *Social Work Research & Abstracts, 16*(3), 21–29.

Hudson, W. W., & Faul, A. C. (1996). *Designer assessment tools using multidimensional assessment groups.* Tempe: AZ: WALMYR.

Hudson, W. W., & Faul, A. C. (1997). *Quality assurance: A system for practice and program evaluation using outcome measures.* Tempe, AZ: WALMYR.

Hudson, W. W., Faul, A. C., & Sieppert, J. D. (1996). Gate Control Pain Management Inventory. Tempe, AZ: WALMYR.

Hudson, W. W., & McMurtry, S. L. (1997). Comprehensive assessment in social work practice: The Multi-Problem Screening Inventory. *Research on Social Work Practice, 7*(1), 79–98.

Nunnally, J. C., & Bernstein I. H. (1994). *Psychometric theory.* New York: McGraw-Hill.

Nurius, P. S., & Hudson, W. W. (1993). *Human services practice, evaluation, and computers: A practical guide for today and beyond.* Pacific Grove, CA: Brooks/Cole.

Perlman, H. (1957). *Social casework: A problem solving process.* Chicago: University of Chicago Press.

Pike, C. K., & Hudson, W. W. (1997). Second order factors in examining multiple client problems. *Research on Social Work Practice.* In press.

Chapter 20

EMPIRICAL APPROACHES TO CASE MANAGEMENT

Patricia G. Moseley
Kevin L. Deweaver

INTRODUCTION

In the nineteenth century, social casework and public health nursing were sanctioned to coordinate services to the poor and sick and to steward public funds. The two early professions first used case management to accomplish those goals (Brennan & Kaplan, 1993).

In the past century, national programs for health and the care of the vulnerable have advanced the use of case management for access to services, to ensure service effectiveness, and to contain costs (Weils & Karls, 1985). In the 1990s, public financial limitations, advanced technologies of medicine and industry, and emerging health and social conditions have influenced and expanded the complex tasks of case management (Rose & Moore, 1995).

Social work case management is defined by the National Association of Social Workers as:

> . . . a method of providing services whereby a professional social worker assesses the needs of the client and the client's family, when appropriate, and arranges, coordinates, monitors, evaluates, and advocates for a package of multiple services to meet the specific client's complex needs.

Brennan and Kaplan (1993) identified that not only is the client's biopsychosocial status significant, but also of importance is the state of the social system within which case management operates.

American society values its members' participation, contributions, and talents. Environments for the restoration, healing, rehabilitation, and protection of vulnerable members have been created. This chapter is organized to reflect the different environments of care and consumer participation in case management. Targeted populations are those consumers requiring specific interventions due to their debilitating conditions (e.g., lifelong chronic illnesses). Environments of care are those organizations of skilled groups (e.g., hospices, hospitals, halfway houses) providing the interface of services and case management interventions to dependent populations.

Populations and organizations reciprocally impact one another and, moreover, are impacted upon by their sociocultural contexts and diverse geographical, ecological, and physically constructed environments. All operate in a framework of time, and all experience unique strengths and limitations (Bloom, 1996).

In the present time frame, policies that were enacted years ago continue to function through case management utilization. Clients, the public, and delegated funding sources require an account of stewardship of the sick and the poor, along with the conservation of funds. Studies of case management interventions and their assessment methods provide an account of effective services.

ASSESSMENT METHODS

Case management is a process incorporated by numerous programs to help individuals, groups, and families with debilitating conditions. Case managers require knowledge of the extent of change in clients and their biopsychosocial settings and feedback on the usefulness of interventions. The efficacy of case management interventions in assisting different populations can be determined by measurement and evaluation (e.g., adjustment to the community for homeless people) with chronic mental illness.

Assessment methods, scales, and instruments for outcome research are not static, but will vary with each agency and population served. The unique aspects of some client populations may require specially designed instruments. Advanced technologies for computerized assessment methods have been developed to train and assist case managers.

This section identifies some measures used for specific populations in the research of case management. Reviewed first are assessments of domains affected by case management, such as quality of life and adjustment to the community, consumer satisfaction, instrumental role functioning, and the burden of psychiatric illness on the family. Tables 20.1 and 20.2 provide the dimensions of assessment, measurement instruments, and references by categories of the clients' conditions. These are all drawn from the empirical studies noted in the following section.

Quality of Life

Quality of life is a difficult concept to assess because of the many concepts incorporated into the measurement. One commonly used and adapted assessment tool is the Oregon Quality of Life Questionnaire (OQLQ; Bigelow, Brodsky, Stewart, & Olson, 1981). This multidimensional, fixed-response instrument is administered by a trained interviewer. The personal life domains measured by this questionnaire are psychological distress, interpersonal interaction, and meaningful use of leisure time. The OQLQ has been standardized for a variety of populations that use mental health services. To measure quality of life for clients of mental health clinics who are at risk for hopitalization, Bond, Miller, Krumwied, and Ward (1988) used a 32-item self-report scale adapted from studies of similar populations. Other authors measuring quality of life are Modrcin, Rapp, and Poertner (1988) and Bigelow and Young (1991). Jordan and Franklin (1995) caution that, in general, multidimensional scales may be vague and at times poorly operationalized.

Consumer Satisfaction

Two frequently used methods of measuring consumer satisfaction with case management are self-reporting scales and questionnaires. Jordan and Franklin (1995) describe self-reporting as a form of measurement for clinical assessment and treatment in which clients record their feelings, thoughts, and behaviors.

One self-report scale specially designed to measure the responses of adult consumers with serious mental illnesses is the Self-Report Inventory (Macias & Jackson, 1990). The tool is composed of twelve 5- to 10-point composite scales that measure four consumer resource variables: (a) help received, (b) level of personal liability, (c) family support, and (d) personal income. The five consumer outcome variables also include the following: (a) global mental and physical health, (b) problems with thinking, (c) emotional problems, (d) level of social support, and (e) competence in daily living. Three service satisfaction variables are also measured: (a) satisfaction with primary therapy, (b) general satisfaction with the mental health center, and (c) experimental group satisfaction with case management.

Questionnaires are quantitative assessment tools that allow a simple method to gather data, plus provide flexibility for gathering either specific or global information on clients (Jordan & Franklin, 1995). Goering, Farkas, Wasylenki, Lancee, and Ballantyne (1988) devised and administered a questionnaire to learn about consumer satisfaction for rehabilitation case management clients. A rating scale by Larsen, Attkisson, and Hargreaves (1979) was adapted as a questionnaire to assess client satisfaction with intervention for people with chronic mental illness in an urban environment (Morse, Calsyn, Allen, Tempelhoff, & Smith, 1992).

Instrumental Role Functioning

Rating scales are assessment tools used to obtain information about a client's presenting problem. These tools are completed by someone other than the client, as clients do not always observe their own behavior in the same manner as another does (Jordan & Franklin, 1995).

In one study Goering, Wasylenki, Farkas, Lancee, and Ballantyne (1988) used several measures to examine instrumental role functioning for clients with psychiatric disabilities. The authors chose the Brief Follow-up Rating Scale (Soskis, 1970) to determine patients' overall mental health functioning. Ratings are obtained on four areas: hospitalizations, work, family, and social life. The numerical ratings are based on nine questions, which may be asked of the client, a friend, or a family member. Answers may be gathered over the phone, in a personal interview, or by question-naire. The scale is quantitative, relatively inexpensive, and usable by personnel with various levels of training. Jordan and Franklin (1995) affirm that rating scales can add to the view of the client's functioning and confirm treatment progress.

MEASURING THE BURDEN OF PSYCHIATRIC ILLNESS ON THE FAMILY

Several instruments measure the impact of the burden of psychiatric illness on the family. One empirical study uses the 11-item Utah Family Burden Scale (Macias, Kinney, & Vos, 1991), which is composed of three subscales reflecting: (a) the direct impact of consumer functioning on the emotional well-being of family members, (b) the degree of worry and responsibility assumed by the family mem-ber for the consumer's welfare, and (c) objective reports of consumer disruptions of normal family functioning. Platt (1985) clearly defines the term *burden.* The author provides criteria for evaluating rating scales measuring the burden of psy-chiatric illness on families, reviews the major rating scales of burden, and adds methodological improvements.

Case Manager Assessment of the Consumer

One qualitative assessment method studying processes and relationships is partic-ipant observation (Jorgensen, 1989). This method requires the client's permission and can give an inside view of a participant's daily life experience (Jordan & Franklin, 1995). An example is the 12-item scale, the Utah Case Management Consumer Assessment Record (Utah CCAR), developed by Carter et al. (1990).

The Utah CCAR is applied in this study by the professional having primary responsibility for the welfare of the consumer with severe and persistent mental ill-ness. Based on actual consumer behavior and everyday life events, the Utah CCAR evaluates mood, rationality, social behavior, self-care, management of environment, money management, family relations, friendship relations, education, vocational or daily activity, physical health, substance use, and legal problems. Each item is scaled from 1 (*extreme dysfunction*) to 6 (*above average function*) and each scale level is labeled (Carter et al., 1990).

Assessment tools are numerous, address diverse dimensions, and can be used in many environments of care: shelters, halfway facilities, clinics, hospitals, case man-agers' offices, or the clients' natural environments and social networks. A listing of specific instruments used in research studies noted in this chapter are presented in Tables 20.1 and 20.2.

EMPIRICAL APPROACHES TO CASE MANAGEMENT INTERVENTION

Case management intervention is provided in diverse environments for clients with various conditions. Movement through specialized, structured settings may be necessary due to natural, imposed, or accidental changes in an individual's level of physical health, cognitive or psychological status, financial resources, or the ability of supporters to care for the person with a disability. Processes are initiated for stabilizing, maintaining, or transitioning an individual from one setting to another.

Table 20.1.   Measures Mainly Used with People with Chronic Mental Illness

Dimension	Instrument	Reference
Adjustment to environment	Uniform Client Data Instrument	Bernstein, Love, & Davis, 1981
Housing	Housing Scale	Clare & Cairns, 1978
Consumer satisfaction	Self-Report Inventory	Macias & Jackson, 1990; Larsen et al., 1979
Social functioning	Social Functioning Schedule	Remington & Tyrer, 1979
Adjustment and social performance	Katz Social Performance Scale	Katz & Lyerly, 1963
Social desirability	Social Desirability and Approval	Crowne & Marlow, 1965
Social networks	Psychosocial Kinship Model	Hurd, Pattison, & Smith, 1981
Mental functioning	Brief Follow-up Rating Scale	Soskis, 1970
	Brief Psychiatric Rating Scale	Overall & Gorham, 1962
	Symptom Checklist (SCL 90-R)	Derogatis, Lipman, & Covi, 1973
Positive affect	Bradburn Positive Affect Scales	Bradburn, 1979; Beiser, 1974
Quality of life	Oregon Quality of Life Questionnaire	Bigelow et al., 1981
Well-being	Brief Psychological Well-Being Index	Macias & Kinney, 1990
	Psychological General Well-Being (PGWB)	Dupuy, 1984
	Health and Daily Living Form	Moos, Cronkite, & Finney, 1984
Case manager assessment of the consumer	Utah Case Management Consumer Assessment Record (Utah-CCAR)	Carter et al., 1990
Family burden	Utah Family Burden Scale	Macias et al., 1991
	Family Burden Scale	Platt, 1985

Table 20.2.   Measures Mainly Used with Homeless People with Mental Illness

Dimension	Instrument	Reference
Psychological distress	Brief Symptom Inventory	Derogatis & Spencer, 1973
Mental functioning	Structured Clinical Interview for *DSM-III-R* (SCID)	Spitzer, Williams, & Gibbon, 1988
Self-esteem	Rosenberg Self-Esteem Scale	Rosenberg, 1979
Social network	Personality and Social Network Adjustment Scale	Clark, 1968
Alcohol abuse and alcoholism	National Institute on Alcohol Abuse and Alcoholism Index Form	Hargreaves, Attkisson, & Sorensen, 1977
Alienation	Bahr and Caplow's Alienation Measure for Homeless Men	Bahr & Caplow, 1973
Client satisfaction	Client Satisfaction Questionnaire	Larsen et al., 1979

Each environment of care evaluates clients' needs and teaches participants skills to function in the immediate environment or to negotiate other areas of life.

The interactional settings of the family, friends, kinship system, coworkers, and community impact one another. Each setting will be impacted by the debilitating changes in a person. Participants in case management vary in their abilities to negotiate the changing roles of independence, interdependence, or dependence for either surviving or thriving in different environments. Programs will vary in the specific interventions applied to assist consumers of case management. This review of empirical approaches to case management will provide information to case managers seeking to help persons with disabling conditions.

Eleven studies from the literature of empirical approaches to case management are organized in this section in the following manner: (a) aspects of the client's interaction with the environment of care (e.g., environmental adjustment, instrumental role functioning, or improved quality of life), (b) supportive networks in the environments of care (e.g., networks facilitating community adjustment or family members linking formal and informal support networks), and (c) case management interventions adapted to client condition (e.g., homeless people with mental illness in urban areas, people with developmental disabilities and hospitalization, and people with mental illness in urban, metropolitan, and rural areas). Each study's intervention, assessment tools or outcome variables, results, and limitations or implications are delineated.

EFFECTIVE CASE MANAGEMENT INTERVENTIONS

Adjustment to Community Living

One experimental study assessed adjustment to community living for people with chronic mental illness. Procedures were specified for the systematic monitoring of case management (Modrcin et al., 1988). A mental health center randomly assigned participants referred for community support services to either an experimental group ($n = 19$) or a control group ($n = 19$) during a 4-month period of time.

Intervention.   The experimental group used a five-step process of engagement, assessment, case planning, resource acquisition, tracking, and evaluation. Client strengths and self-determination were emphasized in directing the intervention. The comparison group received normal case management services.

Measurement.   The Oregon Quality of Life Questionnaire (OQOL) was administered as a pretest to determine the perception of quality of life (Bigelow, Gareau, & Young, 1982). After 4 months of intervention, the OQOL was applied as a posttest. The Uniform Client Data Instrument (UCDI) scales for adjustment to the environment (Bernstein et al., 1981) were given by both case managers and either a family member, a friend, or a relative of the participant. Case records were used to collect data on five other dependent measures: medication compliance, hospitalization, number of days hospitalized, employment, and vocational training.

Results.   The participants in the experiment were rated by significant others as better adjusted on community living skills and appropriate community behaviors. Members of the experimental group were more likely to be involved in vocational training, and to show increased tolerance of stress, and they perceived their use of leisure time as more meaningful. Case managers of the experimental group had more total contacts with clients and more contact with them in their own environments than did the case managers of the comparison group.

Implications.   A limitation of the study seen by the authors was that case management interventions were not well defined. A lack of behavioral terms increases the difficulty of future research replication. The population with chronic mental illness is diverse; therefore, generalization is limited. Alternative models of case management may demonstrate differential results with different subgroups of people with chronic mental illness. Further refinement of the assessment tools was advised.

Instrumental Role Functioning

The instrumental role function of clients with severe psychiatric disabilities who participated in a case management program was studied by Goering, Farkas, et al. (1988). Seventy clients were randomly selected for a longitudinal study. The predictors and correlates of improved instrumental role functioning during the first year after hospital discharge and program entry were examined. Clients who moved into a high-functioning group ($n = 38$) were contrasted with those who remained in low- ($n = 13$) and moderate-functioning groups ($n = 19$).

Intervention. All participants were provided continuity of care and coordination, rehabilitative assessment and planning, community service linkage and coordination, continuous interpersonal support, strengthening of individual support networks, and resource development. Case managers supported clients dealing with crises, coping with bureaucratic confusion, and acquiring personal and social skills.

Measurement. Clients advancing to a high-functioning group were contrasted with those remaining in low- and moderate-functioning groups. Data were gathered at 1-, 6-, and 12-month follow-ups on six items: aftercare service use, patient characteristics, symptoms, housing, and social adjustment. Instruments designed by the authors examined outcomes of discharge plans, amount and type of service use, and consumer satisfaction. Also applied were the Brief Follow-up Rating Scale (Soskis, 1970), a housing scale (Clare & Cairns, 1978), the Social Functioning Schedule (Remington & Tyrer, 1979), and the Brief Psychiatric Rating Scale (Overall & Gorham, 1962).

Results. The measurement of instrumental role functioning allowed the recognition of improvement for more than half of the clients with moderate to severe impairments. Sustained involvement with the rehabilitation case manager was related to improved instrumental role functioning. Program involvement had an effect on instrumental role functioning through the specific type of referrals made to vocational and educational services. Involving clients in the referral process and systematically supporting their use of the service may have made successful participation in the referred service more likely. Improved instrumental role performance was associated with lower symptom levels and a better quality of life.

Implications. Replication of the study would be useful, particularly for people with disabilities in other categories of conditions, such as people with developmental disabilities, or elderly people.

Improved Quality of Life

In an experimental study of improved quality of life, 167 clients at risk for psychiatric rehospitalization received case management intervention through three community mental health centers for a 6-month period (Bond et al., 1988). The study used random assignment, which compared members in an experimental group ($n = 84$) that received assertive case management and a comparison group ($n = 83$) that received all other public mental health aftercare services at the center.

Intervention. Case management included frequent contact with clients in their own homes and communities, addressing problems of daily living, and advocacy to ensure assertive outreach and service coordination.

Measurement.   Outcome measures included the clients' use of the following: (a) psychiatric hospitalizations (state, private-contracted), (b) participation in community mental health centers (outpatient, partial hospitalization, residential, and substance abuse treatment), (c) law enforcement involvement (contacts with police and number of days in jail), and (d) quality of life (measured by a 32-item self-report instrument). Data were gathered at 6 months and were obtained from intake forms, hospital records, service log sheets, and 6-month client interviews.

Results.   At the 6-month follow up, clients who participated in the experiment had received an average of one visit a week from the assertive case management team either in the home or in a community setting. These clients were rehospitalized an average of 9.2 days, significantly less than the 30.8 days for those in the comparison groups. Treatment effects were especially strong for state facilities.

Implications.   This case management intervention program appeared to have the greatest impact on clients who were in the greatest need (e.g., frequent hospitalization and refusers of aftercare services). Replication is suggested for traditional mental health systems.

Support Networks for Community Adjustment

One case management evaluation studied support networks and their facilitation of community adjustment for chronic mental health patients (Cutler, Tatum, & Shore, 1987). The study used comparison groups to examine the social support networks of case management consumers to the networks of consumers attending community social centers. Ten participants each from three different programs provided a total sample of thirty patients.

Intervention.   Three programs for adults with schizophrenia and their intervention services included: (a) a medication group in a community aftercare clinic without community support, but with ongoing aftercare and psychotropic medication monitoring, (b) a socialization group in an aftercare clinic and a voluntary church-based socialization center, and (c) a case management group in a community support demonstration site with a high staff-to-patient ratio offering an intensive program, which integrated patients into community resources and activities and provided day activities and family treatment. Satellite housing for patients previously identified with high utilization of hospital bed days was provided.

Measurement.   All participants were given the following structured interviews at study inception and 1 year later: the Symptom Checklist (SCL 90-R; Derogatis et al., 1973), the Bradburn positive affect scales (Bradburn, 1979; Beiser, 1974), the self-report version of the Katz Social Performance Scale (Katz & Lyerly, 1963), the Crowne and Marlow (1965) social desirability scale, and the Pattison Psychosocial

Kinship System Inventory (Hurd et al., 1981). Study participants provided feedback about program involvement, aftercare services, and medications.

Results.   The case management group had perfect program attendance and hospitalizations. The medication-monitoring-only group had the densest networks, significantly less program contact, and twice the average annual hospitalization rate. The members of the socialization group, who were older, were more satisfied with their levels of functioning, had more friends, had twice the number of network members than either the case management or the medication group, and had the least program attendance. The data implied that patients who formed better developed networks over time have a greater likelihood of adjustment to and satisfaction with their lives, despite continued low levels of functioning.

Limitations.   The similar demographic variables of the clients cause questions regarding generalizability of the findings. All but one of the participants were White males between ages 20 and 30. There were no females, there was only one minority-group member, and only two members were married. The study compared types of programs, but did not show how cooperation with other community support programs increased social network support. The study noted that further research could focus on the long-term efforts of intensive programs for younger chronic patients to identify beneficial factors and time determinants for functional network development.

Support Networks for Elderly Persons

Elderly persons often remain in their own environments or live with extended family. One study of a case management intervention examined urban family members who were trained as case managers (Seltzer, Ivry, & Litchfield, 1987). In the study, 157 elderly persons were randomly assigned to either an experimental group ($n = 81$) or a control group ($n = 76$).

Intervention.   The experimental group was provided a partnership-relationship between the formal and informal support systems via family-centered training. Training involved a family member assuming a case management task; a case management service plan being developed; dissemination of information on community resources and entitlements; and systematic telephone contacts for consultation, monitoring, supportive counseling, and reassessment of the elderly client's needs. The comparison group received counseling, crisis intervention, and concrete services. No agency program services were withheld from the comparison group.

Measurement.   The Barthel Index (Mahoney & Barthel, 1965) was used to determine a functional evaluation of the elderly participants. The extent of case management was assessed in ten areas, and the duration of services and unmet service needs were measured.

Results.   Family members in the experimental group were more likely to perform at least one case management task more than control group family members. The duration of service was significantly shorter for the experimental group than for the comparison group. No differences were found in the two groups for health, functional abilities, mortality rates, and residential arrangements.

Limitations.   The authors noted that an elderly person, with impaired functional skills and less frequent contact with a family member, may require a social worker to take primary responsibility for case management. Elderly persons in this study did not experience extreme mental impairments, had family members, and were of middle-class income and the same religious affiliation. These conditions would not be ordinarily applicable to all service-delivery situations. The authors noted that further research is needed to determine the durability of family-centered training, continued family member responsibility for case management, and the generalizability of these findings to the general population of elders.

ADULTS WITH DEVELOPMENTAL DISABILITIES WHO ARE AT RISK FOR HOSPITALIZATION

The outcomes of case management intervention provided for adults with developmental disabilities at risk for hospitalization for physical health problems were studied by Criscione, Kastner, Walsh, and Nathanson (1993). Eighty-six study participants, noted by hospital discharge records for ICD-9 codes for mental retardation, were placed in either the experimental care coordination group ($n = 36$) or a control group of inpatients, the usual care group ($n = 50$).

Intervention.   The experimental group received health care coordination services through a developmental disabilities center, including consistent monitoring and health maintenance functions, diagnostic services, and subspecialty consultations on an outpatient basis. Inpatient hospitalizations for procedures and treatments were reserved for patients truly requiring hospital admission. The comparison group did not receive services from the developmental disabilities center.

Measurement.   Hospital and practice variables, cost variables, and readmission rates were outcome measures in this study. Data were gathered from several sources, including a retrospective chart review, a clinically based, computerized grouping system that analyzed objective indicators of anatomic disease and physiologic dysfunction, discharge information, and the hospital database.

Results.   Health care service coordination was associated with fewer hospitalizations. Results suggested that inpatient hospitalization is cost-effective when the health care for people with developmental disabilities is managed and coordinated in a community setting. Additionally, when hospital admission is required, patients with developmental disabilities entered the inpatient setting in a less severe status than those patients not receiving coordinated care.

Limitations.   Health care coordination services reduce the costs of inpatient services for persons with mental retardation who live in the community; however, the authors identified that the impact of these services on total health care costs remains unknown. Managed health care coordination services for improving outpatient care should be studied further.

HOMELESS ADULTS WITH MENTAL ILLNESS AND EFFECTIVE CASE MANAGEMENT

Homelessness is a problem encountered by clients with mental illness who are discharged from inpatient hospitalization. One study, a longitudinal experimental design (Morse et al., 1992), compared the effectiveness of three community-based treatment programs serving 178 homeless clients with mental illness in an urban environment. The clients were randomly assigned to the three programs.

Intervention.   One group ($n = 64$) received traditional outpatient treatment from a mental health clinic, to include psychotherapy, psychiatric medication, and linkage to social services. The second group ($n = 62$), participants at two drop-in centers, received respite from street life, food, clothing, showers, limited recreational activities, and referral to social services. The third group ($n = 64$) received continuous treatment from case managers for intensive outreach and service activities for individual change, environmental change, supportive connections for the clients' needs, and environmental resources and demands.

Five continuous treatment case management interventions included help with building ongoing therapeutic relationships and coping abilities, linking clients with psychiatric medication services, teaching community living skills and interpersonal skills, and giving crisis intervention. Casework advocacy promoted environmental change by securing resources from agencies allocating welfare, housing, and health care. Intervening with landlords and shelters stimulated more beneficial reactions toward clients. Also involved were transportation, medication management, money management, and assistance in keeping apartments clean.

Measurement.   Seven outcome measures, assessed at baseline and at 12 months, included homelessness, income, psychiatric symptoms, self-esteem, alienation, interpersonal adjustment, and alcohol abuse. Other outcome measures, not assessed at baseline, included treatment program contact, client satisfaction, and resource utilization. Measurement tools used were the Structured Clinical Interview for *DSM-III-R* (SCID; Spitzer et al., 1988), Brief Symptom Inventory (Derogatis & Spencer), the Rosenberg self-esteem scale (Rosenberg, 1979), the Personality and Social Network Adjustment Scale (Clark, 1968), National Institute on Alcohol Abuse and Alcoholism index forms (Hargreaves et al., 1977), a client's satisfaction questionnaire (Larsen et al., 1979), and Bahr and Caplow's (1973) alienation measure for homeless men.

Results.   At the 12-month follow-up the following were noted: Attrition occurred, but did not compromise the quality of research. Clients receiving case management intervention had more frequent contact with their program than clients in other programs, regarding (a) housing, (b) entitlements, (c) counseling, (d) inpatient drug abuse treatment, (e) other mental health treatment, (f) life skills training, and (g) practical support. These clients were more satisfied with their program and were less likely to be homeless at the 12-month follow-up. Clients in all treatment programs had enhanced scores on days per month of homelessness, financial status, psychiatric symptoms, self-esteem, and interpersonal adjustment. No changes were found over time on the variables of alienation and alcohol consumption. Clients in all three conditions improved over time in most areas, after being linked to some form of mental health service. Client engagement with mental health services and other community-based services demonstrates a positive improvement in the intrapersonal, interpersonal, and social well-being of homeless people with mental illness (Morse et al., 1992).

Implications.   This study identified the efficacy of the individual programs. Further study could combine their effective aspects. For example, the drop-in centers' client contact approach for inpatient drug treatment could be utilized in the case management group to explore further the problem of alcohol consumption. The authors noted that the study examines the efficacy of programs for the homeless; however, it cannot end the national problem of homelessness. Social policies relevant to the supply of low-income housing require examination and change.

URBAN ADULTS WITH MENTAL DISABILITIES AND REHABILITATIVE CASE MANAGEMENT

The effectiveness of rehabilitation-oriented case management to improve patients' functioning was assessed for hospital-discharged psychiatric patients by Goering, Wasylenki, et al., (1988). Patients who suffered from chronic psychiatric illnesses, social isolation, poor employment history, and residential instability participated in psychiatric rehabilitation. Each participant ($n = 82$) attended a 6-month outpatient program and was assigned to one of eight case managers. Participants were matched to 82 control patients who had been discharged from the same inpatient settings before the case management program was established.

Intervention.   Case management intervention included person-centered interviews, rehabilitation assessments, development of rehabilitation plans, linkages to community services, and support in dealing with crises, coping with bureaucracies, and teaching personal and social skills.

Measurement.   The patients' functional improvements were measured by a range of survey instruments at 1, 6, 12, and 24 months after entering the program. At the 2-year interview, the Brief Follow-up Scale (Soskis, 1970) was administered.

Results.   Two years after discharge, the patients' outcomes were compared with the outcomes of the 82 matched control patients. The patients in the rehabilitation program had higher occupational functioning than did the control group. Three indicators of social isolation were compared 24 months postdischarge. Patients in the control group had become more isolated and the patients in the program were less isolated. Two years after the program, 90% of the patients in the program reported having someone in whom to confide, while 76% of the control group members reported the same; 48% of the patients in the program and 73% of control patients had fewer than two visits a month with persons other than family. Recidivism rates for hospitalization did not differ between the groups at either the 6-month or the 24-month follow-up. The program's focus was on improving patients' functioning rather than preventing hospitalization.

In all, the relationship between the case manager and the patient was the most potent therapeutic factor in the program. The ongoing relationship, focusing on rehabilitation assessment, programming, and service coordination, influenced patient outcomes toward improved occupational functioning, decreased social isolation, and more independent living. Improvement in the quality of life is an important benefit and was a primary goal of treatment efforts (Goering, Wasylenki, et al., 1988).

Implications.   Further research is warranted in reducing the rate of rehospitalization among persons with severe mental disabilities. A scarcity in the service system exists for alternative methods of treating acute psychotic episodes for this study population. Case managers for persons with severe mental disabilities have limited influence on the control of the patients' medical and other kinds of therapeutic care. Goering et al. (1988) noted that studies determining successful outcomes for rehabilitation programs may be influenced by cost-effectiveness in the reduced use of hospitalization; however, reducing reliance on inpatient care must also be considered on equal footing with improvement in the patients' quality of life.

RURAL ADULTS WITH MENTAL DISABILITIES: COMBINED CASE MANAGEMENT AND PSYCHOSOCIAL REHABILITATION

One study reported the successful integration of case management into an existing community support program of psychosocial rehabilitation (Macias, Kinney, Farley, Jackson, & Vos, 1994). Forty-two adult consumers with serious mentally illness were randomly assigned to either the experimental case management program ($n = 20$) or a control-like condition ($n = 21$). One consumer refused participation.

Intervention.   Both groups participated equally in psychosocial rehabilitation and primary therapy from the mental health center. The experimental group received in vivo counseling and teaching, practical problem solving experience, direct instruction in life skills, consumer autonomy, and required individualized goal setting experience, and established strong consumer–case manager relationships. Case managers provided linkage and brokerage of social and medical services, monitoring of consumer functioning, and advocacy in community affairs.

Results.   Consumers who received case management in conjunction with psychosocial rehabilitation functioned at higher levels of competency and had lower levels of psychiatric symptomatology than consumers who received only psychosocial rehabilitation. Rates of hospitalization and incidence of crisis center contacts were reduced for case management consumers, but not for the comparison-group consumers. Family members in the case management group reported lower emotional burdens.

Implications.   Macias, Kinney, Farley, Jackson, & Vos (1994) encourage the replication of integrated case management with existing community support programs. In vivo counseling and teaching have the potential to augment other programs in a community support system.

METROPOLITAN ADULTS WITH MENTAL DISABILITIES AT RISK FOR REHOSPITALIZATION

In a metropolitan area, a study was conducted regarding the impact of case management on hospitalization (Bigelow & Young, 1991). The case management utilization evaluation of two comparison groups contrasted an experimental case management group ($n = 21$) with a control-like group ($n = 21$).

Intervention.   The case-managed group discharged from inpatient psychiatric care could receive services from the following 10 areas: mental health, nutrition, housing, home management, public assistance, money management, physical health, transportation, social and recreational services, and employment. The comparison group, identified after discharge, received standard treatment.

Measurements.   At 3 months after discharge, a sample of 21 case-managed and 21 comparison clients was interviewed using a protocol adapted from the Quality of Life Questionnaire (Fixed Response Alternative versions). The instrument rated the client's living situation and asked open-ended questions about events since the hospitalization.

Results.   The case management group received more services when needed than are otherwise received by people with chronic mental illness. Adjustment by the case management clients was maintained or improved by the case management group, as indicated by quality of life reports for persons with chronic mental illness. The members of the sample group reported less psychological distress, a greater sense of well-being, more social support, and time spent in more meaningful, satisfying ways than did the comparison group. Living situations were rated as more stable, comfortable, structured, and supportive. Clients in the case management group used hospitals less often: 29.5% of the comparison group spent some time in hospital, as contrasted to 9.0% of the case-managed group. The findings were consistent with the hypothesis that the adequacy of mental health services in the community is associated with quality of life in the community, which is associated with reduced use of state hospitals.

Implications.   The study added to social work knowledge; however, some might argue about the indicators of quality of life or the use of a comparison method rather than random assignment to an experimental or control group. The study touts use of community mental health services to reduce psychiatric hospitalization, but does not indicate just how or how well case management worked in conjunction with community support programs.

URBAN ADULTS WITH MENTAL DISABILITIES AND IMPROVED COMMUNITY LIVING

Another study identifying the reduced use of mental hospitals and improved community living was conducted by Bush, Langford, Rosen, and Gott (1990). Twenty-eight adults with severe mental illness in an urban area were randomly assigned to either an experimental or a control-like group to receive outreach by case managers from a rehabilitation center and a mental health center. The study used a two-group, repeated-measures experimental design.

Intervention.   The experimental group ($n = 14$) received intensive help in members' natural environments with problems of living, the anticipation and prevention of crises, obtaining safe shelter, adhering to individual service plans, and maintaining medication schedules. The control group ($n = 14$) received the same case management and rehabilitation services as it had before the study (e.g., medication checkups and counseling), but at less intensive levels and only in the offices of the case managers.

Results.   Intensive outreach by case managers resulted in improved community living, adherence to service plans, decreased admissions to mental hospitals, fewer days spent in mental hospitals, and fewer contacts with crisis and emergency services. Clients in the experimental group had an average of ten fewer hospital days and better adherence to medication regimens and agreed-upon service plans during the project.

Implications.   The study provided information about a socially diverse group of participants, which included Black and White males and females from ages 25 to 56. Intensive outreach case management can facilitate clients' use of service plans and improve community living for adults with severe psychiatric disabilities who would otherwise experience difficulty with service plans and living arrangements.

CONCLUSIONS

In summary, specific types of case management interventions have proven to be helpful with elderly people, people with developmental disabilities, and people with mental illnesses. Some forms of case management were successfully used in conjunction with rehabilitation programs. It is important to note that the programs that more frequently and intensively applied case management interventions to clients were more effective in helping them. Case management was beneficial in specific domains, improving quality of life, support networks, instrumental functioning, and adjustment to the community. In some studies, the ongoing relationship between the case manager and the client was a powerful therapeutic factor for positive changes. The numerous national programs for health and vulnerable populations have incorporated case management as the common form of intervention. Yet this is a vastly understudied area with more new questions than answers from empirical research. Therefore, even greater efforts toward identifying, evaluating, and replicating successful case management interventions are needed. This chapter is an empirical start to the further research that has been identified as being necessary. Regarding case management effectiveness research, the starting gate is closer than the capstone; however, research efforts appear to be on the right track, as indicated by the studies reviewed here and the number of assessment tools that are being developed, adapted, and now computerized.

REFERENCES

Bahr, H. M., & Caplow, T. (1973). *Old men drunk and sober.* New York: New York University Press.

Beiser, M. (1974). Components and correlates of mental well-being. *Journal of Health and Social Behavior, 15,* 320–327.

Berstein, A., Love, R., & Davis, G. (1981). *Collaborative data collection and analysis for community support program demonstration projects.* Washington, DC: Public Sector Research Group Market Facts.

Bigelow, D. A., Brodsky, G., Stewart, L., & Olson, M. (1981). The concept and measurement of quality of life as a dependent variable in evaluation of mental health services. In G. J. Stahler & W. R. Tash (Eds.), *Innovative approaches to mental health education.* New York: Academic Press.

Bigelow, D., Gareau, M., & Young, D. (1982). *Interrater reliability of a quality of life interview for chronically mentally ill people* (Contract No. 278-79-0053). Salem, OR: Oregon State Mental Health Department.

Bigelow, D., & Young, D. (1983). *Effectiveness of a case management program.* Unpublished manuscript, University of Washington, Graduate School of Nursing, Seattle, Washington.

Bigelow, D. A., & Young, D. J. (1991). Effectiveness of a case management program. *Community Mental Health Journal, 27*(2), 115–123.

Bloom, M. (1996). *Primary prevention practices. Issues in children's and families' lives* (Vol. 5). Sage: Thousand Oaks, CA.

Bond, G. R., Miller, L. D., Krumwied, R. D., & Ward, R. S. (1988). Assertive case management in three CMHCs: A controlled study. *Hospital and Community Psychiatry, 39*(4), 411–418.

Bradburn, N. M. (1979). *The structure of psychological well-being.* Chicago: Aldine.

Brennan, J. P., & Kaplan, C. (1993). Setting new standards for social work case management. *Hospital and Community Psychiatry, 44*(3), 219–222.

Bush, C. T., Langford, M. W., Rosen, P., & Gott, W. (1990). Operation Outreach: Intensive case management for severely psychiatrically disabled adults. *Hospital and Community Psychiatry, 41*(6), 647–649.

Carter, C., Heugly, B., Jackson, R., Kirkman, D., Macias, C., & Saderholm, Z. (1990). *The Utah case management consumer assessment record (Utah CCAR).*

Clare, A., & Cairns, V. (1978). Design, development and use of a standardized interview to assess social maladjustment and dysfunction in community studies. *Psychological Medicine, 8,* 589–604.

Clark, A. W. (1968). The personality and social network adjustment scale, *Human Relations, 21,* 85–96.

---

* The views expressed in this article are those of the author and do not reflect the official policy or position of the United States Air Force, Department of Defense, or the U.S. Government.

Criscione, T., Kastner, T. A., Walsh, K. K., & Nathanson, R. (1993). Managed health care services for people with mental retardation: Impact on inpatient utilization. *Mental Retardation, 31*(5), 297–306.

Crowne, D., & Marlow, D. (1965). *The approval motive.* New York: Wiley.

Cutler, D. L., Tatum, E., & Shore, J. H. (1987). A comparison of schizophrenic patients in different community support treatment approaches. *Community Mental Health Journal, 23*(2), 103–113.

Derogatis, L., & Spencer, P. (1973). *Administration and procedures: BSI Manual 1.* (Available from the authors, 1228 Wine Spring Lane, Towson, MD)

Derogatis, L. R., Lipman, R. S., & Covi, L. (1973). SCL-90: An outpatient psychiatric rating scale: Preliminary report. *Psychopharmacology Bulletin, 9* 13–27.

Dupuy, H. J. (1984). The Psychological General Well-Being (PGWB) Index. In N. K. Wenge, M. E. Mattson, D. D. Furberg, & Elinson, J. (Eds.), *Assessment of quality of life.* Le Jacq Publishers.

Field, G., & Yegge, L. (1982). A client outcome study of a community support demonstration project. *Psychosocial Rehabilitation Journal, 6,* 15–22.

Goering, P. N., Farkas, M., Wasylenki, D. A., Lancee, W. J., & Ballantyne, R. (1988). Improved functioning for case management clients. *Psychosocial Rehabilitation Journal, 12*(1), 3–17.

Goering, P. N., Wasylenki, D. A., Farkas, M., Lancee, W. J., & Ballantyne, R. (1988). What difference does case management make? *Hospital and Community Psychiatry, 39*(3), 272–276.

Hargreaves, W., Attkisson, C., & Sorensen, J. (1977). *Resource materials for community mental health program evaluation.* Rockville, MD: National Institute of Mental Health.

Hurd, G., Pattison, E. M., & Smith, (1981, February 20–21). Test-retest reliability of social network self-reports: The Pattison Psychosocial Kinship Inventory (PPI). Paper presented to the Sun Belt Social Network Conference, Tampa, Florida.

Jordan, C., & Franklin, C. (1995). *Clinical assessment for social workers: Quantitative and qualitative methods.* Chicago: Lyceum Books.

Jorgensen, D. L. (1989). *Participant observation: A methodology for human studies.* Newbury Park, CA: Sage.

Katz, M. M., & Lyerly, S. B. (1963). Methods for measuring adjustment and social behavior in the community: Rationale, description, discrimination, validity and scale development. *Psychological Reports, 13,* 503–507.

Larsen D., Attkisson, C., & Hargreaves, W. (1979). Assessment of client/patient satisfaction development of a general scale. *Evaluation and Program Planning, 2,* 197–207.

Macias, C., & Jackson, R. (1990). The self-report inventory: An interview schedule for adults with serious mental illness. From *Community Mental Health Journal,* (1994), 30(4), 329.

Macias, C., & Kinney, R. (1990). The brief psychological well-being scale. From *Community Mental Health Journal,* (1994), 30(4), 329.

Macias, C., Kinney, R., and Vos, B. (1991). The Utah family burden scale. From *Community Mental Health Journal,* (1994), 30(4), 330.

Macias, C., Kinney, R., Farley, O. W., Jackson, R., & Vos, B. (1994). The role of case management within a community support system: Partnership with psychosocial rehabilitation. *Community Mental Health Journal, 30*(4), 323–338.

Mahoney, F. I., & Barthel, D. W. (1965). Functional evaluation: The Barthel Index. *Maryland State Medical Journal, 14,* 61–65.

Modrcin, M., Rapp, C. A., & Poertner, J. (1988). The evaluation of case management services with the chronically mentally ill. *Evaluation and Program Planning, 11,* 307–314.

Moos, R. H., Cronkite, R. C., & Finney, J. W. (1984). *Health and Daily Living Form.* Palo Alto, CA: Department of Veterans Affairs and Stanford University Medical Centers.

Morse, G. A., Calsyn, R. J., Allen, G., Tempelhoff, B., & Smith, R. (1992). Experimental comparison of the effects of three treatment programs for homeless mentally ill people. *Hospital and Community Psychiatry, 43*(10), 1005–1009.

Overall, J. E., & Gorham, D. R. (1962). The brief psychiatric rating scale. *Psychological Reports,* 799–819.

Platt, S. (1985). Measuring the burden of psychiatric illness on the family: An evaluation of some rating scales. *Psychological Medicine, 15,* 383–393.

Remington, M., & Tyrer, P. (1979). The social functioning schedule: A brief semi-structured interview. *Social Psychiatry, 14,* 151–157.

Rose, S. M., & Moore, V. L. (1995). Case management. In R. L. Edwards, (Ed.), *Encyclopedia of social work.* (19th ed., pp. 335–340). Washington, DC: NASW Press.

Rosenberg, M. (1979). *Conceiving the self.* New York: Basic Books.

Seltzer, M. M., Ivry, J. I., & Litchfield, L. C. (1987). Family members as case managers: Partnership between the formal and informal support networks. *The Gerontologist, 27*(6), 722–728.

Spitzer, R. L., Williams, J. B., & Gibbon, M. (1988). *Structured clinical interview for* DSM-III-R. New York: State Psychiatric Institute, Biometrics Research Department.

Soskis, D. A. (1970). A brief follow-up rating. *Comprehensive Psychiatry, 11*(5), 445–449.

Weil, M., & Karls, J. M. (1985). Historical origins and recent developments. In M. Weil & J. M. Karls and Associates (Eds.), *Case management in human service practice: A systematic approach to mobilizing resources for clients.* (pp. 1–28). San Francisco: Jossey-Bass.

Chapter 21

EMPIRICAL APPROACHES TO SOCIAL WORK SUPERVISION

Thomas A. Artelt
Bruce A. Thyer

> The quality of services you offer should be enhanced by the supervision
> you receive and supervisors should be evaluated by reviewing the out-
> comes achieved by those whom they supervise.
>
> Eileen Gambrill (1983, pp. 400–401)

INTRODUCTION

After quoting Gambrill, let us pose two questions:

1. Do social workers who receive supervision act any differently toward their clients than ones who are not supervised?
2. Do clients whose social workers are being supervised experience better clinical outcomes than clients whose social workers are not supervised?

Would you be surprised to learn that neither question can be clearly answered in the affirmative? Sad but true. The point of supervision is to change the behavior of practicing social workers, hopefully in a more constructive and therapeutic direction. However, as is common in many areas of our field, the literature on social work supervision is very long on description and exhortation, and short on data. Given the central importance that competent supervision has been given in social work education and practice, it is rather astonishing to troll through the supervisory literature and find so much opinion buttressed by so few facts. In this chapter we present a brief overview of the nature of supervision and some practices that can be undertaken to ground the practice of supervision on a more empirical foundation.

The Definition of Supervision

The word *supervision* is derived from two Latin words: *super,* meaning "over," and *videre,* meaning "to watch" and "to see." *Supervision* refers to the transactional process whereby one professional social worker watches over the work of another social worker within an officially sanctioned and supported oversight role. In essence, the supervisor is interested in and responsible for the work of the social workers within his or her realm of influence and responsibility (Kadushin, 1992).

Munson (1993) linked the definition of social work supervision to the definition of social work practice. He defined social work practice as the assistance offered to persons by graduates of accredited social work schools that helped them overcome any physical, financial, social, or psychological barrier to psychosocial functioning. Social work supervision was defined as the interactional process whereby a supervisor was designated to assist or direct the social work practice of a supervisee in the disciplines of teaching, administration, and helping.

Social work supervision may involve administrative, educational, and supportive functions (cf. Kadushin, 1992). The educational functions of supervision involve the supervisor's sharing of knowledge and insights about social work practice with a less experienced social worker. The administrative functions of social work practice concern meeting the agency's goals, serving the agency's constituents, and maintaining organizational control and accountability. The supportive function of supervision means that supervisors influence the morale of their staff members, help explore and resolve workers' job-related discouragements, promote the social workers' sense of worth as helping professionals, promote a sense of belonging within the agency, and encourage staff members to develop a certain sense of security and trust in the performance of their jobs.

Kadushin (1992) considered the administrative function of social work supervision as the area in which the supervisor achieves the goal of adhering to agency policies and procedures through the correct, appropriate, and effective implementation of established policies and procedures. The educational functions of social work supervision overcome the problem of staff ignorance or incompetence through the transmission of knowledge and the development of skills that enable workers to perform the duties of their job. The supportive function of social work supervision confronts the issues of low employee morale or low job satisfaction through intentional actions that improve these dynamics. Following are some examples of empirically based supervision that focus on education and administrative concerns.

Two Examples of Educationally Focused Clinical Supervision

The bug-in-the-ear (BITE) device is a hearing-aid-like device worn by a therapist during actual treatment sessions. Treatment is observed via a one-way mirror by the supervisor, who can communicate to the therapist through the BITE by speaking into a microphone. The idea is that supervisory suggestions may be more effective if delivered in the actual context of live therapy than if delayed some hours or days later during formal, nonlive supervision.

Although the focus of much laudatory literature (see review by Gallant & Thyer, 1989), there is actually little evidence that the BITE effectively alters therapist behavior during treatment. Paul Gallant, a social worker completing his PhD in marital and family therapy at Florida State University, undertook one study to investigate this matter (Gallant, Thyer, & Bailey, 1991).

Therapists wore the disconnected BITE device and conducted therapy viewed through a one-way mirror by a supervisor. Regular supervisory processing of these sessions was provided some time afterward. All sessions were videotaped and the therapist's use of some selected clinical skills (e.g., facilitation, support) was reliably coded. After baseline sessions of this regular supervision and recording of selected therapy skills, the BITE was activated and live supervision took place during actual treatment sessions, with the supervisor providing the usual prompts and suggestions unobtrusively (at least to the client) via the BITE. Illustrative data from two therapists is presented in Figure 21-1. The skill being monitored was the use of *supportive statements.* For both therapists 1 and 2, the use of this supportive skill was minimal during the baseline. Following implementation of BITE supervision, the number of supportive statements dramatically increased. These data are

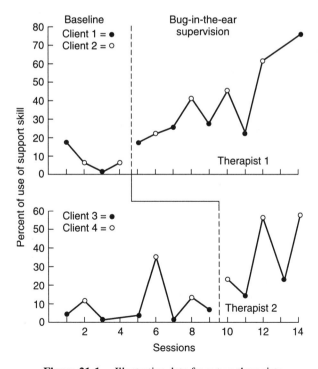

Figure 21-1.   Illustrative data from two therapists.

formatted in a multiple-baseline design across the therapists' design (see Thyer, 1993, for a discussion of this research method) and provide at least some evidence that supervision provided by a social worker actually produces a change in the behavior of supervisees.

Less intrusive clinical supervision was evaluated by Isaacs, Embry, and Baer (1982). Five therapists (including one MSW student) provided family therapy for the families of noncompliant children. Selected clinical skills were reliably baselined and a supervisory intervention was sequentially provided to the therapists. The supervision consisted of direct instruction, a training manual, and instructional videotapes, centered around having the therapist do a better job of conducting parent training. Pre- and posttreatment supervisory feedback was also provided, regarding the therapists' clinical skills. In each case, the therapists' targeted clinical skills impressively improved only following the supervisory intervention, as documented by the data graphed in a multiple-baseline-across-five-therapists design. More important, child noncompliance during therapy sessions was reduced only after structured supervision was implemented.

The preceding examples are some initial steps toward demonstrating empirically that, yes, supervision does make a difference. However, the social work field is a long way from achieving the goal noted by Ford (1979, p. 91): "Ultimately, it will be essential to demonstrate that changes in trainees' functioning that are generated by training interventions do, in fact, produce therapists who consistently provide effective therapy."

Two Examples of Administratively Focused Supervision

Shoemaker and Reid (1980) conducted an evaluation study of a supervisory technique intended to reduce excessive absenteeism among direct care workers at a state residential facility for persons with severe developmental disabilities. Fifteen workers were identified by supervisors as being chronically absent, and attendance was systematically monitored in a prospective manner using time clock data. During the baseline, the usual, existing administrative practices for dealing with excessive absenteeism remained in effect. The supervisory intervention consisted of a three-pronged approach involving *systematic counseling,* periodic *commendation letters* for perfect attendance, and a *lottery* system. At the end of every 4 weeks, workers with perfect attendance had their names enrolled in a lottery, wherein four randomly chosen winners received one of several possible awards (e.g., free lunches or relief from certain onerous duties). The details of the intervention package are not as important as is the general approach.

The attendance of 10 workers was base-lined for about 20 weeks, and then the intervention was implemented. Concurrently, 5 workers' attendance was base-lined for about 30 weeks, then the same supervisory intervention was put into place. For both groups, absenteeism was high during the baseline periods, and greatly reduced when the new procedures were implemented. The data were graphed for each individual and formatted into a multiple-baseline-across-two-groups design. It was very clear that the new supervisory intervention was effective in reducing absenteeism among this group of human service workers. The intervention was based on some prior research that suggested that this approach would be helpful.

Jones, Morris, and Barnard (1986) worked with the supervisors of a hospital emergency room to improve the staff completion of legally required civil commitment forms. The staff included 9 psychiatrists, 11 psychiatric medical residents, 8 clinical social workers, and 6 psychiatric nurses. The problem was that, when a patient was involuntarily admitted to the hospital, there were three forms to be completed by the staff and included in the patient's record. Unfortunately, the busy staff often neglected to complete these forms, which held unpleasant consequences for the hospital's administrators and supervisors during periodic quality assurance reviews of medical records.

Separate, unobtrusive baseline recordings were made of the percentage of charts that contained each of the required civil commitment forms. A supervisory intervention was implemented first for completion of one of the required forms, then the second, and then the third. The intervention consisted of instructions and performance feedback (publicly displayed graphed data depicting the percentage of charts containing the completed form). The intervention was implemented for the first form after about 20 weeks of baseline data, for the second form after about 23 weeks, and for the third form after about 26 weeks. Proper completion of each form dramatically increased only after each form was the focus of intervention. At the end of the study some months later, nearly 100% of the required forms were being properly completed and included in the charts, up from 54% to 67% during the baseline phases.

Both of the preceding examples—basing the interventions on prior research that suggested they would be helpful and evaluating the actual outcomes—exemplify an empirically based approach to administrative supervision.

Clinical supervision and the practice of psychotherapy share some common features (Toukmanian, 1996): The therapist and the supervisor are both agents of change; theirs is a dyadic intervention that presumes the active involvement of both parties; it is assumed that an open, trusting, and collaborative relationship between the participants is essential for success. Such a view does not really differentiate clinical practice from clinical supervision. In operationalizing supervision, Toukmanian (1996) stressed the heavily didactic component and function of supervision that rests upon an individual's experiences, knowledge base, and beliefs about treatment intervention. He believed that there are desirable behaviors that the supervisor seeks to instill and strengthen within the supervisee so that the supervisee develops into an effective practitioner. Such skills and behaviors are taught, modeled, and explored through structured supervisory sessions.

Wetchler (1990) viewed supervision within a constructionist framework and encouraged supervisors to focus on the trainees' successes in supervisory sessions. He defined supervision as a process of strengthening the trainees' clinical intervention skills and knowledge base. This is done by looking at what the trainees are doing and emphasizing the continuation of effective behaviors. The supervisor is not the person to teach the "correct" solution that the trainee simply applies to a client's problem or issue. Wetchler emphasized the constructionist view that the trainee and client should focus on the methods or interventions that successfully contribute to client health and avoid a problem-focused treatment plan.

Solution-focused supervision is defined by its two components: a focus on strengths or solutions, and clinical education (Wetchler, 1990). A focus on the trainee's successes leads to a trainee's greater sense of clinical competence, more effective interventions by the trainee, and the setting of goals he or she may set for supervisory sessions. By looking at solutions, the trainee looks at the client's strengths for change and the definition of what a "successful" outcome for that client might be. Further, the educational focus of supervision deals with increasing a trainee's success with a client by imparting clinical knowledge.

Wetchler (1990) encouraged supervisors to avoid a problem-focused model of supervision because such an approach confuses trainees and emphasizes their ineffectiveness. Solution-focused supervision is defined as a model that includes four areas. First, trainees describe and discuss the successful interventions and components of their sessions with the clients. Wetchler believes that this act compels trainees to deal with their successes as it also reinforces or *ritualizes* the positive outcomes. Next, the supervisor identifies and discusses with trainees those aspects of their contact with clients that were successful. This positive feedback reinforces the trainees' effectiveness with the clients and reduces the trainees' sense of defensiveness with the supervisor. This also encourages the trainees to become more self-aware and confident in discussing their interventions. Third, the *solution-focused* supervisory time aims to resolve the trainees' problems within the client contact. Such a debriefing strengthens the trainees' skills and begins to explore what they might do differently to gain positive outcomes with the clients in the future. Finally, the education phase of the supervisory session enables trainees to apply the knowledge they learned in the sessions with the supervisor so that future client contacts are more successful. Wetchler (1990) defines supervision as a process of growth that seeks to build up and empower trainees through its focus on trainees' abilities, clinical successes, and knowledge. It avoids the supervisory approach that focuses on trainees' mistakes and problems.

The solution-focused perspective described here seems to be quite consistent with behavioral models of supervision that advocate changing behavior using positive reinforcement of successive approximations, also called *shaping,* in lieu of punitive practices (see Follette & Callaghan, 1995; Komaki, Deselle, & Bowman, 1989; Strosahl & Jacobson, 1986).

RECOMMENDED PRACTICES FOR SUPERVISORS

The empirical clinical practice (ECP) model of social work practice has engendered a lively debate among social work educators and practitioners (see Thyer, 1996). This discussion has touched on issues related to social work assessment, intervention, and the evaluation of outcomes, and has articulated some principles for educators, students, and supervisors. Empirically based social work supervision should involve supervisors implementing some of the following practices:

1. Supervisors should encourage social workers to use, as first-choice assessment options, empirically supported methods of assessment, where such knowledge is available.

Supervisors should encourage practitioners to become competent in the use of relatively reliable and valid methods of assessment, such as the *Diagnostic and Statistical Manual of Mental Disorders,* fourth edition (American Psychiatric Association, 1994); rapid assessment instruments useful in supplementing clinical judgment pertaining to clients' affective states, behavior, and thoughts (see, for example, Fischer & Corcoran, 1994; Hudson & Thyer, 1987; McDowell & Newell, 1996; Sederer & Dickey, 1996); and methods of directly assessing behavior (see Polster & Collins, 1992). By using reliable and valid assessment instruments and practices to supplement clinical judgments, the social worker is in a better position to gain a comprehensive, accurate understanding of the client's frame of reference than through the use of clinical judgment alone or by alternative assessment techniques lacking much of an empirical basis (e.g., genograms and ecomaps).

2. Supervisors should encourage social workers to repeatedly gather quantitative and qualitative data on the client's situation throughout the course of treatment. This information should be presented in records as an up-to-date graph.

This is actually a very old notion, perhaps first articulated by Mary Richmond when she recommended that "... special efforts should be made to ascertain whether abnormal manifestations are increasing or decreasing, in number and intensity, as this often has a practical bearing on the management of the case" (Richmond, 1935/1917, p. 435). In these contemporary times, some social work education standards even mandate that students shall be taught research designs (see Thyer, 1993) to evaluate their own practices. Extending this concept, whereby in actual practice supervisors require a discussion of graphs of credible data on the client's condition (just as process recordings used to be required in bygone days), to post-MSW training as a part of the supervisory session seems long overdue. A future standard of practice could read as follows:

Clinicians should routinely gather empirical data on clients' relevant behavior, affect, and reports of thoughts, using reliable and valid measures, where such measures have been developed. These measures should be repeated throughout the course of treatment, and used in clinical decision making to supplement professional judgments pertaining to the alteration or termination of treatment. (Thyer, 1995, p. 95)

Aubrey Daniels's (1989) fine book, *Performance Management,* is a delightfully readable exposition of using systematic measures and feedback as supervisory and intra-agency interventive tools in organizations. It is most highly recommended.

3. Supervisors should encourage social workers to use as first-choice treatment options empirically supported methods of intervention, where such knowledge is available.

Thirty years ago, perhaps, when there was little knowledge about what constituted truly effective social work practice, the aforementioned standard would not have been a practical recommendation. The intervening decades have seen a number of remarkable advances in clinical research, to the point where many psychosocial interventions are well established as effective for a variety of problem areas of concern to social workers (see Giles, 1993). Among these conditions are certain clinical disorders such as severe depression, various anxiety disorders, alcohol and other substance abuse, chronic mental illness, and various childhood disorders (e.g., enuresis, encopresis, elective mutism, sleep terror disorder, conduct problems). Selected psychosocial problems of a more complex nature are receiving their share of attention from practitioner-researchers, resulting in a corresponding growth in knowledge about what is really effective in alleviating problems such as chronic unemployment, violence, racism, spouse abuse, child maltreatment, and sexism (see Mattaini & Thyer, 1996).

It certainly makes sense now for the profession to move toward the adoption of a standard of practice along the lines of the following:

Clients should be offered as a first choice treatment, interventions with some significant degree of empirical support, where such knowledge exists, and only provided other treatments after such first choice treatments have been given a legitimate trial and have been shown not to be efficacious. (Thyer, 1995, p. 95)

Clients should be seen to have a *right* to be provided with effective treatments (cf. Myers & Thyer, 1997), where such empirically based knowledge exists. Where the knowledge base is underdeveloped, then sole reliance on practice wisdom, clinical judgment, intuition, theory, and so forth (the traditional standards guiding the selection of interventions) remains justifiable. It can be difficult to rationalize a social worker providing a treatment that has been shown not to be effective (e.g., Rogerian counseling for persons with schizophrenia) and not providing one known to be more helpful (e.g., behavior analysis and therapy, or antipsychotic medication). We do recognize that, in social work practice as in medicine, plausible clinical, practical, or theoretical rationales may exist to justify *not* providing a so-called first-choice treatment. However, this does not blunt the essential thrust of the principle any more than it does in medicine.

4. Supervisors should encourage social workers to focus their continuing education activities on becoming proficient in empirically supported methods of assessment and treatment.

The field of post-MSW continuing education in social work is a morass of options, with training possible in "holotropic breathwork," "alchemical hypnotherapy," "inner child work," "core energetics," "creating mandalas," "hot monogamy," "Reichian therapy," "neurolinguistic programming," and a host of other bogus interventions (these are all real examples collected by one of the authors). This borders on the criminal, and the allocation of training resources to such topics seems professionally irresponsible. To the extent that social work supervisors can influence supervisees choices of continuing education options, gently guiding them into taking workshops and participating in other training programs which appear to provide training in empirically based methods of assessment and intervention is advocated.

DO VARIOUS MODELS OF SUPERVISION MAKE A DIFFERENCE?

Supervision can be provided to social workers using a number of modalities. One-to-one versus small-group supervision is but one example. Another is expert consultant versus peer supervision. Perhaps the most common approach is for the social worker to see clients, to meet with his or her supervisor some time later (often days or even weeks), provide a verbal report of what transpired with selected cases, discuss the management of the cases, and perhaps receive suggestions or admonitions from the mentor, presumably such that will guide the social worker's future discourse with the client. Variations on this approach are to tape-record or videotape selected client sessions and to share these with the supervisor and or with peer social workers. Again, discussion ensues and opinions are shared. A disadvantage of these methods is that feedback is *delayed,* as the length of time between behavior and feedback directly impacts the efficacy of feedback in effecting change (longer times yield weaker impact).

Live supervision, whereby the supervisor directly observes the social worker's therapy as it transpires with real clients in real time, can mitigate these delays (Kaplan, 1987). In some models the supervisor sits in the same room as an observer; in others the supervisor sits behind a one-way mirror. Feedback may be immediate or it may be provided directly after a therapy session. The supervisor in the same room may actually interject comments during a live session. The supervisor behind the one-way mirror may tap on the mirror to signal the therapist to take a break for a private consultation, call the therapist on the telephone, or use the bug-in-the-ear device. All these methods have their strengths and limitations. Live supervision would, on the face of it, seem to be more effective, but the practical difficulties of arranging for three parties to be present (as opposed to only two) can be immense. The intrusive nature of some forms of live supervision can be off-putting to some clients and overly intimidating to some social workers. For example, imagine informing a paranoid client that he or she is being watched from behind a one-way-mirror!

Follette and Callaghan (1995) advocate moving beyond traditional supervisory or didactic models toward a more empirically based approach. They assume that a therapist in training would be taught a particular theory of behavior and behavior change. This leads the student to learn to ". . . apply a distinct set of basic principles, and develop the ability to apply an analytic method to understanding behavior problems in vivo" (Follette & Callaghan, 1995, p. 414). This leads the authors to conclude that the behavior therapist is expected to be able to actively assess the client's problem(s), apply principles of behavior therapy to the client's problem(s), and explain how the appropriate theoretically driven intervention would work within the framework of behavior therapy's guiding principles.

These training methods may reinforce ". . . rule-governed behavior where the therapist assiduously follows the supervisor's agenda regardless of what new problems may emerge in the next session" (Follette & Callaghan, 1995, p. 414). This rigid adherence to learned rules and behaviors may also interfere with the dynamic exchanges within the session between the therapist and the client, and thereby dull the therapist's senses to the various and changing circumstances as they occur. While rule adherence relative to a code of professional ethics is commendable, just, and expected, an inflexible use of rule application and adherence places the dynamic transactions of therapy at risk. Therefore, Follette and Callaghan (1995) encourage supervisors to move beyond a rule-dominated approach to supervision by attending to what is happening between the client, the supervisee, and the supervisor during the session. This encourages interaction among all participants within the session. It also helps to prevent the imposition of an artificial agenda upon the client by the supervisor or the supervisee. The trainee and supervisor are less distracted from the client's problem(s) and are focused on providing an effective intervention.

No one particular model of supervision presently enjoys a particularly stronger foundation in terms of research support than any other. Virtually all the supervisory literature invokes opinion, theory, and personal anecdote, with little reliance on empirical research. Is live supervision more effective than delayed supervision?

Does reviewing videotapes of actual sessions improve upon using process recordings? Is directive supervision superior to nondirective oversight? Is behaviorally based supervision more helpful than that guided by psychodynamic principles? None of these important issues are resolved at present.

OBSTACLES TO EMPIRICALLY BASED SUPERVISION

As with other models, empirical approaches to supervision may encounter common obstacles. Here are a few that have been mentioned in the literature.

The Barrier of Punitiveness

Allen, Szollos, and Williams (1986) concluded that an authoritarian supervisory style does not support the provision of quality supervision. They also concluded that ineffective supervision is usually identified as being ill-defined, harshly judgmental, or inappropriately intrusive into the personal issues of the trainee. In addition, Marmor (1953) stated that supervisors could spoil their work with supervisees if they constantly point out the trainees' errors in an attempt to demonstrate their own knowledge.

The Barrier of Ignorance

A major, yet certainly preventable, barrier to empirical supervision is supervisor ignorance. Given the pace at which information is made available and research is published, it is crucial that the supervisor maintain the regular practice of reading and evaluating the studies presented in various research journals. Further, it is important to attend seminars and conferences that discuss empirically validated interventions.

The Barriers of Inadequate Training and Research

Holloway and Neufeldt (1995) stated that a major obstacle to empirical supervision is the lack of standardized and empirically validated training programs specifically developed for supervisors. They noted that research on supervision has

> . . . provided information on supervisors' and trainees' theoretical orientation, experience in supervision, interpersonal style, and interactional behaviors as related to trainees' satisfaction with supervision and in a few cases client factors. There is no research on standardized training in supervision and how it may mitigate the effects of these more personal and professional characteristics of the supervisor, trainee, or both. (Holloway & Neufeldt, 1995, p. 211)

They cited only one manual that has been developed and used for training supervisors (see Neufeldt, Iversen, & Juntunen, 1993). Saba and Liddle (1986) also noted the limited resources for training supervisors and considered the training resources and literature in this area of practice as fragmented and disorganized. According to Holloway and Neufeldt (1995, p. 211), "The lack of attention to this area may be a holdover from the early days of therapy training in which it was assumed that a trained therapist was a good supervisor."

In addition, Holloway and Neufeldt (1995) stated that another obstacle to empirical supervision is the fact that the majority of treatment efficacy outcome studies focus upon the perceptions of the trainees and supervisors regarding the effectiveness of supervision. In essence, the consumer of the supervisor's intervention, namely the trainee, has become the authoritative opinion as to a supervisor's effectiveness. Holloway and Neufeldt (1995, p. 211) asked, "To what extent can a learner know what they [sic] need to know?" Given the interactional and developmental aspects of the trainee-supervisor relationship, the authors noted that:

> Although more advanced professionals learning new skills would be more skilled in recognizing their deficits, it still remains that the supervisor offers the perspective of a trained professional with the expertise to implement these skills in therapeutic practice. (Holloway & Neufeldt, 1995, p. 211)

They concluded that, if supervisors were not instructed in learning how to teach trainees as a part of their own supervisory training, their skills in this area would be limited.

The Barrier of Specialized Knowledge

Munson (1993) explored the broad area of practice in which social workers are usually employed. Practice within medical, geriatric and gerontology, criminal justice, and rural practice sites may call for and presume a unique and specialized knowledge base, specialized clinical training, and the ability to work on interpersonal and intrapersonal levels with clients and peers. The knowledge and skills needed to effectively help persons with bipolar disorder and their families are quite distinct from those necessary to assist victims of domestic violence. Is it possible to truly effectively supervise a number of social workers if they are employed in disparate agencies serving vastly differing clientele?

The Barriers of Personal Circumstances

Munson (1993) also noted that issues of a social worker's personal situation (e.g., pregnancy, degree of physical disability, social workers who are themselves in therapy, state of recovery), the availability of resources (space, furniture, one-way viewing mirrors, bugs-in-the-ear, audio and video recording equipment, etc.), the use of a cotherapist, and gender issues and bias may also impact the scope and effectiveness of supervision.

The Barriers of Interpersonal Difficulties

Inevitably, practitioners will react in various ways to those who supervise them. Sometimes these reactions are not helpful. The reverse is also true: A supervisor may have an aversive reaction to a particular supervisee. Munson (1993) addressed the issue of a supervisee's resistance to supervision and noted a number of possible negative reactions the supervisee might offer. Among these are the following:

1. *Reasoned neutrality.* The social worker resists the supervisor's recommended intervention because it makes the social worker look like he or she is taking sides and is not impartial toward the client. The supervisor must distinguish between overall patterns in practice and those of the social worker's interactional patterns with the client.

2. *Perceived organizational constraints.* A therapist may resist implementing a particular intervention because the agency would not support a recommended intervention. The supervisor must be aware of and sensitive to institutional obstacles, as he or she helps the worker to see distinctions between the organization and those who compose it.

3. *Overwhelming clinical evidence.* The social worker presents so much information on the client's limitations and dysfunction that the case seems hopeless and, when the supervisor suggests an intervention, the worker replies with more information that makes the case seem still more hopeless. The supervisor should ask the worker to organize data on the client's problem areas, prioritize them, and develop strategies to intervene. The supervisor may ask the worker if the case is hopeless. If the answer is no, the worker can focus on problems and interventions. If yes is the answer, the supervisor may ask the worker to explain the rationale for such a conclusion and explore the worker's insights on the case.

4. *Persistent diagnosis.* The social worker continues to gather client data as if to try to reach a point at which enough information will make interventions and solutions obvious. The supervisor should advise the worker to move from diagnostic to intervention activities even if it seems as though there is a gap in information. If the supervisor allows the worker to continue to gather information on the client, too much information may make this case look hopeless. A lack of supervisory attention to such a case may mean that the client is not helped.

5. *Oversimplification response.* When a social worker presents a complex case, the data and dynamics of the case may bewilder him or her. When the

supervisor tries to focus on a particular aspect of the case, he or she is told by the social worker that the supervisor's perception is an oversimplification. If the supervisor agrees with the social worker, he or she is drawn into the deeper, broad issues of the case and is overwhelmed with persistent diagnosis dilemmas. The supervisor may ask the social worker to suspend his or her judgment of oversimplification and help the trainee target an issue and begin an intervention with the client. The supervisor may monitor the case to see if the social worker communicated the impression that the intervention is based upon an oversimplified view of his or her case.

6. *Theoretical speculation.*   A practitioner may focus heavily on the theoretical implications of a case to the point at which the theory becomes the main point of the case. In such a case, the supervisor may help the social worker maintain his or her theoretical base, but redirect the focus to what the social worker does to help the client.

7. *Self-analysis.*   Too much self-analysis on a difficult case may immobilize the social worker and divert attention from the client's dynamics and problem. The supervisor must focus on the client's issues with the supervisee, provide understandable and constructive feedback on the case to the worker, and prevent self-analysis from clouding case and treatment issues. The supervisor must avoid giving the worker personal therapy.

Munson (1993) summarized much of this content on supervisee resistance into three questions the supervisor may ask as the focus of supervision is refined: (a) What are the major areas in which the client needs help? (b) What are the genuine problems the client has encountered? (c) What are the positive and negative patterns of relating that the patient demonstrated? Such questions, while not exhaustive, enable a supervisor to focus on client issues and begin an intervention.

EVALUATING SUPERVISION

Given the depth and breadth of the supervisory relationship, how are the supervisor and supervisee going to evaluate their work and, if indicated, improve it? Robiner, Fuhrman, and Ristvedt (1993) stated that supervisory evaluation provides feedback on the therapist's skill levels and competencies and an objective assessment of the social worker's competence and progress. The evaluation process should be an ongoing, administrative function for the supervisor that assesses the quality and quantity of work the practitioner is expected to complete (Kadushin, 1992; Shulman, 1993). Such a process enables the supervisor to review the practitioner's performance and give the worker some constructive, evaluative feedback on his or her work performance. Munson (1993) stated that one of the most important questions supervisees can ask the supervisor is How do you think I am doing in my work?

(Munson, 1993, p. 204). The supervisor's response to the social worker facilitates the development of the practitioner's clinical skills and the supervisory relationship.

The evaluation process may cause feelings of guilt for the supervisor, because the negative evaluation of a staff member may reveal that the supervisor did not train the social worker adequately and is partly responsible for the poor evaluation (Shulman, 1993). Further, supervisors may avoid a negative evaluation and the worker's possible anger and legal concerns by being lenient on the worker's evaluation, because a worker's incompetence may not be operationalized or documented adequately (Robiner et al., 1993). Despite the pitfalls and responsibilities of the evaluation process, it is a valuable tool for the social worker, the agency, the supervisor, the client population, agency funding sources, and society at large.

The supervisee benefits from the evaluation because it enables social workers to know whether their performance measures up to the job description. Workers can discuss their work within the context of the supervisor's expectations. The evaluation should discuss the workers' abilities, weaknesses, professional growth, and plans for improvement (Kadushin, 1992). It is also an opportunity for the supervisor and practitioner to strengthen or repair their work relationship. Descriptions of the format and dynamics of the evaluation process and simple assessment instruments are available within the professional literature, among agencies, and through social work practitioners (See Kadushin, 1992; Munson, 1993; Shulman, 1993).

Of course, it is appropriate to evaluate the services provided by the *supervisor* to the social worker under supervision. In somewhat of a role reversal, it is useful for the supervisor to periodically ask the supervisee, How am I doing? Are there any areas of our work with which you are not satisfied? How can I be a better supervisor for you? More systematically, it is possible to make use of a number of rapid assessment instruments designed to measure the supervisee's appraisals of the supervisor. Vonk and Thyer (1997) provided a recent selective review of these instruments and short pencil-and-paper forms to be completed by the social worker, including the Supervision Perception Form (Heppner & Roehlke, 1984), the Supervisor Styles Inventory (SSI; Friedlander & Ward, 1984), the Supervision Feedback Form (Williams, 1994), the Supervision Questionnaire: Worker's Version (cited in Shulman, 1982), and the Supervisory Questionnaire (Worthington & Roehlke, 1979). Of these, Vonk and Thyer (1997) recommended the SSI as most appropriate for use by social workers. The SSI could be completed every few months (in long-term supervisory relationships), for incorporation by the supervisor into his or her own self-evaluation efforts with a particular social worker. For shorter term supervision, the SSI could be administered at the termination of a supervisory relationship simply as a feedback tool for the supervisor.

Periodic administration of one or more rating scales designed to assess supervisee perceptions of supervision would seem to be a sound practice, one compatible with the empiricist principles outlined in this chapter. This information could be garnered by supervisors themselves or by agency administrators (with due regard for the possible intrusive nature of such assessments) and used to supplement standard interview-based assessments of how supervision is going. Of course, Gambrill's gold standard, cited at the beginning of this chapter, should not be overlooked as the primary method of evaluating supervision: *"Supervisors should be evaluated by reviewing the outcomes achieved by those whom they supervise"* [italics added] (Gambrill, 1983, p. 401). This is a lofty ideal, which needs to take into account clinical difficulties, but it certainly makes a good deal of sense. A good supervisor is one whose supervisees can demonstrate that they have effectively helped their clients.

THE ETHICS OF EMPIRICALLY BASED SUPERVISION

The principles of empirically based supervision as described in this chapter are completely consistent with current ethical standards and practice guidelines. For example, the new Code of Ethics developed by the National Association of Social Workers clearly states:

> Social workers who function as educators, field instructors for students, or trainers . . . should provide instruction based on the most current information and knowledge available in the profession (NASW, 1996, p. 19). . . . Social workers should critically examine and keep current with emerging knowledge relevant to social work. . . . Social workers should *base practice on recognized knowledge, including empirically based knowledge,* [italics added] relevant to social work. . . . Social workers should monitor and evaluate . . . practice interventions. . . . Social workers should . . . fully use evaluation and research evidence in their professional practice. (NASW, 1996, p. 20)

The NASW document, *Standards for the Practice of Clinical Social Work,* states that social workers should have ". . . knowledge . . . required for effective clinical intervention . . ." and that "the social worker should base practice upon recognized knowledge relevant to social work" (NASW, 1989, p. 6). Similar themes can be found in other NASW practice guideline documents. While these recommendations are subject to a number of interpretations, it seems clear that the model of empirically based supervision being advocated in this chapter is certainly consistent with such guidelines.

CONCLUSION

Empirical approaches to supervision can promote the quality and effectiveness of social work services to clients. Social worker practitioners and their supervisors who have reached a level of professional development that respects the use of research data in practice will live up to the profession's explicit foundation of basing practice on empirically based knowledge. Clients seeking help expect nothing more and they deserve nothing less.

REFERENCES

Allen, G. J., Szollos, S. J., & Williams, B. E. (1986). Doctoral students' comparative evaluation of best and worst psychotherapy supervision. *Professional Psychology: Research and Practice, 17,* 91–99.

Daniels, A. C. (1989). *Performance management.* Tucker, GA: Performance Management Publications.

Fischer, J., & Corcoran, K. J. (1994). *Measures for clinical practice* (2nd ed.). Englewood Cliffs, NJ: Prentice Hall.

Follette, W. C., & Callaghan, G. M. (1995). Do as I do, not as I say: A behavior-analytic approach to supervision. *Professional Psychology: Research and Practice, 26,* 413–421.

Ford, J. D. (1979). Research on training counselors and clinicians. *Review of Educational Research, 49,* 87–130.

Friedlander, M. L., & Ward, L. G. (1984). Development and validation of the Supervisory Styles Inventory. *Journal of Counseling Psychology, 31,* 541–557.

Gallant, J. P., & Thyer, B. A. (1989). The bug-in-the-ear in clinical supervision: A review. *The Clinical Supervisor, 7*(2/3), 43–58.

Gallant, J. P., Thyer, B. A., & Bailey, J. S. (1991). Using bug-in-the-ear feedback in clinical supervision: Preliminary evaluations. *Research on Social Work Practice, 1,* 175–187.

Gambrill, E. (1983). *Casework: A competency-based approach.* Englewood Cliffs, NJ: Prentice Hall.

Giles, T. R. (Ed.). (1993). *Handbook of effective psychotherapy.* New York: Plenum Press.

Heppner, P. P., & Roehlke, H. J. (1984). Differences among supervisees at different levels of training: Implications for a developmental model of supervision. *Journal of Counseling Psychology, 31,* 76–90.

Holloway, E. L., & Neufeldt, S. A. (1995). Supervision: Its contributions to treatment efficacy. *Journal of Consulting and Clinical Psychology, 63,* 207–213.

Hudson, W. W., & Thyer, B. A. (1987). Research measures and indices in direct practice. In A. Minahan (Ed.), *Encyclopedia of social work* (pp. 487–498). Washington, DC: National Association of Social Workers.

Isaacs, C. D., Embry, L. H., & Baer, D. M. (1982). Training family therapists: An experimental analysis. *Journal of Applied Behavior Analysis, 15,* 505–520.

Jones, H. H., Morris, E. K., & Barnard, J. D. (1986). Increasing staff completion of civil commitment forms through instructions and graphed group performance feedback. *Journal of Organizational Behavior Management, 7*(3/4), 29–43.

Kadushin, A. (1992). *Supervision in social work.* New York: Columbia University Press.

Kaplan, R. (1987). The current use of live supervision within marriage and family therapy training programs. *The Clinical Supervisor, 5*(3), 43–52.

Komaki, J. L., Deselles, M. L., & Bowman, E. D. (1989). Definitely not a breeze: Extending an operant model of effective supervision to teams. *Journal of Applied Psychology, 74,* 522–529.

Marmor, J. (1953). The feeling of superiority: An occupational hazard in the practice of psychotherapy. *American Journal of Psychiatry, 110,* 370–376.

Mattaini, M. A., & Thyer, B. A. (1996). *Finding solutions to social problems: Behavioral strategies for change.* Washington, DC: American Psychological Association Press.

McDowell, I., & Newell, C. (1996). *Measuring health: A guide to rating scales and questionnaires.* New York: Oxford University Press.

Munson, C. E. (1993). *Clinical social work supervision.* New York: Haworth Press.

Myers, L. L., & Thyer, B. A. (1997). Do social work clients have the right to effective treatment? *Social Work, 42,* 288–298.

National Association of Social Workers. (1989). *NASW standards for the practice of clinical social work.* Silver Spring, MD: Author.

National Association of Social Workers. (1996, November). The National Association of Social Workers Code of Ethics. *NASW News,* pp. 17–20.

Neufeldt, S. A., Iversen, J. N., & Juntunen, C. L. (1993). *Supervision strategies for the first practicum.* Alexandria, VA: American Counseling Association.

Polster, R. A., & Collins, D. (1992). Structured observation. In R. M. Grinnell, Jr. (Ed.), *Social work research and evaluation* (4th ed., pp. 244–261). Itasca, IL: F. E. Peacock.

Richmond, M. (1935). *Social diagnosis.* New York: Russell Sage Foundation. (Original work published in 1917)

Robiner, W., Fuhrman, M., & Ristvedt, S. (1993). Evaluation difficulties in supervising psychology interns. *The Clinical Psychologist, 46,* 3–13.

Saba, G. W., & Liddle, H. A. (1986). Perceptions of professional needs, practice patterns and critical issues facing family therapy trainers and supervisors. *American Journal of Family Therapy, 14,* 109–122.

Sederer, L. I., & Dickey, B. (Eds.). (1996). *Outcomes assessment in clinical practice.* Baltimore, MD: Williams & Wilkins.

Shoemaker, J., & Reid, D. (1980). Decreasing chronic absenteeism among institutional staff: Effects of a low-cost attendance program. *Journal of Organizational Behavior Management, 2,* 317–328.

Shulman, L. (1982). *Skills of supervision and staff management.* Itasca, IL: Peacock.

Shulman, L. (1993). *Interactional supervision.* Washington, DC: NASW Press.

Strosahl, K., & Jacobson, N. S. (1986). Training and supervision of behavior therapists. In F. Kaslow (Ed.), *Supervision and training: Models, dilemmas, and challenges* (pp. 183–206). New York: Haworth Press.

Thyer, B. A. (1993). Single system research designs. In R. M. Grinnell (Ed.), *Social work research and evaluation* (4th ed., pp. 94–117). Itasca, IL: F. E. Peacock.

Thyer, B. A. (1995). Promoting an empiricist agenda within the human services: An ethical and humanistic imperative. *Journal of Behavior Therapy and Experimental Psychiatry, 26,* 93–98.

Thyer, B. A. (1996). Guidelines for applying the empirical clinical practice model to social work. *Journal of Applied Social Sciences, 20*(2), 121–127.

Toukmanian, S. G. (1996). Clients' perceptual processing: An integration of research and practice. In W. Dryden (Ed.), *Research in counselling and psychotherapy* (pp. 184–210). London: Sage.

Vonk, M. E., & Thyer, B. A. (1997). Evaluating the quality of supervision: A review of instruments for use in the field instruction. *The Clinical Supervisor, 15,* 103–113.

Wetchler, J. L. (1990). Solution-focused supervision. *Family Therapy, 17,* 129–138.

Williams, L. (1994). A tool for training supervisors: Using the Supervision Feedback Form (SSF). *Journal of Marital and Family Therapy, 20,* 311–315.

Worthington, E. L., & Roehlke, H. J. (1979). Effective supervision as perceived by beginning counselors-in-training. *Journal of Counseling Psychology, 26,* 54–73.

Chapter 22

OBSTACLES TO CONDUCTING EMPIRICALLY BASED PRACTICE

Michael J. Holosko
Donald Leslie

As evidenced by the numerous testimonials provided in this text, empirically based social work practice is alive and well. Current trends in social work that hold the promise of increased organizational accountability (Hersey & Blanchard, 1988; Latting, 1996; Martin & O'Conner, 1989; Ott, 1989; Perrow, 1979), greater practice relevance (Bloom, Fischer, & Orme, 1995; Blythe, Tripodi, & Briar, 1994; Fischer & Corcoran, 1994), case management (Austin, 1996; Gorin & Moniz, 1996; Paulson, 1996;), cost-effectiveness (Gabor & Grinnell Jr., 1994; Patton, 1988; Yates, 1994, 1996), managed care (Holosko & Feit, 1996; Rosen, 1996), and the need for practitioner and consumer-driven research to enhance knowledge (Gingerich & Green, 1996; Holosko, 1997; Ingersoll-Dayton & Jayaratne, 1996) all suggest that empirically based practice (EBP) will hold even greater prominence in future professional social work education, training, and practice (Fischer, 1993; Reid, 1994; Thyer, 1989, 1996).

Coupled with the ubiquitous and increasing demands for social and health services in North America and a decrease in proportionate funding dollars to meet these demands, EBP seems well positioned to provide legitimacy to the programs and services offered to clients and, at the same time, presents the profession of social work a viable avenue to developing its own professional autonomy (Holosko, 1996; Raffoul & McNeese, 1996). Indeed, as even the harshest critics of EBP agree, research that guides social work practice can do nothing more than enhance social work practice.

Three hurdles to the current development, acceptance, and use of EBP in social work are: (a) the uniqueness of social work research, (b) its definition of practice effectiveness, and (c) the organizational context in which EBP takes place. Neither of these present insurmountable obstacles to the growing EBP movement afoot

Note: We would like to acknowledge the contributions of Ann Holosko in the preparation of this manuscript.

(Reid, 1994), but failure to address their concerns may inhibit the potential for social work to meet its professional obligation to provide competent, ethical, accountable, and effective practice.

THE UNIQUENESS OF SOCIAL WORK RESEARCH

Since the inception of social work, generally deemed to be around the sixteenth century with the advent of the Elizabethan Poor Laws in England (Lubove, 1973), the business of social work has largely been face-to-face practice with individuals, small groups, and families. Historically, social work research has reflected but lagged behind emerging issues in practice (Dunlap, 1993; Teare & Sheafor, 1995; Witmer, 1942). It has also been focused primarily on the problems of clients rather than the problems of society. C. Wright Mills in *The Sociological Imagination* (1959) defined social problems as "the personal troubles of the milieu" or "the public issues of social structure" (p. 8). Meyer (1992) similarly dichotomized social work research into "research in practice" (her word choice), meaning evaluation research, practice effectiveness, or outcome research, versus "substantive research," which is about broader social issues or concerns. Despite her rather convincing plea for the latter, she concurred that the vast majority of research conducted and published in our core professional journals falls into the research in practice category. Thyer (1989) indicated that, even if we are to separate social work research into practice versus nonpractice categories as such, both have either applications or implications for practice overall.

Despite this dichotomy, all social work research is decidedly client focused by its very nature. Thus, regardless of its purpose, methods, or results, at the core of all social work research is the central question: How does this study relate to the problems of clients? Emanating from this question is another set of related questions, such as: How does this study help us to better understand our clients and their problems? How does it better help us to treat clients? How does it help in developing theories or knowledge to guide our practice? Consequently, it may be argued that, because all social work research is client focused, it can be deemed applied research in the broadest sense of this term (Witkin, 1991; Wolfe, 1959).

Further, since social work research is conducted in either direct or indirect practice settings, its client focus and applied perspective can be conceptualized across the continuum of micro, meso, and macro domains as indicated in Figure 22-1.

Examples of the types of social work research conducted in the various domains presented in Figure 22-1 include: (a) a single-subject evaluation of one's practice, (b) a program evaluation, (c) a community needs assessment, and (d) a policy analysis. Thus, the transcending and applied nature of all social work research trickles in to a client-centered core regardless of where on the continuum (in Figure 22-1) it is conducted. As a result, it is not surprising that the majority

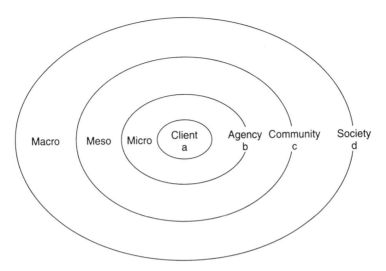

Figure 22-1. Practice domains for the conduct of social work research.

of social work research conducted and disseminated is client-centered research in practice.

A second unique feature of social work research is that its orientation works directly out from the research problem or question to a particular methodology. Thus, once the research problem (or question) is determined by the social work researcher, he or she then utilizes a range of eclectic and available methods or approaches to study this problem (Jayaratne, 1982; Reid, 1987). Such approaches are usually practical and resource determined, and they often involve multiple strategies. Fischer (1993) stated, "Thus, the question should not be which is the best philosophy, method or perspective for social work in general, but, given a particular research question, what is the best method and design . . . whether quantitative or qualitative or a combination of both—for addressing that particular question" (p. 27). In this regard, it is incumbent upon the social work researcher to craft or tailor the subsequent method or approach to the particular research problem he or she is addressing. Given the fact that core social work professional journals are likely to publish studies about EBP and their methods—for example, single-subject design (SSD; Holosko, Moore, & Gaul, 1996)—educational resources and materials reflecting these methods or designs are more likely to be available, widely used, and accepted by social work researchers, in general (Fischer & Corcoran, 1994).

The application of methodologies post hoc has the unintended effect of researchers utilizing methods or instruments of convenience, that is, those that are available to them. This, in turn, encourages research studies that are typically: (a) hypothetically deductive and reductionistic in their orientation, (b) point-in-time as opposed to longitudinal investigations, (c) quantitative rather than qualitative, (d) atheoretical rather than theory-building research, and (e) supportive of the applied client-centered research in practice previously described. The extent to which this methodological feature truly promotes the potential range of research assumptions and methodologies and actually enhances our knowledge development in social work remains questionable (Fischer, 1993). However, it is clear that, at some point in the future, the profession must evolve its research assumptions and methodologies to expand beyond the parameters of its current orientation (Tutty, Rothery, & Grinnell, 1996).

The final (and more disparaging) unique feature of social work research relates to the schism that exists between social work researchers and practitioners. The past 40 years have encompassed a proliferation of numerous social work research publications; the availability of more resources, materials, and forums to both conduct and disseminate research; BSW, MSW, and PhD curriculum developments in North America that encourage more research education and training; the coming of age of the empirical practice movement; models and orientations within the profession that promote research and practice concurrently, such as the "practitioner-researcher"; and the profession's acknowledgment of the necessity for research to enhance both its own knowledge base and professional autonomy. Despite all of this, the fact that social work researchers and practitioners remain divided today undermines the capacity for social work research to fully develop its potential within the profession. The primary issues of this divisiveness relate to who conducts social work research, how it is disseminated, and how it is utilized.

Since the working definition of social work practice was first espoused (Bartlett, 1958; Gordon, 1962) and because social work research was historically appended to practice, the issue of how research can be better incorporated into practice has been the subject of some concern (Siegel, 1988; Thomas, 1990). At the heart of this issue is the realization that those who conduct social work practice do not conduct social work research (and vice versa). Ironically, Compton and Galaway (1979), in their effort to bridge the gap of this reality, actually perpetuated this divisiveness when they indicated that "social work researchers need to generate and test new knowledge that has been developed by social work practitioners such as the development of various social work models, theories, methods or techniques" (p. 38). Indeed, some 14 years ago, Grinnell and Royer (1983) reported that 41.5% of the social work articles in their review were written by university college professors, 21% by government officials, 24.3% by private agency personnel, 4% by medical personnel, 1.9% by research centers, and 1.2% by private practitioners. Similarly, Karger (1983) succinctly concluded that social work researchers basically write for each other and not for social work practitioners. More recent reviews about who conducts social work research (Penka & Kirk, 1991) have concluded with the same finding.

In terms of dissemination, despite the fact that social work has evolved from a rather vague, haphazardly derived, knowledge-based profession into a more systematic, rational, and empirically based profession (Fischer, 1993, p. 19), social work practitioners are unlikely to have the time, inclination, support, or resources to either read research or integrate it into their day-to-day practice. (The literature on this phenomenon is related to the previously described issue of who conducts social work research, in that 20 years of investigation about the issue have yielded the same conclusion.) More than a quarter of a century ago, Rosenblatt (1968) reported that only 9% of the respondents in his study of private practitioners read research articles published in social work journals. Similarly, Kirk, Osmalov, and Fischer (1976) reported that less than half of the social work practitioners in their sample read journals that contained substantial research content and 57% of these did not consult research when confronted with difficult practice situations (p. 122). More recent reviews of this phenomenon (Penka & Kirk, 1991; Richey, Blythe, & Berlin, 1987) have reached the same conclusion. In short, despite the proliferation of dissemination and technological forums for social work research, such as publications, conferences, workshops, and the Internet, and the use of methods that promote and encourage dissemination, such as SSDs, program evaluations, and outcome studies, direct service practitioners who can benefit most from social work research rarely have the occasion to read or even hear about such research.

Finally, although somewhat offset by the accountability demands of funding bodies (requiring more data on clients and their programs) and the overarching integrating function (between research and practice) of EBP (Reid, 1994), in general, social work practitioners do not utilize social work research in their day-to-day practice. Rosen (1983) described five barriers to utilization that included: (a) the knowledge to be used, (b) the practice situation and setting, (c) the characteristics of the practitioner, (d) the medium through which knowledge is being communicated, and (e) the social context (e.g., the language of the text, whether research is supported by peers or supervisors). Kirk (1990), who similarly assessed this phenomenon over a number of years, concluded that such barriers were apparent and formidable; however, some progress was being made in this area. Fischer (1993) concurred with this sentiment when he indicated:

> There are signs that researchers increasingly are sensitive to "beginning where the practitioner is," that qualitative studies may be able to provide information of more immediate relevance to practice, that technology needs to be and can be modified to meet more adequately the needs of practitioners, and that work in developmental research and social research and development (R&D) . . . has great potential for increasing the use of research derived modes of practice. (p. 33)

Thus, the historic and ongoing schism between social work researchers and practitioners is a prevalent and unique feature of social work research. It appears that, until social work researchers and practitioners can work together in collaborative partnerships conducting knowledge-based research, this divisiveness will continue to plague the potential for both research and practice development. In this regard, however one examines this issue, unfortunately the EBP movement and research venues that have developed along with it—namely SSD and the practice-researcher model—have not delivered on the promises for actualizing social work research that the profession had hoped for (Fischer, 1993; Hess & Mullen, 1995; Reid, 1994; Witkin, 1996).

THE DELIMITING NATURE OF EMPIRICAL PRACTICE EFFECTIVENESS

Although the social work research literature has historically touted a multifaceted and eclectic view of EBP (Fischer, 1973, 1978, 1986, 1992; Gambrill, 1990; Lazarus, 1986; Thyer, 1989), this view is one that is delimited, for it holds that EBP is either about practice interventions or the outcomes of these interventions (Reid, 1994; Thyer, 1981), or it is about their methodologies, specifically SSDs (Gottlieb & Hideki, 1987; Thyer & Boynton, 1989). In turn, this has led to an evolving and even narrower perception of practice effectiveness—as being almost exclusively concerned with research on the effectiveness of specific direct practice interventions (Gorey, 1996). The point here is that such a perception of EBP and practice effectiveness (derived from the published social work research literature) never gives the profession its just deserts in terms of acknowledging the true character of generalist social work practice, or, more simply, what transpires in everyday practice. Arguably, such a skewed perception may have resulted in the frequent and often dubious concerns held about social work's effectiveness overall, which has been troubling to the profession ever since Joel Fischer (1973) first begged the question, "Is casework effective?"—and then asked for some corroborating empirical evidence to answer this concern.

It appears that, for a variety of reasons, intervention and outcome research about social work practice that is largely behavioralistic, quantitative, atheoretical, client-focused, and methodologically neat (i.e., employing objective, practical, and feasible designs and available instruments to assess phenomena) is more likely to be published in core professional social work journals. However, Siegel (1984), in her attempt to present a more comprehensive conceptual and operational definition of EBP, specified seven criteria incorporated by this term, which include the following:

> 1) makes maximum use of research findings, 2) collects data systematically, 3) demonstrates empirically whether or not interventions are effective, 4) specifies problems, interventions, and outcomes in terms that are concise, observable, and measurable, 5) uses research ways of thinking and research methods in defining client's problems, formulating questions for practice, collecting assessment data, evaluating the effectiveness of interventions, and using evidence, 6) views research and practice as part of the same problem-solving process, and 7) views research as a tool to be used in practice. (p. 329)

Thus, a much broader view of EBP, extending well beyond intervention or outcome assessments, characterizes EBP, and if we are concerned with promoting this view, then both the profession and social work research literature should reflect this reality.

In addition to the delimited definition of EBP and practice effectiveness, a number of social work authors studying empirical practice effectiveness have stated that day-to-day practice activities, not necessarily neatly tied to specific interventions or outcomes, need to be more thoroughly considered if we are to understand what EBP and practice effectiveness really mean. For example, Berlin and Marsh (1993) stated that "despite the importance of empirical knowledge, it is insufficient for guiding practice" (p. 22). Cheetham (1992) indicated that "a first and often ignored priority is some focus on the content and manner of the service being delivered. . . . Furthermore, all bets about the relationship between outcome and intervention are pointless unless you know what social workers did" (p. 276). Reid (1994), in a comprehensive review of EBP, concluded that "controlled SSD's had been seen as a major breakthrough in effectiveness testing. So far they have not added substantially to the knowledge base of social work, although they still have the potential to do so." Later he added "significant advances have been made in the incorporation of research-based interventions into education and practice, but such interventions provide only a portion of the knowledge that is needed, and the extent of their use has not been adequately described" (p. 181). Meyer (1992), in describing day-to-day practice in an ecosystems framework, indicated that

> among the most difficult issues for researchers is the requirement in this perspective [ecosystems] to include, rather than exclude, extraneous variables. Such an encompassing perspective implies a broadening and generality of practice tasks . . . exactly contrary to the narrowing and specifying tasks that are favored by current research methodology. (p. 299)

Finally, Gorey (1996), in his metanalysis of the effectiveness of social work intervention over 4 years of social work literature (1990 to 1994), concluded by indicating that his review and analysis would have been more meaningful if the studies he sampled had more information on day-to-day practice experiences about clients, workers, and intervention characteristics (p. 125).

In summary, both the definition of EBP and practice effectiveness presented in the social work literature have had a mitigating effect in acknowledging the nature of day-to-day social work practice, empirical practice, and practice effectiveness. The extent to which such a limited perception renders the profession and its programs and services vulnerable to federal, state, and municipal budget cuts remains to be seen. Certainly, the profession has an ethical responsibility to promote itself through practice and research that characterize and reflect its current practice realities.

THE ORGANIZATIONAL CONTEXT OF SOCIAL WORK PRACTICE

The evolving EBP movement has a rich history rooted in social work practice. Most notably, the basis for EBP can be traced to Mary Richmond's legitimizing social work practice text, *Social Diagnosis* (1917), to Helen Perlman's (1957) delineation of the problem-solving process in practice, to Florence Hollis's (1963) psychoanalytic casework model, to Carol Meyer's (1987) call for an ecosystems approach to assessments and interventions, and to Louise Johnson's (1989) operationalization of the generalist problem-solving process. Thus, the social and health care settings in which the majority of social work is practiced in North America clearly provided both the impetus and rationale for more scientifically based practice in the sense of its being more systematic, rational, objective, and problem solving in its orientation. Ironically, it has been these very same domains of practice that have not been able to adapt, promote, use, or enhance the development of EBP to any great extent. Reid (1994) concluded his review of the history of the EBP movement in America with the following paragraph:

> As the historical review suggested, the empirical practice movement was instigated by research-minded academics who were involved in direct practice and committed to its improvement. Academics continue to dominate the movement. If it is to realize in any substantial way of making practice more effective, the movement must become better rooted in agency soil. It badly needs agency-based advocates, implementers, and, of course, practitioner-researchers. For this to happen, more extensive collaboration between our academic and agency establishments must occur, but the focus it should take are by no means clear. (p. 181)

The empirical practice literature clearly demonstrates the importance of the organizational context in understanding the conduct of practice effectiveness research. However, relying upon human service organizations (HSOs) to provide the framework for any social work research places serious constraints upon the conduct of such research (Bar-On, 1994). These constraints at best bracket or delineate the nature and scope of EBP and at worst create a number of obstacles to the actual conduct of such activities (Hudson, 1987; Reid, 1987).

As discussed earlier in this chapter, it can no longer be assumed that problems or difficulties in conducting EBP are attributed solely to issues of practitioner preparation or commitment, or to the acquisition of research resources. Explanations for such difficulties must be sought by examining the nature of HSOs themselves. While it is clear that HSOs are complex, with a myriad of interrelated functions and aspects (Hasenfeld, 1992), it is important to view those functional areas that serve as distinct contributors to obstacles in EBP. These areas include the organizational domain and external environment in which they operate, the organizational culture, and the structure of human service organizations and their service-delivery systems.

Practice effectiveness issues are significantly constrained by the fact that HSOs must function in an external environment and interorganizational domain (Reid, 1988). The ability for an HSO to function effectively as such requires that it meet or respond to multiple expectations and criteria emanating simultaneously from funders, government bureaucracies, community stakeholders, and client constituencies (Baum & Oliver, 1991; Gronbjerg, 1992; Hasenfeld, 1983; Singh & Lumsden, 1990; Tucker, Baum, & Singh, 1992). In recent times, the majority of these external stakeholders have insisted upon higher levels of accountability and more rigorous outcome evaluations (Biggerstaff, 1977; Carter, 1987; Feinstein, 1985). However, the specification of these criteria remains imprecise and quite diverse in nature, with the focus remaining upon organizational goals and objectives, rarely including practice effectiveness criteria (Hudson, Mayne, & Thomlinson, 1992). Empirical evidence indicates that most elements in an organization's external environment still pay more attention to issues of organizational reputation, service-delivery quantity and efficiency, and the emotional appeal of providing assistance to the client population or system, more so than anything else (Handy, 1995; Hasenfeld, 1983).

Even organizational effectiveness research proposals requiring commitments of significant funds or public resource allocations tend to be given low priority no matter how rigorous their methodology (Carter, 1987). Generally, evaluation and accountability in this context are viewed as something that should be accomplished within existing resources or with one-time grant funding. Provision is rarely made for long-term evaluation processes and, thus, establishment of a stable environment for any consistent evaluation is not cultivated, let alone one that would provide nurturance for practice effectiveness research (Love, 1991). This environment is further eroded by the failure of major stakeholders to pay attention to evaluation results even when they do exist (Brawley & Martinez-Brawley, 1988; McNeece, DiNitto, & Johnson, 1983; Rapp & Poertner, 1986; Rossman, Hobber, & Ciarlo, 1979). For instance, Holosko (1997) pointed out that inclusion of client input in program evaluation outcomes (the current trend) has become an almost universal requirement, but the failure of organizations and funders to act upon the information provided by the consumers is tantamount to abuse of the consumers or at least to patronization of them. Again, this is hardly an inducement for HSOs to get excited about undertaking the onerous task of practice effectiveness research.

The sociopolitical context in which most HSOs operate may be best illustrated through the backdrop of chaos theory. This theory posits the external environment of HSOs to be characterized by sudden leaps or reversals in an atmosphere of randomness. Consequently, the external environment undergoes rapid changes, which produce paradoxes and disconnectedness within organizational and interorganizational domains (Briggs & Peat, 1989; Gregerson & Sailer, 1993; Holosko & Taylor,

1989; Prigogine & Stengers, 1984; Ramsey, 1991). While demands for outcome evaluation indicators and accountability are made by elements in the external environment, in today's reality, organizational managers find themselves faced with unclear, contradictory, and irrational rewards and penalties for their successes or failures in this accountability process (Aiken & Hage, 1968; DiMaggio, 1988; Meyer & Scott, 1983; Scott & Meyer, 1983). Indeed, many HSOs live hand-to-mouth with short-term and tentative funding guarantees, while, ironically, others experience relatively secure funding without respect to their accountability performance. These latter organizations are reluctant to become involved in comparative studies of practice effectiveness, since the outcomes will not likely enhance their position within their organizational domain and may have the impact of destabilizing their privileged status (Grasso & Epstein, 1987). Similarly, those struggling HSOs are much more concerned about developing a reputation as being caring of their target population, committed to efficient service delivery, and able to meet program objectives in the eyes of their stakeholders in the external environment, rather than as contributing to the development of practice knowledge in the social work profession (Baum & Oliver, 1991; Handy, 1995; Singh, Tucker, & House, 1986). Both sets of organizations have learned through past experience that functioning in an environment of chaos makes it more important to tell external stakeholders what they *want* to hear, rather than what they *need* to hear (Cutt, Bragg, Balfour, Murray, & Tassie, 1996). The trick here is in knowing the difference. Currently, the ability of HSOs to respond to the ever changing evaluation criteria and tentative political context of service delivery appears far more important than the systematic evaluation of either program objectives or practice effectiveness.

The culture of most HSOs also tends toward a deemphasis of practice effectiveness information. For instance, most HSOs are highly mission driven and sprang into existence through the energy and commitment of groups of individuals within the proximal community (Holland, Leslie, & Holzhalb, 1993; Sheehan, 1996). The culture of such HSOs evolves around the delivery of services to some identifiable, vulnerable, or disadvantaged population. This service mission focus results in an overly emphasized commitment to perceiving service delivery as the major area of mission fulfillment in this regard.

As a result, the time and energy of direct service practitioners is viewed and presumably valued as being most appropriately spent in effecting this service-delivery mandate. Thus, the organizational culture reinforces the social work practitioner's view that direct, tangible, visible, and immediate "body count" work with client populations (i.e., how many clients came in for service last month) is a much higher priority than systematically evaluating one's own work with such populations. Further, since client needs normally outstrip available intervention resources and the nature of professional intervention often involves unplanned crises, it is difficult to maintain a commitment to organized professional practice methodologies. Thus, the rigor imposed upon methodology in many research studies conflicts with the existing culture and practitioner and client expectations (Grasso & Epstein, 1987). This poses an even greater obstacle, because the differing needs of evaluating organizational effectiveness fit more clearly into the organizational culture.

The mission statements of HSOs are usually expressed in some form of delineation of goals. Further, each program developed through the organization is required to have its own set of goals, objectives, and services that are consistent with the overarching mission and goals of the HSO. Consistent with this is the practice of program evaluations and evaluators to focus upon criteria that relate to the achievement of these goals and objectives (Hadley & Mitchell, 1995; Holosko, 1989; Rossi & Freeman, 1989). Thus, time, energy, and resources spent in evaluating program goals and objectives are supported through the culture of the organization, because these criteria relate directly to mission fulfillment. Unfortunately, these evaluative criteria relate only tangentially, if at all, to practice effectiveness criteria.

While there are compelling arguments for including practice effectiveness as a bona fide area of concern for HSOs and, even though other disciplines have successfully modeled this approach (Joss & Kogan, 1995), social work practice settings continue to be unsuccessful in accomplishing this task. The general cultures of the major medical disciplines have demonstrated an ability to view practice effectiveness and the development of effective service technologies as a major aspect of their overall effectiveness evaluation process irrespective of their delivery organizations. HSOs, on the other hand, have failed to incorporate adequately this aspect of effectiveness into their cultures, possibly because of the grassroots nature of mission development and the core values of the social work profession, which enhance the commitment to this client-centered, mission-driven style of organization development and operation.

Further, the basic structures of HSOs have been influenced greatly by service-delivery expectations and by service technologies (Hasenfeld, 1983; Mills & Simmons, 1995). Despite marked changes in service technologies in the delivery of human services overall, HSO structures continue to be most impacted by social work practice's commitment to accounting for cases and case study methods of practice knowledge building, resulting in a consultation or mentoring model of supervised practice. As such, social work's commitment to a core consultative methodology for practice has neatly fit in a variety of hierarchical types of HSO organizational structures. In turn, these hierarchical structures contribute to differing foci or emphasis upon evaluation criteria appropriate at different levels of the organizational process (Grasso & Epstein, 1987). These authors also point out that supervisors require information on quality control and improvement of program technology rather than direct service outcomes. Program or middle managers require systematic and reliable information on program outcomes, while executives need more global measures of client outcomes. Consequently, frontline and supervisory levels of HSOs show some commitment to practice effectiveness evaluation, while upper management structures show a clear bias toward program evaluation and the meeting of goals and objectives in terms of program implementation. This difference in focus becomes problematic because, in a hierarchical structure, more power and control over resource allocation rests with upper management positions and functions (Levine & White, 1961).

Given this structural power imbalance and the focus of senior management upon program evaluation criteria, it is not surprising that an emphasis upon practice effectiveness evaluation gets lost in the shuffle. Further, in order for HSOs to compete in today's business-oriented environment, managers require information that allows them to demonstrate organizational effectiveness and efficiency (McIntyre Hall & Hall, 1996). While this type of information is deemed essential to the survival of most HSOs, it differs clearly from the information and data required for practice evaluation. This creates a tendency for emphasis to shift from the appropriate matching of interventions to assessed client or system needs to issues of amount of service units delivered and the efficient delivery of social work hours (Bielawski & Epstein, 1984; Conrad, 1985).

Evidence abounds to show that most evaluative research is ignored by organizational managers for the purpose of program planning and decision making (Brawley & Martinez-Brawley, 1988; McNeece, DiNitto, & Johnson, 1983; Rossman, Hober, & Ciarlo, 1979). In the nonprofit sector, which encompasses a large proportion of HSOs, evaluative research is rarely used by governing boards to inform their policymaking and priority-setting functions (Love, 1991; Rossi & Freeman, 1989; Tripodi, 1983; Van Maanen, 1979). Similarly, evaluative research is rarely conducted and designed with respect to the practice effectiveness needs of frontline social workers, and equally rarely are results disseminated in such a way as to inform the effective practice of these workers (Grasso & Epstein, 1987; Reid, 1987). The bulk of research undertaken in HSOs fails to provide sufficient methodological rigor to evaluate practice effectiveness or fails to disseminate evaluative results in a way that informs and guides social work practice. In fact, most evaluative research studies remain unpublished. The literature is replete with articles extolling the virtues of program evaluation and examining program evaluation methodology (Biggerstaff, 1977; Feinstein, 1985; Rossi & Freeman, 1989; Van Maanen, 1979) but shows a distinct scarcity of articles reflecting the practice effectiveness associated with particular intervention approaches.

Issues arising from the chaotic external environments, the culture of the organization, and the organizational structures all contribute to obstacles to conducting empirically based social work practice effectiveness research. While these obstacles are understandable when viewed from the perspective of the organizational context, they nonetheless pose a significant challenge to social work practitioners, researchers, and administrators alike. In order to meet the needs of the organization and to establish EBP effectiveness outcomes, it will be necessary to forge clear partnerships combining concerns for organizationally necessary outcome measures with those appropriate to social work practice effectiveness. These partnerships will require input and cooperation from all stakeholders in order to accomplish mutually desirable objectives of EBP and program effectiveness outcomes.

CONCLUDING REMARKS

Three obstacles stand in the way of the development of EBP in social work: (a) the uniqueness of social work research, (b) a delimited view of practice effectiveness, and (c) the organizational context of EBP. In order for EBP to realistically develop its potential for knowledge enhancement in social work, such obstacles need to be addressed. Furthermore, the profession of social work includes the necessary knowledge, values, skills, and resources to not only overcome such obstacles, but develop new ways of operationalizing EBP and practice effectiveness—for, as the various chapters in this handbook indicate, EBP is not just about intervention or outcome assessments, but also includes a critical analysis of research methods, accurate descriptions of day-to-day practice activities, the development of easy-to-use instruments and scales to assess practice, the development and systematic use of meaningful outcome measures to assess practice, case recording and monitoring for assessment purposes, and the use of data to develop theories, frameworks, and approaches to practice. Such a view of EBP is broader than that currently presented in the effectiveness literature and necessitates a range of methods that can be empirically and readily used by researchers and practitioners alike to guide practice and simultaneously enhance social work knowledge about practice.

In regard to the organizational context of practice, the HSOs in which mainstream social work is practiced presently do not encourage or promote EBP to any extent. They simply do not have the time, resources, or inclination to do so. Also, as was presented, they have a number of inherent organizational impediments to promoting, conducting, or using EBP. As many of the proponents of the EBP movement contend, much work (by the profession) needs to be done in social work agencies to change this reality. As a result, this chapter offers evidence to suggest that perhaps a new approach to implementing EBP in HSOs should be developed. This approach would not necessarily be grounded in the two main elements of EBP—namely, the practitioner-researcher model and SSD, per se—but even more would involve a collaborative partnership between academic researchers and frontline practitioners, each doing what they do best, research *or* practice. That is, academics would liaise with agencies and communities and listen to practitioners describe their research needs, and then work from there to design their research studies together. Thus, a dynamic and proactive approach to EBP that is practice driven and research determined is suggested as a way to offset some of the long-standing problems in evolving EBP in our agencies. The extent to which this approach or others can enhance EBP remains to be seen, but we are convinced that the profession has to be more creative and take more initiative in implementing a broader view of EBP than currently exists if it is to develop its research and practice potential.

REFERENCES

Aiken, M., & Hage, J. (1968). Organizational interdependence and intraorganizational structure. *American Sociological Review, 33,* 912–931.

Austin, C. (1996). Case management practice with the elderly. In M. J. Holosko & M. D. Feit (Eds.), *Social work practice with the elderly* (2nd ed., pp. 151–178). Toronto, Ontario: Canadian Scholar's Press.

Bar-On, A. A. (1994). Boundaries of social work. *Journal of Sociology & Social Welfare, 21(3),* 53–67.

Bartlett, H. (1958). The working definition of social work practice. *Social Work, 3(2),* 1028–1030.

Baum, J. A. C., & Oliver, C. (1991). Institutional linkages and organizational mortality. *Administrative Science Quarterly, 36,* 187–218.

Berlin, S., & Marsh, J. (1993). *Informing practice decisions.* New York: Macmillan.

Bielawaski, B., & Epstein, I. (1984). Assessing program stabilization: An extension of the differential evaluation mode. *Administration in Social Work, 8,* 13–23.

Biggerstaff, M. A. (1977). The administrator and social agency evaluation. *Administration in Social Work, 1(1),* 71–78.

Bloom, M., Fischer, J., & Orme L. (1995). *Evaluating practice: Guidelines for the accountable professional* (2nd ed.). Needham Heights, MA: Allyn & Bacon.

Blythe, B., Tripodi, T., & Briar, S. (1994). *Direct practice research in human service agencies.* New York: Columbia University Press.

Brawley, E. A., & Martinez-Brawley, E. E. (1988). Social programme evaluation in the USA: Trends and issues. *British Association of Social Workers, 18,* 391–413.

Briggs, J., & Peat, D. (1989). *Turbulent mirror: An illustrated guide to chaos theory and the science of wholeness.* New York: Harper & Row.

Carter, R. K. (1987). Measuring client outcomes: The experience of the states. *Administration in Social Work, 11,* 3(4), 73–89.

Cheetham, J. (1992). Evaluating social work effectiveness. *Research on Social Work Practice, 2(3),* 265–287.

Compton, B., & Galaway, B. (1979). *Social work processes.* Homewood, IL: Dorsey Press.

Conrad, K. (1985). Promoting quality of care: The role of the compliance director. *Child Welfare, 64,* 639–649.

Cutt, J., Bragg, D., Balfour, K., Murray, V., & Tassie, W. (1996). Nonprofits accommodate the information demands of public and private funders. *Nonprofit Management & Leadership, 7(1),* 45–67.

DiMaggio, P. J. (1988). Interest and agency in institutional theory. In L. G. Zucker (Ed.), *Institutional patterns and organizations: Culture and environment* (pp. 3–21). Cambridge, MA: Ballinger.

Dunlap, K. (1993). A history of research in social work education: 1915–1991. *Journal of Social Work Education, 29*(3), 293–301.

Feinstein, K. W. (1985). Innovative management in turbulent times: Large-scale agency change. *Administration in Social Work, 9*(3), 35–47.

Fischer, J. (1973). Is casework effective?: A review. *Social Work, 18,* 5–21.

Fischer, J. (1978). *Effective casework practice: An eclectic approach.* New York: McGraw-Hill.

Fischer, J. (1986). Eclectic casework. In J. C. Norcross (Ed.), *Handbook of eclectic psychotherapy* (pp. 320–352). New York: Bruner/Mazel.

Fischer, J. (1992). *Whatever happened to eclecticism? An analysis of psychotherapy integration, the latest psychotherapeutic fad.* Paper presented at 1st International Congress on Integrative and Eclectic Psychotherapy, Mazatlan, Mexico.

Fischer, J. (1993). Empirically-based practice: The end of an ideology? *Journal of Social Service Research, 18*(1), 19–64.

Fischer, J., & Corcoran, K. (1994). *Measures for clinical social work practice* (2nd ed., Vols. 1 & 2). New York: Free Press.

Gabor, P., & Grinnell, Jr., R. (1994). *Evaluation and quality improvement in the human services.* Boston: Allyn & Bacon.

Gambrill, E. (1990). *Critical thinking in clinical practice.* San Francisco: Jossey-Bass.

Gingerich, W., & Green, R. (1996). Information technology: How social work is going digital. In P. Raffoul & C. A. McNeece (Eds.), *Future issues for social work practice* (pp. 19–26). Boston: Allyn & Bacon.

Gordon, W. (1962, October). A critique of the working definition. *Social Work, 7*(4), 3–13.

Gorey, K. (1996). Effectiveness of social work intervention research: Internal versus external evaluations. *Social Work Research, 20,* 119–129.

Gorin, S., & Moniz, C. (1996). From health care to health: A look ahead to 2010. In P. Raffoul & C. A. McNeece (Eds.), *Future issues for social work practice* (pp. 58–64). Boston: Allyn & Bacon.

Gottlieb, N. (Ed.), Hideki, A., & editorial committee (1987). *Perspectives on direct practice evaluation.* Seattle, WA: Center for Welfare Research, School of Social Work, University of Washington.

Grasso, A. J., & Epstein, I. (1987). Management by measurement: Organizational dilemmas and opportunities. *Administration in Social Work, 11,* 3(4), pp. 89–100.

Gregerson, H., & Sailer, L. (1993). Chaos theory and its implications for social science research. *Human Relations, 46*(7), 777–802.

Grinnell, R., Jr., & Royer, M. (1983). Authors of articles in social work journals. *Journal of Social Service Research, 6*(3/4), 150–164.

Gronbjerg, K. (1992). Nonprofit human service organizations: Funding strategies and patterns of adaptation. In Y. Hasenfeld (Ed.) *Human services as complex organizations,* (pp. 73–97). Newbury Park, CA: Sage.

Hadley, R., & Mitchell, L. (1995). *Counseling research and program evaluation.* Pacific Grove, CA: Brooks/Cole.

Handy, F. (1995). Reputation as collateral: An economic analysis of the role of trustees of nonprofits. *Nonprofit and Voluntary Sector Quarterly, 24*(4), 293–305.

Hasenfeld, Y. (1983). *Human service organizations.* Englewood Cliffs, NJ: Prentice Hall.

Hasenfeld, Y. (Ed.). (1992). *Human services as complex organizations.* Newbury Park, CA: Sage.

Hersey, P., & Blanchard, K. (1988). *Management of organizational behavior: Utilizing human resources* (5th ed.). Englewood Cliffs, NJ: Prentice Hall.

Hess, P., & Mullan, E. (Eds.). (1995). *Practitioner-researcher partnerships: Building knowledge from, in, and for practice.* Annapolis, MD: National Association of Social Workers.

Holland, T. P., Leslie, D., & Holzhalb, C. (1993). Culture and change in nonprofit boards. *Nonprofit Management & Leadership, 4*(2), 141–155.

Hollis, F. (1963). Contemporary issues for caseworkers. In H. Pasad & R. Miller (Eds.), *Ego-oriented casework* (pp. 13–33). New York: Family Association of America.

Holosko, M. (1996). Research and autonomy [Guest editorial]. *The Beacon.* The Ontario Association of Social Workers, Windsor-Essex Branch, pp. 2–3.

Holosko, M. (1997). Service user input—fact or fiction? A case example of the Trauma Program, Department of Rehabilitation, Sault Ste. Marie, Ontario. *The Canadian Journal of Program Evaluation, 11*(2), 111–126.

Holosko, M. J. (1989). Prerequisites for EAP evaluations: A case for more thoughtful evaluation planning. In M. J. Holosko, & M. D. Feit (Eds.), *The Evaluation of Employee Assistance Programs,* (pp. 56–67), Binghamton, NY: Haworth Press.

Holosko, M., & Feit, M. D. (Eds.). (1996). *Social work practice with the elderly* (2nd ed.). Toronto, Ontario: Canadian Scholar's Press.

Holosko, M. J., Moore, B., & Gaul, R. (1996). *An analysis of research methods used in core professional social work journals (1992–1996).* Unpublished manuscript, University of Windsor, Ontario.

Holosko, M., & Taylor, P. (1989). *Social work practice in health care settings.* Toronto, Ontario: Canadian Scholar's Press.

Hudson, W. W. (1987). Measuring clinical outcomes and their use for managers. *Administration in Social Work, 11,* 3(4), 39–57.

Hudson, J., Mayne, J., & Thomlinson, R. (Eds). (1992). *Action-oriented evaluation in organizations.* Toronto, Ontario: Wall & Emerson.

Ingersoll-Dayton, B., & Jayaratne, S. (1996). Measuring effectiveness of social work practice: Beyond the year 2000. In P. Raffoul & C. A. McNeese (Eds.), *Future issues for social work practice* (pp. 29–35). Boston: Allyn & Bacon.

Jayaratne, S. (1982). Characteristics and theoretical orientations of clinical social workers: A survey. *Journal of Social Service Research, 4,* 17–30.

Johnson, L. (1989). *Social work practice: A generalist approach* (3rd ed.). Needham Heights, MA: Allyn & Bacon.

Joss, R., & Kogan, M. (1995). *Advancing quality: Total quality management in the National Health Service.* Buckingham, England: Open University Press.

Karger, H. (1983). Science, research and social work: Who controls the profession? *Social Work, 28,* 200–205.

Kirk, S. (1990). Research utilization: The substructure of belief. In L. Videka-Sherman & W. Reid (Eds.), *Advances in clinical social work research* (pp. 233–250). Silver Springs, MD: National Association of Social Workers.

Kirk, S., Osmalov, M., & Fischer, J. (1976). Social worker's involvement in research. *Social Work, 21*(2), 121–132.

Latting, J. (1996). Human service organizations of the future. In P. Raffoul & C. A. McNeese (Eds.), *Future issues for social work practice* (pp. 214–225). Boston: Allyn & Bacon.

Lazarus, A. (1986). Multimodel therapy. In J. C. Norcross (Ed.), *Handbook of eclectic psychotherapy* (pp. 65–93). New York: Bruner/Mazel.

Levine, S., & White, P. (1961). Exchange as a conceptual framework for the study of interorganizational relationships. *Administrative Science Quarterly, 5,* 583–601.

Love, A. J. (1991). *Internal evaluation: Building organizations from within.* Newbury Park, CA: Sage.

Lubove, R. (1973). *The professional altruist.* New York: Harvard University Press.

Martin, P., & O'Conner, G. (1989). *The social environment: Open systems application.* New York: Longman.

McIntyre Hall, L., & Hall, M. F. (1996). Big fights: Competition between poor people's social movement organizations. *Nonprofit and Voluntary Sector Quarterly, 25*(1), 53–72.

McNeece, C. A., DiNitto, D. M., & Johnson, P. J. (1983). The utility of evaluation research for administrative decision-making. *Administration in Social Work, 7*(3/4), 77–87.

Meyer, C. (1987). Direct practice in social work: Overview. In *Encyclopedia of Social Work* (18th ed., pp. 409–422). Silver Spring, MD: National Association of Social Workers.

Meyer, C. (1992). Social work assessment: Is there an empirical base? *Research on Social Work Practice, 2*(3), 297–305.

Meyer, J. W., & Scott, W. R. (1983). Centralization and the legitimacy problems of local government. In J. W. Meyer & W. R. Scott (Eds.), *Organizations environment: Ritual and rationality* (pp. 199–215). Beverly Hills, CA: Sage.

Mills, A., & Simmons, T. (1995). *Reading organization theory: A critical approach.* Toronto, Ontario: Garamond Press.

Mills, C. Wright (1959). *The sociological imagination.* London: Oxford University Press.

Ott, J. (1989). *The organizational culture perspective.* Homewood, IL: Irwin.

Patton, M. Q. (1988). Integrating evaluation into a program for increased viability and cost-effectiveness. In J. McLaughlin, J. Weber, R. Covert, & R. Ingle (Eds.) *Evaluation utilization: New directions for program evaluation* (No. 39, pp. 85–94). San Francisco: Jossey-Bass.

Paulson, A. (1996). Swimming with the sharks or walking in the garden of Eden: Two visions of managed care and mental health practice. In P. Raffoul & C. A. McNeece (Eds.) *Future issues for social work practice* (pp. 85–96). Boston: Allyn & Bacon.

Penka, C., & Kirk, S. (1991). Practitioner involvement in clinical evaluation. *Social Work, 36,* 513–518.

Perlman, H. H. (1957). *Casework: A problem-solving process.* Chicago, IL: University of Chicago.

Perrow, C. (1979). *Complex organizations: A critical essay* (2nd ed.). Glenview, IL: Scott, Foresman.

Prigogine, I., & Stengers, I. (1984). *Order out of chaos.* New York: Bantam Books.

Raffoul, P., & McNeece, C. A. (1996). *Future issues for social work practice.* Boston: Allyn & Bacon.

Ramsey, R. (1991). Preparing to influence paradigm shifts in health care strategies. In P. Taylor & J. Devereux (Eds.), *Social work administrative practice in health care settings,* (pp. 29–44). Toronto, Ontario: Canadian Scholar's Press.

Rapp, C. A., & Poertner, J. (1986). The design of data based management reports. *Administration in Social Work, 10*(4), 53–64.

Reid, W. (1987). Research in social work. In A. Minahan, R. Becerra, S. Briar, C. Coulton, L. Ginsberg, J. Hopps, J. Longres, R. Patti, W. Reid, T. Tripodi, & S. Khinduka, (ex-officio), et al. (Eds.), *Encyclopedia of social work* (18th ed., pp. 474–487). Silver Spring, MD: National Association of Social Workers.

Reid, W. (1988). Service effectiveness and the social agency. *Administration in Social Work, 11,* 3(4), 39–57.

Reid, W. (1994). The empirical practice movement. *Social Service Review, 68*(2), 165–184.

Richey, C., Blythe, B., & Berlin, S. (1987). Do social workers evaluate their practice? *Social Work Research and Abstracts, 23,* 14–20.

Richmond, M. (1917). *Social diagnosis.* New York: Russell Sage Foundation.

Rosen, A. (1983). Barriers to utilization of research by social work practitioners. *Journal of Social Service Research, 6,* 1–15.

Rosen, A. (1996). The scientific practitioner revisited: Some obstacles and prerequisites for fuller implementation in practice. *Social Work Research, 20*(2), 105–113.

Rosenblatt, A. (1968). The practitioner's use and evaluation of research. *Social Work, 13*(4), 55–65.

Rossi, P. H., & Freeman, H. E. (1989). *Evaluation: A systemic approach* (4th ed.). Beverly Hills, CA: Sage.

Rossman, B. B., Hober, D. I., & Ciarlo, J. A. (1979). Awareness, use and consequences of evaluation data in a community mental health center. *Community Mental Health Journal, 15*(1), 7–16.

Scott, W. R., & Meyer, J. W. (1983). The organization of societal sectors. In J. W. Meyer & W. R. Scott (Eds.), *Organizational environment: Ritual and rationality* (pp. 129–153). Beverly Hills, CA: Sage.

Sheehan, R. M., Jr. (1996). Mission accomplishment as philanthropic organization effectiveness: Key findings from the Excellence in Philanthropy Project. *Nonprofit and Voluntary Sector Quarterly, 25*(1), 110–123.

Siegel, D. (1984). Defining empirically based practice. *Social Work, 29*(4), 325–337.

Siegel, D. (1988). Integrating data gathering techniques and practice activities. In R. M. Grinnell (Ed.), *Social work research and evaluation* (3rd ed., pp. 465–482). Itasca, IL: F. E. Peacock.

Singh, J. V., & Lumsden, C. J. (1990). Theory and research in organizationl ecology. *Annual Review of Sociology, 16,* 161–195.

Singh, J. V., Tucker, D. J., & House, R. J. (1986). Organizational legitimacy and the liability of newness. *Administrative Science Quarterly, 31,* 171–193.

Teare, R., & Sheafor, B. (1995). *Practice sensitive social work education: An empirical analysis of social work practice and practitioners.* Alexandria, VA: Council on Social Work Education.

Thomas, E. (1990). Modes of practice in developmental research. In L. Videka-Sherman & W. J. Reid (Eds.) *Advances in clinical social work research,* (pp. 202–217). Silver Spring, MD: National Association of Social Workers.

Thyer, B. (1981). Behavioural social work: A bibliography. *International Journal of Behavioural Social Work and Abstracts, 1,* 229–251.

Thyer, B. (1989). First principles of practice research. *British Journal of Social Work, 19,* 309–323.

Thyer, B. (1996). Social work practice in the year 2006: A developing empirical clinical science. In P. Raffoul & C. A. McNeece (Eds.), *Future issues for social work practice* (pp. 77–84). Boston: Allyn & Bacon.

Thyer, B., & Boynton, K. (1989). Single subject research designs in social work practice: A bibliography. Unpublished manuscript [Mimeo], School of Social Work, University of Georgia, Athens, GA.

Tripodi, T. (1983). *Evaluation Research for Social Workers.* Englewood Cliffs, NJ: Prentice Hall.

Tucker, D. J., Baum, J. A. C., & Singh, J. V. (1992). The institutional ecology of human service organizations. In Y. Hasenfeld (Ed.) *Human services as complex organizations* (pp. 47–72). Newbury Park, CA: Sage.

Tutty, L., Rothery, M., & Grinnell, R. Jr., (1996). *Qualitative research for social workers.* Toronto, Ontario: Allyn & Bacon.

Van Maanen, J. (1979, January/February). The process of program evaluation. *The Grantsmanship Center News,* pp. 30–73.

Witkin, S. (1991). Empirical clinical practice: A critical analysis. *Social Work, 36,* 158–163.

Witkin, S. (1996). If empirical practice is the answer, then what is the question? *Social Work Research, 20*(2), 69–77.

Witmer, H. (1942). *Social work: An analysis of a social institution.* New York: Farrar & Rinehart.

Wolfe, D. (Ed.). (1959). *Symposium on basic research.* Washington, DC: Association for the Advancement of Science.

Yates, B. (1994). Cost-effective analysis, cost-benefit analysis, and cost-benefit analysis into clinical research. *Journal of Consulting and Clinical Psychology, 62,* 729–736.

Yates, B. (1996). *Analyzing costs, procedures, processes and outcomes in human services.* Thousand Oaks, CA: Sage.

Author Index

Aase, J. M., 12
Abbott, R. D., 368
Abel, E. L., 12
Abidin, R. R., 37
Abrami, P. C., 61
Abrams, D. A., 132, 136
Abrams, D. B., 131
Accardo, P., 182
Achenbach, T. M., 228
Ackerman, N., 19
Acklin, J. D., 276
Acosta, F. X., 252
Adams, H. B., 135
Addington-Hall, J., 321–323
Adelson, C., 365
Adey, M. B., 263
Ager, J. W., 92
Ageton, S., 159
Aging America: Trends and Projections, 261
Ahmed, S., 263
Aiken, M., 442
Ajzen, I., 209
Aktan, G. B., 143
Aldarondo, E., 231–233, 235
Alden, L. E., 135
Aldwin, C., 277, 279
Alemi, F., 93
Allen, D. M., 106
Allen, E. A., 200, 216–217
Allen, G., 395, 404, 405
Allen, G. J., 423
Allen, J. P., 129, 132–133, 136
Allen-Hagen, B., 157
Alleyne, E., 110
Allman, K., 110
Alter, J., 95
Alterman, A. I., 132–134
Amar, D. F., 328, 332–333
Ambinder, A., 271
Amenta, M., 323–324
American Medical Association, 5–8, 58, 86

American Psychiatric Association, 123, 124, 127, 343–344, 419
American Psychological Association, 67, 226, 343–344, 368
Ames, D. L., 185
Ammerman, R. T., 36
Amundsen, A., 135
Amundson, N. E., 204, 206
Andersen, R., 292
Anderson, K. R., 279
Anderson, L., 186, 300–301, 309
Angel, J. L., 284, 289
Angel, R. J., 284
Anglin, M., 164
Annis, H. M., 128, 131, 136
Anton, R. F., 132, 134
Antonucci, T. C., 282
Appleborne, P., 243
Applegate, J., 320
Aral, S. Q., 108
Aranalde, M., 249
Arbuthnot, J., 229
Ards, S., 34
Argeriou, M., 128
Arkinson, M. K., 47
Armistead, L., 227
Armstrong, B., 109
Armstrong, E., 5, 6, 27, 86, 87
Arndt, I. O., 135
Arnetz, B. B., 204, 206
Arnold, E. L., 59
Arnold, S., 320, 328
Arsham, G. M., 304, 309
Ashby, M. R., 363
Ashworth, C. S., 110
Askew, M., 324
Assal, J., 309
Astor, R., 80
Atchley, R., 279–280
Atkins, R., 323

Attala, J. M., 232
Attkisson, C., 395, 397, 398, 405
Auerbach, S. M., 265
Auslander, W., 94, 96, 110
Austin, C., 433
Austin-Murphy, J., 269
Averill, J. R., 341, 345
Avery, L. S., 47
Azar, S. T., 37
Azrin, H. H., 137, 138
Azrin, N., 210, 215

Babor, T. F., 133
Bachman, J. G., 58, 69, 94–95
Back, A. S., 143
Badger, G. J., 139
Baer, D. M., 416
Bagarozzi, D. A., 4, 59, 227
Bagley, C., 165
Bahr, H. M., 398, 405
Bailey, J. S., 415
Bailey, S. L., 363
Baird, C., 35, 159, 160
Baker, E., 143
Baker, F., 21
Baker, N., 323
Baldwin, J. A., 245, 256
Baldwin, L. M., 205
Balfour, K., 442
Ballantyne, R., 395, 399, 405, 406
Bamford, C. R., 268
Bandura, A., 364
Bangert-Drowns, R., 140
Banks, S. M., 138
Banspach, S. W., 110, 117
Barber, J. G., 137–139
Barham, J., 79
Barlow, J., 45
Barnard, J. D., 417
Barnes, P. J., 310

Subject Index